Professional
Visual Studio® 2005
Team System

Professional
Visual Studio® 2005
Team System

Jean-Luc David,
Tony Loton,
Erik Gunvaldson,
Christopher Bowen,
Noah Coad,
Darren Jefford

WILEY

Wiley Publishing, Inc.

Professional Visual Studio® 2005 Team System

Published by
Wiley Publishing, Inc.
10475 Crosspoint Boulevard
Indianapolis, IN 46256
www.wiley.com

Copyright © 2006 by Wiley Publishing, Inc., Indianapolis, Indiana

Published simultaneously in Canada

ISBN-13: 978-0-7645-8436-7

ISBN-10: 0-7645-8436-7

Manufactured in the United States of America

10 9 8 7 6 5 4 3 2 1

1B/QZ/QV/QW/IN

Library of Congress Cataloging-in-Publication Data:

Professional Visual studio team system / Jean-Luc David ... [et al.].
    p. cm.
  Includes bibliographical references and index.
  ISBN-13: 978-0-7645-8436-7 (paper/website)
  ISBN-10: 0-7645-8436-7 (paper/website)
  1. Microsoft Visual studio. 2. Web site development—Computer programs. 3. Application software—Development—Computer
programs. I. David, Jean-Luc, 1971-
  TK5105.8885.M57P76 2006
  006.7'86—dc22

                    2005026362

Credits

Executive Editor
Bob Elliott

Development Editor
Brian MacDonald

Contributors
Joe Sango
Etienne Tremblay
Steven Borg
Mike Diehl
Mickey Gousset

Technical Editors
Steven Borg
Jason Camp
Rob Caron
Steve Cook
Mickey Gousset
Bill Essary
Doug Neumann
Bruce Taimana
David Anderson
Sam Guckenheimer
Khushboo Sharan
Tom Patton
Yogita Manghnani
Randy Miller
John Turley
Susan Llewellyn
Dave Schmitt
Shawn Elliott
Rick Rainey
Wayne Ewington
Barry Fridley
Yulin Jin
Georg Drobny
Esther Fan
Ajoy Krishnamoorthy
Dominic Hopton
Carsten Lemm
Cissy Ho
Prasad Kakulamarri
Jenniger Norberg
Bill Gibson

Production Editor
William A. Barton

Copy Editor
Luann Rouff

Editorial Manager
Mary Beth Wakefield

Production Manager
Tim Tate

Vice President and Executive Group Publisher
Richard Swadley

Vice President and Publisher
Joseph B. Wikert

Media Development Specialists
Angela Denny
Kit Malone
Travis Silvers

Project Coordinator
Kristie Rees

Graphics and Production Specialists
Karl Brandt
Andrea Dahl
Mary J. Gillot
Denny Hager
Joyce Haughey
Alicia South

Quality Control Technicians
Laura Albert
Joe Niesen

Proofreading and Indexing
Christine Sabooni, Techbooks

About the Authors

Jean-Luc David is a current Team System MVP and a Toronto-based trainer, consultant, and author. He is also the CEO/Lead Developer for Stormpixel Solutions, a company focused on developing .NET solutions for the desktop, mobile devices, and the web. He has published numerous technical articles on ASPToday.com, C|NET, Builder.com, and XML.COM. He also co-authored *Professional Javascript, Second Edition* and *Professional WinFX Beta* for WROX Press and Wiley Publishing. Jean-Luc has the distinction of being the first Canadian to receive the Microsoft Visual Developer-.NET Most Valuable Professional (MVP) award. His recent activities include presiding over the Toronto Windows Server User Group, a collective of over 853 IT Professionals in the greater Toronto Area. He is also part of the administrative team of the East of Toronto .NET User Group and is a speaker in the MSDN/INETA Canada Speakers Bureau.

Erik Gunvaldson is the Technology Development Manager in the Microsoft Enterprise Partners Group where he is currently focused on process methodologies and driving the Software Factories vision across Microsoft partners. Prior to the fall of 2005, Erik was the first Microsoft Technical Evangelist for Visual Studio 2005 Team System. In this role, Erik was responsible for the Team System Technology Adoption Program (TAP) for partners and enterprise customers. Before coming to Microsoft, Erik worked for several large enterprises in roles ranging from C++ developer and software manager to distributed application architect. Erik's professional goal is to automate the building of software solutions to the point where it is 90 percent inspiration and 10 percent perspiration. When not spending time thinking about software, Erik enjoys spending time with his wonderful wife, Anna, their beautiful daughter, Katrina, and their big black lab, Joe.

Noah Coad is currently a Program Manager in the Developer and Test Tools product unit of Visual Studio Team System. His focus is on developer-driven testing, including unit testing and code coverage. As a community lead for Team System, Noah is responsible for engaging with MVPs, regional directors, and other key influencers. He is a former C# MVP and a developer at heart. While obtaining a B.S. in Computer Engineering from Texas A&M University, Noah worked as a contract programmer, taught .NET, and helped lead the initial C# online community. He enjoys mountain biking, hard-core coding, creating gizmos with microcontrollers, and spending time with his beloved wife, Dawn.

Darren Jefford is an Application Development Consultant working for Microsoft in the U.K. In his spare time (of which there isn't much), he likes to be with his young family, follow Formula 1, play the guitar, and tinker with digital photography.

Tony Loton is a Microsoft Certified Professional for .NET Solution Architectures and MSF 3.0. He works through his company, LOTONtech Limited (www.lotontech.com) as an independent consultant, instructor, and freelance author in addition to holding an appointment as Associate Lecturer for the United Kingdom's Open University. Tony graduated in 1991 with an honors degree in Computer Science with Management, and has authored many published works, including the book *Professional UML with Visual Studio .NET* and a Visual Studio 2005 article series for the MSDN Developer Center.

Christopher Bowen is the Lead Applications Architect at Monster.com in Maynard, Massachusetts, where he works on the design, implementation, and optimization of Monster's applications. Chris is highly involved in the .NET development community, contributes to running the Boston .NET User Group, and speaks on a variety of subjects at area developer events. He is a member of Microsoft's Patterns & Practices Customer Advisory Board and the Microsoft East Region Architect Council. Christopher holds a masters of science in Computer Science and a bachelors of science in Management Information Systems from Worcester Polytechnic Institute in Worcester, Massachusetts.

Acknowledgments

This book is dedicated to my beautiful, loving wife, Miho, for supporting me in a million ways. My family also deserves a loud, big round of applause for their ongoing patience and support. First and foremost, I would like to thank Rob Caron (and the rest of the Team System product group) for providing invaluable technical advice, comments, and resources (even at all hours of the night). Next comes Noah Coad, who is undeniably the nicest guy I've ever met and a great friend. He co-authored a chapter in this book despite his busy schedule, and helped out in countless ways. Erik Gunvaldson has contributed a great deal to this book—his breadth and depth of knowledge on Team System made an indelible impact on its contents. Mickey Gousset, a fellow Team System Most Valuable Professional (MVP) and all-around amazing guy, dedicated hours of his time to provide fantastic technical reviews in record time and really made a positive contribution—thanks, Mickey! Other product team members who have made significant contributions to the book include Sam Guckenheimer, Sean Sandys, Jennifer Norberg, Dominic Hopton, Ajay Sudan, Ayesha Mascarenhas, Buck Hodges, Khushboo Sharan, Bindia Hallauer, Beny Rubenstein, Chris Lucas, Rick LaPlante, Prasad Kakulamarri, Ed Hickey, and countless more. Next, I would like to thank all my co-authors for your amazing chapters—without you this book wouldn't exist: Erik, Noah, Darren Jefford, Christopher Bowen, and Tony Loton. Other MVPs and experts who have authored parts of the book (in its final stages) include Joe Sango, Etienne Tremblay, Steven Borg, Mickey Gousset, and Mike Diehl. Joel Semeniuk and Baryr Gervin provided some great feedback and technical edits on some of the chapters. A very special thanks goes out to the editors and publisher at Wiley Publishing: Robert Elliott for his ongoing support and advice. Other Wiley/Wrox contributors include Helen Russo and Bill Barton. Last, I'd like to thank Chris Dufour for being a great friend and soundboard. —*Jean-Luc David*

Many thanks to Thomas Delrue for providing the SDM sample at the end of Chapter 7. After teaching Microsoft .Net and related technologies in Belgium, Thomas moved to the United States to join the Visual Studio team at Microsoft Corporation. He currently works in the Distributed Systems Designers team as a Software Design Engineer in Test. He can be reached via his personal e-mail at `thomas .delrue@tiscali.be`. —*Erik Gunvaldson*

Special thanks to Dawn Coad, my lovely, sweet wife, who has been my inspiration and support. She is truly God's gift and makes my life a joy. Many thanks to Jean-Luc David, who made this book possible and is one of our top Team System MVPs, and my team, including Chris Lucas, Rob Caron, Tom Arnold, Tom Marsh, and Dominic Hopton, who provided feedback and support for the material. —*Noah Coad*

I'd like to thank my fantastic wife, Julieann, and our wonderful children, Lucy and Toby, for their love, support, and patience. I'd also like to thank Duncan Pocklington, Dave Thomas, and the DSL Tools team in Cambridge, all of whom helped to get the boxes joined together. Last, but not least, thanks to Microsoft, Keith Everitt, Totem, and Simon Dutton, all of whom helped me get to where I am today! —*Darren Jefford*

I'd like to thank Bob Elliot for getting me and Jean-Luc together at the outset, and Brian MacDonald for his professional and friendly editorial advice throughout. I'd also like to thank Simon Williams, a colleague who took no reward for looking through my very first chapter drafts before anyone else saw them. As always, I'd like to acknowledge my close family—Debs, Becky, and Matt. You don't have to live with me; they do! —*Tony Loton*

Thanks and love go to my wife, Jessica, and our daughters, Deborah and Rachel, for their understanding and support throughout the creation of this book. Thanks to my family and friends for their understanding when I had to bow out of activities to research and write. Thanks to the Team System staff at Microsoft for their support and to the reviewers who helped to improve my chapters. Special thanks go to Jean-Luc David for inviting me to join in the creation of this book. Finally, I'd like to express thanks, love, and gratitude to my parents—Peter, my father, and Joan, my mother, in loving memory.
—Christopher Bowen

Contents

Contents

Contents

Contents

Contents

Contents

Contents

Contents

Contents

Contents

Introduction

In June of 1999, Microsoft started to reevaluate how Visual Studio was being used as part of a software development process. Microsoft's Developer Division sustained the developer community at large for years, but did not adequately address all of the challenges of software development within a team environment. For example, what Microsoft tools were out there for architects before Team System? There really wasn't that much—the most notable tool is Microsoft Visio, which is used to design UML diagrams. There are also some other lesser known design tools in Visio. However, there isn't any solid two-way integration between Visio diagrams and code within Visual Studio. Another problem relates to the tools themselves. To effectively set up a software development shop, you have to purchase several third-party tools (or use open-source tools) to handle tasks such as version control and team communications. A mishmash of tools is even more difficult to integrate.

Here is a common scenario: You are compiling a list of tasks or requirements to send out to your team using products such as Microsoft Excel, Word, or Project. You then have to be able to communicate these tasks to the rest of your team and respond when they have completed the task or the status changes. To be able to achieve this, you have to do a lot of cutting and pasting. On top of that, the process is very deliberate—there is no automation or shortcuts. You also have to handle a lot of your communication by e-mail. The problem with e-mail is that your team members can lose messages; there may be a server outage that may prevent your messages from coming through, and so forth.

Before Team System, the only version control product Microsoft had to offer was Microsoft Visual SourceSafe. SourceSafe is an excellent tool for a single developer or a very small team, but it doesn't scale very well if you have a large number of developers working concurrently. In addition, it isn't really designed to be used over the Web.

Visual Studio's Enterprise Tools team launched a project code-named "Burton" to create a team product that would integrate well with Visual Studio and tackle the challenges of integration and scalability.

> "Burton" is named after a very popular snowboard and clothing company based in Vermont. Many Microsoft employees enjoy skiing in their free time and as a result, many of the product code names are based on skiing-related locations and equipment. For example, Windows XP was code-named after Whistler Mountain in British Columbia.

In May of 2004, after five years of research, planning, and development, Microsoft announced and presented Visual Studio 2005 Team System to the public. Team System consists of experience and tools used internally at Microsoft for years, such as PREfast, Product Studio, and Source Depot. Rick LaPlante (the general manager for Team System) delivered a keynote presentation and an end-to-end demo that changed the way people looked at Visual Studio. The first major change in the Visual Studio product is the availability of tools targeted at all roles within an IT organization: architects, developers, testers, and project managers. Another big focus is on the *software development life cycle* (also known as the *SDLC*). Within the product, you can now use the Microsoft Solutions Framework, which not only provides a framework for developing software, but also includes process guidance and integration.

Introduction

Fast forward to today: Team System is now in stores and you've picked up a copy of this book to learn more about it. Professional Visual Studio 2005 Team System will provide you with an end-to-end overview of the important features of the product. In the Wrox spirit, we have included a lot of practical information and hands-on walk-throughs to put Team System through its paces, regardless of your role within your organization.

> *One of the most important aspects of Team System is that it is designed to fit your needs and not the other way around. Unlike other Microsoft products such as Office, Team System isn't designed for out-of-the-box use. You have to spend some time configuring it and applying your policies and best practices—in essence, tailoring it to the way you develop software. Why make changes if you have established a good development process and everything is working well? Alternatively, if your approach is more ad hoc, Team System will provide you with a good framework to work out a suitable and workable process.*

We will make no bones about it—Team System is a *huge* product. Think of this book as your starting point into Team System. Like other *Professional* books by Wrox, we not only dive into the important features, but also the grittier details.

Team System is composed of several logical tiers. Figure 1 features a very high-level logical overview of Team System's architecture.

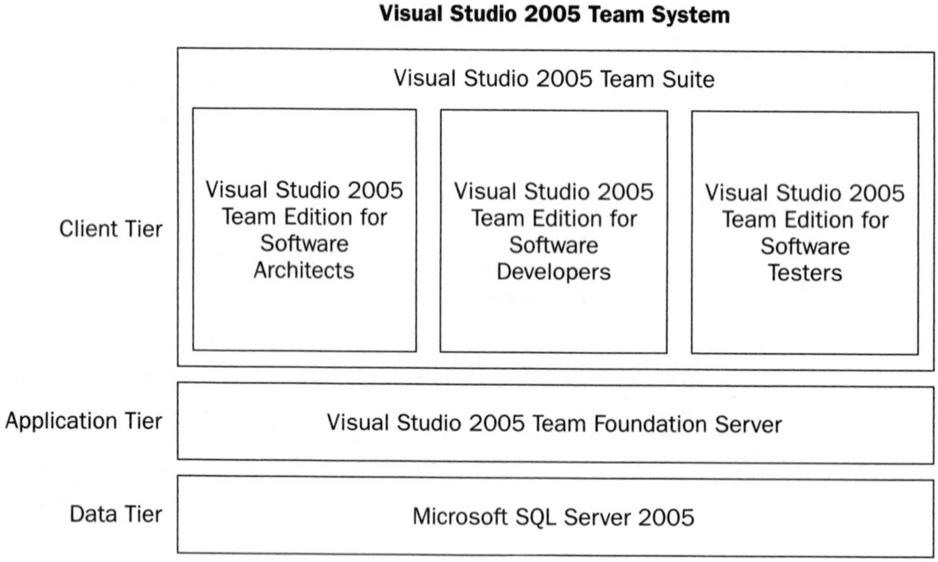

Visual Studio 2005 Team System

	Visual Studio 2005 Team Suite
Client Tier	Visual Studio 2005 Team Edition for Software Architects · Visual Studio 2005 Team Edition for Software Developers · Visual Studio 2005 Team Edition for Software Testers
Application Tier	Visual Studio 2005 Team Foundation Server
Data Tier	Microsoft SQL Server 2005

Figure 1

Following is a detailed explanation of each of the tiers included in Team System.

Client tier

The client tier is composed of several role-based versions of Visual Studio 2005 and other tools that are designed to connect to the application and data tiers of Team System. Here is a description of the four Team System client products:

❑ **Visual Studio 2005 Team Suite** incorporates the functionality of Visual Studio 2005 Team Edition for Software Architects, Visual Studio 2005 Team Edition for Software Developers, and Visual Studio 2005 Team Edition for Software Testers all bundled into one. This product is geared toward team members who want (or need) to take on several roles. The Team Suite product is also useful for installing on the Team Foundation Build server to incorporate the test capabilities of both the Developer and Tester versions of the product.

❑ **Visual Studio 2005 Team Edition for Software Architects** includes tools to support the application and infrastructure architects during the initial design phase and ongoing development of a software project. It includes several designers, such as the Application Modeling, Infrastructure Modeling, and Deployment Modeling tools. This tool should not be confused with the Visual Studio .NET 2003 Enterprise Architect product. The older Enterprise Architect tool was considered the most complete version of Visual Studio .NET 2003. The "equivalent" tool for Team System is the Visual Studio 2005 Team Suite.

❑ **Visual Studio 2005 Team Edition for Software Developers** has Static Code Analyzers for both managed and unmanaged code, Dynamic Code Analyzers (also commonly known as AppVerifier), Unit Testing, Coverage, and Code Profiling tools.

If you want to enforce static code analysis or dynamic code analysis on your build, you have to add these tests to a test task and make sure that the Team Edition for Software Developers version is installed on your build machine (or you can alternatively use Team Suite).

❑ **Visual Studio 2005 Team Edition for Software Testers** has features such as Test Case Management, Performance and Load Testing, Unit Testing, Code Coverage, and Manual Testing. If you want to enable any of these tests in your builds, you have to install this version of Visual Studio 2005 on your build server (or Team Suite).

Once you are finished installing Visual Studio, you need to install the Team Explorer. Team Explorer is a client plug-in that will enable you to connect to Team Foundation Server, create projects, and administer all of the project details. Team Explorer can also be installed as a standalone tool. It has the same "look and feel" as Visual Studio, and it has a light memory footprint. Note that you can't write code within the standalone version of this tool (you still need Visual Studio to be able to do that). You can also use it for source control operations side by side with Visual Studio .NET and other development tools. It's also appropriate for project managers.

Although not officially part of Team System, Microsoft Office Professional 2003 (specifically Word and Excel), and Microsoft Project are used to interface with both the application tier and the data tier. Excel and Project can be used to manage work items and requirements; Word is used to create manual tests. Excel can be used to get a nice view of your project data by connecting directly to the data tier using pivot tables.

Chapters 1 through 17 cover most of the client-based tools. If you are interested in project management and reporting, you should definitely take a look at Chapter 19.

Application tier

Team Foundation Server incorporates the application and data tiers. This server has many integrated and centralized functions, including project management capabilities (a SharePoint-based Team Project Portal site, work item tracking, and reporting), build automation, and a version control system. Team Foundation Server also provides support for fine-grained security, policies, and other administrative capabilities. Chapters 18–24 cover each feature in detail.

One of the topics we won't be covering in detail is the Team Foundation Core Services. The reason we are excluding this information is because the programmability features and API are very much in flux at the time of writing. For current documentation and samples, we highly recommend that you visit the Visual Studio Extensibility Center website at www.vsipdev.com.

Data tier

Team System's data tier is based on Microsoft SQL Server 2005. This product was specifically selected to reduce the complexity of the application and speed up time to market. At this point, Team System is not compatible with third-party data sources and does not integrate with Enterprise Data Services (EDS). Team System's data tier is used to store all of Team System's data, such as source code, work items, reporting data, and project settings. You can find coverage on the data warehouse in Chapter 19. You can also find out about how to back up and recover your data store (and other data-related topics) in Chapter 24.

Modern Software Development Challenges

Software developers share common challenges, regardless of the size of your team. Businesses require a high degree of accountability; software has to be developed in the least amount of time with no room for failure. Some of these challenges include the following:

- ❑ **Integration problems.** Prior to Team System, most of the tools you commonly use to operate software development teams come from third-party vendors. Integrating these tools is a big challenge—in many cases, to make it all work you have to repeatedly copy project data into different software packages. Each application has a learning curve, and transmitting information from one application to another incompatible application can be frustrating and time-consuming.

- ❑ **Geographically distributed teams.** Many development and management tools don't scale for geographically distributed teams. Getting accurate reporting can be difficult, and there is often poor support for communication and collaborative tools. As a result, requirements and specifications can be mapped incorrectly, causing delays and introducing errors. Global teams require solid design, process, and software configuration management all integrated in one. There aren't many software packages that can deliver all of these features, and those that do exist tend to be inordinately expensive.

- ❑ **Segmentation of roles.** Specialization can be a huge problem on a team. Experts can assume that other departments are aware of information, which doesn't end up in the status reports but may greatly affect the project as a whole. Interdepartmental communications is a huge and prevalent problem.

❑ **Bad reporting.** This is an offshoot of the segmentation problem. In most cases, reports need to be generated manually by each team, which results in a lack of productivity. There aren't any effective tools that can aggregate all the data from multiple sources. As a result, the project lead lacks the essential data to make effective decisions.

❑ **Lack of process guidance.** Ad hoc programming styles simply don't scale. If you introduce an off-cycle change to the code, it can cascade into a serious problem requiring hours and days of work. Today's software has a high level of dependencies. Unfortunately, most tools don't incorporate or enforce process guidance. This can result in an impedance mismatch between tools and process.

❑ **Testing as a second-class citizen.** Shorter cycles and lack of testing can introduce code defects late in the process. There aren't many integrated tools for testers for Visual Studio.

❑ **Communication problems.** Most companies use a variety of communication methods, such as e-mail, messengers, memos, and sticky notes, to send information to team members. You can easily lose a piece of paper or delete an important e-mail message if you are not careful. There aren't many centralized systems for managing team communication. Frequent and time-consuming status meetings are required to keep the team on track, and many manual processes are introduced (such as sending e-mail and cutting and pasting reports). Fundamentally, the problem is that there is no communication between the tools and the project leads.

Companies introduce methodologies and practices to simplify and organize the software design process, but these methodologies need to be balanced. The goal is to make the process predictable, because in a predictable environment, methodologies keep projects on track. Conversely, methodologies add tasks to the process, such as generating reports. If your developers spend too much time doing these tasks, they'll be less productive, and your company won't be able to react competitively.

How Team System Fits In

Team System was designed to mitigate or eliminate many of these challenges. There are three founding principles behind Team System: *productivity, integration,* and *extensibility.*

Team System increases productivity in the following ways:

❑ **Collaboration.** Team Foundation Server centralizes all team collaboration. Work items, source code, and builds are all managed from the Team Portal. All the reporting is also centralized, which makes it easy for project leads to track the overall progress of the project regardless of where the metrics are coming from.

❑ **Complexity.** The process and the project plan can be integrated and enforced from within your project in Team System. In addition, the architecture tools reduce the complexity of the service-oriented applications by providing visual designers that simplify the designs.

Integration is improved in the following ways:

❑ Integrated tools facilitate communication between departments. More important, they remove information gaps. Most of the Team System tools report back to the Team Foundation Server.

❑ Many versions of Visual Studio share the same tools. For example, the Unit Testing tool is available in both the Developer and Tester editions of Team System. The tools have been designed to transition and work smoothly between editions.

❏   Team System increases the visibility of a project. Project leads can easily view metrics on the Team Portal and can proactively address problems by identifying patterns and trends.

Team System achieves extensibility through these three avenues:

❏   **Visual Studio Industry Partner Program.** Over 190 partners are participating in an initiative to provide 450 new products that interface with Team System.

❏   **Team Foundation Core Services API.** Most of Team System platform is exposed to the developer, providing many opportunities for extensibility. The Team Foundation Core Services are still under development and are specifically targeted for developers and vendors who are planning to integrate with the platform.

❏   **Meta Data Framework.** This provides a way for partners to develop model-based designers and add-ins for Team System and Visual Studio.

A Software Development Life Cycle Example

How does Team System work in a real-world scenario? To best demonstrate the tools in action, we'll run through a typical scenario with a fictional software development company called eMockSoft. eMockSoft has recently signed a partnership with a distributor to release their catalog of products. The distributor has requested a secure web service to transmit inventory and pricing information over the web. We will look at the scenario as it applies to the software development life cycle and the Team Systems tools.

Figure 2 illustrates the basic phases of the software development life cycle.

The Software Development Life Cycle

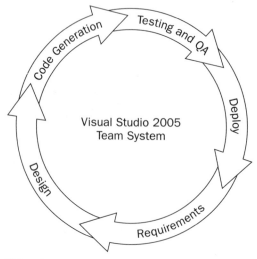

Figure 2

Requirements

The project leads meet with the sponsor to obtain requirements for the project. From these requirements, the project management team creates a list of specifications and templates. In Team Foundation Server, the project lead creates a new project using a variant of the MSF for Agile Software Development process. The Team Portal, reports, and templates are auto-generated on the server. In Microsoft Project, the lead creates a checklist of work items and assignments. The infrastructure architect receives his or her first work item.

System design and modeling

Based on the client specifications, the infrastructure architect uses the Logical Datacenter Designer tool to define the new external service. He needs to open ports on the server to allow outbound web service. The requirements include enabling SSL on port 443. The experts on the operations team conduct a security analysis and approve the changes. The architect then adds the appropriate endpoints and boundaries to allow outbound communication for the service. Finally, he assigns a work item to the solutions architect.

The solutions architect uses the Application Connection Designer to create a model of the secure web service and validates against the network topology using the Deployment Designer. In the past, she would have used Visio for her modeling tasks. Team System enables her to change the design and system in real time and facilitates communication with the infrastructure architects, developers, and project lead. Using the Class Designer, the solutions architect visually sets up the required objects and methods and resolves her work item.

Behind the scenes, the project lead can track the progress of design, including the diagrams that were generated. Based on the specs, he can send tasks to the developers on the team. The project lead has created a project plan on the Team Portal, which reduces the number of required status meetings.

Code generation

The developer receives his work assignments and the class diagrams that were designed by the solutions architect. The required classes have already been auto-generated as class templates—all the developer has to add is the business logic. He checks the specifications on the Team Project Portal Site: This application requires a secure web service using WSE 2.0. The developer writes the necessary code and does some preliminary testing. At the end of the day, the developer checks his code into Team Foundation version control.

Testing and QA

The tester checks her nightly builds and automated tests. She performs Web and load testing, which reveal a few minor coding defects in the developer's work. The tester then fills in a bug work item that is returned to the developer to alert him of the problem.

All the bug reports and work items are tracked by the project lead, who can then provide status reports to eMockSoft's management team. The project lead can instantaneously provide attractive visual reports and metrics thanks to SQL Server 2005 Reporting Services.

Deployment

Once the project is completed, the solution is deployed. From its initial stages, the solutions architect has already tested the application against the constraints within the target infrastructure. It now falls on the hands of the release manager to deploy the application. The deployment occurs smoothly and in record time.

Who Is This Book For?

This book primarily targets teams of professionals in the field of commercial or enterprise software development—in other words, intermediate to advanced users. You are likely to find the book useful if you are any of the following:

- ❑ A developer, tester, or architect who wants to learn about the new Microsoft tools
- ❑ A project manager who wants to set up and administer a project
- ❑ An IT implementer who wants to evaluate Team System as a whole
- ❑ An IT professional who wants to learn how to maintain and set up this new product

This book and product are not designed for the absolute beginner. The focus is on advanced and practical application of the tools, code samples, case studies, scenarios, and automation scripting. The book's organization makes it easy to use as both a step-by-step guide and a reference for modeling, designing, testing, and coordinating enterprise solutions at every level.

Team System is designed for software teams of all sizes, so whether you have a team of five or 2,000 members, this book contains useful information for you. Unlike most Wrox books, this book targets all roles in the IT organization: architects, developers, testers, project leads, and management—not just developers.

What Does This Book Cover?

The book includes a complete overview of Team System from design to deployment. The book is divided into four main parts for each of the roles in a software development team.

- ❑ **Part I:** Team Architect: Infrastructure and Solutions Architects
- ❑ **Part II:** Team Developer: Software Developers
- ❑ **Part III:** Team Tester: Software and QA Testers
- ❑ **Part IV:** Team Foundation: Project Management and Administration

How Is This Book Structured?

Chapter 1 is an introduction to Visual Design and the Distributed System Designers and Class Designer. The chapter outlines the features of Visual Design tools, presenting an overview of all the Distributed System Designers and Class Designer along with the primary integration points between each tool. The highlight of the chapter is a StockBroker case study that puts the designers into action.

Chapter 2 introduces Application Modeling using the Application Designer. The Application Designer enables you to add external applications (such as web services and external databases) to a predefined system. This chapter presents an overview of the AD toolbox and prototypes, the process of designing a distributed system using the toolset, implementing your applications, and adding constraints.

Chapter 3 presents Logical Infrastructure Modeling using the Logical Datacenter Designer. The Logical Datacenter Designer is used to create logical server diagrams representing the structure of a datacenter. This chapter shows you the components of the LDD toolbox and prototypes, and demonstrates how to create a logical datacenter and configure it to work with a predefined system. The examples are illustrated using the StockBroker case study introduced in Chapter 1.

Chapter 4 focuses on the System Designer and Deployment Designer. The first part of the chapter introduces both designers in detail. Later in the chapter, you'll learn how to create a trial deployment using the Application Connection Designer. You will also learn how to define and deploy entire systems and create deployment reports.

Chapter 5 features the Visual Studio 2005 Class Designer. Class Designer isn't a Team System designer per se (it is a feature of Visual Studio 2005 Standard and higher), but it enables you to model objects and create templates (which makes it a very complementary tool in the architect's toolkit). You will learn about the features of the designer and associated tools. You will also learn how to convert class diagrams to code and vice versa. Finally, you will learn about the advanced features within the Class Designer, including code synchronization, pattern modeling, and dynamic modeling.

Chapter 6 presents the Microsoft Domain-Specific Language SDK. The SDK allows you to define domain languages and custom designers built upon the language you defined. These Visual Studio 2005 designers can then be used to generate code or files—in fact, anything.

Chapter 7 features an in-depth introduction to the Dynamic Systems Initiative (DSI). You'll learn about the core DSI principle to reduce the complexity of your infrastructure. The chapter also presents an overview of Team System's DSI tools, which can be used to design, deploy, and operate distributed systems. You'll also learn about the Systems Definition Model (SDM). The Systems Definition Model is an XML document that defines a system from the perspective of hardware and software resources through a deployment life cycle. This chapter features various authoring models, types, and resources. You will also learn how to create SDM and leverage SDM designs as a whole.

Chapter 8 is the first chapter in the Team Edition for Software Developers portion of the book. It focuses on the tool for managed code analysis (also commonly known as FxCop). FxCop is a tool that analyzes the conformance of the .NET managed code assemblies against the .NET Framework Design Guidelines. It looks for defects in security, performance, and several other areas. You will learn about the FxCop UI, how to implement code reviews, and how to assemble FXCop rules.

Chapter 9 features Code Analysis for C/C++ (also known as PREfast). Code Analysis for C/C++ is a tool that checks the reliability of your C++ code and catches errors that aren't typically presented by a compiler. In this chapter, you'll learn how it works, how to configure it, and practical troubleshooting tips.

Chapter 10 targets the Application Verifier. You will learn how to set up and configure the AppVerifier tool to detect heap corruption, check lock usage, and detect invalid handle usage in your unmanaged code. This chapter also provides you with an end-to-end run-through of the product and information that will enable you to programmatically control the dynamic test engine from within Visual Studio.

Chapter 11 features refactoring and code snippets. Refactoring is a technique for incrementally restructuring code to make it more loosely coupled and comprehensible. You'll learn how to refactor diagrams and code in Visual Studio 2005. You will also learn how to use the Code Snippet Manager with samples in both VB.NET and C#.

Chapter 12 is devoted to profiling and performance. You'll learn how to use the Team System Code Profiler to profile your code using sampling and instrumentation. Code profiling is important because it uncovers slow code, which in turn helps the developer optimize the performance of the application.

Chapter 13 presents Test Case Management within the Team System environment. In this chapter, you will find out how to create test projects using the Test Case Manager.

Chapter 14 features unit testing with the Unit Test Framework. This chapter provides an overview of the core concepts of unit testing, including best practices. You'll learn how to create a simple unit test using Team System, and how to administer the results and completely leverage the framework. You will also learn about test-driven development (TDD) and code coverage features.

Chapter 15 deals with Web and load testing. In this chapter, you will learn how to create and configure web and load tests. You will also examine the command-line tools and instructions for setting up a test rig using agents and controllers.

Chapter 16 features manual testing. This chapter describes the difference between test automation and manual tests. You will learn how to create and configure manual tests, and how to design your own custom templates. Finally, you'll learn how to run through the tests and publish the results on Team Foundation Server.

Chapter 17 covers generic testing. In this chapter, you'll learn how to create a generic test and interpret error codes. You will also learn how to create and run an external tool using the Windows Scripting Host, and look at a managed code example.

Chapter 18 will teach you about the architecture of Team Foundation Server. You'll learn the core features of the server, including the clients, components, and architecture.

Chapter 19 tackles the project management tools and Reporting in Team System. You'll learn how to create a Team Project portal site, and how to administer and manage the details of your project. Next, you will get an internal overview of work items. You'll see how Reporting in Team System provides high-level metrics and data to measure the health of your project.

Chapter 20 describes Team Foundation version control. You will learn about its major features, such as performing check-ins and check-outs, shelving, and manipulating your source code store using the Source Code Explorer.

Chapter 21 is about the Microsoft Solutions Framework (MSF). You will get an overview of MSF for Agile Software Development and MSF for CMMI Process Improvement and you will learn about the roles and components of each process.

Chapter 22 targets process templates. This chapter is an in-depth continuation of Chapter 21. You will learn how to modify and design custom process templates from beginning to end.

Chapter 23 covers Team Foundation Build. After an overview of this powerful build engine, you will learn how to implement popular build configurations such as continuous integration (CI).

Chapter 24 describes how to deploy and maintain Team System. This chapter focuses on IT professional topics such as tools migration, backup/recovery strategies, and much more.

Conventions

To help you get the most from the text and keep track of what's happening, we've used a number of conventions throughout the book.

> **Boxes like this one hold important, not-to-be forgotten information that is directly relevant to the surrounding text.**

Tips, hints, tricks, and asides to the current discussion are offset and placed in italics like this.

As for styles in the text:

- ❑   We *highlight* new terms and important words in italics when we introduce them.
- ❑   We show keyboard combinations like this: Ctrl+A.
- ❑   We show filenames, URLs, and other code-related terms within the text like so: `persistence.properties`.
- ❑   We present code in two different ways:

```
In code examples we highlight new and important code with a gray background.

The gray highlighting is not used for code that's less important in the present
context, or has been shown before.
```

Source Code

As you work through the examples in this book, you may choose either to type in all the code manually or to use the source code files that accompany the book. All of the source code used in this book is available for download at `www.wrox.com`. Once at the site, simply locate the book's title (either by using the Search box or by using one of the title lists) and click the Download Code link on the book's detail page to obtain all the source code for the book.

Because many books have similar titles, you may find it easiest to search by ISBN; this book's ISBN is 0-7645-8436-7 (changing to 978-0-7645-8436-7 as the new industrywide 13-digit ISBN numbering system is phased in by January 2007).

Once you download the code, just decompress it with your favorite compression tool. Alternately, you can go to the main Wrox code download page at `www.wrox.com/dynamic/books/download.aspx` to see the code available for this book and all other Wrox books.

Errata

We make every effort to ensure that there are no errors in the text or in the code. However, no one is perfect, and mistakes do occur. If you find an error in one of our books, such as a spelling mistake or a faulty piece of code, we would be very grateful for your feedback. By sending in errata, you may save another reader hours of frustration, and you will be helping us provide even higher quality information.

To find the errata page for this book, go to www.wrox.com and locate the title using the Search box or one of the title lists. Then, on the book details page, click the Book Errata link. On this page, you can view all errata that has been submitted for this book and posted by Wrox editors. A complete book list, including links to each book's errata, is also available at www.wrox.com/misc-pages/booklist.shtml.

If you don't spot "your" error on the Book Errata page, go to www.wrox.com/contact/techsupport.shtml and complete the form there to alert us about the error you have found. We'll check the information and, if appropriate, post a message to the book's errata page and fix the problem in subsequent editions of the book.

p2p.wrox.com

For author and peer discussion, join the P2P forums at http://p2p.wrox.com. The forums are a web-based system for you to post messages relating to Wrox books and related technologies and to interact with other readers and technology users. The forums offer a subscription feature to e-mail you topics of interest of your choosing when new posts are made to the forums. Wrox authors, editors, other industry experts, and your fellow readers are present on these forums.

At http://p2p.wrox.com you will find several different forums that will help you not only as you read this book, but also as you develop your own applications. To join the forums, just follow these steps:

1. Go to http://p2p.wrox.com and click the Register link.

2. Read the terms of use and click Agree.

3. Complete the required information to join, as well as any optional information you wish to provide and click Submit.

4. You will receive an e-mail message with information describing how to verify your account and complete the joining process.

   You can read messages in the forums without joining P2P but in order to post your own messages, you must join.

Once you join, you can post new messages and respond to messages other users post. You can read messages at any time on the web. If you would like to have new messages from a particular forum e-mailed to you, click the Subscribe to this Forum icon by the forum name in the forum listing.

For more information about how to use the Wrox P2P, be sure to read the P2P FAQs for answers to questions about how the forum software works as well as many common questions specific to P2P and Wrox books. To read the FAQs, click the FAQ link on any P2P page.

Part I
Team Architect

Chapter 1: Introducing the Visual Designers

Chapter 2: Application Modeling Using Application Designer

Chapter 3: Logical Infrastructure Modeling Using Logical
Datacenter Designer

Chapter 4: Defining Systems and Evaluating Deployments Using
System Designer and Deployment Designer

Chapter 5: Class Modeling Using Class Designer

Chapter 6: DSL Tools

Chapter 7: Dynamic Systems Initiative and the System Definition
Model

1

Introducing the Visual Designers

In May 2005, Microsoft published its Visual Studio 2005 Team System Modeling Strategy at `http://msdn.microsoft.com/library/default.asp?url=/library/en-us/dnvs05/html/vstsmodel.asp`. In this introductory chapter, we'll draw on the main themes — domain-specific languages (DSLs), model-driven development (MDD), Software Factories, and the Unified Modeling Language (UML) — as they apply to the Visual Studio 2005 Team Edition for Software Architects. We'll summarize what Microsoft has to say on those subjects, and we'll add our own impartial views.

We'll review the evolution of distributed computing architectures — from simple object-oriented development through component and distributed-component design to the service-oriented architectures that represent the current state of the art. That will be our link to the Application Designer that supports a DSL specifically for modeling interconnected Web services applications.

Application Designer is the first in a suite of Distributed System Designers (formerly codenamed "Whitehorse") that also supports system modeling, logical infrastructure modeling, and deployment modeling. We'll introduce each in turn, to be fleshed out in subsequent chapters. To complete the picture in terms of visual design, we'll introduce the Visual Studio 2005 Class Designer, which complements the Distributed System Designers but is not strictly part of that set, and which is available in all Visual Studio editions apart from the Express editions.

Finally, we consider the question "What about UML?" As professional software designers, you may well have been trained in the Unified Modeling Language (UML), the until-now industry standard notation for visual modeling. Like us, you might wonder how — if at all — UML fits into the Visual Studio 2005 Team System scheme; how you can capitalize on your UML skills; and what you do with the UML artifacts you have created.

We'll begin by first establishing the case for undertaking visual modeling — or visual design — at all.

Why Design Visually?

We'd like to divide that question into two parts: Why design at all, rather than just code? And why design visually?

To answer the first question, we can draw on the common analogy of building complex physical structures, such as bridges. Crossing a small stream requires only a plank of wood—no architect, no workers, and no plans. Building a bridge across a wide river requires a lot more: a set of plans drawn up by an architect so that you can order the right materials; planning the work; communicating the details of the complex structure to the builders, and getting a safety certificate from the local authority. It's the same with software. You can write a small program by diving straight into code, but building a complex software system requires some forethought. You must plan it, communicate it, and document it to gain approval.

The four aims of visual design are therefore as follows:

- ❑   To help you visualize a system you want
- ❑   To enable you to specify the structure or behavior of a system
- ❑   To provide you with a template that guides you in constructing a system
- ❑   To document the decisions you have made

Traditionally, design processes like the *Rational Unified Process* have treated design and programming as separate disciplines, at least in terms of tools support. You use a visual modeling tool for design, and a separate IDE for coding. This makes sense if you treat software development like bridge building and assume that the cost of fixing problems during implementation is much higher than the cost of fixing those problems during design. For bridges that is undoubtedly true; but in the realm of software development, is it really more costly to change a line of code than it is to change a design diagram? Moreover, just as bridge designers might want to prototype aspects of their design using real materials, so might software designers want to prototype certain aspects of their design in real code. For these reasons, the trend has been toward tools that enable visual design and coding within the same environment, with easy switching between the two representations, thus treating design and coding as essentially two views of the same activity. The precedent was set originally in the Java space by tools such as Together-J, and more recently in the .NET space by IBM-Rational XDE, and this approach has been embraced fully by the Team Edition for Software Architects.

Now the second part of the question: If the pictorial design view and the code view are alternative but equivalent representations, then why design visually at all? The answer to the second part of the question is simple: A picture paints a thousand words. To test that theory, just look at the figures in this chapter and imagine what the same information would look like in code. Then imagine trying to explain the information to someone else using nothing but a code listing.

Of course, if we're going to use visual modeling as a communication tool, the notation must be commonly understood. In UML terms, this means an industry-standard, general-purpose notation that is all things to all people. In Visual Studio 2005 terms, this means a set of domain-specific notations that are highly tuned for the information they are designed to convey. Nonetheless, the first version notations are familiar enough to be immediately accessible to most UML-trained software designers.

Microsoft's Modeling Strategy

As we stated at the outset, Microsoft's Visual Studio 2005 Team System Modeling Strategy is based on three key ideas: domain-specific languages (DSLs), model-driven development (MDD), and Software Factories.

We consider these three topics together as comprising Microsoft's new vision for how to add value to the software development process through visual modeling. It's this "adding value" that distinguishes the new vision from the old vision, which — to put a label on it — we'll call UML.

First to set the scene: The Object Management Group (OMG) has a licensed brand called *Model-Driven Architecture (MDA)*. MDA is an approach to MDD based on constructing platform-independent UML models (PIMs) supplemented with one or more platform-specific models (PSMs). Microsoft also has an approach to model-driven development, based not on the generic UML but on a set of tightly focused domain-specific languages (DSLs). This approach to model-driven development is part of a Microsoft initiative called *Software Factories,* which in turn is part of a wider Dynamic Systems Initiative.

> *If you would like a more in-depth exploration of software factories, we recommend that you pick up* Software Factories: Assembling Applications with Patterns, Works, Models and Tools, *written by Keith Short and Jack Greenfield (Wiley & Sons Publishing; ISBN: 0471202843).*

Model-driven development

As a software designer, you may be familiar with the "code-generation" features provided by UML tools such as Rational Rose and IBM-Rational XDE. These tools typically do not generate "code" at all but merely "skeleton code" for the classes you devise, so all you get is one or more source files containing classes populated with the attributes and operation signatures that you specified in the model.

> *The words "attribute" and "operation" are UML terminology. In the .NET world, we tend to refer to these as "field" and "method," respectively.*

As stated in Microsoft's modeling strategy, this leads to a problem:

"If the models they supported were used to generate code, they typically got out of sync once the developers added other code around the generated code. Even products that did a good job of 'round tripping' the generated code eventually overwhelmed developers with the complexity of solving this problem. Often these problems were exacerbated because CASE tools tried to operate at too high a level of abstraction relative to the implementation platform beneath. This forced them to generate large amounts of code, making it even harder to solve the problems caused by mixing hand-written and generated code."

The methods that are generated for each class by UML code generation tools typically have complete signatures but empty bodies. This seems reasonable enough because, after all, the tool is not psychic. How would it know how you intend to implement those methods? Well, actually, it could know.

UML practitioners spend hours constructing dynamic models such as statecharts and sequence diagrams that show how objects react (to method invocations) and interact (invocate methods on other objects). Yet that information, which could be incorporated into the empty method bodies, is lost completely during code generation.

We should point out that not all tools lose this kind of information during code generation, but most of the popular ones do. In addition, in some cases UML tools do generate code within method bodies — for example, when you apply patterns using IBM-Rational XDE — but in general our point is valid.

Why do UML tools generally not take account of the full set of models during code generation? In part it's because software designers do not provide information in the other models with sufficient precision to be useful as auto-generated method bodies. The main reason for that is because the notation (UML) and tools simply do not allow for the required level of precision.

What does this have to do with model-driven development? Well, MDD is all about getting maximum value out of the modeling effort, by taking as much information as possible from the various models right through to implementation. As Microsoft puts it:

"Our vision is to change the way developers perceive the value of modeling. To shift their perception that modeling is a marginally useful activity that precedes real development, to recognition that modeling is an important mainstream development task. . . "

Although our example of UML dynamic modeling information finding its way into implemented method bodies was useful in setting the scene, don't assume that model-driven development is only, or necessarily, about dynamic modeling. If you've ever constructed a UML deployment model and then tried to do something useful with it — such as generate a deployment script or evaluate your deployment against the proposed logical infrastructure — you will have seen how wasted that effort has been other than to generate some documentation.

The model-driven development ethos translates into Visual Studio 2005 functionality as follows:

- ❑ Automated validation of application settings against constraints of the hosting environment
- ❑ Generation of Web services wrappers to bridge different implementation technologies
- ❑ Automatic synchronization between source code and class models (therefore, no troublesome code generation and reverse engineering phases)
- ❑ Production of deployment reports in support of automated deployment via external scripting tools

The bottom line? Well, because models are regarded as first-class development artifacts, developers write less conventional code and development is therefore more productive and agile. In addition, it fosters a perception among all participants — developers, designers, analysts, architects, and operations staff — that modeling actually *adds value* to their efforts.

Domain-specific languages

UML fails to provide the kind of high-fidelity domain-specific modeling capabilities required by automated development. In other words, if you want to automate the mundane aspects of software development, then a one-size-fits-all generic visual modeling notation will not suffice. What you need is one or more domain-specific languages (or notations) highly tuned for the task at hand — whether that task is the definition of Web services, the modeling of a hosting environment, or traditional object design.

> A domain-specific language (DSL) is a modeling language that meets certain criteria. For example, a modeling language for developing Web services should contain concepts such as Web methods and protocols. The modeling language should also use meaningful names for concepts, such as fields and methods (for C#) rather than attributes and operations. The names should be drawn from the natural vocabulary of the domain.

The DSL idea is not new, and you may already be using a DSL for database manipulation (it's called SQL) or XML schema definition (it's called XSD).

Visual Studio 2005 embraces this idea by providing domain-specific languages for specific tasks. Domain-specific languages enable visual models to be used not only for creating design documentation, but also for capturing information in a precise form that can be processed easily, raising the prospect of compiling models into code.

In the section labeled "Visual Designers" later in this chapter, we'll introduce the initial set of DSLs that Microsoft has devised for service-based application modeling, logical infrastructure modeling, system modeling, and deployment modeling. But that's not an exhaustive set. We can expect additional visual designers to be incorporated into future versions of Visual Studio — perhaps to support business process modeling or Web-services contract design. In addition, Microsoft has a suite of tools that enables you to devise your own domain-specific languages for your own problem domain.

In that context, "your own problem domain" need not be technology focused, such as how to model Web services or deployment infrastructures, but may instead be business focused. You could devise a DSL that is highly tuned for describing banking systems or industrial processes. And here's an interesting idea: If you really can't live without UML, how about devising a set of DSLs that mirrors the UML?

We'll say more about that at the end of the chapter, and you can also find out more about DSLs in Chapter 7.

Software Factories

In their book *Software Factories* (Wiley, 2004) Greenfield, Short, and others introduce and discuss techniques and tools for adding significant value to the process of turning visual models into functional implementations.

In a nutshell, the Software Factories initiative is all about pulling together the ideas of model-driven development and domain-specific languages to support the following:

❑ Full or partial generation of artifacts (such as source code and configuration files) from other artifacts (particularly models)

❑ Synchronization of related artifacts (such as the model and the code) during development, and validation of artifacts constructed manually

❑ The application of patterns and industry best practices *driven by guidance in context.*

7

The key to all that is a Software Factory Schema, which relates work done at one level of abstraction, in one part of the system or in one phase of the life cycle to work done at other levels or in other parts and phases.

While some of the results of this initiative are already apparent in the Visual Studio 2005 Team System, some of the ideas have yet to be fully realized in tools, and this is not just about Microsoft tools. To quote from Microsoft's published modeling strategy:

". . . we see factories as the basis of a broad ecosystem in which our customers and partners participate, building custom factories on top of foundations we supply, and supplying factory components to other members of the ecosystem."

A concrete example would be a software factory for *banking*. This would include DSL-based modeling tools, process guidance, and architectural frameworks that help to automate the tasks involved in building systems specifically for the banking industry; the point being that all banking systems comprise the same sorts of entities (accounts, interest rates, etc.), the same kinds of processes (bill payments, funds transfers, etc.), as well as being bound by the same regulatory requirements. It makes little sense to reinvent the wheel for each new process.

> **For more information on this initiative, visit the Software Factories Workbench at** `http://lab.msdn.microsoft.com/teamsystem/workshop/sf/.`

From Objects to Services

The design features provided by Visual Studio 2005 Team Edition for Software Architects have been influenced not only by Microsoft's vision for model-driven development, but also by a technological evolution from object-based architectures through (distributed) component-based architectures to the service-oriented architectures (SOA) that represent the current best practice in distributed system design.

This section summarizes that evolution — in part to demonstrate that service orientation is a good idea, and in part as a natural lead-in to the first of the new visual designers, the Application Designer, which provides a DSL specifically for modeling interconnected service-based applications.

Objects and compile-time reuse

When object-oriented programming became popular in the mid-1990s, it was perceived as a panacea. In theory, by combining state (data) and behavior (functions) in a single code unit, we would have a perfectly reusable element: a cog to be used in a variety of machines.

The benefit was clear. No more searching through thousands of lines of code to find every snippet that manipulated a date — remember the Y2K problem? By encapsulating all date manipulation functionality in a single Date class, we would be able to solve such problems at a stroke.

Object orientation turned out not to be a panacea after all, for many reasons, including — but not limited to — bad project management (too-high expectations), poor programming (writing procedural code dressed up with objects), and inherent weaknesses in the approach (such as tight coupling between objects).

For the purposes of this discussion, we'll concentrate on one problem in particular, which is the style of reuse that objects encouraged — what you might call *copy-and-paste reuse*.

Consider the following copy-and-paste reuse scenario: You discover that your colleague has coded an object — call it Book — that supports exactly the functionality you need in your application. You copy the entire source code for that object and paste it into your application.

Yes, it has saved you some time in the short term, but now look a little further into the future.

Suppose the Book class holds fields for Title and ISBN, but in your application you now need to record the author. You add a new field into your copy of the Book source code, and name that field Author.

In the meantime, your colleague has established the same need in his application, so he too modifies the Book source code (his copy) and has the foresight to record the author's name using two fields: AuthorSurname and AuthorFirstname.

Now the single, reusable Book object exists in two variants, both of which are available for a third colleague to reuse. To make matters worse, those two variants are actually incompatible and cannot easily be merged, thanks to the differing representations of the author name.

Once you've compiled your application, you end up with a single executable file (.exe) from which the Book class is indivisible, so you can't change the behavior of the Book class — or substitute it for your colleague's variant — without recompiling the entire application (if you still have the source code, that is!).

As another example (which we'll continue through the next sections), imagine you're writing a technical report within your company. You see one of the key topics written up in someone else's report, which has been sent to you by e-mail. You copy their text into your document, change it a little, and now your company has two — slightly different — descriptions of the same topic in two separate reports.

Components and deploy-time reuse

At this point you might be shouting that individual classes could be compiled separately and then linked together into an application. Without the complete source code for the application, you could recode and replace an individual class without a full recompilation, just link in the new version.

Even better, how about compiling closely related (tightly coupled) classes into a single unit with only a few of those classes exposed to the outside world through well-defined interfaces? Now the entire sub-unit — let's call it a *component* — may be replaced with a newer version with which the application may be relinked and redeployed.

Better still, imagine that the individual components need not be linked together prior to deployment but may be linked on-the-fly when the application is run. No need to redeploy the entire application then; just apply the component updates. In technological terms, we're talking here about DLLs (for those with a Microsoft background) or JAR files (for the Java folks). And in .NET terms, we're talking about assemblies.

Continuing our nonprogramming analogy, consider hyperlinking your technical report to the appropriate section of your colleague's report and then distributing the two documents together, rather than copying his text into your document.

Distributed components and run-time reuse

Continuing with this line of thought, imagine that the components need not be redeployed on client devices at all. They are somehow just available on servers, to be invoked remotely when needed at runtime.

In our nonprogramming example, consider not having to distribute your colleague's report along with your own. In your own report, you would simply hyperlink to the relevant section in your colleague's document, which would be stored — and would remain — on an intranet server accessible to all recipients.

One benefit of this kind of remote linking is that the remote component may be adapted without having to be redeployed to numerous clients. Clients would automatically see the new improved version, and clients constrained by memory, processing power, or bandwidth need not host the components locally at all.

This leads us to a distributed component architecture, which in technology terms means DCOM, CORBA, or EJB. All of these technologies support the idea of a component — or object — bus via which remote operations may be discovered and invoked. In Figure 1-1, the component bus is indicated by the grayed-out vertical bar.

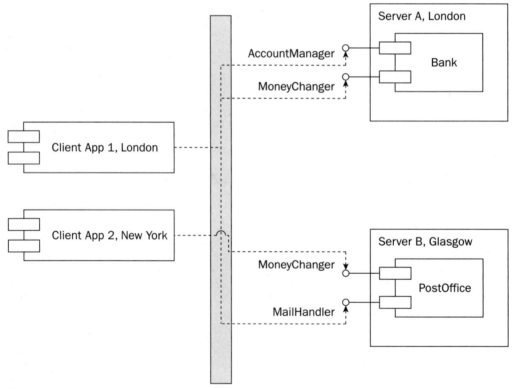

Figure 1-1

In case you're wondering, the notation used in Figure 1-1 is UML. In fact, it's a UML Component Diagram drawn using Visio for Enterprise Architects. We used UML here because we haven't yet introduced you to the new notations.

Of course, as remote components are modified, we must ensure that none of the modifications affect clients' abilities to use those components, which is why we must make a distinction between interfaces and implementations:

❏ **Interface:** A component interface defines the contract between that component and the clients that use it. This contract must never be broken, which in practice means that existing operations may not have parameters added or taken away, though it may sometimes be permissible to add new operations.

❏ **Implementation:** A component implementation may be changed at will in terms of the use of an underlying database, the algorithms used (e.g., for sorting), and maybe even the programming language in which the component is written, as long as the behavior is unaffected as far as the client is concerned.

This distinction between interface and implementation raises some very interesting possibilities. For example, a single component implementation (e.g., Bank) may support several interfaces (e.g., AccountManager and MoneyChanger) whereas the MoneyChanger interface may also be supported by another implementation (e.g., PostOffice).

Moreover, the underlying implementations may be provided by various competing organizations. For example, you could choose your bank account to be managed by the Bank of BigCity or the National Enterprise Bank so long as both supported the AccountManager interface. This idea is revisited in Chapter 2.

Distributed services and the service-oriented architecture

What's wrong with the distributed components approach?

To start with, the same underlying concepts have been implemented using at least three different technologies: the OMG's Common Object Request Broker Architecture (CORBA), Microsoft's Distributed Component Object Model (DCOM), and Sun Microsystems' Enterprise Java Beans (EJB). Though comparable in theory, these approaches require different programming skills in practice and do not easily interoperate without additional bridging software such as DCOM/CORBA bridges and RMI-over-IIOP.

Furthermore, distributed component technologies encourage stateful intercourse between components by attempting to extend the full object-oriented paradigm across process and machine boundaries, thereby triggering a new set of challenges such as how to manage distributed transactions across objects, requiring yet more complex technology in the form of the CORBA Transaction Service or the Microsoft Transaction Server (MTS).

To a certain extent, a service-oriented architecture alleviates these problems by keeping it simple: by making the services stateless if possible, and by allowing services to be invoked using the widely adopted, standard over-the-wire protocol Simple Object Access Protocol (SOAP).

Logically, a representation of Figure 1-1 (distributed component bus) redrawn as Web services would be virtually identical, as shown in Figure 1-2 (distributed Web services). Admittedly, this diagram has been drawn specifically to look as much like the other one as possible; nevertheless, you should note the close correspondence between the various elements.

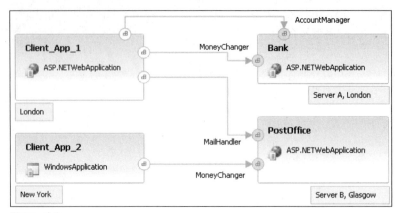

Figure 1-2

Not only does Figure 1-2 show the close correspondence — and logical progression — from distributed components to Web services, it also offers a first glimpse at the kinds of diagrams you'll be drawing in this part of the book. It is a Visual Studio 2005 application diagram drawn using Application Designer.

Before we move on, it's important to understand a key point here: Just because the original object-oriented paradigm has evolved toward the service-oriented architecture, and just because Application Designer (described in the next section) is biased toward service-oriented architectures, that doesn't mean that the earlier object-oriented and component-based approaches have been replaced — they are merely complemented. In fact, in Chapter 5, you'll do some traditional object-oriented design using the Visual Studio 2005 Class Designer.

Visual Designers

Visual design within Visual Studio is not new, hence the name "Visual" Studio. For some time there have been visual designers for Windows forms and web forms so that you can lay out your screen designs without resorting to code, and so that you can add behavior to buttons and other controls without having to remember how to code their event handlers. There are also other visual designers such as the XML schema designer.

The new suite of visual designers complements the existing set by providing capabilities for modeling the static aspects of your application architecture, deployment infrastructure, and lower-level object design. The complete list of new designers that we'll be introducing in this chapter and covering in-depth in this part of the book is as follows:

❑   Application Designer

❑   Logical Datacenter Designer

❑   System Designer

❑   Deployment Designer

❑   Class Designer

As stated earlier, the first four comprise the Distributed System Designers (formerly called "Whitehorse") that are unique to the Visual Studio 2005 Team Edition for Software Architects. Class Designer is not unique to that edition, so you'll find it also in the Team Developer and Team Tester editions. We treat it as a member of the same set — rather than relegate it to another part of the book — because it operates in a similar fashion and contributes to the same overall visual modeling experience.

Each is covered in turn, although System Designer and Deployment Designer are covered together because they are intrinsically linked. Although you can use Application Designer and Logical Datacenter Designer individually, it makes little sense to use Deployment Designer without System Designer.

> *In fact, all of the designers are interrelated in very important ways via the common SDM format, as you'll see later. All we're saying here is that you can — and in fact, should — draw an Application Diagram separately from a Logical Datacenter Diagram, but it makes much less sense (arguably it's not possible) to draw a Deployment Diagram without the benefit of a set of System Definitions.*

Note that the existing designers for forms and XML schemas have a direct correspondence with the underlying code. This is true also of the new designers, which, unlike their UML equivalents, are not merely abstract representations of the underlying code.

As we introduce each of the visual designers, keep in mind that we're doing just that — introducing them. Our aim is to provide only a preview of each of the diagram types, and to place those diagrams relative to one another in the Software Development Lifecycle (SDLC). As it happens, the diagrams that we use in the following preview are all taken from the StockBroker case study that runs through the subsequent chapters, but we're not setting out to explain the details of that running example in this chapter. You'll be introduced to it more formally at the end, as a road map for the chapters that follow.

Application Designer

Application Designer enables you to define the major applications (like components in UML), their endpoints (like interfaces in UML), and their interconnections. An example application diagram based on the StockBroker case study that we'll introduce later is given in Figure 1-3.

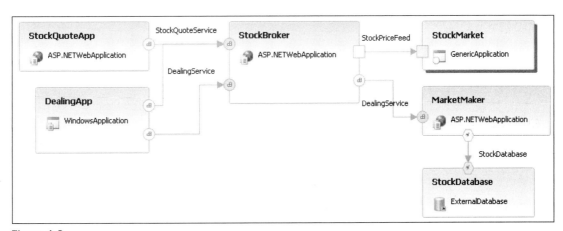

Figure 1-3

You can populate such diagrams by dragging application prototypes from the toolbox onto the diagram. These prototypes, rendered as stylized box shapes, represent ASP.NET web applications, Web services, Windows applications, and other application types. Once placed, the applications are adorned with consumer and supplier endpoints between which connections may be made.

You are allowed only one Application Diagram per solution, because ultimately it defines how your solution is composed of projects. If you implement this diagram (discussed in Chapter 2), you end up with a separate project for each application shown on the diagram, except for the MarketMaker and StockDatabase applications, which cannot be implemented.

> In Chapter 2, you'll see how some applications may be implemented in a solution, whereas some — such as generic applications, external Web services, and databases — may not.

It's no accident that we discussed service-oriented architecture (SOA) immediately before we introduced this designer, because it is biased very much toward designing service-oriented applications. While you'll find good support for adorning applications with Web service endpoints, you'll find no out-of-the-box support for adding .NET Remoting endpoints or COM endpoints as alternative communication mechanisms.

Logical Datacenter Designer

Logical Datacenter Designer enables you to define one or more deployment architectures in terms of communication boundaries, logical servers, and the protocols that interconnect them (see Figure 1-4 for an example taken from our StockBroker case study).

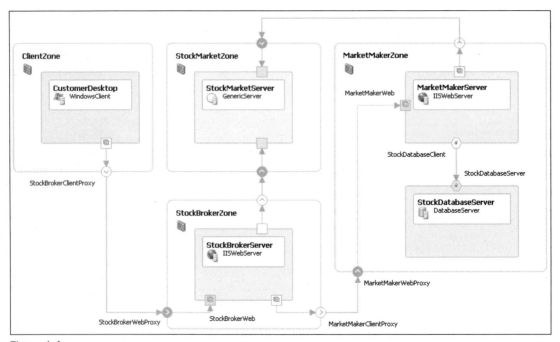

Figure 1-4

You populate such diagrams by dragging zone and server prototypes from the toolbox onto the diagram. Zones are rendered as dashed boxes representing protected network regions, and logical servers are rendered as stylized boxes representing deployment hosts. Zones and servers may be adorned with endpoints between which connections may be made.

Note that that this designer is used for *logical* infrastructure modeling, not *physical* infrastructure modeling. The five servers shown in the diagram could be hosted on five separate machines, across four machines — one in each zone — or even all on one machine, perhaps running in Virtual PCs.

You can have as many logical datacenter diagrams as you like, and the diagrams may be moved freely between solutions.

System Designer and Deployment Designer

We cover System Designer and Deployment Designer together because it makes little sense to show you one without the other. In fact, even in the simplest case of defining a default deployment scenario straight from an application diagram (as you'll see in Chapter 2), a system is created implicitly.

The two design diagrams described so far provide two alternate views of the overall architecture. The application diagram represents a solution-scoped view of the applications that you have designed, and the logical datacenter diagram represents the operations analyst's view of the logical infrastructure on which the system will be deployed. A deployment diagram depicts a deployment of the applications in a system to the logical servers in a logical datacenter. In essence, the System Designer and Deployment Designer serve to tie the two views together.

By default, each application from the application diagram binds onto an individual deployable system, but using System Designer it is possible to specify an alternative binding — for example, two applications can be combined into a single deployable system. Figure 1-5 shows such a system, along with the System View window from which you can select the applications for each system.

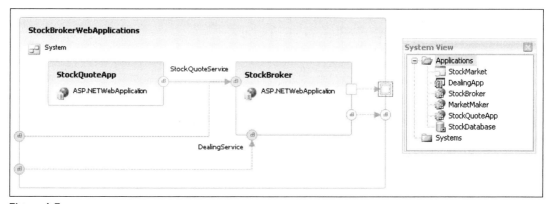

Figure 1-5

At first glance, the design surface of Deployment Designer (see Figure 1-6) looks very much the same as Logical Datacenter Designer. Look closer, however, and you'll see that each of the servers has one or more applications (also taken from the System View) bound onto it.

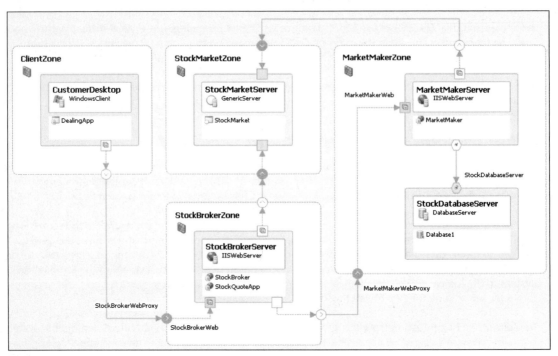

Figure 1-6

Class Designer

If you mention visual modeling to most software developers, the first thing that will spring into their minds is the UML class diagram that shows how object classes are connected together in a persistent sense or to allow navigation between them. Visual Studio 2005 provides a Class Designer most closely resembling its UML namesake.

> *Class Designer is not limited to the Visual Studio 2005 Team Edition for Software Architects. You can do class modeling in the Team Developer and Team Tester editions too.*

Figure 1-7 provides an example Class Designer class diagram showing classes (with fields and methods), interfaces (shown as lollipops), associations, and inheritance.

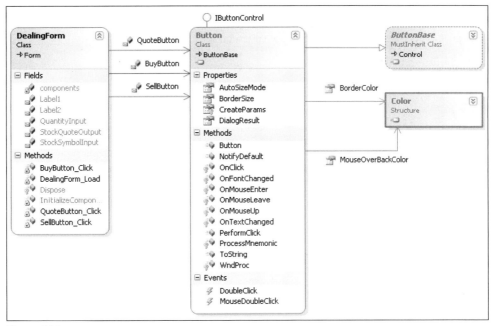

Figure 1-7

Code synchronization

Historically, visual design tools such as Rational Rose were distinct tools, separate from the development tools used for coding. Integration was achieved via a code-generation facility that would produce a one-shot cut of skeleton code as source files that could be loaded up in the IDE. Conversely, existing source files and compiled class libraries could be reverse-engineered into the design tool to document existing code using UML notation.

Some tools — including Rose but excluding Visio EA — provided a degree of round-trip engineering whereby code could be generated from the model in the design tool, modified in the IDE, reverse-engineered back into the model, and so on, ad infinitum. This round-trip engineering was not always as effective as the tool vendor claimed for the following reasons:

❑   It was not always possible for the tool to reconcile every change made outside of the tool. For example, a class renamed in code is indistinguishable — as far as the tool is concerned — from a class being deleted and a new one being created.

❑   Synchronization issues could arise in team scenarios, such as multiple designers and developers modifying portions of the model and the code in incompatible ways, resulting in an intractable merge.

17

A new precedent was set by IBM-Rational XDE, which keeps the two views—model and code—perfectly synchronized with no need to explicitly generate code or reverse engineer. Any changes you make in code are automatically reflected in the model, and vice-versa.

That is the approach taken by Class Designer, which means you won't find any feature labeled "generate code" or "reverse engineer." They're simply not needed. We'll discuss this further in Chapter 5, but for now the main implications of this are as follows:

❑ Unlike UML, which can be rather generic in its class modeling offering, Class Designer uses the data types provided by the underlying implementation language, whether Visual Basic, Visual C#, or Visual J#. The Visual Studio 2005 Class Designer does not support Visual C++.

❑ The three kinds of association defined by UML—ordinary association, aggregation, and composition—are not distinguished on diagrams because they cannot be distinguished in code.

❑ Class Designer is just as useful for visualizing existing classes and other types as it is for defining new ones.

Introducing the StockBroker Case Study

A single example, the StockBroker case study, will be used as a consistent thread running throughout the chapters in this part of the book. We regard the StockBroker scenario as a fair representation of the kind of service-oriented distributed system that you might encounter in the real world, and toward which the Distributed System Designers are targeted. In this context, an example based on the usual personal CD cataloging program simply wouldn't do justice to the tools.

If you refer to our summary of the visual designers previously discussed, you'll notice that the diagrams included items with names such as StockBroker, MarketMaker, DealingApp, and StockDatabase, which are the essential items from which the case study is composed. In the following chapters, you'll meet those figures again in the following contexts:

❑ In Chapter 2, you'll learn how to use Application Designer to sketch out the overall structure of the StockBroker example in terms of applications and the connections between them. You'll also learn how to generate and locally deploy implementation code directly from that design.

❑ In Chapter 3, we'll define a logical datacenter using Logical Datacenter Designer to host the case study example, independent of the application design devised in Chapter 2.

❑ Chapter 4 pulls the two together by showing how a combination of System Designer and Deployment Designer may be used to bind the applications from the application diagram onto the datacenter defined by the LDD.

❑ In Chapter 5, you'll revisit the implementation code from Chapter 2 as a vehicle for learning how Class Designer may be used to model the internal implementations of each application.

Though a single case study example is used for consistency, and to give credibility to the overall process, we will step outside of that example as necessary to demonstrate concepts and mechanisms that do not fit neatly into that scheme.

Designer Relationships and Team System Integration

Being presented with five new visual designers, each representing a different view of the overall system, you might be wondering how they all fit together. This section describes the important relationships between the designers, in the context of who uses which designer.

Traditional methods of teaching visual modeling often present a set of notations that individually represent one aspect — or view — of the system without describing how those various views are interrelated. You might learn, for example, that a UML statechart shows transitions between states triggered by events; and that a UML sequence diagram shows messages being passed between objects; but without further guidance, how do you deduce that the events in the statechart are related to the messages in the sequence diagram?

In Figure 1-8, we have used a Visio UML Activity Diagram for convenience to show how various roles within your software development organization would typically use the visual designers, including the artifacts that would be produced or consumed at each stage.

We've not used a Team System diagram because as yet there is no diagram suited to that purpose. That situation might change with future releases; in the meantime, we see a retained role for Visio in cases such as this.

You can read the diagram shown in Figure 1-8 in one of two ways:

❑ A *process flow diagram* (in bold) showing the activities performed by the various roles — that is, who uses which of the visual designers

❑ An *object flow diagram* (not bold) showing the objects produced and consumed by each activity — that is, the artifacts exchanged between the design tools

The following sections describe each of those perspectives in turn.

Process flow (roles and activities)

The role names that we have used are only indicative, because in reality the exact role names and the scopes of those roles will depend on the process that you follow: MSF for Agile Software Development, MSF for CMMI Process Improvement, the Unified Process, or whatever else you choose. Regardless of process, the order in which the designers are used and their interactions via artifacts are likely to be as shown in Figure 1-8.

Initially, the process flow branches into two parallel activities such that operations analysts may use Logical Datacenter Designer to define the logical infrastructure, and the application solution designer/architect may use Application Designer to define the overall shape of the system, completely independently.

Once the Application Design has been completed, the designer/developer can define the code structure for each application using Class Designer.

Once the Application Design and the Logical Datacenter Design have been completed, the application solution designer/architect can use System Designer to group applications into systems, and then use Deployment Designer to specify and evaluate how the application systems will be deployed on servers of the logical datacenter.

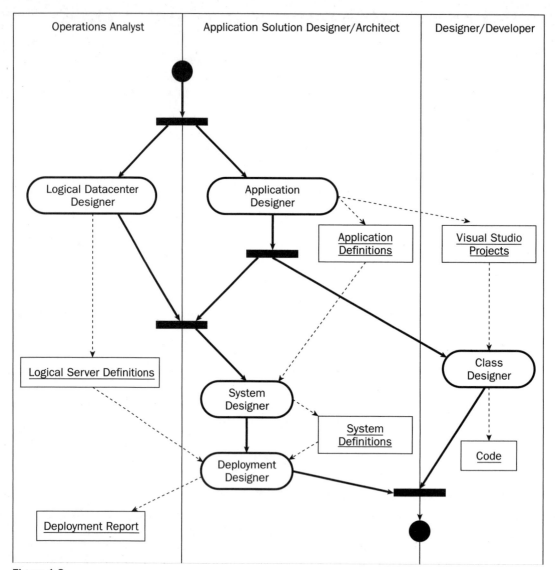

Figure 1-8

Object flow (artifacts)

The output from Application Designer is a set of Application Definitions expressed in SDM syntax and stored in an .ad file. If you generate projects, the SDM files that describe the applications are stored in the projects as .sdm files.

Class Designer may be used to refine and restructure the skeleton projects code and to define new code structures within those projects, resulting in final deliverable code.

System Designer accepts Application Definitions and enables you to compose systems as groups of applications, resulting in a set of System Definitions stored in an .sd file and again expressed in SDM syntax.

The output from Logical Datacenter Designer is a set of Logical Server Definitions expressed in SDM syntax and stored in an .ldd file.

Deployment Designer accepts System Definitions and enables you to map systems onto servers, resulting in a deployment map (as SDM) and a Deployment Report. The Deployment Report may be human-readable (as HTML) or machine-readable (as XML). The latter allows for automated deployment via scripting.

Settings and constraints

When you produce application definitions using Application Designer, you can specify settings and constraints for those applications, and these may be refined when you produce system definitions using System Designer. You can also specify settings and constraints when you produce logical server definitions using Logical Datacenter Designer.

What you need to understand is that the settings and constraints defined using Logical Datacenter Designer work in the opposite manner to those defined using Application Designer and System Designer. Application and System settings must be compatible with the constraints of the Logical Server that will host them. Logical server settings must be compatible with constraints of the applications and systems to be hosted.

By defining constraints on a server, the operations analyst is saying to the application architect, "If you want to host your application on this server of my logical datacenter, then you must satisfy these constraints via your settings." By defining constraints on an application or system, the application architect is saying to the operations analyst, "To host my application, you need to provide me with a server whose settings match the constraints of my application."

Source control and item tracking

Because the diagrams that you draw, and the application and server definitions that you produce, not to mention the project source code, are all stored in files, these may be checked in or out of the source control portion of the Team System and tracked as artifacts, in part to eliminate clashes during team working (i.e., two people trying to work on the same diagram at the same time) and in part to provide a versioned history of certain artifacts. For example, the operations team might want to baseline the logical datacenter diagram at various stages, by version controlling the .ldd files.

When controlling diagrams and files, you need to consider whether those items have an independent life cycle or whether they are intrinsically linked to specific Visual Studio solutions. For example, the .ldd files that define a logical datacenter are truly portable. Therefore, they may be included in any number of solutions or many can be contained within one solution. Conversely, the .ad files that define the application design are limited to one per solution, and tie into a specific solution once implemented. You can have as many class diagrams in a project as you like, but these are tied in absolutely to the source code that they visualize.

Introducing the System Definition Model

It's doubtful whether anyone would attempt to design an application these days without the aid of a modeling tool, using nothing but pencil and paper. That would be like writing this chapter using a type-writer, rather than Microsoft Word! Not so bad if you get it all right the first time, but almost impossible to rework in the light of new ideas or mistakes.

But all you need for visual design is a good drawing package, right? One that will let you redraw as many times as you like? No, because a good modeling tool is more than just a drawing package—it actually understands the design you're creating. For example, if you draw a line between a shape representing a web application and a shape representing a Web service, the tool will be able to deduce the following:

❑   These shapes represent a web application and a Web service, respectively.

❑   The web application references the web service, and communicates with it in some way.

This understanding of your design enables a modeling tool to add value to the Software Development Lifecycle (SDLC) by automating the validation of your design, the generation of code, the deployment of applications, and the production of documentation. To put it another way, the modeling tool must understand your design in order to make model-driven development and Software Factories a reality.

Meta-models

What distinguishes a good visual design (or modeling) tool from a simple drawing package? What is it that makes the tool understand your design? The meta-model.

Rational Rose has a true UML meta-model, accessible programmatically through the Rose Extensibility Interface (REI). Visio for Enterprise Architects ostensibly represents UML elements generically as picto-rial shapes with no true meta-model, but it is possible to dig a little deeper to discover a meta-model of sorts encoded within those shapes.

> Tony Loton's article "Build a Better Design Tool with Visio Automation" at www.asptoday.com/ Content.aspx?id=2051 demonstrates how to extract information from the Visio UML meta-model using VBA macros and .NET programs.

IBM-Rational XDE has a meta-model partially represented in the code itself, as this is continually syn-chronized with the model, and also in an internal form accessible programmatically in a limited way through exposed COM interfaces.

Externally, modeling tools represent their meta-models using a proprietary file format or an industry standard format such as XML Metadata Interchange (XMI).

SDM and the Team System meta-model

Because Class Designer synchronizes perfectly with classes in source code, on a one-for-one basis, the meta-model for this designer is in effect the programming language itself: Visual C#, Visual Basic, and Visual J# class diagram files carry very little additional metadata, a side-effect of which is that concepts which cannot be represented in code cannot be represented on diagrams. Therefore, whereas in Rational Rose class diagrams there is a diagrammatic distinction between associations and compositions, in Class Designer there is not.

With the Distributed System Designers, the situation is slightly different. They encode design information in XML conforming to the System Definition Model (SDM) schema. Try opening any of the application, logical datacenter, system, or deployment diagram files — with extensions `.ad`, `.ldd`, or `.sd` — using Windows NotePad, and you will see the following tag:

```
<SystemDefinitionModel xmlns:xsi="http://www.w3.org/2001/XMLSchema-instance"
xmlns:xsd="http://www.w3.org/2001/XMLSchema" Name="LogicalDataCenter2"
Version="1.0.0.0" Culture="en-US"
xmlns="http://schemas.microsoft.com/SystemDefinitionModel/2003/10">
```

As you progress through the software development life cycle, you will see that some of this information finds its way into separate files with an .sdm extension, again conforming to the same schema.

The good news is that you don't need to understand the SDM schema in order to use the modeling tools. For now, you just need to be aware that such a meta-model is important, and be mindful of the fact that everything you draw is described under-the-covers in the SDM format.

You can refer to Chapter 7 for more detailed information about the SDM.

What about UML?

As a professional software designer, chances are good that you have at least a passing acquaintance with UML. If so, you might want to know the following: How can you capitalize on your investment in UML skills when adopting the new tools? How can you capitalize on your investment in UML artifacts? What if you really want a fully integrated UML capability?

We'll attempt to answer those questions, but first a few words about Microsoft's position regarding UML.

According to the published modeling strategy, Microsoft is not against UML as such. They see UML as a valuable notation for sketching out ideas early in the software life cycle, a task for which you can continue to use Visio in the retained role that we discuss shortly. They also support third-party vendors, some of whom are building UML 2.0 tools for Visual Studio 2005. In addition, where it makes sense to do so, the new set of visual designers will use UML-like notations to ease the transition.

However, Microsoft believes that it can better bridge the gap between design and development (modeling and coding) by providing a set of visual designers — underpinned by DSLs — that enable you to work at a high level of abstraction while providing sufficiently high fidelity for the specific domain being modeled. In this respect, using stereotypes and other mechanisms to extend UML 2.0 would have been overly complex and still too generic.

Capitalizing on your investment in UML skills

A direct comparison between UML and the new visual designers is not valid, not to mention unfair. Microsoft has deliberately eschewed UML in favor of domain-specific languages that are highly tuned for specific tasks, and it's early days for this new vision, so we cannot expect a full end-to-end visual modeling capability in Visual Studio 2005.

However, just because a blow-by-blow comparison is not possible, you can still find similarities that offer opportunities to take advantage of your UML skills.

First, Application Designer enables you to model applications that communicate through endpoints in much the same way as you would use the UML component diagram to model components that communicate through interfaces. Therefore, if you're used to component diagrams, you'll take to application diagrams. In fact, we translated a UML component diagram into an equivalent VSTS application diagram early in this chapter.

Second, Logical Datacenter Design, in conjunction with Deployment Designer, enables you to model a logical infrastructure, and to show which applications will deploy to which servers, in much the same way as you would with a UML deployment diagram. If you're used to deployment diagrams, you'll take to logical datacenter diagrams.

When it comes to Class Designer, the similarities with UML class diagrams are apparent even from the first glance. The rendering of classes (as boxes with compartments) and interfaces (as lollipops) is much the same, as is some of the notation, such as the idea of "associations." In both cases, the purpose is exactly the same: to provide a one-for-one graphical representation of the underlying types in code. You just need to be aware of some terminology differences, such as "operations" and "attributes" in UML ("methods" and "fields" in Class Designer) and "generalization" in UML ("inheritance" in Class Designer).

We hope that those brief points have convinced you that all that UML training has not been a waste of time. You can take at least some of what you know and apply that knowledge when using the new tools.

You might have spotted that Visual Studio 2005 does not offer dynamic modeling capabilities that approximate UML's sequence and statechart diagrams. That situation might change over time as new visual designers are produced to support DSLs specifically for dynamic modeling. In the meantime, you can continue to use Visio (see the following section) or use strategically placed comments on diagrams to convey limited dynamic information.

Capitalizing on your investment in UML artifacts

If you've already designed .NET applications, chances are good that you have some existing models in Visio for Enterprise Architects or IBM-Rational XDE that you'd like to migrate into the Team Architect.

Any attempt to migrate your models as a whole will prove fruitless. Not only because of the lack of XMI exchange features, but also because a significant proportion of the model's contents simply cannot be represented in Visual Studio 2005 — specifically, the use cases and the dynamic diagrams. That need not be a problem if Visio is used in the retained role indicated below, as the best tool for recording analysis-level dynamic information that does not directly affect the generated code.

You can certainly import into Visual Studio 2005 the static information from your existing models' class diagrams, either by generating code from Visio into Visual Studio or by reverse engineering existing deployed applications — including Web services — into Team Architect representations. Thanks to code synchronization, you should be able to quickly build a class diagram and/or application diagram that reflects the Visio-generated or reverse-engineered code base.

Achieving a fully integrated UML capability

This chapter has offered some good reasons why you should not want this at all, and Microsoft can offer many more. However, you may still find yourself wanting to adopt Visual Studio 2005 Team System but unable to live without a UML capability.

One option is to wait for a third-party vendor to provide a UML add-in. Borland has announced an intention to develop UML 2.0 capabilities for the Visual Studio Team System.

The other option is to use Microsoft's DSL tools to grow your own UML designers. We don't recommend that unless you work for an organization that can absorb the development costs of such an initiative, or unless you think you can sell the end product! Having said that, growing your own design notations is considerably easier with the DSL tools than it ever used to be by other means. To prove it, we had a stab at devising a DSL to mirror the UML's activity diagram notation. The result is the Activity Designer shown in Figure 1-9.

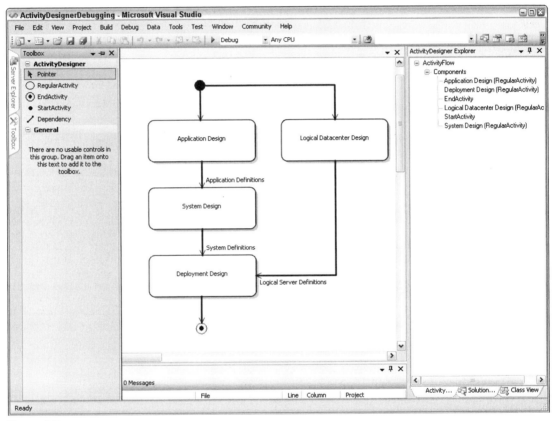

Figure 1-9

It turned out not to be production quality and it supported only a very limited subset of the notation, but when we tell you that it took only days — not weeks or months — to achieve something approaching the diagram we presented in Figure 1-8, you'll appreciate the potential offered by the DSL tools, even for UML stalwarts.

We could have just as easily used the DSL tools to build simulations of the other UML diagram types, such as use case diagrams and collaboration diagrams. And if all that sounds like too much hard work, you'll be pleased to hear that Microsoft's DSL Tools team has provided you with a starting point by bundling sample DSLs for UML use case diagrams, activity diagrams, and class diagrams with the DSL toolkit available at http://lab.msdn.microsoft.com/teamsystem/workshop/dsltools/default.aspx.

A retained role for Visio for Enterprise Architects

Previously, Microsoft bundled Visio for Enterprise Architects with Visual Studio .NET, as the preferred tool for modeling .NET applications. Microsoft will continue to bundle Visio for Enterprise Architects as a complementary tool providing a broad modeling capability, most useful in the early analysis stages, and compliant with UML 1.3.

Here's our advice on how you should continue to use Visio:

What we're *not* advocating is using Visio in combination with the new visual designers for detailed design, implementation, and deployment activities within Visual Studio. The Team Edition for Software Architects is clearly stronger here with its IDE integration, code synchronization, and bias toward creating deployable designs.

What we are advocating is using Visio for the up-front analysis and design activities that may well be undertaken by a business or systems analyst already familiar with working with Visio, rather than a designer/developer familiar with working with Visual Studio. In a nutshell, we propose using the right tool for each job, with little or no overlap, as follows:

❑ Use Visio for the initial analysis activities, which in any case may be performed by people — business analysts or solution designers — more used to working in Visio than in Visual Studio. We're talking about use cases and scenario realizations (e.g., as sequence diagrams) that are in any case not supported by the Team Architect.

❑ Use Visio to generate a one-time-only domain model as code. Because the Team Architect keeps code and model in perfect sync, any Visio-generated classes will be available immediately to your Visual Studio model.

❑ Use the Visual Studio 2005 Application Designer to sketch out the overall shape of the system in terms of interconnected applications and services, analogous to a UML component diagram.

❑ Use the Visual Studio 2005 Class Designer to evolve the Visio-generated domain model (if you have one) into a proper technical design model incorporating the .NET framework classes that are not supported well in Visio.

❑ Develop the code itself, with Visual Studio 2005 automatically ensuring synchronization between the code and the model, analogous to UML round-trip engineering.

❑ Use the Visual Studio Logical Datacenter Designer and Deployment Designer to specify the mappings and constraints for the deployed system, analogous to a UML deployment diagram.

Finally, if you need to do any limited dynamic modeling in support of the detailed designs, do this using strategically placed comments to convey the necessary information without reverting back to Visio.

> **The UML capabilities of Visio are fully documented in *Professional UML with Visual Studio.NET: Unmasking Visio for Enterprise Architects* (Wrox, 2003). This book is based on Visio for Enterprise Architects 2003, but for the retained role we suggest it should be equally applicable to the newer Visio for Enterprise Architects 2005.**

Summary

In this chapter we first set the scene by establishing the case for doing design, specifically visual design, at all. Because Microsoft's new vision for how visual design should work is somewhat different from the old-world view based around UML, we highlighted the three main pillars that support that vision — namely, model-driven development (MDD), domain-specific languages (DSL), and software factories.

Because the underlying technologies have also evolved over time, thereby influencing the kinds of design you'll produce, we also traced that evolution of concepts from the original object-oriented paradigm through components and distributed-components to the service-oriented architectures that represent the current wisdom. We did that for a very good reason — as a lead-in to the Application Designer, which lends itself to service-based application design.

Application Designer is the first in the "Whitehorse" set of Distributed System Designers, which also includes Logical Datacenter Designer, System Designer, and Deployment Designer. We introduced each one and showed the important relationships between them. We also introduced Class Designer, which is not strictly part of the same set but which is complementary — and similar — in use.

Because all of the designers apart from Class Designer are tied together by a meta-model in the form of the System Definition Model (SDM), we introduced the term SDM and invited you to refer to Chapter 7 for further information.

We'd be failing you if we had not paid some attention to the hitherto industry-standard notation for visual modeling (UML). Our aim was not to compare the UML approach with Microsoft's vision, but to help you make the transition by suggesting which skills and artifacts might be transferable. Because Visual Studio doesn't yet provide a complete end-to-end modeling solution, you learned how you might continue to use Visio for Enterprise Architects in the early phases of the software development life cycle.

Having introduced the new visual designers in this chapter, we now devote Chapters 2 through 5 to covering them in detail.

2

Application Modeling Using Application Designer

In this chapter, we introduce and demonstrate Application Designer, the Distributed System Designer that enables you to define and configure applications that provide and consume services in a service-oriented architecture. The application diagram that you create using this designer describes the overall structure of your service-based solution in terms of the following:

❑ The major applications, services, and databases

❑ The endpoints through which those applications communicate

❑ The connections between the endpoints, showing application interdependencies

First we'll introduce the most common toolbox items that are available for use in an application diagram. You construct this diagram, and other diagrams we will introduce in subsequent chapters, by dragging toolbox items (called *prototypes*) onto the diagram.

Next, we'll provide a design overview of the StockBroker scenario that is used throughout subsequent chapters. We'll present the complete application diagram up-front as a means of communicating the overall design of an application system, and we'll briefly compare that diagram to an equivalent UML diagram. You will then learn how to create the diagram yourself.

> *It's important to consider that the Application Definition is used to define the applications and that these are composed in one or more systems that describe the intended deployable systems. In some cases, the Application Definition and resultant System Definition will be similar, but the Application Definition is simply a dynamic view of the solution; it is the System Definition created with a Distributed System Designer that is the rigorously maintained and versioned design artifact that should be focused on as the target of the overall design activity.*

After that, you'll see how easy it is to take the application design right through to a set of executable implementations. This is one of the major differences between the Team Edition for Software Architects and equivalent UML tools. The former pays attention to implementation and deployment issues from the very start, and the latter allows for the design of systems in an abstract sense with little attention paid up-front to the final realization in software.

Finally, you'll learn about the additional features and characteristics of Application Designer, including model-code synchronization, reverse-engineering of existing solutions, the Settings and Constraints Editor, and printing.

This chapter provides a very practical and accessible demonstration of the Application Designer's capabilities in the context of the `StockBroker` example that we will use in upcoming chapters. Using this example, you will get the chance to learn by doing.

Application Designer Toolbox and Prototypes

Initially, the toolbox contains pre-configured reusable application and endpoint prototypes for common applications such as Web services, web applications, Windows applications, and external databases (see Figure 2-1). Your list might not be exactly the same as the one shown in Figure 2-1; and you can add new prototypes to the toolbox yourself, as you'll see later.

Figure 2-1

So that you're familiar with those prototypes as you encounter them, we'll provide a brief description of each one. Our descriptions are arranged into three sets: General Designer, Endpoints, and Applications to match the layout of the toolbox shown in Figure 2-1.

General Designer

The items in this section are not really "prototypes" at all, but "tools." We list them here as items within the same toolbox:

❑ **Connection:** The connection tool is used to connect applications with one another through their endpoints. You can also make connections by pressing the Alt key while the mouse is over an endpoint or application and dragging to connect.

❑ **Comment:** A comment is simply a free text item that you can place anywhere on a diagram to add clarification. You'll see later how you can use comments to add some limited dynamic information to a design.

You will have noticed one toolbox item that is listed in every section of the toolbox, yet we've not listed it as a bulleted point. That is the Pointer tool, which merely deselects whichever prototype or tool the mouse cursor is currently set to and reverts it back to a regular mouse cursor with which you can select items on the diagram.

Endpoints

Endpoints of the various types exist in two flavors: *provider* endpoints and *consumer* endpoints. The toolbox enables you to drag provider endpoints onto applications, to which you can connect clients via corresponding consumer endpoints (although you never add consumer endpoints directly; they are created for you when you connect an application to a provider endpoint):

❑ **WebServiceEndpoint:** This provider endpoint represents a connection point for a Web service that appears by default on an ASP.NETWebService application, an ExternalWebService application, or a BizTalkWebService application. Client connections are made through a corresponding WebServiceConsumerEndpoint.

❑ **WebContentEndpoint:** A WebContentEndpoint appears by default on an ASP.NETWebApplication and represents a connection point at which Web content — such as HTML files or ASP.NET pages — is exposed. Client connections are made through a corresponding WebContentConsumerEndpoint.

❑ **GenericEndpoint:** The GenericEndpoint provides a mechanism for connecting generic applications. An explanation of generic applications is provided in the following section.

Connections on the Application Definition represent the configuration of the applications in your solution. Once you have implemented an application with a consumer endpoint, changing the connection will change the corresponding configuration entry in the applications configuration file. Deleting a connection but not the consumer endpoint will blank that configuration entry, and reconnecting an endpoint will set it to the appropriate value. Configurability of endpoints is the key to making applications configurable on deployment. You should not create hard-coded connections between applications or databases. If you hard-code connections, by and large, these will not appear at all on the Application Definition.

Applications

This section of the toolbox contains a set of application prototypes that define specific application types. In addition to the predefined types detailed in the following list, you'll see later how you can define your own application prototypes and add them to the toolbox:

❑ **WindowsApplication:** Represents a Microsoft Windows application to which you can attach generic provider endpoints and all types of consumer endpoints. This application type can be implemented in the solution.

❑ **ASP.NETWebService:** Represents an ASP.NETWebApplication (see next) with a default WebServiceEndpoint. This application type can be implemented in a solution and can be adorned with additional Web service, web content, and generic provider endpoints plus all types of consumer endpoints.

❑ **ASP.NETWebApplication:** Represents an ASP.NETWebApplication with a default WebContentEndpoint. This application type can be implemented in the solution and can be adorned with additional Web service, web content, and generic provider endpoints plus all types of consumer endpoints.

❑ **OfficeApplication:** Represents a Microsoft Office application and supports Excel, Outlook, and Word templates. This application type supports generic provider endpoints and all types of consumer endpoints. It can be implemented in the solution.

❑ **ExternalWebService:** Represents an external Web service defined by a Web services Description Language (WSDL) file. It displays a default provider WebServiceEndpoint and may be adorned with additional generic provider endpoints plus all types of consumer endpoints. As it represents an existing external service, it is not implemented in the solution.

❑ **ExternalDatabase:** Represents an existing database to which clients can connect through the default database provider endpoint. You can add generic provider endpoints and all consumer endpoints apart from database consumer endpoints. As an external resource, this application type is not implemented in the solution.

❑ **BizTalkWebService:** Represents a BizTalk Web service with a default WebServiceEndpoint. It supports additional generic provider endpoints and all consumer endpoints apart from database consumer endpoints, and as an existing service it is not implemented in the solution.

❑ **GenericApplication:** Represents an unsupported or unspecified application. It has no default provider endpoints but supports generic provider endpoints in addition to all types of consumer endpoints. This application type is not implemented in the solution.

Designing the Distributed System

In this section, we first provide an overview of the StockBroker distributed application design, so that you know what the system is meant to do. We then show you how to draw the diagram representing the design by dragging application prototypes and endpoints onto the diagram. In doing that, we show off as many of the Application Designer features as possible via the running example.

The Design scenario

Figure 2-2 provides a pictorial representation of the distributed service-oriented system we'll be designing (the StockBroker system) in the format we'll be using to design it (as an application diagram), and drawn using Application Designer.

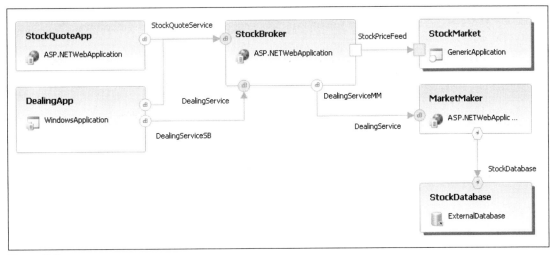

Figure 2-2

Our key application will be the StockBroker application, which exposes two ASP.NET Web services: the StockQuoteService (to report latest stock prices) and the DealingService (to enable stocks to be bought and sold).

Two end-user applications will be provided: a StockQuoteApp ASP.NETWebApplication that may be used for free over the Internet, and a more functional DealingApp WindowsApplication that may be downloaded by paid, registered users. StockQuoteApp will make use of the StockQuoteService, and DealingApp will make use of both the StockQuoteService and the DealingService.

The StockBroker application will take in latest stock prices via a direct feed from the stock market, using non-Microsoft technologies that we model as a GenericApplication. The StockBroker application will also make use of a third-party ASP.NET Web service provided by a *MarketMaker*, so as to place "buy" and "sell" deals.

> *Market Maker is a stock-broking term for a firm that stands ready to buy or sell a particular stock at a publicly quoted price, thereby creating a ready market in which buyers and sellers need not be matched on every deal.*

To complete our design from a full solution perspective, we're showing that the MarketMaker places deals into a StockDatabase.

Design characteristics and UML comparison

This design exhibits some interesting characteristics. First, it shows a layered service-oriented architecture whereby the services provided by the application-specific StockBroker application are supported by more generic business services provided by the MarketMaker application.

Second, while you could add some application-specific behavior into the StockBroker Dealing Service, you will certainly have noticed that it has the same name as a service provided by the

`MarketMaker`. Though the internal implementations will be different, we intend the interfaces (i.e., the list of supported operations) to be the same, which effectively makes the `MarketMaker` version of the `DealingService` definition an ideal prototype for the definition of the same service on the `StockBroker`.

Finally, this design combines several services into a single application, so you have a single `StockBroker` application exposing `StockQuote` and `Dealing` services, rather than separate StockQuote and Dealing applications. This is reminiscent of UML component modeling, which enables you to define a system in terms of components that expose multiple interfaces. This is shown in Figure 2-3, which is an equivalent UML component diagram (drawn using Visio) for the design shown in Figure 2-2.

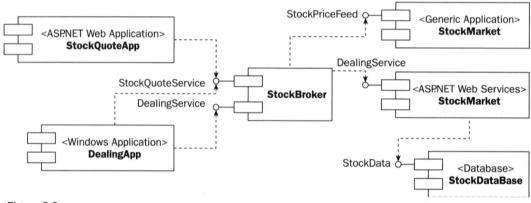

Figure 2-3

If you have a UML background, you will now see how key concepts translate between the two notations. An application in Application Designer is analogous to a component in UML, and an endpoint is equivalent to a UML interface.

You might also have noticed that in the UML representation, we have distinguished between the types of components using stereotypes such as <<ASP.NET Web service>> and <<ASP.NET Web Application>>. This is necessary because UML component notation is not a domain-specific language, whereas Application Designer notation is specific to the .NET Framework.

> *In Chapter 1 we indicated that a DSL for Web service design and assembly should contain concepts such as Web services, web methods, and protocols. Application Designer does this through the mechanism of prototypes, which is much more powerful than the UML stereotype mechanism.*

Reproducing the design using Application Designer

In this section, you'll see how you can set about drawing the diagram shown in Figure 2-2 yourself. As a starting point, you'll need a Distributed System Solution containing an application diagram. Choose File ➪ New Project from the menu and choose the Distributed System template, which you should find under Distributed System Solutions. We named our project/solution "`StockBrokerApplicationDesign`".

The new solution will include a file with the extension .ad to designate it as an application diagram — in this case, named `StockBrokerApplicationDesign.ad`. Remember that you are allowed only one such diagram in your solution.

The other way to begin using Application Designer is to add an application diagram to an existing solution. This will reverse engineer all application types supported by the Application Designer.

The diagram is constructed by dragging application prototypes from the toolbox that was shown in Figure 2-1. You'll need to drag five application prototypes from the toolbox onto the design surface:

- ❏ A GenericApplication prototype, to be named `StockMarket`
- ❏ An ASP.NETWebService prototype, to be named `MarketMaker`
- ❏ An ASP.NETWebService prototype, to be named `StockBroker`
- ❏ An ASP.NETWebApplication prototype, to be named `StockQuoteApp`
- ❏ A WindowsApplication prototype, to be named `DealingApp`

You can name each one by simply clicking its name label on the diagram, or by revealing its properties.

You should connect the applications together via their endpoints positioned around the edges of the application shapes. As you place each application onto the diagram, it will have one or more provider endpoints attached by default, and you can drag additional endpoints from the toolbox onto your applications as needed.

You need a total of four provider endpoints:

- ❏ A GenericEndpoint on the `StockMarket` application, named `StockPriceFeed`
- ❏ A WebServiceEndpoint on the `MarketMaker` application, named `DealingService`
- ❏ A WebServiceEndpoint on the `StockBroker` application, named `StockQuoteService`
- ❏ A WebServiceEndpoint on the `StockBroker` application, named `DealingService`

You can right-click any endpoint and choose Show Label from the context menu to reveal its name; then change the name by clicking the label or via its properties. You will notice the endpoints rendered as different icons according to their types; and as you complete the picture, you will see that provider endpoints are shown filled, whereas consumer (client) endpoints are shown hollow.

Now you need to connect these provider endpoints to their client applications in the configuration shown in Figure 2-2:

- ❏ Connect the `StockPriceFeed` endpoint provided by the `StockMarket` application to the `StockBroker` application.
- ❏ Connect the `DealingService` provided by the `MarketMaker` application to the `StockBroker` application. Rename the resulting consumer endpoint to `DealingServiceMM`.
- ❏ Connect the `StockQuoteService` endpoint provided by the `StockBroker` application to the `StockQuoteApp`.

❏ Connect the `StockQuotesService` endpoint and the `DealingService` endpoint, both provided by the `StockBroker` application, to the `DealingApp`. Rename the consumer end of the `DealingService` to `DealingServiceSB`.

In all cases, you can form a connection by moving the mouse over a provider endpoint, pressing the Alt key to see the mouse cursor change, and then moving the mouse cursor to an appropriate consumer endpoint or client application itself. Alternatively, you can use the Connection tool provided in the toolbox.

> *Note that these instructions encouraged you to name all of the provider endpoints first, and then connect them up to their client applications to create corresponding consumer endpoints. If you had connected the MarketMaker DealingService endpoint to the StockBroker application immediately after adding that provider endpoint, you would have created a consumer endpoint on the StockBroker with a default name of DealingService, which would prevent you from subsequently adding a DealingService provider endpoint to the StockBroker. Another way around that problem is to rename the StockBroker DealingService consumer endpoint to DealingServiceMM as soon as you place it—as we have in Figure 2-2.*

Your final result should match ours from Figure 2-2 except that at this point your diagram will not show the `StockDatabase`. That's because placing an ExternalDatabase on the diagram requires some additional effort beyond simply dragging the appropriate prototype from the toolbox, as we'll now describe.

Specifying database connection properties

We've included an ExternalDatabase in our design for illustration, but to keep it simple for you and to stick to the main focus of this chapter—which is not database modeling—we won't be taking it any further into implementation, so you can regard that as optional.

However, on the assumption that curiosity is bound to get the better of you, we should at least tell you what will happen if you drag an ExternalDatabase prototype onto the diagram and try to connect to it.

You can drag an ExternalDatabase prototype onto the diagram and rename it StockDatabase to match ours. You will see that the default provider endpoint for the database will also rename automatically to StockDatabase.

So far so good, until you attempt to connect the provider endpoint to the `MarketMaker` client application, which will require you to configure a connection.

A Connection Properties dialog box will appear, as shown in Figure 2-4. From here you must select a data provider (such as SQL Server or ODBC) and a set of connection properties (as shown).

> **Here's a tip: If you've installed Visual Studio 2005 with the SQL Server 2005 Express Edition, you can create an empty database to use in this dialog by right-clicking Data Connections and choosing Create New SQL Server Database. In the dialog that appears, enter *YourComputerName*\SQLEXPRESS as the server name and StockDatabase as the database name. Once the database has been created, you can use the same server name and database name in this dialog.**

Though the figure shows connection properties for a SQL Server database, your connection properties may well be for an Access, Oracle, or any other database depending on your provider selection.

In fact, this Connection Properties dialog is the same one that appears if you connect to a database from Server Explorer. In many cases, application prototypes you use are effectively pictorial routes into the existing Visual Studio wizards and features, and the same is true of ASP.NET websites and Web services.

Figure 2-4

The connection to the database will appear on the diagram after you confirm your settings. However, if you really don't want to configure your database connection at this point, you can simply cancel the Connection Properties dialog.

Keep in mind that this necessary restriction on not being able to visualize certain connections on the diagram until you have configured them also applies to external Web services (described later) and BizTalk services.

Application definitions do not contain hard-coded connection information, making it possible to specify the database connection during deployment.

Specifying endpoint details

By clicking one of the WebServiceEndpoints on the diagram, you can gain access to the Web service Details window, which is where you define the operations provided by the Web service. Figure 2-5 gives an indication of what you might see when you click the `DealingService` provider endpoint.

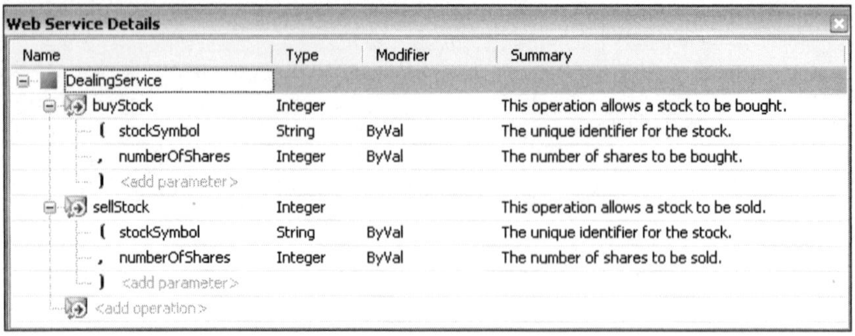

Figure 2-5

Of course, it won't look exactly like that for you because you've not yet added the operations. Do that now by clicking the <add operation> and <add parameter> indicators as appropriate, making sure that the result matches Figure 2-5. Everything you enter here will find its way into the implementation code, which in Visual C# will ultimately include the following method declarations:

```
public int buyStock(string stockSymbol, int numberOfShares)

public int sellStock(string stockSymbol, int numberOfShares)
```

The endpoint details for the MarketMaker DealingService should be made identical but don't rush in and do that just yet. For now, just add an operation to the StockQuoteService endpoint to match this Visual Basic signature:

```
Public Function getQuote(ByVal stockSymbol As System.String) As System.Double
```

We've shown the method signatures here in two different languages for good reason. The DealingService methods will be implemented in Visual C#, and the StockQuoteService methods will be implemented in Visual Basic. The operation and parameter types shown in the Web service Details window will reflect the implementation language, which by default will be Visual Basic for each application. You can enter Web service details using Visual Basic types at this stage yet still change the implementation language later to Visual C#.

Defining your own endpoint prototype

Our design allows for the two applications, Stockbroker and MarketMaker, to expose the same service — that is, the same service interface with different underlying implementations. As you've just entered the endpoint details for the DealingService endpoint located on the StockBroker application, it seems a shame to do all that work again for the benefit of the MarketMaker application, doesn't it?

Fortunately, you don't have to do all that work again because you can use the endpoint from one application as a prototype for an identical endpoint on another application. Right-click the DealingService endpoint and select Add to Toolbox from the context menu to launch the Add to Toolbox dialog box shown in Figure 2-6.

You can also copy and paste the application or copy the endpoint from one application to another. You don't need to create a toolbox entry to do this.

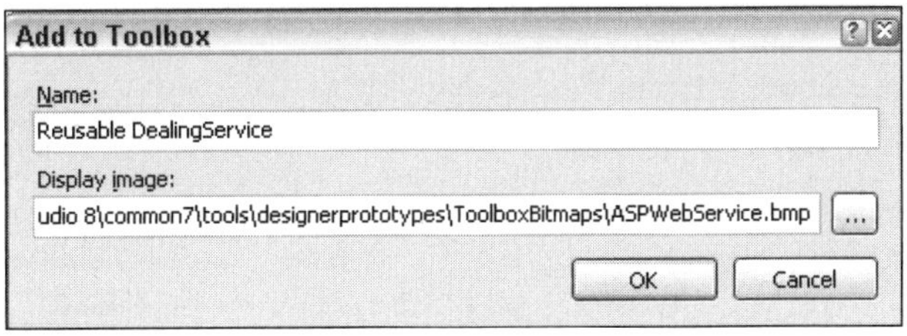

Figure 2-6

Upon completing that dialog box, you will be prompted to save the prototype into a file named `ReusableDealingService.adprototype`, alongside other files with the same extension representing the prototypes already included in the toolbox. Storing prototypes in files enables you to share them between Visual Studio users by distributing the files.

Once the file is saved, a new prototype — `ReusableDealingService` Endpoint — will be added automatically to the toolbox. Just drag it from the toolbox to the `MarketMaker` application on the diagram.

If you think about it, this mechanism is really very powerful. Not only does it facilitate the addition of the same service onto many applications, but it also allows you to define a common set of operations that all your services must implement. Imagine a `getServiceVersion` operation defined on a BusinessService prototype, to which you may add additional service-specific operations when the prototype is placed onto an application.

> *Tip:* **You can achieve something similar simply by copying and pasting (CTRL+C, CTRL+V) application and endpoints, though using that technique you would not have a prototype to use in other solutions or to share with other developers.**

Representing an existing service

In the initial discussion, we hinted that the `MarketMaker` application might actually be a third-party application accessible only via a Web service URL. In that case, you could represent it on the design service in the form of an ExternalWebService that you'll find in the toolbox.

After you add an external Web service to the diagram, the Add Web Reference dialog box would appear, as shown in Figure 2-7, enabling you to specify the URL supplied by the third party.

Later in this chapter, you'll implement and deploy a DealingService, which will provide you with a URL to insert into that dialog box as though it were supplied by a third party. That's what we (the authors) did, and you might like to do the same by revisiting this section after completing the chapter.

Alternatively, you could try this out by creating a Web service in a separate running instance of Visual Studio as you would when not using these design tools and reference that service. That's not such a crazy idea because a local "dummy" version of an external service could easily be replaced with the real one later. The URLs of external Web services are not hard-coded within the application and may be specified at deployment.

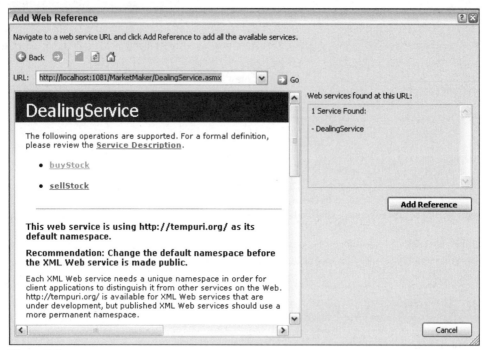

Figure 2-7

To simply try out this feature outside of the context of our running example, you could use the URL for any sample Web service that you happen to find on the web. At this point, we just want you to try out the feature; we won't be asking you to build on this result.

Suppose that one way or another you have added an external DealingService onto your diagram, and suppose you did that before adding the other applications to the diagram. Wouldn't that service have made a great prototype for the same-named service on your StockBroker application?

As an alternative to adding an ExternalWebService and then creating a prototype from it, you could instead simply right-click an application — such as the StockBroker application — and choose Create Web service Endpoints from WSDL from the pop-up menu to launch the Add Web Reference dialog (refer to Figure 2-7). The result would be the same except that there will be no separate ExternalWebService on the design surface and no additional new prototype in the toolbox.

These techniques are similar to what you might have seen referred to as *reverse engineering* in a UML tool, but in both cases you have reverse-engineered the interfaces only, not the internal implementations. In addition, with a Web service reverse-engineered onto an existing application (just described), you will be able to go ahead and implement the service, whereas for an ExternalWebService you won't. It is "external," after all, and all you've done is reference it.

One of the key principles behind the Common Object Request Broker (CORBA) standard for distributed systems, which preceded Web services, is the separation of interfaces from implementations. The idea is that vendors can cooperate on interfaces while competing on the quality-of-service of their implementations. Therefore, reverse-engineering the interface of a third-party component and then using its prototype to front a better quality implementation seems a very logical thing to do.

Implementing the Applications

One of the major strengths of Application Designer and the other Distributed System Designers is that they encourage the design of systems that can actually be implemented and deployed. In this section, we'll show you just how easy it is to move rapidly from a design to an implemented and locally deployed system.

> *UML tools in particular encourage the design of applications in an abstract sense, and from a user perspective, with little regard up-front for whether those applications can actually be built. We have witnessed too many projects where that has turned out to be the case. The use-case-driven analysis-first approach is fine up to a point, which is where we currently see a retained role for Visio alongside Team System, but once the handover has occurred from the business analysts to the designers/developers, it's time to take advantage of Team Edition for Architects' real strengths.*

It's precisely because of the Distributed System Designers' strengths in this area that we'll be devoting plenty of attention to coding, in what you might have expected to be purely a "design" chapter. Don't worry as it won't be too taxing and we won't be asking you to work with complex database schemas, XML files, and the like. You'll do just enough to get the design up and running to the point that you could credibly take it forward.

Before you implement the design, we'll invite you to set the implementation languages for the various applications by clicking each one in turn and selecting the relevant language in the Properties window:

❑ StockQuoteApp should be set to Visual C#.

❑ DealingApp should be set to Visual Basic.

❑ StockBroker should be set to Visual Basic.

❑ MarketMaker should be set to Visual C#.

Of course, you're free to choose whatever languages you wish, but the subsequent discussion of the generated code will make more sense if you stick to our choices.

> **Provided files:** The accompanying file StockBrokerApplicationDesign.zip includes a Visual Studio 2005 solution containing the application diagram for our example, so you have the option of performing the following implementation steps using our diagram if you have not successfully created your own. A separate file, StockBroker ApplicationDesignImplemented.zip, contains the full solution as we implemented it, so wherever we ask you to enter code in the following sections, you could simply copy the code from the files in that solution.

To implement an entire design, you can simply right-click an empty portion of the diagram and choose Implement All Applications...from the context menu. The phrase "empty portion of the diagram" is important because if you click a specific application, you will implement just that one.

> You cannot reverse the process that generates project files for applications, which means you cannot subsequently modify some implementation properties such as the language. It's always a good idea to save the application diagram (i.e., Stock BrokerApplicationDesign.ad) as soon as you've drawn it and before you implement it, so that you can roll back and start again.

A Confirm Application Implementation dialog box will appear showing the applications to be implemented. Clicking OK will cause Visual Studio to begin generating code and creating deployment websites. At the end of this process, you will see several new projects in the Solution Explorer, one for each implementable application.

> By default, Web service applications will be deployed as file-based Web services that run in the ASP.NET Development Server, rather than being deployed in full to IIS. This can be very convenient during development, but if you want to deploy properly to IIS, then you can do this by selecting the application on the application diagram and changing its Project property (in the Implementation section) to `http://localhost/WebServiceName`.

The StockMarket application will not have an implementation in the Solution Explorer because it's a generic application; and as mentioned earlier, generic applications cannot be implemented.

If you had represented the MarketMaker third-party application as an ExternalWebService (we told you how in the "Representing an existing service" section earlier in this chapter), it too would not have been implemented; but as there was no such service in existence already, we modeled it as a conventional ASP.NETWebService to demonstrate the service layering. This means it will have an implementation project. Obviously, the database will not have been generated as an implementation project, but it will be represented as a connection in its client application.

You can represent applications that are referenced by other applications but that are not implemented in your solution nor planned for deployment as part of any application systems that you design and compose from applications in the solution. Though these applications are called *external* because they are technically external to a system in the context of implementation and deployment, you can still include these applications as part of a system design. Including external applications in a system makes it possible for you to validate communication pathways to and from these applications when you define and validate deployment for the system. When the system is eventually deployed, references to external applications must be resolved with the actual deployment location of these applications. Don't underestimate what has happened here. While your UML tool may well be able to generate code skeletons from a design, would you really expect it to deploy new websites directly into IIS in a form that you can run with no additional configuration and virtually no extra coding?

A note about SDM files

In the discussions that follow, we'll invite you to examine some of the implementation files that have been generated, and to modify those files in order to complete the implementations. In addition to those files, a number of System Definition Model (.sdm) files may also have been created. We won't discuss those files in this chapter as they are not crucial to the implementation of our design, but you will learn about the structure and purpose of SDM files in Chapter 7.

All you need to know right now is that prior to implementation, the application diagram (.ad) file itself stores the definitions of the applications. During implementation, an additional SDM file will have been generated for each application to contain the definitions. These files should not be modified except through Application Designer.

The MarketMaker implementation

The MarketMaker project will appear in Solution Explorer under location C:\...\MarketMaker\ (for file-based deployment) or http://localhost/MarketMaker (for IIS deployment), and will contain several automatically generated files. The important files for our discussion are as follows:

```
App_Code/
    DealingService.cs
DealingService.asmx
```

The file DealingService.cs contains the implementation code for the service of that name exposed by the MarketMaker application. You will modify this file.

The file DealingService.asmx defines the DealingService Web service that you added as a provider endpoint. You won't modify this file, but you will use it to test the service, and it's worth noting its content, which hooks up to the DealingService.cs code-behind file:

```
<%@ webservice class="MarketMaker.DealingService" language="c#"
codebehind="~/App_Code/DealingService.cs" %>
```

Modifications to DealingService.cs

The following listing shows the code that was generated for the MarketMaker.cs file. Notice how the Summary texts that we entered into the Web service Details window have found their way into comments in code. All of this code was generated automatically, except for the highlighted lines. You should add those manually to provide basic implementations of the web methods:

```csharp
namespace MarketMaker
{
    [System.Web.Services.WebServiceBinding(Name = "DealingService", ConformsTo =
System.Web.Services.WsiProfiles.BasicProfile1_1, EmitConformanceClaims = true),
System.Web.Services.Protocols.SoapDocumentService()]
    public class DealingService : System.Web.Services.WebService
    {
        /// <summary>
        /// This operation allows a stock to be bought.
        /// </summary>
        /// <param name="stockSymbol">The unique identifier for the stock.</param>
        /// <param name="numberOfShares">The number of shares to be bought.</param>
        [System.Web.Services.WebMethod(),
System.Web.Services.Protocols.SoapDocumentMethod(Binding = "DealingService")]
        public int buyStock(string stockSymbol, int numberOfShares)
        {

            System.Random rnd = new System.Random(numberOfShares);
            if (rnd.NextDouble() > 0.5) return numberOfShares;
            else return 0;
```

```
        }

        /// <summary>
        /// This operation allows a stock to be sold.
        /// </summary>
        /// <param name="stockSymbol">The unique identifier for the stock.</param>
        /// <param name="numberOfShares">The number of shares to be sold.</param>
        [System.Web.Services.WebMethod(),
    System.Web.Services.Protocols.SoapDocumentMethod(Binding = "DealingService")]
        public int sellStock(string stockSymbol, int numberOfShares)
        {
            System.Random rnd = new System.Random(numberOfShares);
            if (rnd.NextDouble() > 0.5) return numberOfShares;
            else return 0;

        }
      }
    }
```

If you really did want to place stock deals into a database, that is where your database access code would go. To keep it simple, you're just returning the number of shares sold (if the deal went ahead) or 0 (if it didn't) on a random basis. Client applications need not know that you've used such a stubbed-out implementation.

Test-running the MarketMaker application

Once you have made the code modifications highlighted in the preceding section, you are in a position to take the MarketMaker application — specifically, its DealingService Web service — for a test drive. Just right-click the `DealingService.asmx` file, choose View in Browser, and Internet Explorer will open at the URL for the service.

You'll see options for the two operations. If you choose buyStock, you will then be able to fill in the form shown in Figure 2-8.

Remember that the buyStock operation returns the number of shares actually bought, or 0 if the deal could not be processed. Given the input data of stockSymbol=MSFT, and numberOfShares=12, the response in XML is as follows:

```
<?xml version="1.0" encoding="utf-8" ?>
<short xmlns="http://tempuri.org/">12</short>
```

If you enter 5 as the numberOfShares, then you get the following response, demonstrating how we've simulated failed deals using the random number generator:

```
<?xml version="1.0" encoding="utf-8" ?>
<short xmlns="http://tempuri.org/">0</short>
```

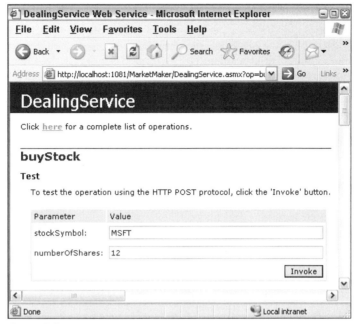

Figure 2-8

We think that one of the great features of Web services, compared with other distributed technologies, is that you can test them in this way independently and irrespective of whether you have yet coded their clients.

The StockBroker implementation

The MarketMaker project will appear in the Solution Explorer under location C:\...\StockBroker\ (for file-based deployment) or URL http://localhost/StockBroker (for IIS deployment) and will contain several automatically generated files. The important ones for our discussion are as follows:

```
App_Code/
  DealingService.vb
  StockQuoteService.vb
DealingService.asmx
StockQuoteService.asmx
```

Between them, the files DealingService.asmx and StockQuoteService.asmx contain the following Web service definitions with links to the code-behind file:

```
<%@ webservice class="StockBroker.DealingService" language="vb"
codebehind="~/App_Code/DealingService.vb" %>

<%@ webservice class="StockBroker.StockQuoteService" language="vb"
codebehind="~/App_Code/StockQuoteService.vb" %>
```

StockQuoteService.vb

This code simulates the action of the getQuote operation by simply returning a random number between 0 and 100 as the latest stock price, regardless of the stockSymbol passed in. Remember that you're implementing this method purely to test the interconnectedness of the overall design, not to create a fully functional stockbroking system.

```vb
Namespace StockBroker

  <System.Web.Services.WebServiceBinding(Name:="StockQuoteService",
ConformsTo:=System.Web.Services.WsiProfiles.BasicProfile1_1,
EmitConformanceClaims:=True)> _
  <System.Web.Services.Protocols.SoapDocumentService()> _
  Public Class StockQuoteService
    Inherits System.Web.Services.WebService

    ''' <summary>
    ''' This operation returns the current share price for a given stock.
    ''' </summary>
    ''' <param name="stockSymbol">The unique identifier for the stock.</param>
    <System.Web.Services.WebMethod()> _

<System.Web.Services.Protocols.SoapDocumentMethod(Binding:="StockQuoteService")> _
    Public Function getQuote(ByVal stockSymbol As String) As Double

        Dim randomPrice As Integer
        randomPrice = Rnd() * 10000
        Return randomPrice / 100

    End Function
  End Class

End Namespace
```

DealingService.vb

In the code that follows, the buyStock and sellStock operations are implemented by delegating to the same-named services of the (third-party) MarketMaker application. The remote services are accessed via local Web service proxies that for our purposes are identical but which hide the technical details of sending SOAP messages to those services.

A proxy is a client-side representation of a remote object, component, or service. A method invoked on a local proxy triggers the same method to be invoked on the remote service, with the details of how that happens — for example, by sending a SOAP message — being hidden within the proxy itself.

```vb
Namespace StockBroker

  <System.Web.Services.WebServiceBinding(Name:="DealingService",
ConformsTo:=System.Web.Services.WsiProfiles.BasicProfile1_1,
EmitConformanceClaims:=True)> _
  <System.Web.Services.Protocols.SoapDocumentService()> _
  Public Class DealingService
    Inherits System.Web.Services.WebService

    ''' <summary>
```

```
''' This operation allows a stock to be bought.
''' </summary>
''' <param name="stockSymbol">The unique identifier for the stock.</param>
''' <param name="numberOfShares">The number of shares to be bought.</param>
<System.Web.Services.WebMethod()> _
    <System.Web.Services.Protocols.SoapDocumentMethod
(Binding:="DealingService")> _
    Public Function buyStock(ByVal stockSymbol As String, ByVal numberOfShares As
Integer) As Integer

    Dim MarketMakerDealingService As New
StockBroker.WebServiceProxies.DealingService()
    MarketMakerDealingService.UseDefaultCredentials = True
    Return MarketMakerDealingService.buyStock(stockSymbol, numberOfShares)

End Function

''' <summary>
''' This operation allows a stock to be sold.
''' </summary>
''' <param name="stockSymbol">The unique identifier for the stock.</param>
''' <param name="numberOfShares">The number of shares to be sold.</param>
<System.Web.Services.WebMethod()> _
    <System.Web.Services.Protocols.SoapDocumentMethod
(Binding:="DealingService")> _
    Public Function sellStock(ByVal stockSymbol As String, ByVal numberOfShares As
Integer) As Integer

    Dim MarketMakerDealingService As New
StockBroker.WebServiceProxies.DealingService()
    MarketMakerDealingService.UseDefaultCredentials = True
    Return MarketMakerDealingService.sellStock(stockSymbol, numberOfShares)

    End Function
  End Class

End Namespace
```

> **The code line** `MarketMakerDealingService.UseDefaultCredentials = True` **is included to overcome a problem with accessing remote Web services in a file-based deployment. If you deploy properly to IIS (we told you how), then that code will not be required.**

With that code in place, you're now ready to test the `StockBroker` application.

Test-running the StockBroker application

Test-running the DealingService on this application will produce the same results as when you tested the same service on the MarketMaker application; but as you test this service yourself, bear in mind that something quite different is happening under the covers: a Web service delegating to another Web service.

One of the guiding principles of a Service Oriented Architecture (SOA) is that services may be designed in layers, with application-specific services calling on generic business services and/or technology-bound services.

The StockQuoteService is new in this application, and Figure 2-9 shows it in action.

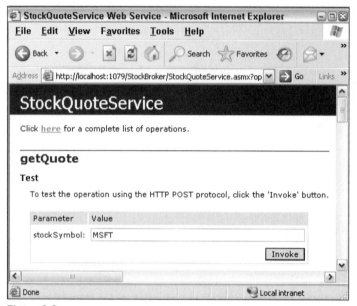

Figure 2-9

For stockSymbol MSFT (Microsoft), the resulting XML response is as follows:

```
<?xml version="1.0" encoding="utf-8" ?>
<double xmlns="http://tempuri.org/">70.55</double>
```

Each time you run it, the result will be different because you implemented this method with Rnd() to simulate the volatility of share prices. (Of course, it's only a fictional share price, so don't go investing on the back of this information!)

That's the last of the Web services that we designed. You have tested them independently, and if you're happy that they're all running correctly, you can now proceed to look at the end-client applications shown on the application design diagram.

The StockQuoteApp implementation

The StockQuoteApp project will appear in the Solution Explorer under location C:\...\StockQuoteApp\ (for file-based deployment) or URL http://localhost/StockQuoteApp (for IIS deployment), and will contain several automatically generated files, of which two are important for our discussion: Default.aspx (the main web page for the application) and Default.aspx.cs (the code-behind file).

Default.aspx

The following listing shows the code that will have been generated for the `Default.aspx` file, with the additions you should make highlighted:

```
<%@ Page Language="C#" AutoEventWireup="true" CodeFile="Default.aspx.cs"
Inherits="_Default" %>

<!DOCTYPE html PUBLIC "-//W3C//DTD XHTML 1.1//EN"
"http://www.w3.org/TR/xhtml11/DTD/xhtml11.dtd">

<html xmlns="http://www.w3.org/1999/xhtml" >
<head runat="server">
    <title>Untitled Page</title>
</head>
<body>
  <form id="form1" runat="server">
  <div>

    <asp:Label ID="Label1" Runat="server" Text="Enter Stock Symbol"></asp:Label>
    <asp:TextBox ID="StockSymbolInput" Runat="server"></asp:TextBox>
    <asp:Button ID="QuoteButton" Runat="server" Text="Get Quote"
OnClick="QuoteButton_Click" />
    <br />
    <asp:Label ID="Label2" Runat="server" Text="Latest Stock Price"></asp:Label>
    <asp:TextBox ID="StockPriceOutput" Runat="server"></asp:TextBox>

  </div>
  </form>
</body>
</html>
```

That code defines a user interface comprising two labels, two text boxes, and a button. Actually, we didn't write the code by hand but generated that too from a UI design drawn using the web forms designer. You can design the form (which you'll see soon) or enter the preceding code as you see fit.

Default.aspx.cs

The code-behind file handles the button press, as shown in the following code. Again, the code you should enter is shown highlighted:

```
public partial class _Default : System.Web.UI.Page
{
  protected void QuoteButton_Click(object sender, EventArgs e)
  {

    StockQuoteApp.WebServiceProxies.StockQuoteService QuoteService = new
        StockQuoteApp.WebServiceProxies.StockQuoteService();
    QuoteService.UseDefaultCredentials = true;
    StockPriceOutput.Text =
        QuoteService.getQuote(StockSymbolInput.Text).ToString();

  }
}
```

A proxy to the `StockBroker`'s StockQuoteService is created and its getQuote operation code invoked with the text supplied by the user in the StockSymbolInput text box; the result is displayed in the StockPriceOutput text box.

Test-running the StockQuoteApp web application

The functionality provided by the StockQuoteApp is pretty much identical to that provided by the auto-generated test form for the StockQuoteService, except that this time it's a proper client ASP.NET web application that you have designed and implemented.

Figure 2-10 shows what will happen if you enter a stock symbol and press the Get Quote button. Of course, the latest stock price will be different each time you run it.

Figure 2-10

Note that we have now completed the client-server pair of the StockQuoteApp ASP.NET web application and the `StockBroker` Web service.

The DealingApp implementation

As a Windows application, the DealingApp will be represented as a folder in the Solution Explorer, with generated files stored locally in the solution directory, so there will be no URL associated with this project. Only one file in this project requires further investigation, `DealingForm.vb`, which represents the application's main Windows Form.

We renamed this form from its auto-generated name to make it more meaningful.

To complete the implementation of this application you'll need to open the file in design view and use the Windows Form designer to come up with something like what is shown in Figure 2-11.

Figure 2-11

The first text box (named StockSymbolInput) enables you to enter a stock symbol for which the user can obtain the latest price by pressing the button marked Get Latest Price (and named QuoteButton). The result is to be displayed in the second text box, named StockQuoteOutput.

Once the user has obtained the latest stock price, he or she can enter a number of shares into the third text box (named QuantityInput) and initiate a deal by pressing the Buy button (named BuyButton) or the Sell button (named SellButton).

Once you've designed the form, you'll need to add some code behind each of the buttons, which you can do easily by double-clicking each button in Design view.

DealingForm.vb code

The code behind each of the buttons should be as follows (note that in each case, one of the operations on one of the Web services of the StockBroker application is invoked):

```
Public Class DealingForm

    Private Sub QuoteButton_Click(ByVal sender As System.Object, ByVal e As
System.EventArgs) Handles QuoteButton.Click

        Dim QuoteService As New DealingApp.StockQuoteService.StockQuoteService
        StockQuoteOutput.Text = QuoteService.getQuote(StockSymbolInput.Text)

    End Sub

    Private Sub BuyButton_Click(ByVal sender As System.Object, ByVal e As
System.EventArgs) Handles BuyButton.Click

        Dim DealingService As New DealingApp.DealingService.DealingService
        MsgBox(DealingService.buyStock(StockSymbolInput.Text, QuantityInput.Text), ,
"Number of Shares Bought")

    End Sub

    Private Sub SellButton_Click(ByVal sender As System.Object, ByVal e As
System.EventArgs) Handles SellButton.Click

        Dim DealingService As New DealingApp.DealingService.DealingService
        MsgBox(DealingService.sellStock(StockSymbolInput.Text, QuantityInput.Text), ,
"Number of Shares Sold")

    End Sub
End Class
```

For the Buy and Sell buttons, the result is not written to an output text box but displayed in a pop-up message box with the title "Number of Shares Bought" or "Number of Shares Sold."

Test-running the DealingApp Windows application

For this application, we've already shown you what happens when it is run. Figure 2-11 showed not only the layout of the form, but also the data used to test the stock price functionality. When the user enters a number of shares — in this case, 100 — the outcome will be a message box with the following information:

```
Number of Shares Bought: 100
```

or

```
Number of Shares Sold: 100
```

That completes the implementation of the second client application — this time a Windows application that demonstrates the end-to-end connectivity of the design. The application invokes an application-specific Web service, which delegates to a (third-party) business service, which in turn would write to the database if we had set one up.

Application Designer Additional Features

Having spent some time looking at the important implementation features, we'll round off this chapter by returning to the core design features of Application Designer. We'll tie up a few loose ends by covering some of the additional capabilities that did not fit neatly into our running example.

Model and code synchronization

One of the key features of the Distributed System Designers that distinguishes them from some precursor modeling tools such as Visio for Enterprise Architects and Rational Rose is its tight model and code synchronization. This ensures that any changes made in the code can be reflected in the design diagrams, and vice-versa, without any further code or model mitigation, thus breaking down the artificial barrier between design and coding. You'll look at this feature in more detail when considering Class Designer, but the principle can be demonstrated quickly here in the context of Application Designer.

Suppose you decide that the sellStock and buyStock methods provided by your dealing services are not sufficient because they return only the number of shares bought or sold. You'd now like those methods to return the price at which the shares were dealt and maybe the exact time that the deal was transacted. You could conceive two new classes — StockPurchase and StockSale — to encapsulate these details, and change the signatures of the two DealingService methods from

```
public int sellStock(string stockSymbol, int numberOfShares)
public int buyStock(string stockSymbol, int numberOfShares)
```

to

```
public StockSale sellStock(string stockSymbol, int numberOfShares)
public StockPurchase buyStock(string stockSymbol, int numberOfShares)
```

Make that change in code in the file DealingService.cs. Then click the MarketMaker's DealingService endpoint on the diagram to determine whether the changes are reflected immediately in the Web service Details window.

Reverse engineering existing solutions

This chapter has focused on creating an application design from scratch, with the possible incorporation of some existing (external) Web services and databases. That is the approach you would usually take.

Of course, we all know that it doesn't always work like that. You may well encounter a system that has been implemented without a design, at least without a formal documented design based on Team Edition for Architects notations or UML. In addition, you may well be charged with documenting the design of that system after the fact. Furthermore, even for a so-called "new development," you might find that in fact this is a modification to an existing deployed system, in which case you will need a representation of the existing applications and services before you start.

To address these problems, Application Designer enables you to reverse engineer existing solutions as follows:

❑ Add an application diagram to an existing solution, in which case application definitions will appear automatically on the diagram.

❑ Add a suitable existing project or website to a Distributed System Solution — that is, a solution that has an application diagram.

Thanks to synchronization between the model, the code, and the other solution items, other changes you make will also be reflected in the application diagram, such as adding a web reference in the Solution Explorer, or adding a database connection entry in the configuration file.

Settings and Constraints Editor

By right-clicking any application in Application Designer and choosing Settings and Constraints, you launch the Settings and Constraints Editor. Do that now, or look ahead to Figure 2-12 to see what the Settings and Constraints Editor looks like.

We'll cover that in more detail in the next two chapters, where you'll learn how constraints in one layer are created against settings in another layer. For example, constraints can be set from the application layer (Application Designer, this chapter) against settings in the hosting layer (Logical Datacenter Designer, next chapter). The idea is that the infrastructure architect can constrain the application layer while allowing the application architect to request a set of features in the target deployment environment. Ultimately, the application design will be validated against the constraints and topology defined for the logical datacenter.

In Figure 2-12, we have launched the Settings and Constraints Editor for the StockBroker application, which by default is constrained to being hosted on an IIS Web Server. If that application is subsequently bound to a logical server (see Chapter 4) that does not have the appropriate IIS Web Server settings, then the constraint will not be satisfied, and a warning will occur on validation, indicating that the application cannot be successfully deployed to that server.

Furthermore, the settings and constraints information specified at the application level may be redefined or overridden in System Designer, prior to being evaluated for deployment; as you'll learn in Chapter 4.

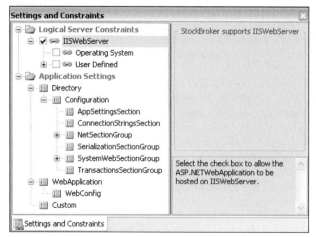

Figure 2-12

Printing and copying diagrams

You can print your application diagram by selecting the File ➪ Print menu option, which seems to work quite well. Be sure to check the page setup properties (by choosing File ➪ Page Setup) first, as by default these might be set to print your diagram across several pages.

The other obvious way to reproduce your diagram as hardcopy is to copy the shapes from the design surface and paste them into Microsoft Word. Just press Ctrl+A (select all) followed by Ctrl+C (copy) in Visual Studio, and then Ctrl+V (paste) in Word.

> *You can also use the right menu option, Copy Image, which will make the copy a vector image. This can be pasted into most graphics programs, Microsoft Word, and so on. This results in higher quality, as it can be rescaled and manipulated without loss of quality.*

This enables you to include the diagram in a design document, and you could use the same technique to paste the diagram into Visio — as long as you bear in mind that all you would be pasting is a bitmap, not a Visio interpretation of the application details.

> *In Chapter 5, you will discover that Class Designer allows class diagrams to be exported as image files. Unfortunately, this feature is currently not supported by Application Designer.*

Application Designer Limitations and Workarounds

While Application Designer is an excellent tool for visually modeling connected service-based applications, and is one of the most promising of the new batch of visual designers to come out of Microsoft, it's not yet perfect. What it does, it does well, but there are a couple of areas in which we would like it to do more.

Modeling .NET Remoting and DCOM applications

In Chapter 1, we described the evolution of distributed computing concepts from object-oriented programming through component-based and distributed-component-based development to Web services and the service-oriented architecture.

In focusing version one of Application Designer on service-oriented designs, Microsoft did not provide a way for designers and developers working with precursor (but not yet obsolete) distributed technologies such as DCOM and .NET Remoting. You won't find prototypes for .NET Remoting applications or DCOM applications in the Application Designer toolbox.

Currently, you have three (to four) options: throw away your existing distributed design in favor of Web services (a great idea, but not practical), use the GenericApplication and GenericEndpoint prototypes to model the other distributed technologies (not ideal, but simple and useful for documentation purposes), or use the SDM SDK to model your own remoting consumer and provider endpoints (for the experts). None of these options results in support for generated code and reverse engineering. Of course, a fourth option is to maintain your unsupported (Visio) models in parallel with Application Designer.

If you choose the second option — using the GenericApplication and GenericEndpoint prototypes — then you can take advantage of the features provided by the Settings and Constraints Editor, plus the Add to Toolbox functionality. For example, you could place a GenericEndpoint on an application diagram, navigate to Endpoint Hosting Constraints ➪ GenericServerEndpoint ➪ User Defined, and set the communications protocol to the value Remoting, as shown in Figure 2-13.

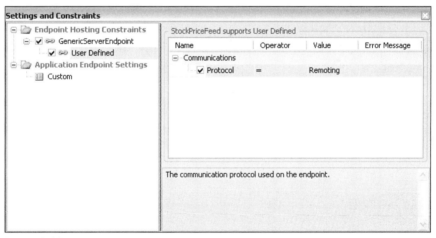

Figure 2-13

You could then right-click the endpoint on your diagram and select Add to Toolbox to create a RemotingEndpoint prototype.

The situation is bound to change over time as Microsoft enables richer modeling support for distributed system design in the area of Indigo — code name for a unified programming model and runtime for building service-oriented applications with managed code, business process orchestration, and data. It's always worth checking to see whether Microsoft has made additional types available to represent other kinds of applications and endpoints before inventing your own.

Modeling Windows services and console applications

For some other application types—for example, a windows service—the situation is rather different from that just described. While Application Designer appears not to support this application type, you can, in fact, add a Windows application from the toolbox and change its Template property in the Property window to Windows Service. You won't see any difference on the diagram but the correct project type will be created when the application is implemented.

The same applies to console applications. Just change the Template property from Windows Application to Console Application.

Dynamic Modeling

One of the limitations of the Team Architect visual designers as they stand is that they do not support dynamic modeling, which in UML terms means sequence diagrams and collaboration diagrams. Though true dynamic modeling belongs for the time being in the realm of Visio, it might be useful and informative for some limited dynamic information to be indicated on our diagrams. (*Note*: Microsoft or third parties may provide support for dynamic modeling [e.g., sequence diagrams] via the DSL tool in the near future.)

You can take advantage of the fact that a UML collaboration diagram is essentially a static diagram—like a class diagram or component diagram—by using numbered labels showing the sequence of interactions in a typical scenario. In Figure 2-14, we've used Comments (from the toolbox) as sequence labels for a "Buy Stock" scenario.

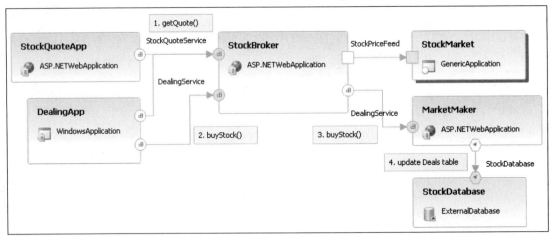

Figure 2-14

The sequence of interactions for this scenario, now reflected in the diagram, is as follows:

1. The DealingApp invokes the getQuote operation on the StockBroker StockQuoteService.
2. The DealingApp invokes the buyStock operation on the StockBroker DealingService.
3. The StockBroker delegates the request to the buyStock operation on the MarketMaker DealingService.

4. The MarketMaker updates the Deals table of StockDatabase.

For any serious dynamic modeling, such as realizing full use cases as object interactions, we recommend that you use Visio, but this technique is a feasible workaround for showing limited dynamic behavior without switching tools.

The only real restriction on our workaround is the fact that you are limited to just one application diagram per solution, so in effect you can model only one scenario at a time. To overcome that problem, you might consider this idea again when you read about the System Designer in Chapter 4, because you can have as many system diagrams as you like and you could devise a set of diagrams purely to show how applications interact in various scenarios.

In Chapter 5, you'll revisit the same technique again using class diagrams, the benefit there being the fact that you can have as many class diagrams as you like.

Summary

In this chapter we've shown what a typical service-oriented application design will look like when drawn using Application Designer. You learned how to draw this design yourself by placing application prototypes, endpoints, and connections onto the design diagram. In doing so, you also learned how to perform some useful tasks:

❑ How to reference an external database

❑ How to reverse engineer an external Web service

❑ How to add your own reusable prototype to the toolbox

Our design made use of the most common application prototypes: WindowsApplication, ASP.NETWebService, ASP.NETWebApplication, ExternalDatabase, and Generic Application. We also discussed how one of our services could in reality take the form of a third-party service modeled using the ExternalWebService prototype. Two additional prototypes were not used: the OfficeApplication (which could represent an Excel application that extracts web content from an ASP.NETWebApplication using the Excel's Web Query feature) and the BizTalkWebService (which would be used in much the same way as ExternalWebService). In fact, we could never hope to cover every application prototype that you might find in the toolbox because this list is sure to increase over time — as Microsoft, various third parties, and you yourself introduce new application types.

Having drawn up the static design, we identified the dynamic modeling limitation and suggested a technique for adding limited dynamic information in the form of numbered comments.

Because the major strength of Application Designer lies in its ability to quickly translate a design into a deployable implementation, we have given a lot of attention to that aspect. By making only very minor changes to the auto-generated code and deployment websites, we have — by the end of the chapter — created a working end-to-end system.

Additional examples of using Application Designer to construct a distributed system design and take it right through to implementation can be found in Tony Loton's MSDN article "Introduction to the Visual Studio 2005 Application Designer," parts 1 and 2, at http://msdn.microsoft.com/ library/default.asp?url=/library/en-us/dnvs05/html/introappdesigner1.asp

and `http://msdn.microsoft.com/library/default.asp?url=/library/en-us/`
`dnvs05/html/introappdesigner2.asp`.

Toward the end of the chapter, we tied up a few loose ends by describing the synchronization between the model and code, the ability to reverse engineer existing solutions, the existence of the Settings and Constraints Editor (which we'll revisit in the next chapter), and the ability to reproduce your design diagrams in hardcopy format.

Though we've taken a design all the way through to implementation and deployment, we've done this very simply by not specifying any deployment configuration details at all. That served for the purposes of this chapter, but if you're serious about using the Visual Studio 2005 Team Edition for Software Architects to design deployable systems, you'll need to read on.

In the next chapter, you'll learn about the Logical Datacenter Designer, which enables you to design the logical infrastructure against which your applications will be deployed; and after that you'll learn how to map applications designed with Application Designer onto the logical datacenter using System Designer and Deployment Designer so that you can evaluate your deployment.

3

Logical Infrastructure Modeling Using Logical Datacenter Designer

In this chapter, we'll look at Logical Datacenter Designer, the distributed system designer that you can use to define the logical servers, protected zones, and communication pathways of the target deployment environment, along with the meta-data and configuration requirements of that deployment environment.

The logical datacenter may be devised independently of the applications that will be deployed to it, with a diagrammatic representation of the deployment environment — the logical datacenter diagram — being delivered to the applications team so that they have a view of that environment before being exposed to the deployment environment itself. In addition, that need not be limited to a single target deployment environment because Logical Datacenter Designer enables you to create several diagrams representing alternative deployment infrastructures.

The important link between Application Designer (discussed in the previous chapter) and Logical Datacenter Designer (this chapter) will be described in the next chapter, where we'll show how applications grouped into systems may be mapped to, and validated against, the logical servers of a datacenter using System Designer and Deployment Designer. That's an important concept, one we know as *design for deployment*.

In this chapter, we'll first give you an overview of the Logical Datacenter Designer toolbox and the prototypes it provides. Then we'll give you a couple of examples: first a simple diagram based on a real .NET deployment infrastructure, and then the logical datacenter for the StockBroker applications. We'll close with a discussion of how you can gain fine-grained control of the deployment environment characteristics via the Settings and Constraints Editor.

To work through this chapter, you need to be familiar with the design of the StockBroker running example introduced in Chapter 2, but you need not have implemented it.

Logical Datacenter Designer Toolbox and Prototypes

As with Application Designer, initially the Logical Datacenter Designer toolbox will provide a set of pre-configured prototypes to which you can add your own. In this case, the prototypes are for servers, zones, and endpoints, as shown in Figure 3-1.

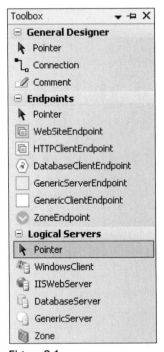

Figure 3-1

The following sections describe each prototype shown in Figure 3-1 in turn, though the set of prototypes available to you might be slightly different from those shown.

General

The first item you'll see in the General Designer section of the toolbox, and in the other sections for that matter, is Pointer. This is not an item to place on a diagram, but a mechanism for reverting the mouse cursor to a general selection pointer, thereby deselecting the prototype to which the mouse cursor is currently set:

❑ **Connection:** Just as with the same-named item in the Application Designer toolbox, the Connection item enables you to connect endpoints together. However, the endpoints that you connect on Logical Datacenter Designer belong to servers and zones, rather than applications.

❑ **Comment:** Once again, a Comment is just a free text note that adds clarity to your diagrams.

Endpoints

As will become clear later, communication pathways between servers are defined through the endpoints on those servers or through the zone endpoints that act as proxies to the server endpoints. Endpoints are typically "server" endpoints (for incoming communication) or client "endpoints" (for outgoing communication with those servers), but it is possible to alter the properties of an endpoint to make it bi-directional.

The endpoint prototypes provided by the toolbox shown in Figure 3-1 are as follows:

- ❑ **WebSiteEndpoint:** This is a strongly typed endpoint through which a client may communicate with an IIS Web Server using the HTTP protocol. Our StockBroker example presented later includes two such endpoints.

- ❑ **HTTPClientEndpoint:** This is the client-side counterpart of the server-side WebSiteEndpoint. Every connection to a WebSiteEndpoint will have a HTTPClientEndpoint, as you will see in our StockBroker example.

- ❑ **DatabaseClientEndpoint:** This client endpoint represents the client side of a connection to a database server, such as SQL Server. Our StockBroker example will incorporate such a connection.

- ❑ **GenericServerEndpoint:** The GenericServerEndpoint is a generalized endpoint for those situations in which a generic server accepts incoming communications via an unspecified protocol.

- ❑ **GenericClientEndpoint:** This is the client-side counterpart of the GenericServerEndpoint.

- ❑ **ZoneEndpoint:** This prototype represents an endpoint that constrains the type of communication that can travel into or out of a zone. In our StockBroker example, client and server endpoints will typically be coupled using zone endpoints as proxies, rather than being connected directly together.

Logical servers

Each of the logical server prototypes provided by the toolbox (refer to Figure 3-1) has specific settings and constraints appropriate to that server type. As you place logical servers onto a diagram, each will have, by default, zero, one, or more of the aforementioned endpoints. The prototypes are as follows:

- ❑ **WindowsClient:** The WindowsClient prototype represents a machine running a Windows operating system, to which a Windows application may be deployed. You'll encounter one of these in our StockBroker example.

- ❑ **IISWebServer:** This prototype represents an IIS Web Server instance capable of hosting ASP.NET web applications and Web services. We'll use this prototype twice in our StockBroker example.

- ❑ **DatabaseServer:** This represents a database server such as Microsoft SQL Server.

- ❑ **GenericServer:** The GenericServer represents a server in the broadest sense and is useful when you need to show a host to which a non-Microsoft-technologies application will be deployed.

- ❑ **Zone:** A Zone represents a network region for which communication to and from the servers in that region is restricted to a specific set of protocols — by a firewall, a physical boundary, or both. There may in reality be no actual restriction mechanism; the zone describes a configuration constraint that, in effect, defines policy about connections that are permitted. This might be realized by a firewall or physical boundaries but may only exist logically as a means to constrain deployments. In our StockBroker example, we will place servers within zones.

Sample Logical Datacenter

Having introduced the various prototypes that make up a logical datacenter diagram, we'll now show what a typical logical datacenter might look like. The diagram in Figure 3-2 is based on the deployment configuration of a real-life .NET project that went live in 2003, and we'll describe the diagram in general before demonstrating how you can create a similar diagram specifically for our StockBroker running example.

As you look at Figure 3-2, note that client endpoints are shown hollow and server endpoints are shown solid, with connection arrows flowing in the direction client-to-server. At this stage, we're keeping it simple by showing servers, zones, and the connections between them with no additional information about the required communication protocols.

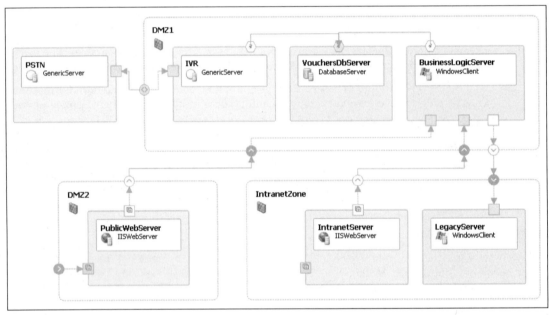

Figure 3-2

For your information, this datacenter was designed to host a "virtual vouchers" system that enables electronic representations of mobile airtime vouchers, book tokens, meal vouchers, and so on to be issued and redeemed without any paper artifacts changing hands. (Actually, the nature of the system to be deployed matters very little to this discussion, but we wanted to satisfy your curiosity nonetheless.)

This datacenter comprises three zones:

❑ **DMZ1:** A perimeter zone protected by an internal firewall, containing the core servers for business logic and the database

❑ **DMZ2:** A separate perimeter zone protected by an external firewall, containing the public-facing web server

❑ **IntranetZone:** The company-wide intranet providing a nonpublic web server and a legacy platform

Logical Datacenter Designer does not oblige you to place servers within zones, and we've illustrated that by placing the PSTN server (representing the telephone network) outside of any zone.

Datacenter zones

Now we'll take each of those zones in turn. For each zone, we describe the server(s) within the zone and the connections between the servers and the zone perimeter.

DMZ1

This zone represents the core protected zone, separated from all other zones by an internal firewall. The zone encloses the following key servers that are crucial to the operations:

❑ The Interactive Voice Response (IVR) server handles incoming and outgoing telephone-based interactions via the Public Switched Telephone Network (PSTN). This proprietary server has been modeled as a generic server, which for clarity only has been connected bi-directionally to a generic server outside the zone; this second server is a placeholder for the PSTN network itself. The IVR server takes voice prompts from, and writes its results to, the SQL Server directly, which is the only link with the other servers in the data center.

❑ The VouchersDbServer is the central database server, acting not only as the repository for data accessed by the BusinessLogicServer, but also as the integration point between the BusinessLogicServer and the IVR server.

❑ The BusinessLogicServer hosts the core business logic in the form of .NET Remoting components accessible to clients in the DMZ2 and the IntranetZone. This server is logically connected to the SQLServer within the same zone, and — as well as being a server itself — is connected as a client of the LegacyServer in the IntranetZone.

DMZ2

The PublicWebServer delivers ASP.NET applications to users over the Internet. This server is connected to the BusinessLogicServer within the DMZ1 zone, the BusinessLogicServer providing common business logic to various presentation layers. Notice how servers are connected via outgoing and incoming zone endpoints, rather than being connected directly, so that all network traffic is subject to firewall scrutiny.

In this zone, the PublicWebServer has a website endpoint connected to a (solid) zone endpoint, thus providing an incoming connection point for clients of this server.

IntranetZone

This zone is similar to the DMZ2 because it includes a web server, the IntranetServer that will host a set of ASP.NET applications providing an alternative presentation layer for the common business logic hosted by the BusinessLogicServer. However, this server and the zone that contains it will be subject to a different set of constraints so that clients may connect from within the same company network but not over the public Internet. For this reason, a WebSiteEndpoint has been provided on the server but not connected to an incoming endpoint on the zone; therefore, all connected clients must be added within the same Intranet zone.

The IntranetZone also contains a LegacyServer that hosts an existing application that may have directly connected legacy clients (not shown). All new client applications — provided by the PublicWebServer in DMZ2 and the IntranetServer in the IntranetZone — are decoupled from the legacy server as a consequence of the BusinessLogicServer in DMZ1 that is connected as a client to the LegacyServer.

Endpoint styles

Though we did not label communication protocols explicitly in Figure 3-2, you can deduce much of that information from the style in which the endpoints are rendered. Server endpoints are shown solid, client endpoints are shown hollow. Generic endpoints, website endpoints, and database endpoints are distinguished pictorially.

On each zone endpoint, an arrow shows whether the communication flow is outgoing (the arrow points outward from the zone), incoming (the arrow points in toward the zone), or bi-directional (with inward and outward pointing arrows).

The UML deployment diagram: Similar, but not the same

At this level, a logical datacenter diagram is rather like a UML deployment diagram in that it shows deployment nodes and the connections between them. Figure 3-3 shows the same logical datacenter drawn as a UML deployment diagram.

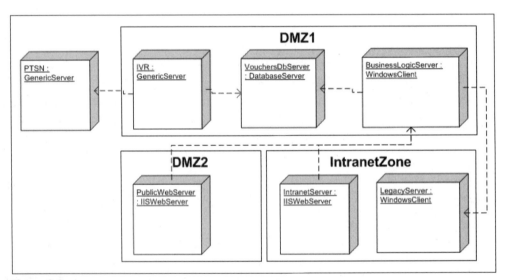

Figure 3-3

An important distinction is that whereas the UML deployment diagram is biased toward modeling physical deployment nodes, the logical datacenter diagram is strictly logical. Therefore, an LDD may show three logical servers of different kinds, all of which map to a single physical machine, or across two physical machines; it makes no difference as long as the required communication pathways (discussed later) are all in place.

In practice, UML deployment diagrams are limited in two important respects: Much of the information they show (such as IP addresses) is of no real use to developers intending to deploy on that infrastructure, and the lack of tight integration between the UML deployment view and the other UML views means that information about the datacenter's requirements and capabilities cannot be communicated effectively. That's not the case with the Visual Studio 2005 Distributed System Designers, which use a common metamodel (SDM) as the vital link between the logical infrastructure and the application architecture.

In UML, the deployment diagram actually serves two purposes: to model the infrastructure — therefore equivalent to Logical Datacenter Designer — and to allow the mapping of application components onto deployment nodes. The latter purpose is equated in the Team System with the System Designer/ Deployment Designer combination described in the next chapter. Thus, the Visual Studio 2005 Team Edition for Software Architects decouples the logical infrastructure design from the deployment design such that it is possible to map a single application design onto various logical datacenters representing alternative deployment scenarios — or, indeed, map various application systems onto a single logical datacenter.

Defining a Logical Datacenter for the StockBroker Applications

Figure 3-2 was provided as a gentle introduction to logical datacenter design, based on a real-life datacenter described in terms of zones, servers, and connections. Now we'll devise a logical datacenter against which we can validate the deployment of the StockBroker running example that was designed using Application Designer in Chapter 2. For this one, we'll tell you how to draw the diagram yourself and then we'll use it to introduce some more advanced ideas.

First, you need to add a Logical Datacenter Diagram to your solution, which you can do by right-clicking the solution in Solution Explorer and choosing Add ⇨ New Item. Select the Logical Datacenter Diagram from the Distributed System Diagrams category and name the new diagram `StockBrokerDatacenter.ldd`.

> Note that because logical datacenter diagrams are stored as separate files with the extension .ldd, these files could be signed and versioned in a real-life scenario as base-lined representations of the datacenter. These diagrams may be created in — or imported to — any Visual Studio solution. They aren't limited to "Distributed System" solutions such as our StockBroker solution.

The application design from Chapter 2 includes not only our own suite of applications — the StockBroker, the StockQuoteApp, and the DealingApp — but also representations of what could be third-party applications (the MarketMaker and the StockMarket) that we need to interface with. For a complete picture, we'll specify in the LDD how we expect those third-party applications to be hosted, and that will be our starting point.

The MarketMaker Zone

In the preceding chapter, we suggested that the MarketMaker application would most likely be an external application. Though technically outside our control, we have created a representation of that application within the application design and we need to show it hosted somewhere.

We'll create a zone named MarketMakerZone containing a server named MarketMakerServer. Let's be clear that as a third-party hosted application, the server and zone in which it is hosted would really be outside our control, but from an operational point of view we'll need to understand — or indeed specify — the constraints of that hosting if we are to be able to connect to the application.

Figure 3-4 shows our design for the MarketMakerZone, or rather, what we expect the third-party zone to look like. We expect there to be an IISWebServer (which we've named MarketMakerServer) supporting incoming communication to a WebSiteEndpoint (which we've named MarketMakerWeb) through a zone endpoint (which we've named MarketMaketWebProxy) via HTTP so that we can invoke the Web services.

In our application design, we envisioned that the MarketMaker application would communicate with a StockDatabase, so for completeness we've shown a SQLServer named StockDatabaseServer. We've used the names StockDatabaseClient and StockDatabaseServer to distinguish the client and server endpoints of the database connection.

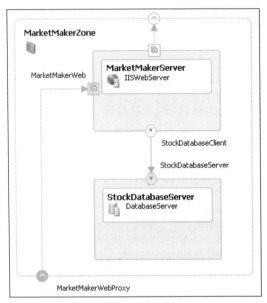

Figure 3-4

Figure 3-4 demonstrates that a zone may include one or more servers — in this case, a database server as well as a web server.

To draw the MarketMakerZone, first drag a zone prototype from the toolbox onto the diagram. Initially it will have one incoming endpoint and one outgoing endpoint, as indicated by the arrows. It will also have a default name — such as Zone1 — that you can change to MarketMakerZone.

Next, drag an IISWebServer prototype from the toolbox to inside the zone boundary. Be sure to place this item inside the zone boundary, not outside of it. Change the name of this server to MarketMakerServer.

Click the solid provider endpoint on the MarketMaker server and choose Show Label from the pop-up menu. Whatever text appears (most probably WebSiteEndpoint1) change it to MarketMakerWeb. Now hover over that endpoint and press the Alt key until the connection cursor appears; click and drag a connection to the incoming endpoint on the MarketMaker zone. You could also relabel that zone endpoint as MarketMakerWebProxy to match our diagram.

What you've just done is indicate that clients can communicate with the MarketMaker IISWebServer through the zone via HTTP.

Now you should drag a DatabaseServer prototype into the MarketMaker Zone. Rename it to StockDatabaseServer, rename its solid provider endpoint to StockDatabaseServer, and connect it to the MarketMaker server. Make a connection to the MarketMaker server itself, not to the existing hollow consumer endpoint that we'll make use of shortly. Relabel the new database consumer endpoint that appears to StockDatabaseClient, and show its label.

You've now enabled direct communication between the MarketMaker web server and the StockDatabase database server within the zone, not from outside the zone. The only communication allowed into the zone from the outside is HTTP.

To complete this picture, you can connect the spare consumer endpoint of the MarketMaker server to the spare outgoing zone endpoint. This shows that we'll be communicating from the MarketMaker server, out through the zone, via HTTP. Although it's not crucial for this design, for completeness we'll be showing how this server may ultimately become a client of the StockMarket server, described next.

> You can resize zones and servers, and move endpoints around their peripheries, to make your diagrams look better. You can also zoom out to see the complete picture as your diagram grows.

Your result should match what is shown in Figure 3-4.

The StockMarket Zone

For the StockMarket zone, we'll adopt the same rationale we used for the MarketMaker zone. While the StockMarket application — which we modeled as a generic application in Application Designer — will be outside of our control, we'll allocate a zone to it and specify the characteristics of that zone in order to complete the infrastructure picture.

Figure 3-5 shows the StockMarket zone alongside the MarketMaker zone created in the previous step. Because we modeled the StockMarket application as a generic application in Application Designer, all we need to host it is a GenericServer.

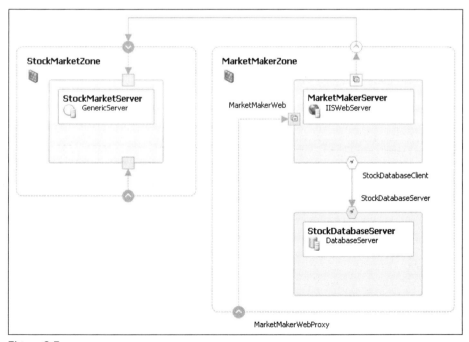

Figure 3-5

We'll anticipate that this server will accept two kinds of incoming communications:

❑ One from the MarketMaker, which will presumably need to communicate with the StockMarket at some point, though the exact details are outside of our core application design

❑ One from the StockBroker, for which we've not yet provided a host in the figure, but for which we've shown a spare incoming endpoint in anticipation

Drawing the StockMarketZone is much simpler than the previous example. The steps to complete the drawing of that zone are as follows:

1. Drag a new zone onto the design surface and rename it StockMarketZone.

2. Ensure that the zone has only two incoming endpoints, if necessary, by dragging ZoneEndpoint prototypes from the toolbox.

3. Drag a new GenericServer prototype from the toolbox onto the zone, rename it StockMarketServer, and make sure it has two provider endpoints, if necessary, by dragging GenericServerEndpoints from the toolbox onto the server, or by using the Properties window to change the Communication Flow property of one of the default endpoints from Outbound to Inbound.

4. Connect each of the zone endpoints to one of the provider endpoints you've just created.

We won't display the endpoint labels on this zone and server, or rename them, because — to be frank — our knowledge of the StockMarketServer is sketchy and we're only showing this server and zone for illustration and to complete the overall picture. The minimum we need to show is that there will be some kind of generic server, located within its own zone and accepting connections from two other zones: the MarketMaker zone (described previously) and the StockBroker zone (described next).

Your result should match Figure 3-5.

The StockBroker Zone

Our Web services application, the StockBroker, will be hosted by a StockBroker IISWebServer within a StockBroker zone over which we have complete control. The Stockbroker Server will communicate out of its zone and into the MarketMaker zone via HTTP, as you would expect because the StockBroker application (defined previously using Application Designer) will invoke Web services of the MarketMaker application (also defined using Application Designer). It will also communicate with the StockMarket server via some other generic protocol that has not yet been specified.

Finally, the StockBroker server will accept incoming Web services requests as HTTP via a WebSiteEndpoint named StockBrokerWeb, the clients of which we have not yet specified (see Figure 3-6).

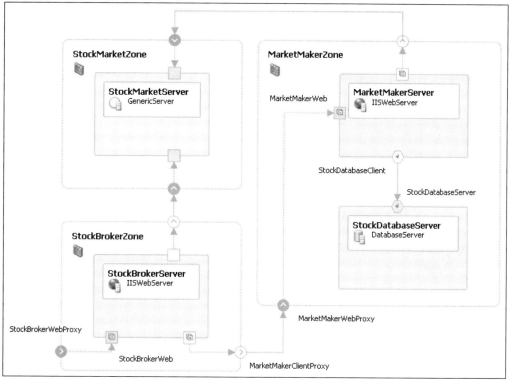

Figure 3-6

The steps to complete the drawing of the StockBroker zone are as follows:

1. Drag a new zone onto the design surface and rename it StockBrokerZone.

2. Ensure that this zone has two outgoing endpoints, if necessary, by dragging ZoneEndpoint prototypes from the toolbox, or by changing the Communication Flow property of one of the default endpoints from Inbound to Outbound. Rename one of them MarketMakerClientProxy.

3. Ensure that the zone has one incoming endpoint named StockBrokerWebProxy.

4. Drag a new IISWebServer prototype from the toolbox into the StockBroker zone and rename it StockBrokerServer.

5. Ensure that this server has a WebSiteEndpoint, if necessary, by dragging one from the toolbox. Rename it StockBrokerWeb and connect it to the StockBrokerWebProxy endpoint on the zone.

6. Ensure that the server has a HTTPClientEndpoint, if necessary, by dragging one from the toolbox. Rename it MarketMakerClient and connect it to the MarketMakerClientProxy endpoint on the zone.

7. Finally, ensure that the server has a GenericClientEndpoint, if necessary, by dragging one from the toolbox. Connect this endpoint to the unlabeled outgoing endpoint on the zone.

Your result should match Figure 3-6.

The Client Zone

Our final zone will be a ClientZone to represent the scope of our client deployments. As our application design includes a Windows application, we'll populate the ClientZone with a WindowsClient server—named CustomerDesktop—which will host that application. As shown in Figure 3-7, client applications will connect from the ClientZone, through the StockBroker zone, to the StockBroker server via HTTP.

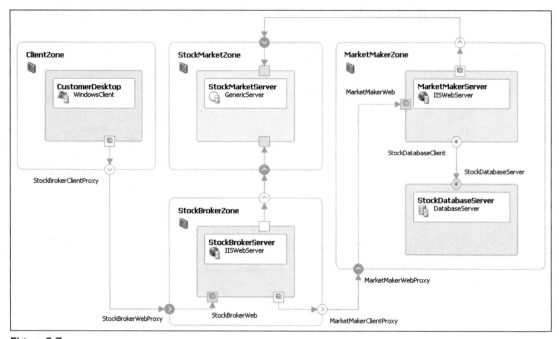

Figure 3-7

That completes the picture of our Logical Datacenter.

> *Although we've used only one-to-one connections between provider and consumer endpoints, the notation does not mandate this. It would be perfectly possible, but not advisable in this case, to connect the HTTPServer endpoint of the MarketMaker to the ClientZone, thereby establishing two consumer endpoints for the same provider endpoint.*

You should be able to draw the Client zone easily by now. The final steps to complete this logical datacenter diagram are as follows:

1. Drag a new zone onto the diagram and rename it ClientZone, ensuring that this zone has only one outgoing endpoint named StockBrokerClientProxy.

2. Drag a new WindowsClient prototype from the toolbox onto the ClientZone, renaming this server CustomerDesktop.

3. Ensure that this server has an outgoing HTTPClientEndpoint (add one if necessary) connected to the endpoint on the Zone.

4. Finally, ensure that the StockBrokerClientProxy endpoint of the ClientZone is connected to the StockBrokerWebProxy endpoint of the StockBrokerZone.

> The logical datacenter that we have drawn represents just one possible deployment scenario for the StockBroker suite of applications. You could create another logical datacenter diagram to reflect an alternative deployment scenario, and you could even try embedding one zone within another, which is certainly possible.

Settings and Constraints

In addition to creating a high-level picture of a logical datacenter, you can also dig deeper into the specific settings and constraints for the individual servers and endpoints. The constraints will ultimately determine the kinds of applications that may be bound to specific servers, the communication pathways that are allowed between servers, and the policy specifying which kinds of traffic can pass along those communication pathways.

This discussion moves us away from the core topic of visual design and into the realms of, for example, IIS configuration. While it's not possible to step you through every setting and constraint — there are tens if not hundreds of them — we can at least show you how to access the Settings and Constraints window to give you an idea of what you'll see there.

You can right-click any server and choose Settings and Constraints to invoke the Settings and Constraints window. We'll do that for a GenericServer (as the simplest case), for an IISWebServer (as a more complex case), and, to show it's not limited to servers, for a WebSiteEndpoint and a ZoneEndpoint.

For completeness, we should tell you that you can also access the settings and constraints for zones, not just their endpoints. Zone constraints determine which types of servers you can add to a zone.

Before we access the settings and constraints specific to our example, we'll first say a few words about the important relationship between settings and constraints, and the interplay between the two.

Constraints versus settings

Constraints are created in one layer against settings in another layer. For example, constraints can be set from the application layer (using Application Designer) against settings on the hosting layer (the Logical Datacenter) and vice versa. The idea is that the operations team can constrain the application layer while allowing the developers to request a set of features in the target deployment environment. The operations team may or may not decide to accommodate those requests in the logical datacenter.

To see an example of this interplay between settings and constraints, you can view the settings of the StockBrokerServer in the logical datacenter diagram, and then compare them with the constraints of the StockBroker application in the Application Diagram. You will notice that where the StockBrokerServer has a setting for the operating system, the StockBroker application has a matching constraint.

> A constraint is a requirement that must be met by an application deployed on a particular logical server.

The Settings and Constraints Editor provides control over predefined constraints and user-defined constraints, both of which you'll see as our discussion progresses. A third kind of constraints — *implicit constraints* — are inherent in the elements placed on the diagram from the toolbox. These cannot be edited using the Settings and Constraints Editor but may be authored using the System Definition Model SDK.

GenericServer settings and constraints

Figure 3-8 shows the Settings and Constraints window for a generic server — actually, the StockMarketServer of our example. Note that there are no predefined settings for a generic server, and the only available constraint is whether or not (checked or unchecked) this generic server can host a generic application.

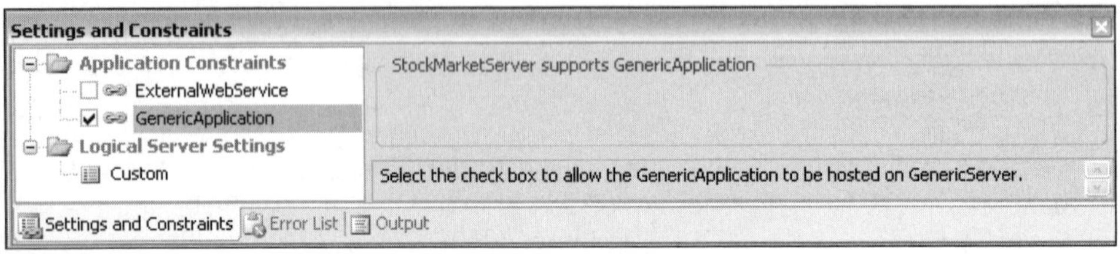

Figure 3-8

The constraints determine what kinds of applications you can bind to servers using Deployment Designer, which you'll meet in the next chapter. For a generic server, the only kind of application you can bind — if you check the box — is a generic application.

The generic server exposes the simplest grouping of settings and constraints, which is why we covered that one first.

IISWebServer settings and constraints

An IISWebServer enables a richer set of settings and constraints to be specified — so many that we couldn't cover the complete set in any detail without moving away from the core topic of visual design and into the realm of IIS configuration. We can at least provide a starting point in terms of how and where to manipulate these settings, and in this case we'll consider the two aspects — the setting and the constraints — separately.

Figure 3-9 shows a subset of the constraints for an IISWebServer — actually, the StockBrokerServer of our ongoing example.

As you can see, several checkboxes are provided so that you can constrain the server to host any combination of ASP.NET services and applications, External BizTalk Web services, and External Web services. In Figure 3-9, we have expanded the ASP.NETWebApplication so that you can see the additional constraints that may be specified. For illustration, we have checked the ASP.NET Session State box, thereby enabling us in the main pane to further specify the Session State Mode as SQLServer and the HttpCookie Mode as Auto Detect.

Figure 3-10 shows a subset of the settings for an IISWebServer — once again the StockBrokerServer of our ongoing example.

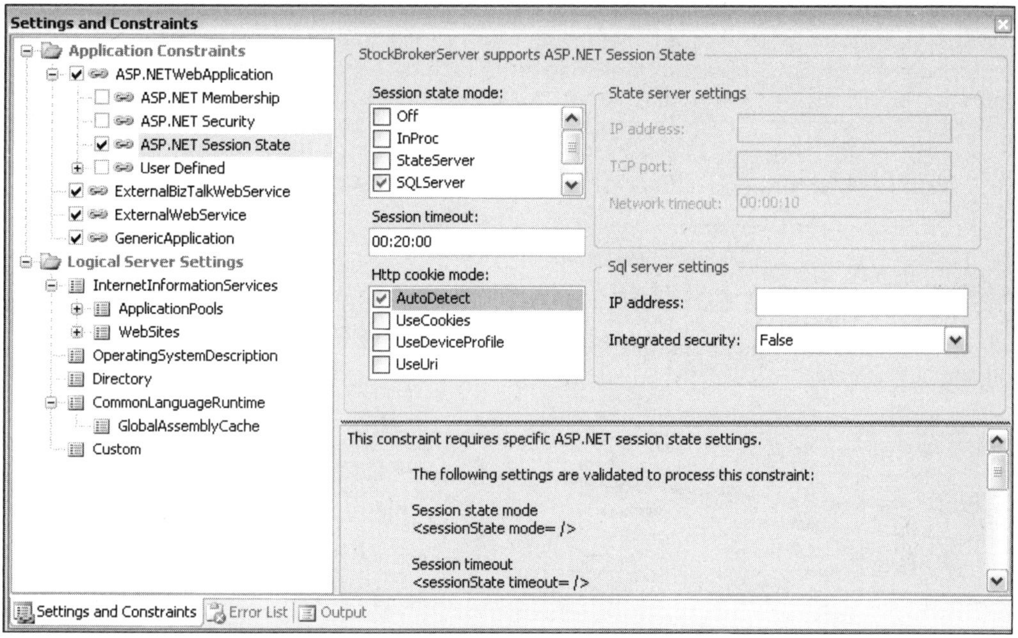

Figure 3-9

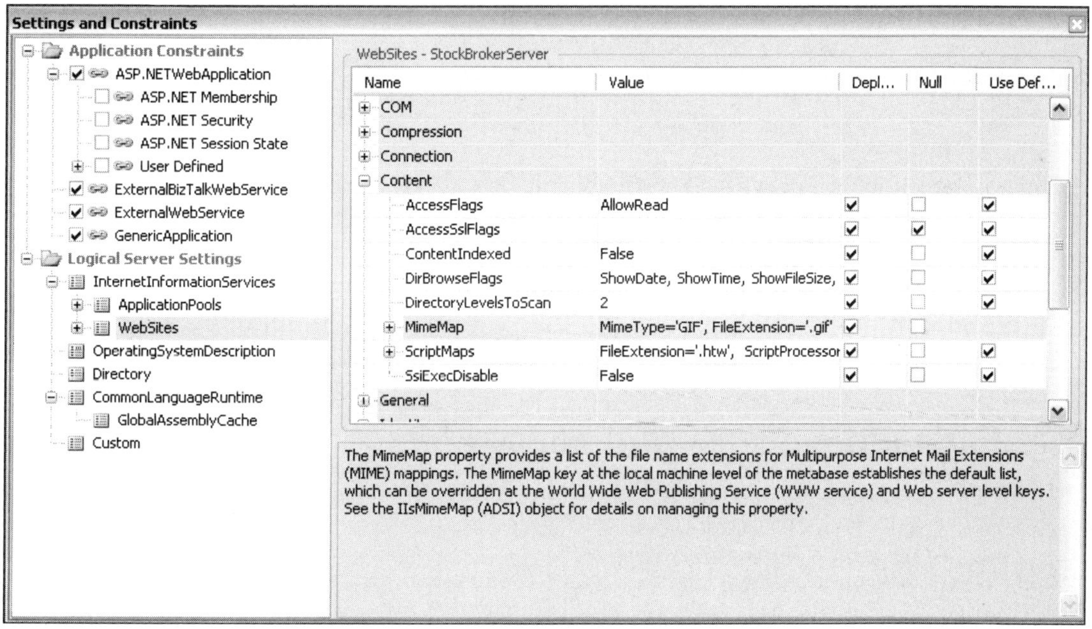

Figure 3-10

In Figure 3-10, the InternetInformationServices ⇨ WebSites category has been selected, thereby enabling us to specify settings for the operation of the IIS HTTP server. In the main pane, we've expanded the Content category in order to set up MimeMap for the allowable MIME types to be handled by the server.

> Look in the IIS documentation for more information about the effect of configuring various settings, along with how those settings are stored in Metabase.

WebSiteEndpoint settings and constraints

Settings and constraints are not limited to servers, so you can also specify these for an endpoint — such as WebSiteEndpoints — as we have in Figure 3-11.

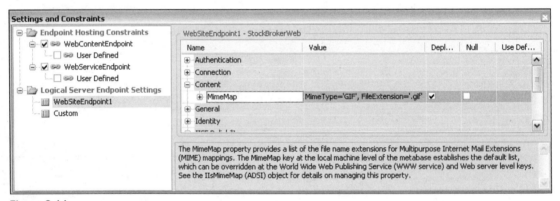

Figure 3-11

We have expanded the Content subcategory within the main pane in order to show the correspondence between this setting on the WebSiteEndpoint and the same setting on the IISWebServer shown earlier. Effectively, a WebSiteEndpoint provides a subset of the settings and constraints for an IISWebServer.

You can constrain this kind of endpoint to be a WebSiteEndpoint (obviously) and to handle web content. What effect might this have? Well, an HTTPClientEndpoint constrained to allow only web content traffic cannot be bound to a WebSiteEndpoint configured to allow only Web service traffic.

ZoneEndpoint settings and constraints

To complete the picture regarding settings and constraints, we'll consider zone endpoints. Figure 3-12 shows how a zone endpoint may be constrained.

Notice that the WebSiteEndpoint checkbox allows the zone endpoint to accept communications to an internal WebSiteEndpoint if checked. The zone endpoint may also allow for communication to an internal DatabaseServerEndpoint if that box is checked.

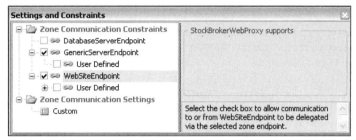

Figure 3-12

Custom settings and user-defined constraints

The settings and constraints we've just considered are predefined. In addition to those, you can define your own custom settings and user-defined constraints.

Custom settings

You can create custom settings for zones, endpoints, applications, systems, and logical servers in order to provide additional meta-data about your development or deployment environment.

To create a custom setting:

1. Select the zone, endpoint, application, system, or server for which you want to provide the custom setting.

2. In the Settings and Constraints Editor, expand the Settings node, right-click Custom, and choose Add Custom Settings.

3. Enter the required information in the Custom Settings dialog box that appears.

As a concrete example, you could create a new setting that specifies a server as being "Test" or "Live" by populating the fields as follows:

Name	Category	Type	List	Value
Environment	OurCompanySpecific	String	False	Live

Note that we chose "OurCompanySpecific" as the category in order to group this setting with other company-specific settings. You could choose another category or leave that field blank.

Custom settings cannot be used to define constraints, so when checking the User Defined (constraints) checkbox — described in the next section — you will not be able to gain access to settings that you have defined as described here. However, custom settings can be used in custom deployment scripts because they are captured in the deployment report; and unlike other settings, custom settings can be displayed in the Properties window.

User-defined constraints

User-defined constraints enable you to specify constraints that fall outside the group of predefined constraints. Because constraints are the counterpart of settings, which they constrain, you can specify them from the available pool of settings.

An example given in the Visual Studio 2005 documentation is that of HTTP KeepAlive functionality, for which there is no predefined constraint. You can author a user-defined constraint for the connection settings on the website, and you can specify for that constraint a custom error message and a help URL.

You can create a user-defined constraint as follows:

1. Select the application or logical server for which you want to define the constraint.
2. Open the Settings and Constraints Editor.
3. Select the User Defined checkbox.
4. In the tree view under User Defined, select additional checkboxes as needed to specify groups of settings to include in the constraint.
5. For each group of settings, select the checkbox for individual settings to include in the constraint.
6. Enter setting values in the Value column.

For each setting value, you have the option to specify a custom error message that will appear if the constraint fails as a result of this setting. To set a custom error message:

1. Under Error Message, click the ellipsis. The Error Text dialog box appears.
2. Enter the text of the custom error message using the macros provided to enter placeholders for items such as setting name, required value, Help URL, and current value.
3. Click OK to set the custom error message.

The full text of the custom error message will include the text specified for the error message, including the Help URL if you added it to the error message text using the Help URL macro.

Import IIS Settings Wizard

It can be difficult to manage the overwhelming number of settings that are available, so help is at hand in the form of the Import IIS Settings Wizard. This wizard guides you through the process of importing settings from an existing IISWebServer into an IISWebServer shown in Logical Datacenter Designer.

You launch the wizard by right-clicking an IISWebServer on the diagram and choosing Import Settings. Using the various checkboxes, you can choose to import the web server global configuration, applications pools, plus the settings for already deployed websites. In the latter case, each will become a new endpoint on the server.

Defining Your Own Reusable Prototypes

In the previous chapter, you learned how to add your own application prototypes to the Application Designer toolbox by selecting one or more items on the diagram and choosing the Add to Toolbox pop-up menu option. You can do exactly the same thing with Logical Datacenter Designer — for example, to add combinations of configured zones and servers to the toolbox as reusable prototypes.

When you define a zone or logical server using the prototype you created, it will be identical to your original, apart from the name. Connections from outside a zone will have been removed, but connections within a zone will have been retained, as will all settings and constraints applied to servers within the zone.

> You can achieve something similar simply by copying and pasting (Ctrl+C, Ctrl+V) zones between diagrams, although by using that technique you would not have a prototype to use in other modeling sessions or to share with other developers.

When you invoke the Add to Toolbox feature, a dialog box will prompt you to name the new prototype. This name will determine the file (with extension `.lddprototype`) in which the prototype is stored; and just as with Application Designer, these prototype files may be shared with other users simply by distributing the files.

The new item will be added to the toolbox under the currently active node — for example, under Endpoints (if you previous used an Endpoint item) or under Logical Servers (if you previously used a Logical Server item). This can take some getting used to as you can easily create a reusable server prototype inadvertently under the Endpoints node.

You might take advantage of this feature as an aid to building multiple logical datacenter diagrams representing alternative deployment scenarios. Though these diagrams would have subtle — or substantial — differences, they would most likely share a high degree of commonality in terms of key zones and servers. You don't want to draw and configure the otherwise identical aspects on every diagram individually, do you?

StockBrokerZone prototype

In the context of our running example, we can identify the StockBroker zone as being an essential element of any deployment scenario for our application. Whereas the MarketMakerZone, the StockMarketZone, and even the ClientZone may well be outside of our control and in the hands of external organizations, the StockBrokerZone and its StockBrokerServer will surely be a consistent feature as the host for our core business logic.

For that reason, we'll use that zone as a good candidate for a new prototype and we'll add it to the toolbox by right-clicking the zone and choosing Add to Toolbox from the pop-up menu. If you do that now, you'll be prompted for a name, so use "StockBrokerZone".

You'll then be prompted to save the prototype definition in a file named `StockBrokerZone` `.lddprototype`, in a folder populated with other prototype definitions.

Once you've added that new prototype to the toolbox, you could trying creating a brand-new logical datacenter diagram, onto which you could place the new prototype as a starting point.

Team-working with prototypes

Once you've developed some useful prototypes, why keep them to yourself? Because prototypes are stored in files with extension `.lddprototype`, you can share the prototypes with your team by exchanging those files. They will appear in the toolbox the next time a distributed system solution is opened.

Alternatively, you can copy the prototype files to a shared folder on the network, thus making them accessible to everyone. To make this work, you will have to add a registry entry as follows:

1. Run `regedit` from the Windows Start menu.

2. Navigate to the key `HKEY_LOCAL_MACHINE\SOFTWARE\Microsoft\VisualStudio\` `8.0\EnterpriseTools\DesignerPrototypeFolders`.

3. Look at the entry `PrototypesFolder1=C:\Program Files\...` and add a new entry `PrototypesFolder2=\YourSharedFolderPath\`.

You can test the principle without a network simply by specifying an additional folder on your local machine, such as `C:\Prototypes\`, where you have placed one or more `.lddprototype` files.

> **You must include a trailing slash (\) in the folder name; otherwise, the shared prototypes will not appear in the toolbox.**

Summary

After introducing the Logical Datacenter Designer toolbox and the prototypes that it provides, we presented a sample logical datacenter diagram based on a real-life deployment configuration that one of the authors has encountered. That was to get you used to the idea of logical datacenter modeling and the style of the diagrams.

We then turned our attention to the StockBroker running example as a vehicle for specifying a logical datacenter in more detail.

Our original application design involved a number of applications, but some—such as the MarketMaker and StockMarket—we regarded as external and outside of our core design. You might wonder, therefore, why we modeled servers to host those applications in the logical datacenter. In part, we did that because the datacenter is defined by the operations team, which has less concern about which applications will be developed in house and which externally. If the external components are to be hosted in house (even if not developed in house), then operations will need to specify servers to host them. Otherwise, operations may need to model the characteristics of the third-party remote servers and zones on which they will be hosted, or maybe even specify to the third parties the characteristics that those servers and zones should exhibit — as part of the service-level agreement.

You saw how the settings and constraints for any server or endpoint may be accessed and manipulated, and you looked at some examples (although coverage of the full range of settings and constraints for every server type was not practical here).

Finally, you learned how to add your own prototypes to the toolbox, and how to share your prototypes in a team environment.

In Chapter 4, we'll pull together the application design from Chapter 2 and the logical datacenter design from this chapter by mapping the applications onto the datacenter.

Defining Systems and Evaluating Deployments Using System Designer and Deployment Designer

Having discussed how to design a set of distributed applications using Application Designer in Chapter 2, and how to design one or more logical datacenters using Logical Datacenter Designer in Chapter 3, we'll now pull those two strands together and demonstrate how an application design may be mapped onto a logical datacenter for deployment.

Specifically, in this chapter we'll demonstrate the following:

❑ How to define a default deployment directly from Application Designer, as a quick-start route into learning about deployment design without having to define systems explicitly

❑ How to define systems explicitly, by combining groups of applications into systems that may be bound to logical servers in your datacenter using Deployment Designer

We'll contrast the two approaches and discuss important topics such as validating the deployment, specifying and overriding settings and constraints, nesting systems, and generating deployment reports.

Finally, we'll compare the Visual Studio 2005 Deployment Designer with the equivalent UML deployment diagram. It's similar, but not the same.

Introducing System Designer and Deployment Designer

Because we're presenting two designers in this chapter, the following sections introduce each one, with a particular emphasis on the coupling between the two.

Introducing System Designer

System Designer takes as input the application definitions that are created with Application Designer (Chapter 2) and produces as output a set of system definitions that will be evaluated for deployment using Deployment Designer. These system definitions are constructed using *system diagrams*.

In Visual Studio 2005 Team Edition for Software Architects, a *system* is a deployment unit comprising a number of applications (from Application Designer) and/or previously defined subsystems. The embedding of systems within systems enables large-scale distributed system scenarios to be defined as a hierarchy of nested systems.

System definitions allow deployment configurations—the settings and constraints discussed previously—to be defined independently of the development configurations described by the application design so that deployment configurations are fully decoupled from application designs. Application settings may be overridden by system settings, enabling various configurations of a single application design for different logical datacenters, different geographical locations, and even different customers.

Introducing Deployment Designer

Deployment Designer allows a system—defined previously using System Designer and comprising applications from Application Designer—to be evaluated for deployment to a logical datacenter defined previously using Logical Datacenter Designer. Applications are taken from the system and bound to the servers of the logical datacenter.

Once the applications constituting the system are bound to the servers of the logical datacenter, the deployment may be validated. This validation ensures that the bound applications meet the application constraints defined by the logical datacenter and that the logical servers meet the hosting constraints specified by the application design and/or system design.

> Settings defined using Application Designer may be overridden by constraints specified using System Designer.

Validation also ensures that communications pathways exist and are compatible between applications and servers.

Finally, a deployment report may be generated in human-readable format, or in XML as a feed to automated deployment scripting tools. The Deployment Report describes all the required application and datacenter configuration settings.

Toolbox and System View

The System Designer toolbox does not play as big a part in constructing diagrams as do the Application Designer and Logical Datacenter Designer toolboxes. It contains only two items: Comment and Connection. There are no prototypes because systems are composed of existing applications taken from the application design, so aside from establishing connections there is no need for toolbox items.

The System View (see Figure 4-1) provides the set of applications that you can drag onto diagrams in order to compose systems, so in that respect the System View acts as a kind of toolbox for System Designer.

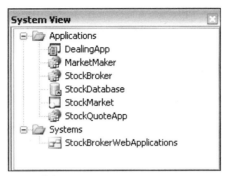

Figure 4-1

In the case of Deployment Designer, it is also meaningless to show a toolbox comprising prototypes from which diagrams are created. Deployment diagrams are based entirely on existing logical datacenter diagrams, onto which applications are bound by dragging them from the System View.

The items available to you in the System View will depend on the applications you have defined using Application Designer and any systems you have already defined using System Designer. In addition, the contents of System View will vary according to what kind of diagram you're constructing. When using System Designer, the System View will show the list of application definitions and system definitions available in the solution, whereas when using Deployment Designer the System View will show only those applications belonging to the system that you're evaluating for deployment.

Defining a Default Deployment from Application Designer

The standard sequence of events is to construct a System by drawing a system diagram using System Designer, and then evaluate that system against a logical datacenter using Deployment Designer. We describe that sequence of events in detail in the section "Defining and Deploying Systems."

There is a quick way to get started, which is to define a default deployment directly from Application Designer. We'll discuss that first, but keep in mind that this technique is intended only to allow for a quick evaluation of your deployment and, in this case, as a convenient way to introduce the concepts.

> *Provided Files:* **The file** `StockBrokerSystemDeployment.zip` **contains a Visual Studio solution incorporating the application diagram (**`StockBrokerApplicationDesign.ad`**) and logical datacenter diagram (**`StockBrokerDatacenter.ldd`**) that you will need for this chapter.**

With the StockBroker application diagram (StockBrokerApplicationDesign.ad) open, you can right-click an unpopulated region of the diagram and choose Define Deployment. You will be prompted for a logical datacenter diagram to deploy against, and you should choose the diagram StockBroker Datacenter.ldd, as shown in Figure 4-2.

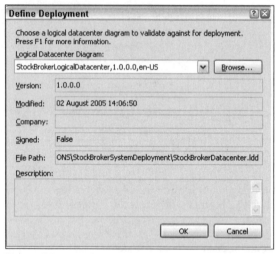

Figure 4-2

The result will be a new deployment diagram with a default name like DefaultSystem1.dd, shown in the Solution Explorer within the Default System folder. Displayed, the diagram will look like what is shown in Figure 4-3.

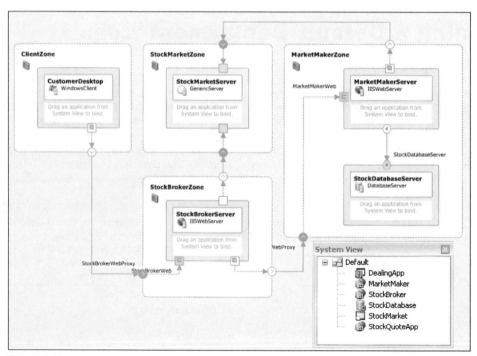

Figure 4-3

That diagram looks rather like the logical datacenter diagram itself, doesn't it? If you look closely, however, you'll see that each server representation contains the instruction "drag an application from System View to bind," which is exactly what you'll do next.

The System View

The System View should appear automatically, and will provide the following list of applications grouped under the heading Default, which is the name of the default system into which the applications have been grouped:

❑ StockBroker

❑ MarketMaker

❑ StockQuoteApp

❑ DealingApp

❑ StockDatabase

❑ StockMarket

You will learn later how applications can be grouped more logically into systems of your choice, with names that are more meaningful than "default."

> If the System View does not appear automatically, you can display it at any time by right-clicking the deployment diagram and choosing System View.

Binding applications to servers

Given a deployment diagram (refer to Figure 4-3) and a set of applications grouped into systems (described previously), you can set about mapping the applications onto the servers. This mapping process is called *binding* and is performed simply by dragging applications from the System View onto the servers that will host them.

In general, logical servers may host applications as follows:

❑ An IISWebServer may host Web services, web applications, external Web services, or BizTalk Web services.

❑ A DatabaseServer may host ExternalDatabase applications.

❑ A WindowsClient may host Window applications.

❑ A GenericServer may host generic applications.

You can try out the binding process by dragging the applications onto the servers according to the following scheme:

❑ DealingApp application to be hosted by the CustomerDesktop

❑ StockMarket application to be hosted by the StockMarketServer

❑   MarketMaker application to be hosted by the MarketMakerServer

❑   StockDatabase to be hosted by the StockDatabaseServer (optional)

❑   StockBroker application to be hosted by the StockBrokerServer

❑   StockQuoteApp application to be hosted by the StockBrokerServer

The similarity between the application names and server names is simply for convenience and clarity in our example. Servers need not have names similar to the applications they host, and the binding of applications onto servers need not be one-to-one. That fact is demonstrated by our final bindings, which result in two applications — StockBroker and StockQuoteApp — being bound to a single server.

You may want to observe that any number of systems may be bound to a single logical datacenter — a common real-world scenario. You not only bind each application to a server on which it is to be hosted, but also bind each of its endpoints to an endpoint on that logical server. In simple cases, where there is no ambiguity, this binding is automatic. If not, you must resolve the endpoint selection manually.

When you bind the StockMarket application to the StockMarketServer, a Bindings Details dialog box will ask you to choose one of the StockMarketServer's incoming server endpoints as the endpoint to which the application's StockPriceFeed endpoint should be bound. If you placed them initially without renaming them, your options will be ServerEndpoint1 or ServerEndpoint2. We bound to ServerEndpoint2, as the endpoint ultimately connected to the StockBrokerServer as a client.

Obviously, you could be more meticulous about assigning meaningful names to all endpoints when constructing a logical datacenter diagram, or even rename the endpoints on the LDD immediately prior to using Deployment Designer.

When all of the applications have been bound, you will end up with what is shown in Figure 4-4.

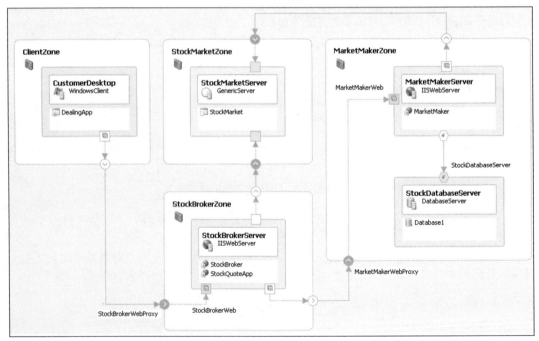

Figure 4-4

In our list of bindings, we indicated the binding between the StockDatabase and the StockDatabaseServer as optional because you won't be able to perform that binding using the supplied files without first creating an ExternalDatabase in Application Designer. We have shown that binding in Figure 4-4, however, for completeness.

Prohibited bindings

As you experiment with Deployment Designer, you will find that in some cases you are prevented from binding an application to a server. This will be indicated by the cursor changing to a no-entry symbol and a message "Bind application to a compatible logical server."

If this occurs, you will have to check the compatibility of the applications and endpoints on your Application Diagram against the zones, servers, and endpoints on your Logical Datacenter Diagram. For example, you might have tried to bind a web application onto a server that is not an IISWebServer, or which does not have a WebSiteEndpoint. Or you might have used the Settings and Constraints Editor to constrain a web server to allow only external Web services to be hosted.

Validating the deployment

Once you have bound applications onto servers, you can then validate your deployment by right-clicking the diagram and choosing Validate Diagram. The settings and constraints specified in the system will be validated against the settings and constraints specified in the logical datacenter. Although we have successfully bound the applications to the datacenter definition, this does not imply that the configuration of the system and the datacenter are compatible. Please note that validation will confirm that connection pathways exist in the datacenter between the servers that you use to host applications connected in the system definition.

> We told you earlier about the interplay between settings in the application/system layer and constraints in the hosting layer, and vice-versa. In a nutshell, by defining constraints on the hosting layer (via the LDD) the operations analyst is saying to the application developers, "If you want to deploy in my datacenter, your application systems must have settings that are compatible with the constraints I have set." The levying of requirements can go the other way as well. The application developer or architect can require that the datacenter have a hosting environment compatible with the requirements of the application (e.g., Windows Server 2003).

Validation errors, if any, will be displayed in the Error List window. You can double-click a validation error in the error list to navigate to the setting that violates the constraint.

> Thinking about the Team System in a wider sense, this situation might present an ideal opportunity to create a work item for the error, to ensure that it is addressed.

For demonstration, you can cause a validation error by following these steps:

1.   Select the incoming StockBrokerWeb WebSiteEndpoint of the StockBrokerZone on the Logical Datacenter Diagram.

2.   In the Settings and Constraints Editor, uncheck the WebServiceEndpoint constraint.

3.   Validate the existing deployment diagram again by right-clicking the diagram and choosing Validate Diagram.

You will see the following validation error:

```
The WebSiteEndpoint StockBrokerWeb can only host the following types:
WebContentEndpoint.
```

Obviously, you can fix it by rechecking the WebServiceEndpoint constraint of the StockBrokerWeb endpoint in the Settings and Constraints Editor.

You can cause further validation errors simply by not binding some of the applications from the System View, as shown in the following example:

```
The application StockMarket from system DEFAULT is not bound in the deployment
diagram DEFAULT1.
```

> **You can clear the validation errors from the error list by right-clicking the deployment diagram and choosing Clear Validation Messages. Be aware that this only clears the messages; it does not resolve the errors!**

Differences between default deployments and system deployments

Having described how to create a default deployment directly from an application design, we will describe how to define systems as groups of applications for deployment. What's the difference?

As you saw, a default deployment always creates a default system, which has configurations and connections taken from the application diagram. Thus, the configuration and connections reflect your development environment, rather than the final system deployment, so this technique is most useful when the development environment and deployment environment are in fact identical. Even so, Microsoft recommends that you not use default deployments to finalize a deployment definition, even in the case of identical environments.

Microsoft's specific advice is as follows:

"Finalizing a deployment definition from deployment diagrams or deployment reports generated from default systems is not recommended. Default systems are useful for quickly evaluating individual applications within the datacenter, but should not be used for final deployment. No system diagram (.sd) files are generated for default systems. Therefore, except for the information included in the deployment report, no record of the default system actually exists, for example, to check into source code control. It is recommended that you use deployment diagrams created using default systems to quickly evaluate applications for configuration and connection issues. You should then use System Designer to create your system designs and use these instead to create deployment diagrams and the corresponding deployment reports."

The default system mirrors the application diagram to the extent that if you change the applications and connections in Application Designer, these changes will be incorporated automatically in the default system. The application diagram mirrors the solution; there are several scenarios in which the solution diagram may contain more than you want to include in a system for deployment: test, test-service stubs, alternative applications (such as geographic variations of the same function that will be substituted in the system, depending on the target of the system), or functional elements that might be excluded, perhaps if defining a down-level configuration, perhaps as a down-level product. For deployments based on explicitly defined systems, you might need to incorporate changes in the application design manually in those systems. Specifically, what is not incorporated is the configuration of connections from the application diagram. Any underlying structural changes do get reflected in the system diagram by default—endpoints added or removed, for example, or the configuration of settings and constraints defined in the solution, which is considered part of the application definition.

With that in mind, we'll now demonstrate how to define systems explicitly.

Defining and Deploying Systems

We have demonstrated the key principles for binding applications onto servers, using the default deployment as our vehicle. That resulted in an automatically generated system—named Default— which collected all applications together.

Now you'll see how to define your own systems from groups of applications.

System definition for the full application design

You can define a new system combining all of the applications shown on an Application Diagram by right-clicking the diagram surface (with nothing selected) and choosing the Design Application System option.

In the Design Application System dialog that appears, you can enter a name for the system; for example, for a system based on the StockBroker application design, you could enter **FullStockBrokerSystem**. A new diagram will appear in the Solution Items folder with the extension .sd—in this case, `FullStockBrokerSystem.sd`.

The resulting system will contain the same set of applications as the default deployment, except that in this case when you subsequently use Deployment Designer, the System View would list the applications under the more meaningful FullStockBrokerSystem heading, rather than the Default heading.

On the face of it, this technique achieves little more than what was achieved using the Define Deployment function, but this approach need not be limited to defining a system for the whole application design. You can define a system for a subset of the application design.

System definition for a subset of the application design

We'll follow the same procedure just described, but this time we'll select two specific applications to be combined as a system. On the StockBrokerApplicationDesign diagram, click the StockBroker application, and then hold down the Ctrl key and click the StockQuoteApp application. With those two applications selected, right-click and choose Design Application System. When the Design Application System dialog appears, you can enter StockBrokerWebApplications as the name of the system.

The result will be the new system diagram named StockBrokerWebApplications.sd, which is shown in Figure 4-5. Initially, you won't see the connections between the StockBroker endpoints and the system boundary, so you must add these by right-clicking the endpoints on the StockBroker and selecting Add Proxy Endpoint.

Alternatively, you can simply click an application endpoint, hold down the Alt key, and drag to the system boundary.

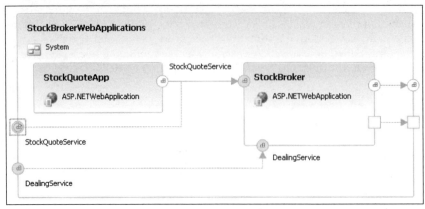

Figure 4-5

To connect to a system, that system must expose a proxy endpoint, through which communication can occur into the system. When you read the "Nested Systems" section later, you will understand why we needed to create the proxies here.

It makes sense to combine the two applications — StockQuoteApp and StockBroker — into a single system because we intend to supply them together as our software release, whereas the MarketMaker and StockMarket applications are design representations of external, or third-party, applications. On that basis, we could consider also including the DealingApp within the same system, but we have chosen not to in this example because, besides forming part of our core product, we also intend StockBroker and StockQuoteApp to be deployed to the same server type (i.e., an IISWebServer) and possibly on the very same server instance. Therefore, in this case we have defined the scope of our system based on deployment constraints, rather than commercial product groupings.

> *Note that there is no requirement to define in a system applications that must be deployed to a single server. You can potentially reuse the subsystem on other systems or in isolation.*

Having defined a new system using System Designer, we can now define a deployment of that system using Deployment Designer.

Defining deployment

Start by right-clicking the StockBrokerWebApplications system shown in Figure 4-5, and choose Define Deployment. When the Define Deployment dialog appears, browse to the `StockBrokerDatacenter.ldd` diagram to deploy against.

A new deployment diagram (e.g., `StockBrokerWebApplications1.dd`) will be created; and when displayed, this diagram will be the same as the one shown in Figure 4-3. This time, the System View window will provide the two applications — StockBroker and StockQuoteApp — that comprise the StockBrokerWebApplications system (see Figure 4-6).

> *If you chose Define Deployment for the FullStockBrokerSystem mentioned earlier, the System View would list all applications, as with the default deployment. The applications would be grouped under the heading FullStockBrokerSystem, rather than the heading Default.*

Figure 4-6

To bind the StockBrokerWebApplications onto servers, you can simply drag the applications onto the server representations of the deployment diagram, just as before.

Nested systems

When defining the StockBrokerWebApplications system, we defined the scope of our system based on deployment constraints, rather than commercial product groupings. In doing so, however, we acknowledged the case for combining the DealingApp into a system along with the StockBroker and StockQuoteApp applications — perhaps as a "release" of our software.

One way to achieve that, while preserving the integrity of the original StockBrokerWebApplications system, is to include a system within a system, as shown in Figure 4-7. You can see there that we have created a new system — named StockBrokerRelease1 and containing the DealingApp — to which we have added the StockBrokerWebApplications system itself.

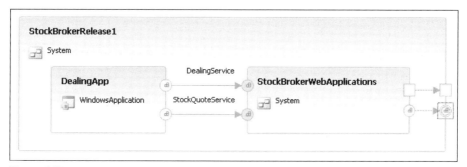

Figure 4-7

As a starting point for that diagram, we selected DealingApp in Application Designer, right-clicked and chose Design Application System, and named the new system StockBrokerRelease1. We then dragged the StockBrokerWebApplications system straight from the System View onto the StockBrokerRelease1 system.

At that point, the diagram would not show connections between the DealingApp consumer endpoints and the StockBrokerWebApplications provider endpoints (which we delegated earlier), so we added those connections in the usual way.

When attempting this yourself, you might wonder how we knew which of the provider endpoints to connect to which of the consumer endpoints. One way would be to reveal the provider endpoint labels — right-click and choose Show Label. Another way would be to simply let the designer warn you of an incorrect connection, which it will with the following message:

```
Warning: The Binding Name and Namespace of the endpoints do not match
```

There is no practical limit to the number of systems that can be nested within one another or the depth of nesting, but a system cannot directly or indirectly contain a use of itself, which would result in a circular reference. Please note that this is just a warning; you can ignore it if you are not using binding names and namespace to identify the type of a Web service endpoint.

Creating System Diagrams from Scratch

For simplicity in our examples, we have encouraged you to create system diagrams by pre-selecting applications in Application Designer. You can also create brand-new system diagrams from scratch that you populate from the System View without using Application Designer at all.

As you experiment with System Designer, you may at some point encounter the problem of an application being shown with a dashed red outline on a system diagram, which indicates that the definition of the application (required by the system) is missing. The most likely causes for you to check are as follows:

❑ The application has been removed from the application diagram.

❑ The project for the application is unloaded or not part of the solution.

❑ The application definition on the application diagram was renamed while the system diagram was closed; thus, the two diagrams could not be synchronized. All you have to do is locate or rename the missing application or system, and the references will resolve correctly. Renaming an application or system that is referenced in a system while that system diagram is open is fine, as it will rename the reference.

System Settings and Constraints

Just as you can launch the Settings and Constraints Editor from Application Designer and Logical Datacenter Designer, so can you launch it from System Designer. Right-click an application or endpoint and choose Settings and Constraints.

Remember that the settings and constraints in Application Designer and Logical Datacenter Designer are interrelated so that logical datacenter constraints apply to application settings, and application constraints apply to logical datacenter settings. System Designer settings and constraints operate in the same way they do in Application Designer. In fact, System Designer provides an opportunity to override the application settings prior to final deployment. Changing settings from the System Designer overrides settings defined on the underlying application definition. These overridden settings will be used in the deployment.

Figure 4-8 shows a subset of the settings that you will see if you selected the StockQuoteApp in System Designer while viewing the Settings and Constraints window. We have highlighted the LogonMethod setting, for demonstration only, to change it from the default value (ClearText) to one of the other possible values (Interactive, Batch, or Network).

That is possible only because the same setting in Application Designer was set to Overridable. To see what we mean, Figure 4-9 was created by selecting the StockQuoteApp in Application Designer while viewing the Settings and Constraints window. Notice the boxes checked in the Overridable column.

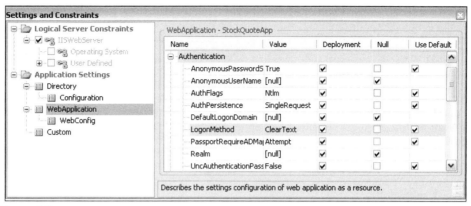

Figure 4-8

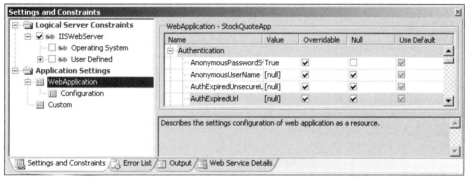

Figure 4-9

A system can contain multiple instances of a given application definition, with each instance having different settings. To test this out, you can open an existing system diagram and drag an item already shown on the diagram from the System View as a new instance. Open the Settings and Constraints Editor on the new instance, change a setting, and then open the Settings and Constraints Editor on the original instance to confirm that it isn't reflected in that instance.

> *Additional examples of using System Designer to construct deployable systems from groups of applications can be found in Tony Loton's MSDN article "Introduction to the Visual Studio 2005 System Designer" at* http://msdn.microsoft.com/library/default.asp?url=/library/en-us/dnvs05/html/vstssysdesigner.asp.

Deployment Reports

In the preceding coverage of the System Designer and Deployment Designer, we haven't actually deployed anything. What we've done is evaluate the deployment of our application systems against the requirements of the logical datacenter. In order to deploy properly, we need a deployment report that describes what to deploy, where, and how.

Deployment Designer provides a Deployment Report feature, which produces a document containing SDM meta-data from the application and application hosting layers. This information tells you what software needs to be deployed where, and how the applications and hosts need to be configured to support the deployment.

Right-click a deployment diagram and choose Generate Deployment Report. Two new files will appear in Solution Explorer with the same names as the deployment diagram: an .html file (the human-readable version, discussed in the next section) and an .xml file (the machine-readable version, covered in the section "Machine-readable deployment reports and automated deployment").

Human-readable deployment reports

Generating a deployment report for the default system deployment (file `DefaultSystem1.dd`) that we created at the outset will result in a file named `DefaultSystem11.html` containing the deployment information as human-readable HTML.

The companion file `DefaultSystem1.xml` is discussed in the next section.

The human-readable version comprises a number of sections that provide information on Errors (listed first to get your attention), Bindings (see Figure 4-10), the deployment diagram (identical to Figure 4-4), the logical datacenter diagram (the target of the deployment), systems (see Figure 4-11), and the system diagram (for the full suite of applications), followed by a number of sections describing the deployment resources in detail such as IIS6 settings.

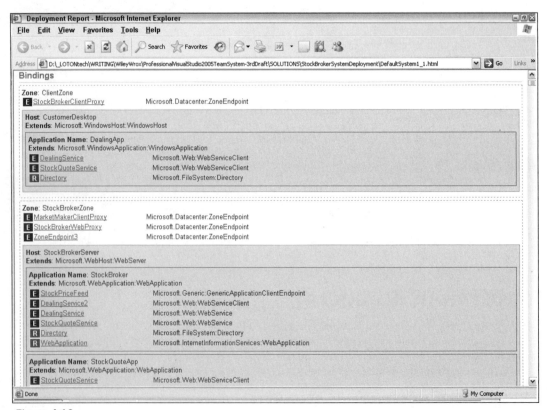

Figure 4-10

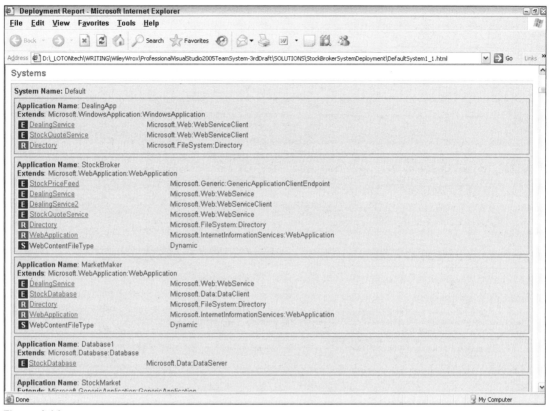

Figure 4-11

Machine-readable deployment reports and automated deployment

What you achieved by using Deployment Designer is matching up the configurations of the applications and systems to be deployed with the hardware and software resources available to host them in the deployment environment. You also matched the logical resources referenced by the applications with the actual access points in the deployment environment.

Ultimately, we'd like to be able to use that model-based information to provision or configure resources on demand, and this aspiration is made feasible thanks to the XML version of the deployment report, which is not intended for human interpretation. Because the format is XML, it raises the possibility of transforming the output, using XSLT, into an in-house format suitable for generating an automated deployment script.

> *Remember that where an automated deployment is neither possible nor desirable, the same deployment report may be generated as human-readable HTML.*

The XML output can be very large (measured in megabytes), so it is impossible to list here in its entirety, but it's easy enough for you to reproduce as described. Figure 4-12, in which we have collapsed some of the XML elements to show the overall structure, gives you a feel for the information it contains.

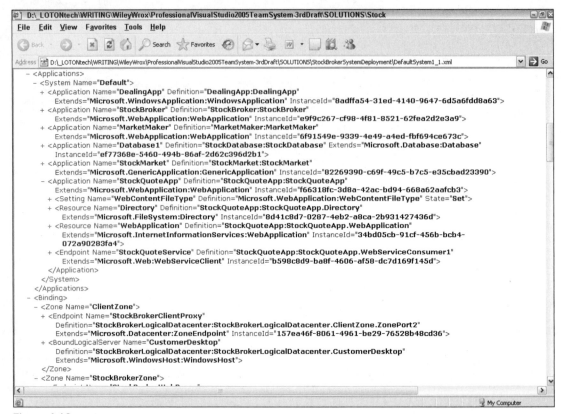

Figure 4-12

You can see two XML tagged elements, <Applications> and <Binding>, that correspond with sections of the HTML report. If you could scroll down, you would see more such sections.

Within the <Applications> element is a <System> element (named Default because this is a report for our default deployment); and within the <System> element are <Application> elements representing each of the applications within that system. We have expanded the <Application> element corresponding with the StockQuoteApp so that you can see further details of the settings, resources, and endpoints of that application.

Within the <Binding> element, we have expanded the <Zone> element corresponding with the ClientZone so that you can see — among other things — that the CustomerDesktop logical server is contained within that zone.

To clarify the overall structure just described, and in case it's difficult to see that detail in Figure 4-12, here is a simplified version of that hierarchy:

```
<Applications>
  <System Name="Default">
    <Application Name="DealingApp">
    </Application>
    <Application Name="StockBroker">
    </Application>
```

```
    <Application Name="MarketMaker">
    </Application>
    ...
    <Application Name="StockQuoteApp">
      ...
      <Endpoint Name="StockQuoteService">
    </Application>
  </System>
</Applications>
<Binding>
  <Zone Name="ClientZone">
    <Endpoint Name="StockBrokerClientProxy">
    <BoundLogicalServer Name="CustomerDesktop">
...
```

That should serve to whet your appetite to investigate further the syntax of the deployment reports. The point is that you—or more likely a third-party vendor—can devise tools that automate the deployment by interpreting and transforming the information contained therein.

The UML Deployment Diagram: Similar, but Not the Same

The name Deployment Designer inevitably conjures up a comparison with the UML deployment diagram. Indeed, Figure 4-13, an equivalent deployment diagram drawn in UML, bears a striking resemblance to the Visual Studio 2005 deployment diagram shown in Figure 4-3.

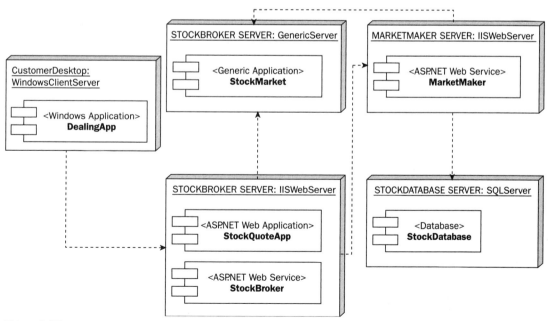

Figure 4-13

You can see that we have used UML components to represent the applications, an analogy that we first established in Chapter 2. UML nodes have been used to represent logical servers, and the binding of components onto nodes (refer to Figure 4-13) is equivalent to the binding of applications onto servers (refer to Figure 4-4). Dependencies between nodes in Figure 4-13 reflect the connections between servers in Figure 4-4.

Thus, the correlation between the two notations is high, with some notable anomalies such as the lack of support for zones in the UML notation.

Despite that high correlation, the two notations are not exactly equivalent in the sense of a one-to-one correspondence. As discussed previously, the single UML deployment diagram actually maps to a combination of two distributed system designers — Logical Datacenter Designer and Deployment Designer. Thus, the distributed system designers provide greater flexibility by decoupling the logical datacenter definition from the binding of application components onto logical server nodes.

Furthermore, System Designer allows anticipated deployment settings and constraints (specified using Application Designer and, in the case of settings, overridden in System Designer) to be defined separately from the actual deployment settings and constraints specified using Logical Datacenter Designer.

Dynamic Modeling

While on the subject of UML we'll revisit the topic of dynamic modeling. You might remember that in Chapter 2 we indicated that the Distributed System Designers do not (yet) provide dynamic modeling capabilities analogous to the UML sequence and collaboration diagrams.

We suggested that you could simulate a UML collaboration diagram by adding numbered comments to the links between applications on an application diagram — to show the sequence of calls or messages between the application services. Refer back to Chapter 2 to see a sample application diagram marked up in that way. The main problem with that idea is that you are allowed only one application diagram per solution, so unless you create multiple solutions simply for documentation purposes, you can only ever show one interaction scenario.

The good news is that System Designer has no such limitation; you can create as many system diagrams as you like. In addition, because system diagrams are visually very similar to application diagrams, you can apply the same technique. Better still, because a system diagram can contain a subset of the complete application set, you can create a separate diagram for each set of collaborating applications in each scenario.

That's perhaps not what System Designer was intended for, but as a handy workaround it's the closest you'll get to model the dynamic (runtime) behavior of your applications using the current set of distributed system designers.

Summary

This chapter introduced Deployment Designer, which enables applications defined using Application Designer to be bound to logical servers defined using Logical Datacenter Designer.

Initially, we used the Define Deployment feature of Application Designer to demonstrate this binding process for a default system based on the application design. We indicated some of the errors that could occur when binding applications to servers and told you how the final deployment could be validated.

We highlighted the difference between default deployments and (explicit) system deployments, leading into a discussion about grouping applications into systems explicitly for deployment to the logical data-center. In the context of user-defined systems, we discussed the role of the Settings and Constraints Editor and the idea of nested systems.

We demonstrated how to generate deployment reports in human-readable HTML format and in machine-readable XML format. We also offered a head start on how to navigate the structure of the XML file, suggesting that this format lends itself to automated deployment through scripting.

Finally, we contrasted the Visual Studio 2005 Deployment Designer with the UML deployment diagram, noting the one-to-many correspondence between the UML notation and the set of Visual Studio notations.

This chapter concludes our coverage of the four Distributed System Designers: Application Designer, Logical Datacenter Designer, System Designer, and Deployment Designer. One more visual designer is included for the first time in the Visual Studio 2005 Edition for Software Architects, as well as in some of the other Visual Studio 2005 editions. Though not strictly one of the Distributed System Designers, *Class Designer* operates in a similar way and is complementary in its usage. If you have a visual modeling background — for example, using UML — our coverage of visual design would be incomplete without a discussion of Class Designer, so that's the topic of Chapter 5.

5

Class Modeling Using Class Designer

In this chapter, we'll look at Class Designer, which provides a design surface for visualizing the classes and other types that you define in code. Looking at it from that perspective, Class Designer provides an up-to-date window on the code, thanks to automatic synchronization. Conversely, this designer enables you to define your class structure diagrammatically prior to using the code editor. If you have a background in UML, you will recognize this as the raison d'être for a class designer.

We'll look at Class Designer from both angles—visualization of existing code and design of new type hierarchies.

In the section headed "From Code to Class Diagrams," we introduce class diagrams as a pictorial way of representing code. For continuity, we draw on the running StockBroker example for inspiration, and to provide a code base. We invite you to retrofit some new ideas into that example, but that's not compulsory and you'll learn a lot simply by reading that section.

In the section headed "From Class Diagrams to Code," we show how class diagrams should be used to drive the high-level design and overall structure of your code, rather than as a convenient mechanism for documenting it after the event. In that section, we take each of the modeling concepts—such as inheritance and association—in turn.

We'll use the Visual Basic .NET Class Designer to introduce the notation and to demonstrate the main features in a consistent manner. Keep in mind that the majority of the features are equally applicable to Visual C# and Visual J# as well as Visual Basic, and indeed we'll use C# toward the end as a vehicle for introducing some more advanced ideas. Unfortunately, C++ is not supported by this first version of Class Designer.

As you read this chapter, you should be aware of the distinction between the terms *type* and *class*. By *type* we mean any type supported by Class Designer, such as a class, an interface, a structure, or a delegate. By *class* we mean specifically the class type, though discussions about classes may well apply to some of the other types too. This distinction between the terms used is important because Class Designer could be regarded in a wider sense as a "Type Designer" not limited to class design, although the term *Type Designer* would be less familiar to the object modeling—and especially UML—community.

> *Provided Files:* **You will find the sources files and class diagrams for this chapter in a solution contained within the** StockBrokerClassLibrary.zip **file provided on the book's Website. That will be useful to you as a reference point and a quick route through the chapter, though of course we encourage you to take the time to build the examples yourself from scratch.**

Class Designer Toolbox and Types

Because Class Designer is coupled tightly with the underlying code, the available toolbox items depend to some extent on the language of the project to which you add a class diagram. Figure 5-1 presents the Class Designer toolbox for Visual Basic, which differs from the C# toolbox in only two respects:

- ❏ There is an additional VB-specific type: the Module.
- ❏ The Structure type is named Struct in the C# toolbox.

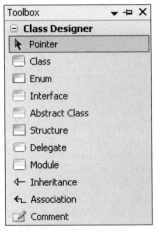

Figure 5-1

You may already have noticed our use of the word *type,* rather than *prototype.* Whereas the toolbox items of Application Designer and Logical Datacenter Designer are referred to as prototypes, those of Class Designer are referred to simply as types. We'll offer a brief description of each type in turn, and later we'll dig deeper into each one:

- ❏ **Class:** This type provides a diagrammatic representation of a class in code, synchronized with the code so that code changes are reflected in the diagram and vice versa. The notation is similar to UML in that a class representation has compartments for members such as fields (attributes in UML) and methods (operations in UML), as well as domain-specific compartments for events and properties.

- ❑ **Enum:** This type provides a diagrammatic representation of an enumeration in code.

- ❑ **Interface:** The Interface type provides a diagrammatic representation of an interface in code. Inheritance relationships may be drawn between classes and interfaces, rendering the interfaces as lollipop shapes attached to the classes that implement them.

- ❑ **Abstract Class:** This type represents an abstract (`MustInherit`) class in code. The abstract class may provide concrete implementations of some methods, with other methods left to be implemented in derived concrete classes. An abstract class is rendered on the design surface with a broken-line boundary to distinguish it from a concrete class.

- ❑ **Structure (Struct in C#):** The Struct type provides a diagrammatic representation of a struct (value type) in code, with compartments to show fields, methods, and so on.

- ❑ **Delegate:** The Delegate type provides a diagrammatic representation of a delegate method, with the delegate parameters shown as members.

- ❑ **Module (Visual Basic only):** This type represents a Visual Basic module and is not available in the Visual C# Class Designer.

- ❑ **Inheritance:** The inheritance toolbox item represents a relationship, or connection, between types, rather than a type itself. The relationship connects a derived type to a base type (a subclass to a superclass) and is equivalent to the UML generalization relationship.

- ❑ **Association:** This toolbox item also represents a relationship — between a class and the type of one of its members. Unlike most UML tools, the Visual Studio Class Designer allows any member to be shown within a type, or as an association to another type, completely interchangeably according to your preference. Unlike UML, the stronger forms of association — aggregation and composition — are not distinguished on diagrams because they are not distinguishable in code.

- ❑ **Comment:** As in previous chapters, a Comment is just a free text note that adds clarity to your diagrams. Unfortunately, it is not possible to attach comments to other elements on class diagrams.

From Code to Class Diagrams

As described earlier, the purpose of Class Designer can be stated in two ways: as a tool for visualizing existing code, and as a tool for defining the structure of that code in the first place. In this section, we'll look at the visualization of existing code.

> *In fact, version 1 of Class Designer has been optimized for several usage scenarios, including visualization of existing code (this section), refactoring (Chapter 11), and drawing diagrams for documentation purposes. In addition, of course, is top-down class design, which is the subject of the section "From Class Diagrams to Code."*

As a representation of types, the class diagram offers a pictorial alternative to the Object Browser for examining types. You can visualize types that are not your own — i.e., those from third-party assemblies, including the .NET Framework itself — and you can tailor the visualization to show more or less detail, including the important relationships between the types. The selection and arrangement of types on diagrams should communicate something extra, over and above what would be deduced from the Object Browser.

StockBroker revisited — from code to class diagrams

The StockBroker example that runs through the previous chapters will provide a basis for visualizing existing code using class diagrams. We'll start by drawing a pictorial representation of the UI classes for one of the StockBroker client applications: DealingApp.

DealingApp class diagram

Figure 5-2 is a class diagram based on the UI components of the DealingApp Windows application implemented in Chapter 2.

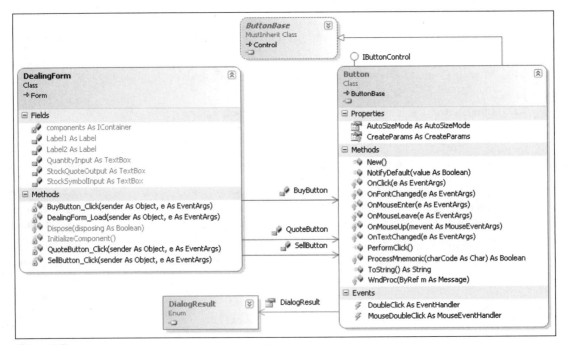

Figure 5-2

You don't need to follow these steps yourself, but they demonstrate how we created that diagram. Here's what we did:

1. Within our fully implemented StockBroker solution, we created a new blank class diagram by right-clicking the DealingApp project and choosing Add ➪ New Item from the context menu.

2. We dragged the DealingForm.vb file from the Solution Explorer to the class diagram, resulting in the DealingForm class shape being displayed.

3. We expanded the DealingForm class shape to reveal its members, and for the three Button members — BuyButton, QuoteButton, and SellButton — we right-clicked and chose Show As Association... to reveal three links to instances of the separate Button class.

4. We right-clicked the Button class shape and chose Show Base Type to reveal the ButtonBase superclass from which Button inherits.

5. We expanded the `Button` class shape to reveal its members, right-clicked the `DialogResult` member, and chose Show As Association... to reveal a link to an instance of the `DialogResult` Enum.

We'll tell you about the Show as Association and Show Base Type features more formally later. The important thing to understand now is that Class Designer has been used as a tool for inspecting types and their relationships, very much as you would use the Object Browser, although in this case we have specifically drawn a picture showing only the types we want to show, to the level of detail we are interested in, and in a form that we can share with other developers as printed copy.

We have built a picture of the UI classes in our application merely by exploring relationships from the single starting point of the `DealingForm`, a class that was generated originally from our Application Design, and whose members are instances of .NET or other library types — not types of our own making.

We can use Class Designer to provide a diagrammatic representation of auto-generated classes and those belonging to compiled assemblies, but what about new classes of our own making?

StockDeal classes: Code and Class Diagram

You might recall that in Chapter 2 we invited you to change the return types of the `DealingService` `buyStock` and `sellStock` web methods from integers to `StockSale` and `StockPurchase` types. That was to demonstrate the synchronization between the code and the model, whereby changes that you made in code were reflected in Application Designer's Web Service Details window.

We'll take that idea further by conceiving three new classes: `StockPurchase`, `StockSale`, and `StockDeal`, which provides a common base class for both kinds of deal. Let's look at the code for the three `StockDeal` classes.

The `StockPurchase` class would be returned by the `buyStock` web method of the DealingService. The code for that class would be as follows:

```
Public Class StockPurchase
    Inherits ClassLibrary.StockDeal

    Private mNumberOfSharesBought As Integer

    Public Sub New(ByVal stockSymbol As String, ByVal numberOfShares As Integer)
        MyBase.New(stockSymbol)
        mNumberOfSharesBought = numberOfShares
    End Sub

    Public ReadOnly Property NumberOfSharesBought() As Integer
        Get
            Return mNumberOfSharesBought
        End Get
    End Property

    Public Overrides ReadOnly Property NumberOfShares() As Integer
        Get
            Return NumberOfSharesBought
        End Get
    End Property

End Class
```

The main points to note in the preceding code are as follows:

- ❑ The `StockPurchase` class inherits from the `StockDeal` base class (defined later).

- ❑ There is a member variable—`mNumberOfSharesBought`—to hold the number of shares bought in the purchase.

- ❑ The constructor takes in a `stockSymbol` and `numberOfShares`, storing the number of shares in the local member variable and passing the `stockSymbol` through to the base class constructor.

- ❑ There is a read-only property named `NumberOfSharesBought` that returns the contents of the `mNumberOfSharesBought` member variable.

- ❑ An additional read-only property named `NumberOfShares` returns the value of the `NumberOf SharesBought` property, thereby implicitly also returning the value of the `mNumberOfShares Bought` member variable. Take note of the name of this property—`NumberOfShares` rather than `NumberOfSharesBought`—and note the inheritance modifier of Overrides.

The `StockSale` class would be returned by the `sellStock` web method of the DealingService. The code for that class would be as follows:

```
Public Class StockSale
    Inherits ClassLibrary.StockDeal

    Private mNumberOfSharesSold As Integer

    Public Sub New(ByVal stockSymbol As String, ByVal numberOfShares As Integer)
        MyBase.New(stockSymbol)
        mNumberOfSharesSold = numberOfShares
    End Sub

    Public ReadOnly Property NumberOfSharesSold() As Integer
        Get
            Return mNumberOfSharesSold
        End Get
    End Property

    Public Overrides ReadOnly Property NumberOfShares() As Integer
        Get
            Return NumberOfSharesSold
        End Get
    End Property

End Class
```

That code is pretty much identical to the code of the `StockPurchase` class except that the member variable is named `mNumberOfSharesSold` and its wrapper property is named `NumberOfSharesSold`.

The two classes that we've reviewed both inherit from the base class `StockDeal`, the code for which is as follows:

```
Public MustInherit Class StockDeal

    Private mStockSymbol As String

    Public ReadOnly Property StockSymbol() As System.String
```

```
        Get
            Return mStockSymbol
        End Get
    End Property

    Public Sub New(ByVal stockSymbol As String)
        mStockSymbol = stockSymbol
    End Sub

    Public MustOverride ReadOnly Property NumberOfShares() As Integer

End Class
```

The main points to note in the preceding code are as follows:

❑   The `StockDeal` class is defined as `MustInherit`, thus making it an abstract class.

❑   There is an `mStockSymbol` member variable to hold the symbol of the stock to which a deal relates, with a read-only property that returns it. This functionality is provided entirely by this base class, on behalf of the `StockPurchase` and `StockSale` subclasses.

❑   The constructor takes a `stockSymbol` and sets the member variable, with this constructor invoked from the constructors of the subclasses.

❑   A read-only property named `NumberOfShares`, with inheritance modifier `MustOverride`, is declared but not implemented. The idea is that any kind of `StockDeal` — whether `StockSale` or `StockPurchase` — can report the number of shares involved in the deal regardless of whether they are shares bought or shares sold. The subclasses take care of returning the correct value in each case.

> **If you like, you can attempt to retrofit those classes into your implementation of the StockBroker application and its clients. It's not compulsory, of course, and for the purposes of this chapter it is sufficient to simply create a new Visual Basic Class Library project containing those classes, as we have.**

Now we'll create a class diagram to show those classes diagrammatically.

Assuming you have the three classes contained within a class Visual Basic Class library, you can create a new class diagram simply by right-clicking the project and choosing Add ➪ New Item from the pop-up menu. Select the Class Diagram item and name it `StockDeal.cd`, the .cd extension marking this as a class diagram file.

> *You could also do this from the StockBroker project if you decided to follow the optional exercise and retrofit these classes into your StockBroker application.*

Now all you need to do is drag the three classes from the Class View, or the three source files from the Solution Explorer, onto the diagram, for the result shown in Figure 5-3. You could also build that diagram by multiple-selecting the three classes in Class View or Solution Explorer, right-clicking, and choosing View Class Diagram from the context menu — without having pre-created the blank diagram at all. In that case, the diagram will be given a default name.

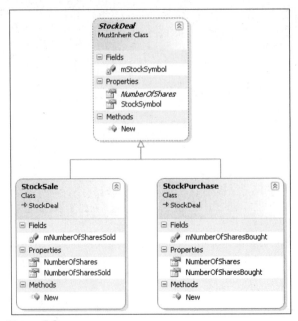

Figure 5-3

You can also create an auto-populated diagram to show all of the classes in a particular project, or all of the classes within a specific namespace. Just right-click the project or namespace as appropriate and choose View Class Diagram from the context menu.

The main points to note on the diagram are as follows:

❑   Each class is shown with compartments for its Fields (i.e., member variables), Properties, Methods, and Events in a style similar to the UML notation for attributes and operations on a class. If you don't see those compartments, try clicking the scroll-up and scroll-down buttons (shown as chevrons in the top-right corner of each class).

❑   The inheritance relationships between the two subclasses and the base class have been drawn automatically, using notation similar to UML generalization notation.

❑   Because the StockDeal base class must be inherited, it is rendered with a dashed outline to distinguish it as an abstract class.

What you've achieved by dragging those classes onto the diagram is equivalent to reverse engineering a set of source code classes into a class diagram, except that you haven't had to perform any explicit "reverse engineering" step at all. Whereas some modeling tools require you to invoke a specific reverse-engineer option to achieve this, Visual Studio 2005 does not. All classes shown in the Class View are immediately available for representation on class diagrams; and for classes taken from compiled assemblies, the original source code need not even be present.

Visualizing members

Members of types are displayed in compartments according to what kind they are. Figure 5-3 shows members grouped as Fields, Properties, and Methods. Alternatively, you can choose to group members by access modifier; or sort them alphabetically, simply by selecting the menu option Class Diagram ⇨ Group Members ⇨ Group by Access or Class Diagram ⇨ Group Members ⇨ Sort Alphabetically.

You can hide selected members by right-clicking a member and choosing Hide; then right-click the member's compartment heading and choose Show all Members to see it again. You can also collapse and expand entire compartments, such as all fields or all methods, or all public members or all private members, depending on what is on view. Choosing to hide members, or to collapse compartments, has no effect on the underlying code whatsoever, so these operations are fully reversible.

As you work with visualizing members, you will notice that the set of compartments varies according to the language of the underlying code.

Historically, UML notation does not provide separate compartments for some kinds of members such as properties, so UML tools such as Visio for Enterprise Architects and Rational XDE indicate properties as stereotyped attributes, or as pairs of get/set methods. This demonstrates one of the benefits of Class Designer's domain-specific notation over a generic design notation such as UML.

On some of the class diagrams in this chapter, such as Figure 5-3, member names are shown but member types are not. On other figures, such as Figure 5-4, the type of each member is shown along with its name. In Figure 5-2, method members are shown with their full signatures. You can toggle these display settings by selecting Class Diagram ⇨ Change Members Format and choosing Display Name, Display Name and Type, or Display Full Signature.

If you choose to save space on diagrams by showing only member names, you can still see the complete type and signature information for a member by hovering over a member to see that additional information as a tooltip.

From Class Diagrams to Code

Now that we've demonstrated how to visualize existing code using a Class Diagram, we'll now take a step back and look at this from another angle — how to design your code types from scratch using Class Designer, before undertaking the hardcore programming using the code editor.

There is no benefit in attempting to design some types up-front using Class Designer, because it's more effective to let Visual Studio generate them automatically. Specifically, we're referring to the application classes that are generated when you implement an application directly from Application Designer, or the classes that you get when you create a new project from a template. In addition, the UI classes for forms, buttons, and so on are better designed using the web/windows forms designers — to be visualized subsequently using Class Designer as we did in Figure 5-2.

> *Some notations and processes, particularly the UML/RUP combination, encourage a "user experience modeling" activity that involves defining screens, forms, and fields in an abstract sense before coding them in any language. This may have some limited benefit during the analysis phase, but serves no useful purpose during design — specifically, .NET design — where more suitable tools are provided.*

So what kinds of classes should be designed initially using Class Designer, rather than in code? Consider the three classes StockDeal, StockPurchase, and StockSales, that we visualized in Figure 5-3. These classes could not be generated automatically by Visual Studio, nor could they be designed using one of the other designers such as the forms designer. Those classes — which we'll refer to as *domain classes* — are conceived mentally, or in a team brainstorming session, according to a narrative like the following:

"We need to represent two kinds of deals: purchases and sales. These have common attributes, such as the number of shares and the stock symbol for the deal, which could be recorded in a base class. That base class would also facilitate a DealHistory, which would list previous deals regardless of whether they are sales or purchases. Obviously, there would be no StockDeal that was neither a purchase nor a sale, so the base class would be abstract."

While working through that narrative, you might have drawn a mental picture of how these classes would fit together; and in the brainstorming scenario, you may well have drawn up that mental picture informally with lines and boxes. Using Class Designer enables you to formalize the mental picture in a way that is accessible to noncoders as well as coders, and without having to worry about the exact syntax for defining the classes in code using various languages.

> *Additional examples of using Class Designer to model a set of domain classes in support of an API can be found in Tony Loton's MSDN article "Designing an API with the Visual Studio 2005 Class Designer" at* `http://msdn.microsoft.com/library/default.asp?url=/library/en-us/dnvs05/html/vstsclassdesigner.asp`.

Designing the StockDeal classes using Class Designer

To begin the process of designing the `StockDeal` classes using Class Designer you need to do the following:

1. Create a new Visual Basic Class Library project in Visual Studio, and add a Class Diagram to it named `StockDeal.cd`.

2. Drag an Abstract Class type from the toolbox to the design surface and name it `StockDeal`. A dialog will force you to name the class when placing it on the design surface.

3. Drag a Class type from the toolbox to the design surface and name it `StockPurchase`.

4. Drag a Class type from the toolbox to the design surface and name it `StockSale`.

> *Note that wherever the steps say "drag a class type from the toolbox" you can also use the context menu of the diagram (right-click an empty portion) to the same effect. However, to add relationships (see the following section) you have to use the toolbox.*

Adding inheritance relationships

To show that the `StockPurchase` and `StockSale` classes derive from the `StockDeal` base class, you need to draw in two inheritance relationships. Click the Inheritance item in the toolbox, click the `StockPurchase` class, and drag the connection to the `StockDeal` class. Then do the same for the inheritance between `StockSale` and `StockDeal`.

Your diagram should be starting to look like Figure 5-3, at least in outline. Already you have modeled the essential relationships, which have been reflected automatically in the code as follows:

```
Public MustInherit Class StockDeal
```

```
Public Class StockSale Inherits ClassLibrary.StockDeal
```

```
Public Class StockPurchase Inherits ClassLibrary.StockDeal
```

> The process for drawing inheritance relationships using Class Designer is the same regardless of which programming language you're using, so you don't need to remember whether the syntax is "Must Inherit" (Visual Basic) or "abstract" (Visual C#).

We have demonstrated how to draw an inheritance relationship between two classes. You can also draw inheritance relationships between two interfaces, or between a class and an interface. In the latter case, the interface will be visualized independently on the design surface and as a lollipop shape emanating from the class shape. It will also auto-generate stubs that implement the interface.

Now we need to populate those classes with members.

Adding members

To add new members to a type, you can right-click the shape on the diagram and choose Add from the pop-up menu. You will be able to add a Method, Property, Field, Event, Constructor, Destructor, or Constant. Attempting to add a member will display the Class Details window.

Note that you cannot add members in this way to types that are referenced in other assemblies, such as the Button class that was visualized on the Class Diagram in Figure 5-2.

The Class Details window is rather like the Web Service Details window that you met in Chapter 2. When you click a type on the diagram, this window shows the following information for every member of the type: the member name, its type, its modifier, and any comments you have entered. You can edit any of those things providing the member is not read-only; and in the case of member types, you can take advantage of the full Intellisense support. You can also add new members by clicking the <add property>, <add method>, <add field>, or <add event> indicators as appropriate.

Method and Property members may be expanded to reveal additional indicators for <add parameter>.

The following table gives an example entry for a StockSymbol property as it would appear in the Class Details window.

Name	Type	Modifier	Summary
StockSymbol	String	Public	Unique identifier for the stock

There is one further column, Hide, which we have not shown. This additional column has checkboxes that enable you to selectively hide members on the diagram.

Use the Class Details window to populate the StockDeal, StockPurchase, and StockSale classes with their members, in order to reflect the diagram shown in Figure 5-3 and the final code listed earlier. Pay particular attention to the NumberOfShares property that is present in all three classes.

You may remember that in the "From Code to Class Diagrams" section we coded that property in the abstract base class (StockDeal) as follows:

```
Public MustOverride ReadOnly Property NumberOfShares() As Integer
```

In the `StockSale` derived class we defined it this way:

```
Public Overrides ReadOnly Property NumberOfShares() As Integer
    Get
        Return NumberOfSharesSold
    End Get
End Property
```

The definition in the `StockPurchase` derived class was the same except for the `Return` statement, which was `Return NumberOfSharesBought`.

When working in the opposite direction, from class diagrams to code, you can specify such overriding of members using Class Designer as follows:

1. Once you've added the member (in this case, the `NumberOfShares` property) to the base class, change the Inheritance Modify setting in the Properties window to `MustOverride`.

2. Right-click the derived class (`StockSale` or `StockPurchase`) and choose Intellisense ➪ Override Members from the context menu.

3. Select the member to override, which in this case is `NumberOfShares`.

Adding association relationships

Having looked at the inheritance relationship, we'll now turn our attention to the other kind of relationship that you can draw between classes — namely, association. An association shows that a class holds a reference to another class such that instances of the two classes are linked via a member variable.

> *If you have a UML background, you may be familiar with the stronger forms of association called aggregation and composition, which are not supported in Class Designer. This is good news in that, when implemented, aggregation and composition are usually indistinguishable because most programming languages — apart from C++ — do not distinguish between "by reference" members (association) and "by value" members (aggregation/composition). Furthermore, the stronger forms of association are defined imprecisely, leading to debate and misinterpretation even among the experts.*

As a practical example of association, we'll introduce a new class named `Customer` that will hold a reference to the last deal placed by the customer:

1. Add a new Class Diagram named `CustomerStockDealClasses.cd`.

2. Drag a new class from the toolbox onto the design surface, and name that class `Customer`.

3. Drag the `StockDeal` class from Solution Explorer onto the design surface.

4. Choose Association from the toolbox, click the `Customer`, and drag to `StockDeal`.

5. In Properties — or on the diagram — rename it `lastDeal`.

The result should be as shown in Figure 5-4, which — among other things — demonstrates that the same class (in this case, `StockDeal`) may be shown on more than one class diagram.

> *Placing a class on more than one diagram does not create a copy of the class.*

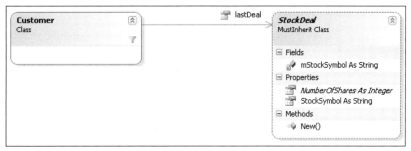

Figure 5-4

Naming the association `lastDeal` causes a property of that name to be added as a member to the `Customer` class, as shown here:

```
Public Class Customer


    Public Property lastDeal() As ClassLibrary.StockDeal
        Get

        End Get
        Set(ByVal value As ClassLibrary.StockDeal)

        End Set

    End Property
End Class
```

That property is the realization of the association in code.

If you think about it, this is just a property like any other, so there's no logical reason why it could not be represented simply as a member of the `Customer` class, with no association line at all. Indeed, that is the case, and you can choose that alternative representation by right-clicking the association line and selecting Show as Property from the pop-up menu. You can also reverse that action at any time by right-clicking the `lastDeal` property member and selecting Show as Association. You can even multiple-select properties or fields prior to invoking the Show As Association feature.

> *UML tools typically do not allow such easy switching between representations. For example, in Rational Rose, you configure the tool to treat certain objects such as Strings as basic types, so that during reverse engineering/code generation, they are rendered as attributes (i.e., member fields), rather than associations.*

> *Note also that unlike UML tools you may have used, Class Designer does not support bi-directional associations. If you want a reciprocal link between the `StockDeal` class and the `Customer` class, you'll have to add a new association explicitly.*

The purpose of adding that association was to record against a `Customer` the `lastDeal` that he or she placed, and by associating with the `StockDeal` abstract class we can record the last deal regardless of whether it was a `StockSale` or a `StockPurchase`.

One-to-many associations

The `lastDeal` association is a one-to-one association — for each `Customer`, there is only one `lastDeal` (i.e., the last purchase or last sale). What if we wanted to record a history of all deals made by a customer? That would imply a list, collection, or array, or — in UML parlance — a one-to-many association.

In Class Designer, it is not possible to draw a one-to-many association at all, unfortunately. Suppose, however, you already have a one-to-many relationship represented in Visual Basic code, like this:

```
Dim dealHistory(12) As StockDeal
```

Or this:

```
Public Property dealHistory() As StockDeal
```

Or in Visual C# code that takes advantage of the Generics feature, like this:

```
private List<StockDeal> deals;
```

Including such a member in the `Customer` class would enable that class to hold a list of previous deals performed by that customer, but how will that relationship be rendered by Class Designer?

Class Designer will render an association line between the `Customer` and `StockDeal` classes in the fashion of the `lastDeal` association shown in Figure 5-4, except that this time the association will be named `dealHistory` and will have a double arrow at the "many" end of the association line, as you can see in Figure 5-5.

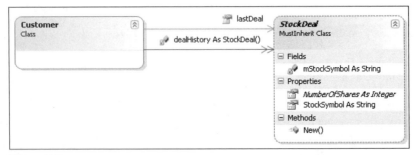

Figure 5-5

Whereas with one-to-one associations you have two options for visualization, Show as Property and Show as Association, for one-to-many associations you have a third option: Show as Collection Association. That's how we caused the double arrowhead to appear in Figure 5-5; and in the case of our Visual Basic examples, that double arrowhead is the only notational difference you'll see between the "Show as Association" and the "Show as Collection Association" display modes. In the case of the C# generics example that we gave, however, the effect will be as follows:

❑ Show as Collection Association will render an association between the `Customer` and `StockDeal` classes pretty much as shown in Figure 5-5, with a double arrow at the "many" end of the association.

❑ Show as Association will render an association line between the `Customer` class and a new Generic Interface type labeled `IList<T>` — with a single arrow because the association is to a single "list" of stock deals even though it was to "many" of the stock deals themselves.

You can find out more about how Visual Studio 2005 determines one-to-many associations by reading R. Ramesh's weblog entry"Collection associations in Class Designer" at `http://blogs.msdn.com/r.ramesh/archive/2005/02/01/364862.aspx`.

Working with methods

The `StockDeal`, `StockPurchase`, and `StockSale` classes represent the entity classes of our problem domain. These may well be refinements of entities identified during analysis (perhaps modeled in Visio), and they may well be candidates for persisting away in a database.

Those classes will not be at all useful unless we have a set of methods — an API — to manipulate them. You can define a very simple API in the form of a `StockBroker` class with two methods that have the following signatures:

```
Public Function buyStock(ByVal stockSymbol As String, ByVal numberOfShares As
Integer) As StockPurchase

Public Function sellStock(ByVal stockSymbol As String, ByVal numberOfShares As
String) As StockSale
```

You can add a `StockBroker` class to a class diagram and use the Class Details window to define those methods, as shown in Figure 5-6. Click the <add parameter> indicators to fill out the method signatures, and notice that the return types of these methods are the `StockPurchase` and `StockSale` domain classes that were defined previously.

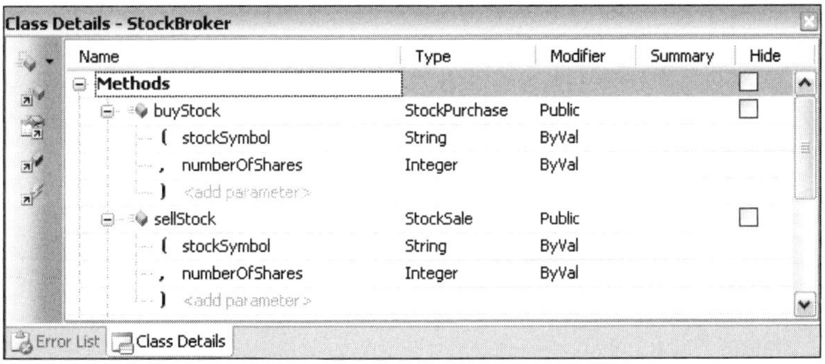

Figure 5-6

If you think back to Chapter 2, you'll recognize these method signatures as almost identical to those provided by the `StockBroker DealingService` Web service, apart from those structured return types that we had not yet conceived of when devising the Web services originally because we hadn't used Class Designer.

For a pure Web services implementation, the StockBroker API library class just defined is not strictly necessary because you could modify the return types of the Web services to match, and then insert into the Web service methods whatever implementation code would go into the methods defined above. However, we like the idea of a separate API class that encapsulates the underlying implementations and which may be fronted by the Web services or any other façade, such as a .Net Remoting object, or even invoked directly in cases where no remote invocations are required.

Remember that you can choose to see method names, names and types, or full method signatures on Class Diagrams by selecting Class Diagram ⇨ Change Members Format.

Working with other types

The bulk of our discussion so far has been centered on class types, which is hardly surprising as this is Class Designer. However, this designer provides the capability to represent language types other than classes, and in that respect it might be thought of more properly as a Type Designer.

Figure 5-7 gives examples of the other types that may be represented on a class diagram: Structure (or Struct), Enum, Delegate, and Module.

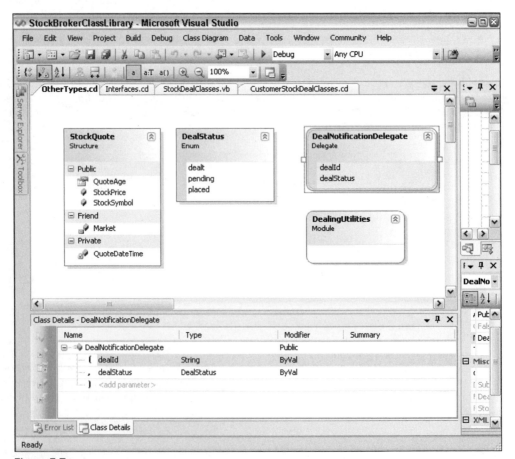

Figure 5-7

The following sections describe each of those additional types in turn.

StockQuote structure

Chances are good that when designing a StockQuoteService in real life, you would want that service to return not only the latest stock price, but also the following:

❑ The StockSymbol to which the quote relates, which would have been passed as input to the service

❑ The QuoteAge, so that we have an indication of how current — or not — that quote is

❑ An indication of the Market (LSE, NYSE, etc.) from which the quote was obtained, as a single company may trade shares in more than one market

You could therefore create a StockQuote structure to be returned as a value type from the getQuote Web service defined in Chapter 2.

Structures may contain many of the same members as classes, as you can see in Figure 5-7. There is a QuoteAge public property, actually derived from a QuoteDateTime private field. There are public fields indicating the StockSymbol and StockPrice. Finally, there is Market field, marked as *friend* because we want to account for the market within our implementation but not make this information generally available.

DealStatus enum

Earlier in this chapter we introduced the idea of a StockDeal class to record each deal that has been enacted for a customer. A deal will pass through a number of stages: placed (the customer has placed the deal instruction and could still cancel it), pending (the deal has not yet been done but is in a queue and cannot be canceled), and dealt (the customer has now bought or sold the shares).

Crucially, these status changes occur in a set order, so they could be coded numerically as 1 (placed), 2 (pending), and 3 (dealt). It's far better to use an enum that allows meaningful names as well as an implicit ordering. This is the DealStatus enum in the figure, the underlying code for which is as follows:

```
Public Enum DealStatus
    placed = 1
    pending = 2
    dealt = 3
End Enum
```

DealingNotificationDelegate delegate

In a full commercial implementation of a stockbroking system, you might expect one or more classes to be notified, in callback fashion, when a deal has changed status from placed to pending or pending to dealt. This functionality could be provided through a delegate such as the DealNotificationDelegate shown in Figure 5-7.

A delegate is essentially a method signature that must be implemented by any classes that wish to receive the notification. In that respect, you might expect a delegate to be visualized as a member with parameters, but in fact it is visualized as a type having members that correspond with the delegate parameters.

DealingUtilities module

For completeness, Figure 5-7 includes a module type that is only applicable to Visual Basic. This `DealingUtilities` module has a corresponding source file named `DealingUtilities.vb`.

Working with interfaces

An interface may be represented as a lollipop shape emanating from a class, or as a type shape in its own right. Figure 5-8 shows both representations: a lollipop emanating from the `Control` class annotated with the names of all the interfaces implemented by that class; and three of those interfaces — `IDisposable`, `IComponent`, and `IDropTarget` — rendered separately as shapes with member lists.

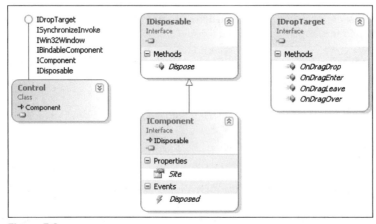

Figure 5-8

You can toggle to your preferred representation as follows:

❑ To view an interface in full as a separate shape, right-click the interface name on the lollipop (not the lollipop itself) and choose Show Interface.

❑ To remove an interface from your diagram simply right-click the shape and choose Remove from Diagram. This does not delete the interface code itself or remove the interface name from the lollipop.

UML tools will typically show an inheritance relationship between a class and an interface that it implements, if the two are on the same class diagram. With this Class Designer, the only indication that an interface is implemented by a particular class is its presence on the lollipop.

Showing an interface separately is beneficial in terms of visualizing the interface members, and to see relationships between interfaces themselves; such as `IComponent` and `IDisposable` in the figure. The downside is that it takes up more space on the diagrams and is unnecessary if all you really want to see is the list of interfaces supported by a class.

You can save more space in diagrams by collapsing the interface lollipop completely. Just right-click the lollipop itself (not one of the interface names) and choose Collapse. The result will be an unlabeled lollipop indicating that the class supports one or more interfaces, but you have to guess which ones. To see which ones, you can right-click again and choose Expand.

When you add interfaces to a diagram, along with classes that implement them, the designer is quite clever. Drawing an inheritance relationship between a class and an interface not only attaches that interface to the class, but also copies the interface members down to the class automatically.

Reproducing class diagrams in hard copy

After you have fine-tuned one or more class diagrams, you can copy them into Microsoft Office documents and print them. You can copy one, several, or all the shapes from a class diagram into other documents. Whether the copy operation duplicates the visual image of the shape or its underlying code depends on the type of document into which you paste it:

- ❑ **To copy a single element:** Right-click the shape and choose Copy to place the shape on the Clipboard.

- ❑ **To copy several elements:** On the diagram surface, drag the pointer to select the shapes you want to copy, right-click one of the selected shapes, and choose Copy to place all selected shapes on the Clipboard.

- ❑ **To copy all the elements in a class diagram:** Right-click the diagram surface and choose Select All. Then click the Copy icon on the standard toolbar or select Copy from the Edit menu to place all of the diagram's shapes on the Clipboard.

Once you have copied your selection, paste it using the Paste command in the destination program.

Text-oriented programs will display the code behind the selected shape or shapes, while graphics-oriented programs will display the image of the shape or shapes that you copied.

To print a class diagram directly from Visual Studio 2005, just click Print on the File menu and the entire class diagram will print.

Another way to reproduce class diagrams in a format suitable for printing or inserting into documents is to choose the Class Diagram ➪ Export Diagram As Image menu option; or right-click an empty portion of the diagram and choose this option from the context menu. The resulting Export Diagram As Image dialog is slightly misnamed because it actually allows you to multiple-select from all of the available class diagrams in your solution. An interesting way in which this feature could be used is as follows:

1. Export image files to a folder.
2. Insert the images into your design document using Word's Insert ➪ Link to Image feature.
3. Export the diagrams to the same folder at regular intervals so that the images in Word are kept automatically up-to-date.

Although Class Designer has much the same look-and-feel as the Distributed System Designers (Chapters 2 through 4), the Export Diagram as Image feature is peculiar to Class Designer. It is not possible to export images from Application Designer, Logical Datacenter Designer, System Designer, or Deployment Designer in this way.

Advanced Topics

In Chapter 1, we described how visual modeling tools are more than simply drawing tools. As well as enabling you to draw pictures, such tools have an understanding of what those pictures actually mean. Visio for Enterprise Architects marked a transition from Visio as a drawing tool to Visio as a (UML) modeling tool, yet it fell short of the capabilities offered by contemporary UML tools by not providing support for the following:

❑ **Code Synchronization:** The capability to see changes made in code reflected immediately on diagrams, and vice versa, with no explicit code generation or reverse engineering steps

❑ **.NET Framework Classes on class diagrams:** The capability to visualize and explore the relationships between .NET Framework classes themselves using class diagrams

Class Designer supports both code synchronization and the capability to visualize .NET Framework classes on diagrams, so we'll discuss that support in this section.

We'll also discuss the following features that you may have encountered in other visual design tools, but for which there is not yet any explicit support in Visual Studio 2005:

❑ **Patterns:** This is the capability to load standard patterns from a catalogue as a mechanism for standardizing designs. Some modeling tools such as IBM-Rational XDE provide this feature. Class Designer provides no explicit support but offers some possibilities.

❑ **Dynamic Modeling:** This is the capability to express the expected dynamic (runtime) behavior of a system as well as its static structure. This is fundamental to UML design tools but is (as yet) unsupported in the Visual Studio 2005 editions (but keep an eye on the DSL Toolkit). For some dynamic modeling, you can defer to Visio, but — as with Application Designer, described in Chapter 2 — Class Designer supports a potential workaround for limited dynamic modeling.

Though these are not supported explicitly, we can offer some workarounds to tide you over.

Code synchronization

A class diagram can provide a view of your code that shows the types (classes, interfaces, and the like), the type members (fields, properties, etc.), and the relationships between the types (including inheritance and association). Though class diagrams provide views of the code, to the extent that you can have more than one diagram reflecting the same set of classes, those views are fully synchronized with the code, so any changes you make in code are reflected automatically in the diagrams, and vice versa.

If you like, you can try this out again to satisfy yourself that it works, perhaps using the file in our sample solution if you have not built your own. Make a change to the StockDeal class in the source file StockDealClasses.vb and see that change reflected automatically in the two class diagrams showing that class (Figure 5-3 and Figure 5-4). Then make a change to that class on *one* of the class diagrams to see the change reflected in source code *and* on the other diagram.

Unlike tools such as IBM Rational XDE, which require you to synchronize manually after each change, or which synchronize automatically on saving a file, Class Designer synchronizes immediately when a change is made. However, note the following proviso: References to types in other projects cannot be displayed in class diagrams until you build the referenced project, and changes to the code of external entities are not reflected until the project is rebuilt. Class Designer does not have the concept of deferred implementation that Application Designer has (see Chapter 2). Each and every change to the model is immediately reflected in code, and each change to the code is immediately reflected in the model. In this way, it can be said that "the code is the model, and the model is the code."

.NET Framework classes on Class Diagrams

We've suggested that one of the key capabilities provided by any credible visual design tool should be the representation of language and framework classes themselves. For example, Rational Rose provides UML representations of the J2SE (Java 2 Standard Edition) and J2EE (Java 2 Enterprise Editions) class libraries, and Rational XDE provides UML representations of the .NET Framework classes, but Visio for Enterprise Architects provides only language types with no representations of .NET Framework classes themselves.

> It is possible to import representations of the .NET Framework classes into Visio for Enterprise Architects using the RE.NET reverse engineering utility described at http://www.lotontech.com/visualmodeling/RENET.html.

Visual Studio 2005 Class Designer enables the classes from the .NET Framework assemblies or any third-party assemblies to be represented on class diagrams. This can be achieved in various ways.

One way is to right-click a class that inherits from a .NET Framework class or from any other class in a referenced assembly, and then choose Show Base Type from the pop-up menu. The base class will appear on your diagram with an inheritance connector between it and the derived class.

Another way is to right-click a field whose type is that of a .NET Framework class or a third-party referenced class, and then choose Show As Association from the pop-up menu. The type of that field will be shown explicitly on the design surface as a separate class, with an association line between it and the containing class.

> Remember that showing members as fields or associations in Visual Studio 2005 Class Diagrams is fully reversible because the representation in code is the same either way. This is in contrast to tools such as Rational Rose that establish members as attributes (like fields) or associations according to the reverse-engineering settings, by allowing you to designate certain object classes (such as String) as basic types for which associations should not be established.

A third way of showing .NET Framework classes and other referenced classes on a class diagram is simply to drag those classes from the Class View or the Object Browser onto the design surface. This is the most flexible technique because the classes you choose need not be referenced by existing classes in your design, but their containing assemblies must be referenced by your project.

We've used the word "class" throughout the foregoing discussion for consistency, but rest assured that you can represent other .NET Framework types on class diagrams just as easily — whether they are interfaces, enums, or delegates.

Patterns

In our introduction to this section, we suggested that patterns support is a desirable feature in a visual design tool, but not supported explicitly as a visual modeling capability of Class Designer. Unlike some earlier visual design tools, Class Designer is fully integrated with the Visual Studio 2005 IDE, and the IDE itself has some patternlike features, including the following:

❑ The template wizards accessible via the Add New Item dialog, which allows items conforming to a standardized structure — or pattern — to be added to your project or solution. These templates may be the default ones, or supplied by third parties, or even devised by you.

❑ Access to .NET Framework classes and other classes from referenced assemblies to be used as base classes in your design

❑ The refactoring mechanisms for retrofitting patterns into your code. Refactoring is discussed in Chapter 11.

❑ The insertion of code snippets that standardize the implementation of certain operations in code. Code snippets are discussed in Chapter 11.

In other words, Visual Studio 2005 does provide some pattern or patternlike facilities, but they are not directly accessible from Class Designer.

Template wizards cannot currently be initiated from Class Designer, though this capability might be provided in future releases as a mechanism for incorporating patterns into class diagrams. Another possibility is that future releases will allow combinations of classes (representing patterns) to be added to the toolbox as prototypes, to mirror the same functionality provided by Application Designer and Logical Datacenter Designer.

As described earlier, any combination of .NET Framework classes or other classes from referenced assemblies may be shown on the design surface. Therefore, where these represent base classes or interfaces defined by patterns — such as an `AbstractFactory` class or a `State` interface — then effectively you can present those patterns in a class diagram.

Certain refactoring types may be applied directly from Class Designer — for example, Implement Abstract Class or Extract Interface. In this respect, Class Designer does indeed support some patternlike features directly.

Because code snippets are inserted within methods, it makes little sense to drive this functionality from a Class Designer that represents method signatures without internal implementations. As an important technique in its own right, the code snippets mechanism is discussed in Chapter 11.

Having surveyed the limited degree of support for patterns provided by Class Designer, we'll now provide some practical examples that show how you could create your own pattern library, at least as a short-term measure until Visual Studio incorporates explicit patterns support.

Building your own pattern library

In this section, we'll show you how to construct a project containing C# implementations of common patterns, with supporting class diagrams. To save on the effort of implementing each pattern yourself, you can find a ready supply of pattern implementations on the web.

For demonstration purposes we took some sample pattern implementations from the Data and Object Factory "Software Design Patterns" at `www.dofactory.com/patterns/Patterns.aspx`. We chose that site mainly because the sample implementations may be used freely as long as the original copyright notices are displayed as shown in the code that follows:

```
// Proxy pattern -- Structure example

//----------------------------------------------------------
// Copyright (C) 2001 - 2002, Data & Object Factory
// All rights reserved. www.dofactory.com
//
// You are free to use this source code in your
// applications as long as the original copyright
// notice is included.
//
// THIS CODE AND INFORMATION IS PROVIDED "AS IS" WITHOUT
// WARRANTY OF ANY KIND, EITHER EXPRESSED OR IMPLIED,
// INCLUDING BUT NOT LIMITED TO THE IMPLIED WARRANTIES OF
// MERCHANTABILITY OR FITNESS FOR A PARTICULAR PURPOSE.
//----------------------------------------------------------

using System;

// "Subject"

abstract class Subject
{
  // Methods
  abstract public void Request();
}


// "RealSubject"

class RealSubject : Subject
{
  // Methods
  override public void Request()
  {
    Console.WriteLine("Called RealSubject.Request()");
  }
}

// "Proxy"

class Proxy : Subject
{
  // Fields
  RealSubject realSubject;

  // Methods
  override public void Request()
  {
    // Uses "lazy initialization"
    if( realSubject == null )
      realSubject = new RealSubject();

    realSubject.Request();
  }

}
```

As you may have deduced already, this C# code implements the Gang of Four (GoF) proxy pattern.

If you're familiar with UML, then you'll be used to seeing that pattern in the form of a Class Diagram. If you're not familiar with UML, and you've never met that pattern before, then it might take you a while to figure out the relationships between the three classes. Figure 5-9 shows how much clearer those relationships become when shown as a class diagram.

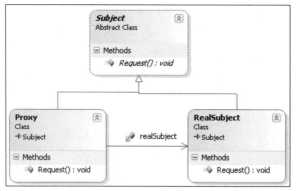

Figure 5-9

That diagram was drawn simply by dragging the source file `Proxy_Structure.cs` onto the diagram. Because that source file contains three class definitions, all three classes appear on the diagram.

> **Dragging a source file onto the design surface causes all of the classes within that source file to be shown on the diagram, so defining several interconnected classes within a single source file is a convenient way to encode a pattern.**

The inheritance relationships from the `Subject` class to the `Proxy` and `RealSubject` classes appeared automatically, whereas the association relationship between the `Proxy` and the `RealSubject` did not. By default, the `Proxy` included a field of type `RealSubject`, which was rendered as an association when we right-clicked the field and chose Show as Association.

Remember that Show as Field and Show as Association are completely interchangeable and do not affect the code at all. They are merely alternate display notations.

The proxy pattern is important because it underpins many distributed computing technologies, such as Web services and .NET Remoting, not to mention CORBA and Enterprise Java Beans. A remote object (the `RealSubject`) may need to be represented by a local client-side class (the `Proxy`) that appears to behave exactly the same because the `RealSubject` and the `Proxy` both implement the same interface or abstract class. The sleight of hand is that the `Proxy` passes on requests to the `RealSubject` over the network, thus hiding the tricky networking issues from the developer.

When you begin to use this pattern, you'll want to substitute the names of the participating classes with names that are meaningful in the context of the problem you're solving. For example, you might substitute the name `Subject` with `Bank`, the name `RealSubject` with `BankImplementation`, and the name

`Proxy` with `BankProxy`. A convenient way to do this is by using the Rename refactoring that is covered in Chapter 11, as it will not only rename that classes themselves but also the references between the classes.

If you've used a pattern engine such as the one in IBM Rational XDE, you will recognize this as pattern expansion, with the renaming process equivalent to the binding of values to template parameters.

Dynamic modeling

If you're familiar with UML, you know that class diagrams represent the static structure of the classes in your application. The dynamic behavior — that is, how instances of classes react and interact over time — has traditionally been modeled in UML using statechart diagrams (for how classes react) and collaboration diagrams (for how classes interact).

Because Visual Studio 2005 does not support dynamic modeling, we'll now offer some workarounds that you could use to simulate those additional diagram types.

Simulating Statechart Diagrams using the state pattern

When designing classes using UML, it is possible to create for each (stateful) class a statechart diagram that shows the following:

❑ The possible states in which an instance of that class may find itself

❑ The allowable transitions between states, which occur in response to events if certain conditions are met

❑ The events that an instance of that class may respond to in each state

An example statechart in UML for an `Account` class is shown in Figure 5-10.

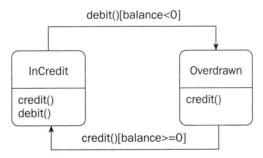

Figure 5-10

This diagram shows that an account may be in state `InCredit` or state `Overdrawn`. In state `InCredit`, the account can accept credits and debits (which are events), but in state `Overdrawn`, only credits are allowed. If the account receives a debit event while in state `InCredit` that causes the balance to fall below zero, then the account transitions into state `Overdrawn`. Conversely, if the account receives a credit event while in state `Overdrawn` and that credit takes the balance above zero, then the account transitions back to state `InCredit`.

The problem is that, currently at least, the Visual Studio 2005 editions do not provide these statecharts.

It turns out that our discussion of patterns in the previous section provides a workaround here. There is a well-known design pattern for representing an object's possible states as a set of classes. Applying the State pattern to an `Account` class would result in the class diagram shown in Figure 5-11.

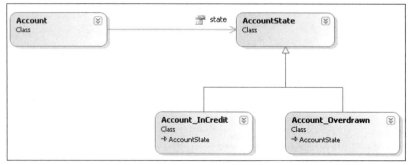

Figure 5-11

Remember that class diagrams are merely views of the underlying classes, so we can draw as many Class Diagrams as we like showing various combinations of classes. Suppose we draw a new class diagram to show only the `Account_InCredit` and `Account_Overdrawn` classes that represent states. By adding some events and associations, we can come up with the diagram shown in Figure 5-12. Are you experiencing any déjà vu yet?

Figure 5-12

Essentially, this diagram contains all of the information contained in the earlier statechart, and it looks very similar too. Events represent events, as they should; and associations represent transitions, which is not unreasonable because you would need a navigable association between the (state) classes in order to make a transition. Because the notation is not quite powerful enough to distinguish events (debit) and conditions (balance<0), we have encoded those semantics into the association role names. That makes sense when you consider that the implementation code for that transition would be something like the following:

```
if (event==debit && balance<0)
  nextState=currentState.debit_balanceLessThanZero;
```

It's not ideal, but while we wait for true statecharts to be provided, this technique offers a very feasible workaround, especially if you would manage object states using the recognized State pattern anyway. We've not resorted to using comments, and where we have used specific constructs — such as Events — we've used them exactly for the purpose they are intended.

Simulating collaboration diagrams using comments

UML collaboration diagrams are essentially static structure diagrams — like class diagrams — with additional adornments showing the sequence of messages between those classes in a typical scenario. Those collaboration diagrams will often be accompanied by a participating classes diagram; a class diagram showing only those classes that participate in the collaboration.

Taking those two ideas together, in Figure 5-13 we have drawn a participating classes diagram for a "Buy Stock" scenario, and used comments to indicate a numbered sequence of messages that pass between the classes as that scenario plays out.

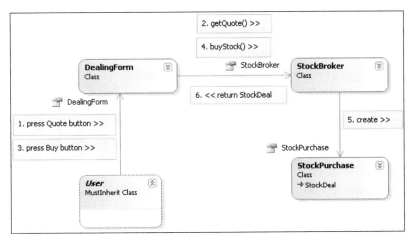

Figure 5-13

If you've read Chapter 2, you know that we first introduced this idea in the context of application diagrams, the problem there being that you can only have one application diagram per solution, so you can only show one scenario at a time. Using class diagrams, there is no such restriction because you can have as many class diagrams as you like, and therefore as many simulated collaboration diagrams as you like.

UML purists will point out that collaboration diagrams do not show interactions between classes at all; they show interactions between object instances. Well, our workaround is exactly that, a workaround, so it's not perfect; but in practice we find that the majority of collaboration diagrams are drawn as though they show classes, rather than instances. For those scenarios in which you must distinguish between two instances of the same class — for example, when transferring funds from one bank account to another — you can include an instance name with the message comments in order to set the context.

Consider the following two messages that would appear as two separate comments next to a single association line to an `Account` class:

```
1. sourceAccount.withdrawFunds()
2. destinationAccount.depositFunds()
```

127

Comparison with UML Class Diagrams

Class diagrams drawn using the Visual Studio 2005 Class Designer are basically the same as their UML equivalents, save for a few minor issues. Class Designer is limited in the following respects:

❏ Bi-directional associations are not supported.

❏ Association names and end roles are not distinguished, and indeed associations are not distinguished from compositions and aggregations.

❏ Inheritance relationships between classes and interfaces are not visualized.

❏ There is no notion of a simple dependency between classes.

❏ .NET namespaces (similar to UML packages) cannot be visualized on class diagrams.

That's not an exhaustive list, but it gives you an idea. Many of those apparent limitations arise from the fact that Class Designer provides a direct representation of the underlying code, rather than an abstract representation as provided by UML. Aggregations, compositions, and regular associations cannot be distinguished in code so cannot be distinguished on diagrams. Simple dependencies cannot be represented in code, so cannot be represented on diagrams.

> *Actually, in a sense, dependencies are represented in source code, as* Imports *statements (VB) or* using *statements (C#). The problem is that generally these statements are used to refer to packages (namespaces), rather than individual classes. The current version of Class Designer does not support the rendering of namespaces on class diagrams, so these dependencies between packages cannot be visualized.*

Aside from those issues, if you redrew any of the preceding figures using Visio, you would be conveying pretty much the same information in the same way. In fact, of all the Visual Studio 2005 designers, this one is the closest match with UML.

Figure 5-14 shows a UML class diagram reverse-engineered into Visio for Enterprise Architects from the Visual Studio solution on which Figures 5-3 and 5-4 were based.

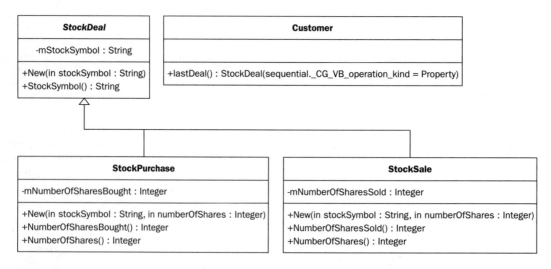

Figure 5-14

Remember in Chapter 1 that we indicated the importance of domain-specific languages (DSLs). Class Designer provides a DSL for class modeling. In keeping with Microsoft's focus on deployment, and with the developer in mind, Class Designer handles Common Language Runtime (CLR) types directly, whereas UML notation typically uses more abstract types that must translate (map) to CLR types during code generation and reverse engineering.

This makes Class Designer code synchronization much more effective than the round-trip engineering features of the previous generation of UML tools, and with an added benefit for the developer. Traditionally, UML tools generated large amounts of superfluous source code simply to support the round-trip engineering process, which overwhelmed developers and encouraged them to write code manually, rather than generate code from models. Class Designer adds little or no additional meta-data to your code.

As good as Class Designer is, we're not suggesting that you throw out your UML tool straightaway. As we indicated in Chapter 1, we do see a retained role for Visio Enterprise Architect for devising entities at the analysis stage that will ultimately become classes at the design stage. The idea is that business and systems analysts, who have no need for the Visual Studio suite and in any case have no requirement for code synchronization, can whiteboard various usage scenarios using analysis entities (key abstractions) in Visio. The Visio code-generation facility can then be used to provide a starting set of classes in Visual Studio, for refinement using Class Designer.

Summary

We began this chapter by introducing the Class Designer toolbox and the types it provides. Unlike the visual designers described in Chapters 2 through 4, the items in the Class Designer toolbox are "types" rather than "prototypes." Furthermore, because these types represent interfaces, enumerations, structures, and other types besides classes, we can think of this designer more accurately as a Type Designer (though, of course, Class Designer sounds better and in any case is consistent with UML).

Class Designer may be used as a means to visualize existing code (a picture is worth a thousand words), and as a means of creating and structuring new code. Both uses were demonstrated, in the "From Code to Class Diagrams" and "From Class Diagrams to Code" sections, respectively. We showed that various types — not just classes — may be represented in Class Designer, and demonstrated the relationships that may exist between them, including inheritance and association.

Having covered the basics, we then discussed some advanced topics such as model-code synchronization, representation of .NET Framework classes on diagrams, patterns, and dynamic modeling. In the case of dynamic modeling, we suggested some workarounds that enable you to simulate UML statechart diagrams and collaboration diagrams, as a stopgap until Visual Studio provides dynamic modeling capabilities.

Finally, we highlighted some of the similarities and differences between Visual Studio 2005 class diagrams and the class diagrams that you might have seen in other UML tools.

6

DSL Tools

DSL Tools is the first tools release from Microsoft to start making the Software Factories vision a reality. It leverages the modeling platform developed by the Visual Studio team for the Visual Designers shipped with Visual Studio 2005. DSL Tools enables developers to create design tools to automate tedious and complex parts of your software project.

Using DSL Tools, you can define domain-specific languages (DSL) and graphical modeling tools based upon these languages; the resulting designer is then hosted inside Visual Studio 2005, and users can use the graphical modeling surface to indirectly construct an in-memory representation of the domain-specific language.

The resulting in-memory domain-specific language is typically called a *domain model*; this domain model can then be used to generate C# code, XML files — in fact, anything. You don't have to generate code from this domain model, but code tends to be the most common output form.

Domain-Specific Languages

A domain-specific language (DSL), quite simply, is a specific language targeted at a specific problem space rather than a general-purpose language used to solve everything.

Consider the following examples of DSLs in use today by Microsoft Tools: The Class Designer available in Visual Studio 2005 enables developers to visualize the classes within their projects and understand relationships between them; this designer is based on a CLR Type DSL that describes classes, methods, properties, and so on. The Class Designer is covered in Chapter 5.

The Visual Designers available in Visual Studio 2005 enable software architects and infrastructure architects to model their view of a software architecture through the use of two different designers that are based on the System Definition Model (SDM), which is part of the Dynamic Systems Initiative (DSI).

Another potential example could be the XML Schema editor. You could build a DSL based on the XML Schema standard and then render a graphical design surface to allow easy modification, although the current XML Schema designer is not built using the DSL Tools release.

Figure 6-1 provides an example of a Visual Studio 2005 SDM Designer in action, showing the components of an application and how they interact. You can then generate Visual Studio 2005 projects and any appropriate boilerplate code from this domain model.

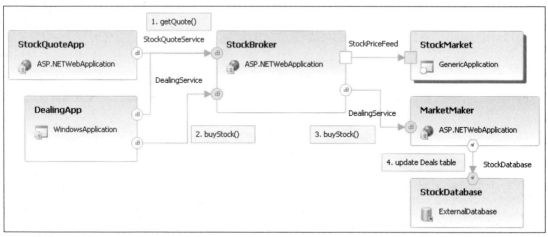

Figure 6-1

Creating a Designer

This chapter will walk you through the creation of a Navigation Designer, which enables a business user to express the navigation of an Internet site or application using a custom designer built using the DSL Tools.

This chapter is based on the February 2006 CTP build of the DSL Tools; further changes are expected in later releases, mainly around the way you express your domain model and the designer definition. (See the Wiley website at www.wiley.com for future updates.) The latest release of the DSL Tools can be found at http://msdn.microsoft.com/vstudio/OSLTools/.

Navigation — say, of an Internet site — can be highly complex, and the semantics are typically wrapped up inside code, making the navigation hard to understand and change as the site evolves. At the initiation of such a project, a developer could spend weeks creating all of the pages and the links between them. The developer would reference documentation of the navigation during this stage, which can lead to errors as he or she "transcribes" from documentation to code. Generating the pages, code, and links directly from the model avoids this problem, and ensures that the model is always the primary source moving forward.

Consider the scenario in which your chosen technology vendor releases a new vision for site development. This typically requires you to rewrite much of the application.

Once the business user has expressed the navigation semantics graphically using the designer, you can then generate code from the model. In this case, you generate ASP.NET pages directly from the in-memory model as generated by the graphical designer.

Then, when Microsoft releases Windows Presentation Foundation, for example, you can modify the designer to emit XAML and instantly retool the application against a brand-new software technology. You're effectively abstracting yourself from the implementation technology, enabling your business to be more agile.

Another possible scenario is having this navigation domain model, but different users within your organization who wish to view and change the domain model in different ways. You can have two different designers who target the same navigation model but provide a different graphical designer. Perhaps a business user wishes to annotate the diagram to identify auditing points that are used during the code-generation phases to add code to write to an audit trail.

Creating the Project

To create a new DSL Designer, choose the Domain Specific Language Designer project type under the Extensibility branch of Other Project Types, as shown in Figure 6-2. Click OK.

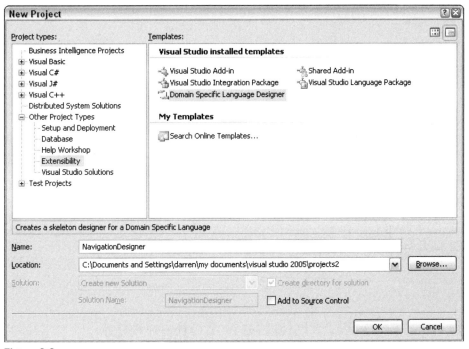

Figure 6-2

The Domain Specific Language Designer wizard is then displayed. For this project, you want to define your own language, so select the Minimal Language template as shown in Figure 6-3. Other templates are included as examples to demonstrate how you might construct your language. Selecting one of these templates will give you a completed Language Model and Designer, enabling you to run the designer immediately by pressing F5.

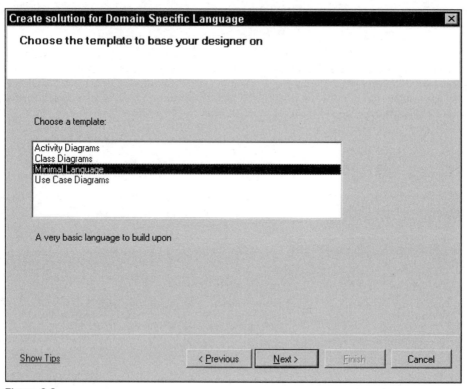

Figure 6-3

Click the Next Button on the wizard and set Company Name, Designer Name, and File Extension as appropriate. The designer name is used for the namespace and code files, and the file extension is used by VS to identify the designer for a given extension so files can be opened in the correct designer. The remaining steps enable you to de-register any other designers using the file extension, specify a key file that will be used to code sign your designer assembly, and provide a name for the Visual Studio SDK package that will host your designer.

Creating the Navigation Language

You now need to define the language used to describe the navigation domain. The wizard creates a sample .DSLDM file that will contain the language definition. Double-click the <YourDesignerName> .DSLDM file located in the DomainModel section of your project to open the Domain Model Designer.

You will see that a sample language is already present in this file. It was defined by the template selected during the wizard process. For the purposes of this designer, we will start from scratch, so delete all boxes from the design surface by selecting them and pressing the Delete key.

For this simple Navigation Designer, we have two concepts: a *page* and a *site*.

A page will be a number of properties such as Name and Title, and optionally holds a collection of child pages that are used to store references to other pages, enabling you to model the nested nature of navigation. We also have a parent concept called Site, and all its pages are members.

To create the concept of a Site, drag a class from the toolbox onto the design surface and change the Name property to Site, as shown in Figure 6-4.

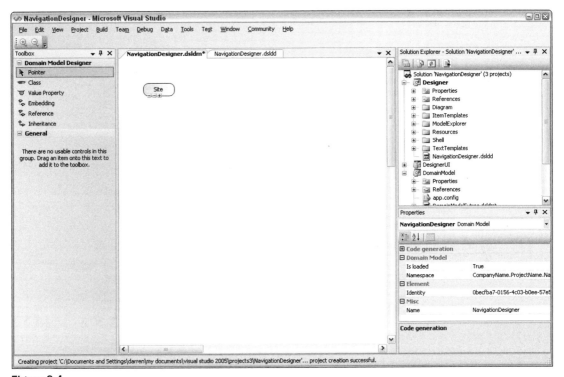

Figure 6-4

You now need to create the concept of a Page, which will be linked to the site. Drag a class from the toolbox onto the design surface and change the Name property to Page, as shown in Figure 6-5.

Then use an Embedding Connector from the toolbox to create the parent/child relationship between Site and Page. Draw the connector between Site and Page to create the language model depicted in Figure 6-6.

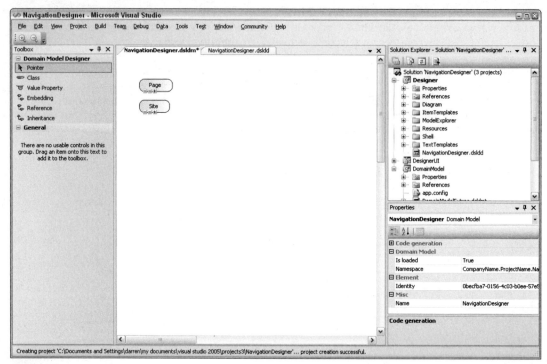

Figure 6-5

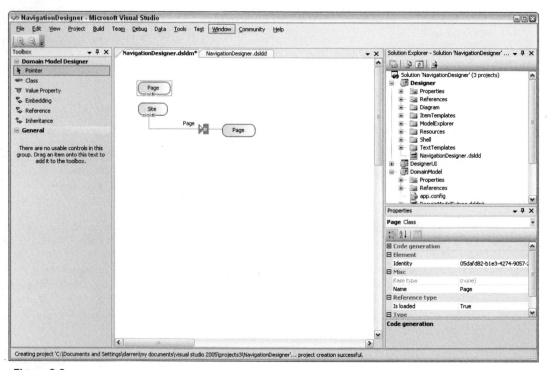

Figure 6-6

There is now a relationship between Site and Page, as you can see a new Page class has been displayed, which is connected to the Site. This is just a visual reference to the Page class that appears above. You can right-click on the new Page class and choose Bring Definition Here to make the diagram clearer, as shown in Figure 6-7.

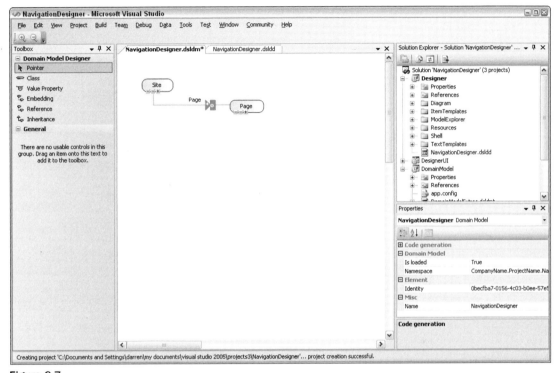

Figure 6-7

A relationship in the Domain Model Designer is represented by a line connecting two classes together. A relationship always has two symbols in the center representing roles.

The left-hand role, shown as a triangle, represents the left-hand side of the relationship. The character contained within the triangle indicates the cardinality of the relationship. In this case, * means *unbounded,* so a Site can have many pages. You can change this by modifying the Min and Max properties on the role.

The right-hand role, shown as a rectangle, represents the right-hand side of the relationship. Again, the character within the rectangle indicates the cardinality of the relationship — in this case, it defaults to 0 or 1, meaning a page can be a member of zero or one sites.

The domain model designer assigns default names to these roles, which in some cases are unsuitable for your domain model. Click the left triangle and change the name property to SitePages to reflect that this role represents the pages within a site. The right rectangle role is already set to Site, which is correct and reflects the Site where this page is a member.

As it stands, this language model enables you to express multiple Pages, but not the nested behavior of navigation whereby pages refer to other pages. To express this in your language, use the Reference Connector from the toolbar, and draw a connection from the Page concept back to the Page concept, effectively making it self-referencing, as per Figure 6-8.

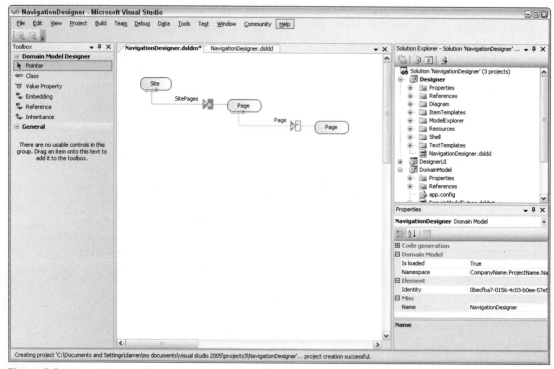

Figure 6-8

This relationship allows a Page to refer to another Page, thus enabling us to express navigation. By default, however, the left-hand side of this relationship will only allow a page to reference one other page, instead of multiple pages as we require.

The cardinality of this relationship is modeled using roles on the domain model as discussed previously. In this case, we want to modify the left-hand side of the relationship to enable us to link to many pages. Click the triangle and change the Min and Max properties to 0 to indicate unbounded, and change the name of the role to ChildPages.

The cardinality of the right-hand side of the relationship is correct, but click the rectangle and change the Name property to ReferringPages, which makes the language easier to navigate later and reflects which pages are linked to a given page. By default, this role will not generate a property linked to the Referring Page in the object model, which is required for the connector to work in the next section, so set the Is Property Generator property to true.

The relationship between the two page classes is given a default name of PageHasPage. Click the relationship and change the Name property from PageHasPage to Transition, thus making the language model clearer.

The next step for this stage is to click on the SitePages role and set the `Accepts` property to `All`. This enables the graphical designer to merge `Page` classes into the model at this point as they are dragged onto the surface. If you forget this step, you will be warned at compile time.

Finally, the current build of the DSL Tools requires an XML Root to be defined on the root element of your language designer for serialization purposes. Right-click the Site concept and choose Make XML Root. Your domain model should mirror the diagram shown in Figure 6-9.

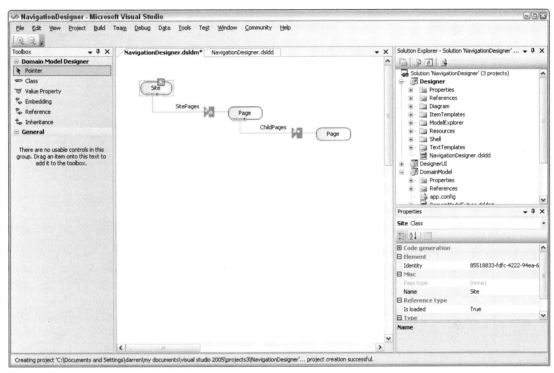

Figure 6-9

All classes on the designer inherit a `Name` property, which we will use to store the Page Name. For this simple designer we'll also add a `Title` property. You can create properties on a class by dragging the Value Property toolbox item onto the class and changing the name of the property to `Title` via the `Name` property in the properties window (see Figure 6-10).

The last step for our navigation language is to add a `Name` property to the relationship between the Pages. Connectors don't have a name by default, but you can add one. Right-click the Transition relationship, choose Show as Class, drag a `Value` Property from the toolbox onto the `Transition` class, and call it `Name`, as shown in Figure 6-11.

The navigation language is now complete. You can generate the object model behind this language by right-clicking on the `<YourDesignerName>.dsldm.dsldmt` file and choosing Run Custom Tool. A C# file is created by the DSL Tools, which produces the classes, as shown in Figure 6-12. You can see this C# file by clicking Show All Files on Solution Explorer and expanding the `<YourDesignerName>.dsldm.dsldmt` entry in Solution Explorer.

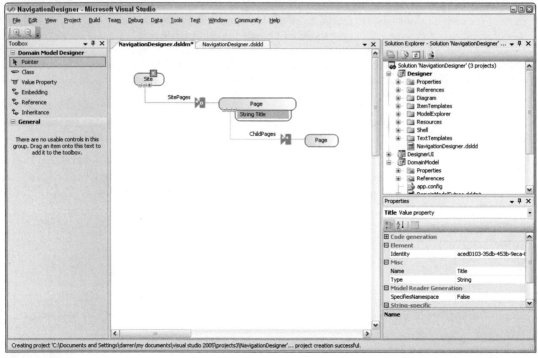

Figure 6-10

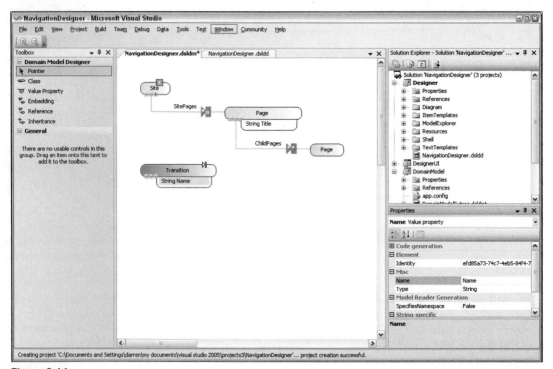

Figure 6-11

This is the object model that will be created as the user uses the diagram. New `Page` classes will be initialized for each Page dropped onto the diagram, and these `Page` classes will be added to the `SitePages` collection. When Pages are connected together to form the navigation, references to the pages are added to the `ChildPages` connection. This code is generated by the DSL Tools in the previous step, and you can use it to create an in-memory representation of your domain model. It also allows a strongly typed way to access the contents of the domain model.

The diagram in Figure 6-12 depicts the object model created for your navigation domain model. This diagram was created using the Class Diagram feature of Visual Studio 2005, which uses the same designer framework that we are using — the Class Diagram tools use a CLR Type domain model to represent classes, methods, and so on. Everything you see in this diagram, including the visual compartments that hold Fields and Methods, can be used by your custom designer.

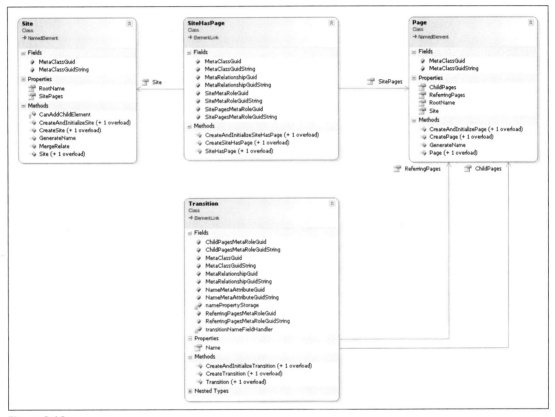

Figure 6-12

Creating the Graphical Language

You now have the underlying navigation domain language. In this case, the graphical presentation of this language is nearly a one-to-one mapping — that is, you expect the user to create pages and create links between them so there are no additional concepts to provide.

This isn't the case in all scenarios. For example, the graphical language for a given user can be completely different from the domain language. Also, a graphical shape dragged onto a designer could (under the covers) have to build a very complex language model instead of a simple one-to-one mapping. For example, if you had a domain model that represented a car and its various component parts, such as Wheels, Engine, and Windows, you could allow the user to just drag a Car onto the designer and automatically create the components of the car in the language model without requiring the user to manually create them all.

The Designer Definition (.dsldd) file defines the graphical language for your designer and specifies the mapping between the graphical and domain language elements. That way, when you drag a graphical element onto the design surface, the corresponding domain language elements will be created automatically and merged into your domain-specific language domain model.

The Designer Definition file is currently implemented as an XML file, but a later release of the DSL Tools will have the two files combined, and one graphical designer will be provided. This will make the development experience far simpler, as you won't need to manually provide mapping between your graphical and domain language elements, with all the obvious brittleness this presents.

The outline of the designer definition is shown here:

```xml
<?xml version="1.0"?>
<designerDefinition namespace="CompanyName.ProjectName.NavigationDesigner.Designer"
name="NavigationDesigner" xmlns="http://schemas.microsoft.com/dsltools/dsldd">
    <explorer>
    <notation>
    <objectModels>
    <propertiesWindow>
    <validationBehavior>
</designerDefinition>
```

Defining the shapes

The first step is to define the graphical shapes that will be used by the diagram. In the case of the Navigation Designer, we only have one graphical shape to represent a page. We don't have a graphical shape to represent a site because the designer will only be used to model one site at a time, so there's no need to provide a graphical shape on the designer, although you could provide one if required.

All designers have one diagram, which you can see defined here:

```xml
<notation>
    <diagramMaps/>
    <diagrams>
        <diagram name="NavigationDesignerDiagram">
            <connectors/>
            <shapes/>
            <toolbox/>
        </diagram>
    </diagrams>
</notation>
```

We start by defining the shapes under the `Shape` element. A number of shapes are supported out of the box, such as Geometry, Image, and Compartment. For the purposes of this designer, we will just use the GeometryShape.

We define one Shape called `PageShape`, as shown below. Apart from the name, this shape is identical to the sample shapes defined in the Designer Definition file. Also defined on the Shape is a decorator that will be used to display the name of the Page:

```
<geometryShape name="PageShape" initialWidth="2.0" initialHeight="0.75"
geometry="Rectangle">
    <decorators>
        <shapeText name="Name" position="Center"
            defaultTextId="PageShapeNameDecorator"/>
    </decorators>
    <fillColor color="blue" variability="User"/>
    <outlineColor color="black" variability="User"/>
</geometryShape>
```

Defining the connectors

Now that you have your Page shape, you need to define the connector that will link Page shapes together to form the navigation. You do this under the `connectors` element.

The key parts of the connector section are the source and target elements that define what shapes a connector can be drawn from and to. The designer will then enforce these rules when the user selects the connector. In our case, the connector is identical to the sample connector, apart from the `permittedShapes` sections, which we change to `PageShape` to specify that Page shapes can only be linked to other Page shapes, as shown below, and the connector `name` property, which we set to `TransitionConnector` to represent a transition between Pages:

```
<connectors>
    <connector name="TransitionConnector">
        <color variability="User" color="black" />
        <dashStyle variability="User" dashStyle="dash"/>
        <decorators>
            <connectorText name="Label" position="TargetBottom"
                defaultTextId="DefaultLabelText"/>
        </decorators>
        <source>
            <permittedShapes>
                <shape>CompanyName.ProjectName.NavigationDesigner.Designer.
                    NavigationDesignerDiagram/Shapes/PageShape</shape>
            </permittedShapes>
        </source>
        <target arrowStyle="EmptyArrow">
            <permittedShapes>
                <shape>CompanyName.ProjectName.NavigationDesigner.Designer.
                    NavigationDesignerDiagram/Shapes/PageShape</shape>
            </permittedShapes>
        </target>
    </connector>
</connectors>
```

Defining the toolbox

Now that you have your Shape and Connecter defined, you need to display these on the designer tool-box to enable a user to select them. You do this under the `toolbox` element as shown below.

The properties `iconId`, `captionId`, and `contextSensitiveHelpId` are all keys to resources held within the project. The wizard generates a sample resources file called `<YourDesignerName>.Resource.resx` located under the Diagram Solution folder.

If you open this resource file, you will see a number of sample resources that you can rename and mod-ify, or replace with your own bitmaps. For the purposes of the designer, we rename the items and reuse the bitmaps as shown in the following code. Under the `ShapeTool` element, you specify the graphical shapes that the toolbox item will be representing, which in our case are PageShape and TransitionConnector, as defined above:

```
<toolbox>
    <items>
        <shapeTool iconId="PageShapeBitmap" captionId="PageShapeToolboxCaption"
            contextSensitiveHelpId="PageShapeHelpId" order="0">
            <shape>CompanyName.ProjectName.NavigationDesigner.Designer.
                NavigationDesignerDiagram/Shapes/PageShape</shape>
        </shapeTool>
        <connectorTool iconId="TransitionBitmap"
            contextSensitiveHelpId="TransitionLinkHelpId"
            captionId="Transition" order="1">
            <connector>CompanyName.ProjectName.NavigationDesigner.Designer.
                NavigationDesignerDiagram/Connectors/TransitionConnector</connector>
        </connectorTool>
    </items>
</toolbox>
```

Providing a Shape Map

The next step is to provide a Shape Map, which maps Domain Model classes to graphical shapes on your designer. This enables the DSL Tools framework to create the appropriate object graph for a given graph-ical shape and merge it into the domain model.

The `class` element of the Shape Map identifies the class in your domain model that you want to map to a graphical element. In this case, it's the `Page` class.

The next section of the Shape Map, called `melCollectionExpression`, specifies the domain model role to which the new `Page` class will be added. In our case, this is the left-hand role of the `SiteHasPages` relationship, which is called `SitePages`. This will cause a new `Page` to be added to the `SitePages` col-lection of the `Site` class.

The `Shape` element defines the graphical shape you wish to map to, which is a `PageShape` in this case. The following sections refer to the decorators used on the graphical shape. All Shapes have a standard decorator called `Name`, and you specify the value to be the value of the `Name` property on the `Page` class, thus displaying a property held in the ObjectModel on the graphical shape:

```
<shapeMaps>
    <shapeMap>
        <class>CompanyName.ProjectName.NavigationDesigner.
              DomainModel.NavigationDesigner/Page</class>
        <iconMaps>
        </iconMaps>
        <melCollectionExpression>
            <roleExpression>
                <role>CompanyName.ProjectName.NavigationDesigner.
                    DomainModel.NavigationDesigner/Site/SitePages</role>
            </roleExpression>
        </melCollectionExpression>
        <shape>CompanyName.ProjectName.NavigationDesigner.Designer.
                NavigationDesignerDiagram/Shapes/PageShape</shape>
        <textMaps>
            <shapeTextMap>
                <textDecorator>CompanyName.ProjectName.NavigationDesigner.
                    Designer.NavigationDesignerDiagram/Shapes/PageShape/
                    Decorators/Name</textDecorator>
                <valueExpression>
                    <valuePropertyExpression>
                        <valueProperty>CompanyName.ProjectName.
                            NavigationDesigner.DomainModel.NavigationDesigner
                            /Page/Name</valueProperty>
                    </valuePropertyExpression>
                </valueExpression>
            </shapeTextMap>
        </textMaps>
    </shapeMap>
</shapeMaps>
```

Providing a Connector Map

The final step is to define a Connector Map, which maps the graphical connector onto a domain model relationship, in the same way as a Shape Map. This enables the domain model to construct the relationship when a connection is made between two shapes.

The connector section defined previously enforces the rules regarding which shapes can be connected to, so this section purely defines the mapping.

The class element of the Connector Map identifies the relationship in our Domain Model that we want to map to a graphical connector — in this case, it's the Transition relationship.

The connectors element defines the graphical connector to which you are mapping, which is called TransitionConnector as defined in the connectors element previously.

The next two sections, SourceMap and TargetMap, define what domain model roles are updated when a connection is made between two pages.

The SourceMap expression refers to the Role on the right-hand side of the relationship (modeled as a rectangle), which in this case is the ReferringPages role; therefore, the TargetMap expression refers to the Role on the left-hand side of the relationship (modeled as a triangle), which is called ChildPages.

The remaining sections refer to the decorators used on the graphical connector. All connectors have a standard decorator called `Name`, and you specify the value to be the value of the `Name` property on the `Transition` class, thus displaying a property held in the ObjectModel on the graphical connector:

```
<connectorMaps>
    <connectorMap>
        <class>CompanyName.ProjectName.NavigationDesigner.
                DomainModel.NavigationDesigner/Transition</class>
            <connector>CompanyName.ProjectName.NavigationDesigner.
                    Designer.NavigationDesignerDiagram/Connectors/
                    TransitionConnector</connector>
            <sourceMap>
                <modelNavigationExpression>
                    <roleExpression>
                        <role>CompanyName.ProjectName.NavigationDesigner.
                                DomainModel.NavigationDesigner/
                                Page/ReferringPages</role>
                    </roleExpression>
                </modelNavigationExpression>
            </sourceMap>
            <targetMap>
                <modelNavigationExpression>
                    <roleExpression>
                        <role>CompanyName.ProjectName.NavigationDesigner.
                            DomainModel.NavigationDesigner/Page/ChildPages</role>
                    </roleExpression>
                </modelNavigationExpression>
            </targetMap>
            <textMaps>
                <connectorTextMap>
                    <textDecorator>CompanyName.ProjectName.NavigationDesigner.
                        Designer.NavigationDesignerDiagram/Connectors/
                        TransitionConnector/Decorators/Label</textDecorator>
                    <valueExpression>
                        <valuePropertyExpression>
                            <valueProperty>CompanyName.ProjectName.
                                    NavigationDesigner.DomainModel.
                                    NavigationDesigner/Transition/
                                    Name</valueProperty>
                        </valuePropertyExpression>
                    </valueExpression>
                </connectorTextMap>
            </textMaps>
    </connectorMap>
</connectorMaps>
```

We've now provided all of the information needed for our designer to be built. The navigation language has been defined, and you've detailed the graphical language that users will interact with to indirectly build this navigation language.

Using the Designer

The DSL Tools automate all of the heavy lifting work to actually produce your designer, which takes advantage of the Designer platform.

This automation is done through the use of templates that use the templating technology included with the DSL Tools. These templates are akin to ASP.NET in that you define the code you wish to be generated and then insert tags to vary the code generated. You can see these templates in your solution as files with an extension of .dslddt.

The first step to generate your designer is to run the templates to generate the code. You can do this by clicking the button to "transform all templates" on the Solution Explorer toolbar. This toolbar button is highlighted in Figure 6-13.

Figure 6-13

The templates are executed and several code files are generated, which you can view in the Solution Explorer nested under the .dslddt files when you click the "show all files" button on the Solution Explorer toolbar.

If you have mistyped any names in the Designer Definition file, errors will be generated during template execution, which should point you at the area that needs to be changed.

Once the designer has been successfully built, you can press F5 to run the Designer. The DSL Tools Project Wizard automatically creates a debugging project within which you can test your designer; pressing F5 launches the designer with this project.

Any designer you write using the DSL Tools is configured to work in the "Experimental" version of Visual Studio that the Visual Studio SDK configures during installation. This is identical to your usual Visual Studio IDE except that it has a different registry hive, so any designer registrations don't affect your core developing environment. To support debugging, your designer can be configured for the normal instance of Visual Studio as required.

When the designer loads, you will see a file in the debugging project called empty.<yourdesigner extension>. Double-clicking this file will display the design surface and the toolbox, with your graphical items listed as shown in Figure 6-14.

You can now drag Pages onto the Diagram and change the name by clicking on the Decorator or using the Properties pane. You can also use connectors to connect shapes together. You can use all the tools together to produce a navigation model, as depicted in Figure 6-15.

During the construction of your language model using the graphical designer, you can view the navigation domain model as it's constructed, using the Explorer that the DSL Tools Project Wizard installs as part of your designer. If the Explorer is not visible, you can make it visible by selecting View ➪ Other Windows ➪ NavigationDesigner Explorer. In Figure 6-16, you can see the domain model for the navigation model defined in Figure 6-15, created by dragging shapes onto the designer.

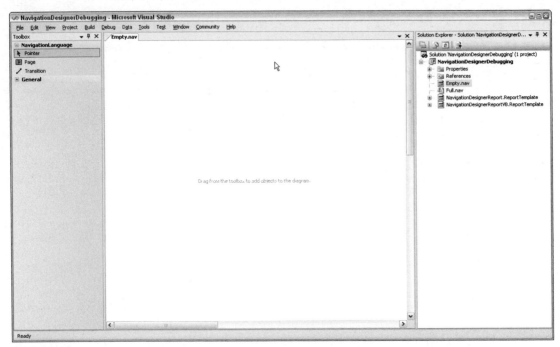

Figure 6-14

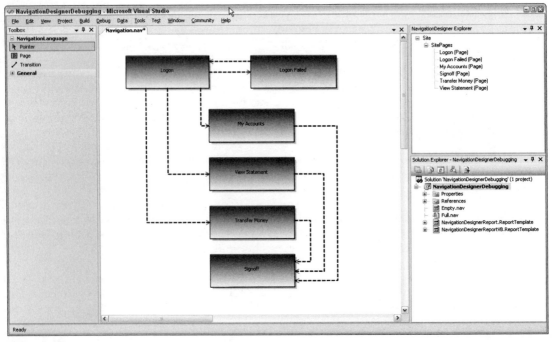

Figure 6-15

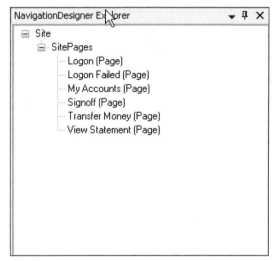

Figure 6-16

All designers leverage the rich designer platform in Visual Studio 2005. You can zoom in and out of the diagram by holding down Ctrl+ Shift and pressing the left mouse button to zoom in or the right mouse button to zoom out. You also get Resize, Undo, and Redo functionality for free.

When you save this navigation model, it is stored as an XML file that contains all of the navigation model information. You can, of course, override the save logic to save to another file format if required, and provide the corresponding load logic to rebuild the navigation model using the object model created for you.

Using the Domain Model

Now that you have a language model, we'll demonstrate how you might use it after a user has used the graphical designer to build a navigation model.

As you've seen previously, a set of .NET classes are constructed to reflect the language model. These classes are created in memory as an object graph as the user constructs the graphical designer.

The object model that is created is strongly typed to the language you defined in the language designer, making it extremely straightforward to use. Consider the following example, which iterates around all of the pages defined in the Navigation model depicted in Figure 6-15 and outputs each page's Name and a list of all the pages to which it links:

```
IList MELPages = this.Store.ElementDirectory.GetElements
                 (DomainModel.Page.MetaClassGuid);
foreach (DomainModel.Page MELPage in MELPages)
{
    Debug.WriteLine( "Page: " + MELPage.Name );
    if (MELPage.ChildPages.Count > 0)
```

```
        {
            Debug.WriteLine("Links to: ");

            foreach (DomainModel.Page MELChildPage in MELPage.ChildPages)
            {
                Debug.WriteLine(MELChildPage.Name);
            }
            Debug.WriteLine("\n");
        }
        else
        {
            Debug.WriteLine("Links to nothing");
        }
    }
}
```

Here's the output:

Page: Logon
Links to:
Logon Failed
My Accounts
View Statement
Move Money

Page: Logon Failed
Links to:
Logon

Page: My Accounts
Links to:
Signoff

Page: View Statement
Links to:
Signoff

Page: Transfer Money
Links to:
Signoff

Page: Signoff
Links to nothing

The code sample uses the in-built `ElementDirectory` to find all of the Page elements in our domain model and then iterates through them. Note that the `ChildPages` collection is the left-hand role of the Transition relationship that we defined in the language model, which gives you access to a collection of references to other pages within the model.

The object model is extremely easy to navigate and is typically used by any extensions you build into your designer. Examples of such extensions include code generation or custom save and load routines for your designer; a custom save routine would persist the contents of a model to a proprietary file format and the corresponding custom load routine would then convert from that file format back into the language model to be viewed using the graphical designer.

Generating Code

The DSL Tools provide a rich templating technology that enables you to generate output based on your domain model; and as discussed previously, this technology is used to create your designer and can be used by your own designer. It can also be used by your designer to generate your output of choice — source code and documentation are common examples.

In the scenario of your Navigation Designer, you want to generate ASP.NET Pages and their associated code-behind files for each of the pages in the language model. As placeholders, you could create buttons on each page that will navigate to any child pages linked using the connector.

At the time of writing, the DSL Tools do not provide a way for a template to output multiple files during execution. In our scenario, we need to generate an .ASPX and ASPX.CS file for every Page defined in our navigation model, so we are unable to generate pages using the templates. This feature is planned in the final product. If you were to use the templating technology, you would define a template of a shell ASPX and ASPX.cs file and provide .NET code to iterate around the object model creating pages.

For the purposes of the book, we will implement the page generation manually using .NET code. The principles are in fact identical to how templates will work, but you have to provide a bit more plumbing.

You start by defining the template for the ASPX and ASPX.cs files by creating a new Web Site project and use the default pages generated as a base for your templates. Any page-specific information has to be replaced with tokens that you can then replace with the page specifics during generation.

The ASPX and ASPX.cs templates are shown in the following code examples. You can see that tokens have been added at key places (highlighted in bold). Where the data is the same, we use the same token identifier, and any curly braces in the code need to be escaped with an extra curly brace. Here is TemplatePage.aspx:

```
<%@ Page Language="C#" AutoEventWireup="true"  CodeFile="{0}.aspx.cs"
Inherits="{0}" %>

<!DOCTYPE html PUBLIC "-//W3C//DTD XHTML 1.1//EN"
"http://www.w3.org/TR/xhtml11/DTD/xhtml11.dtd">

<html xmlns="http://www.w3.org/1999/xhtml" >
<head runat="server">
    <title>Untitled Page</title>
</head>
<body>
    <form id="form1" runat="server">
    <h1>{1}</h1>
    <div>
        {2}
    </div>
    </form>
</body>
</html>
```

Here is the corresponding ASPX.CS template. The number of using statements to import namespaces has been reduced for clarity:

```
TemplatePage.aspx.cs

using System;

public partial class {0} : System.Web.UI.Page
{{
    {1}
}}
```

Now that you have your templates, you need to write the code that will iterate through all of the pages in the domain model and generate the physical implementations. As you create pages, you also need to create buttons on the pages to demonstrate the navigation defined in the domain model, so you have some boilerplate button definitions, which you use to simplify insertion of these buttons into the page code.

The code shown retrieves a collection of all the Pages in your domain model and iterates through each one in turn. You then load the templates into a string so you can replace the tokens with the page-specific information.

For each page, you then obtain any child Pages referenced by the Page and construct a button for each one, enabling the user to navigate to them. You also generate the code-behind file that performs the transfer between pages using `Response.Redirect`.

You then replace any tokens in the two files with the page-specific information and then output the text for the pages to disk. Following its execution, you will see .ASPX and .ASPX.cs files generated:

```
const string ButtonDefinition = "<asp:Button ID=\"{0}\" runat=\"server\"
Text=\"{0}\" OnClick=\"{0}_Click\" />";
const string ButtonCodeDefinition = "protected void {0}_Click(object sender,
EventArgs e)\r\n{{\r\n{1}\r\n}}";

IList MELPages =
this.Store.ElementDirectory.GetElements(DomainModel.Page.MetaClassGuid);
foreach (DomainModel.Page MELPage in MELPages)
{
    // Read the ASP.NET Page Templates into a string so we can customise.
    StreamReader ASPXTemplatePageReader = new StreamReader("TemplatePage.aspx");
    string TemplateASPXPage = ASPXTemplatePageReader.ReadToEnd();

    StreamReader CodeTemplatePageReader = new StreamReader("TemplatePage.aspx.cs");
    string TemplateCodePage = CodeTemplatePageReader.ReadToEnd();

    // We loop around any Child Pages and provide buttons on the ASP.NET Page and
    // Code Behind handlers to move to the child pages

    StringBuilder ASPXButtonDefinitions = new StringBuilder();
    StringBuilder CodeButtonDefinitions = new StringBuilder();

    foreach (DomainModel.Page MELChildPage in MELPage.ChildPages)
    {
        // Variable and type names cannot have spaces so we remove
        string CollapsedChildName = MELChildPage.Name.Replace(" ", "");

        // Create a new ASP.NET Button
        ASPXButtonDefinitions.Append( String.Format(ButtonDefinition,
```

```
                                                CollapsedChildName) );

        // Create the Code behind for the button
        string NavigationCode = String.Format(
                        "Response.Redirect(\"{0}.aspx\");",CollapsedChildName );
        CodeButtonDefinitions.Append(String.Format(ButtonCodeDefinition,
                                    CollapsedChildName,NavigationCode ) );
    }

    // Variable and type names cannot have spaces so we remove
    string CollapsedName = MELPage.Name.Replace(" ", "");

    // Our page templates have the areas that need
    // to change for each page replaced with tokens which we now fill in.
    string OutputASPXPage = String.Format(TemplateASPXPage, CollapsedName,
                    MELPage.Name, ASPXButtonDefinitions.ToString() );
    string OutputCodePage = String.Format(TemplateCodePage, CollapsedName,
                                        CodeButtonDefinitions.ToString() );

    using (StreamWriter ASPXPageWriter = new StreamWriter( CollapsedName +
                                                    ".aspx" ) )
    {
        ASPXPageWriter.Write(OutputASPXPage);
    }

    using (StreamWriter ASPXPageWriter = new StreamWriter( CollapsedName +
                                                    ".aspx.cs" ) )
    {
        ASPXPageWriter.Write(OutputCodePage);
    }
}
```

If you then copy these files into a new ASP.NET website and navigate to Logon.aspx, you should see the logon page as defined in the language model appear as shown in Figure 6-17.

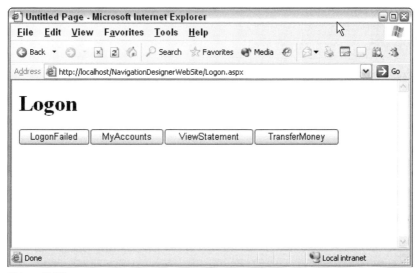

Figure 6-17

Clicking one of the buttons will enable you to navigate to the page as defined in the language model. For example, clicking ViewStatement will take you to the View Statement page (shown in Figure 6-18), which only has a link to the Signoff page.

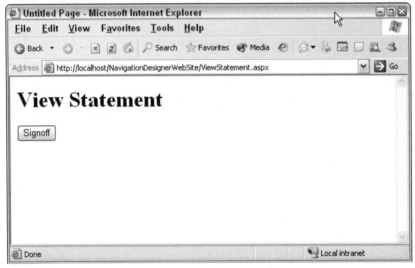

Figure 6-18

As you can see, generating these pages was extremely straightforward, and even a complex navigation model would require much less development effort. The templating support in the DSL Tools makes generation of these pages even easier.

If you wanted to produce an Avalon version of your site or move to another page technology, you could simply replace the templates and regenerate the pages. Using the domain model in this way effectively decouples you from the implementation technology.

Designers and VSTS

This chapter has covered a simplified navigation designer concept that would enable users to model the navigation of an application or website. Abstracting from the end technology, it could be extended in any direction to allow for modeling of different semantics, such as auditing and logging.

In Part IV in this book, we describe how you can build your own custom Work Item types for use by Team System. The process you've already seen is fairly cumbersome in that you have to construct an XML document adhering to the supplied WIT schema.

This in itself is fine, but a Work Item type can become incredibly complex when you have to start modeling the workflow around State Transitions, which is very hard to visualize and understand when it's represented in an XML file format.

You could easily define a language model for Work Item types and construct a designer using the DSL Tools. The only code you would need to write would be code to translate the XML file format of Work Item types into the language model and back again.

This translation section would be very easy to implement; you could use XSD.EXE supplied with the .NET Framework to create a .NET object model from the Work Item Schema, load the XML into this object model, and iterate through all of the concepts, constructing the equivalent language model elements allowing the user to visualize the Work Item structure in the designer. Saving changes would be the same process but in reverse.

Apart from the translation code, you won't have to write any other code, which is very compelling when you consider how much code you would have to write yourself! A screenshot of a prototype WIT designer that one of the authors has developed is shown in Figure 6-19. States are represented by the boxes on the diagrams. Fields in the domain model are not represented as boxes but as dynamic toolbox items, and transitions between states are represented by the lines between states.

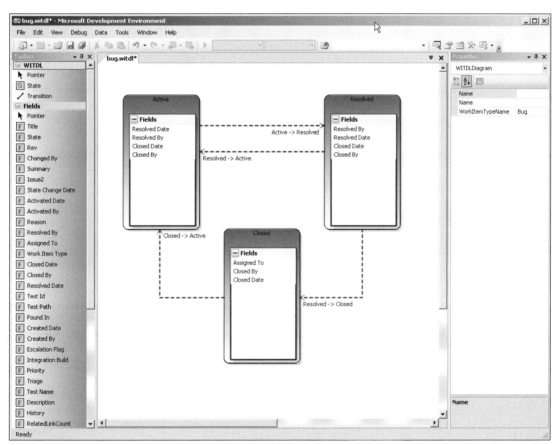

Figure 6-19

Summary

In this chapter, we discussed the background to the DSL Tools and discussed some scenarios whereby a graphical designer could be used to simplify software development and provide a technology abstraction. We detailed the background to our sample Navigation Designer and walked through creating the navigation language and its associated graphical language, resulting in a fully fledged designer integrated with Visual Studio 2005.

With this sample designer, we then detailed how you might use the resulting domain model and demonstrated some code that created a working ASP.NET project from the domain model.

In the next chapter, we cover the Microsoft Dynamic Systems Initiative (DSI) and the System Definition Model (SDM). The SDM Visual Designers in Visual Studio 2005 are built using a domain-specific language.

7

Dynamic Systems Initiative and the System Definition Model

In this chapter, we will show how the Distributed System Designers in Visual Studio Team Edition for Software Architects are the first deliverable of the Dynamic Systems Initiative that are aimed at improving the design and validation of distributed systems. We will also describe the System Definition Model architecture and how it can be used to capture distributed system knowledge. We will conclude this chapter by creating a Windows Mobile Device component, described in SDM, that can be plugged into and extend the Application Design surface.

Industries worldwide are investing in simulation technology. Chip, automobile, and aerospace manufacturers, government agencies, and financial firms are increasingly relying on models to simulate real-world behaviors of their products and services. The payoff is to cheaply predict or uncover design flaws or operational errors in the product or service before they're laboriously produced, tested, and deployed into the real world.

With the industry aimed toward simulating increasingly complex systems, advances in hardware are being pursued at a breakneck pace. Today's supercomputers exercise models at teraflop speeds to simulate rapid crash tests of fenders. In five years, the computing industry hopes to build a supercomputer running at petaflop speeds capable of simulating the impact of the entire car system.

Advances in software tools give users enhanced capability to capture models of complex systems and exercise them within virtual computer environments. For instance, specialized software tools help to create clinical models that enable medical students to virtually visualize and even feel patient procedures.

Yet, for all this virtual computerization, businesses are ill prepared to effectively preempt problems within their own increasingly complex and costly information technology (IT) infrastructure. They are unable to use software to readily understand the often significant effects a change in one part of their system can have on their overall environment.

The rate and intricacies of new business application requirements are swelling. The interdependencies between heterogeneous software and hardware are rising; and as these interdependencies increase, so does the complexity that spans the entire IT life cycle from designing, developing, and deploying to managing and operating these distributed systems.

While developing these new distributed systems is requiring increasing amounts of effort, time-to-market pressures have never been higher. Increased system complexity drives cross-team coordination to new limits. Deploying new systems often requires buying new hardware, and demands numerous development iterations to optimize the system. Once out the door, the manual nature of operations means that some customers spend as much as 75 percent of their IT budget on system maintenance.

In such an environment, the ability to predict failure is daunting — and failure to predict is costly.

So that's the problem we face — but how to solve it? Well, modeling helps, but modeling by itself is insufficient.

The modeling challenge for IT today is not simply to represent the structure and architecture of each system in a distributed environment or to additionally describe the behavior and processes of these systems. Nor is it to bring more computing power to bear on the models and processes already in place. The challenge is to provide a *holistic modeling experience* that can persist beyond design, where models share a *common* definition of IT knowledge and behavior so that they can communicate among themselves, especially within heterogeneous IT environments.

This kind of modeling support is unlikely to come from modeling tools that have little capability to model knowledge and communicate with a system in generic ways. Nor is it likely to come from tools that provide generalized solutions to designing but treat the deployment and operation of these complex distributed systems as an afterthought.

Rather, a new systemic approach is needed, a technology able to shift operational intelligence into the design of the application itself. The Dynamic Systems Initiative, and in particular Systems Definition Modeling, provides that direction. The Dynamic Systems Initiative (DSI) is an effort by Microsoft to deliver, over time, a coordinated set of solutions that dramatically simplify and automate how businesses design, deploy, and operate these distributed systems. At the heart of the DSI is a modeling language called the Systems Definition Model (SDM). SDM is used to create models of distributed systems, which it does by defining system building blocks capable of accurately capturing descriptions and behaviors pertinent to the system's development, deployment, and operation. With SDM, administrators, system integrators, and vendors can create a living blueprint of an entire system, which can be dynamically maintained at any point in the system's life cycle.

This chapter introduces you to the Systems Definition Model (SDM) architecture and describes the runtime environment that allows for modest simulation scenarios, such as validating at design time whether an application can be deployed to a target environment. We then investigate the SDM object model and schema used to author a systems structure and behavior. Lastly, this chapter provides a nontrivial example of Team Architect extensibility using the SDM SDK.

This chapter is developer focused and will not focus on DSI areas such as driving toward more operationally aware Windows platform with virtualization, management technologies and tools, automated deployment, configuration, and monitoring.

It is assumed that the reader has a basic understanding of the XML Schema Definition (.xsd) format.

Dynamic Systems Initiative

The Dynamic Systems Initiative (DSI), announced in mid-2003, is a Microsoft-led multi-year industry initiative to provide a coordinated set of solutions around the Microsoft Windows platform. The goal of DSI is to simplify and automate how businesses design, develop, deploy, manage, and operate distributed systems.

Enterprise solutions often have a mix of Microsoft and non-Microsoft software services running on a wide range of hardware, so it's not surprising that Microsoft is collaborating heavily with partners on the design and development of all aspects of DSI, as well as promoting DSI as the best way for third parties to deliver end-to-end solutions. It is Microsoft's intention to work with partners to leverage DSI to more easily integrate their various application development tools, operating systems, applications, hardware, and management tools around the Windows platform. The result of this initiative will be better reliability, reduced costs, and increased responsiveness throughout the entire IT life cycle.

The Dynamic Systems Initiative is not an effort to create a series of independent discrete software development life cycle technologies. Rather, the goal of DSI is to create a connection from the design of a system to the operation of that system, and on through to the end users using that system. By creating an integrated feedback loop spanning the entire life cycle of a system, Microsoft plans to facilitate the ongoing improvement of IT infrastructure with software.

In short, the Dynamic Systems Initiative is focused on maximizing people resources and delivering software that can decrease labor costs through the entire IT life cycle. For this effort to succeed, systems must be designed with operations in mind and with management a core attribute of the underlying platform. To this end, Microsoft has mapped out three Dynamic Systems Initiative deliverables key to the promise of self-managing dynamic systems (this chapter focuses on the first only):

❑ **System Definition Model (SDM):** The future of DSI is dependent on delivering a unifying XML-driven modeling technology called the System Definition Model (SDM). SDM enables Microsoft and third parties to describe life-cycle components (and tools) for heterogeneous distributed systems. These modeled components will be capable of enabling increased integration, automation, flexibility, and design time validation across the full application's life cycle. Microsoft sees SDM as a core technological differentiator between Windows and competing platforms.

❑ **DSI roadmap:** The first roadmap deliverable for developers can be found in Visual Studio Team Edition for Software Architects whose Distributed System Designers rely on the System Definition Model to support the architecture and design support for applications and data centers. On the Windows server front, Microsoft has already begun delivering on this initiative with Windows 2003 Server R2 WS-Management, System Center Capacity Planner 2006, System Center Reporting Manager 2006, System Center Data Protection Manager 2006, System Management Server (SMS) 2003 SP1, and Microsoft Operations Manager (MOM) 2005. Microsoft's long-term roadmap includes new versions of these products with deeper integration between these products and use of SDM.

❑ **Broad partner ecosystem:** A broad set of Microsoft partners delivering DSI products and solutions. Microsoft has worked hard over the past few years to solicit input and feedback from enterprise customers, partners, and third-party vendors to ensure that a robust SDM schema is captured.

System Definition Model

At the heart of the Dynamic System Initiative is the System Definition Model, an XML-based modeling language used to capture formal representation of systems. More precisely, the SDM is a meta-model used to create models of a distributed system, including all information pertinent to its design, deployment, and ongoing operations.

The SDM provides enterprise customers, vendors, system integrators, and administrators the capability to create a dynamic "living blueprint" of their system. This blueprint can be used not only to describe the system, but also to actively facilitate its development, deployment, and ongoing operations.

The SDM defines the structure of the distributed system and maintains data about its various elements and how they relate to one another. In addition, the behavioral tasks of the system are captured. This includes the operational tasks that can be applied to the system as well as the *constraints* of the system: the rules or policies that must remain true in order for the system to be considered operational.

SDM models of distributed system elements can be defined in advance and made available through Microsoft or (eventually) non-Microsoft tools. For example, Visual Studio Team Edition for Software Architects ships with SDM models for web services, ASP.Net applications, IIS6, SQL Server, and Windows Application, among others. These predefined SDM prototype models may be further modified to support a particular element of a connected system. Along with these models are the necessary supporting tools such as the SDM Compiler (more on this later).

The benefits of SDM are as follows:

- ❑ **Communication:** Using a single systems definition language enables developers and operations teams to communicate on common ground. Developers are able to communicate application requirements of the run-time environment, and operation teams can communicate application runtime, connectivity, and security requirements expressed in the target deployment environment's policies. With the SDM, architects can fully specify systems and polices in their designs. Reducing the level of misinterpretation when systems are implemented mitigates one of the biggest challenges in traditional software modeling: their limited utility to developers in real-world situations.

- ❑ **Extensibility:** SDM is designed to be extensible and makes it possible for users to add or modify any system definitions. Users can add other types of applications, logical servers, or resource types created by Microsoft, third parties, or other users.

- ❑ **Efficiency:** By capturing knowledge of the system at design time and "flowing" that knowledge through the entire life cycle of the system, developers can more readily create and deploy solutions that result in reduced costs, improved reliability, and increased responsiveness across the entire IT life cycle.

- ❑ **Design-time validation:** The most evident benefit of SDM in Team Architect is to facilitate, at design-time, validation of a connected application against its target deployment environment. This *design for deployment* scenario is further described in this chapter and in Chapter 3 in this book.

SDM Architecture

This section provides a high-level overview of the SDM architecture, terminology, and basic elements of SDM and how they relate.

The configuration of connected systems and the interactions between their elements can be modeled using the System Definition Model (SDM) language.

At a high level, SDM is governed by an object-relational model. Objects are used to represent both the physical and logical elements in the modeled system and to specify the links between them. Objects and relationships are further classified to capture semantics important to the SDM. The definitions of these objects and relationships provide a way to create reusable configurations of resources and systems, much like classes in an object-oriented programming language. Abstractions of these objects help describe characteristics common (and largely immutable) to these object and relationships categorizations. For example, a characteristic that all SDM objects must have is support for a containment relationship; that is, an object should be able to contain other objects. This relationship is captured in an abstract definition from which all SDM objects can derive. In this way, abstractions provide meta-modeling support—they help model possible models. More pragmatically, abstract definitions enable tool support for a large number of applications, and are the basis for type checking at design time. There are two abstract definition types: *abstract objects* and *abstract relationships*. Abstract object definitions are the building blocks of a modeled system. Every entity in a modeled system is represented by an abstract object. Abstract relationship definitions model the interactions that can occur between abstract object definitions, and therefore identify the types of the instances that participate in the relationship. Abstract relationships provide a way to bind objects together in order to model, for example, their containment and communication relationships.

All abstract definitions have the ability to expose settings. These settings are basic name-value pairs that use XML schema to define the type or definition of the setting (such as `Name=MyWebApp`). Settings can be static or dynamic. Static settings can only be set during the deployment process. Dynamic settings can be changed after deployment

> *In Chapters 2 through 4, you saw such settings exposed to the user via the Settings and Constraints editor.*

In addition to the meta-modeling support provided by abstract objects and relationship definitions, SDM also supports a set of core models used as the basis for defining real-world application or datacenter objects. Like building blocks, these core models simplify the design process of resources and help ensure consistency in the basic properties and behaviors associated with such basic types as `user`, `file`, and `computer`—a core model that may describe settings, relationships, and operations common to all computers.

Core models are derived from abstract definitions. As such, they cannot be directly instantiated or contain object or relationship members. Nonetheless, they represent real-world (albeit incomplete) types of objects. To emphasize this distinction, we will sometimes use the term *concrete definitions* to describe core models. You can view a concrete definition as a real-world reusable template of the abstract definition. Put another way, you can consider the concrete definition space a subset of the abstract object space. You can use the concrete space to create a reusable configuration based on one or more abstract definitions. Concrete definitions supply implementations for a specific abstract definition that includes extensions to the settings schema, values for settings, declarations for type and relationship members, and constraints on the relationships in which the type can participate.

A real-world *instantiation* of the concrete definition is called an *instance*. A distributed system is then built from collections of these instances. Instances come from a mix of sources and are typically associated with applications or datacenter infrastructure. Instances may result from models that ship with Team Architect—called built-in or prototype definitions (see `C:\Program Files\Microsoft Visual Studio 8\Common7\IDE\ PrivateAssemblies`), they may come from third-party libraries or online depositories, or they may be user defined. Microsoft's goal is to build into the SDM and tools a set of these core models that will entice users to create libraries of refined definitions. For example, under an SDM computer library (in which all models derive from a "computer" core model), you may find SDM descriptions for various models of Dell laptops, HP servers, and Apple devices. Manufacturers, companies, or individuals may refine these computer library models by describing standardized configurations for their datacenter around CPU, memory, and OS. Others may take a set of generic SDM computer component models (perhaps from other libraries) and build a computer for individual use. Each instance of these configured models would be unique. This concept is illustrated in Figure 7-1.

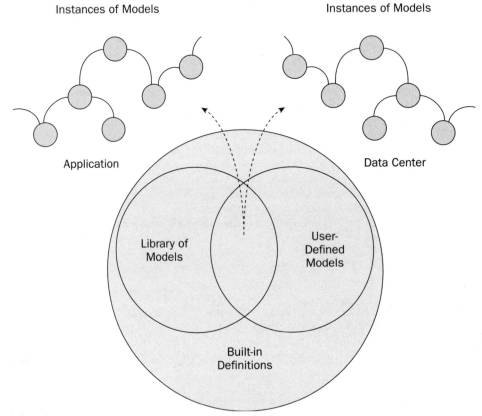

Figure 7-1

Constraints specify restrictions on the permissible set of relationships in which an instance can participate. They capture fine-grained requirements that depend on the configuration of objects involved in a relationship. For example, a constraint can be used to validate that participants on each end of a communication protocol are using compatible security settings.

Managers are used to both provide customized behavior to the runtime and to support interaction between the modeled system and the runtime. Managers are required for custom constraints.

An *SDM document* is the source XML file (.sdm) containing one or more definitions, resources, endpoints, and relationships.

The *SDM Compiler* validates the format, references, and constraints of an SDM document (.sdm). The compiler takes as input one or more SDM documents, executes a set of validation steps, and returns a set of errors. If successful, the compiler outputs a compiled and signed SDM file (.sdmDocument).

After the SDM file passes the compiler's initial load and validation processes, the compiler checks for constraints and flow. It does this by simulating an instance space for the SDM types given. The instance space captures both the current and desired state of the SDM defined application. Changes in the instance space are initiated by *change requests*.

A change request is initiated either through a declarative XML description or through APIs that enable the request to be constructed. A change request represents a set of create, update, or delete requests for objects and relationships associated with specific members of an existing instance.

Finally, the SDM run-time represents an extended version of the SDM Compiler. It provides a set of processes and components responsible for consuming and validating SDM files, loading associated binary information (files) and any third-party Microsoft Windows Installers (MSIs), generating and executing SDM change requests, and deployment of SDM-based applications into target, distributed server environments. The SDM run-time contains the deployment engines, the SDM Object Model APIs, and the Instance Space — the store of types, instances, and relationships relevant to the applications scoped by the current modeled system. By using the version history maintained by each instance, which is linked to each change request, the SDM run-time is able to maintain a complete account of each instance created as well as the relationships between these instances.

Currently, the runtime allows applications and hosting environments described using the SDM to be defined and validated in Team Architect. This is called *design-time validation*. In future Microsoft product releases, the runtime is expected to manage the loading of SDUs, SDM change requests, and deployment to a set of servers.

Design-time validation

Because an SDM model captures the structure of the system, the relationships between a system's components, the settings and constraints of the system, and any operational task that can be performed on the system, SDM-based deployment and operational tools can be created to manipulate the model and not the real world.

Starting with Team Architect, users can model their distributed application and datacenter for design-time validation to ease deployment and operations. Users then request SDM validation within Team Architect during development to further ensure that the application being developed can be deployed.

Future versions of Visual Studio are expected to take SDM beyond design-time validation to help facilitate deployment and provide post-deployment handling of operational requests. Rather than directly manipulate real-world systems, users will have the capability to validate a change request within the simulated SDK environment and rely on adapters to effect the changes to these systems. Figure 7-2 shows the relationship between the system administrator, SDM models, and the real-world systems that future evolutions of DSI will support.

In the near future, you can also expect SDM to assist in the health monitoring of deployed applications. For example, if a problem occurs in the datacenter, adapters can send SDM documents reflecting the current state and configuration of the servers back to the Team System tools for immediate consideration.

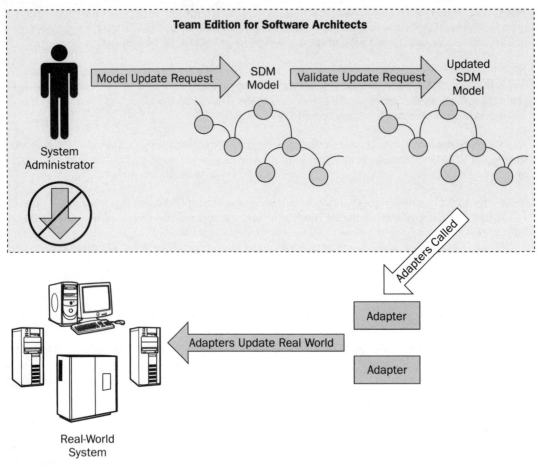

Figure 7-2

SDM in Visual Studio 2005 Team Edition for Software Architects

As you work with SDM, you may wish to extend existing models and develop new models not supported natively in the first release of Team Architect. These new models may describe custom definitions for your connected system or datacenter, or capture third-party products or technologies. If that's the case, you'll want the capability to author Visual Studio Team Edition for Software Architect providers that plug in to the design surfaces and relevant user interfaces for the new models. This will enable you to use the design surfaces to load, compose, extend, and validate—and possibly provide code-generation capabilities with—these new models. This extensibility will enable you to better capture the breadth of your own distributed systems, thereby further reducing the development and operations communication gap. This capability will be provided through the SDM SDK discussed later in this chapter.

Figure 7-3 illustrates the principal flow of SDM in Team Architect.

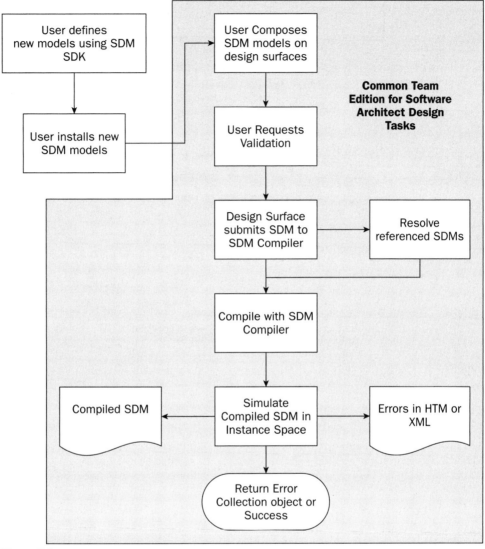

Figure 7-3

Deployment

Although the current SDM tools will not automate the actual deployment and versioning of distributed applications, Team Architect provides the capability to generate a deployment report of all required application and datacenter configuration settings. You can use these reports to create a script for custom deployment. In Figure 7-4, each step of the SDM deployment is presented.

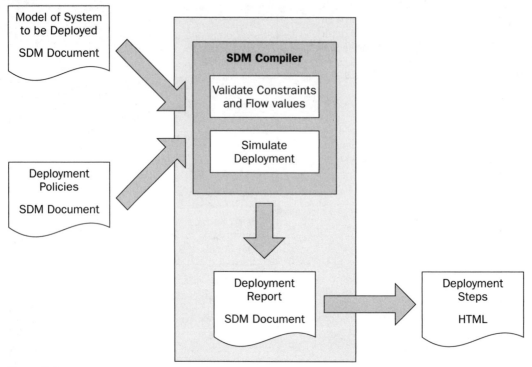

Figure 7-4

Modeling layers of a system

SDM uses a four-layered approach to further represent the structure of distributed systems. These layers include the application, the application hosting environment, the network and operating systems environment, and lastly the hardware. These layers reflect the traditional role boundaries of IT professionals.

Each of these layers represents a set of definitions (resources, endpoints, subsystem) particular to the objects modeled in that layer. For example, the application layer may include web application and database system definitions, while the application hosts layer includes definitions related to IIS or SQL. The operating system layer may further include definitions for file systems and network devices. Some definitions may not be assigned to layers and will instead be usable across a range of layers.

Objects in one layer can describe constraints on the layers above or below. A system at one level is then bound to and validated against a system at the other level. Therefore, an application system defined at the application layer can be bound to or hosted on a logical server defined at the level below, the application host layer. Both the application system and the logical server on which it is hosted can describe constraints on the other. Thus, a mapping of one layer to another — in this instance, referred to as a *system deployment definition* — can be validated. Team Architect includes the SDM Compiler that checks the definitions of each entity defined in each layer and then checks the validity of the bindings between elements in adjacent layers. For example, the SDM Compiler will validate whether an ASP.NET 2.0 web application with a dependency on Windows Server 2003 SP1 is compatible with an IIS6 host deployed on Windows Server 2003 without SP1. This example would result in the compiler issuing an alert to the Visual Studio user that an OS incompatibility exists between the web application and its target host.

Team Architect supports only the top two layers of the DSI model, the application layer and the application host layer. Later releases of DSI supported tools and servers will include support for the remaining two levels, including support for deployment and management of distributed systems. Figure 7-5 illustrates the relationship between the SDM layers.

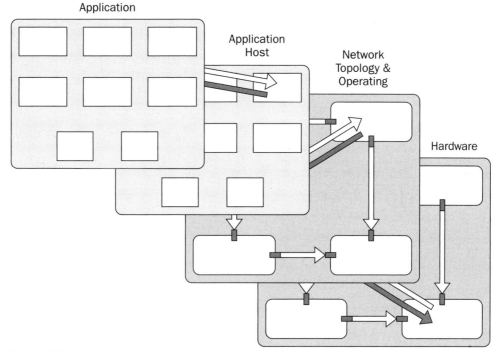

Figure 7-5

In Figure 7-5, the application layer describes the structure and behavior of application systems. The application host layer underneath describes a logical model of the application hosts, such as IIS and SQL Server. The term "logical" is used to indicate that elements described in the application host layer are scale-invariant — a single SDM modeled element, such as an IIS6 host, may represent one physical IIS6 box or a farm of IIS6 boxes, each sharing the same (pre-deployment) settings and constraints. The arrows between layers illustrate that the setting and constraints of an element in the application layer can be compared or validated against those of its intended logical host.

> *It is not yet clear whether future versions will allow comparisons directly between non-adjacent layers. However, it may be the case that such a detail, regardless of implementation, would make little difference in overall validation behavior.*

SDM types

As you would expect with any object-oriented technology, SDM relies on a type system for defining the behavior and structure of instances. At the highest level, the SDM type system categorizes types into *simple types* and *complex types*. Complex types represent those instances that have a unique identity, and thus are comparable to complex types in object-oriented terminology.

Simple type instances have no unique identity and can only exist within the context of a complex type instance. A simple type holds values, so you can generally think of a simple type as being a "value type." An example of a simple type could be a binary representation of data. Simple types are further refined into user-definable predefined simple types, enumeration types, and struct types. Predefined simple types may include integers (such as 4, 5, 9) and strings (such as "Hello, SDM World"). Like the Common Language Runtime (CLR), SDM defines a number of unalterable primitive types that form the basis of all other SDM types. However, through SDM's XML Schema Definition (more on this below) you can define a new SDM simple type to restrict the value space of a predefined type—for example, an integer type whose values lie between 50 and 99.

You can see the simple types the SDM relies on from the CLR by viewing the `System.sdm` document in NotePad (`C:\Program Files\Microsoft Visual Studio 8\Common7\IDE\PrivateAssemblies\ System.sdmDocument`).

Complex types are further categorized into *class types* and *interface types*. As with object-oriented methodology, SDM treats the class type as the most fundamental building block of an SDM system. A class type is a description of a set of objects that have the same structure, behavior, and semantics. An instance of a class type is an object. For example, instances of a `Dir` (i.e., directory) class type are objects (each representing a file or other directories), each with a unique identifier (the directory name and path).

In Visual Studio 2005, most SDM classes are hidden. The developer uses the SDM schema to create instances of these class types. Classes that are accessible (that is, public APIs) are those called by the SDM tools `SdmC.exe`, `SdmG.exe`, the Visual Studio 2005 design surface, and those related to the `Manager` class (more on this later).

Each class can have zero or more *properties*. A property is a named structural feature member of a class. Every property must contain a simple type. The property can manage single or multiple values. For multi-valued properties, lower and upper bounds can be specified via lower and upper attributes (e.g., `MinOccurs`, `MaxOccurs` attributes of the `ObjectMember` complex type).

Each class can also contain zero or more methods. A method represents code that solves a particular problem for a class or supports a particular behavior of a class. A method is defined by a set of formal parameters and a return value. Because SDM is not a programming language, the implementation of class methods must be done in an external programming language such as C# or Visual Basic .NET. (As of this writing, it is not clear yet whether other .NET languages will be supported by Visual Studio 2005.) An example of a method is the C# or Visual Basic .NET `Compile` method defined in the `Compiler` class. This class is part of the `SdmCompile.dll` assembly and is defined by the namespace `Microsoft.SystemDefinition Model.Tools`. The `Compile` method takes no parameters, is used by `SdmC.exe` to compile a SDM document (.sdm), and returns `True` if an error occurred during compilation; otherwise it returns `false`. In C#, the API signature is the public Boolean `Compile()`.

In the SDM world, types are defined through *type definitions*. Like class inheritance, new types are defined based on existing type definitions. Type definitions may be nested, and they rely on enumeration types. Types may also use modifiers to define the characteristics of the type. As an example, the modifier `abstract` signifies that instances cannot be directly created from this type. Only non-abstract types that derive from this type can have direct instances.

In sum, an SDM type definition is similar to a class in that it defines the structure and behavior of an instance of that class.

The following sections describe the definition of these types in terms of their SDM schema. Following that, the instance space of these definitions is explored.

SDM schema structure

XML-based languages follow a set of grammar rules that define, for example, what types are allowed and what child elements a particular element may have. These definitions are captured in a file called (unsurprisingly) an XML Schema Definition, and have the file extension .xsd. The SDM is also an XML-based schema built upon the SDM type system. The SDM schema captures reusable configurations of a modeled system element that can be instantiated to create instances of that configuration. These configurations include definitions for member types and relationships, and define the settings required to act on the modeled instance.

By looking into the SDM schema (`C:\Program Files\Microsoft Visual Studio 8\Common7\Packages\SDM\Schema\SystemDefinitionModel.xsm`), you can see the schema for each SDM type discussed in the architecture section.

All abstract and concrete objects (complex types) derive from a common root-level type definition called `Definition`. Objects, relationships, setting, and constraint definitions all extend from `Definition`. For example, the abstract definitions `ObjectDefinition` and `RelationshipDefinition` derive from `Definition`. `SystemDefinition`, `EndpointDefinition`, and `ResourceDefinition` derive from `ObjectDefinition`. The definitions `HostingDefinition` and `ContainmentDefinition` derive from `RelationshipDefinition`.

The definitions associated with settings and constraints do not use the base `Definition` but instead have their own base definitions, which are discussed in the Settings and Constraint sections that follow. Figure 7-6 relates the `Object` complex type definitions to the Distributed System Designers.

In the top-right box of Figure 7-6, two .NET projects are visualized as boxes in the Application Designer tool of Team Architect. Each is defined by an SDM (.sdm file). Both `My_Web_Application` and `My_DB_Resource` represent Object Instance definitions. They've been created by dragging and dropping the ASP.NETWebApplication concrete object (MicrosoftWebApplication:WebApplication) and ExternalDatabase concrete object (MicrosoftDatabase:Database) from the Application Designer toolbox to the design surface, configuring any and then implementing the design into code. Concrete objects are assembled from Abstract Object definitions of System, Endpoints, and Resources.

In the second row, a relationship is shown between an ASP.NETWebApplication and an ASP.NET WebService. The latter is also extended from MicrosoftWebApplication:WebApplication but with different settings and constraints. Although both are derived from the same concrete object, they are represented as two distinct components in the Application Designer toolbox that can be further customized. Each of these components in the toolbox is therefore called a *prototype*.

Relationships between these object instances can then be described via their endpoint instances. In the center-right box, these endpoints indicate the relationship MyWebService has between My_Web_Application and My_WebService_App.

The last row illustrates meta-data that further defines (configures) the policies or restrictions an object may have. In this example, an IIS Read constraint is placed on My_Web_Application.

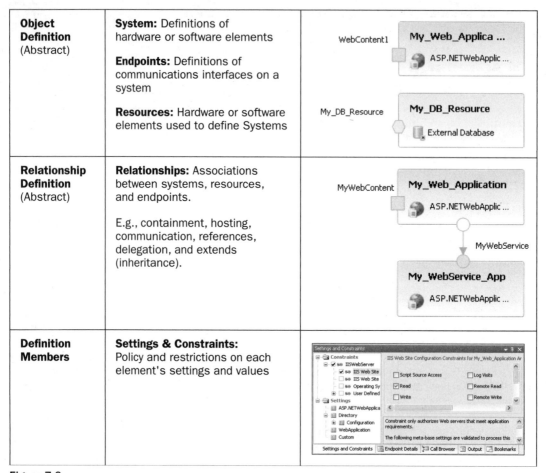

Object Definition (Abstract)	**System:** Definitions of hardware or software elements **Endpoints:** Definitions of communications interfaces on a system **Resources:** Hardware or software elements used to define Systems	
Relationship Definition (Abstract)	**Relationships:** Associations between systems, resources, and endpoints. E.g., containment, hosting, communication, references, delegation, and extends (inheritance).	
Definition Members	**Settings & Constraints:** Policy and restrictions on each element's settings and values	

Figure 7-6

Definition complex type

Each definition is identified by a simple name. These (SDM) names are scoped by the namespace in which they are defined. A namespace is identified by a name, version, language, and public key token, and is contained within a single file. To uniquely identify a persisted definition (a definition "instance"), each identity includes a name, version, culture, platform, and public key token.

The SDM run-time allows namespaces to reference other namespaces by importing them into the *current* namespace and then associating an alias with the *imported* namespace. The imported namespace is referenced by name and version (and possibly by public key token).

The following list describes *some* of the elements in the definition schema that can be set with some simple values. All definitions can include a description, setting members, setting values, and design surface data:

- ❑ **Description:** A text description of the definition.

- ❑ **SettingDeclaration:** Contains the *base* definition for a setting member.

- ❑ **SettingValue:** A value for a setting on the definition or its base definition. A value can only be provided once for a setting declaration within a definition.

- ❑ **SettingValueList:** A list of values of the same type as the setting declaration.

- ❑ **DesignData:** Design-surface-specific information about an object, relationship, constraint, or flow definition.

- ❑ **Name:** A name for this definition that is unique within the scope of the containing SDM file.

- ❑ **Manager:** A reference to the manager declaration for this definition.

- ❑ **ClrClassName:** The name of the CLR class that supports this definition in the runtime. The class must exist in the assembly identified by the manager. The manager attribute must be present if this attribute is present.

The structure of the SDM `Definition` schema looks like this:

```
<xs:complexType name="Definition">
  <xs:sequence>
    <xs:element name="Description" type="Description" minOccurs="0" />
    <xs:element name="DesignData" type="DesignData" minOccurs="0" />
    <xs:choice minOccurs="0" maxOccurs="unbounded">
      <xs:element name="SettingDeclaration" type="SettingMember" />
      <xs:element name="SettingValue" type="SettingValue" />
      <xs:element name="SettingValueList" type="SettingValueList" />
    </xs:choice>
  </xs:sequence>
  <xs:attribute name="Name" type="SimpleName" use="required" />
  <xs:attribute name="Manager" type="QualifiedName" use="optional" />
  <xs:attribute name="ClrClassName" type="xs:string" use="optional" />
</xs:complexType>
<!--
```

The following is an excerpt of the `DesignData` complex type and `ManagerDeclaration` complex type elements from the `Microsoft.Web.sdmDocument` model shipping with Visual Studio 2005:

```
<DesignData>
  <VisualStudio xmlns=
    "http://schemas.microsoft.com/SystemDefintionModel/
      2005/1/DesignData/VisualStudio">
    <ModelElement Type="Microsoft.VisualStudio.EnterpriseTools.
      LogicalInfrastructureDesign.Modeling.HostLayerDocument">
        <PropertyName="DocumentType" Value="AbstractTypes" />
    </ModelElement>
  </VisualStudio>
</DesignData>
<ManagerName="WebManager" AssemblyName="Microsoft.Sdm.Web"
    Version="1.0.41013.0" PublicKeyToken="31B3856AD364E35"
    Culture="neutral" SourcePath="Microsoft.Sdm.Web.dll" />
```

ObjectDefinition complex type

The complex type `ObjectDefinition` provides the abstract and concrete definitions for the objects that form the software and hardware building blocks for systems, and captures structure and behavior at a global level. `ObjectDefinition` is derived from the base definition. It includes elements for object members (derived from `Member` complex type) and object relationships (derived from `RelationshipDefinition` complex type). In addition to these, `ObjectDefinition` types share the ability to constrain the relationships in which the objects participate.

Attributes of this definition are as follows:

❑ **Layer:** Supplies the modeling layer for which this abstract object definition can be used. If there is none, then the abstract object layer can be used in any layer. This attribute helps determine which designer can reference the object. In Visual Studio 2005, valid values are `Application` for the Application Designer and `ApplicationHost` for the Logical Datacenter Designer.

❑ **Extends:** Provides the base object definition from which this object definition derives. If provided, the abstract object definition then inherits the settings and relationship constraints from that base object definition.

❑ **Abstract:** Specifies whether this object can be instantiated. If the object is marked as abstract with Boolean value `true`, then the definition must be extended in order to fill in missing elements. The default value is `false`. Users of Team Architect need never to worry about this distinction. Users can only place abstract objects on the design surface and Visual Studio will automatically promote these objects to concrete upon output (i.e., all SDM objects represented in the Solution Explorer are concrete).

In addition to these attributes are numerous child elements. These elements and respective types define various parent-child, client-server, guest-host, and other relationships this object may have with other complex types. The following code illustrates the structure of the `ObjectDefinition` schema:

```
<xs:complexType name="ObjectDefinition">
  <xs:complexContent>
    <xs:extensionbase="Definition">
      <xs:choice minOccurs="0" maxOccurs="unbounded">
        <xs:element name="Flow" type="FlowMember" minOccurs="0"
            maxOccurs="unbounded"/>
        <xs:element name="RelationshipConstraintGroup"
            type="RelationshipConstraintGroup"/>
        <xs:element name"RelationshipConstraint" type="RelationshipConstraint"/>
        <xs:element name"Constraint" type="ConstraintMember"/>
        <xs:element name"ConstraintGroup" type="ConstraintGroup"/>
        <xs:element name"EndpointDefinition" type="EndpointDefinition"/>
        <xs:element name"SystemDefinition" type="SystemDefinition"/>
        <xs:element name"ResourceDefinition" type="ResourceDefinition"/>
        <xs:element name"CommunicationDefinition" type="CommunicationDefinition"/>
        <xs:element name"ContainmentDefinition" type="ContainmentDefinition"/>
        <xs:element name"DelegationDefinition" type="DelegationDefinition"/>
        <xs:element name"ReferenceDefinition" type="ReferenceDefinition"/>
        <xs:element name"HostingDefinition" type="HostingDefinition"/>
        <xs:element name"Endpoint" type="EndpointMember"/>
        <xs:element name"Subsystem" type="SystemMember"/>
        <xs:element name"Resource" type="ResourceMember"/>
        <xs:element name"Hosting" type="HostingMember"/>
```

```
    <xs:element name"Containment" type="ContainmentMember"/>
    <xs:element name"Connection" type="CommunicationMember"/>
    <xs:element name"Delegation" type="DelegationMember"/>
    <xs:element name"Reference" type="ReferenceMember"/>
    <!--flow -->
    <!--constraints -->
    <!--nested definitions -->
    <!--object / relationship members -->
    <!--flow-->
  </xs:choice>
  <xs:attribute name="Layer" type="xs:string" use="optional"/>
  <xs:attribute name="Extends" type="QualifiedName" use="optional"/>
  <xs:attribute name="Abstract" type="xs:boolean" use="optional"/>
 </xs:extension>
  </xs:complexContent>
</xs:ComplexType>
```

Further classifications of `ObjectDefinition` are provided for systems, resources, and endpoints:

```
<xs:complexType name="SystemDefinition">
  <xs:ComplextContent>
    <xs:extension base="ObjectDefinition">
      <xs:attribute name="SimulationRoot" type="xs:boolean" use="optional" />
    </xs:extension>
  </xs:complexContent>
</xs:complexType
<xs:complexType name="EndpointDefinition">
  <xs:ComplextContent>
    <xs:extension base="ObjectDefinition" />
  </xs:complexContent>
</xs:complexType
<xs:complexType name="ResourceDefinition">
  <xs:ComplextContent>
    <xs:extension base="ObjectDefinition" />
  </xs:complexContent>
</xs:complexType
```

The `SystemDefinition` complex type is derived from `ObjectDefinition` and adds support for the following: endpoint, system, and resource types; endpoint, system, and resource members; and host, containment, connection, delegation, and reference relationships. Examples of a SystemDefinition attribute and schema element are provided as follows.

❑ **SimulationRoot:** Determines how the definition should handle design-time checking (simulation) during compilation of the SDM document. This Boolean attribute is optional and is `false` by default. As such, it may not appear in the output. It is doubtful a beginning Visual Studio 2005 SDM developer will ever need to set it.

❑ **DesignData:** In the following example, the Report element enables this system to be outputted in the Application section of the DeploymentReport.

These additional elements can be seen in the following schema snippet. Note the `Name`, `Description`, `DesignData`, `SettingDeclaration`, and `SettingValue` elements inherited from the `Definition` complex type:

```
<SystemDefinition Name="MySdkSystem" Layer="Application" Abstract="true">
<Description>My Sdm SDK System</Description>
<DesignData>
<Report Type="Application" xmlns="http://schemas.microsoft.com/
SystemDefinitionModel/2005/1/DesignData/DeploymentReport"/>
</DesignData>
<!-- Add Settings (Members) to this System -->
<SettingDeclaration Name="SystemName" Definition="String" CanBeNull="true"/>
<SettingValue Path="SystemName">SDK Authored System</SettingValue>
<SettingDeclaration Name="Version" Definition="String" CanBeNull="true"/>
</SystemDefinition>
```

The `EndpointDefinition` complex type is also derived from `ObjectDefinition` and provides support for abstract endpoint definitions, and facilitates communications within the system. An example of an "abstract" WebService definition (from `Microsoft.Web.sdmDocument`) is provided here:

```
<EndpointDefinition Name="WebService" Layer="Application"
Extends="System:EndpointDefinition" Abstract="true">
<Description>
<Entry Name="DisplayName">WebServiceEndpoint</Entry>
</Description>
<DesignData>
<VisualStudio xmlns="http://schemas.microsoft.com/SystemDefinitionModel/
2005/1/DesignData/VisualStudio">
<ModelElement>
<Property Name="PrimaryRelationshipName" Value="HostingDefinition" />
<Property Name="PrimaryRelationshipRole" Value="Guest"/>
<Property Name="DefaultRootName" Value="WebService1" />
<Property Name="ThemeColor" Value="145, 137, 213" />
<Property Name="ImageFileName" Value="WebServiceEndpoint.emf" />
<Property Name="Geometry" Value="WebService" />
</ModelElement>
</VisualStudio>
</DesignData>
</EndpointDefinition>
```

The preceding properties show that the main relationship between the endpoint described above and its WebService Application is a hosting relationship. Because the object is defined at the application layer, the application is considered the host and the endpoint plays the role of the guest. If the layer were `ApplicationHost`, the roles would be viewed in reverse by the Logical Datacenter Designer. When the endpoint is created (dragged onto the design surface), the default name displayed is "WebService1". The endpoint is displayed as a circle.

The `ResourceDefinition` complex type is also derived from `ObjectDefinition` and adds support for resource type definitions, resource members, and host, containment, and reference relationship members. You should consider `ResourceDefinition` objects if they may be reused in many different configurations, if the resource object is not a stand-alone solution but used with other objects, and/or the object does not have communication relationships with other objects.

An example of a "concrete" Resource declaration found as part of a `WindowsApplication.sdm` file in the Solution Explorer is shown here. The `NetSectionGroup` definition is also used in other SDM definitions:

```
  <Resource Name="NetSectionGroup"
      Definition="WindowsApplication1.Directory.Configuration.NetSectionGroup"
      MinOccurs="1" MaxOccurs="1" Reference="false">
    <DesignData>
      <VisualStudio
          xmlns="http://schemas.microsoft.com/SystemDefinitionModel/
          2005/1/DesignData/VisualStudio">
        <ModelElement>
          <Property Name="DisplayName" Value="NetSectionGroup" />
          <Property Name="CreatedByUser" Value="true" />
        </ModelElement>
      </VisualStudio>
    </DesignData>
  </Resource>
  <Containment Name="NetSectionGroupContainment"
    Definition="MicrosoftConfiguration:ConfigurationContainsNetSectionGroup"
    ChildMember="NetSectionGroup" />
</ResourceDefinition>
```

A `ResourceDefinition`, like any other `ObjectDefinition` derived complex type, may extend from existing definitions, as illustrated by the following example:

```
<ResourceDefinition Name="Directory" Extends="MicrosoftFileSystem:Directory"> ...
```

RelationshipDefinition complex type

The `RelationshipDefinition` complex type defines the associations between systems, resources, subsystems, and endpoints by adding object constraints and flow to the base definition. Relationship members are used to define the relationships that object members will participate in when they are created. Like the `ObjectDefinition` complex type, the `RelationshipDefinition` defines the attributes `Abstract` and `Extends`. It also has similar elements for defining child relationships such as hosting, containment, and delegation, but it includes additional elements and respective types such as `Flow`, which may contain a `FlowMember` complex type instance that provides the instances participating in the transformation of values between themselves. The following example shows the `RelationshipDefinition` complex type schema:

```
<xs:complexType name="RelationshipDefinition">
  <xs:complexContent>
    <xs:extension base="Definition">
      <xs:choice minOccurs="0" maxOccurs="unbounded">
        <xs:element name="ObjectConstraintGroup" type="ObjectConstraintGroup" />
        <xs:element name="ObjectConstraint" type="ObjectConstraint" />
        <xs:element name="Constraint" type="ConstraintMember" />
        <xs:element name="ConstraintGroup" type="ConstraintGroup" />
        <xs:element name="Flow" type="FlowMember" />
        <xs:element name="Connection" type="CommunicationMember" minOccurs="0"
          maxOccurs="unbounded" />
        <xs:element name="Hosting" type="HostingMember" />
        <xs:element name="Delegation" type="DelegationMember" />
        <xs:element name="Reference" type="ReferenceMember" />
        <xs:element name="Containment" type="ContainmentMember" />
```

```
            </xs:choice>
            <xs:attribute name="Extends" type="QualifiedName" use="optional" />
            <xs:attribute name="Abstract" type="xs:boolean" use="optional" />
         </xs:extension>
      </xs:complexContent>
   </xs:complexType>
```

Five relationships are derived from `RelationshipDefinition`:

- ❑ **HostingDefinition:** Captures the requirement that a guest object requires a host object in order to be constructed.

- ❑ **CommunicationDefinition:** This is used to capture possible communication links between endpoint definitions. They are used to describe interactions between independently deployed software elements. Interactions between systems are explicitly modeled using communication relationships. In Visual Studio 2005, the most obvious example of communication is through ASP.NET Web services. (Other communication protocols can be modeled via your own custom SDM application and endpoints or via the GenericApplication and GenericEndPoints in the Application Designer.)

- ❑ **DelegationDefinition:** This captures the fact that the source (outer) member will forward behavior to the (contained) object member. It states how pairs of abstract endpoint definitions can participate in the delegation.

- ❑ **ReferenceDefinition:** A source member object has a dependency on an object member. The dependency captured between systems or resources may not be part of the execution environment of the dependent object, but may be required in order to achieve correct operation.

- ❑ **ContainmentDefinition:** This states that an object member is contained by its parent. It implies that a parent instance can control the lifetime of the member instance.

A few of these relationships between objects located in the Application and Application Host layer are illustrated in Figure 7-7.

In this figure, a customer transaction database is hosted by an SQL 2005 server. The customer database is a guest on the server. It is therefore the server's responsibility to manage the life cycle of the database. A guest can be hosted by a number of (database) servers, as long as the guest has compatible configurations (i.e., behaves itself at the party). This database is also in communication with the ASP.NET application through Web services managed by SQL 2005.

Member complex type

A definition can contain *member* definitions. These member definitions are used to reference other definitions — and, in particular, members reference instances of a certain type. Members associate a definition name with a specific instance definition or array of instance definitions. This name is unique among all the members in the scope of the definition that includes the member.

Member definitions can also be used for setting configuration values, descriptions (`Description`), and data useful for a tools design surface (`DesignData`). Members can reference an array of instances and then specify the array's upper and lower bounds.

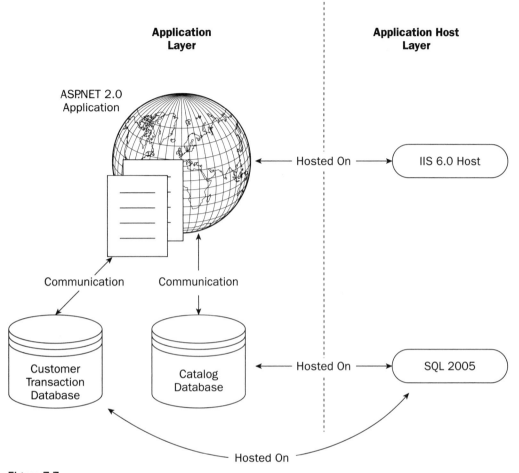

Figure 7-7

The root-level definition for members is the Member complex type. It is not derived from the Definition complex type. It has elements similar to Definition, but without the Manager and ClrClassname elements. Members can be customized depending on the kind of definition they reference. The Member complex type contains two attributes:

❑ **QualifiedName:** This is typically a period-separated string name used to refer to definitions or members defined in an aliased (imported) namespace or an .sdm file's namespace. If the name does not include a period or is not an alias, then it is unqualified and will rely on the scoping rules to resolve. An example of an alias is as follows:

```
<Import Alias="WindowsApp" Name="Microsoft.WindowsApplication"/>
```

❑ **SimpleName:** This may be used to supply names for members in an SDM definition.

Five complex types are derived from Member:

❑ **Object members:** Used to create instances of a particular object definition. Object members reference abstract or concrete object definitions. The member can reference an array of instances that can be described in terms of lower and upper bounds. Values to objects can be obtained by *flowing* the setting values from one object to another.

❑ **Relationship members:** Define the relationships (such as containment or hosting) that object members will participate in when they are created.

❑ **Setting members:** Used to capture a definitions configuration.

❑ **Constraint members:** Used to further define the set of relationships in which a particular object is willing to participate or the set of objects that can participate in a particular relationship.

❑ **Flow members:** Used to define the flow of configuration between members. Flow members gather input values from settings on members, do some processing on that information, and then distribute the results to settings on members — on the same object or other objects.

Here are descriptions for some ObjectMember attributes:

❑ **MinOccurs:** Defines the lower bound on the number of instances associated with this member. If it is zero, then the member is optional. The default is 1.

❑ **MaxOccurs:** Defines the upper bound on the number of instances associated with this member. Must be one or greater. The default is 1.

❑ **Reference:** If this attribute is set to false, the instance is created when the type is created. If it is set to true, the instance that is associated with the member must be explicitly created by the operator or referenced in another type.

❑ **Proxy:** If this attribute is set to true, the object member represents a proxy, rather than a real instance in the target system. The Proxy attribute must be set to true in order to allow the member to participate in delegation relationships.

Following is the schema for the Member, ObjectMember, and RelationshipMember types:

```
<xs:complexType name="Member">
  <xs:sequence>
    <xs:element name="Description" type="Description" minOccurs="0" />
    <xs:element name="DesignData" type="DesignData" minOccurs="0" />
    <xs:choice minOccurs="0" maxOccurs="unbounded">
      <xs:element name="SettingValue" type="SettingValue" />
      <xs:element name="SettingValueList" type="SettingValueList" />
    </xs:choice>
  </xs:sequence>
  <xs:attribute name="Name" type="SimpleName" use="required" />
  <xs:attribute name="Definition" type="QualifedName" use="required" />
</xs:complexType>
<xs:ComplexType name="ObjectMember">
  <xs:complexContent>
    <xs:extension base="Member">
      <xs:attribute name="MinOccurs" type="MinOccurs" use="optional" />
      <xs:attribute name="MaxOccurs" type="MaxOccurs" use="optional" />
      <xs:attribute name="Reference" type="xs:boolean" use="required" />
      <xs:attribute name="Proxy" type="xs:boolean" use="optional" />
    </xs:extension>
```

```
    </xs:complexContent>
  </xs:complexType>
  <xs:complexType name="RelationshipMember">
    <xs:complexContent>
      <xs:extension base="Member" />
    </xs:complexContent>
  </xs:complexType>
  <!--
```

Settings

Settings maintain configuration information for system definitions. Unlike properties, which can be thought of as attributes that affect the design experience, settings are specific values used to control the behavior of the system. For Visual Studio 2005 Application and Logical Datacenter Designers, settings provide behavioral configuration for an application or the application's hosting environment.

You can declare settings when you create a definition by using the `Setting` members. Once declared, a constant value is assigned to define the default behavior of the definition in the system. You can modify these settings later using the Distributed System Designers Settings and Constraints Editor.

Settings are captured in the SDM file or, in the case of a WebApplication, within `web.config` files. When a WebApplication setting (for example, Application Pool) is edited, the changes are persisted back to both the SDM and `web.config` file.

All definitions can expose members for describing configuration values associated with that definition. Methods describe values using setting declarations to define the type of value and any behavioral attributes of the value. The following is the `SettingMember` schema:

```
  <xs:complexType name="SettingMember">
    <xs:complexContent>
      <xs:extension base="Member">
        <xs:choice minOccurs="0" maxOccurs="unbounded">
          <xs:element name="Facet" type="Facet" />
        </xs:choice>
        <xs:attributeGroup ref="SettingsAttributes" />
      </xs:extension>
    </xs:complexContent>
  </xs:complexType>
```

The runtime uses a number of attributes to *describe* the behavior of a particular setting. These attributes are maintained by the SettingAttributes Attribute Group. Here are a few attributes described in this group:

❑ **Access:** Defines whether the setting's value can be read or written to by the SDM run-time or the designer editors.

❑ **Secure:** Defines whether the value of a setting should be encrypted when stored to an SDM document.

❑ **DeploymentTime:** Value used only as part of the deployment process for an instance. Not used for design-time constraints value evaluation.

❑ **Required:** If this attribute is set to `true`, a value must be provided for this setting before deploying an instance.

The following is the `SettingsAttributes` schema:

```
<xs:attributeGroup name="SettingsAttributes">
  <xs:attribute name="List" type="xs:boolean" />
  <xs:attribute name="Access" type="SettingMemberAccess" />
  <xs:attribute name="Secure" type="SettingMemberSecure" />
  <xs:attribute name="DeploymentType" type="xs:boolean" />
  <xs:attribute name="Required" type="xs:boolean" />
  <xs:attribute name="CanBeNull" type="xs:boolean" />
  <xs:attribute name="ElementsCanBeNull" type="xs:boolean" />
  <xs:attribute name="DefaultRead" type="xs:boolean" />
  <xs:attribute name="DefaultWrite" type="xs:boolean" />
</xs:attributeGroup>
<xs:simpleType name="SettingMemberAccess">
  <xs:restriction base="xs:string">
    <xs:enumeration value="ReadWrite" />
    <xs:enumeration value="ReadOnly" />
    <xs:enumeration value="WriteOnly" />
  </xs:restriction>
</xs:simpleType>
<xs:simpleType name="SettingMemberSecure">
  <xs:restriction base="xs:string">
    <xs:enumeration value="Always" />
    <xs:enumeration value="PerInstance" />
    <xs:enumeration value="Never" />
  </xs:restriction>
</xs:simpleType>
```

Setting values

Values are provided for a particular setting declaration using setting value statements. A definition of the setting using `xsd` must be defined before a value is set, and the setting value must match or be able to be converted to the associated setting definition. Here is an example of a setting declaration for a new element `Car`, which must accept a string:

```
<SettingDeclaration Name="Car"
            Definition="String" List="false" CanBeNull="false"/>
```

Single-setting declaration values are provided using the `SettingValue` statement and can be used for both list and non-list values. When a new instance of a definition is created, the setting value statements are evaluated by the runtime to determine the initial values for the instance. For example, if the value is declared fixed, then the value provided will be used in all derived definitions. In the following example, the name of the `SetttingDeclaration` is specified by the `Path` attribute, and the lack of a set `Fixed` attribute specifies that the value `Acura` may be overwritten:

```
<SettingValue Path="Car">Acura</SettingValue>
```

A `SettingValueList` statement is used to provide multiple setting values and may only be used against a setting attribute `List=true` declaration. The following example also signifies that values in this list cannot be changed and will replace, rather than merge with, the existing contents of the target's setting values:

```
<SettingDeclaration Name="Cars"
            Definition="String" List="true" CanBeNull="false"/>
```

```xml
<SettingValueList Path="Cars" Fixed="true" Replace="true">
   <Value>Acura</Value>
   <Value>Volkswagon</Value>
</SettingValueList>
```

The following is the SettingValue, SettingValueList, and SettingValueAttribute schema:

```xml
<xs:complexType name="SettingValue" mixed="true">
  <xs:sequence>
    <xs:any processContents="skip" minOccurs="0" maxOccurs="unbounded" />
  </xs:sequence>
  <xs:attributeGroup ref="SettingValueAttributes" />
</xs:complexType>
<xs:complextType name="SettingValueList">
  <xs:sequence>
    <xs:element name="Value" minOccurs="0" maxOccurs="unbounded">
      <xs:complexType mixed="true">
        <xs:sequence>
          <xs:any processContents="skip" minOccurs="0" maxOccurs="unbounded" />
        </xs:sequence>
        <xs:attribute name="Null" type="xs:boolean" use="optional" />
      </xs:complexType>
    </xs:element>
  </xs:sequence>
  <xs:attributeGroup ref="SettingValueAttributes" />
</xs:complexType>
<xs:attributeGroup name="SettingValueAttributes" />
  <xs:attributename="Path" type="SettingPath" use="required" />
  <xs:attributename="Null" type="xs:boolean" use="optional" />
  <xs:attributename="Fixed" type="xs:boolean" use="optional" />
  <xs:attributename="Unset" type="xs:boolean" use="optional" />
  <xs:attributename="Definition" type="QualifiedName" use="optional" />
  <xs:attributename="Convert" type="xs:boolean" use="optional" />
  <xs:attributename="Secure" type="xs:boolean" use="optional" />
  <xs:attributename="Replace" type="xs:boolean" use="optional" />
</xs:attributeGroup>
<!--
```

Custom settings

You can use custom settings to define additional meta-data required to accurately model the system's development or deployment environment. Custom settings, however, can be used to restrict certain inputs. Rather than allow the SettingDeclaration Cars to take unrestricted strings, it is possible to restrict the strings to certain inputs by defining a new custom simple type that will provide validation for the settings. In the following example, allowable values are specified using the enumeration type:

```xml
<xs:simpleType name="AllowableCarNames">
    <xs:restriction base="xs:string">
        <xs:enumeration value="Acura" />
        <xs:enumeration value="Ford" />
        <xs:enumeration value="Volkswagon" />
        <xs:enumeration value="Other" />
    </xs:restriction>
</xs:simpleType>
```

This example, like all custom setting declarations, requires a manager. Unlike regular settings, custom settings can be displayed in the Properties window.

Constraints

A *constraint* is a requirement for a configuration value to be set in a particular way. These restrictions are evaluated in the instance space by the SDM run-time at both design time and, in future versions, at deployment time. Unlike the custom setting example earlier, all setting constraints use a constraint definition to evaluate the setting values.

Constraints in one SDM model layer may be applied against configuration settings and relationships in another layer. In this way, constraints connect or bind one layer to another. With the Distributed System Designers, constraints are used by developers to state their "requirements" of the datacenter and by operators to convey their "requirements" of the applications.

There are two kinds of constraints: constraints that set restrictions on settings (*setting constraints*) and those that are constrained by the nature of their SDM structure (*structural constraints*).

Structural constraints define the topology of the concrete object space and constrain the settings of objects participating in particular relationships. The StructuralConstraint complex type is the base type from which the complex types RelationshipsConstraint and ObjectConstraint are derived. The StructuralConstraint contains a description element and a design data element. The description element is returned with error messages should the constraint fail. A ConstraintEvaluation attribute determines when the constraint should be evaluated. The default is at design time. The RelationshipConstraint specifies the elements that constrain the relationships in which an object can participate.

The following RelationshipConstraint example shows a structural constraint whereby the abstract object definition ObjA needs to contain an instance of abstract object ObjB; and ObjA must play the role of parent and the type at the other end of the containment relationship must be of type ObjB:

```
<RelationshipConstraint name = "ObjAContainsObjB"
relationship="ContainmentDefinition" myRole="parent" targetType="ObjB"
minOccurs="1" maxOccurs="1" />
```

Setting constraints are made up of two parts: the *constraint definition* and the *constraint member*. The constraints specify values for a single setting or a group of them. Each setting constraint requires a constraint definition to evaluate the setting values. This evaluation is always done by a manager or code. The constraint definition uses settings declarations to identify the values it constrains.

ConstraintDefinition complex type

A constraint definition specifies a reusable restriction that acts on a defined set of input values. The constraint can specify a set of nested relationships or object constraints that are evaluated in the context in which the constraint definition is being used, or the constraint can identify a manager that provides code to evaluate the input values. If a nested constraint is specified, the parent constraint evaluates to true only if all nested constraints evaluate to true. This is in contrast to constraint groups, where the entire constraint group can be true if only one of the nested constraints evaluates to true. This type has two attributes:

- ❑ **TargetDefinition:** Identifies the definition to which this constraint will be applied. If a target definition is not supplied, the constraint is applicable to any object or relationship definition. A target definition must be supplied if this constraint definition contains object or relationship constraints or groups.

- ❑ **ReturnEarly:** Determines whether a failed constraint should return early if part of a larger group of constraints.

Following are some of the elements associated with `ConstraintDefinition`:

- ❑ **Constraint:** Identifies a list of input values for a particular constraint definition. Static values may be used for the settings along with input statements to bind a constraint setting to a path.

- ❑ **Input:** Represents a list of inputs to the constraint. An input provides a path to the source setting value that will be sent to the constraint and constraint setting that will be set as a result. The source setting type and the constraint setting type must be compatible.

ConstraintMember complex type

A constraint member associates a set of input values with a particular constraint definition. The setting value is transferred to the constraint before the constraint is executed by the SDM Compiler. Two attributes belong to this type:

- ❑ **Evaluate:** A value that determines when the constraint will be evaluated. Possible values are `Design` and `Never`. The former will perform evaluation at design, deployment, or validation time.

- ❑ **RaiseError:** A Boolean value of `true` is returned when the constraint catches an input value; otherwise, `false` is returned.

The following shows the schema for `ConstraintDefinition` and `ConstraintMember`:

```
<xs:complexType name="ConstraintDefinition">
  <xs:complexContent>
    <xs:extension base="Definition">
      <xs:choice minOccurs="0" maxOccurs="unbounded">
        <xs:element name="RelationshipConstraint" type="RelationshipConstraint" />
        <xs:element name="RelationshipConstraintGroup"
            type="RelationshipConstraint" />
        <xs:element name="ConstraintGroup" type="ConstraintGroup" />
        <xs:element name="ObjectConstraint" type="ObjectConstraint" />
        <xs:element name="ObjectConstraintGroup" type="ObjectConstraintGroup" />
        <xs:element name="Constraint" type="ConstraintMember" />
      </xs:choice>
      <xs:attribute name="TargetDefinition" type="QualifiedName" use="optional" />
      <xs:attribute name="ReturnEarly" type="xs:boolean" use="optional" />
    </xs:extension>
  </xs:complexContent>
</xs:complexType>
<xs:complexType name="ConstraintMember">
  <xs:complexContent>
    <xs:extension base="Member">
      <xs:choice minOccurs="0" maxOccurs="unbounded">
```

```
              <xs:element name="Input" type="Input" />
         </xs:choice>
         <xs:attribute name="RaiseError" type="xs:boolean" use="optional" />
         <xs:attribute name="Evaluate" type="ConstraintEvaluation" use="optional" />
     </xs:extension>
    </xs:complexContent>
   </xs:complexType>
   <!--
```

Following is a constraint definition for a simple comparison function that takes an operator and two arguments, evaluates the constraint, and finally returns success or an error:

```
<ConstraintDefinition Name=MyConstraint" Manager="MyManager"
ClrClassName="MyCompany.MyManager.MyConstraint">
<SettingDeclaration Name="Limit" Definition="Int"/>
<SettingDeclaration Name="ActualValue Definition="Int" Nullable="true"/>
</ConstrainDefinition>
```

A constraint member is used to provide the values to the constraint type for evaluation. In this example, a specific constraint called `FileSizeLimit` is used to ensure that each file (guest) does not go beyond a certain limit:

```
<RelationshipConstraint Name="HostedFiles" RelationshipDefinition=" DirHostsForD"
    TargetRole="Guest" >
<Constraint Name="FileSizeLimit" Definition="MyConstraint"
<Input Name="Limit" Path="FileSizeRestriction"/>
<Input Name="realValue" Path="HostedFiles.Guests"/>
</Constraint>
</RelationshipConstraint>
```

FlowMember complex type

Another type of member called `FlowMember` is used to flow or pass parameters between members of an object definition and between objects participating in a relationship. This enables the user to transform another member or object's setting values. `FlowMember` defines two elements: `Input` and `Output`. `Input` contains a list of setting value paths used as input to the flow. `Output` contains a list of settings that contain the results of this process flow.

Each setting flow member must use a flow definition type to implement the transformation. This `FlowDefinition` uses the `Definition` complex type to define the input settings, the output settings, and a description for those browsing the .sdm file. As with all `Definition` objects, a flow definition is identified by name within the namespace in which it is defined, and identifies a manager that will support the runtime when it evaluates the flow.

Following are the `FlowDefinition` and `FlowMember` schema:

```
<xs:complexType name="FlowDefinition">
  <xs:complexContent>
    <xs:extension base="Definition" />
  </xs:complexContent>
</xs:complexType>
<xs:complexType name="FlowMember".
```

```
      <xs:complexContent>
        <xs:extension base="Member">
          <xs:choice minOccurs="0" maxOccurs="unbounded">
            <xs:element name="Input" type="Input" />
            <xs:element name="Output" type="Output" />
          </xs:choice>
        </xs:extension>
      </xs:complexContent>
    </xs:complexType>
    <!--
```

The following is an example of a flow definition using three settings. The first two are `Input` settings and define input into the flow; the third is an `Output` setting that provides the path of the setting value that will receive the transformed flow output. This flow definition is used to calculate the full path name using the directory path and directory or filename. In addition, the `Flow` definition identifies the manager code and CLR class within the manager used to calculate the transformation:

```
<HostingDefinition Name="DirHostsForD" GuestDefinition="MyFile"
Hostdefinition="MyDir" SimulationRoot="false">
<Flow Name="CreatePath" Definition="MyPathFlow">
// Find Path by going to the host
<Input Name="DirPath" Path="Host.FullPath"/>
// Find File or Dir by going to the Guest
<Input Name="FileOrDirName" Path="Guest.Name"\>
// Assign fullpath to guest in the hosting
relationship
<Output Name="FullPath" Path="Guest.FullPath" />
</Flow>
</HostingDefinition>
```

ManagerDeclaration complex type

Managers provide the mechanism by which objects and relationships can introduce custom behavior into the runtime environment. An object or relationship can use a manager in any number of ways. For example, a manager may provide the implementation for more involved constraints and flows. They may help in the object's installation, or they may be called upon to handle policy decisions regarding how bindings between types are resolved. The following is the `ManagerDeclaration` schema:

```
<xs:complexType name="ManagerDeclaration:">
  <xs:sequence>
    <xs:element name="Description" type="Description" minOccurs="0" />
  </xs:sequence>
  <xs:attribute name="Name" type="SimpleName" use="required" />
  <xs:attribute name="AssemblyName" type="xs:string" use="required" />
  <xs:attribute name="Version" type="FourPartVersionType" use="optional" />
  <xs:attribute name="PublicKeyToken" type="PublicKeyTokenType" use="optional" />
  <xs:attribute name="Culture" type="CultureNeutral" use="optional" />
  <xs:attribute name="Platform" type="xs:string" use="optional" />
  <xs:attribute name="SourcePath" type="xs:string" use="optional" />
</xs:complexType>
<!--
```

All object managers are exposed through the CLR as entry points into strongly named classes. Object managers are packaged and versioned in the same manner as other types in the SDM; they are distributed in system distribution units and their version and strong name are derived from the .sdm file in which they are declared.

SDM documents

SDM elements are declared within a source SDM XML document (.sdm). The .sdm document contains one or more definitions, resources, endpoints, and relationships. This document is then compiled to an immutable document (.sdmDocument). Both document types represent a unit of versioning and distribution of SDM definitions and are the cornerstone of every building block created in the SDM SDK. Each SDM document produced uses the SystemDefinitionModel XML schema (see C:\Program Files\ Microsoft Visual Studio 8\Common7\Packages\SDM\Schema\SystemDefinitionModel.xsd). A few of the many elements of this schema are provided here:

- ❑ **Information:** General information about this document.
- ❑ **Import:** References to other SDM documents (.sdmDocument).
- ❑ **DesignData:** Design-surface-specific data.
- ❑ **SettingDefinitions:** An XML schema document that contains setting definitions.
- ❑ **Definitions:** The object, relationship flow, and constraint definitions that are contained in this document.
- ❑ **NamespaceIdentity:** The attributes that form the identity of the document.
- ❑ **DocumentLanguage:** The language of the description elements within the document.
- ❑ **CompilationHash:** A unique value for the document. The hash value will change if any character in the document is changed. The SDM run-time will fail to load a referenced document if an incorrect hash value is detected.

The basic SDM document schema is presented here. Figure 7-8 gives a visualization of the expanded schema groups.

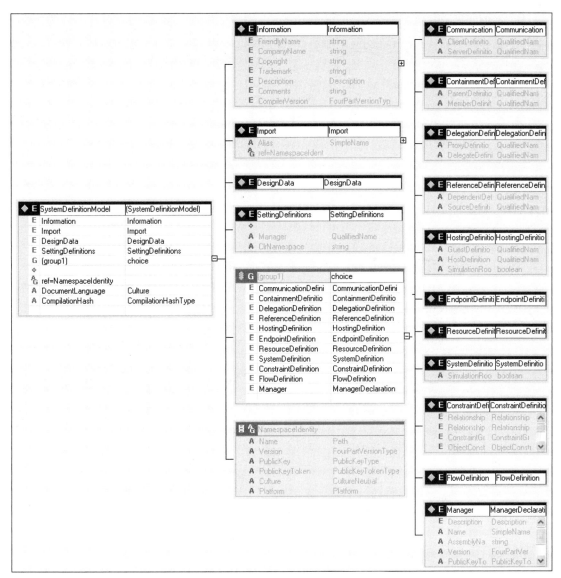

Figure 7-8

The following are top-level schema elements:

```
<?xml version="1.0" encoding="utf-8" ?>
<xs:schema targetNamespace="http://schemas.microsoft.com/
    SystemDefinitionModel/2005/1"
  xmlns:xs="http://www.w3.org/2001/XMLSchema"
  xmlns:xsi="http://www.w3.org/2001/XMLSchema-instance"
  xmlns="http://schemas.microsoft.com/SystemDefinitionModel/2005/1"
  elementFormDefault="qualified" blockDefault="#all" version="1.1"
      id="SystemDefinitionModel">
  <!--
  ========================================================================
  <!-- SDM root element -->
  <!--
  ========================================================================
  <xs:element name="SystemDefinitionModel">
    <xs:complexType>
      <xs:sequence>
        <xs:element name="Information" type="Information" minOccurs="0" />
        <xs:element name="Import" type="Import" minOccurs="0"
            maxOccurs="unbounded" />
        <xs:element name="DesignData" type="DesignData" minOccurs="0" />
        <xs:element name="SettingDefinitions" type="SettingDefinitions"
            minOccurs="0" />
        <xs:choice minOccurs="0" maxOccurs="unbounded">
          <xs:element name="CommunicationDefinition"
              type="CommunicationDefinition" />
          <xs:element name="ContainmentDefinition" type="ContainmentDefinition" />
          <xs:element name="DelegationDefinition" type="DelegationDefinition" />
          <xs:element name="ReferenceDefinition" type="ReferenceDefinition" />
          <xs:element name="HostingDefinition" type="HostingDefinition" />
          <xs:element name="EndpointDefinition" type="EndpointDefinition" />
          <xs:element name="ResourceDefinition" type="ResourceDefinition" />
          <xs:element name="SystemDefinition" type="SystemDefinition" />
          <xs:element name="FlowDefinition" type="ConstraintDefinition" />
          <xs:element name="ContainmentDefinition" type="FlowDefinition" />
          <xs:element name="Manager" type="ManagerDeclaration" />
        </xs:choice>
        <xs:any namespace="http://www.w3.org/2000/09/xmldsig#"
            processContents="skip" minOccurs="0" />
      </xs:sequence>
      <xs:attributeGroup ref="NamespaceIdentity" />
      <xs:attribute name="DocumentLanguage" type="Culture" />
      <xs:attribute name="CompilationHash" type="CompiliationHashType" />
    </xs:complexType>
  </xs:element>
  <!--
```

Every compiled SDM document (.sdmDocument) contains SystemDefinitionModel elements. For example, the following code shows the first part of the compiled SDM Microsoft.FileSystem.sdmDocument (see, for example, C:\Program Files\Microsoft Visual Studio 8\Common7\IDE\PrivateAssemblies):

```
<?xml version="1.0" encoding="utf-8"?>
<SystemDefinitionModel xmlns:xsi="http://www.w3.org/2001/XMLSchema-instance"
xmlns:xsd="http://www.w3.org/2001/XMLSchema" Name="Microsoft.FileSystem"
```

```
Version="1.0.41013.0"
xmlns="http://schemas.microsoft.com/SystemDefinitionModel/2005/1"
CompilationHash="3D96173B92DB35CF305A2F449378FDA878E84065">
<Information>
<CompanyName>Microsoft Corporation</CompanyName>
<Description>
<Entry Name="Description">
This is an SDM model for simple files and directories. The model contains abstract
resources for files and directories, abstract hosting relationships for files-
&gt;files, files-&gt;directories and directories-&gt;directories.</Entry>
</Description>
<CompilerVersion>1.0.41013.0</CompilerVersion>
</Information>
<Import Alias="Flow" Name="System.Flow" Version="1.0.41013.0" Culture="neutral" />
<Import Alias="System" Name="System" Version="1.0.41013.0" Culture="neutral"/>
```

This example includes a reference to the `SystemDefinitionModel` schema version used, a unique hash code used to verify that an SDM file is a valid compiled document, a description of the definition, the version of the `SdmC.exe` compiler used to produce this .sdmDocument, and Import elements to necessary namespaces.

Prototypes and the Distributed System Designers

The distributed system designer tools of Team Architect use a core set of abstract definitions to define common characteristics of a class of applications, servers, and endpoints. Abstract applications, abstract servers, and abstract endpoints are all examples of abstract system definitions in SDM.

These abstract definitions can be predefined and persisted as SDM documents, and added to the toolboxes of the Distributed System Designers or distributed for use by other users.

The toolboxes of the Distributed System Designers use abstract SDM definitions with Visual Studio–dependent information to create and deploy distributed systems. This combination of abstract definitions and Visual Studio–specific information is called a *prototype*. Prototypes may also be referred to as *subsystems* because they can be nested within other prototypes

A prototype of these systems is required before they can appear in the toolbox in Team Architect designers. To create these toolbox-compatible abstract definitions, the `ProtoGen.exe` tool is used.

An abstract application definition is created by the Application Designer, and serves as a design-time description of an independently deployable application layer system that offers or consumes services. Web applications and Window applications are examples of abstract application definitions.

Each application that you define (that is, each prototype that you drag and drop on the Application Design surface) must conform to its abstract application definition. For example, the application definition `MyWebService` must conform to the prototype ASP.NET WebService, which in turn must conform to the web application abstraction. While you can think of an application definition as a self-contained SDM system, it may include a number of resources that must be deployed with it in order to be functional.

You create an abstract server definition with Logical Datacenter Diagram by dragging and dropping a prototype from the LDD toolbox, and it conforms to an application hosting system within a logical datacenter. LDD only uses the definition of a hosting server in the logical datacenter, as opposed to the definition of a particular server. However, because the abstract server is the only access point, logical servers

189

will be considered both abstract and concrete. Hence, an IISWebServer is an example of both an abstract system definition and a subsystem definition.

The Distributed System Designers also rely on prototypes for endpoints. An endpoint prototype is created from an abstract definition, such as a Web service, and can have "consumer" or "provider" type. Examples include `WebServerEndpoint` and `HttpClientEndpoint`.

Figure 7-9 shows application, server, and endpoint prototypes exposed in each Designer's toolbox.

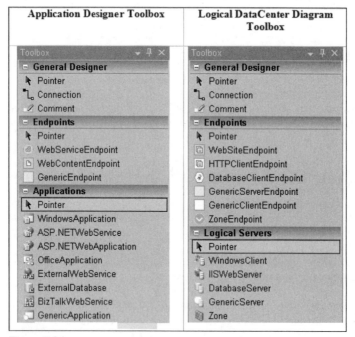

Figure 7-9

Users or third parties can define additional abstract and prototype definitions for different kinds of applications and logical application servers, and load them into these Designer toolboxes using the SDM SDK.

The SDM SDK

This first offering of the SDM SDK enables users to define their own application or hosting models, with relationships between existing host and application models supported in Team Architect. Future releases will introduce SDM infrastructure for the IT shop and use of the SDM to manage Windows and applications running on Windows.

The System Definition Model SDK is part of the Visual Studio 2005 SDK. Please see `http://lab .msdn.microsoft.com/teamsystem/workshop/default.aspx` for details.

The SDM SDK contains the tools, schema, classes, and documentation required to extend the base System Definition Models of the Distributed System Designers. The tools consist of the Prototype Generator, SDM Compiler, and SDM Generator. The SDM schema supports the creation of SDM objects such as systems, endpoints, and resources. In addition, the SDK provides tool classes that are part of the public API of the SDM tools and manager classes that enable users to write the custom constraints and flows for an SDK object. The documentation enables users to quickly ramp up using Get Started User documentation, reference materials, walkthroughs, and samples and code snippets.

The SDM SDK is part of Visual Studio 2005 SDK (VSIP SDK), which ships with Visual Studio 2005. More information about the SDK can be found at `http://lab.msdn.microsoft.com/teamsystem/workshop/sdm/default.aspx`.

You can create and manipulate an SDM model using the SDM authoring tools found in the SDK. After the model is created and deployed, the SDM Service maintains the model, ensuring consistency between the model and the real-world system.

The authoring tasks can be described in the following five high-level steps:

1. Author the model of your system in SDM using your favorite editor and any available SDM SDK documentation, walkthroughs, and samples.

2. Take the .sdm document that describes your model and compile it using the SDM command-line compiler tool. (It's interesting to note that the SDM Compiler uses the same DLLs as Team Architect when compiling SDM documents.) The output is a .sdmDocument document that describes an immutable form of your new model. This document may reference models (.sdmDocuments) that ship in Visual Studio or elsewhere. If your model is evaluating custom constraints or flows, you will also need to use a manager C# code-generation tool to produce your new manager DLL. You may author models that don't require managers.

3. Compile a `Prototype.xml` file using a prototype-generation tool. This will produce a `Prototype.xml` file that is required in order for you to install your model in the Team Architect design surface toolbox.

4. Build an install package. This includes your compiled model (.sdmDocument), any manager DLLs, the `Prototype.xml`, and registry key settings for the model.

5. The user of Team Architect can load the package into the toolbox.

These steps are illustrated in Figure 7-10.

The SDM command-line compiler

The SDM Compiler will only be accessible to SDK users through the command line with the `SdmC.exe` tool. Although the SDM Compiler is the same compiler used by Team Architect, users will not be able to author, compile, and package models using the Team Architect user interface.

The SDM filename to compile is the only required argument. The remaining parameters are all optional. If there are no errors or warnings within the error level, `SdmC.exe` will return a value of 0; otherwise, the return value will be 1. The compiler command-line options are listed here:

```
SdmC.exe file.sdm [/Reference:ref1,ref2,...]
         [/Output:file] [/KeyFile:file]
         [/KeyContainer:name] [/WarningAsError:level]
         [/WarningReported:level] [/SearchPath:dir1,dir2,...]
         [/Help] [/InstanceOutput:file] [/ConfigReport:file]
         [/ErrorLimit:max] [/MaxComplexity:max]
         [/NoLogo] [/StopOnError]
         [@file1[@file2...]]
```

191

Step 1: Model Technology in SDM.

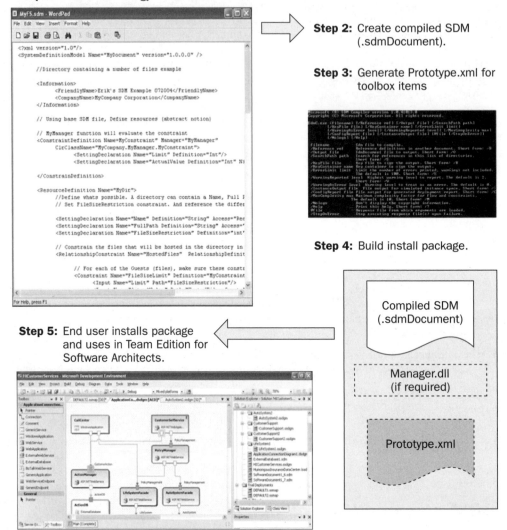

Step 2: Create compiled SDM (.sdmDocument).

Step 3: Generate Prototype.xml for toolbox items

Step 4: Build install package.

Step 5: End user installs package and uses in Team Edition for Software Architects.

Compiled SDM (.sdmDocument)

Manager.dll (if required)

Prototype.xml

Figure 7-10

Walkthrough: SDM Sample

Now that you have a conceptual understating of SDM, you can explore a more practical example. In the following sample, we will create the following setup:

Many thanks to Thomas Delrue, Software Development Engineer on the Team Architect product SKU team at Microsoft for providing the following SDM example.

On the Application Designer layer (AD layer), we'll have a WindowsMobile Application with two accessibility-related settings. This application contains two (IRda) endpoints: one server endpoint and one client endpoint. These endpoints will be able to communicate with each other, and they both contain a setting specifying the size of the buffer on which they operate. We'll also allow the application to be a client of a web service, so we'll make sure the application can also contain a `WebServiceClientEndpoint`.

On the LDD side of things, we'll create a MobileDevice. This will represent any kind of device that is part of the WindowsMobile family (such as a SmartPhone, PDA, or related device). This server system will host the WindowsMobileApplication. The system will also contain both a server endpoint and client endpoint for communication over IrDA. In order to host the `WebServiceClientEndpoint` on the AD side, we'll allow a `HTTPClientEndpoint` to be placed on this logical server.

As this is a MobileDevice, we'll also specify that this system must contain at least one Common Language Runtime (which is the .NET 2.0 runtime).

In order to define a System Definition Model (SDM), we have to create a new XML file that will contain our model. This will be the SDM file (as opposed to the SDM document), which is the result of compiling the SDM file:

```xml
<?xml version="1.0" encoding="utf-8"?>
<SystemDefinitionModel Name="Microsoft.SDM.Samples.Mobile" Version="0.1.0.0"
DocumentLanguage="en" Culture="en-US"
xmlns="http://schemas.microsoft.com/SystemDefinitionModel/2005/1">
    </SystemDefinitionModel>
```

Note a couple of interesting things in this `<SystemDefinitionModel/>` tag. First of all, there is the namespace that we use for this XML file, `xmlns="http://schemas.microsoft.com/systemDefinition Model/2005/1`. This indicates that we are using the SDM Schema and that it will be validated by the compiler when we compile the SDM file.

Secondly, there is the Document Identity Information. This information is contained in the attributes `Name` (which states the name of the document after compilation), `Version` (which indicates the version), and `Culture`. Just as with .NET assemblies, these values make up the identity of the document.

When the SDM file is compiled to an SDM document, the compiler computes a `CompilationHash` and adds this to the Document Identity Information. This `CompilationHash` is basically nothing more than a hash of the contents of the file. Upon validation of the SDM document, the content of the file is hashed and compared to the value in this attribute. This enables the compiler to detect whether or not somebody has modified the compiled SDM document. You can consider this hash value to perform the same task that the `PublicKeyToken` value performs in .NET assemblies. After adding this hash information, the document identity information is complete (and is then made up of `Name`, `Version`, `Culture`, and `CompilationHash`).

There is also a `DocumentLanguage` attribute, which specifies the language of the information contained in the document.

SystemDefinitions

To define the systems in our System Definition Model, we add following code to the SDM file:

```xml
<SystemDefinition Name="WindowsMobileApplication" Layer="Application"
                  Abstract="true">
</SystemDefinition>
```

193

This defines our application system named `WindowsMobileApplication`. When defining this system, we immediately specify the layer on which it will live; in this case, it is the application layer (which is the SDM way of pointing to the AD). We are also creating "descriptions" of the system, so we have to specify that this is not an instance of WindowsMobileApplication, but a definition of that type. This is what the `Abstract="true"` does. It informs the compiler that this is an abstract type (as opposed to a concrete type, which is the instance of the abstract type on the Distributed System Designers).

Likewise, we create a `SystemDefinition` for the MobileDevice that will live on the LDD:

```
<SystemDefinition Name="MobileDevice" Layer="ApplicationHost" Abstract="true">
</SystemDefinition>
```

The only difference with the system for the AD is the value for the `Layer` attribute. In this case, this system lives on the LDD, so in order to specify this in SDM, we use the value `ApplicationHost` for the `Layer` attribute.

In order for the systems defined to show up in the deployment report, we have to add a `DesignData` section within the `<SystemDefinition>` of the application:

```
<DesignData>
    <Report Type="Application" xmlns="http://schemas.microsoft.com/
    SystemDefinitionModel/2005/1/DesignData/DeploymentReport" />
</DesignData>
```

This ensures that the application will show up in the deployment report. For the logical server, we need to add this section inside of it:

```
<DesignData>
    <Report Type="LogicalServer" xmlns="http://schemas.microsoft.com/
    SystemDefinitionModel/2005/1/DesignData/DeploymentReport" />
</DesignData>
```

If this information is not added, the application and logical server and the information they contain will not show up in the deployment report.

You can also add additional DesignData information to the SystemDefinition for aesthetic purposes:

```
<DesignData>
    <VisualStudio xmlns="http://schemas.microsoft.com/
        SystemDefinitionModel/2005/1/DesignData/VisualStudio">
        <ModelElement>
            <Property Name="PrimaryRelationshipName" Value="HostingDefinition" />
            <Property Name="PrimaryRelationshipRole" Value="Host" />
            <Property Name="ThemeColor" Value="61, 107, 206" />
            <Property Name="ImageFileName" Value="OfficeApplication.emf" />
            <Property Name="ErrorImageFileName" Value="OfficeApplicationError.emf" />
        </ModelElement>
    </VisualStudio>
</DesignData>
```

Both `PrimaryRelationshipName` and `PrimaryRelationshipRole` are properties used by the Settings and Constraints Editor. The value for `PrimaryRelationshipRole` for an application system is `Guest`, whereas for a server system it is `Host`.

`ThemeColor` provides a means to give color to the shape that will appear on the Distributed Systems Designers in the HSL (Hue, Saturation, Luminescence) format.

Both `ImageFileName` and `ErrorImageFileName` point to files that will be used as the icon of the shapes (normal and error view) on the Distributed Systems Designer. The normal icons of the Application and Application Host results are shown in Figure 7-11. Note that this is not the value for the icon used for the shape in the toolbox.

Figure 7-11

Settings

As described previously, we want some settings in the system, which will live on the application layer. We can specify this by adding `<SettingDeclaration />` elements between the `<SystemDefinition />` tags of the system that will contain these settings. Add the following SettingDeclarations to the WindowsMobileApplication system:

```
<SettingDeclaration Name="SupportsHighContrast" Definition="System:Boolean"
                    CanBeNull="false" />
<SettingDeclaration Name="SupportsScreenReader" Definition="System:Boolean"
                    CanBeNull="false" />
```

Obviously, the `Name` attribute specifies the name of the setting. `CanBeNull` specifies whether or not this setting is nullable (meaning it does not contain a value). If a setting is declared as `CanBeNull="true"`, a checkbox will appear in the Settings and Constraints Editor that allows users to nullify the value for the setting (in other words, it removes the value for the setting).

In order for both the compiler and the Distributed System Designers to understand what kind of information you can store in the setting, you also have to provide a definition — this will be the datatype of the setting.

In this case, both settings are of type `Boolean`. However, the `Boolean` type is not defined in this SDM file; it is defined in another SDM document, so you will have to import this other SDM document and point the definition of the settings the right way. The SDM document containing the definition for `Boolean` is the `System` document. Add the following code to the top of your SDM file:

```
<Import Alias="System" Name="System" />
```

This `Import` statement will import an SDM document that has the document name `System`; this is specified by the `Name` attribute. If you want, you can specify additional elements making up the document identity information (such as `Culture`, `Version`, or `CompilationHash`), thus making more specifications about which system SDM document is to be imported.

You also provide an alias for the document. This alias will be used every time you reference something defined in this imported document.

This statement makes all definitions in the `System` document available in the SDM file you are currently editing. However, in order to use any definition in this document, you need to prepend the definition with the alias and a colon. This explains the `System:Boolean` value for the `Definition` attributes of the `SettingDeclarations` you just created.

You want these settings to have a default value too, so add the following SDM code to the `WindowsMobileApplication SystemDefinition`:

```
<SettingValue Path="SupportsHighContrast">false</SettingValue>
<SettingValue Path="SupportsScreenReader">false</SettingValue>
```

These elements will set the default value for both the `SupportsHighContrast` and `Supports ScreenReader` settings to be `false`, as shown in Figure 7-12. Note that you use the `Path` attribute to target the setting for which you wish to set a default value. (*Note*: In this stage of the sample, we are defining the definition of the `WindowsMobileApplication` prototype and illustrating what it will look like with an existing `WindowsApplication` prototype. Later, you will see how these settings come together and describe the `WindowsMobileApplication` on the design surface.)

Figure 7-12

Endpoints

You will need to define four new endpoints: a server endpoint on both the AD and LDD layer and a client endpoint on both the AD and LDD layer.

Application layer

Add this information to create a `ClientEndpoint`:

```
<EndpointDefinition Name="ApplicationIrDAClientEndpoint" Layer="Application"
                    Abstract="true">
    <DesignData>
        <VisualStudio xmlns="http://schemas.microsoft.com/
            SystemDefinitionModel/2005/1/DesignData/VisualStudio">
            <ModelElement>
                <Property Name="PrimaryRelationshipName" Value="HostingDefinition" />
```

```
                    <Property Name="PrimaryRelationshipRole" Value="Guest" />
                    <Property Name="Direction" Value="Client" />
                    <Property Name="Geometry" Value="General" />
                </ModelElement>
            </VisualStudio>
        </DesignData>
    </EndpointDefinition>
```

This defines an endpoint named `ApplicationIrDAClientEndpoint` that will live on the Application (AD) layer.

Note how this `EndpointDefinition` also contains the `DesignData`. In this case, you add some `DesignData` properties to the ModelElement representing the definition on the Distributed System Designers.

`PrimaryRelationshipName` and `PrimaryRelationshipRole` contain information for the Settings and Constraints Editor that enables it to determine what kind of constraints are to be displayed. As we are dealing with an endpoint on the AD layer, the values here respectively are `HostingDefinition` (the AD endpoint will be hosted on an LDD endpoint) and `Guest` (the AD endpoint is the `Guest` in that `HostingDefinition`).

The `Direction` property tells your designer the direction of the communication. Note that SDM does not contain this concept of direction (apart from `Server` vs. `Client` in `CommunicationDefinitions` or `Host` vs. `Guest` in `HostingDefinitions`), but our designers do. This property determines what end of the connection on the designer will contain the arrow. As this is a client endpoint, it gets the value `Client`.

The AD designer has a couple of geometries that can be used. This geometry determines the shape of the endpoint. The value `General` in the `Geometry` property uses the default squared display of the endpoint, as shown in Figure 7-13.

Figure 7-13

Likewise, you can create a server endpoint for the AD layer:

```
<EndpointDefinition Name="ApplicationIrDAServerEndpoint" Layer="Application"
                    Abstract="true">
    <DesignData>
        <VisualStudio xmlns="http://schemas.microsoft.com/
            SystemDefinitionModel/2005/1/DesignData/VisualStudio">
            <ModelElement>
                <Property Name="PrimaryRelationshipName" Value="HostingDefinition" />
                <Property Name="PrimaryRelationshipRole" Value="Guest" />
```

```
                <Property Name="Geometry" Value="General" />
                <Property Name="ThemeColor" Value="145, 137, 213" />
            </ModelElement>
        </VisualStudio>
    </DesignData>
</EndpointDefinition>
```

Note the subtle differences between a server endpoint and a client endpoint: the server endpoint does not contain the `Direction` property, but in exchange it does contain a `ThemeColor` property.

This `ThemeColor` property takes a color specification in the HSL (Hue, Saturation, Luminescence) format, as shown in Figure 7-14. (This difference may appear slight in this publication.)

Figure 7-14

Settings

Both this client and server endpoints will contain a setting called `BufferSize`, which will be of definition `Int` (defined in the `System` document) and not nullable. On the server endpoint, this will look like the following:

```
<SettingDeclaration Name'"BufferSize" Definition="System:Int" CanBeNull="false" />
<SettingValue Path="BufferSize">1024</SettingValue>
```

As you already imported the `System` document, you can reference anything within it without any need for an `Import` statement, as shown in Figure 7-15.

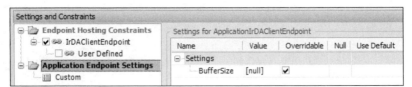

Figure 7-15

On the client endpoint, you will add a more complex setting because it will be used later in a flow and a constraint:

```
<SettingDeclaration Name="BufferSize" Definition="System:Int" CanBeNull="false"
                    DefaultRead="Default" DefaultWrite="Assigned">
    <Facet Name="Default" />
    <Facet Name="Assigned" />
    <Facet Name="Resultant" />
```

```
        </SettingDeclaration>
```

The setting defined in the client endpoint contains *facets*. The setting has three facets (`Default`, `Assigned`, and `Resultant`), which will enable you to put multiple values in this setting.

Next to the usual `SettingDeclaration` attributes are two extra ones: `DefaultRead` and `DefaultWrite`; these respectively point toward the facet used when grabbing the value from the setting, without specifying the facet name to read from, and the facet used when storing a value in the setting, without specifying the facet in which to store it.

In the Settings and Constraints Editor, these facets will not show up; the setting appears as a unity with no default value (as you did not assign one to it), as shown in Figure 7-16.

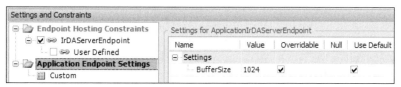

Figure 7-16

Application Host Layer

We have previously defined the endpoints for the ApplicationLayer; likewise, we will define the endpoints that will live on the ApplicationHost layer:

```xml
<EndpointDefinition Name="IrDAServerEndpoint" Layer="HostLayer" Abstract="true">
    <DesignData>
        <VisualStudio xmlns="http://schemas.microsoft.com/SystemDefinitionModel/
            2005/1/DesignData/VisualStudio">
            <ModelElement>
                <Property Name="PrimaryRelationshipName" Value="HostingDefinition" />
                <Property Name="PrimaryRelationshipRole" Value="Host" />
                <Property Name="ThemeColor" Value="145, 137, 213" />
                <Property Name="Geometry" Value="General" />
            </ModelElement>
        </VisualStudio>
    </DesignData>

    <SettingDeclaration Name="MaxAllowedBufferSize" Definition="System:Int"
        CanBeNull="false" />
    <SettingValue Path="MaxAllowedBufferSize">2048</SettingValue>
</EndpointDefinition>

<EndpointDefinition Name="IrDAClientEndpoint" Layer="HostLayer" Abstract="true">
    <DesignData>
        <VisualStudio xmlns="http://schemas.microsoft.com/SystemDefinitionModel/
            2005/1/DesignData/VisualStudio">
            <ModelElement>
                <Property Name="PrimaryRelationshipName" Value="HostingDefinition" />
                <Property Name="PrimaryRelationshipRole" Value="Host" />
                <Property Name="Direction" Value="Client" />
                <Property Name="ThemeColor" Value="145, 137, 213" />
```

```
        <Property Name="Geometry" Value="General" />
      </ModelElement>
    </VisualStudio>
  </DesignData>

  <SettingDeclaration Name="MaxAllowedBufferSize" Definition="System:Int"
                      CanBeNull="false" />
  <SettingValue Path="MaxAllowedBufferSize">2048</SettingValue>
</EndpointDefinition>
```

On the LDD layer, we now have defined two endpoints. There is a server endpoint named
`IrDAServerEndpoint`, which will live on the ApplicationHost layer. This endpoint contains a
SettingDeclaration `MaxAllowedBufferSize` of type `Int`, which will indicate the maximum allowed
value for the value of `BufferSize` in an `ApplicationIrDAServerEndpoint` that is hosted on
`IrDAServerEndpoint`. This setting also has as a default value of `2048`.

We also defined a client endpoint named `IrDAClientEndpoint`, which has the same SettingDeclaration
with the same default value.

Communication and delegation

We have defined two endpoints on each side, but without the possibility of communication between
them, there is not much use for them there, so we'll add that possibility to the SDM file:

```
<CommunicationDefinition Name="AppIrDACommunication"
                         ServerDefinition="ApplicationIrDAServerEndpoint"
                         ClientDefinition="ApplicationIrDAClientEndpoint" />
<CommunicationDefinition Name="IrDACommunication"
                         ServerDefinition="IrDAServerEndpoint"
                         ClientDefinition="IrDAClientEndpoint" />
```

This ensures that on each layer, the client and server endpoint can communicate with each other, as
shown in Figure 7-17.

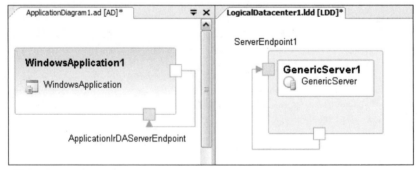

Figure 7-17

When application systems are contained in different systems (SDs in Distributed System Designers) and they need to communicate with each other, this communication needs to occur through the boundary of that system. To allow this, we need to delegate the powers of the server endpoint to the boundaries of the system in which it is contained, as shown in Figure 7-18. Likewise, for the client endpoint, this delegation is also needed:

```
<DelegationDefinition Name="AppIrDAClientEndpointDelegation"
                      DelegateDefinition="ApplicationIrDAClientEndpoint"
                      ProxyDefinition="ApplicationIrDAClientEndpoint" />
<DelegationDefinition Name="AppIrDAServerEndpointDelegation"
                      DelegateDefinition="ApplicationIrDAServerEndpoint"
                      ProxyDefinition="ApplicationIrDAServerEndpoint" />
```

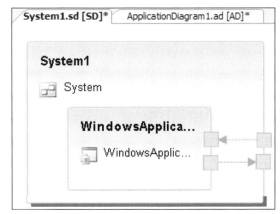

Figure 7-18

Containment

We have now defined two systems, four endpoints, and the communication definitions between them. However, this does not yet allow them to take part in the Distributed Systems Designers experience. You have to explicitly enable these systems and components to be contained in the systems that are represented by the Distributed System Designers. This is where a `ContainmentDefinition` comes in. SystemDefinitions that will live on the application layer need a `ContainmentDefinition` with a system called `DistributedApplication`, which is defined in the `Microsoft.DistributedApplication` SDM document. Therefore, you need an additional `Import` statement that imports this SDM document, and we can define the `ContainmentDefinition`:

```
<Import Alias="DA" Name="Microsoft.DistributedApplication" />
```

After adding this to the Imports section, you can continue with the `ContainmentDefinition` for the Application System (see Figure 7-19):

```
<ContainmentDefinition Name="DAcontainsWMA"
                       ParentDefinition="DA:DistributedApplication"
                       MemberDefinition="WindowsMobileApplication" />
```

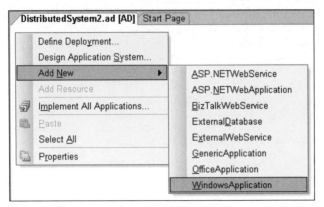

Figure 7-19

Similarly, you need to enable the ApplicationHost System to be contained in the datacenter. For this, you need a `ContainmentDefinition` between your ApplicationHost system on one side and the HostLayer (which is the system representing the LDD and defined in the `Microsoft.Datacenter` SDM document) on the other side (as shown in Figure 7-20):

```
<Import Alias="DC" Name="Microsoft.Datacenter" />
<ContainmentDefinition Name="DCcontainsWMD" ParentDefinition="DC:HostLayer"
                MemberDefinition="WindowsMobileDevice" />

<ContainmentDefinition Name="ZoneContainsWMD" ParentDefinition="DC:HostZone"
                MemberDefinition="WindowsMobileDevice" />
```

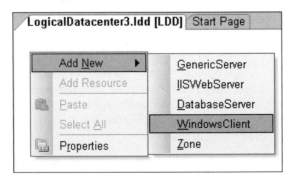

Figure 7-20

That last `ContainmentDefinition` enables the `WindowsMobileDevice` to be placed within a `Zone` on the LDD, as shown in Figure 7-21.

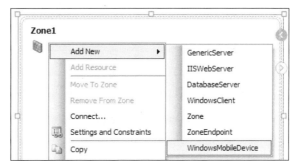

Figure 7-21

You also have to enable your endpoints to be placed — or contained, if you will — on the appropriate systems. This enables the endpoints on the application layer to be contained on the WindowsMobileApplication (as shown in Figure 7-22):

```
<ContainmentDefinition Name="WMAcontainsIRClientEndpoint"
                       ParentDefinition="WindowsMobileApplication"
                       MemberDefinition="ApplicationIrDAClientEndpoint" />
<ContainmentDefinition Name="WMAcontainsIRServerEndpoint"
                       ParentDefinition="WindowsMobileApplication"
                       MemberDefinition="ApplicationIrDAServerEndpoint" />
```

Figure 7-22

As we have allowed delegation from an ApplicationIrDAClientEndpoint to an endpoint of the same type and an ApplicationIrDAServerEndpoint to an endpoint of the same type, we also have to allow these endpoints to be contained within a DistributedApplication (as shown in Figure 7-23):

```
<ContainmentDefinition Name="DAcontainsIRServerEndpoint"
                       ParentDefinition="DA:DistributedApplication"
                       MemberDefinition="ApplicationIrDAServerEndpoint" />
<ContainmentDefinition Name="DAcontainsIRClientEndpoint"
                       ParentDefinition="DA:DistributedApplication"
                       MemberDefinition="ApplicationIrDAClientEndpoint" />
```

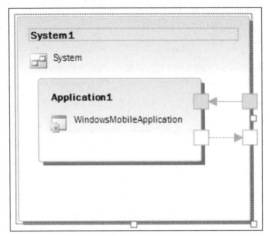

Figure 7-23

The following code enables the endpoints on the ApplicationHost layer to be contained on the `WindowsMobileDevice` system (as shown in Figure 7-24):

```
<ContainmentDefinition Name="WMDcontainsIrDAServerEndpoint"
                       ParentDefinition="WindowsMobileDevice"
                       MemberDefinition="IrDAServerEndpoint" />
<ContainmentDefinition Name="WMDcontainsIrDAClientEndpoint"
                       ParentDefinition="WindowsMobileDevice"
                       MemberDefinition="IrDAClientEndpoint" />
```

Figure 7-24

In addition, we will also allow the following three things:

❑ The Application system can contain a `WebServiceClientEndpoint` (defined in the `Microsoft.Web` SDM document) to consume Web services.

❑ The ApplicationHost system will contain an `HttpClient` endpoint so that it can communicate with IIS Servers — for instance, to query a Web service. (This endpoint is also defined in the `Microsoft.Web` SDM document.)

❑ We can ensure that the `WindowsMobileDevice` will be .NET-ready by enabling it to contain a `CommonLanguageRunTime` (defined in the `Microsoft.CommonLanguageRuntime` SDM document).

To accomplish this, we need to add these two SDM documents to the Imports list:

```
<Import Alias="CLR" Name="Microsoft.CommonLanguageRuntime" />
<Import Alias="Web" Name="Microsoft.Web" />
```

Now you can define the `ContainmentDefinition` between these definitions (as shown in Figures 7-25, 7-26, and 7-27):

```
<ContainmentDefinition Name="WMAcontainsWebServiceClient"
                       ParentDefinition="WindowsMobileApplication"
                       MemberDefinition="Web:WebServiceClient" />
```

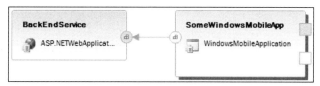

Figure 7-25

```
<ContainmentDefinition Name="WMDcontainsHTTPClient"
                       ParentDefinition="WindowsMobileDevice"
                       MemberDefinition="Web:HttpClient" />
```

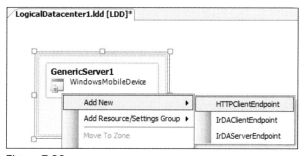

Figure 7-26

```
<ContainmentDefinition Name="WMDcontainsCLR"
                       ParentDefinition="WindowsMobileDevice"
                       MemberDefinition="CLR:CommonLanguageRuntime" />
```

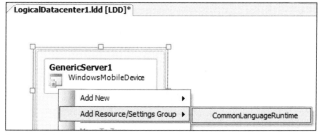

Figure 7-27

Hosting

As you are defining systems and endpoints on different layers, you need to provide the information that describes what types of hosting are allowed. After all, you deploy the systems and endpoints on the AD to the systems and endpoints on the LDD using the Deployment Designer (DD), so for this you need to define `HostingDefinitions`. These `HostingDefinitions` enable the application layer system to be hosted on the ApplicationHost layer system. This box-within-a-box hosting relationship using the DD is shown in Figure 7-28.

```
<HostingDefinition Name="WMDhostsWMA" HostDefinition="WindowsMobileDevice"
                   GuestDefinition="WindowsMobileApplication" />
```

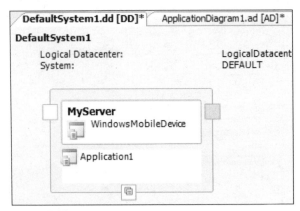

Figure 7-28

Likewise, you need to host your endpoints on their counterparts on the other layer (as shown in Figure 7-29):

```
<HostingDefinition Name="IrDAServerEndpointHostsApplicationIrDAServerEndpoint"
                   HostDefinition="IrDAServerEndpoint"
                   GuestDefinition="ApplicationIrDAServerEndpoint" />
<HostingDefinition Name="IrDAClientEndpointHostsApplicationIrDAClientEndpoint"
                   HostDefinition="IrDAClientEndpoint"
                   GuestDefinition="ApplicationIrDAClientEndpoint" />
```

Note that you do not have to provide hosting information for the `WebServiceClientEndpoint` (which will be hosted onto an `HttpClient` endpoint). This information is already defined in the Microsoft.Web SDM document.

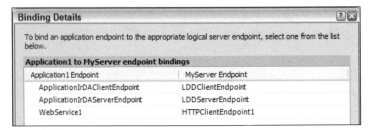

Figure 7-29

Flows

Flows enable values from one layer or object to flow to another. We will use this mechanism to flow a default value through the `HostingDefinition` that specifies that an `IrDAClientEndpoint` can host an `ApplicationIrDAClientEndpoint`. The flow will copy the value for `MaxAllowedBufferSize` of the `IrDAClientEndpoint` into the setting `BufferSize` on the `ApplicationIrDAClientEndpoint` if this endpoint did not provide a value itself. There is an `InheritanceFlow` defined in the `System.Flows` SDM document that will assist you with that. First you have to import that SDM document:

```
<Import Alias="Flow" Name="System.Flow" />
```

You now can access the `InheritanceFlow` defined in this SDM document.

This will flow the values from one layer (LDD layer) to another layer (AD/SD Layer), and will thus operate on a `HostingDefinition`. To be more precise, it will act on the `HostingDefinition` between the `ApplicationIrDAClientEndpoint` and the `IrDAClientEndpoint` named `IrDAClient` `EndpointHostsApplicationIrDAClientEndpoint`. The following statements need to be added within the `HostingDefinition`:

```
<Flow Name="ApplicationClientEndpointUsesMaxAllowedBufferSize"
      Definition="Flow:InheritanceFlow">
  <Input Name="Assigned" Path="Guest.BufferSize@Assigned" />
  <Input Name="Default" Path="Host.MaxAllowedBufferSize" />
  <Output Name="Resultant" Path="Guest.BufferSize@Resultant" Cast="true" />
</Flow>
```

This flow takes two inputs: `Assigned` and `Default`. It takes `Assigned` from the `Guest` in the `HostingDefinition` (which is the `ApplicationIrDAClientValue`) and `Default` from the `Host` in the `HostingDefinition` (which is the `IrDAClientEndpoint`). The result of the flow will be stored in the output, which is located on the `Guest`. In order to store the output in the correct format, you have to cast it to the type of the output (`Cast="true"`).

This is where the facets come in handy. By default, the value for the `Assigned` facet is empty, or null, but as soon as you put a value in the setting (without specifying a facet), it is stored in the `Assigned` facet, as defined by the `DefaultWrite` attribute on the `SettingDeclaration`. Therefore, if no specific value was specified, `Assigned` is null.

The other side of the equation comes from the `Host`; you read the value for `MaxAllowedBufferSize`.

`InheritanceFlow` does the following: It checks whether `Assigned` is null, and if it is, then the result is `Default`; if it is not null, then the result is `Assigned`.

The result is then stored in the `Resultant` output, which in this case maps to facet `Resultant` (the `DefaultRead` facet) of setting `BufferSize` on the `Guest` of the `HostingDefinition`.

This flow has the following effect: If no explicit value is set for the `BufferSize` setting on the `ApplicationIrDAClientEndpoint`, then it will use the maximum value allowed it finds on the host in `MaxAllowedBufferSize`.

Constraints

We have previously defined the possibilities that are allowed. Now it is time to rule out some situations. For this, SDM provides *constraints* in multiple forms.

RelationshipConstraints

We will constrain the relationship `WMDcontainsCLR`, which indicates that a `WindowsMobileDevice` can contain a `CommonLanguageRuntime`. The constraint we will place on this relationship is that it must contain at least one `CommonLanguageRuntime`. In order to do this, we need to add the following statements in the `WindowsMobileDevice` definition:

```
<RelationshipConstraint  Name="WMDMustContainAtLeastOneCLR"
                         RelationshipDefinition="WMDcontainsCLR"
                         TargetRole="Member"
                         TargetObjectDefinition="CLR:CommonLanguageRuntime"
                         MinOccurs="1" />
```

It is imperative that this is added within the `<SystemDefinition>` of the `WindowsMobileDevice` as we are changing its very definition; we are imposing a constraint on this definition, so it must be defined within it. If this would be defined outside of the `SystemDefinition` for the `WindowsMobileDevice`, it would have no effect whatsoever.

The different parts of this `RelationshipConstraint` are the name (or type, if you will) of the relationship we are constraining against (`RelationshipDefinition`), which player in that relationship we are targeting (`TargetRole`), and the definition of that player (`TargetObjectDefinition`).

Lastly, we also have `MinOccurs`, which indicates that at least one instance of this relationship must occur. However, there is no upper limit. If we wanted to impose an upper limit, we could also have added the `MaxOccurs`-attribute to the `RelationshipConstraint`. Leaving either `MinOccurs` or `MaxOccurs` out indicates that for the attribute(s) that is/are left out, there is no limit.

When this constraint fails, it will show up in the Error List, as shown in Figure 7-30.

Figure 7-30

Both `EndpointDefinitions` contain a setting `BufferSize`. In order to have everything in working order, we want to constrain the `CommunicationDefinition` between the application server endpoint and the application client endpoint in such a way that the application client endpoint always has a value for `BufferSize` that is equal to or larger than the value for `BufferSize` on the Server endpoint. Therefore, we have to modify the `CommunicationDefinition` between these endpoints (`AppIrDACommunication`). For this, we will use an existing `ConstraintDefinition` (`SimpleComparison`) defined in the `System.Constraints` SDM document. This requires the following `Import` statement:

```
<Import Alias="Constraints" Name="System.Constraints" />
```

This gives us access to all of the definitions in `System.Constraints`.

The constraint that we will create validates that the values on both ends of the `CommunicationDefinition` meet the requirements, so in effect we have to "walk" the `CommunicationDefinition`. To do this, add the following code within the `CommunicationDefinition` named `AppIrDACommunication`:

```
<ObjectConstraint Name="GetServer"
                  PrimaryObjectDefinition="ApplicationIrDAServerEndpoint"
                  PrimaryRole="Server">
  <RelationshipConstraint Name="GetClient"
                          RelationshipDefinition="AppIrDACommunication"
                          TargetObjectDefinition="ApplicationIrDAClientEndpoint"
                          TargetRole="Client" DelegationAware="true"
                          RaiseError="true">
  </RelationshipConstraint>
</ObjectConstraint>
```

The `ObjectConstraint GetServer` is our point of insertion. It targets one of the players in the relationship we are constraining. It declares that the object we are targeting plays the `Server` role (`PrimaryRole`) and that this object is of type `ApplicationIrDAServerEndpoint` (`PrimaryObjectDefinition`). This `ObjectConstraint` will make all settings of this targeted `ObjectDefinition` available through `GetServer.[SettingName]`.

From the object playing the Server role, we have to walk to the client so we can grab the values there also. We do this using a `RelationshipConstraint` named `GetClient`. It specifies the relationship we are walking (`AppIrDACommunication`) and where we are walking to—namely, the object playing the role of `Client` in that relationship, which is of type `ApplicationIrDAClientEndpoint`. Additionally, we specify that this `RelationshipConstraint` is delegation-aware, which means that if communication passes through delegated endpoints on subsystems, the compiler will determine which actual endpoint on what Application system is talking to which other actual endpoint on another Application system.

The `RaiseError` attribute informs the compiler that the constraint we are building can raise effective constraint errors.

By defining this `RelationshipConstraint`, we can now access all `SettingDeclarations` on the client of relationship `AppIrDACommunication` by using `GetClient.Client.[SettingName]`.

Constraint Validation

We have just provided the path that we will walk in order to grab the settings on both ends of the `CommunicationDefinition` between the `ApplicationIrDAClientEndpoint` and the `Application IrDAServerEndpoint`. We now have to add the actual constraint that will perform the comparison between the values on both sides. Within the path we have just provided (within the inner `Relationship Constraint` named `GetClient`) we will add the actual constraint that validates whether the `Client Endpoint` has a buffer that is at least the size of the buffer on the `ServerEndpoint` or bigger:

```
<Constraint Name="ValidateClientBufferCanHandleServerBuffer"
            Definition="Constraints:SimpleComparison">
  <Input Name="ActualValue" Path="GetClient.Client.BufferSize@Resultant" />
  <Input Name="DesiredValue" Path="GetServer.BufferSize" />
</Constraint>
```

This constraint (defined in `System.Constraints` as `SimpleComparison`) takes three inputs, and the `ActualValue`, the `DesiredValue`, and the `Operator` are applied to these values. As described earlier, we provided two inputs already: the `ActualValue` coming from the client in the `CommunicationDefinition` (`GetClient.Client.BufferSize@Resultant`, which is the value after the flow defined earlier has occurred) and the `DesiredValue` coming from the server in the `CommunicationDefinition` (`GetServer.BufferSize`).

The value for the operator will be a constant, so it will not come from one of the two players in the `CommunicationDefinition`. Instead, we will have it come from the `CommunicationDefinition` itself, where we will define it and give it a default value. Therefore, to the `CommunicationDefinition` `AppIrDACommunication` we will add the following `SettingDeclaration`:

```
<SettingDeclaration Name="Operator" Definition="System:String" CanBeNull="false" />
<SettingValue Path="Operator">&gt;=</SettingValue>
```

This creates a setting `Operator` in the `CommunicationDefinition` with the default value `&gt;=` (which indicates "greater than or equal to"). With this setting in place, we can use it inside the constraint by calling it directly (as it is directly available) through an `Input` in the constraint:

```
<Input Name="Operator" Path="Operator" />
```

This concludes this constraint; it reads the value from the Client Endpoint (`GetClient.Client.BufferSize@Resultant`), which is the result of the flow defined earlier, reads the value from the Server Endpoint (`GetServer.MaxBufferSize`) into `DesiredValue`, and computes that it must be larger than or equal to ActualValue as instructed by the value of `Operator`.

When this constraint it triggered and fails, it will show up in the ErrorList as shown in Figure 7-31.

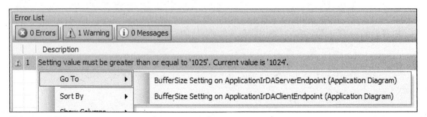

Figure 7-31

We will do something similar with the `HostingDefinition`, which defines that an `IrDAServerEndpoint` can host an `ApplicationIrDAServerEndpoint`. In the `HostingDefinition` named `IrDAServerEndpointHostsApplicationIrDAServerEndpoint`, we will state that the value for `BufferSize` on the Application endpoint cannot exceed the value of `MaxAllowedBufferSize` on the `ApplicationHost` endpoint:

```
<SettingDeclaration Name="Operator" Definition="System:String" />
<SettingValue Path="Operator">&gt;=</SettingValue>

<Constraint Name="AppEndpointCannotExceedServerValue"
            Definition="Constraints:SimpleComparison">
  <Input Name="DesiredValue" Path="Guest.BufferSize" />
```

```
    <Input Name="ActualValue" Path="Host.MaxAllowedBufferSize" />
    <Input Name="Operator" Path="Operator" />
</Constraint>
```

A failure of this constraint will show up in the ErrorList as shown in Figure 7-32.

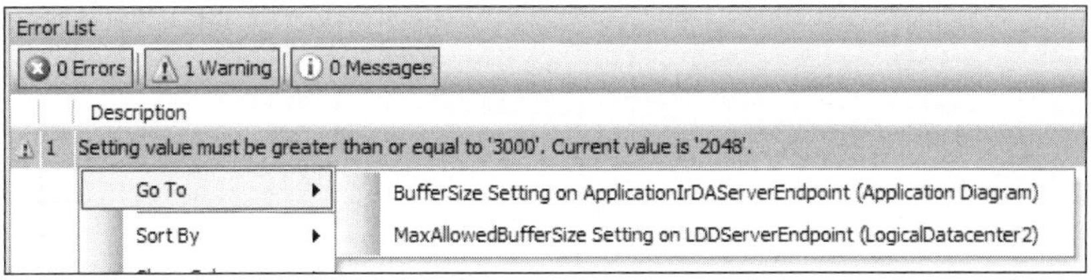

Figure 7-32

Likewise in `HostingDefinition IrDAClientEndpointHostsApplicationIrDAClientEndpoint`, which defines that an `IrDAClientEndpoint` on the ApplicationHost layer can host an `ApplicationIrDAClientEndpoint` from the application layer. In this relationship, we already defined a flow, but we can define this constraint nicely next to the flow and have them co-exist:

```
<SettingDeclaration Name="Operator" Definition="System:String" />
<SettingValue Path="Operator">&gt;=</SettingValue>

<Flow Name="ApplicationClientEndpointUsesMaxAllowedBufferSize"
      Definition="Flow:InheritanceFlow">
  <Input Name="Assigned" Path="Guest.BufferSize@Assigned" />
  <Input Name="Default" Path="Host.MaxAllowedBufferSize" />
  <Output Name="Resultant" Path="Guest.BufferSize@Resultant" Cast="true" />
</Flow>

<Constraint Name="GuestCannotExceedMaxAllowedBufferSize"
            Definition="Constraints:SimpleComparison">
  <Input Name="DesiredValue" Path="Guest.BufferSize@Resultant" />
  <Input Name="ActualValue" Path="Host.MaxAllowedBufferSize" />
  <Input Name="Operator" Path="Operator" />
</Constraint>
```

All we have to do is add the `SettingDeclaration`, the `SettingValue`, and the `Constraint`.

Creating your own constraints

In the `SystemDefinition` for the Application system (`WindowsMobileApplication`), we defined two settings: `SupportsHighContrast` and `SupportsScreenReader`. We want to define some logic validating that both values are set to `true`; otherwise, the application might not fully support the accessibility features available and we wish to fire off a warning to users when they validate the DD.

However, there is no constraint defined yet that takes two values and ensures that both are set to a specific value, so we will have to define this constraint ourselves. Because we are defining a constraint that will make a call back into compiled code, we need to "reference" that code (similar to when we import another SDM document). To reference compiled code, you declare a `Manager`:

211

```
<Manager Name="AccessibilityManager"
         AssemblyName="Microsoft.SDM.Samples.Mobile.AccessibilityManager"
         SourcePath="Microsoft.SDM.Samples.Mobile.AccessibilityManager.dll" />
```

This definition contains a `Name`, which will be used whenever you point to something within that code; an `AssemblyName` that follows the same format as any other full-fledged .NET `AssemblyName` (`name`, `version`, `culture`, and `publicKeyToken`), and a `SourcePath`, informing the compiler where (`filename`) this code can be located.

Now you can define your constraint:

```
<ConstraintDefinition Name="EnsureAccessibilitySupport"
                      Manager="AccessibilityManager"
                      ClrClassName="Microsoft.SDM.Samples.AccessibilityManager.
                      CEnsureAccessibilitySupport">
    <SettingDeclaration Name="SupportsHighContrast" Definition="System:Boolean" />
    <SettingDeclaration Name="SupportsScreenReader" Definition="System:Boolean" />
</ConstraintDefinition>
```

As with any definition, this `ConstraintDefinition` needs a `Name` (`EnsureAccessibilitySupport`), which you will use later to indicate what type of constraint you want; a `Manager`, which points you toward the assembly containing the manager code; and a `ClrClassName`, which informs the compiler what class in the manager assembly should be used to execute this constraint.

Next to that, you provide `SettingDeclarations`, which provide a way for SDM values to be passed into the compiled code.

As you create the Manager and `ConstraintDefinition`, it is obvious that there is no assembly named `Microsoft.SDM.Samples.Mobile.AccessibilityManager.dll`...yet!

This is where the tools in the SDM SDK come into play for the first time.

SdmG

SdmG (SDM Manager Generator) is a tool delivered with the SDM SDK that is capable of generating a skeleton for your manager code based on SDM that you provide to the tool. By running your SDM file through SdmG, SdmG will generate (in this case) a partial class that contains the basic framework to implement the manager. Unfortunately, you need to provide not only the SDM file that contains the `ConstraintDefinition` for which to generate the manager, but also all SDM documents referenced by that SDM file and all the SDM documents referenced in those SDM documents, and so on.

This is how the call to SdmG will look:

```
$> SdmG Microsoft.SDM.Samples.Mobile.sdm /Classes+ /Constraints+ /S "C:\program
files\microsoft visual studio 8\common7\ide\PrivateAssemblies"
/R Microsoft.DistributedApplication.sdmDocument
/R Microsoft.Datacenter.sdmDocument /R System.Constraints.sdmDocument
/R Microsoft.CommonLanguageRuntime.sdmDocument
/R System.Flow.sdmDocument
/R Microsoft.Web.sdmDocument
/R Microsoft.FileSystem.sdmDocument
```

Using the /Classes+ and /Constraints+ switches, you instruct SdmG to generate classes for the ConstraintDefinitions in the SDM file (Microsoft.SDM.Samples.Mobile.sdm) you provided. You also provide all referenced SDM documents using the /R switches and a search path whereby SdmG will look for these documents using /S.

The following command provides you with a complete view of all of SdmG's switches:

```
$> SdmG /?
```

The result of our original SdmG command will be a file named Microsoft.SDM.Samples.Mobile.cs as specified by the ClrClassName attribute of the ConstraintDefinition. If you open this file, the content will look like this:

```
//------------------------------------------------------------------------
// <auto-generated>
//     This code was generated by a tool.
//     Runtime Version:2.0.50426.0
//
//     Changes to this file may cause incorrect behavior and will be lost if
//     the code is regenerated.
// </auto-generated>
//------------------------------------------------------------------------
/// This file was generated using SdmG.exe, version=1.0.50000.0
namespace Microsoft.SDM.Samples.AccessibilityManager
{
    using System;


    public partial class CEnsureAccessibilitySupport :
                        Microsoft.SystemDefinitionModel.Manager.IConstraint
    {

        public bool SupportsHighContrast;

        public bool SupportsScreenReader;
    }
}
```

The first important thing to notice is that the class generated by the tool is a partial class. This enables you to add the logic in a different file and then compile both files into one class. If this were not a partial class and you re-generated your manager using SdmG, it would blow away the implementation code you have already added to the file. Therefore, it is good practice to use this C# 2.0 feature; leave the code generated by SdmG alone and perform the implementation in a separate file, which will then be compiled with the generated file into one assembly.

To implement the manager code, create a new .cs file (called Microsoft.SDM.Samples.Mobile.CEnsureAccessibilitySupport.cs) and place the following code in it:

```
//This file contains the 'second part' of the manager code class
using System;
using System.Collections.Generic;
using Microsoft.SystemDefinitionModel.Manager;

namespace Microsoft.SDM.Samples.AccessibilityManager
```

```
{
    //IConstraint can be found in Microsoft.SystemDefinitionModel.Manager
    public partial class CEnsureAccessibilitySupport : IConstraint{

    public ConstraintError[] Evaluate (){
        List<string> lstViolators = new List<string> ();

        if (!SupportsHighContrast)
            lstViolators.Add ("SupportsHighContrast");
        if (!SupportsScreenReader)
            lstViolators.Add ("SupportsScreenReader");

        return ( SupportsHighContrast && SupportsScreenReader ?
                null :
                new ConstraintError[] {
                    new ConstraintError (       2005 /*errorID*/ ,
                    "No good Accessibility Support!" /*Error Description*/ ,
                    lstViolators.ToArray () /*Inputs causing the error*/ )
                                }
            );

    }
  }
}
```

Here again you define a partial class CEnsureAccessibilitySupport, which will be merged with the CEnsureAccessibilitySupport in the Microsoft.SDM.Samples.Mobile.cs file by the compiler, which contains the implementation for the IConstraint interface — namely, the Evaluate() method.

This method will perform the actual logic required for the constraint. In this case, it creates a list of violating settings (which are the exact same names of the settings as defined in SDM) that will contain one entry for every setting that this constraint deems inappropriate.

If the value of SupportsHighContrast is not true, it will add the name of that setting (as defined in the ConstraintDefinition) to the list of violators. Similarly, it will add the name of the setting SupportsScreenReader to that same list if it is not set to true.

Lastly, it performs a check: If both values were indeed set to true it returns null, indicating that all is well. If any of these settings were not set to null, it returns an array of ConstraintErrors (defined in Microsoft.SystemDefinitionModel.Manager), which — in this case — contain just one ConstraintError.

The ConstraintError object takes three parameters: the ID of the error; a description of the error, which is the description that will appear in the ErrorList after validating the DD in Visual Studio; and an array of strings (System.String) of settings causing this ConstraintError. For each element in this array of strings of offending settings, Visual Studio will create a MenuItem under the GoTo menu item of the context menu that appears when you right-click on the error in the Visual Studio ErrorList that enables you to navigate to this offending setting.

Note that the names of the offending settings are the names of the SettingDeclarations in the ConstraintDefinition, not the name of the path filling in the values of this input.

After the implementation of this manager code, you need to compile both files into one assembly using the C# Compiler (csc.exe):

```
$> csc /out:Microsoft.SDM.Samples.Mobile.AccessibilityManager.dll /target:library
/r:%SDMSDK%\Microsoft.Sdm.Manager.dll Microsoft.SDM.Samples.Mobile.cs
Microsoft.SDM.Samples.Mobile.CEnsureAccessibilitySupport.cs
```

This compiles both files into an assembly named
Microsoft.SDM.Samples.Mobile.AccessibilityManager (as specified by the SourcePath attribute of the Manager declaration). In order for the compiler to resolve all references, you provide the path to the Microsoft.Sdm.Manager.dll assembly as a referenced assembly (you will need to replace %SDMSDK% with the path to this file on your machine; or populate this environment variable with the appropriate value). You also specify that you want a library assembly as output (.dll) through the /target switch.

This results, as expected, in the assembly that you specified in the declaration AccessibilityManager.

Enforcing your constraint

Just as you created a <Constraint/> from a ConstraintDefinition predefined in System.Constraint, you can now create a <Constraint /> from the ConstraintDefinition you defined earlier in your SDM file.

This constraint restricts the SystemDefinition for the WindowsMobileApplication, so you need to place this constraint within that SystemDefinition:

```
<Constraint Name="EnsureApplicationSupportsAccessibility"
            Definition="EnsureAccessibilitySupport">
   <Input Name="SupportsHighContrast" Path="SupportsHighContrast" />
   <Input Name="SupportsScreenReader" Path="SupportsScreenReader" />
</Constraint>
```

You define this constraint and instruct it to use the definition named EnsureAccessibilitySupport, which requires two inputs: SupportsHighContrast and SupportsScreenReader. The value for these inputs can come from the SettingDeclarations that are directly available in this SystemDefinition (and are, coincidentally, named the same).

If your application fails this constraint, you will find an error message in your ErrorList like the one shown in Figure 7-33.

Figure 7-33

If only `ScreenReader` is set to false, the error will look like the one shown in Figure 7-34.

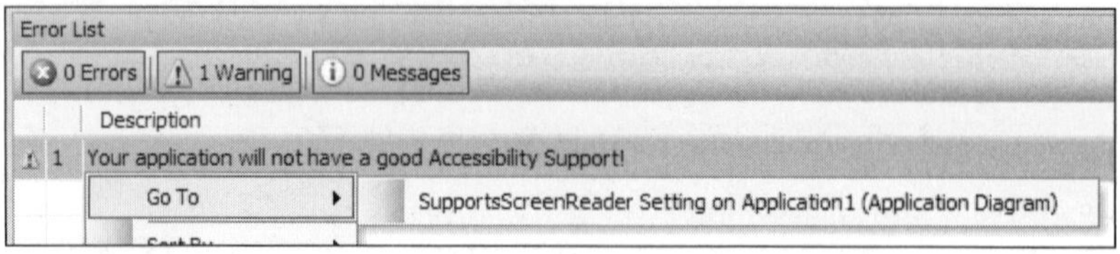

Figure 7-34

SdmC

Before you can use the SDM file you have been authoring in the Distributed Systems Designers (DSDs), you need to run it through the SDM Compiler (SdmC). By running your SDM file through SdmC, you are guaranteed that if the compiler does not report any errors, the resulting SDM document does not contain any semantic or syntactic errors. However, SdmC obviously does not point out errors in logic. You can get a full list of commands for SdmC by executing this command:

```
$> SdmC /?
```

To compile the SDM file you have been authoring, execute this command:

```
$> sdmc Microsoft.SDM.Samples.Mobile.sdm /S "C:\program files\microsoft visual
studio 8\common7\ide\PrivateAssemblies"
/R Microsoft.DistributedApplication.sdmDocument
/R Microsoft.Datacenter.sdmDocument
/R System.Constraints.sdmDocument
/R Microsoft.CommonLanguageRuntime.sdmDocument
/R System.Flow.sdmDocument
/R Microsoft.Web.sdmDocument
```

Similarly to SdmG, you provide the file you wish to compile (`Microsoft.SDM.Samples.Mobile.sdm`); a search path in which SdmC will look for referenced files (`/S`); and the list of referenced files (`/R`).

The result of this statement will be a file named `Microsoft.SDM.Samples.Mobile.sdmDocument` that can be used by the DSDs (unless a different filename was specified using the `/output` switch).

ProtoGen

You have defined two `SystemDefinitions` and four `EndpointDefinitions` in the SDM file that you just compiled to an SDM document. In order to make those accessible to the DSDs and enable Visual Studio to ensure that these are represented in the toolbox so that they can be dragged onto the designer, you need to create prototypes. To do this, you can use another SDM SDK tool called *ProtoGen*. For a full list of options, execute this command:

```
$> ProtoGen /?
```

To generate the prototypes for the two systems, execute these two commands:

```
$> ProtoGen /Type System /Layer Application /Document Microsoft.SDM.Samples.Mobile
/TypeName WindowsMobileApplication
$> ProtoGen /Type System /Layer Host /Document Microsoft.SDM.Samples.Mobile
/TypeName WindowsMobileDevice
```

In its purest form, ProtoGen takes four parameters: the type of SDM element on which you operate (/Type), which can be either System or Endpoint; the layer on which this SDM element lives (/Layer) or, in other words, in which toolbox it appears, the application layer (AD) or the host layer (LDD); the document identity information of the SDM document in which this system is defined (/Document); and the name of the SDM element for which to create a prototype (/TypeName).

The preceding command will result in two prototype files: WindowsMobileApplication.adPrototype, which is a prototype that will appear in the AD toolbox, and WindowsMobileDevice.lddPrototype, which will appear in the LDD toolbox. You can specify a different name for the prototype file by using the /output switch.

Likewise, you can create the prototypes for your four EndpointDefinitions:

```
$> ProtoGen /Type Endpoint /Layer Application /Document
Microsoft.SDM.Samples.Mobile /TypeName ApplicationIrDAServerEndpoint
$> ProtoGen /Type Endpoint /Layer Application /Document
Microsoft.SDM.Samples.Mobile /TypeName ApplicationIrDAClientEndpoint
$> ProtoGen /Type Endpoint /Layer Host /Document Microsoft.SDM.Samples.Mobile
/TypeName IrDAServerEndpoint
$> ProtoGen /Type Endpoint /Layer Host /Document Microsoft.SDM.Samples.Mobile
/TypeName IrDAClientEndpoint
```

These commands will generate four files:

- ❑ ApplicationIrDAServerEndpoint.adPrototype

- ❑ ApplicationIrDAClientEndpoint.adPrototype

- ❑ IrDAServerEndpoint.lddPrototype

- ❑ IrDAClientEndpoint.lddPrototype

When you are done compiling and generating prototypes, you are almost ready to use your freshly compiled SDM document with prototypes in the DSDs.

The registry

Before you can use these prototypes you have to place them in a location Visual Studio knows about.

To instruct Visual Studio to load your compiled SDM file (the SDM document) upon opening the first Distributed Designer Diagram, you need to register this file in the registry at [HKLM\Software\ Microsoft\VisualStudio\8.0\EnterpriseTools\Sdm\InitializationFiles].

You need to add a new string value pointing to the location of the SDM document. Add the following string value to this registry key:

```
Name= [500 Microsoft.SDM.Samples.Mobile.sdmDocument]
Value= [%directory%\Microsoft.SDM.Samples.Mobile.sdmDocument]
```

Be sure to replace `%directory%` with the directory location of the SDM document.

When you use values for `ErrorImageFileName` and `ImageFileName` in the `<DesignData/>` section of the `SystemDefinitions`, make sure that the filenames specified there point to files that reside in the same directory as the SDM document.

The same is true for the value of `SourcePath` in the `Manager` declaration — the path specified in that attribute must point to a filename that is accessible from within the directory in which the SDM document resides.

You also need to put the prototypes in a location Visual Studio can access. When navigating to `[HKLM\Software\Microsoft\VisualStudio\8.0\EnterpriseTools\DesignerPrototype Folders]`, you will find an entry for every directory Visual Studio will query when trying to load all prototypes into the toolbox. Add the following string value to this registry key:

```
Name= [Microsoft.SDM.Samples.Mobile Prototypes]
Value= [%directory%\]
```

Be sure to replace `%directory%` with the directory location of the prototypes. In addition, be sure to terminate this directory with a backslash (\). Without this backslash, Visual Studio will fail to pick up the prototype files in that directory.

Visual Studio

If you start Visual Studio now and create a Distributed Systems Solution, these prototypes will appear in the AD and LDD toolbox, as shown in the two parts of Figure 7-35, respectively.

You have created a System Definition Model of a Windows Mobile Application that can be hosted on a Windows Mobile Device. It can consume WebServices through a `WebServiceClientEndpoint` and can communicate with other Windows Mobile Applications through IrDA. A constraint enforces that when this happens, the client will have a buffer that is at least as big as the buffer on the server side. However, if the Client endpoint on the application layer did not specify its buffer size, a flow makes sure that it is granted the maximum buffer size allowed by the hosting logical server.

When this Windows Mobile Application is hosted on a Windows Mobile Device, you enforce that the buffers used by the application do not exceed the maximum allowed buffer size.

In addition, the Windows Mobile Device must contain at least one `CommonLanguageRuntime` resource so that it can run managed code. It can contain multiples, but we enforce that it contains at least one.

On the application side, you have two settings on the application that specify what support the application delivers for some accessibility features: `ScreenReaders` and `HighContrast` mode. If either of these are not supported (i.e., set to `false`), a constraint you create yourself will be fired, informing the user that the application does not fully utilize and support accessibility. Through the Visual Studio ErrorList, the user will be capable of navigating to the offending settings through the Go To functionality for which your custom-defined constraint provides the names of the offending settings.

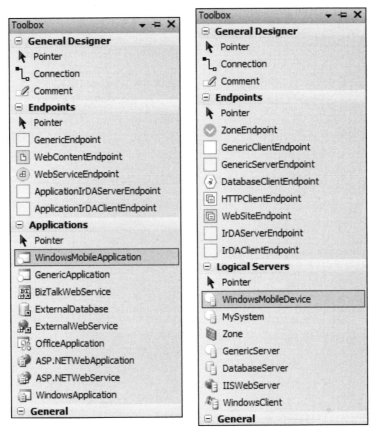

Figure 7-35

Summary

The SDM captures the basic invariant structure and behaviors of a system in a self-contained model. It provides the scaffolding to which other information can be applied. This may include deployment information, installation procedures, configuration schemas, automation tasks, events and instrumentation, health models, and operational policies. Additional information can be added across the lifetime of the distributed system by vendors, the operations staff, and/or management.

Through the SDK, the SDM encourages the creation of reusable, prescriptive models that can be easily incorporated into the application or hosting environment of Team Architect.

Visual Studio will extend *design for deployment* by enabling production deployment and operations management of distributed applications.

Part II
Team Developer

8

Managed Code Analysis

In this chapter and the next, we describe the code analysis features included with Visual Studio Team System. These tools can quickly and easily inspect your code to find common mistakes, suggestions for improvements, and even violations of standards.

In this chapter, we'll focus on analyzing managed code, such as C# and VB.NET. If you're working with C or unmanaged C++, turn to Chapter 9, where you will learn how to analyze native code.

We begin by discussing the origins of the Static Code Analysis tool. We'll introduce Microsoft's .NET Design Guidelines for Class Library Developers and describe how it is related to the tools.

Then we will describe the tool itself and how to take advantage of its full integration with Team System. This includes enabling Static Code Analysis review for your projects, selecting rules to apply, and working with the results of the analysis.

However, using the IDE is not always an option and sometimes you need additional flexibility. The Static Code Analysis tool is available to you from the command line. You will also learn how to use the command line for code analysis and how to include code analysis with your automated builds.

The Static Code Analysis rules that ship with Team System will probably not be sufficient for the specific standards and practices of your own projects. To address this, we will also describe how you can create and integrate new custom rules. We begin by describing the mechanics of rules, introducing the new Introspection engine. You will then create an example rule using introspection and call it from the Visual Studio IDE.

The Need for Analysis Tools

Ensuring that developers follow best practices and write consistent code is a major challenge in today's software development projects. The act of documenting standards and practices is often skipped or overlooked. However, even in projects for which standards have been established, getting developers to read and follow those practices is another major challenge.

One of the best resources available for .NET developers is Microsoft's .NET Framework "Design Guidelines for Class Library Developers." These guidelines document Microsoft's (formerly) internal practices for developing class libraries and are freely available at http://msdn.microsoft.com/library/en-us/cpgenref/html/cpconnetframeworkdesignguidelines.asp.

The guidelines cover a wide range of subjects, including naming conventions, usage guidelines, and performance and security considerations. The importance of these guidelines cannot be overstated. When put into practice, they help ensure that your approach will be consistent with that of other developers. In addition, they have evolved over a number of years to reflect a considerable amount of knowledge, best practices, and lessons learned.

As useful as the design guidelines are, the reality of software creation is that many developers, due to lack of time or perhaps of interest, will not be familiar with their contents. The desire to automate the process of evaluating code for compliance with these guidelines led to the creation of *FxCop*.

Using Managed Code Analysis

FxCop is a tool used to analyze managed code against a library of rules. You can create rules for almost any purpose: naming conventions, security, attribute usage, and so on. FxCop contains nearly 200 rules, based on the .NET Framework Design Guidelines described earlier.

FxCop has been available from Microsoft on the GotDotNet.com site for several years. Before then, it had been used internally at Microsoft for analysis of their own frameworks to help ensure predictable and consistent interfaces. Previous versions of FxCop have been stand-alone applications, separated from the Visual Studio IDE.

With Team System, FxCop is now called the Managed Code Analysis tool, and is fully integrated with the IDE, enabling analysis to be performed with a simple build of your application. The FxCop heritage of Managed Code Analysis is generally hidden when you're using the IDE, but as you'll see, the FxCop name still appears when creating new rules and using command-line options.

We'll follow an example project through this chapter. Create a new C# Class Library project and name it "SampleLibrary." Rename the Class1.cs file to PayCalculator.cs and insert the following code, which, as you'll soon see, has several problems:

```
using System;

namespace SampleLibrary
{
    public class PayCalculator
    {
        public enum Pay_Level
        {
            EntryLevel = 20,
            Normal = 35,
            Senior = 50
```

```
        }

        public static int MaximumHours;
        public const double BONUS = 0.10;

        static PayCalculator()
        {
            MaximumHours = 100;
        }

        public static double ComputePayment(int hours, Pay_Level level)
        {
            if (hours > MaximumHours)
            {
                throw new ArgumentOutOfRangeException("Employee works too much");
            }

            return ((int)level * hours);
        }
    }
}
```

While this code will compile and run as expected, you can make several improvements to it, and the Code Analysis tool will help you find them.

Built-in Managed Code Analysis rules

As mentioned, Team System ships with nearly 200 rules for Managed Code Analysis, each helping to enforce the practices documented in the .NET Framework Design Guidelines and other practices recommended by Microsoft. This section briefly describes each of the eleven rule groups, so you have an understanding of when you might apply them to your projects.

The groups of rules included with Team System are described in the following table.

Rule Group (# of Rules)	Description
Design (60)	Typically focused on the interfaces and structure of code. These enforce proper implementation of common concepts such as classes, events, collections, namespaces, and parameters.
Globalization (7)	Practices to support the internationalization of code. This can include avoiding strings of literal text, correct use of `CultureInfo`, and formatting.
Interoperability (16)	Focused on the correct use of COM Interop. Includes rules for proper use of `PInvoke`, the `ComVisible` attribute, and marshalling.
Maintainability (3)	Rules to help make your code easier to maintain. Identifies potential problems such as complexity and overuse of inheritance.
Mobility (2)	Rules to help detect code that will not run effectively in mobile or disconnected environments

Table continued on following page

Rule Group (# of Rules)	Description
Naming (20)	Enforces naming standards as described in the Design Guidelines. Using these rules verifies that names of items such as assemblies, classes, members, and variables conform to standards. Some rules will even help to detect misspellings in your assigned names.
Performance (19)	These rules help to detect places in your code that may be optimized for performance. They detect a wide variety of wasteful or extraneous code.
Portability (2)	Rules to find code that might not be easily portable between operating environments.
Reliability (5)	The rules in this group will help to detect problems with your code that may lead to intermittent failures, including failure to dispose of objects, improper use of the garbage collector, bad threading use, and more. These rules can be extremely useful because intermittent errors are frequently the most difficult to identify and correct.
Security (24)	These rules help to identify insufficient or incorrect security practices. Rules exist to find missing attributes, improper use of permissions, and opportunities of SQL injection attacks.
Usage (40)	These rules cover a broad spectrum of recommended practices. Whereas the design group rules typically involve API structure, these rules govern the methodologies of code. Practices include proper exception management, handling of arithmetic overflow, serialization, and inheritance.

Of course, the rules that ship with Team System are only a starting point. Microsoft and others will certainly make additional rules available, and you can add your own custom rules and rule groups as well. You'll learn how to create custom Managed Code Analysis rules later in this chapter.

Enabling Managed Code Analysis

By default, code analysis is disabled for projects in Visual Studio. To enable analysis, open your project's Properties window and select Code Analysis from the left-hand side tabs. You will then see a collapsed list of rules, as shown in Figure 8-1.

> To enable and configure Code Analysis for ASP.NET applications, select Website ➪ Code Analysis Configuration. Code Analysis may also be enabled, but not configured, from the Build page of the ASP.NET project's Property Pages.

Check the box labeled Enable Code Analysis. You can also expand the Rules groups to see specific rules. Rules or entire groups of rules can be disabled by unchecking their boxes. Save your settings via Save Selected Items on the File menu or by pressing Control+S.

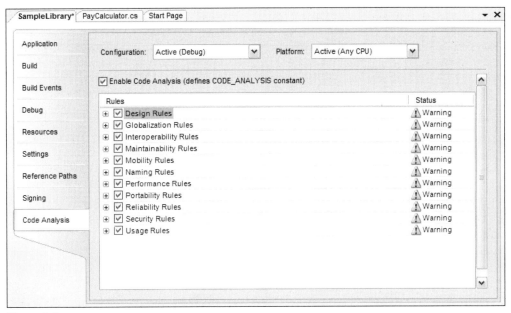

Figure 8-1

In addition, each rule can be set to either Warning (the default) or Error. Warnings serve as an advisory that something may need to be corrected, but they will not prevent the project's build from succeeding. You may want to set certain rules or groups of rules to Error if they are critically important, thus preventing a build when those rules are violated. Double-click on the entry under the Status column to toggle the value between Warning and Error. As with enabling rules, this can be done for specific rules or entire groups of rules.

Figure 8-2 illustrates how to enable and disable specific rules and how each can be set to Warning or Error as necessary.

Finally, you can specify different sets of code analysis properties for each configuration. By default, settings apply to the Active build configuration, but you can be more specific. For example, you may wish to treat certain critical rules as errors in your Release builds, but as warnings in Debug. You might instead decide to disable code analysis entirely for your Release builds. Simply choose a build type from the Configuration drop-down menu and then review your settings. To make changes affecting all build configurations, select the All Configurations option, and then modify and save your settings.

Executing static code analysis

Once you have enabled code analysis and configured the rules to reflect your development standards, code analysis will be performed each time you build your project. Go ahead and build your sample project now.

You can also execute code analysis on your project by choosing Build ⇨ Run Code Analysis on [Project Name].

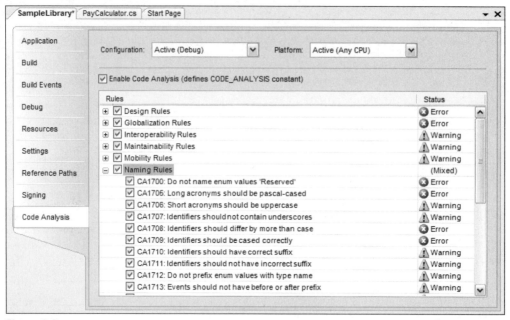

Figure 8-2

The output window will include details about your build, including results from calling code analysis. After the build, the Error List window may appear, displaying a number of warnings and possibly some errors. The Error List does not automatically open if there are only warnings. If you do not see the Error List, choose View ⇨ Error List.

Figure 8-3 is a screenshot of the Error List, displaying code analysis results for the SampleLibrary assembly.

		Description	File	Line
⚠	1	CA2209 : Microsoft.Usage : No valid permission requests were found for assembly 'SampleLibrary'. You should always specify the minimum security permissions using SecurityAction.RequestMinimum.		
⚠	2	CA2210 : Microsoft.Design : Sign 'SampleLibrary' with a strong name key.		
⚠	3	CA1014 : Microsoft.Design : 'SampleLibrary' should be marked with CLSCompliantAttribute and its value should be true.		
⚠	4	CA1053 : Microsoft.Design : Remove the public constructors from 'PayCalculator'.	PayCalculator.cs	5
⚠	5	CA1810 : Microsoft.Performance : Initialize all static fields in SampleLibrary.PayCalculator when those fields are declared and remove the explicit static constructor.	PayCalculator.cs	18
⚠	6	CA1705 : Microsoft.Naming : Correct the capitalization of member name 'PayCalculator.BONUS'.	PayCalculator.cs	15
⚠	7	CA2208 : Microsoft.Usage : Calls to System.ArgumentOutOfRangeException's constructor 'ArgumentOutOfRangeException.ArgumentOutOfRangeException(String)' should contain one of the method's parameter names instead of 'Employee works too much'. Note that the provided parameter name should have the exact casing as declared on the method.	PayCalculator.cs	26
⚠	8	CA2211 : Microsoft.Usage : Consider making 'MaximumHours' non-public or a constant.	PayCalculator.cs	14
⚠	9	CA1008 : Microsoft.Design : Add a member to 'Pay_Level' that has a value of zero with a suggested name of 'None'.	PayCalculator.cs	7
⚠	10	CA1707 : Microsoft.Naming : Remove all underscores from type 'Pay_Level'.	PayCalculator.cs	7

Error List
🔴 0 Errors ⚠ 10 Warnings ⓘ 0 Messages

Figure 8-3

Analysis of the SampleLibrary code indicates 10 potential rule violations. Each item in the list has a full description indicating how your code is in violation of a rule. The Error List has File and Line columns that indicate, when appropriate, specific source files and code related to each warning. Some warnings do not relate to specific code, but perhaps to a lack of an attribute or security setting. In such cases, there will be no value in the File column. Others may refer directly to problem code, perhaps naming violations or performance issues. You can double-click on the warning and the code editor will switch to the related code.

Each time you run code analysis, the results are stored in an XML file. This file is named `<Project Name>`
`.CodeAnalysisLog.xml` and is located in your project's `\bin\Debug` or `\bin\Release` directory, depending on the current build configuration. For the SampleLibrary project, the file will be `SampleLibrary.dll.CodeAnalysisLog.xml`.

If you open the file from within the IDE, you will see the raw, unformatted XML. However, the XML has an associated XSL template that formats the data into HTML, similar to what is shown in Figure 8-4. To see this view, open the XML file with Internet Explorer. To customize rendering, you can supply your own XSL templates. We recommend you make a copy of the included template and modify the copy to suit your needs. The base template is found in your Visual Studio installation directory as `\Team Tools\Static Analysis Tools\FxCop\Xml\CodeAnalysisReport.xsl`.

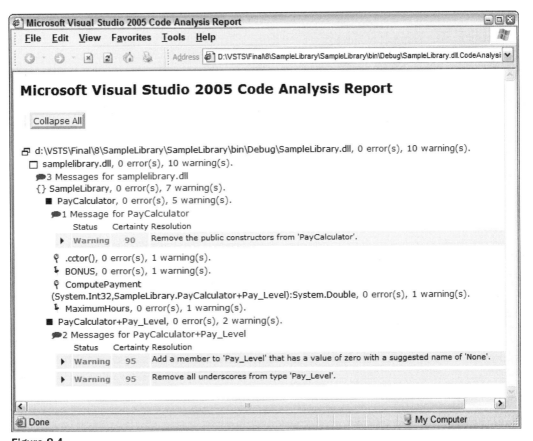

Figure 8-4

Working with rule violations

Several issues should be addressed in the sample `PayCalculator` class. For each warning or error, you need to determine whether the rule actually applies to your project or a specific section of code. If it does, you need to modify the project to address the issue; otherwise, you may choose to ignore the rule. In this section, we'll describe how to act on identified issues and how to ignore, or suppress, a given rule.

We'll immediately go into the code and make corrections as necessary, but your organization or project may require the use of work items to track any changes. Or, alternatively, perhaps you don't have time to immediately address an identified problem but would like to use a work item as a reminder. Fortunately, you can easily create work items directly from Code Analysis rule violations. Simply right-click on the warning or error and choose Create Work Item from the menu. Choose the correct Team Project and you will be shown the New Work Item dialog. Make any necessary changes and save your new work item.

Correcting problems

Looking through the Error List shown in Figure 8-3, you should see item CA1810, with a description of "Initialize all static fields in SampleLibrary.PayCalculator when those fields are declared and remove the explicit static constructor."

Right-click on this warning and choose Show Error Help. This will display the documentation for the rule that triggered this warning, including suggestions for resolving the issue. We are currently assigning the value of 100 to `MaximumHours` inside the static constructor of `PayCalculator`. The rule's Help text states that our code may perform more efficiently if we make that assignment when the variable is defined.

To address this issue, double-click on this warning and you'll be brought to the static constructor of the `PayCalculator` class. Change the code to assign the value in the declaration as follows:

```
public static int MaximumHours = 100;
```

Next, delete the static `PayCalculator` constructor entirely. Build the project and look at the Error List window. The specific warning should no longer be in the list. Your code is better already!

There is another easy problem to correct. Many of the code analysis rules relate to standard naming conventions. Find the warning "Remove all underscores from type Pay_Level" and double-click. The rule helps to enforce the naming convention that underscores should not be used in type names. Use the built-in refactoring support to rename it (see Chapter 10 for details). Right-click on the `Pay_Level` enumeration and choose Refactor ➪ Rename. Change the name to `PayLevel` and apply.

Another warning says "Remove the public constructors from PayCalculator." There aren't any constructors in the code, so why is this violation included? If you don't specify a constructor, a parameterless public constructor is compiled into your code automatically. The `PayCalculator` class has only static members, so creating an instance is not going to be useful. This rule lets you know that you should specifically prevent this by adding a private constructor. Add the following code to `PayCalculator`:

```
private PayCalculator() { }
```

Once you make this change and rebuild, a new warning will appear in the Error List window: "Mark PayCalculator as sealed." This indicates that because all members of the class are static and there are no public constructors, you can improve runtime efficiency by sealing the class. Because a sealed class cannot be inherited from, .NET can make some assumptions about the class, which optimizes performance. Mark the PayCaclulator class definition sealed as follows:

```
public sealed class PayCalculator
```

In C# 2.0, you can go one step further. Instead of using sealed, *you could use the new* static *keyword to mark the entire class as static. This can be applied only to classes that have only static members and no instance constructors, public or private. In our example, you would need to remove the private instance constructor in order to use the* static *keyword.*

Rules can also help ensure that you're using the Framework correctly. You can see from the warning "Calls to System.ArgumentOutOfRangeException's constructor... should contain one of the method's parameter names..." that the rule has detected that you might not be creating the ArgumentOutOfRangeException correctly. To fix this, change the line that throws the exception to the following:

```
if (hours > MaximumHours)
{
    throw new ArgumentOutOfRangeException("hours", "Employee works too much");
}
```

One of the remaining warnings, "SampleLibrary should be marked with CLSCompliantAttribute and its value should be true," is a fairly common suggestion. Consider addressing this when creating a reusable library assembly that might be consumed by code of more than one .NET language. CLS compliance specifies that your assembly must meet the common structure and syntax supported by all .NET languages as defined in the Common Language Specification (CLS). Keep in mind that there may be times when CLS compliance is not possible, such as when exposing unsigned types.

To address this warning, open AssemblyInfo.cs and add the following line:

```
[assembly: System.CLSCompliant(true)]
```

The assembly: notation is used because the attribute applies to the entire assembly, and not to a specific class or member. Other assembly-level attributes can be found in the AssemblyInfo.cs file.

Another change to the AssemblyInfo.cs file will satisfy the "No valid permission requests were found for assembly SampleLibrary" warning. Best practices for security indicate that assemblies should always specify the permissions they require. The SampleLibrary does not require any special permissions, so you'll add an attribute to indicate this. You'll need the System.Security.Permissions namespace, so add the using statement to AssemblyInfo.cs:

```
using System.Security.Permissions;
```

Then add the attribute:

```
[assembly: SecurityPermission(SecurityAction.RequestMinimum, UnmanagedCode=false)]
```

Now, build the project. The violations you corrected should no longer generate messages in the Error List. We'll address some of the other warnings in the next section.

Suppressing messages

Team System ships with many rules, but not all of them are appropriate for every project. There is a chance that some rules will trigger warnings that simply don't apply to certain parts of your project. To prevent these irrelevant messages from recurring, right-click on the rule violation and choose Suppress Message(s).

When you suppress a message, Visual Studio automatically adds an attribute to your code to indicate that a rule should not apply. The `SuppressMessage` attribute can be applied to a code construct, such as a field, method, or class, and to an entire assembly.

> **Suppressing a message is not the same as disabling a rule. Suppression prevents the specific violation of a rule from recurring, but other violations of the same rule will still be identified. You should disable a rule only if you're certain it could never be meaningfully applied to any part of your project.**

Let's continue with the SampleLibrary example and use message suppression to clean up more of the code analysis violation messages.

One of the warnings states "Correct the capitalization of member name PayCalculator.BONUS." Assume that your organization has different naming conventions for constants and you know that this rule will not apply to this BONUS constant. Right-click on the message and choose Suppress Message. The message will be crossed out in the Error List and the `PayCalculator` class will be modified to include the following attribute immediately before the declaration of BONUS:

```
[System.Diagnostics.CodeAnalysis.SuppressMessage(
    "Microsoft.Naming",
    "CA1705:LongAcronymsShouldBePascalCased",
    MessageId = "Member")]
```

The next time Code Analysis is run, the engine will recognize this attribute. Moreover, even when the CA1705 rule is violated at this point, no message will be created. Messages for any other violations of this rule elsewhere in the code will still be reported as normal.

In many cases, especially in ASP.NET applications, Visual Studio will automatically generate helper or wrapper code. Previous versions of FxCop had difficulty working with such generated code and often flagged many warnings — for example, naming convention violations, which would have to be investigated and generally excluded. Fortunately, the .NET Framework 2.0 offers a new attribute, GeneratedCodeAttribute, that the Managed Code Analysis tool uses to identify code that it does not need to analyze.

Two more messages don't apply to the project. "Consider making MaximumHours non-public or a constant" reminds us that external users of the class could change its value. This is the behavior you want, so right-click on the message and choose Suppress Message. The message "Add a member to PayLevel that has a value of zero with a suggested name of None" also does not apply, as all employees are required to have an employee level. Suppress this message as well.

As you can see, suppressing messages can quickly add a number of attributes to your code. If you find that you always suppress a given message, it is probably better to exclude the rule altogether; then your code will not require the additional SuppressMessage attributes. However, as noted above, use caution when doing this because you could unintentionally be missing valid violations that should be addressed.

A new warning appeared after we corrected the ArgumentOutOfRangeException issue earlier. Rule CA1303 warns that we should not embed literal strings in our code. The recommended approach is to use a resource table with all such strings and to load each value using System.Resources .ResourceManager. Too keep this example simple, we'll suppress this message as well.

The warning "Sign 'SampleLibrary' with a strong name key" applies to the overall assembly. If you know that you'll never use this assembly in the Global Assembly Cache and will have no other need for strong names, you can suppress this message. However, because there is no specific code to which the SuppressMessage attribute can be applied, a new file, GlobalSuppressions.cs, will be added to the project with the following code:

```
[assembly: System.Diagnostics.CodeAnalysis.SuppressMessage(
    "Microsoft.Design",
    "CA2210:AssembliesShouldHaveValidStrongNames")]
```

Build the project and you should now see an empty Error List. This indicates all enabled Code Analysis rules have either been passed or suppressed.

The effect of assembly-level suppression is basically the same as if you had excluded the rule altogether. The advantage of the attribute-based approach is that it is easy to see which rules have been suppressed project-wide by viewing the GlobalSuppressions.cs file. In addition, you could add comments to that file to indicate the reason for suppressing the rule to other developers. Excluding a rule by not selecting it in the Code Analysis section of the project's properties has the same effect, but does not offer a way to document why certain exclusions were made.

Using the Command-Line Analysis Tool

Like the versions of FxCop that preceded Team System, a command-line interface is available for static code analysis. This tool, called FxCopCmd.exe, can be found in your Visual Studio 2005 installation directory under Team Tools\Static Analysis Tools\FxCop.

FxCopCmd can perform any of the code analysis functions that are available to you in the Team System IDE. In fact, the IDE uses FxCopCmd under the covers to execute analysis and generate reports.

FxCopCmd options

The following are some of the options that FxCopCmd.exe supports:

Option	Description
/f[ile]: <directory/file>	Assembly file(s) or directory(ies) to analyze. If a directory is used without a filename, Code Analysis will try to analyze all files in that directory with .dll or .exe extensions. You can specify this option more than once. It is required unless you specify a project file with the /project option.
/r[ule]:<directory/file>	A rule assembly file or a directory to browse for rule assemblies. If a directory without a filename is supplied, Code Analysis will look for rules in any files with a .dll extension. You can specify this option more than once.
/r[ule]id:<[+|-] Category#CheckId>	Enables or disables a specific rule, supplying its Category and CheckId values — for example, /rid: +!Microsoft.Usage#CA2225.
/o[ut]:<file>	Names a file in which the results of the analysis will be stored in XML form. Required unless the /console option is used.
/p[roject]:<file>	Loads a project file that contains the settings for FxCopCmd to use (discussed in the next section). Required if you do not use both the /file and /rules options.
/t[ypes]:<type list>	Used to constrain analysis to only the specified type(s). Supply a list of comma-delimited type names. Wildcards can be used to specify multiple types. Optional.
/i[mport]:<directory/file>	Loads analysis reports or project files to exclude items from the current test that appear as excluded in the imported file. You may specify a file or a directory. If a directory is specified, Code Analysis will attempt to load all files with an .xml extension. Optional.
/s[ummary]	Displays a summary after analysis. Optional.
/v[erbose]	Gives more detailed status output. Optional.
/q[uiet]	Suppresses output of status details. Optional.
/u[pdate]	Saves the results of the current analysis to the specified project file. Ignored if you do not supply the /project option. Optional.
/c[onsole]	Uses the console to display the analysis results. This is required unless you have specified the /out option.
/c[onsole]xsl:<file>	Applies an XSL file to transform XML output before displaying.
/plat[form]:<directory>	Location of platform assemblies. Optional.
/d[irectory]: <directory>	Location to search for assembly dependencies. Optional.
/help (or) /?	Help about command-line options.

Notice that most of the commands have long and short forms available. For example /summary and /s are equivalent. Arguments support using wildcards (*) to specify multiple items. Arguments with spaces in them must be surrounded with double quotes.

For example, to conduct analysis of a single assembly `CustomLibrary.dll`, use the following command:

```
FxCopCmd /f:CustomLibrary.dll /o:"FxCop Results.xml" /s
```

The `/f` (or `/file`) argument indicates which assembly to analyze and the `/o` (or `/output`) option indicates that analysis output should be stored as XML in `FxCop Results.xml`. Finally, the `/s` (or `/summary`) option will display a short summary of the results of the analysis.

FxCopCmd project files

`FxCopCmd`'s command-line options offer a good deal of flexibility, but to fine-tune your analysis, you should consider using a *project file*. A project file enables you to set options such as targets and rule assemblies, exclusions, and output preferences. You can then simply use the `/project` option to tell `FxCopCmd` to use those settings instead of supplying a detailed list of arguments.

We recommend you create a default `FxCopCmd` project file that you can copy and customize for each project. Create a new file named `EmptyCodeAnalysisProject.fxcop` and enter the contents as follows:

```xml
<?xml version="1.0" encoding="UTF-8"?>
<FxCopProject Version="8" Name="Temporary FxCop Project">
        <ProjectOptions>
                <SharedProject>False</SharedProject>
                <CompressProjectFile DefaultTargetCheck="True" DefaultRuleCheck=
"True">True</CompressProjectFile>
                <PermitAnalysis>True</PermitAnalysis>
        </ProjectOptions>
        <Targets>
        <Target Name="$(TargetFile)" Analyze="True" AnalyzeAllChildren="True" />
        </Targets>
        <RuleFiles>
        </RuleFiles>
        <FxCopReport Version="8" LastAnalysis="2004-04-20 22:08:53Z">
        </FxCopReport>
</FxCopProject>
```

Copy this to a new file and add your project's settings. The rules and files specified in your project file serve as the basis for `FxCopCmd` execution. Additional rules and target files can be specified on the command line with the `/rules` and `/file` options.

For example, here is a simple project file that specifies a target assembly, `SampleLibrary.dll`, and includes one rule assembly, the default Code Analysis naming conventions assembly:

```xml
<?xml version="1.0" encoding="UTF-8"?>
<FxCopProject Version="8" Name="Sample Library Code Analysis Project">
        <ProjectOptions>
                <SharedProject>False</SharedProject>
                <CompressProjectFile DefaultTargetCheck="True" DefaultRuleCheck=
                  "True">True</CompressProjectFile>
                <PermitAnalysis>True</PermitAnalysis>
        </ProjectOptions>
```

```
        <Targets>
                <Target Name="C:\SampleLibrary\bin\Debug\SampleLibrary.dll"
    Analyze="True"
                AnalyzeAllChildren="True" />
        </Targets>
        <RuleFiles>
                <RuleFile Name="$(FxCopDir)\Rules\NamingRules.dll" Enabled="True"
                AllRulesEnabled="True" />
        </RuleFiles>
        <FxCopReport Version="8" LastAnalysis="2004-04-20 22:08:53Z">
        </FxCopReport>
</FxCopProject>
```

Save the above to a file named `SampleLibrary.fxcop`. To execute Code Analysis for SampleLibrary using this project file, use the following command:

```
FxCopCmd /p:SampleLibrary.fxcop /o:"FxCop Results.xml" /s
```

Build process code analysis integration

You have now seen how to use `FxCopCmd` from the command line to analyze your code and report potential defects. However, with the full integration of code analysis with the Team System IDE, why would you need to use `FxCopCmd`?

One of the main reasons is for automated batch operations. A common use of `FxCopCmd` is to enable automated code analysis from a build process. You can do this with Team System's Team Build, Visual Studio 2005's MSBuild, or one of many other build automation packages available, such as NAnt.

Whichever package you use for your periodic builds, the same basic flow will apply:

1. Build the assemblies you wish to analyze (e.g., by invoking the C# or VB.Net compilers).

2. Call `FxCopCmd.exe`, specifying the `/f[ile]` option pointing to your freshly built assemblies.

3. If `FxCopCmd` outputs any notices of violations, configure your build to stop and display appropriate messages.

4. Review the reasons for the build failure.

5. If any of the rules are false positives that can be safely ignored, update your Code Analysis project file to exclude them. Save your project file and rebuild.

6. If there are any remaining warnings, make the appropriate code changes to comply with the rules.

With Team Build, you can easily enable managed code analysis. Open a build configuration by choosing Team ➪ Team Project Settings, and then click Build Configurations. Open Build Steps and check the Perform Static Analysis option. The next time your build runs, a post-build step will invoke the Code Analysis tool and include the results with the build report.

By integrating Code Analysis with your builds, you can ensure that your entire team's work is being evaluated against a consistent set of rules. You will quickly discover when a developer has added nonstandard code. Developers will quickly learn those rules and practices because they don't want to be the person responsible for "breaking the build."

Creating Code Analysis Rules

Team System includes many code analysis rules, but no matter how comprehensive the rules from Microsoft are, they can never fully cover the specific requirements of your own projects. Perhaps you have specific naming conventions or a standard way to load database connection strings. In many cases, you can create a custom code analysis rule to help diagnose the issue and help developers take corrective action.

Reflection and Introspection

Many static analysis tools use simple source-code inspection to identify issues. However, with FxCop, Microsoft decided to leverage the inherent functionality of .NET itself as the basis for creating rules. A very useful feature of .NET is called *reflection*. Using reflection, you can programmatically inspect other assemblies, classes, and members. You can even invoke methods or access fields, public or private, given appropriate security settings. Reflection is done without establishing a link to the target assembly at compilation time, a practice known as *late binding*.

Initial versions of FxCop relied on reflection as the basis for rules. However, a newer option is available, called *introspection*. Similar to reflection, introspection can inspect a target assembly to discover its types, and details about those types. It can also invoke members of those types. Introspection does this in a much faster manner than reflection and supports multi-threaded operations. Furthermore, introspection does not lock the files under analysis, a problem suffered by previous versions of FxCop that needed to use reflection. Given the clear advantages of introspection over reflection, Microsoft has leveraged introspection with the rules that are shipped with Team System. We'll also use introspection in this section for our custom rule.

Creating a new rule

Creating a new rule can be challenging, so we will walk through the creation of one in this section. We'll continue working with the SampleLibrary created earlier in this chapter. You'll recall that when you ran code analysis on the SampleLibrary, a number of potential issues were flagged. There is actually another problem with the code that is not detected by the set of rules included with Team System.

In this section, we'll create a fairly simple rule to help correct a potentially serious issue. Exposing constant values from an assembly is a normal and expected practice, but with .NET there is a surprising side effect. When a second assembly references a source assembly that exposes a constant value, the value of that constant is actually stored directly in the IL of the referencing assembly. This means that even when you change and recompile the original assembly, the value is not changed in the referencing assembly. This can lead to extremely difficult-to-diagnose problems, and will require you to recompile all referencing assemblies even though those assemblies have not changed.

To address this, we'll create a new rule, `AvoidExposingPublicConstants`, which searches a target assembly for publicly visible constant values. Begin by creating a new C# Class Library project named "CustomCodeAnalysisRules."

Code Analysis loads designated assemblies and searches them for rule classes. Code Analysis rules implement a core interface called `IRule`. Rules that use introspection also implement `IIntrospectionRule`. However, these and other related interfaces and classes are wrapped by the helpful `BaseIntrospectionRule` class. We'll use this class as the basis for our own rules. To use this base class, add a reference in the `CustomCodeAnalysisRules` project to the `FxCopSdk.dll` and `Microsoft.Cci.dll` assemblies found in the `\Team Tools\Static Analysis Tools\FxCop` directory.

Creating a base rule

As mentioned before, most of the included code analysis rules inherit, typically indirectly, from a base class called `BaseIntrospectionRule`. While each custom rule could inherit directly from this class, it's easier to create a common base class that inherits from `BaseIntrospectionRule`. This is because the constructor to `BaseIntrospectionRule` requires three arguments. The first argument is the name of the rule, and the second is the name of the XML file containing rule data. The final argument is a reference to the rule assembly type.

If you created a rule assembly with multiple rules, each rule would have to supply those three arguments each time. However, with a new base class, you can abstract away the last two arguments and keep your rule code streamlined.

Create a new file called `BaseStaticAnalysisRule.cs` and add the following code:

```
using System;
using Microsoft.FxCop.Sdk.Introspection;

namespace CustomCodeAnalysisRules
{
    public abstract class BaseStaticAnalysisRule : BaseIntrospectionRule
    {
        protected BaseStaticAnalysisRule(string name) :
            base(name,
                "CustomCodeAnalysisRules.Rules",
                typeof(BaseStaticAnalysisRule).Assembly ) { }
    }
}
```

Because the values of the second and third parameter to the `BaseIntrospectionRule` constructor will be the same for all rules in your assembly, you use this simple class as a wrapper in which those values can be set. The second argument, `CustomCodeAnalysisRules.Rules`, needs further explanation and is described in the section "Creating Rules. XML."

Implementing the rule

Now that you have a base class to use for all of your custom rules, you can create a rule. A rule has two main components:

❑ **Rule implementation code:** This is the code that analyzes the target assembly and determines whether the standard or guideline it is trying to enforce has been violated.

❑ **Rule descriptive XML:** Having the implementation code is not enough. An embedded XML fragment is required in order to help Managed Code Analysis display the rule and provide details such as descriptions and resolutions to the user.

Before you can create the rule's implementation, you need to have an approach for evaluating and inspecting a target assembly. While there are many ways you could write code to do this, Microsoft has made the job much easier by including the `Microsoft.Cci` assembly with Team System. You'll learn what this assembly is and how to use it in the following section.

Using the Microsoft.Cci assembly

The `Microsoft.Cci` assembly, or Common Compiler Infrastructure, originated from Microsoft Research and contains classes that provide features for language-based tools, such as compilers. This assembly is especially helpful for code analysis because it offers many classes that map directly to common programming constructs such as classes, fields, members, and methods. You'll use these classes to inspect target assemblies to identify the places where your rule applies.

> *You may be familiar with the* `System.CodeDom` *namespace. It is very useful for creating intermediate representations of programming constructs and then using a language provider to generate code in a desired language, such as VB.NET.* `Microsoft.Cci`, *conversely, offers additional features for reading and inspecting existing code, exactly the task we face when creating a code analysis rule.*

The following table lists the major classes offered by `Microsoft.Cci`, organized by programming concept.

Programming Concept	Related `Microsoft.Cci` Classes
Assembly	`CompilationUnit`
Namespace	`Namespace`
Types	`Class, Struct, Interface`
Type Member	`Member`
Member	`Method, Field, Property, Event, EnumNode`
Method	`Method, InstanceInitializer, StaticInitializer`
Statement	`Block, AssignmentStatement, If, For, ForEach, DoWhile, While, Continue, ExpressionStatement, VariableDeclaration, Return, Switch, Lock`
Expression	`Variable, AssignmentExpression, UnaryExpression, BinaryExpression, NaryExpression, Literal, Parameter, Local`
Exception-Related	`ExceptionHandler, Throw, Try, Catch, Finally`
Instructions and Operations	`Instruction, OpCode`

The members of the `Microsoft.Cci` namespace are organized in a hierarchical structure, with related classes organized under a parent type. For example, the `Member` class is the parent for the types of things you'd expect to have as class members, `Method`, `Property`, `Field`, `Event`, and others. If you have a `Method` instance, you can use its members to obtain references to the items it contains. For example, the `Instructions` property returns an `InstructionList` that you can use to loop through the operations of the method. Similarly, the `Method` class also has a `Pamameters` field, returning a `ParameterList` instance that can be used to inspect each parameter to the method.

To use the `Microsoft.Cci` assembly, add a reference to the `Microsoft.Cci.dll` assembly in the `\Team Tools\Static Code Analysis\FxCop` directory.

The IIntrospectionRule interface

As mentioned earlier, one of the abstractions our base class makes is the implementation of the `IIntrospectionRule` interface. This interface gives you a chance to specify the conditions under which you want your rule to be invoked. `IIntrospectionRule` contains the following members:

```
ProblemCollection Check(Member member);
ProblemCollection Check(Module module);
ProblemCollection Check(Parameter parameter);
ProblemCollection Check(Resource resource);
ProblemCollection Check(TypeNode type);
ProblemCollection Check(string namespaceName, TypeNodeList types);
```

These overloads of the `Check` method give you a chance to indicate that your rule should be called when a specific kind of programming construct is currently the focus of the code analysis engine. You do not need to implement all of the `Check` methods in your custom rules, only the ones that expose the constructs you need.

In our example, we're looking for constants in an assembly, so we need to observe the various members of each class, looking for those that are constants and exposed publicly. Therefore, we need to use the `Check(Member member)` overload. This method will be called each time the analysis engine finds any type member, be it a constant, method, field, property, or other member type.

Writing the rule implementation code

You now have a base class for your rule and an understanding of the `Microsoft.Cci` namespace and `IIntrospectionRule` methods that will help you write the implementation. Create a new class file, `AvoidExposingPublicConstants.cs`. First, add `using` statements for the namespaces you'll use:

```
using System;
using Microsoft.Cci;
using Microsoft.FxCop.Sdk;
using Microsoft.FxCop.Sdk.Introspection;
```

Now, create the class, inheriting from the `BaseStaticAnalysisRule` you created earlier:

```
namespace CustomCodeAnalysisRules
{
    public class AvoidExposingPublicConstants : BaseStaticAnalysisRule
    {
        public AvoidExposingPublicConstants() :
                base("AvoidExposingPublicConstants") {}

        public override ProblemCollection Check(Member member)
        {
            Field f = member as Field;
            if (f == null)
            {
                // Not a field
                return null;
```

```
            }

            if (member.DeclaringType is Microsoft.Cci.EnumNode)
            {
                // Inside an enumeration
                return null;
            }

            if (member.IsVisibleOutsideAssembly && f.IsLiteral)
            {
                // Is publicly visible and is a constant
                Problems.Add(new Problem(GetResolution(member.Name.Name)));
            }

            return Problems;
        }

        public override TargetVisibilities TargetVisibility
        {
            get { return TargetVisibilities.ExternallyVisible; }
        }
    }
}
```

The constructor only has to supply the name of the rule to the base class constructor, which will forward the name of your XML data store and the assembly type reference automatically to the BaseIntrospectionRule.

As we determined before, we need to implement the Check(Member member) overload from the IIntrospectionRule and search each member for constants. The first thing we do is attempt to convert the Member to a Field instance. If this fails, we know the member was not a field and we can move on to the next member. If it is a Field, we check the Member to determine whether it was declared inside of an enumeration. We're not interested in enumerations, so we also return null in this case.

Finally, we verify that the member is publicly visible with the IsVisibleOutsideAssembly property, and that it is a constant, or literal, value with the IsLiteral property. If these expressions are true, you have a publicly visible constant, and your rule has been violated.

When a rule has been violated, you must create a new Problem instance and add it to your rule's Problems collection, provided by the BaseIntrospectionRule class. The argument to a Problem constructor is a Resolution instance. The BaseIntrospectionRule class offers a GetResolution helper method that loads the resource data from the embedded XML data for the current rule. Arguments to GetResolution are automatically inserted into any placeholders such as {0} and {1} in the rule's resolution text, in the same manner as String.Format.

The new Problem is added to the Problems collection and the Problems collection is returned, indicating to the Code Analysis tool that a new violation has been added.

The final item in the rule implementation is the TargetVisibility property. This property is used by the Code Analysis tool to determine when items should be fed into the rule's Check method(s). The TargetVisibilities enumeration has values such as All, ExternallyVisible, NotExternallyVisible, and Overridable that can be combined to indicate when the rule should be tested. In our case, we only care about publicly visible members, so we return TargetVisibilities.ExternallyVisible.

Creating Rules.XML

With the implementation written, you now need to create an XML node that describes the rule and provides text to help the user understand and address rule violations. The outer `Rules` node specifies the name of the group of rules — for example, `Performance Rules`. It contains one or more `Rule` nodes, each describing a single rule.

Add a new XML file to the project. Name the file `Rules.xml` and enter the following content:

```xml
<?xml version="1.0" encoding="utf-8" ?>
<Rules FriendlyName="Custom Code Analysis Rules">
  <Rule TypeName="AvoidExposingPublicConstants" Category="Wrox.Custom"
   CheckId="CS0001">
    <Name>Avoid exposing public constants</Name>
    <Description>The values of public constants are compiled into any referencing
assemblies.  Should that value change, it is not sufficient to recompile the source
assembly because that value will also be stored in those referencing assemblies.
Avoid public constants for this reason.</Description>
    <Resolution>Change public constant '{0}' to a readonly variable, or mark it as
     private or internal.</Resolution>
    <MessageLevel Certainty="99">Warning</MessageLevel>
    <FixCategories>NonBreaking</FixCategories>
    <Url>/Custom/AvoidExposingPublicConstants.html</Url>
    <Email>yourname@yourcompany.com</Email>
    <Owner>Contact Person's Name</Owner>
  </Rule>
</Rules>
```

> You must embed the XML into the rule assembly, or the Code Analysis tool will not
> be able to load the XML and your rule will fail. Set this by right-clicking on the
> XML field and choosing Properties. Under the Advanced section, find the Build
> Action property and select Embedded Resource. When you build the assembly, the
> XML will be included in the meta-data.

The `Rule` node has a `TypeName` attribute, which should match the name of the rule class; a `Category`, which is used when displaying violations; and a `CheckId`, which uniquely identifies that rule — for example, in `SuppressMessage` attributes. `Name` is a short but friendly version of the rule name. `Description` contains the full description of what the rule is detecting.

`Resolution` is the full text shown to users to help them correct the violation. It may contain placeholders, such as `{0}`, which will automatically be replaced with values from the implementation code, as discussed in the previous section. This is extremely useful to help users quickly identify where problems exist. `Resolution` also supports an optional `Name` attribute, which enables you to specify multiple resolutions for the same rule, which can be selected at analysis time by your rule. To do so, instead of using the `GetResolution` method, use `GetNamedResolution`, supplying the name you wish to match.

`MessageLevel` provides a `Certainty` that the rule is applicable, with values from 0 to 99. A 99 indicates there is little doubt the rule has been violated and should be addressed. A lower value means violations of the rule are difficult to detect with great certainty. Use this value to indicate to the user how likely it is that a specific member or assembly has violated the rule. The element value of the `MessageLevel` can be any of the `Microsoft.Tools.FxCop.Sdk.MessageLevel` enumeration values, including `Information`,

Warning, CriticalWarning, Error, or CriticalError. Use these to indicate the relative severity of violating a rule. You can see this and the MessageLevel value in practice when you open the XML report from a Code Analysis run, as shown in Figure 8-4.

FixCategories indicate whether the changes needed to correct a rule violation should generally be considered breaking or nonbreaking. Values come from the Microsoft.Tools.FxCop.Sdk.FixCategories enumeration and can be Breaking, NonBreaking, or DependsOnFix. DependsOnFix ties back to the concept of multiple named resolutions. For example, a custom rule has two named resolutions, each used for different rule-violation scenarios. One resolution is easy to implement and considered nonbreaking, but the other is complex to correct, requiring a breaking change.

The Url is the path to an optional file that will show full details of the rule to the user, beyond what is given in the IDE. Email is the optional address of a contact person for help on the rule. Owner is the optionally provided name of a contact person for the rule.

Deploying a rule

You now have a complete rule assembly with embedded XML containing the supporting data for the contained rule(s). The easiest way to get Team System to use the contained rules is to move the assembly into the \Team Tools\Static Code Analysis\FxCop\Rules subdirectory of your Visual Studio installation directory. This will cause the IDE to recognize the rule assembly and read the contained rules so you can select them for inclusion.

However, you need to make a one-time change in order to get the Code Analysis engine to load custom rule assemblies at analysis time. MSBuild needs to be configured to load the custom rule assemblies so they can be applied. To do this, open the file Microsoft.CodeAnalysis.Targets in the C:\Program Files\MSBuild\Microsoft\VisualStudio\v8.0\Code Analysis directory. Find the CodeAnalysisRuleAssemblies node and replace it with the following line:

```
<CodeAnalysisRuleAssemblies
    Condition="'$(FxCopRuleAssemblies)'==''">$(FxCopDir)\rules
</CodeAnalysisRuleAssemblies>
```

Now, every time you run code analysis, any custom rule assemblies in the \FxCop\Rules\ directory will be loaded, and any enabled rules will be invoked.

A useful way to debug new rules is to create a single solution containing both the custom rule project and a sample target project with code that violates the rule. Open the Properties window for the rule assembly project and choose the Build Events tab. Add a post-build event command line to copy the rule assembly from the source project to the \Team Tools\Static Code Analysis\FxCop\Rules directory.

A problem with this approach is that if you open the Code Analysis properties window in either project, the custom rule assembly will be loaded and locked by the IDE. When this happens, you'll need to close and reopen Visual Studio. However, this approach will generally make your rule debugging process much easier.

Learning from existing rules

You've now seen how to create your own rules and integrate them into the Code Analysis tool of Team System. You will certainly find many uses for additional rules, but before you begin creating them you should invest some time learning from examples.

Our recommended approach for those wishing to implement custom rules is to look at how the rules that are included with Team System were written. While you don't have direct access to the source code for these rules, there is a tool that can help. "Reflector," written by Lutz Roeder and available at www.aisto.com/roeder/dotnet/, uses the power of .NET's reflection services to peer inside any assembly and generate an approximation of the source code. The target assembly can be any assembly, including those from Microsoft.

After obtaining Reflector, find the existing rules files in your Visual Studio 2005 installation directory under `Team Tools\Static Analysis Tools\FxCop\Rules`. Using Reflector, open one of the rule assemblies, such as `PerformanceRules.dll`. You can then navigate to the `Microsoft.Tools.FxCop.Rules.Performance` namespace, where you will see all of the rules in the Performance category.

Opening each rule will show you the details you've learned earlier in this chapter. The rules inherit from base helper classes, just as you saw with `AvoidExposingPublicConstants` and `BaseStaticAnalysisRule`. Opening the Resources node for any rule assembly enables you to view the XML data that was embedded in the assembly. Opening members such as the `Check` methods will show you code that, while not exactly original, will give you enough detail to determine how you might accomplish the same tasks in your own rules.

Summary

This chapter demonstrated the need for static analysis tools, introducing you to the .NET Framework Design Guidelines for Class Library Developers. These guidelines are a very important resource that Microsoft has made freely available and which are the basis for Team System's included Code Analysis rules.

We described the Managed Code Analysis tool, including how it now integrates with Visual Studio Team System and enables rule analysis to be performed with a simple build. You learned how to configure and execute analysis and how to work with the resulting rule violation messages.

To support projects using a repeatable build process or that need additional flexibility, you learned how to use the command-line Managed Code Analysis tool, and how to create `FxCopCmd` project files to store settings.

Finally, you walked through the process of creating your own rule and integrating it with your analysis process. You created the simple `AvoidExposingPublicConstants` rule as an example of how to use the new introspection engine to create new Managed Code Analysis rules in Team System.

In the next chapter, we introduce the Unmanaged Code Analysis tool. It is similar in purpose to the one described in this chapter, but is instead used for static analysis of native code.

Code Analysis for C/C++

9

Team System ships with several testing tools for C and C++ programmers. For example, AppVerifier provides support for dynamically testing unmanaged applications. Another feature, Code Analysis for C/C++ (also known as PREfast) is an integrated static code analyzer that enables you to detect security and coding defects during compile time. Here is what Code Analysis for C/C++ has to offer:

- ❑ Complete integration with Visual Studio 2005. It can check your code against a collection of memory and program execution rules. The test results window or custom logs enable you to view the list of errors and warnings, making it easy to solve potential problems.

- ❑ The C/C++ Code Analysis engine includes rich annotations and `#pragma` support to help you effectively enable, disable, filter, and manipulate errors and warnings.

- ❑ It can be launched using command-line directives, making it easy to automate and integrate with other components (such as Team Foundation Server).

Code Analysis for C/C++ does not support .NET code. The best static testing tool for .NET code is the Managed Code Analysis tool (best known as FxCop), covered in Chapter 8. Microsoft Research is currently working on a version of PREfast for the C# language called PREsharp. PREsharp information is available on the following Microsoft Research website:
`www.microsoft.com/windows/cse/pa/pa.mspx`.

Code Analysis for C/C++ is an extremely important and useful tool in Microsoft's internal software development process. They have used it extensively in the development and testing of Windows 2000, Windows Server 2003, and Windows XP. It also has been used for application security audits companywide for both the Trustworthy Computing and Secure Windows Initiatives. Code Analysis for C/C++ has been an integral tool for testing and securing the codebase for Windows XP Service Pack 2, and continues to be in wide use for a number of other products.

Code Analysis for C/C++ is only available in Visual Studio 2005 Team Developer and the Team Suite versions of Team System.

Three core versions of Code Analysis for C/C++ are currently available from Microsoft (some are still referred to as PREfast). Each version has its own specific capabilities and documentation:

❑ This chapter focuses completely on Team System's Code Analysis for C/C++.

❑ The driver-specific version (`drvfast.cmd`) is available as part of the Microsoft Windows Server 2003 Service Pack 1 Driver Development Kit (DDK). This kit is available for download from the MSDN Subscriber downloads (`http://subscriptions.msdn.com`). You can obtain a white paper and an accompanying PowerPoint presentation deck at `www.microsoft.com/whdc/devtools/tools/PREfast.mspx`.

❑ PREfast (`prefast.exe`) is available in the Platform Builder for Windows CE 5.0 SDK. Please refer to the following MSDN article for more details: `http://msdn.microsoft.com/library/en-us/wcepbguide5/html/wce50oriPREfastAnalysisTool.asp`.

Team System's C/C++ static code analyzer has been specifically designed for Win32 code on the x86 platform, as 64-bit support is not currently available.

In this chapter, we describe the advantages and challenges of static code analysis. You will learn how to use Code Analysis for C/C++ within Team System, including how to enable it, manage it, control it, and integrate and share the results on Team Foundation Server using check-in policies and bug work items. Finally, you will learn how to extend the C/C++ static code analysis engine using `#pragma` directives and inline annotations.

Understanding Static Code Analysis

Static Code Analysis is a way of analyzing source code to look for flaws in the constructs and semantics of a computer program. Your application is broken down into several flow models that simulate execution within several paths. The technical details are outlined in the section entitled "How the C/C++ Code Analyzer Works."

Static analysis through Team System (or a third-party static code analyzer) can deliver the following benefits:

❑ **Correctness:** Static code analysis checks for bad coding practices, thus improving the quality of your code.

❑ **Machine detection:** Static code analysis will help you hone in on defects that would be hard to find using manual processes.

❑ **Automation:** Static code analysis automates your testing process, enabling you to fix bugs, rather than spend your time doing extensive code reviews.

Code Analysis for C/C++ looks for specific categories of defects. You can easily use these categories to plan or model your tests. These defect categories (covered later in the chapter) can help you develop solid code review methodologies. For a complete list of warnings and errors, please refer to the C/C++ Code Analysis Warnings section in the MSDN Team System documentation.

How the C/C++ Code Analyzer Works

During the normal compilation of a C++ application, the compiler creates an internal representation of the program as objects. The linker then links these objects and converts them into executables (.exe) or Dynamic Link Libraries (.dll). Code Analysis for C/C++ intercepts the build process and attempts to run through every single execution path of your application, one function at a time. Each function is isolated; if defects are found, they are logged and displayed in the Error List within the Visual Studio 2005 IDE (more about this later).

The last three letters in the word "PREfast" stand for Abstract Structure Tree (AST). The compiler must convert your C++ into an AST to transform them into object files. (.obj). Figure 9-1 shows an example of a typical Abstract Syntax Tree. The algorithm represented in the tree is TOTAL = A+B*C/D.

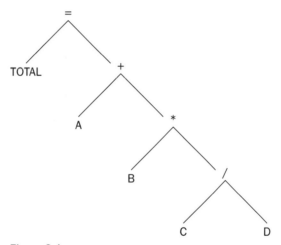

Figure 9-1

An AST can be used for both code optimization and static analysis. The static code analyzer finds bugs by walking through and analyzing the AST using every execution path it can find. If during the inspection of the tree any rules are found to be violated, an error is raised. In the following simple example, the uninitVar variable is uninitialized. As a result, the Team System PREfast analysis tool returns a C6001 warning "using uninitialized memory <variable>":

```
if (NULL != parameter) {
    uninitVar = myFunction(parameter);
}
return uninitVar;
```

Figure 9-2 shows how this code looks represented as an AST structure. You can see precisely where the rule was violated and where PREfast throws a warning or error.

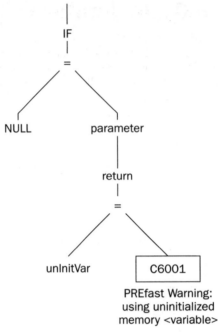

Figure 9-2

Visual Studio 2005 Integration

The incorporation of Code Analysis for C/C++ in Team System is a significant development. Until a few years ago, this feature was only available internally at Microsoft. Now, any C++ developer can benefit from the features of integrated static code analysis for maintaining better and more secure code.

Enabling and disabling C/C++ Code Analysis

Much of the work you will be doing with the C/C++ code analyzer will be within the Visual Studio 2005 test environment. You can access most of the Test windows by selecting Test ⇨ Windows from the main menu. To enable Code Analysis for C/C++, right-click on your C++ project in the Solutions Explorer and select Properties.

The project Property Pages window is shown in Figure 9-3.

1. Expand the Configuration Properties node.
2. Expand the Code Analysis node, and then click General.
3. Under the Enable Code Analysis for C/C++ Option, select Yes (/analyze).

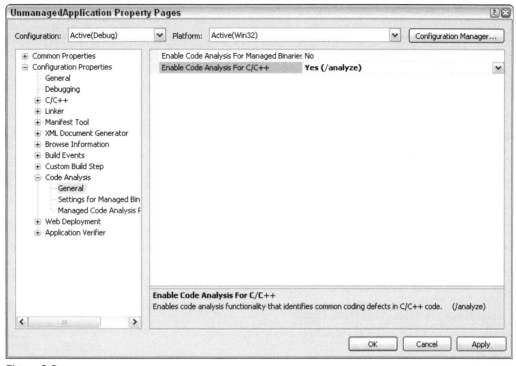

Figure 9-3

You can also enable Code Analysis for C/C++ another way:

1. Right-click on your C/C++ project in the Solutions Explorer and select Properties.

2. Expand the Configuration Properties node.

3. Expand the C/C++ node.

4. Select Advanced.

5. Set Enable Code Analysis for C/C++ to Yes (/analyze), as shown in Figure 9-4.

To disable C/C++ Code Analysis, set any of the above options to No, rather than Yes (/analyze).

Even though there are two ways of enabling C/C++ Code Analysis, you can enable or disable it in one spot, and it will automatically appear enabled or disabled in the other.

Setting warning levels in Visual Studio 2005

You can set warning level options using the Configuration Properties section of the Property Pages window. Follow these steps to change the warning levels from within the Visual Studio 2005 IDE:

1. Right-click on your C++ project and select Properties.

2. Expand Configuration Properties, then C/C++, and then General.

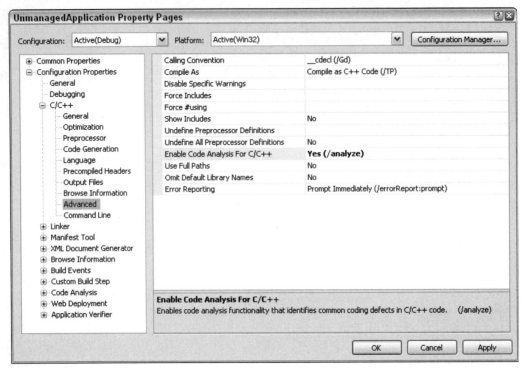

Figure 9-4

Using this window, you can set several options, including the following: Warning Level (/W<n>), Detect 64-bit Portability Issues (/Wp64), and Treat Warnings as Errors (/WX). The C/C++ General options are shown in Figure 9-5.

You can also programmatically set warning levels using #pragma directives and as options when you compile your code with the command-line compiler. Both scenarios are covered in detail later in the chapter.

Viewing code analysis warnings and errors

From this point on, if you compile or build the project, all C/C++ code analysis–related warnings and errors will be logged and displayed on the Error List. Figure 9-6 shows how the warnings are represented in the Error List window.

One of the killer features from the integration of Code Analysis for C/C++ is code highlighting. If you click on any of the warnings, Visual Studio will automatically highlight in yellow the "defect path" (in other words, all the spots in your code) where errors may have occurred. As you can imagine, this greatly facilitates the debugging process.

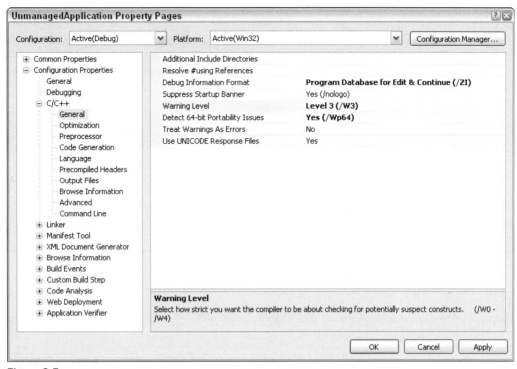

Figure 9-5

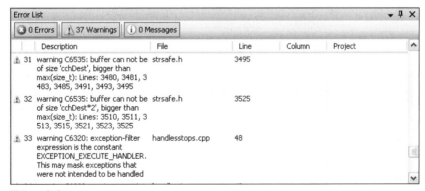

Figure 9-6

Command-line Support

Code analysis for C/C++ is integrated into the command-line compiler (`cl.exe`) that ships with Team System. Please note that code analysis is not available in the compiler included in other products (including the .NET Framework redistributable).

To compile an application using command-line code analysis, simply launch the Visual Studio Command Prompt (Start ⇨ All Programs ⇨ Visual Studio 2005 ⇨ Visual Studio Tools ⇨ Visual Studio Command Prompt). Once the prompt appears, type the following (replacing bug.cpp with the file of your choice and inserting the correct path information):

```
> cl bug.cpp /analyze
```

The /analyze option enables code analysis. If an error or warning is found, the compiler will generate an analysis report that looks something like the following:

```
Microsoft (R) 32-bit C/C++ Optimizing Compiler Version 14.00.50603 for 80x86
Copyright (C) Microsoft Corporation.  All rights reserved.
```

```
bug.cpp
C:\bug.cpp(14) : warning C6230: implicit cast between semantically different
integer types: using HRESULT in a Boolean context
C:\bug.cpp(28) : warning C6282: Incorrect operator: assignment of constant in
Boolean context. Consider using '==' instead
C:\bug.cpp(11) : warning C6014: leaking memory 'domain': Lines: 11, 14, 44
C:\bug.cpp(55) : warning C6001: using uninitialized memory 'i': Lines: 49, 50, 51,
54, 55
C:\bug.cpp(55) : warning C6001: using uninitialized memory 'j': Lines: 49, 50, 51,
52, 55
```

As you can see, Code Analysis for C/C++ will provide you with line numbers and the warning codes. The command-line version of Code Analysis for C/C++ enables you to customize the warning levels. This, in turn, gives you the ability to filter the results, both by escalating serious problems and minimizing inconsequential warnings. The warning-level options are set by adding the appropriate option in the command line. In the following example, all of the C/C++ code analysis warnings generated from testcode.cpp will be replaced by equivalent compiler errors:

```
> cl "C:\testcode.cpp"  /analyze  /WX-
```

Table 9-1 contains a list of warning-level options available via the command line.

Table 9-1

Warning Level Options	Description
/w	Disable all warnings
/wd<n>	Disable a specific warning, indicated by n
/we<n>	Convert a specific warning to an error, for warning n
/wo<n>	Display a warning n one time
/w<l><n>	Set a warning level between 1 to 4, for warning n
/W<n>	Set the warning level, for warning n
/Wall	Enable all warnings
/WL	Diagnose errors one line at a time
/WX	Convert all warnings to errors

As you have learned, you can set different warning levels within the compiler. Later in the chapter, you'll learn how to set these using #pragma directives. Warning levels can help you set the "sensitivity" of the compiler to errors and warnings. Here is a listing of the different warning levels:

- **Level 1:** This is the default level. Level 1 will reveal all critical warnings in your code and will "hide" less severe warnings.

- **Level 2:** This will display severe and moderate warnings in your code. This is the default level for the command-line tool.

- **Level 3:** This is the level that is recommended for testing code that will end up in production.

- **Level 4:** This will display all warnings, even inconsequential ones (very minor warnings are sometimes called *lint-level warnings*). This warning level should rarely be used because of the level of "noise" it generates.

Annotation Support

Annotations enable you to extend and customize the analysis of your source code on top of the built-in rules in Team System's static Code Analysis engine. Annotations are written using the Structured Annotation Language (SAL) and were introduced into the product as a much requested feature within the developer community. The source code annotation API is contained in a header file called SourceAnnotations.h found in the C:\Program Files\Microsoft Visual Studio 8\VC\ include\CodeAnalysis directory. To include this library in your source code, simply use the #include pre-processor command, as shown here:

```
#include <CodeAnalysis/SourceAnnotations.h>
```

In the CodeAnalysis directory, you will also find another header file called Warnings.h that lists all of the code analysis warnings supported in Team System (shown below). To find out the meaning of each warning code, please refer to the MSDN documentation included in Visual Studio.

```
#pragma once
#define ALL_CODE_ANALYSIS_WARNINGS 6001 6011 6014 6029 6031 6053 6054 6056 6057
 6059 6063 6064 6066 6067 6200 6201 6202 6203 6204 6209 6211 6214 6215 6216 6217
 6219 6220 6221 6225 6226 6230 6235 6236 6237 6239 6240 6242 6244 6246 6248 6250
 6255 6258 6259 6260 6262 6263 6267 6268 6269 6270 6271 6272 6273 6274 6276 6277
 6278 6279 6280 6281 6282 6283 6284 6285 6286 6287 6288 6289 6290 6291 6292 6293
 6294 6295 6296 6297 6298 6299 6302 6303 6304 6305 6306 6307 6308 6309 6310 6312
 6313 6314 6315 6316 6317 6318 6319 6320 6322 6323 6324 6326 6327 6328 6329 6331
 6332 6333 6334 6335 6336 6381 6383 6384 6385 6386 6387 6388 6390 6391 6392 6393
 6394 6400 6401 6411 6412 6500 6501 6502 6503 6504 6505 6506 6507 6508 6509 6510
 6511 6512 6513 6514 6515 6516 6517 6518 6519 6520 6521 6522 6523 6524 6525 6526
 6527 6530 6535 6990 6991 6992 6993 6994 6995 6996
```

Annotations provide you with important information about the return types and parameters of your functions. In fact, you can measure a variety of conditions, including testing for Boolean values, proper string formatting, pre- and post-conditions, and read/write conditions. Table 9-2 contains a complete list of the annotations that can be added to your source code.

Table 9-2

Attribute	Description
SA_Yes	This attribute indicates a positive outcome of a condition. For example, `Null=SA_Yes` is used to determine whether the function that is being tested returns a null value during pre- or post-instantiation.
SA_No	This attribute indicates a negative outcome of a condition.
SA_NoAccess	This attribute indicates a condition for which a function has no read/write access — for example, `Access=SA_NoAccess`.
SA_Read	This attribute indicates a condition for which a function has read access.
SA_Write	This attribute indicates a condition for which a function has write access.
SA_ReadWrite	This attribute indicates a condition for which a function has read and write access.
SA_Pre	This attribute indicates that a condition should be tested before a function is instantiated. For example: [SA_Pre(Null=SA_Yes)] `SA_Pre` and `SA_Post` are primarily used as containers to test conditions.
SA_Post	This attribute indicates that a condition should be tested after a function is instantiated. See the preceding description for an example.
SA_InvalidCheck	This attribute will check whether a function is returning a valid value, using the `Value` property.
SA_FormatString	This attribute will provide format information along with the `Style` property.

Working with annotations in C++

Annotations are written as follows in C++:

1. Include the `SourceAnnotations.h` file in your project using the following code:

```
#include <CodeAnalysis/SourceAnnotations.h>
```

2. Use `namespace vc_attributes` and then define your custom class. The namespace will allow you to use multiple attribute types within your applications:

```
using namespace vc_attributes;
class CustomClass{...}
```

Working with annotations in C

To work with annotations in C, you follow similar steps to those for C++ except that you don't have to use the `using namespace vc_attributes`. To add annotation support to your application, simply add the following `include` directive at the beginning of your code:

```
#include <CodeAnalysis/SourceAnnotations.h>
```

Here is an example of simple C application with annotations:

```
#include <CodeAnalysis/SourceAnnotations.h>
#include "customCode.h"
void t( [Post(Valid = SA_No)] int pCProg ){...}
```

#pragma Support

A pragmatic instruction (or directive) is a pre-processor directive recognized by the C++ compiler. These directives are quite practical because they enable you to manipulate and optimize the compilation of an application. Pre-processor directives are typically inserted before your source code.

Microsoft frequently uses `#pragma` directives to debug their code. Assuming you installed Visual Studio 2005 in the default `C:\` directory, you can view and edit header files created by Microsoft staff. This will give you a bit of insight into how PREfast is used internally at Microsoft and what errors tend to come up during the test phase of a Microsoft product. These header files are contained in the following directory:

```
C:\Program Files\Microsoft Visual Studio 8\VC\include\
```

In Team System, `#pragma` is used to programmatically reduce and filter unwanted noise. Let's take a look at how this is done: Warning 6001 indicates that you are trying to use an uninitialized variable somewhere in your application. The following example contains a code defect that will trigger the warning:

```
1   #include <stdio.h>
2
3   int main ()
4   {
5      int myOutput;
6      return myOutput;
7   }
```

The problem occurs at line 6, where the code is trying to return a variable with an undeclared value. If you execute this code, Team System's C/C++ Code Analysis engine will return the following warning message:

```
1   warning C6001: using uninitialized memory 'output': Lines: 5, 6
```

Let's say you are working on a test methodology and you would like to single out defects like these, which can cause corruption and instability in your application. Just add the following `#pragma` directive at the beginning of your application, and warning 6001 will be automatically converted into an error:

```
#pragma warning (error: 6001)
```

The following code shows the result displayed in the Visual Studio Error List. Instead of the yellow yield symbol, you'll get a red X at the beginning of the line. The warning matches the error, but you also get an indication of where the error lies by row and column:

```
1  using uninitialized memory  testOutput.cpp    5, 6    46
```

If you want to disable a warning outright, the `disable` warning specifier enables you to remove warnings from the Error List. To suppress the warning, you can use the following #pragma directive:

```
#pragma warning (disable: 6001)
```

Following is a list of some of the common commands you can use within the #pragma directive (for more information, be sure to take a look at the Pragma Directives article in the MSDN Library):

❑ once: The once specifier causes a warning to appear only once on the Error List. For example: `#pragma warning (once:6011)` will make the C6011 warning appear only once on the list even if there are multiple instances of the warning. This specifier is very useful to reduce the number of warning messages displayed in Visual Studio (thereby reducing unwanted noise).

❑ 1-4: This specifier sets the warning level between 1 and 4. This specifier is used in conjunction with push to set warning levels to a series of warning messages.

```
#pragma warning(push, 4)
#pragma warning(disable:6023)
#pragma warning(disable:6001)
#pragma warning(pop)
```

Both warning 6023 and 6001 are assigned a warning level of 4.

❑ push: The push specifier supresses all warning states. This is useful if you want to disable a series of warnings, as shown in the following example:

```
#pragma warning(push)
#pragma warning(disable:6031)
<Insert C++ Code here>
#pragma warning(pop)
```

❑ pop: The pop specifier restores all warning states.

Here is a cross-section of some of the common warnings you will encounter using Code Analysis for C/C++. You can view the complete list of warnings on the online MSDN Library:

❑ C6001 using uninitialized memory (var): This warning will occur after you've declared a variable's datatype and you forget to provide it with a default value, as shown here:

```
int problemVar;
return problemVar;
```

The obvious solution to this problem is to provide a value to the variable when you declare its datatype, as shown in the following example:

```
int problemVar = 1000;
```

❑ C6014 leaking memory (pointer): This warning will occur if your function returns before you try to free it. Suppose you have a pointer called pLeak; the following line of code will cause a small memory leak, which may grow with time:

```
if (pLeak){
...
return;
free(pLeak);
}
```

To correct this warning, always free your resources before you do a function return, as shown in the following example:

```
if (pLeak){
...
free(pLeak);
return;
}
```

❑   C6031 return value ignored: This warning code occurs if you forget to check for a return value, especially if you are performing a disk, file, or memory resource. The following line of code will cause you problems:

```
fopen("leak.txt","w");
```

To correct this problem, simply check for a return value in your code, as shown here:

```
FILE *textFile;
if((textFile = fopen("noleak.txt","r"))==NULL)
return;
```

Integrating with Team Foundation Server

Once you have generated the errors and warnings, there are many ways you can integrate the results with Team Foundation Server, including the following:

❑   Create a check-in policy to ensure that all members of your team are required to catch and correct all C++ code analysis errors.

❑   Create a check-in note to set who reviews the C++ code before it is checked-in.

❑   Associate a warning to a work item. You can then publish it to the Project Portal, or assign it to another member of your team.

Creating check-in policies using C/C++ code analysis

Check-in policies are essential for controlling the quality of the code entering your source code repository. Team System's source control engine comes with built-in static code analysis. All you need to do is enable it. Here are the steps:

1.   Go to the Team Explorer pane.

2.   Right-click on your Team Project and select Team Project Settings ➪ Source Control. The Source Control Settings dialog box will appear.

3. Click the Check-in Policy tab and then click New. The Add Check-in Policy dialog box appears, as shown in Figure 9-7.

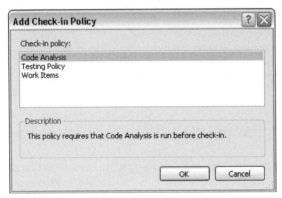

Figure 9-7

4. Now it's time to create a check-in policy that incorporates code analysis. To do this, select the Code Analysis policy in the Create New Check-in Policy dialog box.

5. The Code Analysis Policy Editor will launch, enabling you to fine-tune the policy options. An obvious choice is the Enforce C/C++ Code Analysis (/analyze) option. This will enforce a static code analysis run for all C or C++ code checked into the source repository (illustrated in Figure 9-8).

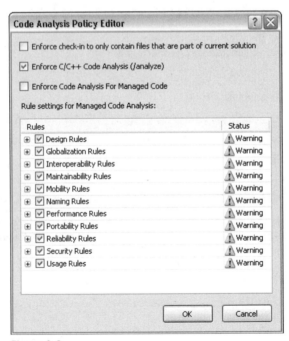

Figure 9-8

6. You can also optionally select "Enforce check-in to only contain files that are part of the solution." This option will ensure that the checked-in code is part of a solution file.

7. When you are done, click OK to enable the policy.

The check-in policy types can be toggled on and off quite easily using the Source Control Settings Check-in Policy Tab. External policies can be migrated over to your current solution by right-clicking on your solution in the Solution Explorer and selecting Migrate Code Analysis Policy Settings to Solution. You will definitely need administrative access to the source control server to create or edit check-in policies. Please refer to Chapter 20 for more details.

Setting check-in notes for your C/C++ code

Check-in notes are primarily used to define who you want to review the code and the information gathered during a check-in. Three predefined roles are allowed to review your code:

❑ **Security Reviewer:** This is a trusted member of your team who will perform a security audit on your source code. You can test the security of an application using a variety of tools, including AppVerifier and Code Analysis for C/C++.

❑ **Code Reviewer:** This is a member of your team (other than you) who is assigned the task of doing a code review. See Chapters 13 and 14 for more information on code review methodologies.

❑ **Performance Reviewer:** This team member will test the performance of your code. You can learn more about performance tweaking in Chapter 12, "Profiling and Performance."

Notes can also be used for a variety of uses, including documenting any changes to the build or your code. The notes can then be compiled into product documentation at a later date. Here are the required steps to create a check-in note for your policy:

1. Go to the Team Explorer pane.

2. Select the Source Control option from the Team Project Settings.

3. Select the Check-in Notes tab from the Source Control Settings dialog box.

4. Select one of the check-in note titles: Security Reviewer, Code Reviewer, or Performance Reviewer, as shown in Figure 9-9.

5. Click the Add button and either select a predefined check-in note in the Name drop-down box or enter a custom role (as shown in Figure 9-10).

6. The notes can be enforced by selecting the Required on Check-ins option.

You can define what notes are mandatory with a great deal of granularity using the Required column. Check-in notes can be removed in a snap using the Remove button.

If you decide to check the Required Check-ins checkbox, please note that your code will not be checked in until the user (in the designated role) enters a note. This policy enforces the good practice of getting your team to document every code review before the code is reintroduced into the source repository. Until the team member in question enters a note, the source code will continue to be checked out on your local machine.

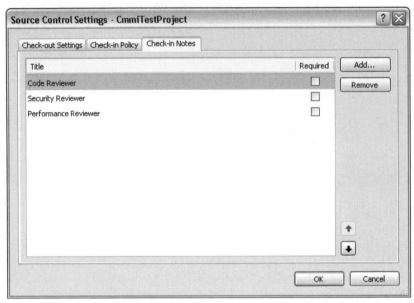

Figure 9-9

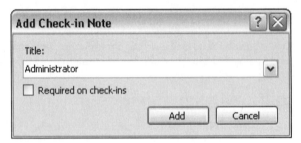

Figure 9-10

Creating work items from code analysis warnings

Once Code Analysis for C/C++ has generated significant errors or warnings, the next logical step is to file a bug. Use the following three steps to effectively manage the C/C++ code analysis within Visual Studio 2005 and Team System:

1. Understand the warning codes generated by the C/C++ code analysis engine.

2. Analyze recurring warnings and errors within the context of your project.

3. Track and resolve problems using work items.

It is in the tracking phase where work items come into play. Here are the steps to file a warning as a work item. Once it is filed, anyone on your team and the project lead will be able to effectively manage the bug:

1. If you can't see the Error List window, select View ⇨ Error List.

2. Right-click on the warning of your choice.

3. A context menu will appear. Select Create Work Item to create a bug. For more information about work items, please refer to Chapter 19.

If you enable C/C++ Code Analysis on your project, these settings will port over to the Team Foundation Build server. Therefore, if there are any static code analysis errors, they will appear in the build server report along with other errors and warnings.

Identifying and Minimizing Noise

Code Analysis for C/C++ is a very verbose tool. Even with tiny bits of code, expect a lot of warning messages. These false positive errors are usually referred to as *noise*. Microsoft devised three primary design goals for the Code Analysis for C/C++ tool:

❑ Extensibility and customization

❑ Wide developer adoption

❑ Reduction of noise

The wide adoption requirement is satisfied through the integration of C/C++ code analysis in Visual Studio 2005. To satisfy the extensibility and noise reduction requirements, Code Analysis for C/C++ offers many customization options to developers. We've examined two of these features earlier in the chapter:

❑ Annotations

❑ #pragma Support

Unlike other versions of PREfast, Team System's C/C++ static code analysis engine does not support custom filters.

Now that you have a firm grasp of the basics, let's look at a common source of noise and use customization techniques to reduce the levels in order to track down the serious errors!

Library header files are known to generate many warnings. These unintentional warnings can cause havoc in your debug process as you try to identify the serious problems in your code. Fortunately, #pragma directives can help you filter out the noise. Here is a practical example:

1. When you compile your application, one of the libraries you are using (libtmp.h) is throwing the following error codes:

```
warning C6031: return value ignored
warning C6059: Incorrect length parameter in call to getprice.
```

2. The library header file is from a trusted source and shouldn't normally be generating warnings. You try to lower the sensitivity of the warning levels to level 4 during compile time using the following command:

```
> cl.exe yourapp.cpp /analyze /W4
```

3. Unfortunately, some of the errors are persisting. In order to block these warnings, you decide to add a couple of #pragma directives in your library file. These directives effectively block the warnings appearing in the Test Explorer:

```
#pragma warning (disable:6031)
#pragma warning (disable:6059)
```

4. When you recompile the code, it runs normally with no warnings or errors.

Tool Limitations

To get the most out of Code Analysis for C/C++, you should be aware of its limitations. Here is a list of important considerations to take into account:

❑ **High noise ratio:** Code Analysis for C/C++ will misidentify a variety of errors because it has been designed to test as many execution paths as possible. You can get around the problem by using Visual Studio 2005 code coverage features to single out the important functions. You can then ignore the errors generated for noncovered code.

❑ **Completeness:** Code Analysis for C/C++ is not the "be all, end all" testing tool. It is most effective when used in combination with AppVerifier, unit tests, and other varieties of tests (see Chapter 13 for more details).

❑ **Programmer skill:** Code Analysis for C/C++ provides a "brute force" approach to finding defects. The true effectiveness of the tool depends on the skill of the programmer to identify noise, filtering the results using annotations, and so on.

❑ **Global state:** Code Analysis for C/C++ cannot recognize problems relating to the global state of an application. See the section "Identifying and Minimizing Noise" earlier in the chapter.

Summary

Code Analysis for C/C++ is a useful static code tool for uncovering errors in unmanaged C++ code. In this chapter, you learned the basics of static code analysis and were presented with a broad overview of the unmanaged code analysis features of Team System. You also learned how to navigate and use Code Analysis for C/C++ from within Visual Studio 2005 Team Developer and command-line tools. Finally, you learned how to customize the tools and found out how the unmanaged code analysis portion of Team System integrates with Team Foundation Server.

What lies in store for unmanaged code analysis in the future? Microsoft is currently working on a unified, extensible compiler framework code-named "Phoenix," which provides a plug-in architecture to create analysis and optimization tools (such as PREfast or FxCop). Phoenix works with both managed and unmanaged code, supports high- and low-level Intermediate Representations (IR), and then outputs code in the format of your choice (.NET or unmanaged executables). You can learn more about Phoenix by visiting http://research.microsoft.com/phoenix/.

Now that you've identified the problems and defects in your code, you'll want to optimize it. Visual Studio 2005 provides a number of tools to assist you in the refactoring process, as discussed in the next chapter.

10

Application Verifier

Have you ever designed an application that works on your development machine but suddenly seems to stop working (or crashes) on another system? Memory corruptions and invalid handles are sometimes hard to detect, especially if you are just looking at the source code. The Microsoft Application Verifier is a dynamic runtime testing tool specifically designed to tackle such issues. It provides a variety of run-time tests for detecting heap, handle, and lock problems.

Application Verifier works by enabling a verification layer between your target application and the Windows operating system, hooking into the instrumentation, and creating a debug environment. Once your application executable runs, key factors, such as memory allocations, are validated. If the process generates any exceptions, they are intercepted and logged in the Team System IDE. Application Verifier also verifies low-level calls to the kernel, API calls, and any DLLs loaded into your project.

Application Verifier comes in two versions: a standalone version and the version that's part of Visual Studio Team Edition for Developers (and the Visual Studio Team Suite). Application Verifier is compatible with Windows XP, Windows 2003, and later Operating Systems. It is not supported on Windows 2000.

Visual Studio's Application Verifier is an important feature of Visual Studio Team Edition for Developers. This new version of Application Verifier requires Windows XP or later (see the system requirements for Visual Studio 2005 in the ReadMe notes). You may need an operating system update to use AppVerifier. If it is not installed on you machine, you will receive a dialog box with download instructions. It is only enabled in the Debug menu when you load in a C or C++ solution (in fact, Application Verifier is not compatible with .NET applications — you'll learn why in a moment). Microsoft has narrowed down the number of tests (in handles, heaps, and locks) in this version to target the issues that affect developers the most, such as buffer overruns.

> *Fundamentally, Application Verifier is designed to test unmanaged Win32 applications. The Start With Application Verifier menu option will appear for all C/C++ projects, but clicking on this will show a message box if the underlying debug engine is anything but the native debug engine. Clicking OK on the message box will show the same behavior as Debug ⇨ Start and the*

application will not be verified. The debug engine can be changed using the project properties. A pure unmanaged project uses native debug engine by default. Managed and mixed-mode C/C++ projects use "Managed Only" and "Mixed" debug engines respectively by default. You can change the debug engine to "Native Only" for managed and mixed-mode projects. By doing so, you can use Start With Application Verifier to verify the application. In this case, it will only verify the native code in your application. If you were able to try it on a managed .NET application by changing the debug engine to "Native Only," you would notice that the tool reports a long list of problems! This is perfectly normal; the Common Language Runtime (CLR) will inevitably generate a lot of noncritical and critical errors. This is because the CLR accesses "protected" portions of the operating system. It also manages memory (via the automatic Garbage Collection routines) and handles process initialization and de-initialization. Because the run-time environment is deeply entrenched in the Windows operating system, the CLR will perform actions that are construed as application errors by Application Verifier.

Also note that you need administrative privileges to run Application Verifier; otherwise, you will receive an error message.

If you are having difficulties running Application Verifier because that option has been grayed out, be sure your C++ project is properly loaded into Visual Studio and you are not currently performing a build or debug operation on your application.

FxCop is an excellent static analysis tool specifically designed to test your .NET applications. You can find out more about FxCop in Chapter 8, "Managed Code Analysis."

Setup and Configuration

The version of Application Verifier that is integrated into Visual Studio 2005 is context sensitive. In other words, the option will only appear in the Debug menu if you create or load a C or C++ project. To start Application Verifier, select Debug ➪ Start with Application Verifier (also accessible by clicking Shift+Alt+F5).

To access the configuration panel for Application Verifier, click on your project in the Solution Explorer, and then select Properties ➪ Configuration Properties ➪ Application Verifier. The Application Verifier Properties Page window will appear, as shown in Figure 10-1.

The project property page has two setting categories: Heap Layer Advanced Settings and Verification Layers Settings. You can configure two settings within the Heap Layer Advanced Settings:

❑ **Conserve Memory:** This option accepts two possible values: Yes or No. *Guard pages* are memory bookends that are placed at the beginning or the end of your application's memory allocation in order to detect any access violations. They are great for uncovering issues such as accesses after the end of the allocated memory block. If you select the No option, guard pages will be inserted in memory and a full page heap will be implemented. As a result, you may find that your overall system performance will temporarily degrade (the overhead is an acceptable trade-off for properly debugging your application). If you don't want memory constraints on your system, select the Yes option to implement a light page heap and conserve memory. However, keep in mind that a light page heap will not catch all of the problems, and finding the root cause of the problem may be difficult

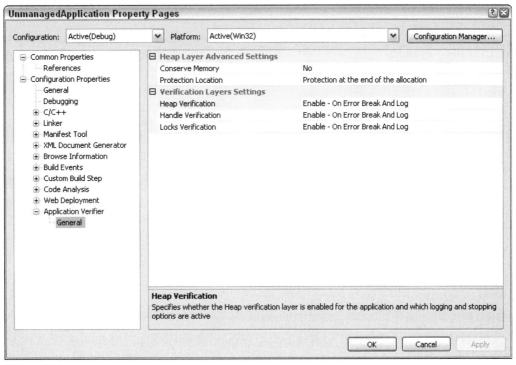

Figure 10-1

❑ **Protection Location:** The two values permitted here include "Protection at the beginning of the allocation" and "Protection at the end of the allocation." In a nutshell, these settings test for buffer underruns (at the beginning) and buffer overruns (at the end). Buffer overruns are a very common problem in unmanaged applications (buffer underruns are a less common problem). Setting the protection at the beginning of an allocation can help you detect issues such as memory accesses before the start of the allocated application memory block. You might be wondering at this point why protection location doesn't place a guard page at both the beginning and end of memory. When full page heap is used (Conserve Memory is set to No), the allocations are aligned with the page boundary. For example, if the application allocates 8 bytes, these 8 bytes are aligned with the end of the page if "Protection at the end of the allocation" is selected, and they are aligned with the beginning of the page if "Protection at the beginning of the allocation" is selected. If there is a buffer overrun or underrun, it may still be in the same page if they are only by a few bytes, which they usually are. So, putting a guard page at the beginning and end of the allocation at the same time is not going to help.

If you are interested in how the heap is structured, Team System's documentation has a great overview of both the light (or normal) heap and the full heap. Search for a document entitled "The Structure of a Page Heap Block" for more details.

You can set up several options for each verification layer on the configuration page:

❑ **Disable:** The disable option will turn off the selected verification layer. Note that if you select Disable, you will not get the full range of run-time tests on your application. Disable a verification layer only when you want to isolate a problem or when it's absolutely required.

❑ **Enable–On Error Break and Log:** By default, this option will be selected for any verification layer you choose to enable. If this option is selected, Application Verifier will show a Verifier stop message and break in to the debugger when an error is detected. It also logs a new item in the Task List (you'll learn more about this feature at the end of the chapter). The Tools window will also provide information to help you evaluate bugs.

❑ **Enable–On Error Break:** This option will also enable a verification layer and break when an error is encountered. Unlike the previous option, no tasks will appear in the Task List as a result of an error.

❑ **Enable–On Error Log and Continue:** This option enables a verification layer, creates an entry in the Task List when an error is encountered, and then the test run will resume (you will not see a Verifier stop message).

Application Verifier uses three verification layers to detect both memory-related and non-memory-related issues. You can enable or disable them at will using the Verification Layer Settings. The three layers include the following:

❑ **Heap Verification:** The heap verification component of Application Verifier looks for corruption issues related to the portion of memory allocated by the running application.

❑ **Handle Verification:** The Handle check ensures that your application doesn't use an invalid handle. This test will also verify that Thread Local Storage (TLS) indexes passed to TLS functions are valid, APIs are not called with handles that have been closed, and handles are valid when passed to APIs that take a handle. If the Handle Verifier encounters a handle with an INVALID_HANDLE_VALUE value or a NULL value, Application Verifier will break and provide you with information to investigate the problem.

❑ **Lock Verification:** The Lock Verifier checks for the correct use of the critical sections. Please refer to the Troubleshooting Locks section to learn more about critical sections.

You'll learn more about these common errors in the rest of this chapter.

Troubleshooting Heaps

In a Windows system, the heap dynamically allocates and manages memory at runtime. Application Verifier specifically checks for access issues and corruption. If you want to detect other kinds of issues, we recommend using the Debug C Run Time (DCRT) library or the Microsoft Foundation Classes (MFC) Debug library. You can learn more on the MSDN website: http://msdn.microsoft.com/library/en-us/vccore98/html/_core_memory_management_and_the_debug_heap.asp.

Another great resource for debugging unmanaged applications is John Robbins's excellent book Debugging Applications for Microsoft .NET and Microsoft Windows *(Microsoft Press, 2003).*

One of the strengths of Application Verifier is that it effectively detects corruption and memory access issues, and does so instantly! The effects of heap corruption are nefarious—a coding mistake can corrupt the heap, which in turn will cause other components to malfunction later because there is a delayed domino effect that is usually difficult to track down. Detecting heap problems without a tool such as Application Verifier can be notoriously difficult.

Depending on the memory conservation settings you picked, you can work with a full or light page heap. The distinction is important because it affects the effectiveness of the heap tests:

- **Full page heap:** This will occur when you select No in the Heap Layer Advanced Options, Conserve Memory option. As explained before, guard pages will be inserted in memory to detect memory corruption. This option enables you to easily find overrun and underrun bugs using the stack trace.

- **Light page heap:** This will occur if you choose Yes to Conserve Memory option. As a result, guard pages are disabled and there will be less consumption of memory. On the downside, although all tests will be enabled, Application Verifier will only be able to detect corruption when a memory block is freed up, which makes it hard to troubleshoot. However, in some circumstances a light page heap is preferable; especially if your application is already using nearly 3GB of memory (see the "Excessive size for the current operation" stop code for more information about Windows built-in memory limitations).

Application Verifier will return specific information about an error, including the heap handle, the block address, the size, and the trace description (in some cases, you will also receive a stack trace to help you track down the error). The following list describes some common heap-related stop codes and the techniques you can use to troubleshoot them:

- **Memory Access Operation in the context of a freed block reuse-after-delete or double-delete:** This error will occur when you try to access a block of memory in the heap after it has been freed or you are trying to repeatedly free a memory block. Once memory has been freed, it is read/write protected and any attempted accesses will result in a break.

    To fix this problem, audit any instances where you are freeing memory in your code (for example, via the `free` operation) and look for duplicates. To rectify this problem, look at the call stack at the point where the target memory has been freed. The call stack will then display where you are trying to access that block of memory in error.

- **Memory Access Operation in the context of an allocated block: heap overrun or heap underrun:** Application Verifier can effectively detect buffer overruns and underruns by inserting guard pages at the beginning or end of memory (see the Conserve Memory Heap Layer options). When these pages are accessed, Application Verifier will break into the "Memory access operation in the context of an allocated block: heap overrun or heap underrun" error.

    A heap overrun can easily be caused by trying to write to a buffer beyond the designated memory allocation. Heap overruns and underruns commonly occur with arithmetic and string operations. To fix this problem, look at the call stack for heap memory allocation information and details about where the memory overrun or underrun is happening.

- **Multithreaded access in a HEAP_NO_SERIALIZE heap:** Heap serialization is a useful feature for managing heaps in a multi-threaded application. If a thread frees a heap block and another thread tries to do the same, you will experience a double-free error. A heap created with HEAP_NO_SERIALIZE flag is not supposed to be accessed simultaneously from two threads. The typical way this situation happens in a program is by linking with a single-threaded version of the C runtime.

If you don't specify the library, the compiler will incorporate LIBC.lib by default. Be sure to add the \MT or \MD switches in your compiler commands (or within the Visual Studio IDE options) to specify multi-threaded runtime libraries. An example is shown here:

```
c:\>cl.exe /MT multithreadedapp.cpp
```

The MT switch will link your application to the static multi-threaded library (LIBCMT.lib). The MD switch compiles your application using the Dynamic Link Library (DLL) CRT library (located in MSVCRT71.DLL or MSVCRTxx.DLL).

As a best practice (unless you are writing a basic single-threaded application that requires a lot of speed), use the dynamically linked multi-threaded library. It will make your application more secure (the .DLL is regularly updated with hot fixes and service packs) and more reusable.

Please note that the single-threaded CRT libraries, libc.lib, licd.lib, msvcrt.lib, and msvcrtd.lib, are no longer supported in Visual C++ 2005.

❑ **Excessive size for the current operation:** You can use the HeapAlloc() and HeapReAlloc() operations to allocate a block of memory from the heap. However, be aware that there are limits to the size of the block, depending on the platform you are using. On the 32-bit platform, the usual value is 0x80000000 (on Windows XP, your total memory allowance is 0x7FFDEFFF — Win32 applications have a realistic upper limit of about 2GB). The 64-bit platform has a much higher limit. The stop code may also be triggered if there are problems calculating the allocation size (which would result in a negative value).

To troubleshoot this problem, perform a code review, specifically looking at the HeapAlloc() and HeapReAlloc() calls. Application Verifier will provide you with a call stack to help you track down the problem.

❑ **Heap handle with incorrect signature:** This error will appear when your heap has been corrupted by random factors, or if you have an incorrect value as a heap handle.

To troubleshoot this problem, do a code review and specifically look at all your handles (with the help of the call stack). Consider the following example:

```
HANDLE hToken = HeapCreate(0,1000,0);
```

Is hToken manipulated or altered anywhere in the rest of your code? That is where you'll find the root of your problem.

❑ **Heap operation performed on an invalid heap handle:** This error is very similar to the "Heap handle with incorrect signature" error. It will occur when you try to access a heap block using the wrong handle. This error is usually accompanied by the following message (which is very useful for tracking down the affected handle):

```
<handle identifier> was expected
```

Looking at the handle in question in your code should help you target the problem. You can use the call stack to pinpoint the problem area. This error can also occur as a result of general heap corruption.

❑ **The heap block object of the current operation is corrupted:** If Application Verifier detects a corrupted heap and can't classify the error using any of the other error codes, it will display the "The heap block object of the current operation is corrupted" stop code. This stop code will also appear when the light page heap can't validate the heap block headers.

The techniques for handling this stop code vary on a case-by-case basis. The stack trace will pinpoint the last operation that accessed the corrupted heap object. You can troubleshoot it using a code review or the CRT Debug Heap. You can learn more at http://msdn.microsoft.com/library/en-us/vsdebug/html/_core_solving_buffer_overwrites_and_memory_leaks.asp.

❑ **Attempt to destroy process heap:** You can't destroy the default process heap — any attempts to do so will result in an access violation. You can access the default heap using the GetProcessHeap() function (without any arguments).

To troubleshoot this error, look at all relevant HeapDestroy calls in your code. The call stack will pinpoint the problem area. One possible problem is that you are passing a handle to the default heap instead of your custom heap.

❑ **Unexpected exception raised in heap code path:** Unless you are validating the heap (using a function call such as HeapValidate()), this stop code indicates that there is a condition that caused an access violation. This stop code can appear, for example, when random heap corruption occurs, because of a "double-free," and when there are problems with the heap blocks. You can find and fix the source of the exception by looking at the exception record information.

❑ **Exception raised while verifying block header:** Sometimes Application Verifier will find corruption from an indeterminate source — for example, when you are trying to free up memory and you pass a pointer to an inaccessible address in memory. The header contains useful information such as user-requested size, real size, owning heap, and, in some cases, a stack trace.

Much like other "indeterminate" errors, your best bet is to look at the stack trace and review your code.

❑ **Corrupted infix pattern for freed block:** Whenever blocks of memory are freed, they are marked. When you are running a full-page heap, these blocks are marked protected and will cause access violation errors.

When you are running in light page heap, the memory blocks are marked with a distinctive infix pattern. Eventually, the block will be freed. If the infix pattern has been modified (the memory block has been corrupted), then you will receive this error and your application will break.

Your best bet for tackling this error is doing a thorough code review based on the information returned by the Application Verifier or enabling a full-page heap by setting Conserve Memory to No.

❑ **Corrupted suffix pattern:** In theory, if your memory is properly managed, it should properly fit in the space allocated to it. A *suffix pattern* is a data integrity pattern added to your application memory space when it is relegated into protected memory. Before finally disposing or reusing memory, the heap manager will look at the suffix pattern. If your application uses more memory than allocated, your suffix pattern will not match up and will throw a "Corrupted suffix pattern" error in Application Verifier.

This type of error is indicative of a buffer overrun. You can use the stack trace and the block address to pinpoint the source, but bear in mind that this particular error may be hard to troubleshoot (because you will be alerted when your application memory is freed, rather than at the source of the corruption). A solid review of the affected code can help; the only information you are provided with is the allocation stack trace and a pointer to your code when the stop code is triggered.

❑ **Corrupted start stamp of block header:** This error is very similar to the "Corrupted suffix pattern" error because it denotes that the integrity of the start stamp of the block header has been compromised. This error is indicative of a buffer underrun.

For this error, apply same recommendations for the previous stop code: Pinpoint the problem space using the stack trace and perform a code review.

❑ **Corrupted end stamp of block header:** This stop code indicates that the end stamp of your memory block header has been corrupted and your application caused a buffer underrun. Refer to the stack trace to determine where the heap allocation occurred. You can then use the call stack to find the buffer underrun.

❑ **Corrupted prefix pattern:** Like the suffix pattern, the prefix pattern can also be corrupted in the case of a buffer underrun, or if there was a buffer overrun from the previous block.

Please follow the troubleshooting guidelines outlined for the "Corrupted suffix pattern" error to solve this problem.

❑ **Process heap list count is wrong:** This stop code will come up when GetProcessHeaps() is used and the page heap manager detects problems with the process address space (sometimes caused by corruption). As mentioned before, heap corruption issues are fundamentally difficult to troubleshoot. An in-depth code review might reveal problems in some cases.

Troubleshooting Handles

Handles are tokens (or pointers) to access resources within an application. The Handle checks ensure that applications do not attempt to use invalid handles. This includes the following:

❑ Ensures that handles are valid when passed to APIs that take a handle. If a NULL value or an INVALID_HANDLE_VALUE value is passed, the handle is clearly invalid and further investigation is necessary.

❑ Ensures that TLS indexes passed to TLS functions are valid.

❑ Ensures that APIs are not called with handles that have been closed.

The following bulleted list shows handle stop codes you will commonly encounter while debugging your application. For each stop code, there is a detailed explanation on how you can troubleshoot each error:

❑ **The handle used for the current operation is invalid:** This stop code will occur in circumstances such as using a handle after closing it using CloseHandle (or trying to use an unassigned NULL handle). This error is usually generated from an application function at the top of the stack.

The easiest way to troubleshoot the error is by looking at the call stack for the operation that used the invalid handle. You can then do a code review to look for all recurrences of that handle to pinpoint the problem, especially when a CloseHandle function is called.

❑ **Invalid parameters passed to a multi-object wait function:** If you pass a NULL/invalid handle to a WaitForSingleObject call or an incorrect number of handles to a WaitForMultipleObjects call, this error is shown. You can solve the problem by looking at the call stack: Simply look for the function that is incorrectly calling the API.

❑ **A NULL handle has been used:** Using NULL handles will invariably cause unpredictable results.

To pinpoint the source of the problem, you should look at the call stack to find the reference to the NULL handle.

❑ **The current thread is performing a wait operating on a thread handle in DllMain:** The DllMain function is primarily used to perform enter/exit operations on a Dynamic Link Library (.DLL). It is used to synchronize and manage both processes and threads.

In a process, if you have a thread that is executing code using DllMain and it calls WaitForSingleObject or WaitForMultipleObjects on a thread handle, you will receive this stop code.

The problem is that the DLL loader lock is owned by the waiting thread. This will likely lead to a deadlock because the thread handle will not get signaled unless that second thread (the thread that is being waited on) is exiting. When the second thread calls ExitThread it will try to acquire the DLL loader lock and then call DllMain (DLL_THREAD_DETACH) for all DLLs in the current process. But the loader lock is owned by the first thread (the one that is waiting on the thread handle) so the two threads will deadlock. To fix this problem, look at the current call stack where the wait operation is being performed and avoid waiting on a thread handle in DllMain.

❑ **Incorrect object type for handle:** Handles are available for a number of thread synchronization mechanisms. For example, you can create handles for semaphores, mutexes, and event objects.

If you try to call a semaphore with, for example, an event object handle, you will receive the "Incorrect object type for handle" stop code. The best way to deal with this error is to look at the call stack to pinpoint the invalid object type in your code.

❑ **Invalid TLS index in the current operation:** Sometimes a programmer makes assumptions about an index value for the Thread Local Storage (TLS) instead of retrieving the value using TlsAlloc. This stop code may also occur if you are trying to pass an uninitialized variable. To solve the problem, look in the call stack for the invalid index.

Troubleshooting Locks

C++ was not originally designed to handle multi-threading. Many performance problems and application hangs can be traced back to thread management routines in your unmanaged code. Fortunately, Application Verifier includes a component called Lock Verifier (also known as the Critical Section Verifier) that checks for common problems that occur when you implement critical sections. In turn, you can troubleshoot and correct the problem from the source.

Critical sections are essential in managing resources in a multi-threaded execution environment. Imagine several applications trying to access the same code block without any management or locking mechanism. You would experience all kinds of problems, including leaks and access violations. For example, thread A might change the value of an operand to zero. Thread B would then be able to change it to some other value. Chaos would ensue.

The locks component of Application Verifier is designed to dynamically monitor all the critical sections in your code. Common errors include repeatedly initializing the same critical section or deleting it multiple times. You can avoid problems by making sure that your threads management is properly sequenced with your memory management. Another common problem that occurs is improperly matching each EnterCriticalSection with a corresponding LeaveCriticalSection.

The following list describes the stop codes generated by Application Verifier, with extra explanations and fixes to help you troubleshoot the problems in your code:

❑ **Critical section over-released or corrupted:** If a critical section is released more times than it is acquired, you may encounter this stop code.

For example, if you call DeleteCriticalSection and then try to reference the critical section object you deleted (by making calls such as LeaveCriticalSection), you run the risk of memory corruption and other problems.

Also watch out for the number of EnterCriticalSection and LeaveCriticalSection calls in your code. For each EnterCriticalSection call, there should be a corresponding LeaveCriticalSection call.

❑ **The thread cannot own a lock in this context:** When a thread is terminated, suspended, or exited, it can no longer own a critical section. This stop code will occur when the thread is in one of these states while owning an active critical section.

To troubleshoot this problem, look at your current thread and avoid calling ExitThread, SuspendThread, or TerminateThread without first exiting or deleting your critical section.

❑ **Module contains an active lock:** This stop is generated if a DLL has a global variable containing a lock and the DLL is unloaded but the critical section has not been deleted. The name of the module that has an active lock is shown in the error message. The Tool Window displays the stack trace for the critical section initialization. Also, check the contents of the current call stack when the DLL with the active lock was unloaded.

❑ **The Lock has already been initialized** or **The lock has been double initialized:** You will likely get one of these stop codes when a critical section has been initialized repeatedly or the structure of the critical section is corrupted. The net effect on your application is that it will start behaving abnormally. To troubleshoot this problem, count all your initialization/exiting calls in the call stack for orphans. You can then use the stack trace to look at the first initialization. Keep in mind that this bug can cause critical section corruption, which may provide inaccurate debug information. In those instances, the stack trace may be inaccurate.

❑ **Released virtual memory containing an active lock:** This stop is generated if the current thread is calling VirtualFree on a memory block that contains an active critical section. The application should call DeleteCriticalSection on this critical section before if frees this memory.

❑ **Released memory containing an active lock:** This stop code is very similar to "Released virtual memory containing an active lock" in that your application is trying to free heap memory that contains a critical section.

Application Verifier detects this problem using the DebugInfo field; if it is pointing to a block of memory that has been freed, a break is called.

You must first call DeleteCriticalSection before releasing memory.

❑ **The lock is corrupted:** This stop normally occurs if the DebugInfo field of the critical section is pointing to freed memory. Another valid DebugInfo structure is found in the active critical section list. Without corruption the two pointers should be identical. You should dump the memory location that is trying to be accessed by the critical section for corruption patterns.

- **The lock count is invalid:** The LockCount field indicates whether a critical section is held within the current context. The default value is -1. If it has a value of 0 or more, the critical section is held, and the OwningThread field will store the corresponding thread ID.

  If the owner is zero, then the critical section is being deleted without initializing. If it is not zero, it is being deleted while a thread still owns the critical section (e.g., LeaveCriticalSection has not been called).

- **The lock has been over released:** If you close the same lock or critical section more than once, you will encounter this stop code. You should verify the stack trace to pinpoint the source of the problem and remove any duplicate exiting routines such as LeaveCriticalSection. This is a very common error.

- **The owner of the lock is invalid, owner was expected:** This stop is generated if the owner thread ID is invalid in the current context. Check the contents of the current call stack where the thread calls EnterCriticalSection or LeaveCriticalSection. Examine the call stacks of the current owning thread and the expected owner thread.

- **The recursion count is invalid:** The recursion count field in a critical section monitors the number of times a thread acquires a lock using EnterCriticalSection or TryEnterCriticalSection. If the field is invalid in the current context, you will get this stop code. The default value for the field is 0, and will increment whenever the thread enters a new critical section. To troubleshoot, look at the call stack for instances of a thread calling LeaveCriticalSection more frequently than EnterCriticalSection.

- **Thread not supposed to be owning a lock:** Whenever a thread enters a critical section, it is noted. If a thread tries a LeaveCriticalSection call without owning the critical section, then this stop code will be raised.

  To avoid this problem, make sure that your lock count is correct. For every EnterCriticalSection, there should be a corresponding LeaveCriticalSection. Many lock errors occur as a result of a mismatch between EnterCriticalSection and LeaveCriticalSection calls.

- **The lock is being used without having been initialized:** If you try to use a critical section without initializing it or after you have exited it, you will receive this stop code. A careful code review will usually help you nail the source of the problem (you can start by looking at the call stack to find out where the lock is being used before it is initialized).

- **The region of memory about to be freed contains an active lock:** This stop is generated if the memory containing a critical section was freed but the critical section has not been deleted using DeleteCriticalSection. Typically, this stop will occur if a previous stop happens to "continue"—for example, if you encountered the *"Memory location at <address> contains an active lock"* stop and then choose to continue running your code. In most cases, the lock verifier immediately detects leaked critical sections contained in a heap allocation, a DLL range, a virtual memory allocation, or a MapViewOfFile mapped memory range. It then issues different stops in each of these cases.

For great information on concurrency, thread management, and creating Windows applications with high availability, please visit Larry Osterman's blog at http://blogs.msdn.com/larryosterman/.

Application Verifier End-to-End

Under the covers, Application Verifier is very rich in functionality, more so than you might expect. In this section, we'll take a look at an end-to-end overview of Application Verifier. Here are the steps to follow:

1. Load in your C/C++ solution (available from this book's page at www.wrox.com) into Visual Studio 2005.

2. Build your solution. Please note that the initial build may not reveal any errors or problems. However, if you have any locks, handles, or heap issues, they will show up when you launch Application Verifier.

   During the build process, you may notice in the Output Window that you are missing symbols. It is recommended that you install the latest debug symbols for your particular platform to get the full mileage from the debug and Application Verifier capabilities in Visual Studio 2005. You can download them from the following website: www.microsoft.com/whdc/devtools/debugging/symbolpkg.mspx.

3. Launch Application Verifier by selecting Debug ➪ Start with Application Verifier.

   In order to use Application Verifier on Windows XP Service Pack 2 or Windows Server 2003, you'll need to apply the update listed in the Microsoft Knowledge Base article KB889016. Otherwise, Application Verifier will not be able to catch all the potential errors in your application (because the required instrumentation API is not installed by default). If the update isn't installed on your machine, a dialog box will appear, along with a link to download it. To learn more information and download the update, please visit the following link: http://go.microsoft.com/fwlink/?LinkId=49500

4. In our example, a critical section error was discovered. Specifically, it appears that an attempt was made to release some code while it was owned by a lock. Immediately, you will see the Application Verifier Stop dialog box (see Figure 10-2). What's interesting is that different stop messages will appear on different operating systems. A general rule of thumb is that you should use the latest Windows operating system to detect the highest number of bugs.

Figure 10-2

5. If you choose the Break option, Visual Studio will provide a complete stack trace in the tool window thanks to the Locks Verification Layer. This tracing is interactive — not only does it visually provide you with information, but double-clicking on the entries will bring you immediately to the problem spots in your code (as shown in Figure 10-3).

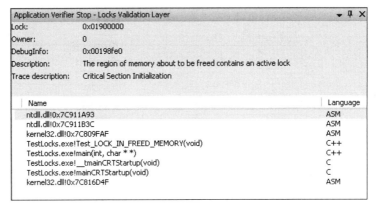

Figure 10-3

6. If you encounter a heap issue, Application Verifier provides information such as the Heap Address, Block, Size, and Description. The breaks are context-sensitive. As shown in Figure 10-4, some of the debug information is contained in your C and C++ code. Application Verifier also provides hooks to Assembly language code (ASM) to give you a wide breadth of information.

Application Verifier Stop - Heap Validation Layer		▾ ↧ ×
Heap:	0x00150000	
Block:	0x00198f00	
Size:	0x00000100	
Description:	Memory access operation in the context of a freed block: reuse-after-delete or double-delete	
Trace description:	Saved Stack Frames for the HeapFree/free/delete operation	

Name	Language
ntdll.dll!0x7C9268AD	ASM
verifier.dll!0x5AD127D1	ASM
TestHeaps.exe!Test_REUSE_AFTER_DELETE_FULL(void)	C++
TestHeaps.exe!main(int, char * *)	C++
TestHeaps.exe!__tmainCRTStartup(void)	C
TestHeaps.exe!mainCRTStartup(void)	C
kernel32.dll!0x7C816D4F	ASM

Figure 10-4

7. A handle stack trace provides you with the handle value (as shown in Figure 10-5, the value is NULL [0x00000000], so the handle is invalid), a description, and some additional information when available.

8. If you right-click on any of the stack trace entries, you can access a variety of information about the source of the problem. An option window will pop up with options for looking at the Memory Lock window, the Source Code window, or the Disassembly window.

If you are working with a handles exception, you can only access the Source Code and Disassembly windows.

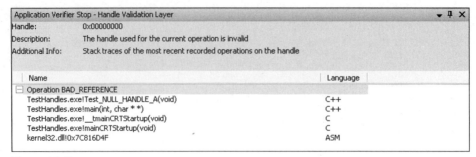

Figure 10-5

9. Figure 10-6 shows the Memory Lock window. It is a hexadecimal representation of an active chunk of memory. This window will sometimes provide you with revealing information about your errors.

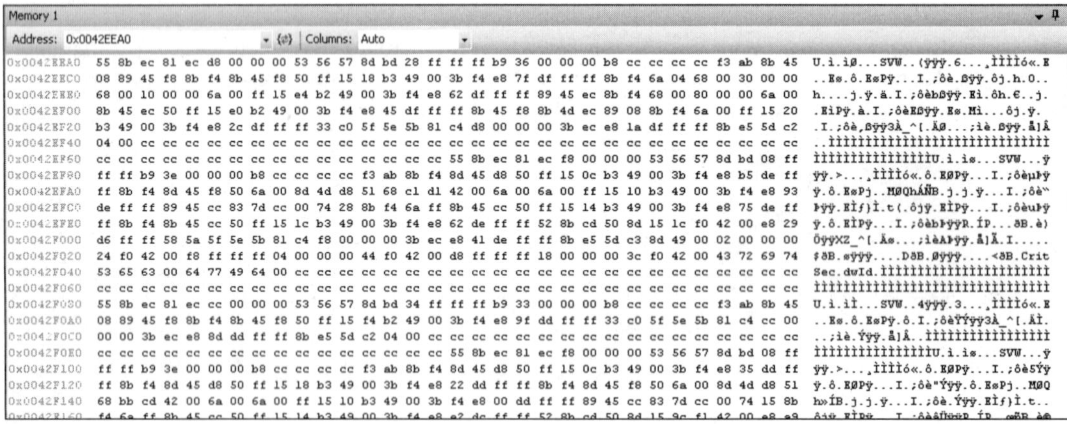

Figure 10-6

10. Figure 10-7 shows the Source Code window. This window will point you exactly to the source of the issue (in this case, a library that is freed while it owns a critical section). Consider this your control center — where you can troubleshoot and fix the code issues in your application.

11. Figure 10-8 shows the Disassembly window. Here you can look at a breakdown of the assembly calls to pinpoint the problem in your code. Microsoft has its own version of assembly language called *MASM*. If you are unfamiliar with MASM, check out the following website: http://msdn.microsoft.com/library/en-us/vcmasm/html/vcoriMicrosoftAssemblerMacroLanguage.asp.

12. Application Verifier conveniently organizes all your errors on the Task List (accessible from the lower tabs). To view the Task List, select View ⇨ Other Window ⇨ Task List. You can view the details by double-clicking on an entry.

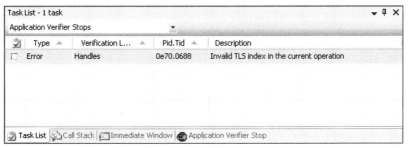

```
lockstops.cpp                                                                    ▾ ×
(Global Scope)                                              ▾  ᪥ Thread_Corrupted_Lock2(PVOID Context)  ▾

        PCRITICAL_SECTION CritSec = (PCRITICAL_SECTION)Context;
        EnterCriticalSection(CritSec);

        PVOID pMem = VirtualAlloc(0,0x1000,MEM_RESERVE|MEM_COMMIT,PAGE_READWRITE);
        VirtualFree(pMem,0,MEM_RELEASE);

        *(ULONG_PTR *)CritSec = (ULONG_PTR)pMem;
        ExitThread(0);
        return 0;
    }
```

Figure 10-7

```
Disassembly   lockstops.cpp                                                      ▾ ×
Address:  Thread_Invalid_Recursion_Count(voi ▾
 0042F242  call       @ILT+3655(__RTC_CheckEsp) (42CE4Ch)
    CritSec.RecursionCount = 0;
 0042F247  mov        dword ptr [ebp-14h],0
    LeaveCriticalSection(&CritSec);
 0042F24E  mov        esi,esp
 0042F250  lea        eax,[CritSec]
 0042F253  push       eax
 0042F254  call       dword ptr [__imp__LeaveCriticalSection@4 (49B2F4h)]
 0042F25A  cmp        esi,esp
 0042F25C  call       @ILT+3655(__RTC_CheckEsp) (42CE4Ch)
    CritSec.RecursionCount = 0;
 0042F261  mov        dword ptr [ebp-14h],0
    LeaveCriticalSection(&CritSec);
 0042F268  mov        esi,esp
 0042F26A  lea        eax,[CritSec]
 0042F26D  push       eax
 0042F26E  call       dword ptr [__imp__LeaveCriticalSection@4 (49B2F4h)]
 0042F274  cmp        esi,esp
```

Figure 10-8

```
Task List - 1 task                                                            ▾ ⤢ ×
Application Verifier Stops                          ▾
 ☑   Type  ▲    Verification L... ▲   Pid.Tid ▲   Description
 ☐   Error       Handles             0e70.0688     Invalid TLS index in the current operation




 ☑ Task List  ▣Call Stack  ▣Immediate Window  ☺ Application Verifier Stop
```

Figure 10-9

13. To view the call stack window, select Debug ⇨ Windows ⇨ Call Stack. A corresponding tab will appear below the Visual Studio 2005 IDE. The call stack provides a list of the functions, scripts, and routines loaded in memory. It can be a helpful tool for troubleshooting your application (see Figure 10-10).

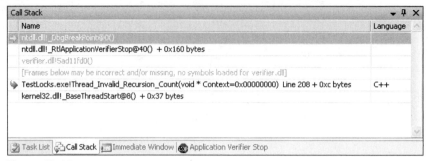

Figure 10-10

14. Once Application Verifier has completed its run, you will receive a report of the errors identified during the debug session, as shown in the following example. You can then manually log these as bug work items for your team to work on, or proceed to fix your application immediately.

```
===========================================================
VERIFIER STOP 00000200: pid 0xB48: Thread is in a state in which it cannot own a
critical section

   00000C14 : Thread identifier
   0012FD40 : Critical section address
   001B7FE0 : Critical section debug info address
   004A315C : Initialization stack trace. Use dds to dump it if non-NULL.
===========================================================
This verifier stop is not continuable. Process will be terminated
when you use the 'go' debugger comm
AVRF: Noncontinuable verifier stop 00000200 encountered. Terminating process ...
The thread 'Win32 Thread' (0xc14) has exited with code -1073741823 (0xc0000001).
The program '[2888] TestLocks.exe: Native' has exited with code -1073741823
(0xc0000001).
```

Programming Application Verifier

Application Verifier has a set of programmable hooks through the Development Tools Extensibility (DTE) model. The purpose of this model is to help you extend and automate tasks within Visual Studio 2005. The main interop assembly that exposes Application Verifier's automation model is `Microsoft .VisualC.ApplicationVerifier.dll`.

Using DTE, you can perform a variety of tasks, including programmatically creating tools and toolbars, responding to events, and launching commands. In many cases, when there is output to be displayed on the screen, it is shown in the Command window. You can access this window by clicking View ➪ Other Windows ➪ Command Window (or CTRL+ALT+A).

In this section, you'll create a Visual Studio 2005 macro that automatically launches Application Verifier. Here are the steps to build your project:

1. Select Tools ➪ Macros ➪ New Macro Project from the main toolbar.

2. This will open the New Macro Project dialog box (shown in Figure 10-11).

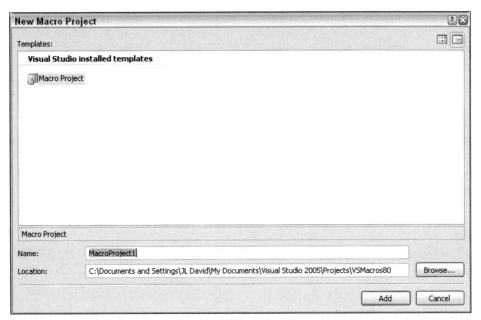

Figure 10-11

3. Select a name for your macro and click the Add button

4. The Macro Explorer window will appear (as shown in Figure 10-12).

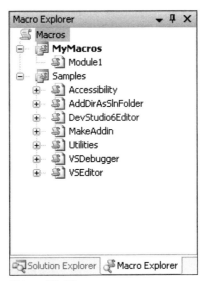

Figure 10-12

5. Double-clicking on Module1 will launch the Visual Studio Macros IDE (as shown in Figure 10-13). It should be split between the Project Explorer window and the Code window. To access the Project Explorer, click View ➪ Project Explorer.

6. Enter the following code and click the Save icon.

```
Imports System
Imports EnvDTE
Imports EnvDTE80
Imports System.Diagnostics

Public Module Module1
    Sub AppVerifMacro()

        DTE.ExecuteCommand("Debug.StartWithApplicationVerifier")
    End Sub
End Module
```

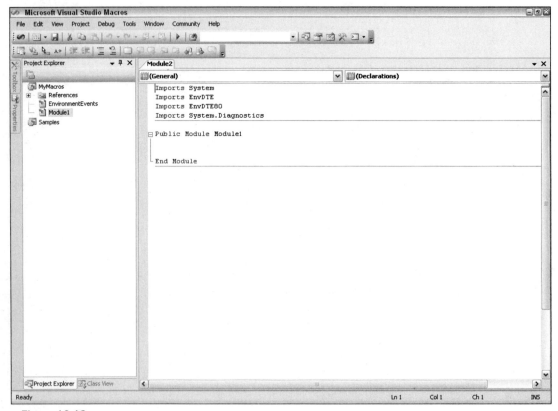

Figure 10-13

When you open the Macro IDE, you'll notice that the `EnvDTE`, `EnvDTE80`, and `System.Diagnostic` namespaces are already in place for you. All you have to add is the `System` namespace. On Line 8 of the application, we execute `Debug.StartWithApplicationVerifier` using the automation model. Note that `Debug.StartWithApplicationVerifier` is an alias for the actual UI command. You can also launch this command using the Command window by typing the following:

```
> Debug.StartWithApplicationVerifier
```

Two major command aliases are available through the Application Verifier automation model. The latter command will open the tool window. This is very useful if you want Application Verifier to output the results of the debug session:

- ❏ `Debug.StartWithApplicationVerifier`
- ❏ `Debug.ApplicationVerifierStopData`

For more information about event handling and programming Application Verifier, you have two primary sources. You can go spelunking into `Microsoft.VisualC.ApplicationVerifier.dll` (using Lutz Roeder's Reflector available at `www.aisto.com/roeder/dotnet/`) to do some trial-and-error exploration (one of the best ways to learn). Alternately, you can refer to the MSDN Library available alongside Visual Studio 2005.

Summary

Application Verifier is an essential tool for developers and testers alike. It dynamically tests your unmanaged applications for memory leaks and handle corruptions. In this chapter, you learned how to launch and configure Application Verifier, the classes of errors Application Verifier detects, including heaps, locks, and handles, and how to identify and correct problems once they occur. A good resource for finding out more about Team System's version of Application Verifier is the Microsoft Team Developer Forums at `http://forums.microsoft.com`.

Future versions of Application Verifier will detect security problems such as encryption key weaknesses and applications that fail to run in a Least-Privilege User Administration (LUA) environment, a key Windows Vista security concept that Microsoft advocates as part of their security initiatives.

11

Refactoring and Code Snippets

Refactoring is the process of changing code retrospectively to make it more comprehensible, maintainable, and efficient. Very often, you perform refactoring to apply good design practice after the fact, once the code has been written; and in that respect, refactoring blurs the edge between design and coding. That edge was getting pretty fuzzy anyway due to Visual Studio 2005's automatic synchronization between class diagrams and code (see Chapter 5); and as you'll see in this chapter, it is perfectly possible to drive some aspects of refactoring straight from Class Diagrams prior to writing a single line of code yourself.

A key principle of refactoring is that it should not change the observable behavior of your code. Following a successful refactoring, your application should work exactly as before; the external behavior should be the same even if the internal implementation is somewhat different.

You can apply refactoring techniques entirely manually, but it can be quite tricky making sure you've taken everything into account — for example, finding every invocation of a method whose parameters you have changed or reordered. It's much better to let the tool — in this case, Visual Studio 2005 — do it for you.

If you've used another IDE, such as the Eclipse, you may already be familiar with automated refactoring.

There are two ways to invoke the various refactoring types: from Class Diagrams (as we've hinted) and from code. We will demonstrate the first two refactoring types — Extract Interface and Implement Abstract Class — using Class Designer, in part because these particular refactorings may be demonstrated very effectively in pictures, and in part to underline the fact that Class Designer, unlike the Distributed System Designers, is not restricted to the Team Architect edition of Visual Studio 2005.

> Here's a tip: If you've not already done so, we recommend that even if you identify
> yourself as a "developer," rather than an "architect," you should read Chapter 5 to
> familiarize yourself with Class Designer.

As a set of code restructuring techniques, all other refactoring types will be demonstrated solely in code, invoked from within the code editor. We'll note the ones that may also be invoked from Class Diagrams.

Be aware that Visual Studio 2005 supports refactoring of C# and J# code out of the box, but not refactoring of Visual Basic code. We'll settle on C# for consistency in our demonstrations, but rest assured that the techniques applied to J# code would be very similar if not identical.

> *Refactoring of Visual Basic code is supported in the form of the "Refactor! for Visual Basic 2005" add-in,*
> *which you can download free at* http://msdn.microsoft.com/vbasic/downloads/2005/
> tools/refactor/. *We don't cover that tool here because it's not core to Visual Studio 2005, but the*
> *principle is the same so it's worth a look if this chapter whets your appetite for refactoring.*

To complete this chapter, we describe another technique for improving the quality of code, called *code snippets*. As you'll see, code snippets help to lock-down standard implementations, thereby ensuring that the same tried-and-tested technique is used throughout development, such as for error handling or logging tasks, which tend to be all pervasive.

We'll use Visual Basic .NET primarily to demonstrate the code snippets feature because it provides the richest set, but it's worth noting that a similar concept is offered to other .NET languages, such as Visual C# and Visual J#. We say "similar," not "the same," because each language offers its own unique set of snippets; and in fact prior to the Visual Studio 2005 Beta 2 release, the equivalent feature in C# was called *expansions,* rather than code snippets.

In the examples that follow, you will see our sample classes prefixed with the namespace `Refactoring`, as in `Refactoring.StockDeal`. That's because we created a Visual Studio project named `Refactoring` to contain all our examples. If you try to recreate our examples from scratch, rather than using our download ZIP, we suggest you do the same.

Refactoring from Class Diagrams

Just two refactoring types are covered in this section: Extract Interface and Implement Abstract Class, which we'll demonstrate using a C# Class Diagram.

Extract Interface

Interfaces enable you to apply polymorphism across hierarchies, namespaces, assemblies, and programming languages. They also enable you to define sets of abstract (that is, not implemented) properties, methods, and events that may be implemented by other types in compliance with a well-defined contract. Sometimes you will devise interfaces up-front, but often the need for an interface will occur to you as you add members to a class and realize that those members have usefulness beyond that one class. In such cases, you can extract those members into an interface retrospectively using the Extract Interface refactoring.

As a concrete example, consider the following scenario: Suppose that in a stockbroking application you conceive a class named StockPurchase, the purpose of which is to hold a record of the number of shares purchased by a customer for a particular stock. That class would have two private members fields, mNumberOfSharesBought and mStockSymbol, each exposed by similarly named properties NumberOfSharesBought and StockSymbol. You might also decide to expose the number of shares involved in the purchase via a shorter-named property NumberOfShares. In addition, because this application will be subject to regulatory scrutiny, you would probably add an audit method to the class, thereby enabling details of that deal to be persisted in an audit trail.

> *If you read Part 1 of this book on Team Architect, you might be experiencing some déjà vu now because we used a stockbroking system as the running example in that section. Though we're returning to that theme here, there is no mandatory link between the two sections and you can treat everything you read here as relevant in its own right.*

Besides stock purchases, you would also want to handle stock sales by devising a StockSale class, and you would correctly deduce that both the StockPurchase and StockSale classes should include a NumberOfShares and a StockSymbol. That commonality could be encoded into an abstract class (as you did in Chapter 5) or as an interface (as you will do here).

Having already devised the common properties as members of the StockPurchase class, you'll be pleased to know about a shortcut you can use to make those members available to other classes via an interface. Just right-click the class and choose Refactor ⇨ Extract Interface to launch the Extract Interface dialog, shown in Figure 11-1.

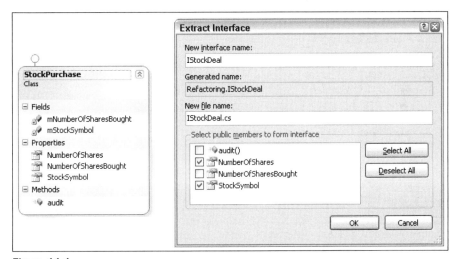

Figure 11-1

Using that dialog, you can create a new interface named IStockDeal, and select the NumberOfShares and StockSymbol properties for extraction into the interface.

You might be wondering why we haven't recommended you extract the audit method into that interface too. After all, you would want to audit sales as well as purchases. However, you might want auditing to be applied more broadly, not limited to stock sales and purchases. Maybe you would be required to audit changes to the state of any object in your application — in which case it makes sense to extract the audit method separately into an IAudit interface, to be implemented by every class.

If you take this discussion to its logical conclusion, the result would be something like what is shown in Figure 11-2.

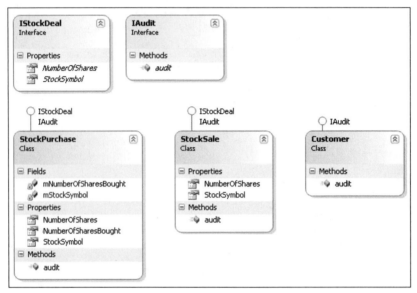

Figure 11-2

❑ The IStockDeal interface, with NumberOfShares and StockSymbol properties, was created automatically by the refactoring, as was the IAudit interface, with its audit method.

❑ The two extracted interfaces are shown emanating as a lollipop (interface) shape from the StockPurchase class.

❑ By adding a StockSale class to the diagram and drawing inheritance relationships between that class and the two interfaces, respectively, the class is populated automatically with the members required by the interfaces.

❑ By adding a Customer class to the diagram and drawing an inheritance relationship between it and the IAudit interface, we have shown that the IAudit interface may be applicable to a wider selection of classes (possibly every class), whereas the IStockDeal interface has a narrower appeal.

An extracted interface specifies only the member signatures, not their implementations, which is why private member mStockSymbol has not been copied automatically into the StockSale class in support of the StockSymbol property.

The following listing shows the result in code of the actions taken on the Class Diagram (note the inherited interfaces and auto-generated regions for properties and methods implementations):

```
public class StockSale : Refactoring.IStockDeal, Refactoring.IAudit
{

    #region IStockDeal Members
    public int NumberOfShares
    {
        get
        {
            throw new Exception("The method or operation is not implemented.");
        }

        set
        {
            throw new Exception("The method or operation is not implemented.");
        }
    }

    public String StockSymbol
    {
        get
        {
            throw new Exception("The method or operation is not implemented.");
        }

        set
        {
            throw new Exception("The method or operation is not implemented.");
        }
    }


    #endregion

    #region IAudit Members

    public void audit()
    {
        throw new Exception("The method or operation is not implemented.");
    }

    #endregion
}
```

Although we used the Class Designer for demonstration, it isn't necessary to initiate this refactoring type from there. You can also select code in the code editor, right-click, and choose Refactor ➪ Extract Interface.

Implement Abstract Class

In the previous example we used an interface (IStockDeal) to factor out the common behavior of different kinds of deals, whereas in Chapter 5 we used an abstract base class to achieve the same effect.

Assuming you took the Abstract Class route, you might conceive the abstract class first and then show one or more concrete classes deriving from it, as shown in Figure 11-3.

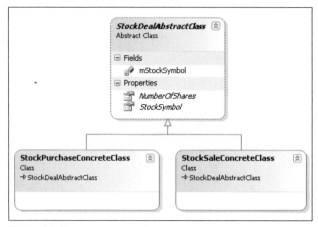

Figure 11-3

Given a diagram like the one shown, you can right-click one of the derived classes — `StockPurchaseConcreteClass` or `StockSaleConcreteClass` — and choose IntelliSense ⇨ Implement Abstract Class to copy the members from the abstract class to the (derived) concrete class.

Note that for the refactoring to take effect the members of the base class, as well as the base class itself, must all be declared as Abstract.

> *You're no doubt wondering why that refactoring type was located under the IntelliSense submenu, rather than the Refactor submenu. In fact, in the early betas of Visual Studio 2005, it did sit as a refactoring type, until Microsoft decided that because it does not truly "refactor" any code, it should reside under a different menu. We still think of it as a kind of refactoring, a counterpart of Extract Interface, and — crucially for this section — one that you can invoke directly from a class diagram.*

Refactoring in Code

As stated earlier, we'll demonstrate the majority of the refactoring types in code. In each of the following cases, we'll be using C# code.

Rename

Renaming is one of the simplest refactorings, and perhaps the most obvious in terms of the result. It's like a global search-and-replace of your sources files that enables you to change the name of a namespace, type, member, or parameter wherever it is used.

Remember the `IStockDeal` interface that was used to demonstrate the Extract Interface refactoring? Suppose you don't like the "I" prefix on interface names, even though it's a Microsoft recommended standard. How could you change the name of that interface to `StockDeal` in every place that it occurs?

Just open the `IStockDeal.cs` source file in the code editor, as shown in the following code, right-click the word `IStockDeal` in the interface definition, and choose Refactor ➪ Rename.

```
interface IStockDeal
{
    int NumberOfShares { get; set; }
    String StockSymbol { get; set; }
}
```

The Rename dialog box will appear, as shown in Figure 11-4, so that you can specify the new name of the interface. Note that in the figure, the checkbox Preview Reference Changes has been checked.

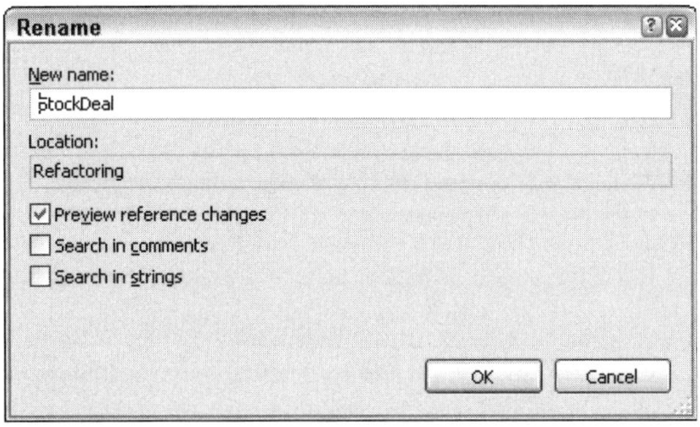

Figure 11-4

Upon pressing the OK button, the Preview Changes–Rename dialog box (shown in Figure 11-5) appears, enabling you to preview the changes that will be made in the source code. If you don't want to review the changes and instead simply want to apply them, you would uncheck the Preview Reference Changes checkbox on the previous Rename dialog.

The upper portion of this dialog shows that, besides the change to the interface definition itself, there will also be changes to the `StockPurchase` and `StockSale` classes that implement the interface. You needn't worry if you get the message "Your project or one of its dependencies does not build. References may not be updated" as shown in the figure. We're only building a set of examples to try out the techniques, not building a functional application that compiles and runs.

> Note that following this refactoring, the interface `IStockDeal` will be changed to `StockDeal` throughout your source files, but the name of the source file, `IStockDeal.cs`, will not change.

You can accept the proposed changes by clicking the Apply button, meaning you are accepting all of the changes you have reviewed — not only the one currently on display.

Before showing the effect in the source code, we suggest one more renaming. Changing the name of `StockSymbol` to `StockIdentifier` will serve to demonstrate that this refactoring type may be applied to members as well as types.

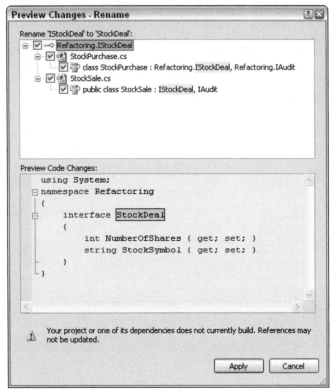

Figure 11-5

The final result of both renamings will be as shown in the following example. We list only the StockSale.cs source file as an example, but rest assured that similar changes will have been made in the StockPurchase.cs file:

```csharp
public class StockSale : Refactoring.StockDeal, Refactoring.IAudit
{

    #region IStockDeal Members
    public int NumberOfShares
    {
        get
        {
            throw new Exception("The method or operation is not implemented.");
        }

        set
        {
            throw new Exception("The method or operation is not implemented.");
        }
    }

    public String StockIdentifier
```

```
        {
            get
            {
                throw new Exception("The method or operation is not implemented.");
            }

            set
            {
                throw new Exception("The method or operation is not implemented.");
            }
        }


        #endregion

        #region IAudit Members

        public void audit()
        {
            throw new Exception("The method or operation is not implemented.");
        }

    #endregion
    }
```

You'll be interested to know that you can also perform this same refactoring from Class Designer. Just right-click the type or member on a Class Diagram and choose Refactor ⇨ Rename.

We demonstrated another use of Rename refactoring in Chapter 5, as a technique for renaming the participant classes of a pattern when applying that pattern.

Encapsulate field

Suppose another developer coded the StockPurchase class, helpfully extracted an IStockDeal interface, and provided this to you as an aid to developing your StockSale class. Without his original implementation, there would be no reason for you not to implement the interface in a slightly different way — for example, by returning the value of a mNumberOfSharesSold field directly via the NumberOfShares property that you have to implement in order to comply with the interface.

The code for your StockSale class would look like this:

```
    public class StockSale : Refactoring.IStockDeal, Refactoring.IAudit
    {

    public int NumberOfShares
    {
      get
      {
        return mNumberOfSharesSold;
      }

      set
      {
```

```
        mNumberOfSharesSold = value;
      }
    }

    ...

    private int mNumberOfSharesSold;
    private String mStockSymbol;
      }
```

There is nothing wrong with this code in terms of complying with the contract defined by the interface.

In a subsequent code review, the original developer points out — constructively, of course — that in his implementation of the StockPurchase class, there is a specifically named NumberOfSharesBought property to return the value of the private mNumberOfSharesBought field. His NumberOfShares property (required by the interface) piggybacks the aforementioned property in order to return the NumberOfSharesBought as NumberOfShares.

You think this is a great idea in terms of encapsulation, so you decide to refactor your code accordingly. You would do this by right-clicking your mNumberOfSharesSold field — in the code editor or on a Class diagram — and choosing Refactor ➪ Encapsulate Field (see Figure 11-6).

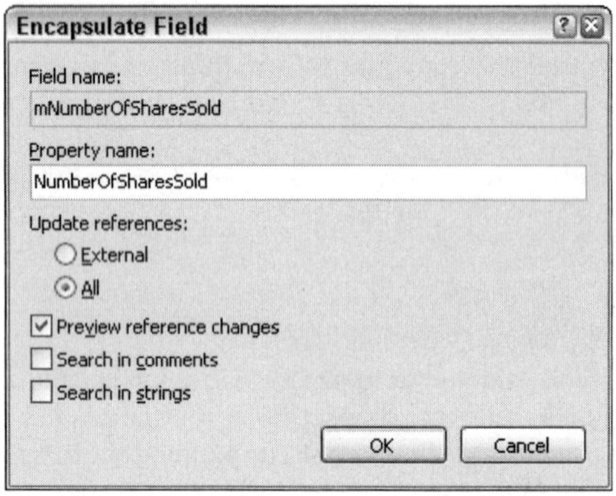

Figure 11-6

The intention is to encapsulate the mNumberOfSharesSold field with a NumberOfSharesSold property, to update all references to the field so that they now use the property, and to preview the changes that will be made before accepting them.

Not only will references be updated automatically within your project, but also across all referenced projects of the same language. If you have a Windows application that references a class library, for example, and you refactor that class library, then references to the refactored items in the class library will be corrected automatically in the Windows application.

Figure 11-7 shows a preview of one of those changes.

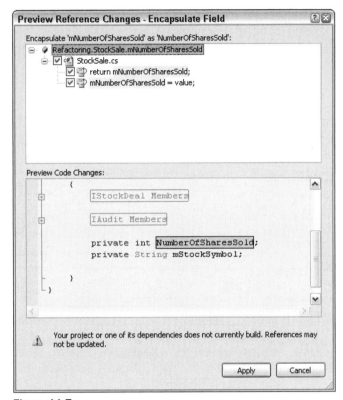

Figure 11-7

The code becomes the following:

```
public class StockSale : Refactoring.IStockDeal, Refactoring.IAudit
{

  public int NumberOfShares
  {
    get
    {
      return NumberOfSharesSold;
    }

    set
    {
      NumberOfSharesSold = value;
    }
  }

  ...
  private int mNumberOfSharesSold;

  public int NumberOfSharesSold
  {
    get
```

```
    {
        return mNumberOfSharesSold;
    }

    set
    {
        mNumberOfSharesSold = value;
    }
  }
}
```

Extract Method

In Chapter 2, we devised a Web service named DealingService, with two web methods: buyStock and sellStock. Though you need not have read that chapter, nor be already familiar with the DealingService class, we have reproduced it here as an ideal example of a class crying out for the Extract Method refactoring:

```
public class DealingService
{
    /// <summary>
    /// This operation allows a stock to be bought.
    /// </summary>
    /// <param name="stockSymbol">The unique identifier for the stock.</param>
    /// <param name="numberOfShares">The number of shares to be bought.</param>
    /// <returns>Returns the number of shares bought.</returns>
    [System.Web.Services.WebMethod(Description = ""),
        System.Web.Services.Protocols.SoapDocumentMethod(Binding = "DealingService")]
    public short buyStock(string stockSymbol, short numberOfShares)
    {
        System.Random rnd = new System.Random(numberOfShares);
        if (rnd.NextDouble() > 0.5) return numberOfShares;
        else return 0;
    }

    /// <summary>
    /// This operation allows a stock to be sold.
    /// </summary>
    /// <param name="stockSymbol">The unique identifier for the stock.</param>
    /// <param name="numberOfShares">The number of shares to be sold.</param>
    /// <returns>Returns the number of shares sold.</returns>
    [System.Web.Services.WebMethod(Description = ""),
        System.Web.Services.Protocols.SoapDocumentMethod(Binding = "DealingService")]
    public short sellStock(string stockSymbol, short numberOfShares)
    {
        System.Random rnd = new System.Random(numberOfShares);
        if (rnd.NextDouble() > 0.5) return numberOfShares;
        else return 0;
    }
}
```

In both web methods, we simulate the action of buying or selling a stock by either of the following:

❏ Returning the number of shares transacted, if we deem the deal to have succeeded

❏ Returning 0 as the number of shares transacted if we deem the deal to have failed

In our simulation, one of those results is chosen according to whether or not a randomly generated number is greater than 0.5.

You will notice that exactly the same code is used in each of the two methods, so to change the probability of a positive result in this simulation, you would need to change the value 0.5 in two places — unless, of course, you factored out the common functionality into a new method (let's call it calculateNumberOfShares) to be invoked from within each web method in place of the original code.

That's exactly what the Extract Method refactoring type enables you to do. To perform that refactoring, you would select one of the segments of code that is highlighted in the preceding code listing. For the sake of argument, we'll use the buyStock method. Right-click and choose Refactor ➪ Extract Method.

The Extract Method dialog (see Figure 11-8) enables you to specify a name for the extracted method, private static, by default because no instance-level variables were included in the code selected.

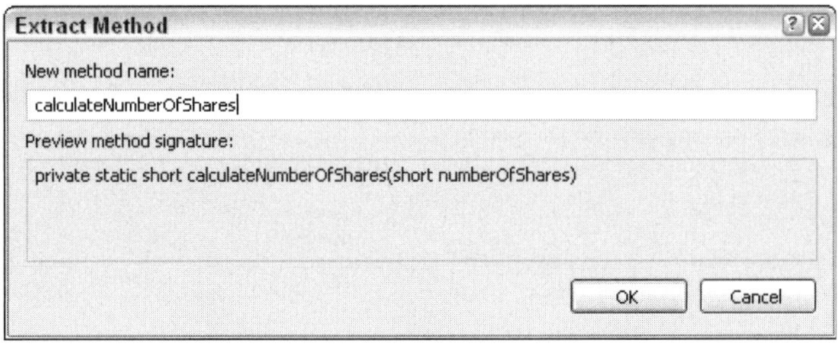

Figure 11-8

Upon accepting that, you would see the result in code as follows:

```
public short buyStock(string stockSymbol, short numberOfShares)
{
   return calculateNumberOfShares(numberOfShares);
}

private static short calculateNumberOfShares(short numberOfShares)
{
   System.Random rnd = new System.Random(numberOfShares);
   if (rnd.NextDouble() > 0.5) return numberOfShares;
   else return 0;
}
```

Notice that the selected code is now encapsulated wholly within the calculateNumberOfShares method, and that an invocation of the new method takes the place of the selected code in the buyStock method. Notice also that the numberOfShares variable, on which the result depends, has been included as a parameter of the extracted method.

The `sellStock` method will not have changed, but obviously it would now make sense to change its implementation to match that of the `buyStock` method, like this:

```
public short sellStock(string stockSymbol, short numberOfShares)
{
  return calculateNumberOfShares(numberOfShares);
}
```

Now, with the simulated result calculated in just one place, you could affect the probability of successful deals by changing this one line of code:

```
if (rnd.NextDouble() > 0.9) return numberOfShares;
```

Obviously, the more places that identical repeated code occurs, the more benefit you will gain from the Extract Method.

Promote local variable to parameter

Often, when coding a method initially, you hard-code values that you later decide should not be hard-coded at all, but rather should be parameters to the method.

Suppose you devise an audit method that writes audit trail information to a log file when invoked. Initially, you might code the method as follows:

```
public void audit()
{
  string logFileName = @"C:\auditLog.txt";
  System.IO.StreamWriter writer = System.IO.File.OpenWrite(logFileName);
  // write the audit information
  // close the file
}
```

Subsequently, you decide that the location of the log file should not be fixed within the method, but should instead be passed in as a parameter so that the location of the logged information may be varied.

To trigger the required refactoring, you can right-click the `logFileName` variable in the code editor and choose Refactor ➪ Promote Local Variable to Parameter. A dialog box will appear warning you that this will result in cascading updates, and the result will show up in code as follows:

```
public void audit(string logFileName)
{
  System.IO.StreamWriter writer = System.IO.File.OpenWrite(logFileName);
  // write the audit information
  // close the file
}
```

Note how the method now takes a parameter `string logFileName`, and how that parameter is used to open the file.

If you try out this example using the `audit` method of the `IAudit` interface (described earlier) you will see that, as warned, the change is propagated (cascaded) through the implementation hierarchy. For example, you could insert your code into the `audit` method implementation within the `StockPurchase` class, and after refactoring you could examine the StockSale class—and the IAudit interface itself—to see the new method signature applied there automatically.

Reorder parameters

This refactoring does exactly what it says on the box—it reorders the parameters of a method. As an example, take a look at the following three overloaded methods that might appear on a Customer class in a stockbroking application:

```
public IStockDeal[] getDeals(String stockSymbol)
{
   // return an array of customer deals for this stockSymbol.
}

public IStockDeal[] getDeals(String stockSymbol, DateTime dateLimit)
{
   // return an array of customer deals for this stockSymbol
   // that occurred before the specified date.
}

public IStockDeal[] getDeals(int qtyLowerLimit, String stockSymbol)
{
   // return an array of customer deals for this stockSymbol
   // where more than qtyLowerLimit shares were traded.
}
```

Though syntactically correct, there is clearly an aesthetic problem. Wouldn't you prefer the stockSymbol to be the first parameter in the last method, to match the other two? Not only that, but imagine the confusion if each method took two parameters of the same type—for example, both strings—and yet one of the methods had them arbitrarily switched around.

To resolve such problems, you can right-click the last getDeals method and choose Refactor ➪ Reorder Parameters. In the Reorder Parameters dialog (shown in Figure 11-9), you can then move parameters up and down in the list to achieve the desired ordering.

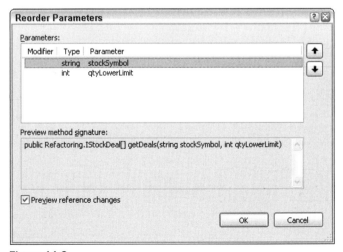

Figure 11-9

For any refactoring that changes a method's signature, it's wise to preview the changes because refactoring will affect all invocations of that method. So we checked the box in Figure 11-9, which triggers the Preview Changes dialog box to appear before you see the result in code.

The result in code, which you will have anticipated, is as follows:

```
public IStockDeal[] getDeals(String stockSymbol)
{
    // return an array of customer deals for this stockSymbol.
}

public IStockDeal[] getDeals(String stockSymbol, DateTime dateLimit)
{
    // return an array of customer deals for this stockSymbol
    // that occurred before the specified date.
}

public IStockDeal[] getDeals(String stockSymbol, int qtyLowerLimit)
{
    // return an array of customer deals for this stockSymbol
    // where more than qtyLowerLimit shares were traded.
}
```

Although we have demonstrated this refactoring type when applied to a method, be aware that the same refactoring may be applied to indexers, constructors, and delegates.

Remove parameters

Suppose you decide that each of the getDeals methods described earlier should not take in a stockSymbol at all. They should simply return a list of either all deals, deals prior to a certain date, or deals over a certain size, regardless of the particular stock.

In that case, you could right-click each method in turn and choose Refactor ➪ Remove Parameters. The Remove Parameters dialog is shown in Figure 11-10.

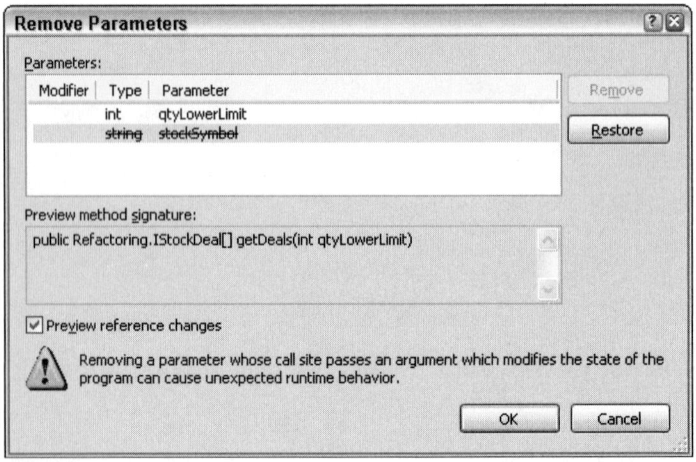

Figure 11-10

This refactoring type can be used to modify indexers, constructors, and delegates as well as methods; and in the case of methods, it's possible to trigger the refactoring from a method invocation, rather than the method declaration as just demonstrated.

Generate Method Stub

Generate Method Stub is not really a refactoring in the sense of code restructuring applied retrospectively, but we include it here as a bridge between the retrospective code improvement techniques (refactoring) described above and the proactive code improvement techniques (code snippets) discussed in the next section.

So how does it help you? Consider the code for the `audit` method described earlier. As you write that method, you might decide to insert comments to show where additional code should be added:

```
public void audit(string logFileName)
{
    System.IO.StreamWriter writer = System.IO.File.OpenWrite(logFileName);
    // write the audit information
    // close the file
}
```

Alternatively, you might go ahead and insert the required code right away, or — with your best design hat on — decide that those pieces of functionality should be factored out into separate methods. Without much thinking, you code the method like this:

```
public void audit(string logFileName)
{
    System.IO.StreamWriter writer = System.IO.File.OpenWrite(logFileName);
    writeToFile(writer, textToWrite);
    closeFile(writer);
}
```

Of course, those methods do not yet exist, which is where Generate Method Stub comes in. Just right-click the `writeToFile` method invocation and choose Generate Method Stub. Then do the same for the `closeFile` method invocation.

Your reward will be just enough code to make it compilable:

```
public void audit()
{
    string logFileName = "C:\auditLog.txt";
    System.IO.StreamWriter writer = System.IO.File.OpenWrite(logFileName);
    writeToFile(writer, textToWrite);
    closeFile(writer);
}

private void writeToFile(System.IO.StreamWriter writer, object textToWrite)
{
    throw new Exception("The method or operation is not implemented.");
}

private void closeFile(System.IO.StreamWriter writer)
```

```
    {
        throw new Exception("The method or operation is not implemented.");
    }
```

Of course, you would now need to complete the implementations of those methods.

Improving Code Quality with Code Snippets

We mentioned in the previous section that Generate Method Stub refactoring is a labor-saving technique during coding, rather than a refactoring applied wholly after the fact. Another labor-saving technique that may be applied while writing code is *code snippets*.

The basic idea is to utilize a library of pre-built tried-and-tested code segments for performing common tasks. Need to parse an XML file but can't remember how? Or not sure how other developers in your team do it? Just find the relevant code snippet.

This idea of pre-built code segments is not unique to Visual Studio 2005 and has analogues, for example, in the IBM Rational XDE Code Templates feature. That feature is described as a mechanism for locking-down implementations for reuse consistently across teams and projects — a description that fits perfectly with code snippets too.

Code snippets can be thought of as developer's equivalent to the architect's *patterns*. Using a combination of patterns (at the architectural level), code snippets (as you write the code), and refactoring (to rework the code), you can significantly improve the quality of your software development.

Using code snippets in Visual Basic

We'll demonstrate this feature using an XML parsing example. Suppose you'd like a general-purpose method that takes in a string containing XML data and displays each of the tagged elements within that string. The only problem is that you can't remember how to do it!

Well, someone else who knew how to do it has helpfully encoded that knowledge into a code snippet that you can reuse.

One way to use that snippet is to create a simple Visual Basic "Console" application project, right-click within the Main method, and choose Insert Snippet from the context menu. You should see a list of code snippet categories (see Figure 11-11) from which you can choose the XML category.

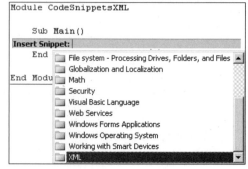

Figure 11-11

Having selected a category by double-clicking, you can then choose a specific snippet from within that category. Figure 11-12 shows the snippet Read XML from a String being chosen.

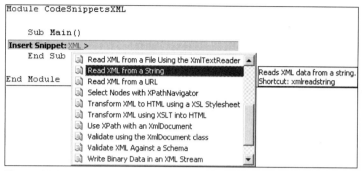

Figure 11-12

Notice in Figure 11-12 that a shortcut for this code snippet is indicated, with the name xmlreadstring. If you know the shortcut name for the code snippet you wish to include, you can simply type that short-cut name in the code editor and press the Tab key to expand the full code automatically. In this case, you would place the cursor at the required place within your code, type xmlreadstring, and press Tab.

Either way, the resultant code will be as follows:

```
Module CodeSnippetsXML

    Sub Main()
        ' Create the reader.
        Dim reader As XmlReader = XmlReader.Create(New StringReader("<book/>"))
        While reader.Read()

        End While
    End Sub

End Module
```

This code is entirely self-sufficient, and because it has been placed within the Main method of a Console application, it can be tested right away simply by running the project. Do that if you like, to confirm that it works.

Actually, that example is not too useful as it stands because the XML string is hard-coded within the example. Much more useful would be a separate method containing the XML processing code, with the XML string passed in as a parameter. That's where refactoring comes in handy.

Using a combination of the Extract Method and Promote Local Variable to Parameter refactorings, you can rework that code as follows:

```
Module CodeSnippetsXML

    Sub parseXML(ByVal xmlData As String)

        ' Create the reader.
```

```
        Dim reader As XmlReader = XmlReader.Create(New StringReader(xmlData))
        While reader.Read()

        End While

    End Sub

    Sub Main()

    Dim xmlData As String

        xmlData = _
          "<book>" & _
          "  <title>Book Title</title>" & _
          "  <price>5.95</price>" & _
          "</book>"

        parseXML(xmlData)

    End Sub

End Module
```

The parsing of the XML is now encapsulated entirely within the parseXML subroutine, thus creating a reusable method. The setting up of the XML data string is retained within the Main method purely as an example, and that code could be reworked — for example, to read the XML data string from a file, perhaps using the "Read text from a File" code snippet!

> *For the record, we created that code listing by refactoring the code manually, because — as we pointed out — the automated refactoring of Visual Basic code is not supported by Visual Studio 2005. You could try using the Refactor! for Visual Basic 2005 add-in referenced earlier.*

To make the parseXML method truly reusable, you might consider refactoring further to separate out the display statements — that is, MessageBox.Show — from the parsing code. Rather than display the elements from the XML string as they are encountered, you might collect these into an array that is returned by the parseXML method.

Using code snippets in Visual C#

The procedure for inserting snippets into Visual C# code is exactly the same as for Visual Basic. Just right-click in code and choose Insert Snippet from the context menu. Or, if you know the shortcode of the snippet, just type that shortcode and press Tab.

The first thing you'll notice is that the available snippets are not C# equivalents of the Visual Basic snippets, which admittedly seems rather inconsistent. The Visual C# snippets are mainly structural in nature and are typified by the foreach snippet that provides template code for a foreach statement. When expanded it looks like this:

```
foreach (object var in collection_to_loop)
{

}
```

Unless you routinely name your collections with the name `collection_to_loop`, that snippet will not be too useful as it stands. Visual Studio treats such variable names as replacement points that you can tab through and type whatever is appropriate for your code. In the case of the `foreach` snippet, you will be prompted initially to replace the `object` item, then (on pressing Tab) the `var` item, and then (on pressing Tab again) the `collection_to_loop` entry.

Some of the more interesting C# code snippets enable the insertion of entirely new methods, rather than code within existing methods. For example, the `equals` snippet inserts the following code, which shows how to override the default equality checking of objects:

```
// override object.Equals
public override bool Equals (object obj)
{

  //
  // See the full list of guidelines at
  //    http://msdn.microsoft.com/library/default.asp?url=/library/
  //    en-us/cpgenref/html/cpconequals.asp
  // and also the guidance for operator== at
  //    http://msdn.microsoft.com/library/default.asp?url=/library/
  //    en-us/cpgenref/html/cpconimplementingequalsoperator.asp
  //

  if (obj == null || GetType() != obj.GetType())
  {
    return false;
  }

  // TODO: write your implementation of Equals() here.
  throw new Exception("The method or operation is not implemented.");
  return base.Equals (obj);

}
```

You might be interested to know that besides inserting code snippets using Insert Snippet, you can also insert some of these same snippets by highlighting a section of code, right-clicking, and choosing Surround With from the context menu. Try this out by surrounding a block of code with a `do / while` construct.

Code Snippets Manager

Whatever language you use, the Code Snippets Manager provides full control over the snippets library. It enables you to manage a set of project-related and inter-project code assets to encourage consistency across implementations.

Choosing Tools ⇨ Code Snippets Manager triggers the dialog shown in Figure 11-13. You can see that we have navigated the VB snippets library to find the "Read XML from a String" snippet demonstrated earlier.

You can change the language from the default Visual Basic in the pull-down list to navigate the available snippets for Visual C# and Visual J#.

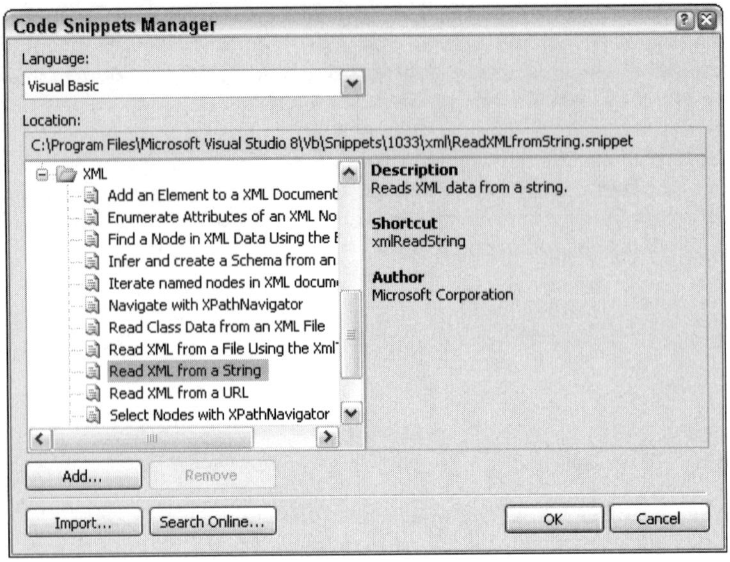

Figure 11-13

Notice that the Code Snippet Manager indicates the location where each snippet is stored, in a file-and-folder structure on disk that corresponds exactly with the hierarchy you see when inserting a snippet. On your machine, the base location for those snippets will be something like `C:\Program Files\Microsoft Visual Studio 8\Vb\Snippets\1033\`.

Each snippet is stored in its own XML file with the extension `.snippet`, such as the file `ReadXMLFrom String.snippet` listed below. Notice in particular the contents of the `<Imports>` tag, which despite its name is language agnostic but ensures that the correct `Imports` statements (VB) or `using` statements (C#) are included with the snippet. Also note the contents of the `<Code>` tag that contains the snippet code itself:

```xml
<?xml version="1.0" encoding="UTF-8"?>
<CodeSnippets xmlns="http://schemas.microsoft.com/VisualStudio/2005/CodeSnippet">
  <CodeSnippet Format="1.0.0">
    <Header>
      <Title>Read XML from a String</Title>
      <Author>Microsoft Corporation</Author>
      <Description>Reads XML data from a string.</Description>
      <Shortcut>xmlReadString</Shortcut>
    </Header>
    <Snippet>
      <References>
        <Reference>
          <Assembly>System.Xml.dll</Assembly>
          <Url />
        </Reference>
      </References>

      <Imports>
        <Import>
```

```
        <Namespace>System.IO</Namespace>
      </Import>
      <Import>
        <Namespace>System.Xml</Namespace>
      </Import>
    </Imports>

  <Declarations>
    <Literal>
      <ID>XmlString</ID>
      <Type>String</Type>
      <ToolTip>Replace with code to initialize string with XML.</ToolTip>
      <Default>"&lt;book/&gt;"</Default>
    </Literal>
  </Declarations>

    <Code Language="VB" Kind="method body"><![CDATA[' Create the reader.
Dim reader As XmlReader = XmlReader.Create(New StringReader($xmlString$))
While reader.Read()

End While]]></Code>

    </Snippet>
  </CodeSnippet>
</CodeSnippets>
```

If you refer back to Figure 11-13, you will notice additional buttons that enable you to import additional snippets and even search for new ones on the web.

If you're comfortable with the XML syntax in the previous listing, then you can even author your own snippets; and if you're not, and you're a VB programmer, then help is at hand in the form of the separate Code Snippet Editor for Visual Basic 2005, which is available for download at http://msdn .microsoft.com/vbasic/downloads/2005/tools/snippeteditor/.

Summary

This chapter described refactoring as a technique for improving the quality, readability, and performance of previously written code.

We showed how the available refactorings may be triggered from Class Designer as well as from the code editor, and in that context clarified that Class Designer is equally accessible to the developer or the architect. As it is essentially a code restructuring technique, we demonstrated the majority of the refactoring directly in code listings.

We demonstrated how the Preview Changes dialog enables you to see the effect of a refactoring before committing to it, and you saw how references to refactored items would be corrected not only within the Visual Studio project but also across all referenced projects in the same language. Be aware, though, that while you can perform refactoring on code that does not even build, there's no guarantee that all references will be updated correctly in that case.

We acknowledged that other mechanisms are available to the developer for improving the quality of code — specifically, the code snippets feature. We demonstrated how code snippets and refactoring may be used in combination and we highlighted the role of the Code Snippets Manager in facilitating the creation and organization of code snippets.

12

Profiling and Performance

One of the more difficult tasks in software development is determining why an application performs slowly or inefficiently. Before Team System, developers needed to turn to external tools to effectively analyze performance. Fortunately, Team System Team Developer Edition includes profiling tools that are fully integrated with both the IDE and other Team System features.

In this chapter, we introduce Team System's profiling tools. You'll learn how to use them to identify problems such as inefficient code, over-allocation of memory, and bottlenecks. You will learn about the two main profiling options, sampling and instrumentation, including how to use each and when each should be applied.

After you learn how to run profiling analyses, you will learn how to use the detailed reporting features that enable you to view performance metrics in a number of ways, including results by function, caller/callee inspection, call tree details, and other views.

Not all scenarios can be supported when using the Team System IDE. For times when you need additional flexibility, you will learn about the command-line options for profiling applications. This will enable you to integrate profiling with your build process and enables some advanced profiling options.

Finally, we introduce Team System's profiling APIs, which enable you to highly customize how specific aspects of your code are profiled.

Introduction to Performance Analysis

Profiling is the process of observing and recording metrics about the behavior of an application. Profilers are tools used to help identify application performance issues. Issues typically stem from code that performs slowly or inefficiently or code that causes excessive use of system memory. A profiler helps you to more easily identify these issues so they can be corrected.

Sometimes an application may be functionally correct and seem complete, but users quickly begin to complain that it seems "slow." Or perhaps you're only receiving complaints from one customer, who finds a particular feature takes "forever" to complete. Fortunately, Team System's profiling tools can help in these situations.

A common use of profiling is to identify *hotspots*, sections of code that execute frequently or for a long duration as an application runs. Identifying hotspots enables you to turn your attention to the code that will provide the largest benefit from optimization. For example, halving the execution time of a critical method that runs 20 percent of the time can improve your application's overall performance by 10 percent.

Types of profilers

Most profiling tools fall into one (or both) of two types: *sampling* and *instrumentation*. A sampling profiler takes periodic snapshots, called *samples*, of a running application, recording the status of the application at each interval, including which line of code is executing. Sampling profilers typically do not modify the code of the system under test, favoring an outside-in perspective. Think of a sampling profiler as being like a sonar system. It periodically sends out sound waves to detect information, collecting data about how the sound refracts. From that data, the system displays the locations of detected objects.

The other type, an instrumentation profiler, takes a more invasive approach. Before running analysis, the profiler adds *tracing markers*, sometimes called *probes*, at the start and end of each function. This process is called *instrumenting* an application. Instrumentation can be performed in source code or, in the case of Team System, by directly modifying an existing assembly. When the profiler is run, those probes are activated as the program execution flows in and out of instrumented functions. The profiler records data about the application and which probes were hit during execution, generating a comprehensive summary of what the program did. Think of an instrumentation profiler as the traffic data recorders you sometimes see while driving. The tubes lie across the road and record whenever a vehicle passes over. By collecting the results from a variety of locations over time, an approximation of traffic flow can be inferred.

A key difference between sampling and instrumentation is that sampling profilers will observe your applications while running any code, including calls to external libraries (such as the .NET Framework). Instrumentation profilers gather data only for the code that you have specifically instrumented.

Team System profiling

Team Developer offers powerful profiling tools that you can use to analyze and improve your applications. The profiling tools offer both sampling and instrumented approaches. Like many Team System features, profiling is fully integrated with the Visual Studio IDE and other Team System features, such as work item tracking, the build system, version control check-in policies, and more.

> *The profiling tools in Team System can be used with both managed and unmanaged applications, but the object allocation tracking features only work when profiling managed code.*

The profiling tools in Team System are based upon two tools that have been used for years internally at Microsoft. The sampling system is based on the Call Attributed Provider (CAP) tool, and the instrumentation system is based on the Low-Overhead Profiler (LOP) tool. Of course, Microsoft did not simply repackage existing internal tools and call it a day. They invested considerable development effort to add new capabilities and to fully integrate them with other Team System features.

Using the Team Developer Profiler

The Team System developers have done a good job making the profiler in Team Developer easy to use. You follow four basic steps to profile your application:

1. Create a performance session, selecting a profiling method (sampling or instrumentation) and its target(s).

2. Use the Performance Explorer to view and set the session's properties.

3. Launch the session, executing the application and profiler.

4. Review the collected data as presented in performance reports.

Each step is described in the following sections.

Creating a sample application

Before describing how to profile an application, we'll create a sample application that you can use to work through the content of this chapter. Of course, this is only for demonstration, and you can certainly use your own existing applications instead.

Create a new C# Console Application and name it DemoConsole. This application will demonstrate some differences between using a simple class and a structure. First, add a new class file called WidgetClass.cs with the following class definition:

```
namespace DemoConsole
{
    public class WidgetClass
    {
        private string _name;
        private int _id;

        public int ID
        {
            get { return _id; }
            set { _id = value; }
        }

        public string Name
        {
            get { return _name; }
            set { _name = value; }
        }

        public WidgetClass(int id, string name)
        {
            _id = id;
            _name = name;
        }
    }
}
```

Now we'll slightly modify that class to make it a value type. Make a copy of the `WidgetClass.cs` file named `WidgetValueType.cs` and open it. To make `WidgetClass` into a structure, change the word `class` to `struct`. Now rename the two places you see `WidgetClass` to `WidgetValueType` and save the file.

You should have a `Program.cs` already created for you by Visual Studio. Open that file and add the following code:

```
using System;
using System.Collections;

namespace DemoConsole
{
    class Program
    {
        static void Main(string[] args)
        {
            ProcessClasses(2000000);
            ProcessValueTypes(2000000);
        }

        public static void ProcessClasses(int count)
        {
            ArrayList widgets = new ArrayList();
            for (int i = 0; i < count; i++)
                widgets.Add(new WidgetClass(i, "Test"));

            string[] names = new string[count];
            for (int i = 0; i < count; i++)
                names[i] = ((WidgetClass)widgets[i]).Name;
        }

        public static void ProcessValueTypes(int count)
        {
            ArrayList widgets = new ArrayList();
            for (int i = 0; i < count; i++)
                widgets.Add(new WidgetValueType(i, "Test"));

            string[] names = new string[count];
            for (int i = 0; i < count; i++)
                names[i] = ((WidgetValueType)widgets[i]).Name;
        }
    }
}
```

You now have a simple application that performs many identical operations on a class and a similar structure. First, it creates an `ArrayList` and adds 2,000,000 copies of both `WidgetClass` and `WidgetValueType`. It then reads through the `ArrayList`, reading the `Name` property of each copy and storing that name in a string array. You'll see how the seemingly minor differences between the class and structure affect the speed of the application, the amount of memory used, and its effect on the .NET garbage collection process.

Creating a performance session

To begin profiling an application, you first need to create a performance session. This is normally done using the Performance Wizard, which walks you through the most common settings. You may also create a blank performance session or base a new performance session on a unit test result. Each of these methods is described below.

Using the Performance Wizard

The easiest way to create a new performance session is to use the Performance Wizard. Select Tools ➪ Performance Tools ➪ Performance Wizard. A three-step wizard will guide you through the creation of your session.

The first step, shown in Figure 12-1, is to select the target for your profiling session.

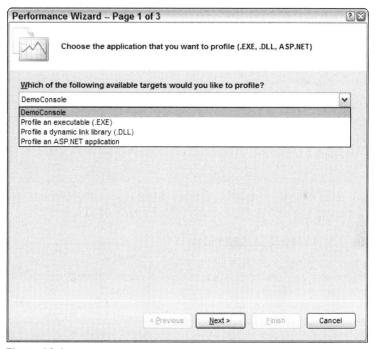

Figure 12-1

By default, the first entries in the list will be any projects in your current solution. You may also choose an executable, an assembly, or a local ASP.NET application. Select the DemoConsole application and click Next.

The second step, shown in Figure 12-2, is to select the profiling method you wish to use, Sampling or Instrumentation. You will usually want to begin with sampling for your applications, so select that for the DemoConsole profiling session.

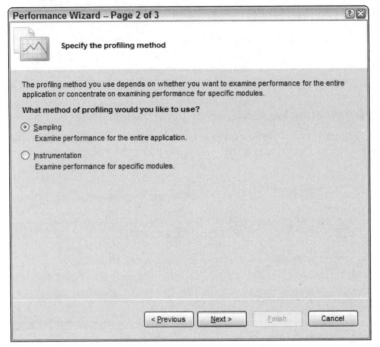

Figure 12-2

The final step is a simple confirmation of your selections. Click Finish to complete the wizard and create your new performance session. Although you can now run your performance session, you may want to change some settings. We describe these settings in the section "Setting general session properties."

Adding a blank performance session

There may be times — for example, when you're profiling a Windows Service — when manually specifying all of the properties of your session is useful or necessary. In those cases, you can skip the Performance Wizard and manually create a performance session.

Create a blank performance session by selecting Tools ⇨ Performance Tools ⇨ New Performance Session. You will see a new performance session, named "Performance1," in the Performance Explorer window. This window is described in detail in the section "Performance Explorer" later in this chapter.

After creating the blank performance session, you will need to manually specify the profiling mode, target(s), and settings for the session. We describe performance session settings in the section "Setting general session properties."

Creating a performance session from a unit test

The third option for creating a new performance session is from a unit test. Refer to Chapter 14 for a full description of the unit testing features in Team System.

There may be times when you have a unit test that verifies the processing speed (perhaps relative to another method or a timer) of a target method. Perhaps a test is failing due to system memory issues. In such cases, you might want to use the profiler to determine what code is causing problems.

To create a profiling session from a unit test, first run the unit test. Then, in the Test Results window, right-click on the test and choose Create Performance Session from the context menu, as shown in Figure 12-3. A unit test does not have to fail for you to create a performance session from it.

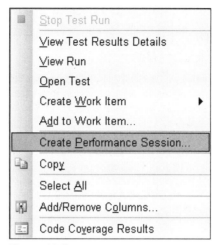

Figure 12-3

Visual Studio will then create a new performance session with the selected unit test automatically assigned as the session's target. When you run this performance session, the unit test will be executed as normal, but the profiler will be activated and collect metrics on its performance.

Performance Explorer

Once you have created your performance session, you can view it using the Performance Explorer. The Performance Explorer, shown in Figure 12-4, is used to configure and execute performance sessions and to view the results of those sessions.

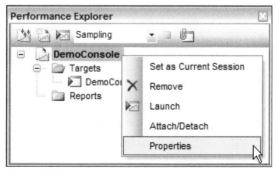

Figure 12-4

The Performance Explorer features two folders for each session: Targets and Reports. Targets specify which application(s) will be profiled when the session is launched. Reports list the results from each of the current session's runs. We describe these reports in detail later in this chapter.

Performance Explorer also supports multiple sessions. For example, you might have one session configured for sampling and another for instrumentation. We recommend you rename them from the default "PerformanceX" names for easier identification.

If you accidentally close a session in Performance Explorer, you can reopen it by using the Open option of the File menu. You will likely find the session file (ending with .psess) in your solution's folder.

Setting general session properties

Whether you used the Performance Wizard to create your session or added a blank one, you may want to review and modify the session's settings. Right-click on the session name (e.g., Performance Session.psess) and choose Properties (refer to Figure 12-4). You will see the Property Pages dialog for the session. It features several sections, described next.

In this section, we focus on the property pages that are applicable to either type of profiling sessions. These include the General, Launch, Counters, and Events pages. The other pages each apply only to one type of profiling. The Sampling page is described in the section "Configuring a sampling session," and the Binary, Instrumentation, and Advanced pages are described in the section "Configuring an instrumentation session," later in the chapter.

General property page

The General page of the Property Pages dialog is shown in Figure 12-5.

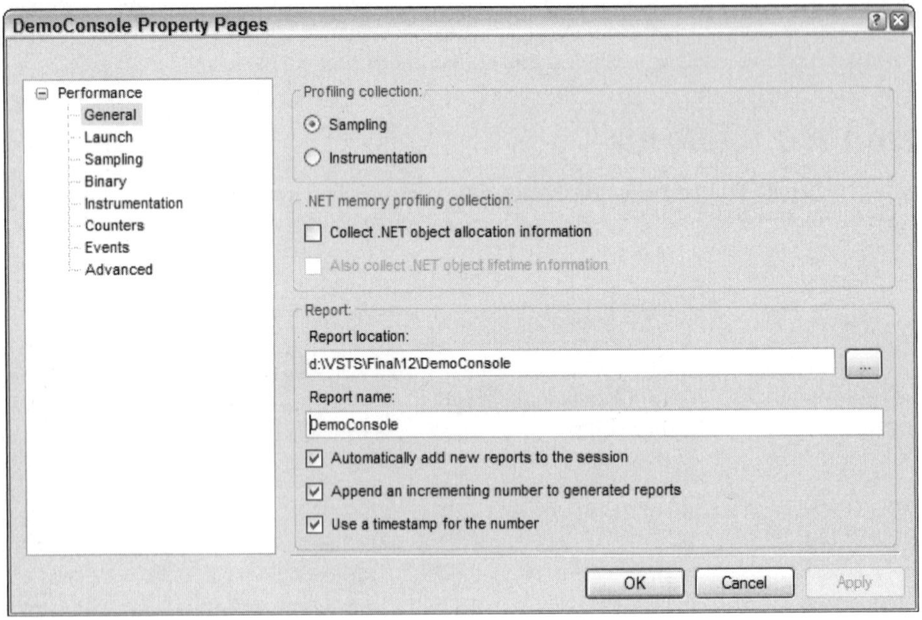

Figure 12-5

The "Profiling collection" panel of this dialog reflects your chosen profiling type (i.e., Instrumentation or Sampling).

The ".NET memory profiling collection" panel enables the tracking of managed types. When the first option, "Collect .NET object allocation information" is enabled, the profiling system will collect details about the managed types that are created during the application's execution. The profiler will track the number of instances, the amount of memory used by those instances, and which members created the instances. If the first option is selected, the second option, "Also collect .NET object lifetime information" will be enabled. If selected, additional details about the amount of time each managed type instance remains in memory will be collected. This will enable you to view further impacts of your application, such as its effect on the .NET garbage collector.

The options in the memory profiling panel are off by default. Turning them on adds substantial overhead and will cause both the profiling and report generation processes to take additional time to complete. When the first option is selected, the Allocation View of the session's report is available for review. The second option enables display of the Objects Lifetime View. These reports are described in the section "Reading and interpreting session reports."

Finally, you can use the Report panel to set the name and location of the reports that are generated after each profiling session. By default, a timestamp is used after the report name so you can easily see the date of the session run. Another default appends a number after each subsequent run of that session on a given day. (You can see the effect of these settings in Figure 12-11 later in the chapter, where multiple report sessions were run on the same day.)

For example, the settings in Figure 12-5 will run an instrumented profile without managed type allocation profiling. If run on November 19, 2005, it will produce a report named "SampleApp051119.vsp." Another run on the same day would produce a report named "SampleApp051119(1).vsp."

Launch property page

While our sample application has only one binary to execute and analyze, your projects may have multiple targets. In those cases, use the Launch property page to specify which targets should be executed when the profiling session is started or "launched." You can set the order in which targets will be executed using the Move Up and Move Down arrow buttons.

Targets are described in the section "Configuring session targets" later in this chapter.

Counters property page

The Counters property page, shown in Figure 12-6, is used to enable the collecting of CPU-related performance counters as your profiling sessions run. Enable the counters by checking Collect Chip Performance Counter Data. Then, select the counters you wish to track from the Available Counters list and click the right-pointing arrow button to add them to the Selected Counters list.

Events property page

The Events property page enables you to collect additional trace information from a variety of event providers. This can include items from Windows itself, such as disk and file I/O as well as the .NET Framework itself. If you're profiling an ASP.NET application, for example, you can collect information from IIS and ASP.NET.

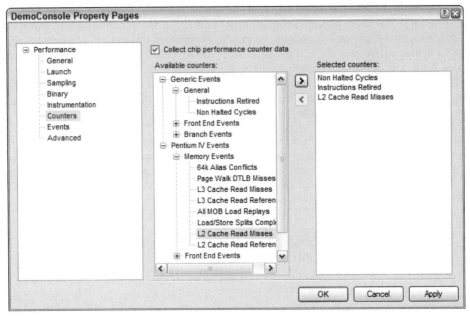

Figure 12-6

Configuring session targets

If you used the Performance Wizard to create your session, you will already have a target specified. You can modify your session's targets with the Performance Explorer. Simply right-click on the Targets folder and choose Add Target Binary, or, if you have a valid candidate project in your current solution, Add Target Project. You can also add an ASP.NET website target by selecting Add Existing Web Site.

Each session target can be configured independently. Right-click on any target and you will see a context menu like the one shown in Figure 12-7.

The properties of a target are different from those of the overall session, so be careful to right-click on a target and not the performance session's root node.

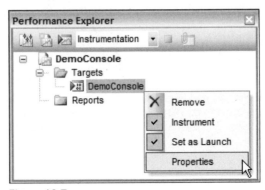

Figure 12-7

If the session's mode is instrumentation, an Instrument option will also be available. This indicates that when you run this session, that target will be included and observed. This option is not shown if your collection mode is set to sampling because sampling automatically observes any executing code.

The other option is Set as Launch. When you have multiple targets in a session, you should indicate which of the targets will be started when the session is launched. For example, you could have several assembly targets, each with launch disabled (unchecked), but one application EXE that uses those assemblies. In that case, you would mark the application's target with the Set as Launch property. When this session is launched, the application will be run and data will be collected from the application and the other target assemblies.

If you select the Properties option, you will see a Property Pages dialog for the selected target, as shown in Figure 12-8. Remember that these properties only affect the currently selected target, not the overall session.

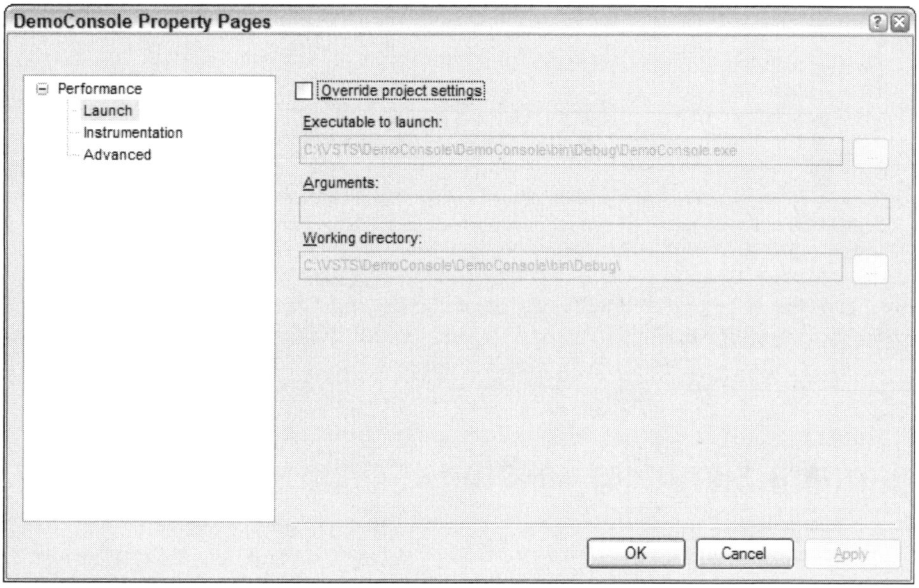

Figure 12-8

If you choose Override Project Settings, you can manually specify the path and name of an executable to launch. You can provide additional arguments to the executable and specify the working directory for that executable as well.

If the selected target is an ASP.NET application, this page will instead contain a "Url to launch" field.

The Instrumentation property page, shown in Figure 12-9, enables you to optionally indicate executables to run before and/or after the instrumentation process occurs for the current target. You may exclude the specified executable from instrumentation as well.

Because instrumenting an assembly changes it, instrumenting signed assemblies will break them because the assembly will no longer match the signature originally generated. In order to work with signed assemblies, you need to add a post-instrument event, which calls to the strong naming tool, sn.exe. In the Command-line field, call sn.exe, supplying the assembly to sign and the keyfile to use for signing. You will also need to check the Exclude from Instrumentation option. Adding this step will sign those assemblies again, allowing them to be used as expected.

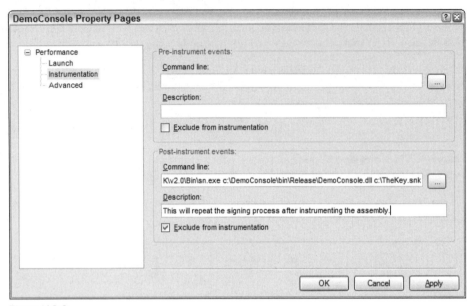

Figure 12-9

The Advanced property page is identical to the one under the General project settings. It is used to supply further command-line options to VSInstr.exe, the utility used by Visual Studio to instrument assemblies when running an instrumentation profiling session. You can see the available switches in the "Command-line Execution" section later in this chapter

Configuring a sampling session

Sampling is a very lightweight method of investigating an application's performance characteristics. Sampling causes the profiler to periodically interrupt the execution of the target application, noting which code is executing and taking a snapshot of the call stack. When sampling completes, the report will include data such as function call counts. You can use this information to determine which functions might be bottlenecks or critical paths for your application, and then create an instrumentation session targeting those areas.

Because you are taking periodic snapshots of your application, the resulting view might be inaccurate if the duration of your sampling session is too short. For development purposes, you could set the sampling frequency very high, enabling you to obtain an acceptable view in a shorter time. However, if you are sampling against an application running in a production environment, you might wish to minimize the sampling frequency to reduce the impact of profiling on the performance of your system. Of course, doing so will require a longer profiling session run to obtain accurate results.

By default, a sampling session will interrupt the target application every 10,000,000 clock cycles. If you open the session property pages and click the Sampling page, as shown in Figure 12-10, you may select other options as well.

You can use the Sampling Interval field to adjust the number of clock cycles between snapshots. Again, you may want a higher value, resulting in less frequent sampling, when profiling an application running in production, or a lower value for more frequent snapshots in a development environment. The exact value you should use will vary depending on your specific hardware and the performance of the application you are profiling.

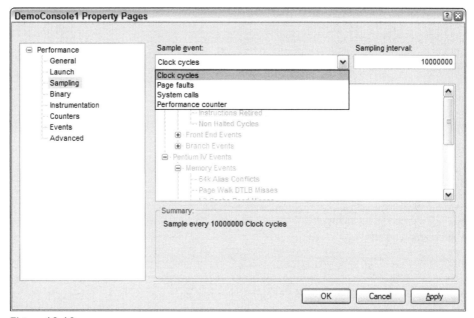

Figure 12-10

Three other sampling methods are available. If you have an application that is memory intensive, you may try a session based on page faults. This causes sampling to occur when memory pressure triggers a page fault. From this, you will be able to get a good idea of which code is causing those memory allocations.

You can also sample based on system calls. In these cases, samples will be taken after the specified number of system calls (as opposed to normal user-mode calls) have been made. You may also sample based on a specific CPU performance counter (such as misdirected branches or cache misses).

These alternative sampling methods are used to identify very specific conditions, so sampling based on clock cycles is what you need most of the time.

Configuring an instrumentation session

Instrumentation is the act of inserting probes or markers in a target binary, which when hit during normal program flow cause the logging of data about the application at that point. This is a more invasive way of profiling an application, but because you are not relying on periodic snapshots, it is also more accurate.

> **Instrumentation can quickly generate a large amount of data, so you should begin by sampling an application to find potential problem areas, or *hotspots*. Then, based on those results, instrument specific areas of code that require further analysis.**

When you're configuring an instrumentation session, three additional property pages can be of use: Instrumentation, Binary, and Advanced. The Instrumentation tab is identical to the Instrumentation property page that is available on a per-target basis, shown in Figure 12-9. The difference is that the target settings are specific to a single target, whereas the session's settings specify executables to run before/after *all* targets have been instrumented.

The Binary property page is used to manage the location of your instrumented binaries. By checking Relocate Instrumented Binaries and specifying a folder, Team System will take the original target binaries, instrument them, and place them in the specified folder.

For instrumentation profiling runs, Team System automatically calls the VSInstr.exe utility to instrument your binaries. Use the Advanced property page to supply additional options and arguments (such as /VERBOSE) to that utility. The available switches are described in the section "Command-line Execution" later in this chapter.

Executing a performance session

Once you have configured your performance session and assigned targets, you can execute, or launch, that session. Use the Performance Explorer window (refer to Figure 12-4), right-click on a specific session, and choose Launch.

> *Before you launch your performance session, ensure that your project and any dependent assemblies have been generated in Release Configuration mode. Profiling a Debug build will not be as accurate because such builds are not optimized for performance and will have additional overhead.*

Because Performance Explorer can hold more than one session, you will designate one of those sessions as the current session. By default, the first session is marked as current. This enables you to click the green launch button at the top of the Performance Explorer window to invoke that current session.

You may also run a performance session from the command line. For details, see the section "Command-line Execution" later in this chapter.

When a session is launched, you can monitor its status via the output window. You will see the output from each of the utilities invoked for you. If the target application is interactive, you can use the application as normal. When the application completes, the profiler will shut down and generate a report.

When profiling an ASP.NET application, an instance of Internet Explorer is launched, with a target URL as specified in the target's "Url to launch" setting. Use the application as normal through this browser instance and Team System will monitor the application's performance. Once the Internet Explorer window is closed, Team System will stop collecting data and generate the profiling report.

> You are not required to use the browser for interaction with the ASP.NET application. If you have other forms of testing for that application, such as web and load tests (described in Chapter 15), simply minimize the Internet Explorer window and execute those tests. When you're done, return to the browser window and close it. The profiling report will then be generated and will include usage data resulting from those web and load tests.

Managing session reports

When a session run is complete, a new session report will be added to the Reports folder for the executed session. For details about how to modify how these report files are generated, see the General property page description in the "Setting general session properties" section.

As shown in Figure 12-11, the Reports folder holds all of the reports for the executions of that session.

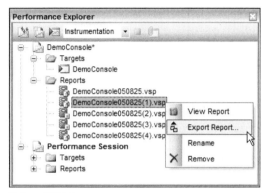

Figure 12-11

Double-click on a report file to generate and view the report. You can right-click on a report and select Export Report, which will display the Export Report dialog box shown in Figure 12-12. You can then select one or more sections of the report to send a target file in XML or comma-delimited format. This can be useful if you have another tool that parses this data, or to transform via XSL into a custom report view.

The items contained in the Reports folders are simply data files. The generation of the reports from that data is performed as you open each file, so expect a delay when viewing a report, especially if it came from a long or highly sampled run.

Reading and interpreting session reports

A performance session report is composed of a number of different views. These views offer different ways to inspect the large amount of data collected during the profiling process. The data in many views are interrelated, and you will see that entries in one view can lead to further detail in another view. Note that some views will have content only if you have enabled optional settings before running the session.

The amount and kinds of data collected and displayed by a performance session report can be difficult to understand and interpret at first. In the following sections, we'll walk though each section of a report, describing its meaning and how to interpret the results.

In any of the report views, you can select which columns appear and their order by right-clicking in the report and selecting Choose Columns. Select the columns you wish to see and how you want to order them using the move buttons.

Figure 12-12

Report statistic types

The specific information displayed by each view will depend on the settings used to generate the performance session. Sampling and instrumentation will produce different contents for most views, and including .NET memory profiling options will affect the display as well. Before describing the individual views that make up a report, it is important to understand some key terms.

Elapsed time includes all of the time spent between the beginning and end of a given function. *Application* time is an estimate of the actual time spent executing your code, subtracting system events. Should your application be interrupted by another during a profiling session, elapsed time will include the time spent executing that other application, but application time will exclude it.

Inclusive time combines the time spent in the current function with time spent in any other functions that it may call. *Exclusive* time will remove the time spent in other functions called from the current function.

> *If you forget these definitions, hover your mouse pointer over the column headers and a tool tip will give you a brief description of the column.*

Summary View

When you view a report, Summary View is displayed by default. There are two types of summary reports, depending on whether you ran a sampling or instrumented profile. Figure 12-13 shows a Summary View from a sampling profile of the DemoConsole application.

The sampled Summary View has two sections: Top Inclusive Sampled Functions and Top Exclusive Sampled Functions. The Samples column shows the number of times the application was actively executing the given function when samples were taken.

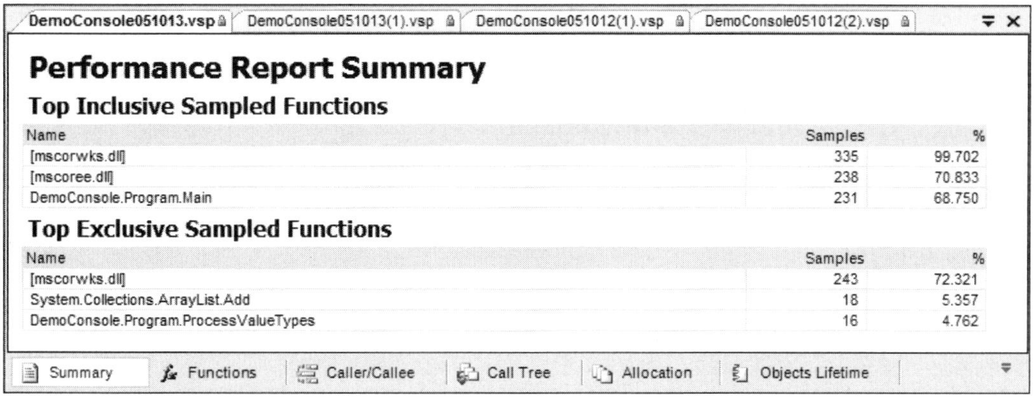

Figure 12-13

A function is considered exclusive if it is the actively running function when a sampling occurs. The functions that are higher than the current function on the call stack — in other words, the functions that called the current function — are counted as inclusive functions.

> *Notice that several of the functions aren't function names, but names of DLLs — for example, [mscor-wks.dll]. This occurs when a function is sampled for which the system does not have debugging symbols. This frequently happens when running sampling profiles and occasionally with instrumented profiles. We describe this issue and how to correct it in the section "Common Profiling Issues" later in the chapter.*

For the DemoConsole application, this view isn't showing much of interest. At this point, you would normally investigate the other views, but because the DemoConsole application is trivially small, sampling to find hotspots will not be as useful as the information you can gather using instrumentation. Let's change the profiling type to instrumentation and see what information is revealed.

In the Performance Explorer window, find the drop-down field on the toolbar that currently reads Sampling and change it to instrumentation. Click the Launch button on the same toolbar to execute the profiling session, this time using instrumentation. When profiling and report generation are complete, you will see a Summary View similar to that shown in Figure 12-14.

The Summary View of an instrumented session has three sections. The three most commonly called functions are first, ordered by the number of calls. Next are the functions with the most individual work. These are the functions that required the most time, not counting the time spent in any other functions they called, similar to the concept of exclusive time. The final list is of the functions that took the longest, including all activity and system time, similar to application inclusive time.

In this view, you can begin to see some interesting results. Note that ArrayList.Add and ArrayList .get_Item were each called 4,000,000 times. This makes sense because ProcessValueTypes and ProcessClasses, which use that method, were each called 2,000,000 times. However, in the Functions Taking Longest section, there is a noticeable difference in the amount of time spent in ProcessingValue Types over ProcessClasses. Remember that the code for each is basically the same — the only difference is that one works with structures and the other with classes. You can use the other views to investigate further.

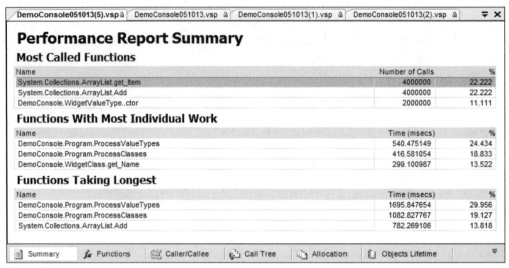

Figure 12-14

Right-click on any function and you will be able to go to that function's source, view it in Functions View, or see the function in Caller/Callee View. You can double-click on any function to switch to the Functions view. You can also select one or more functions, right-click, and choose Copy to add the name, time, and percentage of time to the Clipboard for pasting to other documents.

The Summary View has an alternate layout that is used when the ".NET memory profiling collection" options are enabled on the General page of the session properties. You can see this view in Figure 12-15.

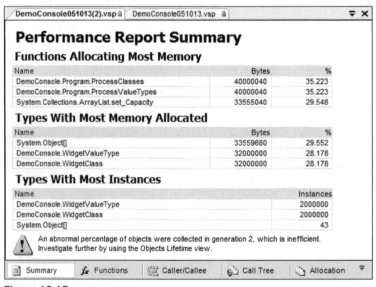

Figure 12-15

Notice that the three main sections are different. The first section, Functions Allocating Most Memory, shows the top three functions in terms of bytes allocated to managed types. The second section, Types With Most Memory Allocated, shows the top three types by bytes allocated without regard to the functions involved. Finally, Types With Most Instances shows the top three types in terms of number of instances, without regard to the size of those instances.

Finally, notice in Figure 12-15 that a warning symbol appears at the bottom of the view, warning you that a large number of objects were collected in generation 2, leading to possible inefficiency. You'll see what this means in the section "Objects Lifetime View" later in this chapter.

Using these three views, you can quickly get a sense for the highest-use functions and types within your application. You'll see in the following sections how to use the other views to dive into further detail.

Functions View

From the Summary View of the instrumented profiling session, choose the DemoConsole.Program .ProcessValueTypes method and switch to Functions View. The Functions View, shown in Figure 12-16, lists all functions sampled or instrumented during the session. For instrumentation, this will be functions in targets that were instrumented and called during the session. For sampling, this will include any other members/assemblies accessed by the application.

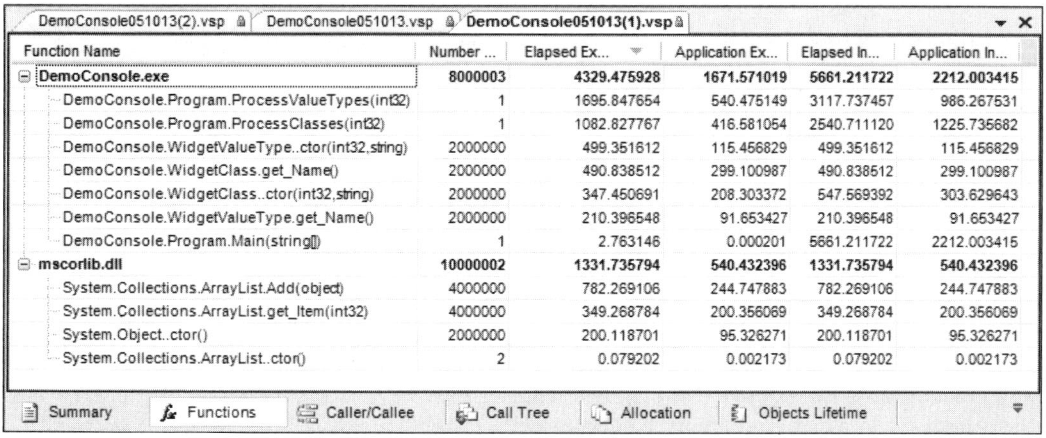

Function Name	Number ...	Elapsed Ex... ▼	Application Ex...	Elapsed In...	Application In...
⊟ DemoConsole.exe	8000003	4329.475928	1671.571019	5661.211722	2212.003415
DemoConsole.Program.ProcessValueTypes(int32)	1	1695.847654	540.475149	3117.737457	986.267531
DemoConsole.Program.ProcessClasses(int32)	1	1082.827767	416.581054	2540.711120	1225.735682
DemoConsole.WidgetValueType..ctor(int32,string)	2000000	499.351612	115.466829	499.351612	115.466829
DemoConsole.WidgetClass.get_Name()	2000000	490.838512	299.100987	490.838512	299.100987
DemoConsole.WidgetClass..ctor(int32,string)	2000000	347.450691	208.303372	547.569392	303.629643
DemoConsole.WidgetValueType.get_Name()	2000000	210.396548	91.653427	210.396548	91.653427
DemoConsole.Program.Main(string[])	1	2.763146	0.000201	5661.211722	2212.003415
⊟ mscorlib.dll	10000002	1331.735794	540.432396	1331.735794	540.432396
System.Collections.ArrayList.Add(object)	4000000	782.269106	244.747883	782.269106	244.747883
System.Collections.ArrayList.get_Item(int32)	4000000	349.268784	200.356069	349.268784	200.356069
System.Object..ctor()	2000000	200.118701	95.326271	200.118701	95.326271
System.Collections.ArrayList..ctor()	2	0.079202	0.002173	0.079202	0.002173

Tabs: DemoConsole051013(2).vsp | DemoConsole051013.vsp | DemoConsole051013(1).vsp

Bottom tabs: Summary | Functions | Caller/Callee | Call Tree | Allocation | Objects Lifetime

Figure 12-16

As with most of the views, you can click on a column heading to sort by that column. This is especially useful for the four time columns. Right-clicking in the Functions View and selecting Group By Module will cause the functions to be grouped under their containing binary.

Reviewing the data for ProcessValueTypes and ProcessClasses, it seems ProcessValueTypes is clearly slower. However, there are some other interesting differences in performance here. Notice that both WidgetClass and WidgetValueType have a get_Name method. This is the Name property get accessor for each. Interestingly, according to Elapsed Exclusive and Application Exclusive time, the system spent over three times longer in the class's version than the structure's. You may wonder why these methods have identical values in the inclusive time columns and the exclusive time columns. Inclusive time is a measure of time spent in a function in addition to the time spent in child functions. Because the Name property get accessors call no other instrumented functions, the time is identical.

Another difference between the value type and class processing can be seen in the last column, Application Inclusive Time. This column shows all time spent in that function as well as functions that it calls, minus system overhead. In this column, the ProcessClasses method takes substantially longer than ProcessValueTypes. The difference is not explained solely by the Name property. The Application Inclusive Time column makes it clear that the constructor for the class also takes longer than the value type's constructor.

To reveal more information, double-click on the ProcessClasses method or right-click and choose Show in Caller/Callee View.

Caller/Callee View

Caller/Callee View, shown in Figure 12-17, displays a particular function in the middle, with the function(s) that call into it in the section above it and any functions that it calls in the bottom section.

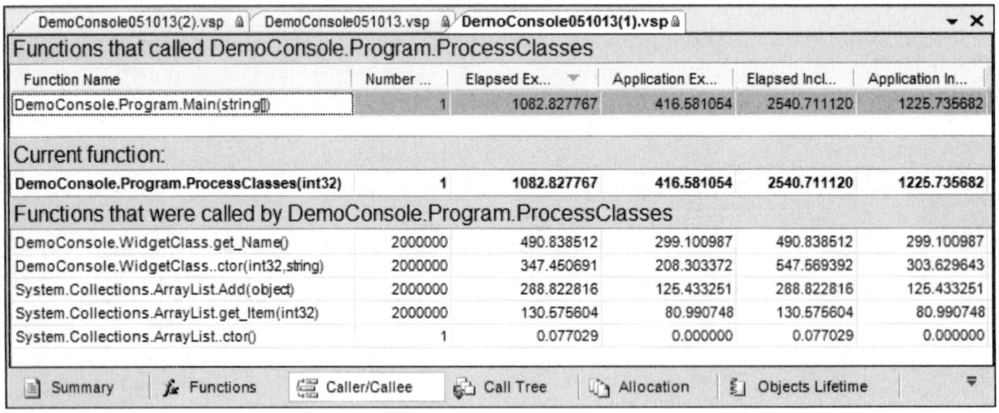

Function Name	Number ...	Elapsed Ex... ▼	Application Ex...	Elapsed Incl...	Application In...
Functions that called DemoConsole.Program.ProcessClasses					
DemoConsole.Program.Main(string[])	1	1082.827767	416.581054	2540.711120	1225.735682
Current function:					
DemoConsole.Program.ProcessClasses(int32)	1	1082.827767	416.581054	2540.711120	1225.735682
Functions that were called by DemoConsole.Program.ProcessClasses					
DemoConsole.WidgetClass.get_Name()	2000000	490.838512	299.100987	490.838512	299.100987
DemoConsole.WidgetClass..ctor(int32,string)	2000000	347.450691	208.303372	547.569392	303.629643
System.Collections.ArrayList.Add(object)	2000000	288.822816	125.433251	288.822816	125.433251
System.Collections.ArrayList.get_Item(int32)	2000000	130.575604	80.990748	130.575604	80.990748
System.Collections.ArrayList..ctor()	1	0.077029	0.000000	0.077029	0.000000

DemoConsole051013(2).vsp　DemoConsole051013.vsp　DemoConsole051013(1).vsp

Summary　Functions　Caller/Callee　Call Tree　Allocation　Objects Lifetime

Figure 12-17

This is particularly useful for pinpointing the execution flow of your application, helping to identify hotspots. In Figure 12-17, the ProcessClasses method is in focus and shows that the only caller is the Main method. You can also see that ProcessClasses directly calls five functions. The sum of times in the caller list will match the time shown for the set function. For example, select the ArrayList.get_ Item accessor by double-clicking or right-clicking and choosing Set Function. The resulting window will then display a table similar to what is shown in Figure 12-18.

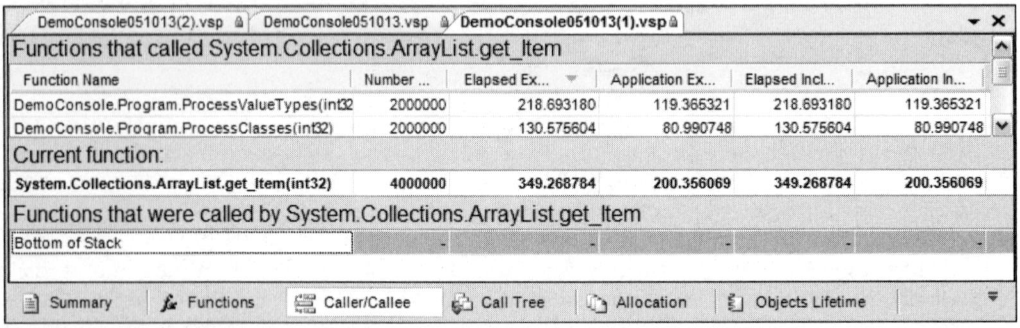

Function Name	Number ...	Elapsed Ex... ▼	Application Ex...	Elapsed Incl...	Application In...
Functions that called System.Collections.ArrayList.get_Item					
DemoConsole.Program.ProcessValueTypes(int32	2000000	218.693180	119.365321	218.693180	119.365321
DemoConsole.Program.ProcessClasses(int32)	2000000	130.575604	80.990748	130.575604	80.990748
Current function:					
System.Collections.ArrayList.get_Item(int32)	4000000	349.268784	200.356069	349.268784	200.356069
Functions that were called by System.Collections.ArrayList.get_Item					
Bottom of Stack	-	-	-	-	-

DemoConsole051013(2).vsp　DemoConsole051013.vsp　DemoConsole051013(1).vsp

Summary　Functions　Caller/Callee　Call Tree　Allocation　Objects Lifetime

Figure 12-18

You saw `ArrayList.get_Item` in the main Functions View, but couldn't tell how much of that time resulted from calls by `ProcessValueTypes` or `ProcessClasses`. Caller/Callee View enables you to see this detail. Notice that there are two callers for this function, and that the sum of their time equals the time of the function itself. In this table, you can see that the `ArrayList.get_Item` method actually took about 67 percent longer to process the 2,000,000 requests from `ProcessValueTypes` than those from `ProcessClasses`.

What could account for this difference in performance? The only real difference between `WidgetClass` and `WidgetValueType` is that one is a reference type and one is a value type. Remember that `ArrayList` works by treating everything it contains as an `object` reference. In order for a value type to behave like an `object`, it must be *boxed*. Boxing creates an object instance and references the value from the value type. After boxing, the value looks like an object and can be used anywhere an `object` reference is necessary, such as when adding members to an `ArrayList`. To read items back from an `ArrayList`, the process must be reversed, called *unboxing*, to access the original value type.

The performance impact of boxing and unboxing is typically minor, but when performed many times, such as with a large collection, the impact can be substantial, as you can see in Figure 12-18. In fact, the cost associated with boxing was a motivating factor for the addition of generics with .NET 2.0.

Call Tree View

The Call Tree View, shown in Figure 12-19, shows a hierarchical view of the calls executed by your application. The concept is somewhat similar to the Caller/Callee View, but in this view a given function may appear twice if it is called by independent functions. For example, in Figure 12-19, `System.Collections.ArrayList.Add` appears under both the `ProcessValueTypes` and `ProcessClasses` nodes. If that same method were viewed in Caller/Callee View, it would appear once, with both parent functions listed at the top. You can quickly switch to Caller/Callee View by right-clicking on a function and choosing Show in Caller/Callee View. The same option is available for Functions View.

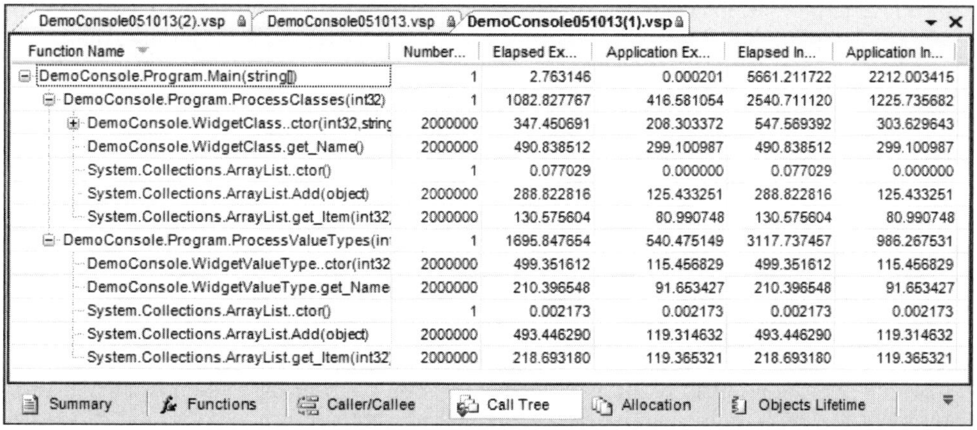

Function Name	Number...	Elapsed Ex...	Application Ex...	Elapsed In...	Application In...
DemoConsole.Program.Main(string[])	1	2.763146	0.000201	5661.211722	2212.003415
DemoConsole.Program.ProcessClasses(int32)	1	1082.827767	416.581054	2540.711120	1225.735682
DemoConsole.WidgetClass..ctor(int32,strinç	2000000	347.450691	208.303372	547.569392	303.629643
DemoConsole.WidgetClass.get_Name()	2000000	490.838512	299.100987	490.838512	299.100987
System.Collections.ArrayList..ctor()	1	0.077029	0.000000	0.077029	0.000000
System.Collections.ArrayList.Add(object)	2000000	288.822816	125.433251	288.822816	125.433251
System.Collections.ArrayList.get_Item(int32	2000000	130.575604	80.990748	130.575604	80.990748
DemoConsole.Program.ProcessValueTypes(in	1	1695.847654	540.475149	3117.737457	986.267531
DemoConsole.WidgetValueType..ctor(int32	2000000	499.351612	115.456829	499.351612	115.456829
DemoConsole.WidgetValueType.get_Name	2000000	210.396548	91.653427	210.396548	91.653427
System.Collections.ArrayList..ctor()	1	0.002173	0.002173	0.002173	0.002173
System.Collections.ArrayList.Add(object)	2000000	493.446290	119.314632	493.446290	119.314632
System.Collections.ArrayList.get_Item(int32	2000000	218.693180	119.365321	218.693180	119.365321

Summary   Functions   Caller/Callee   Call Tree   Allocation   Objects Lifetime

Figure 12-19

By default, the view will have a root (the function at the top of the list) of the entry point of the instrumented application. To quickly expand the details for any node, right-click and choose Expand All. Any function with dependent calls can be set as the new root for the view by right-clicking and choosing Set Root. This will modify the view to show that function at the top, followed by any functions that were called directly or indirectly by that function. To revert the view to the default, right-click and choose Reset Root.

Allocation View

If you configured your session for managed allocation profiling by choosing "Collect .NET object alloca-tion information" on the General property page for your session, you will have access to the Allocation View, shown in Figure 12-20. This view displays the managed types that were created during the execu-tion of the profiled application.

You can quickly see how many instances, the total bytes of memory used by those instances, and the percentage of overall bytes consumed by the instances of each managed type.

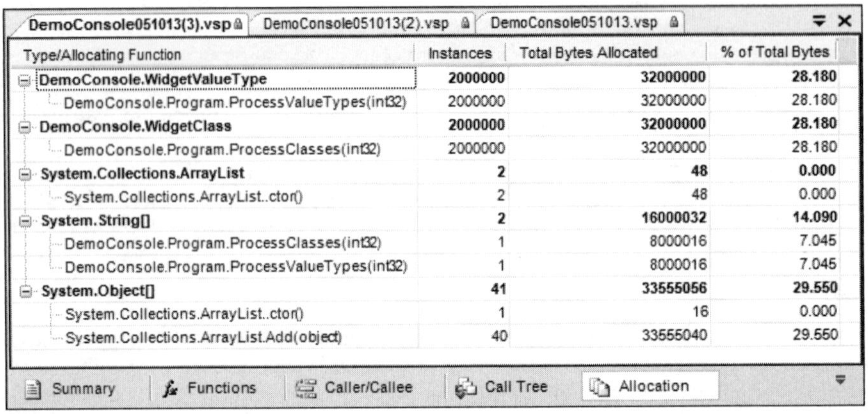

Type/Allocating Function	Instances	Total Bytes Allocated	% of Total Bytes
DemoConsole.WidgetValueType	2000000	32000000	28.180
DemoConsole.Program.ProcessValueTypes(int32)	2000000	32000000	28.180
DemoConsole.WidgetClass	2000000	32000000	28.180
DemoConsole.Program.ProcessClasses(int32)	2000000	32000000	28.180
System.Collections.ArrayList	2	48	0.000
System.Collections.ArrayList..ctor()	2	48	0.000
System.String[]	2	16000032	14.090
DemoConsole.Program.ProcessClasses(int32)	1	8000016	7.045
DemoConsole.Program.ProcessValueTypes(int32)	1	8000016	7.045
System.Object[]	41	33555056	29.550
System.Collections.ArrayList..ctor()	1	16	0.000
System.Collections.ArrayList.Add(object)	40	33555040	29.550

Tabs: DemoConsole051013(3).vsp | DemoConsole051013(2).vsp | DemoConsole051013.vsp

Buttons: Summary | Functions | Caller/Callee | Call Tree | Allocation

Figure 12-20

Expand any type to see the functions that caused the instantiations of that type. You will see the break-down of instances by function as well, so if more than one function created instances of that type, you can quickly determine which created the most. This view is most useful when sorted by Total Bytes Allocated or Percent of Total Bytes. This quickly tells you which types are consuming the most memory when your application runs.

> *An instrumented profiling session will track and report only the types allocated directly by the instru-mented code. A sampling session may show other types of objects. This is because samples can be taken at any time, even while processing system functions, such as security. Try comparing the allocations from sampling and instrumentation sessions for the same project. You will likely notice more object types in the sampling session.*

As with the other report views, you can also right-click on any function to switch to an alternative view such as source code, Functions View, or Caller/Callee View.

In the case of DemoConsole, the details in Figure 12-20 don't indicate any major discrepancies or items of concern. The bytes consumed and instances allocated by both branches of the application seem to be the same. However, we can dig a little deeper into how those instances affected the system by using the Objects Lifetime View, described next.

Objects Lifetime View

The Objects Lifetime View, shown in Figure 12-21, is available only if you have selected the "Also collect .NET object lifetime information" option of the General properties for your session. This option is only available if you have also selected the "Collect .NET object allocation information" option.

> The information in this view becomes more accurate the longer the application is run. If you are concerned about results you see, increase the duration of your session run to help ensure that the trend is accurate.

Several of the columns are identical to the Allocation View table, including Instances, Total Bytes Allocated, and Percent of Total Bytes. However, in this view you can't break down the types to show which functions created them. The value in this view lies in the details about how long the managed type instances existed and their effect on garbage collection.

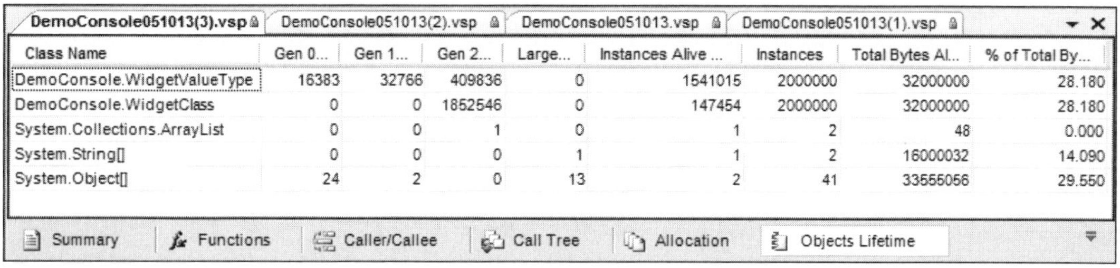

Class Name	Gen 0...	Gen 1...	Gen 2...	Large...	Instances Alive ...	Instances	Total Bytes Al...	% of Total By...
DemoConsole.WidgetValueType	16383	32766	409836	0	1541015	2000000	32000000	28.180
DemoConsole.WidgetClass	0	0	1852546	0	147454	2000000	32000000	28.180
System.Collections.ArrayList	0	0	1	0	1	2	48	0.000
System.String[]	0	0	0	1	1	2	16000032	14.090
System.Object[]	24	2	0	13	2	41	33555056	29.550

Tabs: Summary | Functions | Caller/Callee | Call Tree | Allocation | Objects Lifetime

File tabs: DemoConsole051013(3).vsp | DemoConsole051013(2).vsp | DemoConsole051013.vsp | DemoConsole051013(1).vsp

Figure 12-21

The first three columns show the number of instances of each type that were collected during specific generations of the garbage collector. With COM, objects were immediately destroyed and memory freed when the count of references to that instance became zero. However, .NET relies on a process called *garbage collection* to periodically inspect all object instances to determine whether the memory they consume can be released. Objects are placed into groups, called *generations*, according to how long each instance has remained referenced. Generation zero contains new instances, generation one instances are older, and generation two contains the oldest instances. New objects are more likely to be temporary or short in scope than objects that have survived previous collections, so having objects organized into generations enables .NET to more efficiently find objects to release when additional memory is needed.

The next column is Large Object Heap Instances Collected, which refers to object instances that receive different treatment in the garbage collection process.

The last two columns in Figure 12-21 are Instances Alive At End and Instances. The latter is the total count of instances of that type over the life of the profiling session. The former indicates how many instances of that type were still in memory when the profiling session terminated. This might be because the references to those instances were held by other objects. It may also occur if the instances were released right before the session ended, before the garbage collector acted to remove them. Having values in this column does not necessarily indicate a problem; it is simply another data item to consider as you evaluate your system.

Having a large number of generation-zero instances collected is normal, fewer in generation one, and the fewest in generation two. Anything else indicates there might be an opportunity to optimize the scope of some variables. For example, a class field that is only used from one of that class's methods could be changed to a variable inside that method. This would reduce the scope of that variable to live only while that method is executing.

Looking at the data generated from the DemoConsole application, you can see a number of interesting things. First, the WidgetClass instances are all collected in generation two. By itself, this doesn't indicate a problem, but it does mean that the WidgetClass instances survived collection at least twice. This is likely because the instances of WidgetClass were being referenced by the ArrayList throughout the first part of the program's execution. Once the program began processing the value types, the garbage collector could begin reclaiming the memory allocated to the WidgetClass instances.

Second, note that the WidgetValueType instances were collected in small amounts during generation zero and one, and more were collected in generation two. Most importantly, notice that about 75 percent of them were never collected by the garbage collector and were alive at the end of the session. This can be partially attributed to the fact that value types are based on the stack and not the managed heap, where the garbage collector does its work.

Like the data shown in the other report views, use the data in this view not as definitive indicators of problems, but as pointers to places where improvements might be realized. Also, keep in mind that with small or quickly-executing programs, allocation tracking might not have enough data to provide truly meaningful results.

Command-line Execution

Team System abstracts the process of calling several utilities to conduct profiling. You can use these utilities directly if you need more control or to integrate your profiling with an automated batch process, such as your nightly build. The general flow is:

❑ Configure the target (if necessary) and environment

❑ Start the data logging engine

❑ Run the target application

❑ When the application has completed, stop the logging data engine

❑ Generate the session report

These utilities can be found in your Visual Studio installation directory under \Team Tools\Performance Tools. For help with any of the utilities, supply a /? argument after the utility name.

Configuring instrumentation

If you wish to instrument a binary for profiling, use the VSInstr.exe utility as follows:

```
VSInstr Utilities.dll
```

This will fully instrument all of the methods in the Utilities assembly. If you do not want all of the methods to be instrumented, use the /exclude flag and specify the method you wish to exclude. For example, the following will instrument all Utilities.dll methods except Utilities.Math.LaplaceTransform:

```
VSInstr Utilities.dll /exclude:Utilities.Math::LaplaceTransform
```

Similarly, you can use the /include flag to include only the methods you specify. All others will remain uninstrumented.

The /include and /exclude options can be supplied multiple times, but you cannot use both /include and /exclude options at the same time.

> As mentioned earlier in this chapter, instrumenting a signed assembly will invalidate that assembly because the assembly will no longer match the signature. To remedy this, add a call to the command-line tool sn.exe, supplying the assembly to sign and the keyfile to use.

Setting environment variables

Profiling requires that several Windows environment variables be set. This is important because it allows the profiling subsystem to be invoked in a target process. This is done automatically for you by the Team System IDE, but when using the command line, you need to use the VSPerfClrEnv.cmd utility, which establishes these settings for you.

Instrumentation

If you are running an instrumented session (sometimes referred to as *tracing*,) use the /traceon argument:

```
VSPerfClrEnv /traceon
```

If you also wish to collect allocation data (akin to setting the Allocations Only option in your session's General properties), use the /tracegc argument instead:

```
VSPerfClrEnv /tracegc
```

Remember that specifying this option will cause profiling to have a greater impact on the profiled application's performance.

Sampling

For sampling, you can choose to launch the application from the profiler, in which case you will not need to run VSPerfClrEnv. If you will not launch the application from the profiler, use the /sampleon argument:

```
VSPerfClrEnv /sampleon
```

You can collect managed type allocation details by providing the /samplegc argument instead of /sampleon. If you are not using VSPerfClrEnv, you could supply the /gc argument to the VSPerfCmd utility, described in the section "Executing a profiling session," later in this chapter.

Profiling a Windows service or ASP.NET application

If you need to profile an ASP.NET application or a Windows Service that is automatically run on system startup, use the /globaltraceon options to VSPerfClrEnv. This will set the required variables in the Windows registry so they will automatically be available when Windows starts, which will enable any managed process, including Windows services that automatically start, to hook into the profiling system.

Clearing environment settings

Once profiling is complete, use the `/off` argument (or `/globaloff`) to clear the environment variables:

```
VSPerfClrEnv /off
```

Executing a profiling session

Once the environment has been configured, you need to start the profiling monitor by using the `VSPerfCmd.exe` utility, minimally supplying the `/start` and `/output` arguments. You specify sampling or instrumentation (trace) and a filename in which the profiling data will be stored.

This command will start the logging engine, watching for an instrumented binary:

```
VSPerfCmd /start:trace /output:SampleSession.vsp
```

The following command starts monitoring for a sampled application:

```
VSPerfCmd /start:sample /output:SampleSession.vsp
```

Once the logging monitor has started, run your application. If you are running an instrumented profile, ensure that you are using the instrumented versions of your binaries.

For sampling profiles, you can collect details on managed type allocations by supplying the `/gc` argument. However, in order to use the `/gc` argument, you must also use the `/launch` option, supplying the command to launch the sampled application. Instrumentation-based profiles must use the `/tracegc` argument to `VSPerfClrEnv` as described above. The following command starts monitoring for a sampled application, collecting allocation data for managed types:

```
VSPerfCmd /start:sample /output:DemoConsoleSession.vsp /launch:DemoConsole.exe /gc
```

When the application has completed, shut down the monitoring engine. Do this with the `/shutdown` argument to `VSPerfCmd`:

```
VSPerfCmd /shutdown
```

This will stop the monitor and store all collected data in the file specified with the `/output` argument.

> `VSPerfCmd` *has many advanced options for maximum flexibility. Use the* `/?` *argument to get a full list of available arguments with brief descriptions.*

Generating reports

Once the monitor has completed and created the profile data file (such as `SampleSession.vsp`), you can generate a report by using the `VSPerfReport.exe` utility, supplying the name of the profile data file.

> *You may also import the file directly into the Team System IDE by using the Performance Explorer. Right-click the Reports node and choose Add Report, specifying the data file you wish to import.*

The /summary:<types> argument specifies which report(s) to generate (Module, Function, CallTree, etc.). This can be a comma-delimited list of types or you can use all to generate all report types:

```
VSPerfReport SampleSession.vsp /summary:all
```

You can supply the optional /xml argument to output the report in XML format.

Use the optional /output argument to specify a file for the report.

For example, the following command will generate an XML call tree report to a file named CallTreeReport.xml:

```
VSPerfReport SampleSession.vsp /summary:CallTree /xml /output:CallTreeReport.xml
```

Modifying Instrumentation Programmatically

As mentioned before, instrumentation can quickly generate a lot of data. There are ways to control which parts of your binaries generate this data so you can create reports that are focused only on the areas you wish to observe. This also has the welcome effect of reducing the impact that instrumentation will have on your running application.

Visual Studio features code to help you identify areas that should be included or excluded from instrumentation. For managed code, use the Microsoft.VisualStudio.Profiler assembly, located in your Visual Studio installation directory under \Team Tools\Performance Tools. If you are working with unmanaged code, use the VSPerf.lib and VSPerf.h files, found in the PerfSDK subdirectory. We focus on managed code in this section.

Microsoft.VisualStudio.Profiler features a DataCollection class that can be used to enable and disable profiling. The two methods of greatest interest here are StartProfile and StopProfile. Use these calls to wrap a region of your code for which you want to control profiling. Both methods accept a DataCollection.ProfileLevel enumeration value and an identifier that is related to the chosen ProfileLevel.

In the following code, we wish to profile only the call to GetActiveEmployees, ignoring all other code:

```
using Microsoft.VisualStudio.Profiler;

public class TestApplication
{
  public static void ProcessEmployees()
  {
    // Code here will not be profiled

      DataCollection.StartProfile(DataCollection.ProfileLevel.Global,
                                  DataCollection.CurrentId);

    // Here is the code that will be profiled
```

```
Employees emps = HumanResources.GetActiveEmployees();

DataCollection.StopProfile(DataCollection.ProfileLevel.Global,
                           DataCollection.CurrentId);

    // Code here will not be profiled
  }
}
```

The calls to StartProfile and StopProfile are given a ProfileLevel of Global, indicating this should affect all executions. Because it is global, there is no need for a specific identifier, so the constant DataCollection.CurrentId is passed as the second argument.

The possible values for DataCollection.ProfileLevel are as follows:

- ❑   Global
- ❑   Process
- ❑   Thread

As you can see, you can constrain the profiling to a specific process or thread, supplying the appropriate process or thread ID as the second argument or you can pass DataCollection.CurrentId to reference the currently executing context.

To profile code such as the preceding example, use the same approach as described in the "Command-line Execution" section earlier. However, you will need to include one extra option. By default, the profiler will observe everything. Unless you disable this, all of the code before the StopProfile marker will be profiled, instead of just the code between StartProfile and StopProfile.

VSPerfCmd has an option to disable collection, but you'll typically use it only in this specific case. Follow the same steps as outlined before, but *after* you start instrumentation profiling with VSPerfCmd and *before* you start your profiled application, execute the following command:

```
VSPerfCmd /globaloff
```

By disabling data collection, the profiler relies on your code to call DataCollection.StartProfile in order to begin the collection process.

The Microsoft.VisualStudio.Profiler.DataCollection class supports other methods that can affect profiling.

SuspendProfile and ResumeProfile are used like the StartProfile and StopProfile methods. The difference is that calls to Suspend/Resume are incremented and decremented, similar to the way object reference counting worked in COM programming. For example, if the code you are profiling calls SuspendProfile twice, profiling will not resume until ResumeProfile is likewise called twice. These methods, including calls to StartProfile and StopProfile, return a DataCollection.Profile OperationResult enumeration value that you can verify equals ProfileOperationResult.OK, indicating success.

You can add custom details that will be inserted with the other profiling data:

❑   `MarkProfile` enables you to insert an integer.

❑   `CommentMarkProfile` inserts an integer with a string comment.

❑   `CommentMarkAtProfile` inserts an integer with a string comment at a specified timestamp.

Any data you add with these methods can be seen in the Call Tree View. Each of these operations returns a `DataCollection.MarkOperationResult` enumeration value that you can use to verify success.

Common Profiling Issues

Profiling is a complex topic, and not without a few pitfalls to catch the unwary. This section documents a number of common issues you might encounter as you profile your applications.

Debugging symbols

When you review your profiling reports, you may notice that some function calls resolve to unhelpful entries such as `[ntdll.dll]`. This occurs because the application has used code for which it cannot find debugging symbols, so instead of the function name you get the name of the containing binary.

Debugging symbols, files with the `.pdb` extension (for "program database"), include the details that debuggers and profilers use to discover information about executing code. Microsoft Symbol Server enables you to use a web connection to dynamically obtain symbol files for binaries as needed. Direct Visual Studio to use this server by choosing Tools ➪ Options, and then expand the Debugging section and choose Symbols. Create a new symbol file location, entering the value `http://msdl.microsoft.com/download/symbols`. Because symbols are downloaded, you will also need to choose a local directory to serve as a storage area. Now close and reopen a report; the new symbols will be used to resolve function names.

> *The first time you render a report with symbols set to download from Microsoft Symbol Server, it will take significantly longer to complete.*

If, perhaps due to security restrictions, your profiling system does not have Internet access, you can download and install the symbol packages for Windows from the Windows Hardware Developer Center. At the time of writing, this is `www.microsoft.com/whdc/devtools/debugging/symbols.mspx`. Select the package appropriate for your processor and operating system, and install the symbols.

Instrumentation and code coverage

When running an instrumentation profile, be certain that you are not profiling a target for which you have previously enabled *code coverage*. Code coverage, described in Chapter 14, uses another form of instrumentation that observes which lines of code are accessed as tests are executed. Unfortunately, this instrumentation can interfere with the instrumentation required by the profiler.

If your solution has a test project and you have previously used code coverage, open your Test Run Configuration, under Test ➪ Edit Test Run Configurations, and select the Code Coverage page. Ensure that the binaries you are profiling do not have code coverage enabled. If they do, uncheck them and rebuild your solution. You should then be able to use instrumentation profiling without conflict.

Virtual machines

If you are running your application from within a virtual machine, such as with Virtual PC, VMWare, or Virtual Server, you will not be able to profile that application. Profiling relies upon a number of performance counters that are very close to the system hardware. Some of these counters are unavailable through a virtual instance of an operating system.

ASP.NET profiling

Team System does support the profiling of ASP.NET applications, but they must be based on ASP.NET version 2.0. Version 1.x ASP.NET applications cannot be profiled.

In addition, the ASP.NET application being profiled must be hosted on the same machine that is executing the profiling session. Profiling of remote ASP.NET applications is not supported in this release. Remember that you can also use the command-line tools to execute performance sessions. For an introduction to the command-line tools, see the "Command-line Execution" section earlier in this chapter.

Summary

In this chapter, you learned about the value of using profiling to identify problem areas in your code. Until now, developers needed to use tools outside of Visual Studio to profile for performance issues. Fortunately, Team System now fully integrates profiling tools within the IDE and with other Team System features.

We explained the difference between sampling and instrumentation, when each should be applied, and how to configure the profiler to execute each type. You saw the Performance Explorer in action and learned how to create and configure performance sessions and their targets.

You then learned how to invoke a profiling session and how to work with the reports that are generated after each run. You looked at each of the available report types, including Call Tree, Caller/Callee, and more.

While Visual Studio offers a great deal of flexibility in your profiling, you may find you need to specify further options or profile applications from a batch application or build system. We introduced the command-line tools that are available and explained how to replicate the functionality of Visual Studio from outside the IDE. For additional flexibility, we described how to use the profiling APIs that enable you to exert even more control over the profiling process.

Finally, we described several common scenarios that can cause issues for users of the profiling tools.

Of course, profiling is only one of the tools at your disposal to help ensure that your applications are of the highest quality. You have seen in Chapters 8 and 9 that Team System offers static code analysis to detect common problems. You will see in Part 3 that Team Test enables you to further analyze your applications to see how they perform under load.

Part III
Team Tester

13

Test Case Management

The next several chapters will introduce the testing functionality supported by Team System. Because these testing options are so critical to project success, it is not uncommon for projects to have dozens, sometimes even hundreds, of tests. Fortunately, Team System offers ways to organize and execute tests. In this chapter, you will learn how to use those features to work effectively with your application's tests, whether you have 5 or 5,000 tests to manage.

We begin with an in-depth description of *test projects*, a special project type that you can use to contain tests of any kind. We'll describe the creation of test projects, as well as the various options you can specify when a new test project is created.

Then, we describe the Test View and Test Manager windows. These windows offer effective ways to organize and execute the tests contained in your solutions.

We also explain the management of test results. The Test Results window is described in detail. The files used to store test run results, called *TRX files*, are also discussed. We'll show you how to export and import test run results and how to publish test run results to your Team Foundation Server for reporting purposes.

Finally, an additional test type called an *ordered test* is introduced. Ordered tests are essentially containers of other tests, offering a convenient way to group and execute tests in a specified order.

Test Projects

Visual Studio Team System offers a new project template called "Test Project." Projects of this type provide a convenient way to store tests of any kind. You may decide to have all of the tests in your test project be of one type, or you may mix different types of tests within the same test project.

The types of tests that can be contained in a test project include the following:

❑ **Unit tests:** These are low-level tests verifying that target application code functions as the developer expects. Unit tests are essentially code that tests other code. Because unit tests are normally written by the developer but are also a testing activity, they are available in both the Software Developer and Software Tester editions of Team System. Unit testing is a growing practice and is rapidly becoming an indispensable part of the development process at many companies. Unit testing and the related practice of *test-driven development* are described in detail in Chapter 14.

❑ **Web tests:** Used to verify functionality of a web application, a web test can be created through the IDE or written with code. For example, you may create a web test to verify that a user can create a new account on your site. This web test could be one of a suite of web tests that you run periodically to verify that your website is working as you expect. For more information, see Chapter 15.

❑ **Load tests:** These tests verify that a target application will perform and scale as necessary. A target system is stressed by repeatedly executing a variety of tests. Team System records details of the target system's performance and automatically generates reports from the data. Load tests frequently are based on sets of web tests for verifying web applications. However, non-web applications can be tested by selecting a number of unit tests to execute. For more information, see Chapter 15.

❑ **Manual tests:** These tests allow a manual process, such as one described in a text document, to be carried out, with the results recorded in Team System. A manual test might be a detailed step-by-step use case or scenario that could be difficult to automate. Many companies strongly rely on manually conducted tests. Integration of manual testing enables such companies to continue those practices, with success and failure recorded by Team System, without requiring the expense of conversion. For details, see Chapter 16.

❑ **Generic tests:** These tests enable calling of alternative external testing systems, such as an existing suite of tests leveraging a third-party testing package. Results of those tests can be automatically parsed to determine success. This could range from something as simple as the result code from a console application to parsing the XML document exported from an external testing package. For more information, see Chapter 17.

❑ **Ordered tests:** Essentially containers of other tests, these establish a specific order in which tests are executed and enable the same test to be included more than once. For details, see the section "Using Ordered Tests" later in this chapter.

Placing your tests in a test project has the additional benefit of keeping them separate from your implementation code, reducing the risk that you'll accidentally deploy test code to your production environment.

Later in this chapter, we'll describe test management in detail, including use of the Test Manager and test lists to organize and execute collections of tests.

Creating a test project

There are a number of ways to create a new test project. You can create a test project before you create any tests or you can create one as you are creating a new test.

To create a test project before creating any tests, you can right-click on an existing solution and choose Add ➪ New Project. You may instead use the File menu, also selecting Add ➪ New Project. You will see the Add New Project dialog, as shown in Figure 13-1.

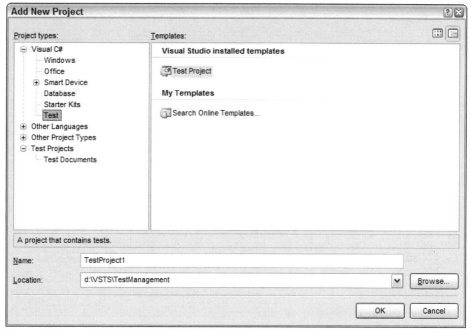

Figure 13-1

Under Project Types, choose the Test category under the language you wish to use for your tests, if applicable. Select Test Project from the Templates list and assign a name to your project. If you do not already have a solution, you will be able to create one as well.

When creating tests, Visual Studio will offer to automatically create a test project for you if you do not already have one. We discuss this later in the chapter.

When your test project is created, Visual Studio adds two files to your solution's Solution Items folder. One is the *test run configuration*, an XML file named `localtestrun.testrunconfig`. This file contains the various settings that determine how your tests will be executed. You can double-click on this file to display those settings. We'll cover test run configuration settings throughout the next few chapters.

The other file, known as the *test meta-data file*, is also XML-based and is named `<ProjectName>.vsmdi`. This file stores information about your solution's test lists and links to any contained tests. Double-clicking this file will open Test Manager. We'll discuss the use of this file later in this chapter.

Setting test project options

You may notice that the test project you have created is not empty. By default, a number of files will be included with your new test project. These include an "About Test Projects" text file that introduces test projects as well as sample unit and manual tests. These serve as helpful starting points to add your tests, but you can safely delete these if you choose. To change what types of files are added to a new test project, select Tools ➪ Options. On the resulting Options dialog, expand the Test Tools category and select Test Project. You will see options as shown in Figure 13-2.

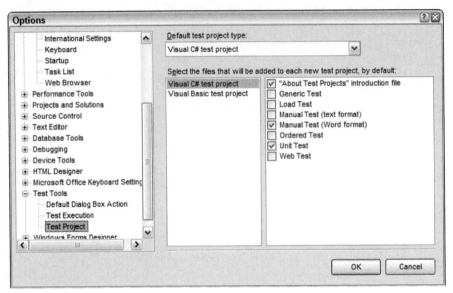

Figure 13-2

You may set the default language for new test projects using the drop-down list at the top. This setting will save you some time later, as you will not need to choose the language each time you create a new test project, though you always have the option to override this setting.

Below that, you will see a list of file types organized by test project language. Notice that several file types are already selected for you. The types of files that are automatically included can be specified by language type. For example, you may wish that VB.NET test projects are always created empty, while your C# test projects include the "About Test Projects" help file. Select which files you wish included, if any, and press OK.

Managing Test Cases

As you start to use the variety of test types supported by Team System, you may quickly find yourself with many tests in your solutions. Team System projects often have dozens and in some cases hundreds of unit tests alone. Add suites of web, load, and other tests and you would quickly have difficulty finding the right tests at the right time.

Fortunately, Team System offers several ways to easily manage, categorize, and locate tests. In this section, we'll cover the Test View and Test Manager windows. These windows are your main interface for organizing and executing all of your tests.

Test Manager

Test Manager, available only in Team Edition for Software Testers, provides many features for organizing, editing, and executing your tests. You can use the Test Manager for all of your solution's tests, regardless of type. To access Test Manager, select Test ➪ Windows ➪ Test Manager or click the Test Manager button on the Test Tools toolbar. You will then see a window similar to that shown in Figure 13-3.

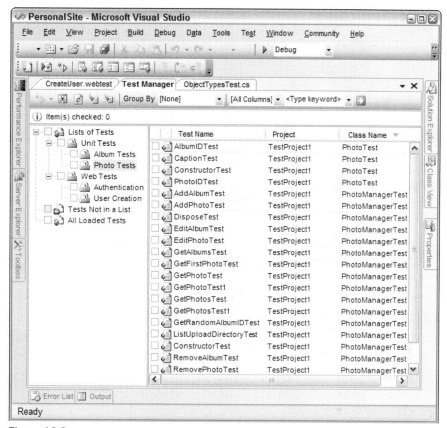

Figure 13-3

Test Manager features two panes. The right pane displays your solution's tests. The left pane is for creating, selecting, and managing groups of tests called *test lists*. We describe these panes in detail in the next section.

Working with tests in Test Manager

To get started, click the All Loaded Tests node of the tree in the left-hand pane. Double-click any test to open it for editing. The appropriate editor will load, depending on the type of test selected. You can also modify properties by right-clicking on a test and choosing Properties. If you already have the Properties window open, simply single-click on a test to view its properties.

Selecting and running tests

Each of your tests has a checkbox next to it. To run tests, check the box next to each test you wish to execute and then press the Run Checked Tests button on the Test Manager's toolbar. This button features another mode, Debug Checked Tests, which can be accessed using the button's drop-down arrow. The debug mode causes execution to pause at any breakpoints you have set, at which point you can debug as you would any other application.

You can also right-click in the test list pane and choose Run Checked Tests or Debug Checked Tests.

Note that Test Manager executes only checked tests. Tests that are highlighted but not checked will not be included in your test runs.

Running tests will activate the Test Results window, where you can track progress and view the results of all executed tests.

Disabling tests

To disable one or more tests, simply highlight the tests (checking them is not required) and then right-click and choose Disable. To restore them, repeat the process, selecting Enable. Disabled tests cannot be checked for execution, even if a containing test list is selected.

Disabling is a useful way to temporarily exclude a test, perhaps one that is flawed and needs correction, without having to remove it from any containing test lists. You can continue to use test lists to quickly select tests to run, knowing that your disabled tests will not be included.

Test lists

Another easy and effective way to organize your tests is by grouping them in test lists. Test lists are groups of tests that you wish to logically associate for any reason, perhaps by type, target, or purpose.

Think of test lists much like playlists of songs in an MP3 player, which are pointers to songs you want to play together. Just as you might load your "Upbeat" playlist for your Friday commute home, you could have a test list called "Offline Tests," which you can run without a network connection.

Creating test lists

To work with test lists, open Test Manager and note the pane on the left side. As shown in Figure 13-3, the left panel includes a tree view containing various groupings of tests. Right-click the Lists of Tests node and choose New Test List. The dialog shown in Figure 13-4 will be shown. You can also create a new test list without opening Test Manager by choosing Test ➪ Create New Test List.

Figure 13-4

Give your test list a name, optionally a description, and then choose a location to place the test list. Click OK and you will see your list in the test list tree.

Test lists and links to the tests they contain are stored as XML in your solution's test meta-data file, the file with an extension of `.vsmdi` *located in the Solution Items folder. This makes it easy to reuse those tests in other solutions. We'll describe importing these files later in this section.*

Note that test lists can contain other test lists. In Figure 13-4, we've created two main grouping lists, "Unit Tests" and "Web Tests." Under these, we created additional lists, such as "Album Tests."

Populating test lists

Once you have created a test list, you can drag tests from Test Manager onto the list. You can also create new tests directly in a test list by right-clicking on the test list and choosing New Test.

Keep two rules in mind when working with test lists. Each test list can contain only one instance of the same test, but tests can appear in more than one test list. By default, dragging tests into a test list is considered a move operation. If that test was dragged from one test list to another, it is removed from the source list and added to the target.

If you want a test to appear in more than one list, you can copy, instead of move, the test. To copy a test, right-click on any test and choose Copy. Then select the target test list and choose Paste. The test will then be in both the source and target lists. You can also hold the Ctrl key down while dragging a test to cause a copy operation.

Working with test lists

Test lists allow you to easily select all related tests for execution by checking the box next to the list name. In the Test List pane, click the checkbox next to one or more test lists you wish to run. All tests in that list, except disabled tests, will be checked. Tests in any child test lists will be selected as well.

As a convenience, if you happen to select all of the tests that comprise a test list through other means, such as the All Loaded Tests list, the containing test list will automatically be checked.

Special-purpose test lists

You've seen how to create your own lists in the Lists of Tests node in the Test List pane's tree. Below that are two other nodes, Tests Not in a List and All Loaded Tests. These are special lists that you cannot directly modify.

All Loaded Tests shows every test in your solution, regardless of their membership in test lists. This view is very useful for an overall picture of your tests. Dragging a test from this group to a test list has no effect on the list of tests in this group.

The other group, Tests Not in a List, shows any tests that have not been included in at least one test list. Use this view to quickly find any tests that might need categorization. If you drag a test from this group to a test list, it will automatically be removed from this group.

Choosing columns to display

By default, Test Manager displays the name, containing project, and type for each test. You can easily add or remove columns by clicking the Add/Remove Columns button or right-clicking in the list pane and choosing Add/Remove Columns.

The Test View window, described later, features similar support for changing which columns display.

Sorting, grouping, and filtering tests

Test lists are only one of the options for handling a large number of tests. The Test Manager and Test View windows both support grouping, sorting, and filtering of tests.

Note that once set, sorting, grouping, and filtering options affect all views of your lists and will remain the same as you switch between test lists or to the View All Tests mode.

Sorting

As mentioned before, you can customize which columns appear in the test listing pane. In addition, you can sort by the values of any of those columns. Simply click on a column name to sort the contents in ascending order. Click again to switch to descending order.

Grouping

By default, tests are displayed as a simple list, perhaps sorted by a column. These lists can get extremely long, especially when you're looking at the All Loaded Tests group in the Test List pane.

The Group By drop-down list enables you to choose a specific column. The lists will then be grouped according to their values for that column. This is especially useful because those groupings can be collapsed to make the list shorter and more manageable.

> *Any column can be used for grouping. The column does not have to be one of the currently displayed columns.*

For example, in Figure 13-5, all of the tests in the current solution are being displayed, but grouped by the name of the test list they are in, if any. Tests with no value for that column are placed together in the No Test List Name group.

To revert to an ungrouped listing, choose the [None] entry in the Group By field.

Filtering

Another powerful option, complementary to grouping and sorting, is *filtering*. Filtering restricts the tests to show only those that match a specified value for a column.

The second drop-down list, Filter Column, by default contains [All Columns], and enables you to select a filter column. You then specify the value to match by typing it in the Filter Text combo box, which contains <Type Keyword> by default. Press the Apply Filter button to the right of the Filter Text box and the list will be updated, showing only tests that match that value.

Tests are considered matching if *any* part of that column's value matches the text you entered. For example, if you enter "web," both "WebTest1" and "TestWebLogout" would match and be displayed.

The Filter Text box maintains a history of values. Use the drop-down list to quickly access previously created filters.

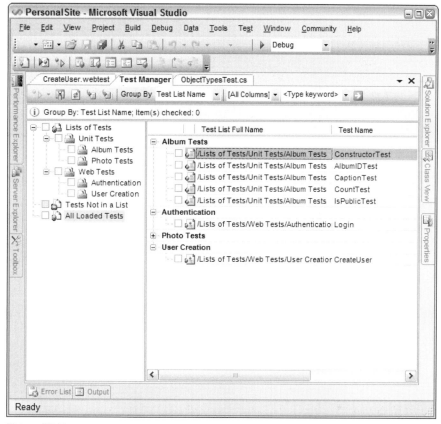

Figure 13-5

Filtering is an excellent complement to grouping. For example, if your solution contained multiple projects with many tests, already grouped by test type, you might find it useful to limit your view to just those tests in a specific project. Select the Project entry in the Filter Column list, enter the name of the project you wish to view, and press the Apply Filter button.

You could achieve similar results grouping by project name and sorting by test type. The final list would be longer, but you could collapse the groups of tests from other projects. You would also need to ensure that the Test Type column is added to the current view in order to perform the sort.

Loading and importing test meta-data files

As mentioned earlier, a solution that contains one or more test projects will have a test meta-data file with an extension of .vsmdi located in the Solution Items folder. This XML file stores details of the test lists in your solution's test projects as well as links to the tests those lists contain. These files can be useful when you want to reuse tests for other purposes — for example, in another solution or in a build environment.

A solution may have only one test meta-data file. If you have a solution without a test project, you can load a test meta-data file by clicking the Load Metadata File button on the Test Manager toolbar. If your project already has a test meta-data file, you can append other test lists by using the Import Meta-data File. Imported meta-data files are merged with the existing solution's meta-data file.

When you load or import a test meta-data file, Visual Studio displays the new test lists and attempts to locate any linked tests. Tests that could not be resolved will be marked with a warning icon. To help resolve these broken links, add the test project that contains those tests to your current solution.

Test View

The Test View window is available in both the Tester and Developer editions of Team System. It offers a streamlined interface very similar to that of Test Manager, but without some of the functionality.

To open the Test View window, choose Test ⇨ Windows ⇨ Test View or click the Test View button on the Test Tools toolbar. You will see a docked window as shown in Figure 13-6.

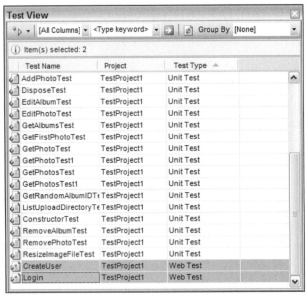

Figure 13-6

There are several differences between Test View and Test Manager. Perhaps most noticeably, listed tests have no associated checkboxes. Another significant difference is that the ability to select and create test lists is not supported in Test View. Finally, the Test View toolbar is slightly simplified, removing some options such as loading and importing test meta-data files.

Selecting and executing tests in Test View is simple and fast. Just highlight one or more tests and press the Run Tests button. You can also right-click and choose Run Selection or Debug Selection. To select multiple tests, hold down Ctrl while clicking on each test. To select a group of consecutive tests, click the first test, hold down Shift, and click on the last test.

Unlike Test Manager, tests in Test View need only be highlighted to be executed.

As with Test Manager, you can double-click on any test to edit it. You may also right-click to access features such as deleting a test, creating a new test, and disabling/enabling a test. You may also choose which columns appear by right-clicking and choosing Add/Remove Columns.

Because Test View does not support test lists, the list of tests can be extremely long. Fortunately, Test View supports the same grouping and filtering options that Test Manager offers. For details, see the "Sorting, grouping, and filtering tests" section.

Working with Test Results

In this section, you'll see how the Test Results window displays the progress and final outcome of test runs. You'll also learn about the secondary uses of the Test Results windows, including exporting and publishing test results.

Test Results window

When a test run is started, the Test Results window is shown, displaying the current status of the run. Each test will update automatically and you can use the control buttons to affect the run, even before it is complete. Click the Pause button to temporarily suspend test execution or click Stop to abort the test run. Whether you pause or stop a run, you will be able to view the results of any completed tests.

As an example, Figure 13-7 shows the Test Results window for a sample test run of four unit tests.

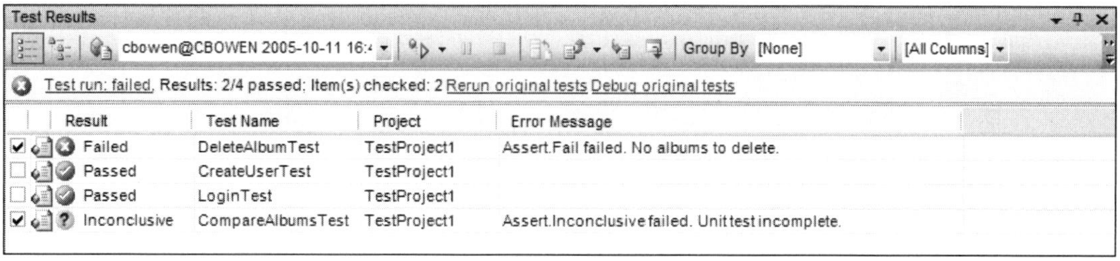

Figure 13-7

The Result Summary for the entire test run can be accessed by clicking the run status hyperlink, which is the first hyperlink in Test Results. In Figure 13-7, the hyperlink has the text "Test run: failed." The test run status hyperlink, may indicate "failed," "aborted," or "succeeded." The Result Summary will show details about the run start and stop time, the configuration used, and the user who submitted the run.

Simply double-click any test to see the detailed results for that test run. For tests that did not pass, you may see additional details such as the error message and a stack trace for the test failure. You can also right-click and choose Open Test to edit each test.

By default, the run's tests are shown as a simple list, but you can press the View Results by Result List button to show a test list pane. This pane functions much the same as it does with Test Manager. As with creating and managing tests, it is also convenient to view results from a large test run organized by those same test lists.

You may notice that the Failed and Inconclusive test results automatically have their checkboxes checked, while the two tests that passed do not. This is to enable the quick rerunning of tests that did not pass. Simply click the Run button and the checked tests will be executed.

As you have seen with Test Manager and Test View, the Run button has a drop-down to select other options, including Debug. In Test Results, the options also include a Run With selection. Use this to run the selected tests using an alternate Test Run Configuration.

Finally, if your run included any tests that did not pass, you will notice two additional hyperlinked options, "Rerun Original Tests" and "Debug Original Tests." Use these to execute the same set of tests again. Note that this will execute the tests as they were when initially run. If you have made any changes to the tests since the original run, those changes will not be included. To include new changes, run your tests with the Run button or by using Test Manager or Test View.

Sorting, grouping, and filtering tests results

The Test Results window supports exactly the same functionality for sorting, grouping, and filtering results that the Test Manager and Test View windows do for test cases.

Click on any column header to sort by ascending value, and again for descending. You can also right-click and choose Add/Remove Columns to modify which columns are displayed.

Notice the Group By, Filter Column, and Filter Text fields on the right-hand side of the Test Results window's toolbar. For details on their use, see "Sorting, grouping, and filtering tests" in the Test Manager section.

Exporting test results

By default, whenever a test is run, statistics on that run are automatically stored in a file on disk. These files are XML files with an extension of .trx. Team System uses these files to store information about which tests were run, when they ran, statistics on that run, and details about the results.

You can use the Test Results window to manually export test run results. This might be useful if you have disabled automatic test results storage or use the database option. To export all results from the current run, click the Export Results button. You can choose to export a subset of test results, perhaps only for tests that passed, by pressing the arrow on the Export Results button and choosing Export Selected Test Results.

Note, however, that these files can contain a lot of data, especially if you have many tests or have any long-running load tests.

Using Test Results XML (TRX) files

Test Results XML, or TRX, files contain all of the details for selected test runs. Team System establishes a Windows file association for the .trx extension, so double-clicking on such a file will automatically load those results into Visual Studio, where the details can be viewed.

In this way, you can easily copy TRX files between systems to view results with full details on a machine other than the one that originally executed the tests. For instance, you may find this useful for transferring details from your testers to your developers.

You can also use the Test Results window to manually import a TRX file to view its contents. Click the Import Test Results button on the Test Results toolbar, and then select the correct TRX file. If the contained run is already loaded in the IDE, then you will see an error message. Otherwise, you will be able to view the results and details from that exported test run.

The following section describes a more powerful option available, called *publishing*.

Publishing results

Exporting test results will store the data in a local TRX file. However, if you have a Team Foundation Server instance configured, you can send those test results to it through a process called publishing.

Publishing your run data is vital to your project's success because it enables your team to view and track testing metrics over time. Published data can be queried through various reports, such as Quality Indicators, Code Coverage Details, and Test Run Details.

Before you can publish results, you must be connected to a Team Foundation Server instance. In addition, that instance must have at least one Team Build configured because published results are associated with a specific build. Because run data is associated with a specific build, you can determine the quality of each build by reviewing the test run data for each to identify trends. Team Foundation and Team Build are described in detail in Part 4 of this book.

To publish a test run, click the Publish button located near the center of the toolbar in the Test Results window. When you click this button, you will see the Publish Test Results dialog shown in Figure 13-8.

> *If the Publish button is disabled, be certain that you are connected to a Team Foundation instance and that your team project has at least one team build.*

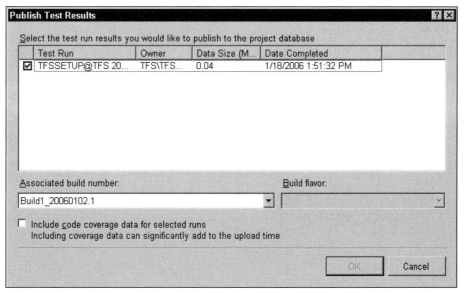

Figure 13-8

Choose one or more test runs to publish. You can then select the build with which to associate the run data. Finally, you can choose to include any code coverage data. Click OK and your results will be published. You will see the Publish View mode of the Test Results window, with details about each publication, including the status and any error message.

When your publication shows a status of Completed, your data has been saved to the operational store for your team project.

> *Published data is not immediately available for reporting. The data can be queried once it has been pulled into the data warehouse. This is done automatically at a frequency you can set in your Team Foundation Server instance.*

You can also publish test run data from the command line using the MSTest console application. See Chapter 15 for more details on command-line testing.

Using Ordered Tests

You've already seen how test lists can be used to easily categorize and organize your tests. However, sometimes you need more control over the members of a test group. Another type of test that Team System supports is the *ordered test*. An ordered test is simply a test that is composed of other logically related tests. As when using test lists, you can add one or more tests as members of an ordered test. Unlike test lists, you can also arrange those tests to execute in a specific sequence. In addition, the same test can be added to an ordered test multiple times.

> *Don't feel constrained by the term "test" when creating your test suites. There may be perfectly valid cases when a "test" doesn't actually test anything. Perhaps you've created a utility method that erases your customer table. Create a unit test to call this method and add it to your ordered test wherever you need that table reset.*

Being able to specify the order of test execution as well as including a test more than once has a wide variety of applications. For example, you may have a Create User web test that, after execution, adds a new user to your database. Your next test, Log User In, may rely on the existence of that new user. By ordering your tests, you ensure that the first test successfully creates the user before the second test attempts to log that user in.

> *Another important reason to create an ordered test is for cases when you wish to profile more than one test at a time. Because you cannot add more than one test to a performance session, an ordered test, containing any number of related tests, is a great way to work around that limitation. See Chapter 12 for more information on profiling.*

Creating an ordered test

An ordered test is simply another type of test, so you create them in much the same way as other tests. Right-click on your test project and select Add ➪ Ordered Test. You will see the Ordered Test Editor, as shown in Figure 13-9.

Using the right and left arrow buttons, add one or more of the tests to the ordered test. The list of tests includes the tests from all projects in the current solution. Multiple tests can be added at the same time by holding the Ctrl key while clicking on each test. As mentioned before, the same test can be added more than once.

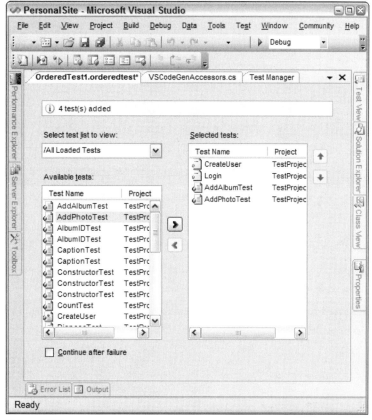

Figure 13-9

You may order the execution of the contained tests by adjusting their position with the up and down arrow buttons. The test at the top of the list will be executed first, proceeding sequentially down the list.

One of the key features of an ordered test is that tests run one at a time in a specified sequence. Using the Continue After Failure checkbox, you can indicate whether the ordered test continues to process remaining tests if a test should fail. By default, this is unchecked, indicating that the ordered test will abort when any test fails. Check the box to cause the ordered test to always execute all contained tests, regardless of success.

Ordered test properties

Find your ordered test in Test Manager or Test View. Right-click and select Properties. You will see the Properties window containing the values for your ordered test, similar to what is shown in Figure 13-10.

You can set the test's Description and temporarily disable the test via the Test Enabled property. Other properties include Timeout, which indicates how long the test should run before failing and the Continue After Failure property, described in the previous section. For descriptions of the Agent Properties and Deployment Items properties, see the "Distributed Load Tests" section of Chapter 15.

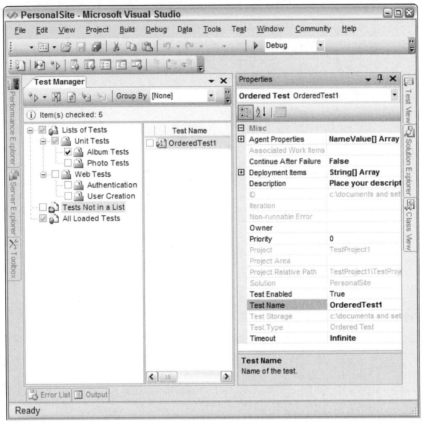

Figure 13-10

Executing and analyzing ordered tests

An ordered test is executed just like other tests. You can use the Test Manager and Test View windows. You can also use the command-line tool, MSTest.exe, as described in the "Command-line Test Execution" section of Chapter 15.

When executed from Visual Studio, the Test Results window will activate, displaying progress as the test is executing and results when it is complete. In the following example, we have an ordered test with four contained tests. As shown in Figure 13-11, the test has been run, but failed.

Notice that the Test Results window indicates "2/5 passed." The ordered test contained four inner tests, but the ordered test itself counts as a test with regard to success or failure. Right-click on the ordered test in the Test Results window and select View Test Results Details. The main window will display Common Results and Contained Tests.

The Common Results show the overall status of the ordered test, including the start and end time and the ultimate result.

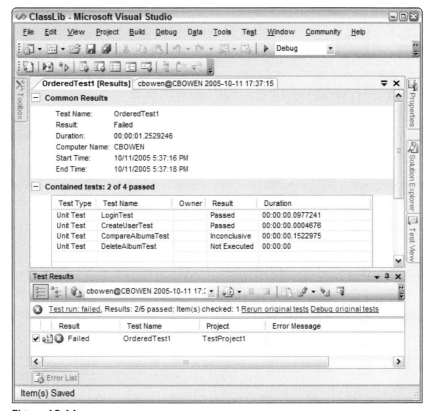

Figure 13-11

However, in this case, we're interested in finding out what happened with the individual tests contained in the ordered test. The Contained Tests section displays each of the contained tests, along with their type, name, result, and how long the test ran.

You can see that the first two tests have passed. However, the third test, CompareAlbumsTest, did not pass. Because our project's Continue After Failure property was set to False, the remaining fourth test was not executed. Double-click on any inner test to see details for that test.

When you are ready to run the test again, you can repeat the selection process via Test Manager or Test View, use the Test Results' Run button, or run the original test(s) by clicking the "Rerun original tests" hyperlink.

Summary

This chapter covered details common to all tests in Visual Studio Team System. We began with an introduction to the new project type, Test Project. You learned about the types of tests that can be added to test projects and how to configure the defaults for test projects you create.

We then covered the Test Manager and Test View windows in detail, showing you how to use the features of each to quickly and easily manage any number of tests.

After explaining the use of the management windows, we detailed some of the less common, but still very important uses of the Test Results window. You've learned how to export and import test run results to TRX files as well as how to publish those results to your Team Foundation Server instance for reporting and tracking purposes.

Finally, we looked at a special test type called the ordered test. Ordered tests are used to group other tests together to be run as a unit. Contained tests are executed in a specified order, and you can optionally indicate that you want the test to abort when any test fails.

The details covered in this chapter should prepare you to effectively manage and orchestrate the testing of your Team System projects. Whether your project has just a few or many hundreds of tests, using the tools and techniques described in this chapter will help you to achieve success.

14

Unit Testing with the Unit Test Framework

Unit testing involves writing code to verify a system at a lower and more granular level than with other types of testing. It is used *by* programmers *for* programmers and is quickly becoming standard practice at many organizations. The Developer and Tester editions of Visual Studio Team System now include unit testing features that are fully integrated with the IDE and with other features such as reporting and source control. Developers no longer need to rely on third-party utilities, such as NUnit, to perform their unit testing, although they still have the option to use them.

In this chapter, we describe the concepts behind unit testing, why it is important, and how to create effective unit test suites. We introduce the practice of *test-driven development,* which involves the creation of tests before writing the code to be tested.

We introduce the syntax of writing unit tests, and you will learn how to work with Team System's integrated features for executing and analyzing those tests. We then go into more detail about the classes available to you when writing your unit tests, including the core `Assert` class and many important attributes. You will also see how easy it is to create data-driven unit tests, whereby a unit test is executed once per record in a data source, and has full access to that bound data.

We also describe the features Team System offers for easily accessing nonpublic members from your unit tests. In addition, you will learn how Team System enables the generation of unit tests from existing code as well as the generation of member structures when writing unit tests.

Team System also provides built-in features to support the unit testing of ASP.NET applications. You will learn how to create ASP.NET unit tests that have full access to the ASP.NET run-time context. This enables actions such as setting and reading form control values and execution of those controls' events.

Finally, we describe how Team System can help measure the effectiveness of your tests. *Code coverage* is the concept of observing which lines of code are used during execution of unit tests. You can easily identify regions of your code that are not being executed and create tests to verify that code. This will improve your ability to find problems before the users of your system do.

Unit Testing Concepts

You've likely encountered a number of traditional forms of testing. Your quality assurance staff may run automated or manual tests to validate behavior and appearance. Load tests may be run to establish that performance metrics are acceptable. Your product group might run user acceptance tests to validate that systems do what the customers expect. Unit testing takes another view. Unit tests are written to ensure that code performs as the *programmer* expects.

Unit tests are generally focused at a lower level than other testing, establishing that underlying features work as expected. For example, an acceptance test might walk a user through an entire purchase. A unit test might verify that a `ShoppingCart` class correctly defends against adding an item with a negative quantity.

Unit testing is an example of *white box testing*, where knowledge of internal structures is used to identify the best ways to test the system. This is a complementary approach to *black box testing*, where the focus is not on implementation details but on overall functionality compared to specifications. You should leverage both approaches to effectively test your applications.

Benefits of unit testing

A common reaction to unit testing is to resist the approach because the tests seemingly make more work for a developer. However, unit testing offers many benefits that may not be obvious at first.

The act of writing tests often uncovers design or implementation problems. The unit tests serve as the first users of your system and will frequently identify design issues or functionality that is lacking. Once a unit test is written, it serves as a form of documentation for the use of the target system. Other developers can look to an assembly's unit tests to see example calls into various classes and members.

Perhaps one of the most important benefits is that a well-written test suite provides the original developer with the freedom to pass the system off to other developers for maintenance and further enhancement. Should those developers introduce a bug in the original functionality, there is a strong likelihood that those unit tests will detect that failure and help diagnose the issue. Meanwhile, the original developer can focus on current tasks.

It takes the typical developer time and practice to become comfortable with unit testing. Once a developer has been saved enough time by unit tests, he or she will latch on to them as an indispensable part of the development process.

Unit testing does require more explicit coding, but this cost will be recovered, and typically exceeded, when you spend much less time debugging your application. In addition, some of this cost is typically already hidden in the form of test console- or Windows-based applications. Unlike these informal testing applications, which are frequently discarded after initial verification, unit tests become a permanent part of the project, run each time a change is made to help ensure that the system still functions as expected. Tests are stored in source control very near to the code they verify and are maintained along with the code under test, making it easier to keep them synchronized.

> Unit tests are an essential element of regression testing. Regression testing involves retesting a piece of software after new features have been added to make sure that errors or bugs are not introduced. Regression testing also provides an essential quality check when you introduce bug fixes in your product.

It is difficult to overstate the importance of comprehensive unit test suites. They enable a developer to hand off a system to other developers with confidence that any changes they make should not introduce undetected side effects. However, because unit testing only provides one view of a system's behavior, no amount of unit testing should ever replace integration, acceptance, and load testing.

Writing effective unit tests

Because unit tests are themselves code, you are generally unlimited in the approaches you can take when writing them. However, we recommend that you follow some general guidelines:

- ❑ Always separate your unit test assemblies from the code you are testing. This separation enables you to deploy your application code without unit tests, which serve no purpose in a production environment.

- ❑ Avoid altering the code you are testing solely to allow easier unit testing. A common mistake is to open accessibility to class members to allow unit tests direct access. This compromises design, reduces encapsulation, and broadens interaction surfaces. You will see later in this chapter that Team System offers features to help address this issue.

- ❑ Each test should verify a small slice of functionality. Do not write long sequential unit tests that verify a large number of items. While creating focused tests will result in more tests, the overall suite of tests will be easier to maintain. In addition, identifying the cause of a problem is much easier when you can quickly look at a small failed unit test, immediately understand what it was testing, and know where to search for the bug.

- ❑ All tests should be autonomous. Avoid creating tests that rely on other tests to be run beforehand. Tests should be executable in any combination and in any order. To verify that your tests are correct, try changing their execution order and running them in isolation.

- ❑ Test both expected behavior (normal workflows) and error conditions (exceptions and invalid operations). This often means that you will have multiple unit tests for the same method, but remember that developers will always find ways to call your objects that you did not intend. Expect the unexpected, code defensively, and test to ensure that your code reacts appropriately.

The final proof of your unit testing's effectiveness will be when they save you more time during development and maintenance than you spent creating them. In our experience, you will realize this savings many times over.

Test-driven development

Test-driven development (TDD) is the practice of writing unit tests before writing the code that will be tested. The logic behind writing tests against code that does not exist is difficult to grasp at first. Our experience has shown that TDD can be a challenge to introduce to developers and that the best way to learn it is by applying it on a small sample or noncritical project. Only after working with TDD will its advantages be fully understood and appreciated.

TDD encourages following a continuous cycle of development involving small and manageable steps. Figure 14-1 illustrates the steps involved in test-driven development.

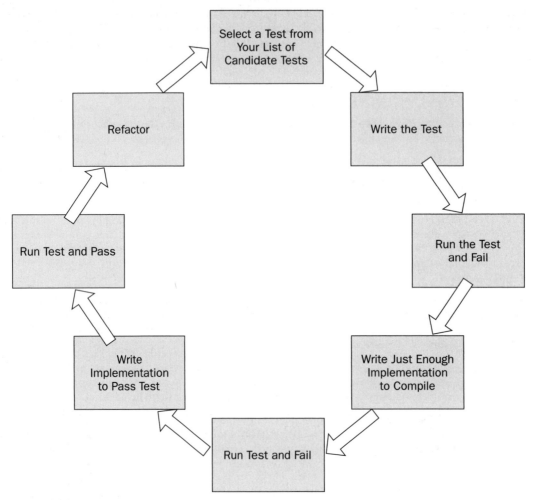

Figure 14-1

First, you generate an initial list of tests that apply to your task. Tests should verify all expected functionality, a variety of inputs, and error handling. Your initial list will rarely, if ever, include all of the tests you will need to write. As you work, you'll realize other inputs or scenarios that need testing. As this happens, simply add them to the list. Think of this list of tests as the requirements of your application. If your code needs to implement a certain behavior, make sure you have one or more unit tests to enforce it.

Once your initial list is ready, you now enter the cycle of TDD, shown in Figure 14-1. As shown at the top of the diagram, select one test from the list and begin writing the unit test. Of course, this cannot compile because the code you're testing does not exist. Write just enough application code to successfully compile and then run the test. As expected, it will fail because the implementation isn't complete. Add enough implementation logic to allow the test to pass. Resist the temptation to write all of the code you think will eventually be needed; instead, focus only on the current test. The code will be completed later as you implement all of the tests.

Once you have a passing test, you can refactor your code. As you learned in Chapter 11, refactoring is the process of making small changes to code that improve the design of the code but do not alter its functionality. Refactoring is critical when following TDD, as your code might not be as clean or organized as it might otherwise be when following a traditional design-first, top-town development model. Refactor to remove duplication and reduce complexity, and to improve maintainability and overall design.

Make sure your refactoring changes are done in small steps, building and running tests with each change. Once refactoring is complete, resume your cycle at the top by selecting the next test. When the list of tests is empty, you're ready to move on to your next task, confident that the functionality you've implemented has been tested and will be much easier to maintain.

This process is often abbreviated to what is known as "red, green, refactor." The "red" means you begin with a failing test. Once the implementation code is written, the test will pass, giving you the "green" result. Finally, the code is refactored to improve design.

You know from Chapter 11 that Visual Studio helps you perform refactoring in efficient and less error-prone ways. Later in this chapter, you'll see how Team System can facilitate a TDD approach through its integrated unit testing features and by offering code generation from within unit tests.

Third-party tools

Unit testing is not a new concept. Before Team System introduced integrated unit testing, developers needed to rely on third-party frameworks. The de facto standard for .NET unit testing has been an open-source package called *NUnit*. NUnit has its original roots as a .NET port of the Java-based JUnit unit testing framework. JUnit is itself a member of the extended xUnit family.

There are many similarities between NUnit and the unit testing framework in Team System. The structure and syntax of tests and the execution architecture are conveniently similar. If you have existing suites of NUnit-based tests, it is generally easy to convert them for use with Team System.

> *James Newkirk, who led development of NUnit 2.0 and is now employed at Microsoft, has written a tool to convert your NUnit tests to Team System's syntax. At the time of writing, this tool, called the "NUnit Converter," is available from GotDotNet at* `http://workspaces.gotdotnet.com/nunitaddons`.

Team System's implementation of unit testing is not merely a port of NUnit. Microsoft has added a number of features that are unavailable with the version of NUnit available at the time of this writing. Among these are IDE integration, code generation, new attributes, enhancements to the `Assert` class, and built-in support for testing nonpublic members. We describe all of these in detail later in this chapter.

Team System Unit Testing

Unit testing is a feature available in the Developer and Tester editions of Visual Studio Team System. In this section, we describe how to create, execute, and manage unit tests.

Unit tests are themselves normal code, identified as unit tests through the use of attributes. Like NUnit 2.0 and later, Team System uses .NET reflection to inspect assemblies to find unit tests.

Reflection is a mechanism by which details about .NET objects can be discovered at execution time. The `System.Reflection` *assembly contains members that help you identify classes, properties, and methods of any .NET assembly. Reflection even enables you to call methods and access properties of classes. This includes access to private members, a practice that can be useful in unit testing, as you will see later in this chapter.*

You will also use attributes to identify other structures used in your tests and to indicate desired behaviors.

Creating your first unit test

In this section, we'll take a slower approach to creating a unit test than you will in your normal work. This will give you a chance to examine details you could miss using only the built-in features that make unit testing easier. Later in this chapter, you'll look at the faster approaches.

In order to have something to test, create a new C# Class Library project named `ExtendedMath`. Rename the default `Class1.cs` to `Functions.cs`. We'll add code to compute the Fibonacci for a given number. The Fibonacci Sequence, as you may recall, is a series of numbers where each term is the sum of the prior two terms. The first six terms, starting with an input factor of 1, are {1, 1, 2, 3, 5, 8}.

Open `Functions.cs` and insert the following code:

```
using System;

namespace ExtendedMath
{
    public static class Functions
    {
        public static int Fibonacci(int factor)
        {
            if (factor < 2)
                return (factor);
            int x = Fibonacci(--factor);
            int y = Fibonacci(--factor);

            return x + y;
        }
    }
}
```

You are now ready to create unit tests to verify the `Fibonacci` implementation. Unit tests are recognized as tests only if they are contained in separate projects called *test projects*. Test projects can contain any of the test types supported in Team System. Add a test project named `ExtendedMathTesting` to your solution by adding a new project and selecting the Test Project template. If the test project includes any sample tests for you, such as `UnitTest1.cs` or `ManualTest1.mht`, you can safely delete them.

> **For full details on creating and customizing test projects, see Chapter 13.**

Because you will be calling objects in your ExtendedMath project, make a reference to that class library project from the test project. You may notice that a reference to the Microsoft.VisualStudio .QualityTools.UnitTestFramework.dll assembly has already been made for you. This assembly contains many helpful classes for creating units tests. We'll use many of these throughout this chapter.

As you'll see later in this chapter, Team System supports the generation of basic unit test outlines, but in this section, we'll create them manually to make it easier to understand the core concepts.

Once you have created a new test project, add a new class file (not a unit test; we'll cover that file type later) called FunctionsTest.cs. You will use this class to contain the unit tests for the Functions class. You'll be using unit testing objects from the ExtendedMath project and the UnitTestFramework assembly mentioned earlier, so add using statements at the top so that the class members do not need to be fully qualified:

```
using ExtendedMath;
using Microsoft.VisualStudio.TestTools.UnitTesting;
```

Identifying unit test classes

To enable Team System to identify a class as potentially containing unit tests, you must assign the TestClass attribute. If you forget to add the TestClass attribute, the unit tests methods in your class will not be recognized.

To indicate that the FunctionsTest class will contain unit tests, add the TestClass attribute to its declaration:

```
namespace ExtendedMath
{
    [TestClass]
    public class FunctionsTest
    {
    }
}
```

Unit tests are required to be hosted within public classes, so don't forget to include the public descriptor for the class. Note also that parentheses after an attribute are optional if you are not passing parameters to the attribute. For example, [TestClass()] and [TestClass] are equivalent.

Identifying unit tests

Having identified the class as a container of unit tests, you're ready to add your first unit test. A unit test method must be public, nonstatic, accept no parameters, and have no return value. To differentiate unit test methods from ordinary methods, they must be decorated with the TestMethod attribute.

Add the following code inside the FunctionsTest class:

```
[TestMethod]
public void FibonacciTest()
{
}
```

Unit test success and failure

You have the shell of a unit test, but how do you test? A unit test indicates failure to Team System by throwing an exception. Any test that does not throw an exception is considered to have passed, except in the case of `ExpectedException` attribute, which we describe later.

The unit testing framework defines the `Assert` object. This object exposes many members, which are central to creating unit tests. You'll learn more about `Assert` later in the chapter.

Add the following code to the `FibonacciTest`:

```
[TestMethod]
public void FibonacciTest()
{
    const int FACTOR = 8;
    const int EXPECTED = 21;

    int actual = ExtendedMath.Functions.Fibonacci(FACTOR);

    Assert.AreEqual(EXPECTED, actual);
}
```

This uses the `Assert.AreEqual` method to compare two values, the value you expect and the value generated by calling the `Fibonacci` method. If they do not match, an exception will be thrown, causing the test to fail.

When you run tests, you will see the Test Results window. Success is indicated with a green checkmark, failure with a red X. A special result, inconclusive (described later in this chapter), is represented by a question mark.

To see a failing test, change the EXPECTED constant from 21 to 22 and rerun the test. The Test Results window will show the test as failed. The Error Message column provides details about the failure reason. In this case, the Error Message would show the following:

```
Assert.AreEqual failed. Expected:<22>, Actual:<21>
```

This indicates that either the expected value is wrong or the implementation of the Fibonacci algorithm is wrong. Fortunately, because unit tests verify a small amount of code, the job of finding the source of bugs is made easier.

Managing and running unit tests

Once you have created a unit test and rebuilt your project, Visual Studio will automatically inspect your projects for unit tests. You can use the Test Manager and Test View windows to work with your tests.

> **For full details on test management and related windows, see Chapter 13.**

The easiest way to open these windows is by enabling the Test Tools toolbar and pressing either the Test View or Test Manager buttons. They are also available by selecting Test ➪ Windows.

Test View

Test View provides a compact view of your tests. It enables you to quickly select and run your tests. You can group tests by name, project, type, class name, and other criteria. Figure 14-2 shows the Test View window.

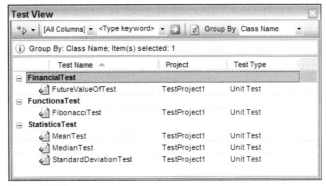

Figure 14-2

Double-click on any test to navigate to that test's code. To run one or more tests, select them and press the Run Selection button.

Test Manager

The Test Manager offers all of the features of the Test View window, but provides more options for organization and display of your tests. Figure 14-3 shows the Test Manager.

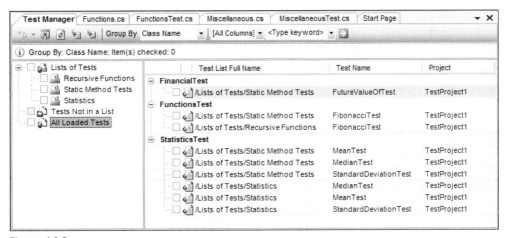

Figure 14-3

By default, all tests are listed, but you can organize tests into lists. In Test Manager, right-click on the Lists of Tests node on the tree on the left-hand side. Select New Test List and the Create New Test List dialog will appear as shown in Figure 14-4. You can also create a new test list by choosing Test ⇨ Create New Test List.

Figure 14-4

Give the list a name and optionally a description. You can also place this list within another list. For example, as shown in Figure 14-4, you might have a top-level Database Required list with a sublist of SQL Server, to which a second sublist for Oracle is being added.

Once you have created a list, you can drag tests from the Test Manager list onto it. The list enables you to easily select all related tests for execution by checking the box next to the list name.

You can also group by test properties. First, click the All Loaded Tests node to ensure that all tests are listed. Then, in the Group By drop-down list, scroll to and select Class Name. You will then see your tests in collapsible groups by class name.

If you have many tests, you will find the filtering option useful. With filters, you can limit the list of tests to only those that match text you enter. Next to the Group By list is a Filter Column drop-down and a text box. Enter the text you wish to match in the text box; you can optionally select a column you would like to match against. For example, if you wish to show only tests from a certain class, enter that class name then select Class Name in the Filter Column list. When you press the Apply Filter button, only tests from that class will be displayed. If the Filter Column is set to [All Columns], tests will display if any of their fields contain the text you enter.

Test run configuration

Whenever you run a set of tests, a group of settings apply to that run. Those settings, called the *test run configuration*, are stored in an XML file with a `.testrunconfig` extension. A test run configuration is created automatically for every new test project, named `localtestrun.testrunconfig`.

The settings include items such as the naming structure of your results files, configuration of remote test execution, enabling of code coverage, and specifying additional files to deploy during your tests.

To edit a test run configuration, choose Test ⇨ Edit Test Run Configurations, and then choose the config-uration you wish to modify. You can also double-click the configuration file in Solution Explorer. Figure 14-5 shows the Test Run Configuration interface.

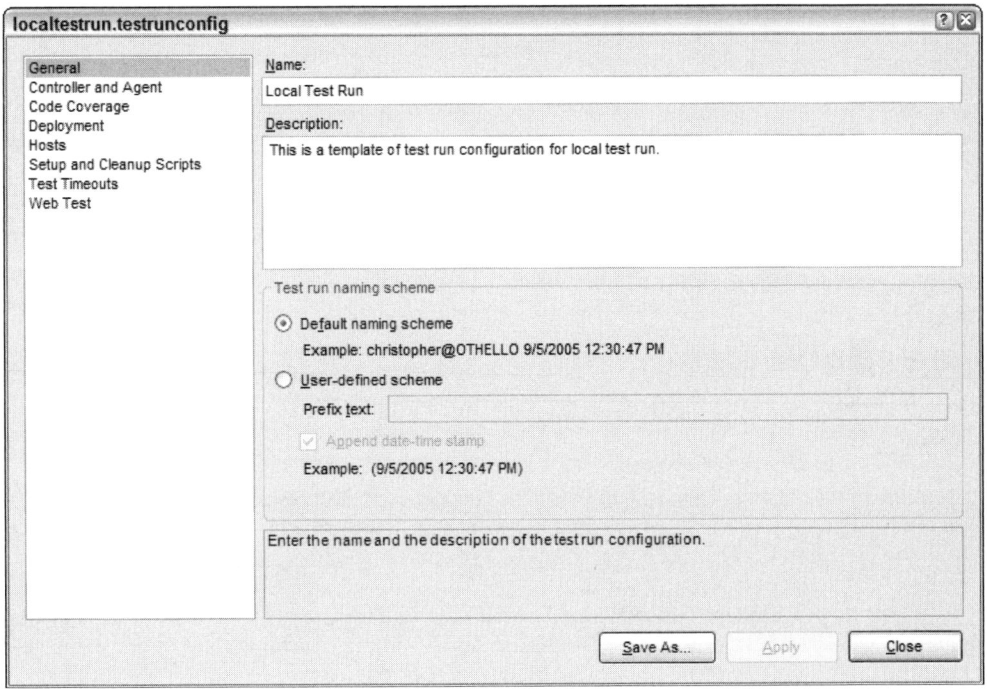

Figure 14-5

You may have more than one test run configuration, perhaps to support different execution environ-ments or code coverage settings, but you must select a single configuration as "active" when you run your tests. To set another configuration as active, choose Test ⇨ Select Active Test Run Configuration, and then choose the correct configuration.

The default configuration settings will generally be fine for your initial unit testing. As you begin to require additional unit testing features, you may need to adjust these settings. For example, later in this chapter, we describe how to monitor code coverage with Team System. In that section, you will learn how to use the test run configuration to enable that feature.

Test results

Once you have selected and run one or more unit tests using the Test View or Test Manager windows, you will see the Test Results window. This window displays the status of your test execution, as shown in Figure 14-6.

You can see that one of the tests has failed, two have passed, and two are inconclusive. The error mes-sage for any nonpassing test is displayed. You can double-click on any test result to see details for that test. You can also right-click on a test result and choose Open Test to navigate to the unit test code.

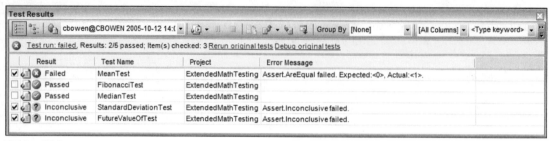

Figure 14-6

Notice that the nonpassing tests are checked. This convenient feature enables you to make some changes and then quickly rerun just those tests that have not passed.

Debugging unit tests

Because unit tests are simply methods with special attributes applied to them, they can be debugged just like other code.

Breakpoints can be set anywhere in your code, not just in your unit tests. For example, the FibonacciTest calls into the ExtendedMath.Fibonacci method. You could set a breakpoint in either method and have execution paused when that line of code is reached.

However, setting program execution will not pause at your breakpoints unless you run your unit test in debugging mode. The Test View, Test Results, and Test Manager windows all feature a drop-down arrow next to the Run button. For example, in Test Manager, click on the arrow next to the Run Checked Tests button. You will see a new option, Debug Checked Tests. If you choose this, the selected unit tests will be run in debug mode, pausing execution at any enabled breakpoints, and giving you a chance to evaluate and debug your unit test or implementation code as necessary.

> *If you have enabled code coverage for your application, you will see a message indicating that you cannot debug while code coverage is enabled. Click OK and you will continue debugging as normal, but code coverage results will not be available. We describe code coverage later in this chapter.*

Keep in mind that the Run/Debug buttons are "sticky." The last selected mode will continue to be used when the button is pressed until another mode is chosen from the drop-down list.

Programming with the Unit Test Framework

In this section, we describe in detail the attributes and methods available to you for creating unit tests. All of the classes and attributes mentioned in this section can be found in the Microsoft.VisualStudio .TestTools.UnitTesting namespace.

Initialization and cleanup of unit tests

Often, you'll need to configure a resource that is shared among your tests. Examples might be a database connection, a log file, or a shared object in a known default state. You might also need ways to clean up from the actions of your tests, such as closing a shared stream or rolling back a transaction.

The unit test framework offers attributes to identify such methods. They are grouped into three levels: Test, Class, and Assembly. The levels determine the scope and timing of execution for the methods they decorate. The following table describes these attributes.

Attributes	Frequency and Scope
TestInitialize, TestCleanup	Executed before (Initialize) or after (Cleanup) any of the class's unit tests are run
ClassInitialize, ClassCleanup	Executed a single time before or after any of the tests in the current class are run
AssemblyInitialize, AssemblyCleanup	Executed a single time before or after any number of tests in any of the assembly's classes are run

Having methods with these attributes is optional, but do not define more than one of each attribute in the same context.

> **Do not use class- or assembly-level initialize and cleanup attributes with ASP.NET unit tests. When run under ASP.NET, these methods cannot be guaranteed to run only once. Because these are static methods, this may lead to false testing results.**

TestInitialize and TestCleanup attributes

Use the TestInitialize attribute to create a method that will be executed one time before each unit test run in the current class. Similarly, TestCleanup marks a method that will always run immediately after each test. Like unit tests, methods with these attributes must be public, nonstatic, accept no parameters, and have no return values.

Here is an example test for a simplistic shopping cart class. It contains two tests and defines the TestInitialize and TestCleanup methods:

```
using Microsoft.VisualStudio.TestTools.UnitTesting;

[TestClass]
public class ShoppingCartTest
{
    private ShoppingCart cart;

    [TestInitialize]
    public void TestInitialize()
    {
        cart = new SomeClass();
        cart.Add(new Item("Test");)
    }

    [TestCleanup]
    public void TestCleanup()
    {
        // Not required - here for illustration
        cart.Dispose();
```

```
        }

        [TestMethod]
        public void TestCountAfterAdd()
        {
            int expected = cart.Count + 1;
            cart.Add(new Item("New Item");)
            Assert.AreEqual(expected, cart.Count);
        }

        [TestMethod]
        public void TestCountAfterRemove()
        {
            int expected = cart.Count - 1;
            cart.Remove(0);
            Assert.AreEqual(expected, cart.Count);
        }
    }
```

When you run both tests, `TestInitialize` and `TestCleanup` are both executed twice. `TestInitialize` is run immediately before each unit test and `TestCleanup` immediately after.

ClassInitialize and ClassCleanup attributes

The `ClassInitialize` and `ClassCleanup` attributes are used very similarly to `TestInitialize` and `TestCleanup`. The difference is that these methods are guaranteed to run once and only once no matter how many unit tests are executed from the current class. Unlike `TestInitialize` and `TestCleanup`, these methods are marked static and accept a `TestContext` instance as a parameter.

The importance of the `TestContext` instance is described later in this chapter.

The following code demonstrates how you might manage a shared logging target using class-level initialization and cleanup with a logging file:

```
        private System.IO.File logFile;

        [ClassInitialize]
        public static void ClassInitialize(TestContext context)
        {
            // Code to open the logFile object
        }

        [ClassCleanup]
        public static void ClassCleanup(TestContext context)
        {
            // Code to close the logFile object
        }
```

You could now reference the `logFile` object from any of your unit tests in this class, knowing that it will automatically be opened before any unit test is executed and closed after the final test in the class has completed.

> *This approach to logging is simply for illustration. You'll see later how the `TestContext` object passed into these methods enables you to more effectively log details from your unit tests.*

The following code shows the flow of execution should you again run both tests:

```
ClassInitialize
    TestInitialize
        TestCountAfterAdd
    TestCleanup
    TestInitialize
        TestCountAfterRemove
    TestCleanup
ClassCleanup
```

AssemblyInitialize and AssemblyCleanup attributes

Where you might use `ClassInitialize` and `ClassCleanup` to control operations at a class level, use the `AssemblyInitialize` and `AssemblyCleanup` attributes for an entire assembly. For example, a method decorated with `AssemblyInitialize` will be executed once before any test in that current assembly, not just those in the current class. As with the class-level initialize and cleanup methods, these must be static and accept a `TestContext` parameter:

```
[AssemblyInitialize]
public static void AssemblyInitialize(TestContext context)
{
    // Assembly-wide initialization code
}

[AssemblyCleanup]
public static void AssemblyCleanup(TestContext context)
{
    // Assembly-wide cleanup code
}
```

Consider using `AssemblyInitialize` and `AssemblyCleanup` in cases where you have common operations spanning multiple classes. Instead of having many per-class initialize and cleanup methods, you can refactor these to single assembly-level methods.

Using the Assert methods

The most common way to determine success in unit tests is to compare an expected result against an actual result. The `Assert` class features many methods that enable you to make these comparisons quickly.

Assert.AreEqual and Assert.AreNotEqual

Of the various `Assert` methods, you will likely find the most use for `AreEqual` and `AreNotEqual`. As their names imply, you are comparing an expected value to a supplied value. If the operands are not value-equivalent (or are equivalent for `AreNotEqual`), then the current test will fail.

A third, optional argument can be supplied: a string that will be displayed along with your unit test results, which you can use to describe the failure. Additionally, you can supply parameters to be replaced in the string, just as the `String.Format` method supports:

```
[TestMethod]
public void IsPrimeTest()
{
    const int FACTOR = 5;
    const bool EXPECTED = true;

    bool actual = CustomMath.IsPrime(FACTOR);

    Assert.AreEqual(EXPECTED, actual, "The number {0} should have been computed as
                    prime, but was not.", FACTOR);
}
```

`Assert.AreEqual` and `AreNotEqual` have many parameter overloads, accepting types such as `string`, `double`, `int`, `float`, `object`, and `generic` types. Take the time to review the overloads in the Object Browser.

When using these methods with two string arguments, one of the overrides allows you to optionally supply a third argument. This is a Boolean, called `ignoreCase`, that indicates whether the comparison should be case-insensitive. The default comparison is case-sensitive.

Working with floating-point numbers involves a degree of imprecision. You can supply an argument that defines a delta by which two numbers can differ yet still pass a test — for example, if you're computing square roots and decide that a "drift" of plus or minus 0.0001 is acceptable:

```
[TestMethod]
public void SquareRootTeset()
{
    const double EXPECTED = 3.1622;
    const double DELTA = 0.0001;
    double actual = CustomMath.SquareRoot(10);

    Assert.AreEqual(EXPECTED, actual, DELTA, "Root not within acceptable range");
}
```

Assert.AreSame and Assert.AreNotSame

`AreSame` and `AreNotSame` function in much the same manner as `AreEqual` and `AreNotEqual`. The important difference is that these methods compare the *references* of the supplied arguments. For example, if two arguments point to the same object instance, then `AreSame` will pass. Even when the arguments are exactly equivalent in terms of their state, `AreSame` will fail if they are not in fact the same object. This is the same concept that differentiates `object.Equals` from `object.ReferenceEquals`.

A common use for these methods is to ensure that properties return expected instances or that collections handle references correctly. In the following example, we add an item to a collection and ensure that what we get back from the collection's indexer is a reference to the same item instance:

```
[TestMethod]
public void CollectionTest()
{
    CustomCollection cc = new CustomCollection();
    Item original = new Item("Expected");
    cc.Add(original);
```

```
Item actual = cc[0];

    Assert.AreSame(original, actual);
}
```

Assert.IsTrue and Assert.IsFalse

As you can probably guess, IsTrue and IsFalse are used simply to ensure that the supplied expression is true or false as expected. Returning to the IsPrimeNumberTest example, we can restate it as follows:

```
[TestMethod]
public void IsPrimeTest()
{
    const int FACTOR = 5;

    Assert.IsTrue(CustomMath.IsPrime(FACTOR), "The number {0} should have been
                    computed as prime, but was not.", FACTOR);
}
```

Assert.IsNull and Assert.IsNotNull

Similar to IsTrue and IsFalse, these methods verify that a given object type is either null or not null. Revising the collection example, this ensures that the item returned by the indexer is not null:

```
[TestMethod]
public void CollectionTest()
{
    CustomCollection cc = new CustomCollection();
    cc.Add(new Item("Added"));
    Item item = cc[0];

    Assert.IsNotNull(item);
}
```

Assert.IsInstanceOfType and Assert.IsNotInstanceOfType

IsInstanceOfType simply ensures that a given object is an instance of an expected type. For example, suppose you have a collection that accepts entries of any type. You'd like to ensure that an entry you're retrieving is of the expected type:

```
[TestMethod]
public void CollectionTest()
{
    UntypedCollection untyped = new UntypedCollection();
    untyped.Add(new Item("Added"));
    untyped.Add(new Person("Rachel"));
    untyped.Add(new Item("Another"));

    object entry = untyped[1];

    Assert.IsInstanceOfType(entry, typeof(Person));
}
```

As you can no doubt guess, IsNotInstanceOfType will test to ensure that an object is not the specified type.

Assert.Fail and Assert.Inconclusive

Use `Assert.Fail` to immediately fail a test. For example, you may have a conditional case that should never occur. If it does, call `Assert.Fail` and an `AssertFailedException` will be thrown, causing the test to abort with failure. You may find `Assert.Fail` useful when defining your own custom `Assert` methods.

`Assert.Inconclusive` enables you to indicate that the test result cannot be verified as a pass or fail. This is typically a temporary measure until a unit test (or the related implementation) has been completed. As described in the section "Code Generation" later in this chapter, `Assert.Inconclusive` is used to indicate that more work is needed to be done to complete a unit test.

> There is no `Assert.Succeed` because success is indicated by completion of a unit test method without a thrown exception. Use a return statement if you wish to cause this result from some point in your test.

`Assert.Fail` and `Assert.Inconclusive` both support a string argument and optional arguments, which will be inserted into the string in the same manner as `String.Format`. Use this string to supply a detailed message back to the Test Results window, describing the reasons for the nonpassing result.

Using the CollectionAssert class

The `Microsoft.VisualStudio.TestTools.UnitTesting` namespace includes a class, `Collection Assert`, containing useful methods for testing the contents and behavior of collection types.

The following table describes the methods supported by `CollectionAssert`.

Method	Description
AllItemsAreInstancesOfType	Ensures that all elements are of an expected type
AllItemsAreNotNull	Ensures that no items in the collection are `null`
AllItemsAreUnique	Searches a collection, failing if a duplicate member is found
AreEqual	Ensures that two collections have reference-equivalent members
AreNotEqual	Ensures that two collections do not have reference-equivalent members
AreEquivalent	Ensures that two collections have value-equivalent members
AreNotEquivalent	Ensures that two collections do not have value-equivalent members
Contains	Searches a collection, failing if the given object is not found
DoesNotContain	Searches a collection, failing if a given object is found
IsNotSubsetOf	Ensures that the first collection has members not found in the second
IsSubsetOf	Ensures that all elements in the first collection are found in the second

The following example uses some of these methods to verify various behaviors of a collection type, `CustomCollection`. When this example is run, none of the assertions fail and the test results in success. Note that proper unit testing would spread these checks across multiple smaller tests.

```
[TestMethod]
public void CollectionTests()
{
    CustomCollection list1 = new CustomCollection();
    list1.Add("alpha");
    list1.Add("beta");
    list1.Add("delta");
    list1.Add("delta");

    CollectionAssert.AllItemsAreInstancesOfType(list1, typeof(string));
    CollectionAssert.AllItemsAreNotNull(list1);

    CustomCollection list2 = (CustomCollection)list1.Clone();

    CollectionAssert.AreEqual(list1, list2);
    CollectionAssert.AreEquivalent(list1, list2);

    CustomCollection list3 = new CustomCollection();
    list3.Add("beta");
    list3.Add("delta");

    CollectionAssert.AreNotEquivalent(list3, list1);
    CollectionAssert.IsSubsetOf(list3, list1);
    CollectionAssert.DoesNotContain(list3, "alpha");
    CollectionAssert.AllItemsAreUnique(list3);
}
```

The final assertion, `AllItemsAreUnique(list3)`, would have failed if tested against `list1` because that collection has two entries of the string `"delta"`.

Using the StringAssert class

Similar to `CollectionAssert`, the `StringAssert` class contains methods that enable you to easily make assertions based on common text operations. The following table describes the methods supported by `StringAssert`.

Method	Description
Contains	Searches a string for a substring and fails if not found
DoesNotMatch	Applies a regular expression to a string and fails if any matches are found
EndsWith	Fails if the string does not end with a given substring
Matches	Applies a regular expression to a string and fails if no matches are found
StartsWith	Fails if the string does not begin with a given substring

Here are some simple examples of these methods. Each of these assertions will pass:

```
[TestMethod]
public void TextTests()
{
    StringAssert.Contains("This is the searched text", "searched");

    StringAssert.EndsWith("String which ends with searched", "ends with searched");

    StringAssert.Matches("Search this string for whitespace",
                    new System.Text.RegularExpressions.Regex(@"\s+"));

    StringAssert.DoesNotMatch("Doesnotcontainwhitespace",
                        new System.Text.RegularExpressions.Regex(@"\s+"));

    StringAssert.StartsWith("Starts with correct text", "Starts with");
}
```

Matches and DoesNotMatch accept a string and an instance of System.Text.RegularExpressions .Regex. In the preceding example, a simple regular expression that looks for at least one whitespace character was used. Matches finds whitespace and the DoesNotMatch does not find whitespace, so both pass.

Expecting exceptions

Normally, a unit test that throws an exception is considered to have failed. However, you'll often wish to verify that a class behaves correctly by throwing an exception. For example, you might provide invalid arguments to a method to verify that it properly throws an exception.

The ExpectedException attribute indicates that a test will succeed only if the indicated exception is thrown. Not throwing an exception or throwing an exception of a different type will result in test failure.

The following unit test expects that an ObjectDisposedException will be thrown:

```
[TestMethod]
[ExpectedException(typeof(ObjectDisposedException))]
public void ReadAfterDispose()
{
    CustomFileReader cfr = new CustomFileReader("target.txt");
    cfr.Dispose();
    string contents = cfr.Read();   // Should throw ObjectDisposedException
}
```

The ExpectedException attribute supports a second, optional string argument. The Message property of the thrown exception must match this string or the test will fail. This enables you to differentiate between two different instances of the same exception type.

For example, suppose you are calling a method that throws a FileNotFoundException for several different files. To ensure that it cannot find one specific file in your testing scenario, supply the message you expect as the second argument to ExpectedException. If the exception thrown is not FileNotFoundException and its Message property does not match that text, the test will fail.

Defining custom unit test properties

You may define custom properties for your unit tests. For example, you may wish to specify the author of each test and be able to view that property from the Test Manager.

Use the `TestProperty` attribute to decorate a unit test, supplying the name of the property and a value:

```
[TestMethod]
[TestProperty("Author", "Deborah")]
public void ExampleTest()
{
    // Test logic
}
```

Now, when you view the properties of that test, you will see a new entry, `Author`, with the value `Deborah`. If you change that value from the Properties window, the attribute in your code will automatically be updated.

TestContext class

Unit tests normally have a reference to a `TestContext` instance. This object provides run-time features that might be useful to tests, such as details of the test itself, the various directories in use, and several methods to supplement the details stored with the test's results. `TestContext` is also very important for data-driven and ASP.NET unit tests, as you will see later.

Several methods are especially useful to all unit tests. The first, `WriteLine`, enables you to insert text into the results of your unit test. This can be useful for supplying additional information about the test, such as parameters, environment details, and other debugging data that would normally be excluded from test results. By default, information from the test run is stored in a *test results file*, an XML file with a `.trx` extension. These files can be found in the TestResults subdirectory of your project. The default name for the files is based on the user, machine, and date of the test run, but this can be modified via the test run configuration settings. See Chapter 13 for more information on test results files.

Here is a simple example of a unit test that accesses the `TestContext` to send a string containing the test's name to the results:

```
[TestClass]
public class TestClass
{
    private TestContext testContextInstance;

    public TestContext TestContext
    {
        get { return testContextInstance; }
        set { testContextInstance = value; }
    }

    [TestMethod]
    public void TestMethod1()
    {
        TestContext.WriteLine("This is test {0}", TestContext.TestName);
    }
```

The `AddResultFile` method enables you to add a file, at runtime, to the results of the test run. The file you specify will be copied to the results directory alongside other results content. For example, this may be useful if your unit test is validating an object that creates or alters a file and you would like that file to be included with the results for analysis.

Finally, the `BeginTimer` and `EndTimer` methods enable you to create one or more named timers within your unit tests. The results of these timers are stored in the test run's results.

Creating data-driven unit tests

An excellent way to verify the correct behavior of code is to execute it using realistic data. Team System provides features to automatically bind data from a data source as input to unit tests. The unit test is run once for each data row.

A unit test is made data-driven by assigning attributes for connecting to and reading from a data source. The easiest way to do this is to modify an existing unit test's properties in the Test Manager window. Begin with a normal unit test outline, and then open Test Manager. Select the unit test and view its properties.

First, establish the connection to the data source by setting the Data Connection String property. You may either enter it manually or click the button labeled with ellipses ("...") to use dialogs to create the connection string. Once the connection is specified, select the table you wish to use in the Data Table Name property.

As mentioned before, the unit test will be called once per row in the data source. You can set how rows are fed into the unit test via the Data Access Method property. Sequential will feed the rows in exactly the order returned from the data source, whereas Random will select random rows. Rows are provided to the unit test until all rows have been used once.

Setting these properties will automatically decorate the selected unit test with the appropriate attributes. You do not need to use the Properties window to create data-driven tests. For example, you may wish to copy attributes from an existing data-driven test to quickly create another.

To access the data from within the unit test, use the `DataRow` property of the `TestContext`. For example, if you bound to a table with customer data, you could read the current customer's ID from the CustomerID column with the following:

```
long customerID = TestContext.DataRow["CustomerID"];
```

Besides a column name, the `DataRow` property also accepts a column offset. If CustomerID were the first column in the table, you could supply a zero as the argument with the same result.

Because the unit test is run once per row in the data source, you want to be able to tell which rows caused certain results. Fortunately, this detail is already tracked for you. In the Test Results window, right-click on the test result and choose View Test Results Details. You will see a list of pass/fail results for each record in the database, enabling you to easily see which rows caused your test to fail.

Team System makes it very easy to write comprehensive tests against actual data. However, keep in mind that it is not enough to test only valid data, such as your real customer data. You will also want to have unit tests that verify your code's behavior when invalid data, perhaps in this case a negative number, is supplied.

Accessing Nonpublic Members from Tests

What if you want to test a class member that is not public? For example, suppose you're writing a private function that is never publicly accessed and is only used internally by other members. You'd like to test this method, but your test code does not have access to private members (or to internal members if the code is in a separate assembly).

There are three main approaches for addressing this issue:

- ❑ Make the private members you need to test public.
- ❑ Ensure that the private members are reachable through a public member and test via those public members.
- ❑ Use .NET reflection in the tests to load and directly invoke the nonpublic members.

With Team System, this final approach is abstracted for you. The following two sections describe how Team System helps to automate this previously manual task.

> **Testing private members is a controversial subject. Some people prefer to test only via public members to allow for easier refactoring. Others argue that an API should never be modified just for the sake of easier testing. If you agree with the former opinion, you can safely skip the remainder of this section.**

Using PrivateObject to access nonpublic instance members

Suppose you'd like to test the private field and method of the following class:

```
public class Example
{
    public Example() {}

    private string password = "letmein";

    private bool VerifyPassword(string password)
    {
        return (String.Compare(this.password, password, false) == 0);
    }
}
```

Because the field and method are marked `private`, a unit test will not have the ability to directly access them. How can you ensure that `VerifyPassword` is working correctly?

Team System introduces the `PrivateObject` class, which is a wrapper around reflection code that enables you to access nonpublic members in a fairly straightforward manner.

The following table summarizes the methods supported by `PrivateObject`.

Method	Description
GetArrayElement	Returns the selected item from a private array member. Supports multidimensional arrays with additional arguments.
GetField	Returns the value of the target field
GetFieldOrProperty	Returns the value of the target field or property
GetProperty	Returns the value of the target property
Invoke	Invokes the target method, optionally passing parameters
SetArrayElement	Assigns the given value to the indicated element of a private array Supports multidimensional arrays with additional arguments
SetField	Assigns the supplied object to the target field
SetFieldOrProperty	Assigns the supplied object to the target field or property
SetProperty	Assigns the supplied object to the target property

To use it, you first create an instance of the `PrivateObject` class, passing a `Type` object for the class you wish to work with:

```
using System;
using Microsoft.VisualStudio.TestTools.UnitTesting;

namespace Explorations
{
    [TestClass]
    public class ExampleTest
    {
        private PrivateObject privateObject;
        const string PASSWORD = "letmein";

        [TestInitialize]
        public void TestInitialize()
        {
            privateObject = new PrivateObject(typeof(Example));
        }
    }
}
```

Now you can create your tests. Use the `GetField` method of the `PrivateObject` instance to access non-public fields, supplying the name of the desired variable. Similarly, use `Invoke` to call methods, supplying the method name as the first argument, followed by any parameters to that method:

```
using System;
using Microsoft.VisualStudio.TestTools.UnitTesting;

namespace Explorations
{
    [TestClass]
    public class ExampleTest
    {
```

```
        private PrivateObject privateObject;
        const string PASSWORD = "letmein";

        [TestInitialize]
        public void TestInitialize()
        {
            privateObject = new PrivateObject(typeof(Example));
        }

        [TestMethod]
        public void ComparePrivatePassword()
        {
            string password = (string)privateObject.GetField("password");
            Assert.AreEqual(PASSWORD, password);
        }

        [TestMethod]
        public void TestPrivateVerifyPassword()
        {
            bool accepted = (bool)privateObject.Invoke("VerifyPassword", PASSWORD);
            Assert.IsTrue(accepted);
        }
    }
}
```

Because `PrivateObject` uses reflection, you need to cast the results of these calls from the generic `Object` type back to the correct underlying type.

Using PrivateType to access nonpublic static members

`PrivateObject` is used to access instance-based members of a class. If you need to access static nonpublic members, you use the `PrivateType` class, which has a very similar interface and is a wrapper of reflection code.

The following table summarizes the methods exposed by `PrivateType`.

Method	Description
GetStaticArrayElement	Returns the selected item from a private static array member. Supports multidimensional arrays with additional arguments.
GetStaticField	Returns the value of the target static field.
GetStaticProperty	Returns the value of the target static property.
InvokeStatic	Invokes the target static method, optionally passing parameters.
SetStaticArrayElement	Assigns the given value to the indicated element of a private static array. Supports multidimensional arrays with additional arguments.
SetStaticField	Assigns the supplied object to the target static field.
SetStaticProperty	Assigns the supplied object to the target static property.

The usage is very similar to the `PrivateObject`. Create an instance of the `PrivateType`, indicating which type you wish to work with, and then use the methods to access members as with `PrivateObject`. Suppose you added a private static count of password failures with a wrapping private property called `FailureCount`. The following code could read and test that property:

```
[TestMethod]
public void TestPrivateStaticFailureCount()
{
    PrivateType example = new PrivateType(typeof(Example));
    int failureCount = (int)example.GetStaticProperty("FailureCount");
    Assert.AreEqual(failureCount, 0);
}
```

Again, you create an instance of `PrivateType`, passing the type reference for the class you wish to access. Then you use that instance, invoking `GetStaticProperty` to retrieve the value you wish to test. Finally, you ensure that the value is zero as expected.

> *Use caution when testing static data. Because static data is shared and is not automatically reset between your tests, sometimes the order of your tests will affect their results. In other words, if you test that a value is initialized to zero in one test and then set it to a test value in another test, if the order of those tests is reversed, the zero test will fail. Remember that you must be able to run your tests in any order and in any combination.*

Code Generation

Remember the work you did earlier in this chapter to create your first unit test? Depending upon the degree to which you practice TDD, you might not create many of your unit tests in that manner. We created the first unit tests manually to help convey basic concepts, but Team System has support for automatically generating code. You may generate unit tests from your implementation code or generate limited implementation code when writing your tests.

Generating tests from code

If you have ever needed to add unit testing to an existing project that had none, it was likely a frustrating experience. Fortunately, Team System has introduced the capability to generate outlines of unit tests based on selected implementation code.

> *If you are practicing test-driven development, described earlier, be aware that generating tests from existing code is considered a very non-TDD practice. In pure TDD, no implementation code should exist before unit tests are created.*

Let's begin with the `Functions` class we used earlier in this chapter. Open `Functions.cs` and ensure it contains the following code:

```
using System;

namespace ExtendedMath
{
    public sealed class Functions
    {
```

```
        private Functions() {}

        public static int Fibonacci(int factor)
        {
            if (factor < 2)
                return (factor);
            int x = Fibonacci(--factor);
            int y = Fibonacci(--factor);

            return x + y;
        }
    }
}
```

If you have been following the examples in this chapter, delete your existing `FunctionsTest.cs` file. Now you can right-click in your code and choose Create Unit Tests or choose the Create Tests button from the Test Views toolbar. The Create Unit Tests dialog will appear, as shown in Figure 14-7.

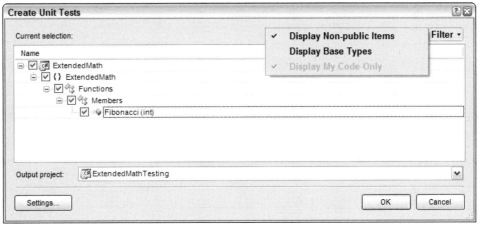

Figure 14-7

Right-clicking in code is context-sensitive and the dialog will default appropriately based on where you clicked. For example, if you click from your class definition, all of that class's members will be selected for generation by default. Clicking on a method will default with only that method selected.

Select the members for which you would like to generate unit tests and then click the Settings button. The Test Generation Settings dialog will appear, as shown in Figure 14-8.

This dialog enables you to choose the behavior and naming conventions that will be used to generate your unit test code. For this first run, leave the settings at their defaults and click OK.

Team System will create a new class file, `FunctionsTest.cs`, if it does not already exist. Inside, you will find a class, FunctionsTest, marked with [TestClass] attribute.

Figure 14-8

At the top of the class is a `TestContext` field initialized to `null`, with a `TestContext` property to enable you to access context from your tests:

```
private TestContext testContextInstance;

public TestContext TestContext
{
    get
    {
        return testContextInstance;
    }
    set
    {
        testContextInstance = value;
    }
}
```

Next, you will find commented-out placeholder methods for `ClassInitialize`, `ClassCleanup`, `TestInitialize`, and `TestCleanup`, wrapped in a region:

```
#region Additional test attributes
//
//You can use the following additional attributes as you write your tests:
//
//Use ClassInitialize to run code before running the first test in the
class
//
```

```
//[ClassInitialize()]
//public static void MyClassInitialize(TestContext testContext)
//{
//}
//
//Use ClassCleanup to run code after all tests in a class have run
//
//[ClassCleanup()]
//public static void MyClassCleanup()
//{
//}
//
//Use TestInitialize to run code before running each test
//
//[TestInitialize()]
//public void MyTestInitialize()
//{
//}
//
//Use TestCleanup to run code after each test has run
//
//[TestCleanup()]
//public void MyTestCleanup()
//{
//}
//
#endregion
```

Finally, you will see the actual generated unit test:

```
/// <summary>
/// A test for Fibonacci (int)
/// </summary>
[TestMethod()]
public void FibonacciTest()
{
    int factor = 0; // TODO: Initialize to an appropriate value

    int expected = 0;
    int actual;

    actual = ExtendedMath.Functions.Fibonacci(factor);

    Assert.AreEqual(expected, actual, "ExtendedMath.Functions.Fibonacci did
not return the expected value.");
    Assert.Inconclusive("Verify the correctness of this test method.");
}
```

The generated code defines a basic structure that depends on the signature of the member being tested. In this example, it recognized that Fibonacci accepts an integer and returns an integer, including an Assert.AreEqual for you. The TODO indicates that factor and expected are only default values and need to be adjusted by you to ensure correct test values.

Keep in mind that generated code will often benefit from careful refactoring, and your generated unit tests will be no exception. For example, look for ways to consolidate common tasks into shared functions. Refactoring is covered in Chapter 11.

Optionally, but by default, generated tests end with calls to `Assert.Inconclusive` to indicate that the unit test needs further inspection to determine its correctness. See the "Using the Assert methods" section for more information.

Generating code from tests

As you have just seen, generating tests from existing code can be very useful. It can be invaluable when you've taken ownership of a system that has no unit tests. However, adherents of test-driven development discourage such approaches, preferring to write test code before implementation code.

Fortunately, Visual Studio also has some support for this approach. You can write unit tests, including calls to classes and methods that do not exist, and the IDE will help you define outlines of their implementations automatically.

Begin by creating a new Class Library project called `ResourceExample`. While TDD purists prefer to avoid writing any implementation code before tests, Team System requires an existing class in which to place generated code. All you need is a basic class definition, so add a new class file called `ResourceLoader.cs` containing the following code:

```
using System;

namespace ResourceExample
{
    public class ResourceLoader
    {
    }
}
```

Now you can write your unit test. It will verify that a call to the `ResourceLoader` class's `GetText` method with an identifier returns the expected resource string. Create a new test project named `ResourceExampleTesting` and set a reference to the `ResourceExample` project. Next, add a new class file called `ResourceLoaderTest.cs` with the following code:

```
using Microsoft.VisualStudio.TestTools.UnitTesting;
using ResourceExample;

namespace ResourceExampleTesting
{
    [TestClass]
    public class ResourceLoaderTest
    {
        [TestMethod]
        public void GetTextTest()
        {
            const int RESOURCE = 100;
            const string EXPECTED = "Result for 100";
            string actual = ResourceLoader.GetText(RESOURCE);

            Assert.AreEqual(EXPECTED, actual);
```

```
            }
        }
    }
```

In the code editor, click on `GetText`. It should be underscored with a small rectangle indicating that one or more options are available. Hover the mouse pointer over the rectangle, click on the resulting button, and you will see "Generate method stub for 'GetText' in 'ResourceExample.ResourceLoader.'" Alternately, you can right-click on `GetText` and choose Generate Method Stub. *If you have trouble finding these options, make sure that you have set a reference from the test project to the ResourceExample project.*

Choose either of these options and then switch to `ResourceLoader.cs`, where you will now see the following:

```
using System;

namespace ResourceExample
{
    public class ResourceLoader
    {
        public static string GetText(int RESOURCE)
        {
            throw new Exception("The method or operation is not implemented.");
        }
    }
}
```

You will notice that Visual Studio inferred the best signature for the method from the context of its use in the unit test. Also notice that the only action in the method is throwing an `Exception`. This is to remind you that there is work left to do. Replace the `throw` with whatever implementation code you need to make your test(s) pass, and then refactor and continue with your next test.

Unit Testing ASP.NET Applications

A common problem for developers prior to Team System was the challenge of unit testing ASP.NET applications. Most of the behavior of ASP.NET applications relies on having a web request context — for example, querystrings, cookies, and server variables. To effectively test this code, a web environment needed to be simulated. While some frameworks, such as NUnitASP existed, the task was still difficult and not integrated with the Visual Studio environment.

Team System enables developers to write unit tests that have access to an active ASP.NET context. The unit testing framework connects to the target ASP.NET application, executes a request, and provides the context of that request to the unit test.

ASP.NET unit test attributes

An ASP.NET unit test looks much like any other unit test, except that it is decorated with additional attributes to indicate details about the target ASP.NET application. The following table summarizes common ASP.NET unit testing attributes.

Attribute	Description
HostType	Identifies the type of host that will run the unit test. Typically, this will be ASP.NET.
UrlToTest	The URL that will be requested. The context of this request will be made available to the unit test via TestContext.
AspNetDevelopmentServerHost	Specify this attribute when the host for the web application will be the built-in ASP.NET Development Server. The first argument is the physical directory of the web application. The second is the name of the application root.

These attributes exist in the `Microsoft.VisualStudio.TestTools.UnitTesting.Web` namespace, and, as with all unit tests, a reference to the `Microsoft.VisualStudio.TestTools` `.UnitTestFramework` assembly is required. Ensure that you add the associated `using` statements as well:

```
using Microsoft.VisualStudio.TestTools.UnitTesting;
using Microsoft.VisualStudio.TestTools.UnitTesting.Web;
```

Now that you have an understanding of the attributes for ASP.NET unit tests, we'll describe your options for creating them.

Creating ASP.NET unit tests

One way to create an ASP.NET unit test is to generate one from a class or method of your web application. You saw in the previous section how simple Team System makes this.

First, open your web application project. Then, open the class containing methods you wish to test. Right-click and choose Create Unit Tests. Select the specific methods for which you wish to generate unit tests and click OK.

The unit tests, already decorated with the appropriate attributes for your web application, are created in a test project in your solution. If you don't already have a test project, one will be created automatically for you.

> ASP.NET unit test generation is only available to classes in your web application's `App_Code` folder. For other items, such as code-behind implementations, we suggest you copy the attributes from a previously generated ASP.NET unit test to another unit test for the code you wish to test.

Whether you generated your ASP.NET unit test or converted a unit test by adding attributes, you are ready to tap into the ASP.NET context in order to verify behavior. The `TestContext` object features a `RequestedPage` property. This is actually an instance of a `System.Web.UI.Page` object appropriate for your web application. Assign this to a local variable and you can use it to access controls of the page.

In order to read and set values of the controls on the page, you will need to obtain a reference to the control using the `Page` object's `FindControl` method.

Frequently, you will need to access nonpublic methods of the page. For example, most button submit methods are not public. As you saw earlier in this chapter, Team System provides a simple way to wrap objects in order to access their nonpublic members. To access such methods, use a `PrivateObject` pointing to the `Page` instance. Once you have that `PrivateObject`, use its `Invoke` method to call the target nonpublic method.

Here is an example ASP.NET unit test, using a local ASP.NET development server, which enters a stock ticker symbol and requests a quote:

```
[TestMethod]
[HostType("ASP.NET")]
[AspNetDevelopmentServerHost("%PathToWebRoot%\\StockTicker", "/StockTicker")]
[UrlToTest("http://localhost/StockTicker")]
public void VerifyCompanyTickerLookup()
{
    Page page = TestContext.RequestedPage;
    TextBox stockName = (TextBox)page.FindControl("txtStockSymbol");
    stockName.Text = "MSFT";

    PrivateObject po = new PrivateObject(page);
    Button getCompanyName = (Button)page.FindControl("cmdGetCompanyName");
    po.Invoke("cmdGetCompanyName_Click", getCompanyName, EventArgs.Empty);

    Label result = (Label)page.FindControl("lblResults");
    Assert.AreEqual("Microsoft", result.Text);
}
```

The attributes indicate how to connect to the local `StockTicker` ASP.NET web application. First, the `Page` reference is obtained from the `TestContext`. Then, the value of the `txtStockName` control is set to `MSFT`. Access to the Submit button is not public, so a `PrivateObject` is used to access the `Page`. After invoking the button's click method, the `txtResult` control is read to ensure that the ticker `MSFT` was correctly returned as "`Microsoft`".

Code Coverage

The unit testing features in Team System have full support for code coverage. Code coverage automatically inserts tracking logic, a process called *instrumentation*, to monitor which lines of code are executed during the execution of your tests. The most important result of this is the identification of regions of your code that you have not reached with your tests.

Often, you may have branching or exception-handling logic that isn't executed in common situations. It is critical to use code coverage to identify these areas because your users certainly will. Add unit tests to cause those areas of code to be executed, and you'll be able to sleep soundly at night.

> *Code coverage is a useful tool, but it should not be relied upon as an exclusive indicator of unit test effectiveness. It cannot tell you the manner in which code was executed, possibly missing errors that would result with different data or timing. A suite of unit tests based on a variety of different inputs and execution orders will help to ensure that your code is correct, complete, and resilient. Use code coverage to help identify code your tests are missing, not to tell you when your tests are complete.*

A tenet of effective unit testing is that the removal of any line of code should cause at least one unit test to fail. This is, of course, an ideal, but worth keeping in mind as you develop your systems.

Enabling code coverage

Code coverage is activated via a setting in the Test Run Configuration. Open the configuration for editing by choosing Test ⇨ Edit Test Run Configuration and selecting the configuration. Once you have the Edit Test Run Configuration dialog active, select the Code Coverage page.

Select the assemblies you wish to instrument from the Select Artifacts to Instrument list. If you don't see an assembly you'd like to instrument, you can click Add Assembly to manually add it. Figure 14-9 is a screenshot of the Code Coverage page of the Test Run Configuration editor.

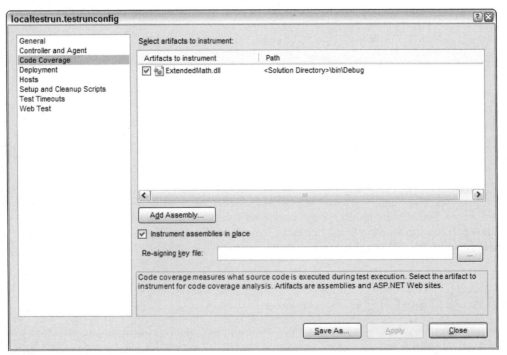

Figure 14-9

The instrumentation process modifies your original assemblies, invalidating original signatures. If you are working with signed assemblies, use the Re-signing key file field to specify a key file with which to sign the instrumented assembly.

Viewing code coverage results

Once you have enabled coverage and selected the assemblies to instrument, run your unit tests as normal. You will then be able to see results of the coverage in the Code Coverage Results window. This window will show counts of lines and percentages of code covered and uncovered. You may expand the view by clicking the plus signs to see details at the assembly, class, and member levels.

To quickly determine which areas of code need attention, enable code coverage highlighting of your code by pressing the Show Code Coverage button on the Code Coverage toolbar. Executable lines of code will be highlighted in red if they have not been run by your tests and in blue if they were. Code that is purely structural or documentation will not be highlighted. Figure 14-10 illustrates the results of a code coverage test.

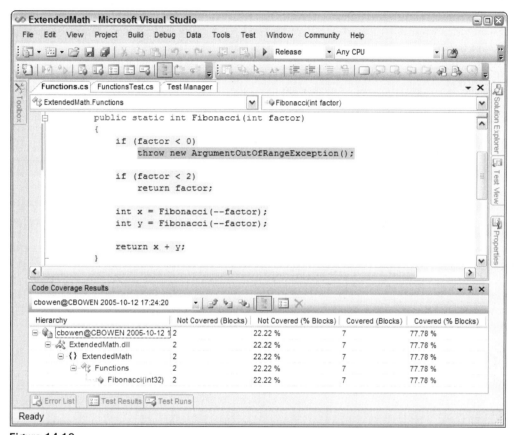

Figure 14-10

In this example, we added two lines to our previous `Fibonacci` implementation that check for a negative `factor` and throw an exception. Code Coverage has colored the line throwing the exception red. This means that none of the unit tests we executed caused that line to run. This is a clear indication that we need another unit test. Create a new unit test—for example, `FibonacciOfNegativeFactorsNotSupportedTest`—and test calling `Fibonacci` with a `factor` less than zero. Decorate the test with the `ExpectedException` attribute, indicating that you expect the `ArgumentOutOfRangeException` in order for the test to pass. Rerun the unit tests and the `Fibonacci` method should now have 100 percent coverage.

Again, keep in mind that 100 percent code coverage does not mean you have finished writing your unit tests. Proper testing may involve multiple executions of the same code using different data. Code coverage is one measure of effectiveness, but certainly not the only one. Consider adopting test-driven development, plan your testing cases up front, and then use code coverage to alert you to scenarios you forgot to test.

Summary

The Developer and Tester editions of Visual Studio Team System bring the advantages of unit testing to the developer by fully integrating features with the development environment. If you're new to unit testing, this chapter has provided an overview of what unit testing is, how to create effective unit tests, and some of the principles behind test-driven development. We covered the creation and management of unit tests and detailed the methods and attributes available in the unit test framework. You should be familiar with attributes for identifying your tests as well as many of the options that the Assert class offers for testing behavior of code.

You've learned how to generate code with Team System, either by generating tests from code or code from tests. As you saw, it is also very easy to bind unit tests to a data source to create data-driven tests. This chapter also showed that Team System offers a simple way to access private members for testing, addressing a need that previously required manual workarounds.

You've also seen that ASP.NET developers can now create unit tests against web applications without relying on external tools and frameworks. Finally, you learned how to use code coverage to help identify where your unit tests may have missed some scenarios.

If you have been using other frameworks for your unit testing to date, you'll enjoy not having to leave the IDE to work with your tests, as well as the familiar options and syntax that Team System offers.

We strongly encourage you to become familiar with the benefits of unit testing, keeping in mind that unit tests are not a replacement for other forms of testing, but a very strong supplement.

Over the next three chapters, we'll continue our look at those other forms of testing that Team System Team Tester Edition supports. You'll learn about load and web tests in Chapter 15, manual tests in Chapter 16, and custom tests in Chapter 17.

15

Web and Load Testing

In the previous chapter, you saw that Visual Studio 2005 Team System includes many features for the creation and execution of unit tests. In this chapter, we continue our coverage of the testing features of Team System by describing web and load tests.

With web testing, you can easily build a suite of repeatable tests that ensure your web application functions as expected. Team System enables you to easily create a web test by recording your actions as you use your web application. In this chapter, you will learn how to create, edit, and run web tests, and how to execute and analyze the results.

> **Please note that web and load testing are available only in Visual Studio 2005 Team Edition for Software Testers.**

Sometimes you need more flexibility than a recorded web test can offer. You will learn how to use coded web tests to create flexible and powerful web tests using any .NET language and leveraging the web testing framework.

Verifying that an application is ready for production involves additional analysis. How will your application behave when (it is hoped that) many people begin using it? The load testing features of Team System for Software Testers enable you to execute one or more tests repeatedly, tracking the performance of the target system. You will learn how to create a load test using the Load Test Wizard and how to use the information Team System collects to identify problems before your users do.

Finally, because a single machine may not be able to generate enough load to simulate the number of users your application will have in production, you'll learn how to configure your environment to run *distributed load tests*. A distributed load test enables you to spread the work of creating user load across multiple machines, called *agents*. Details from each agent are collected by a controller machine, enabling you to see the overall performance of your application under stress.

Web Tests

Web tests enable verification that a web application's behavior is correct. They issue an ordered series of HTTP requests against a target web application and analyze each response for expected behaviors. You can use the integrated web test recorder to create a test by observing your interaction with a target web site through a browser window. Once the test is recorded, you can use that web test to consistently repeat those recorded actions against the target web application.

> **Although you will likely use web tests with ASP.NET web applications, you are not required to do so. In fact, while some features are specific to testing ASP.NET applications, any web application can be tested via a web test, including applications based on classic ASP or even non-Microsoft technologies.**

Previously, Visual Studio Enterprise Edition included a product called *Application Center Test (ACT)*. Like Team System web tests, ACT could be used to record and replay tests against a target web application. Unfortunately, those tests were driven using interpreted scripts, and lacked support for many common scenarios. Team System web tests address those limitations by offering automatic processing of redirects, dependent requests, and hidden fields, including Viewstate. Furthermore, they feature full support for HTTPS communications. In addition, coded web tests can be written in any .NET language, enabling you to take full advantage of the power and flexibility of such languages.

There is no direct support for conversion of web tests from other frameworks such as Application Center Test. For most tests, simply re-recording the tests with Team System is the best option. However, if you have a large suite of complex tests, you might delay conversion and wrap execution of those tests as generic tests. For details on generic tests, see Chapter 17.

Later in this chapter, you will learn how to add your web tests to load tests to ensure that a web application behaves as expected when many users access it concurrently.

Creating a sample web application

Before we create web tests, we'll need a web application to test. While we could create a web test by interacting with any live web site such as Google, Monster, or Microsoft, those sites can certainly change and will likely not be the same at the time you read this chapter. Therefore, we'll base the remainder of this chapter on a sample site that we'll quickly create using one of the starter sites included with Visual Studio.

Start with an empty solution and create a new project by right-clicking on the solution and choosing Add ➪ New Web Site. Choose Personal Web Site Starter Kit, enter the name "SampleWeb," and then press OK.

Visual Studio will then create a new personal website, with full support for users and authentication and features such as a photo album, links, and a place for a resume.

We'll use this site as the basis of some recorded web tests. Later, we'll use these web tests from a load test to put stress on this site to determine how well it will perform when hundreds of friends and family simultaneously converge to view our photos.

Creating users for the site

Before we create tests for our website, we need to create a few users for the site. We'll do this using the Web Site Administration Tool that is included with ASP.NET applications created with Visual Studio. Select Website ⇨ ASP.NET Configuration.

On the resulting page, select Security, and then Create or Manage Roles. Enter "Administrators" as the role name, and then click Add Role. Repeat this process to add a role named "Friends."

Note that the first time the site is run, the application start event will also create these roles for you.

You now have two roles into which users can be placed. Click the Security tab again, and then click Create user. You will then see the window shown in Figure 15-1.

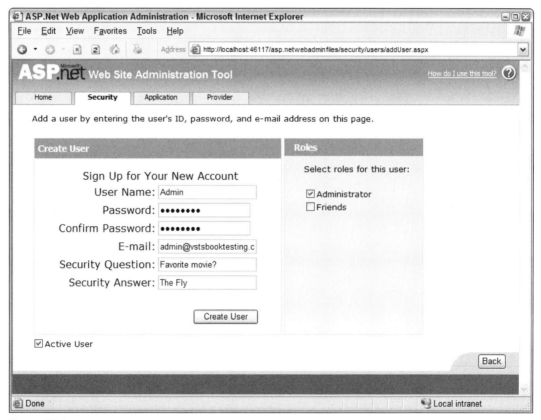

Figure 15-1

Our tests will assume the following users have been created:

- ❑ Admin, in the Administrator role
- ❑ Ken, in the Friends role
- ❑ Mike, in the Friends role
- ❑ Dave, in the Friends role

Enter any values you wish for the Password, E-mail, and Security Question fields.

> *Choosing a valid password can be tricky, and the help text is somewhat cryptic. By default, passwords must be at least seven characters long and have at least one non-alphanumeric character. In this example, we use "@qwerty@". You can modify these settings through the membership provider settings of* `machine.config` *or* `web.config`*.*

Configuring the sample application for testing

It is common, but certainly not required, to run web tests against a website hosted on the local development machine. If you are testing against a remote machine, you need to create a virtual directory or website and deploy your sample application. You may also choose to create a virtual directory on your local machine.

Visual Studio 2005 includes a new feature called the ASP.NET Development Server. This is a lightweight web server, similar to but not the same as IIS, that chooses a port and temporarily hosts a local ASP.NET application. The hosted application accepts only local requests and is torn down when Visual Studio exits.

The Development Server defaults to selecting a random port each time the application is started. In order to execute web tests, you'd have to manually adjust the port each time it was assigned. To address this, you have two options.

The first option is to select your ASP.NET project and choose Properties. Change the Use Dynamic Ports property to `false`, and then select a port number, such as 5000. You can then hard-code this port number into your local web tests.

The second, and more flexible, option is to use a special value, called a *context parameter*, which will automatically adjust itself to match the server, port, and directory of the target web application. You'll learn how to do this shortly.

Later in this chapter, you'll see that unlike web tests, load tests are typically run against sites hosted on machines other than those conducting tests.

Creating and configuring web tests

There are three main methods for creating web tests. The first, and by far the most common, is to use the web test recorder. The second method is to create a test manually, using the Web Test Editor to add each step. Finally, you can create a coded web test that specifies each action via code. You can also generate a coded web test from an existing web test. We describe coded web tests later in this chapter.

To create a new web test, you may either create a test project beforehand or allow one to be created for you. If you already have a test project, right-click on it and select Add ➪ New Test. If you don't have a test project, choose Test ➪ New Test. You will see the Add New Test dialog, as shown in Figure 15-2.

You have several test types from which to choose. Select Web Test and give your test a name. Web tests are stored as XML files with a `.webtest` extension.

> **See Chapter 13 for more details on creating and configuring test projects.**

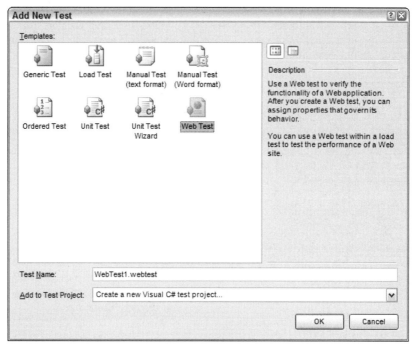

Figure 15-2

Finally, you can either choose an existing test project or specify that a new one be created. After clicking OK, if you opted to create a new test project, you will be prompted to enter a name for that test project. In this example, we'll use "SampleWebTestProject."

Once you have a test project, you can quickly create other web tests by right-clicking on your test project and selecting Add ⇨ Web Test. This automatically creates a new web test with default settings, named "WebTest1.webtest," incrementing the number if that name already exists, and launches the web test recording browser.

Recording a web test

Once your web test is created, an instance of Internet Explorer will be launched with an integrated Web Test Recorder docked window. Begin by typing the URL of the application you wish to test. For the SampleWeb application on a local machine, this will be something like `http://localhost:5000/SampleWeb`. Remember that supplying a port number is only necessary if you're using the built-in ASP.NET Development Server, and is generally not necessary when using IIS.

Recording a web test is straightforward. Using the integrated web browser, simply use the web application as if you were a normal user. Team System automatically records your actions, saving them to the web test.

First, log in as the Admin user (but do not check the "Remember me next time" option). The browser should refresh, showing a "Welcome Admin!" greeting. This is only a short test, so click Logout at the upper-right corner.

Your browser should now appear as shown in Figure 15-3. The steps have been expanded so you can see the details of the Form Post Parameters that were recorded automatically for you. You'll learn more about these later in this chapter, but for now notice that the second step automatically includes Viewstate, as well as the User Name and Password form fields we used to log in.

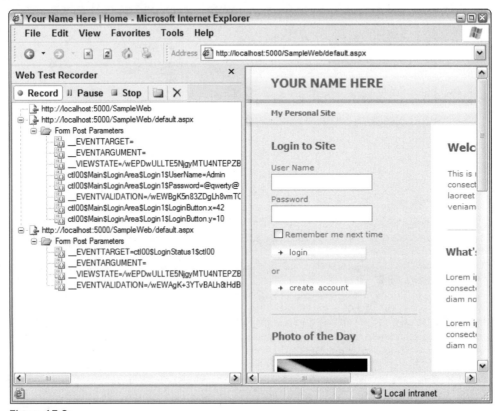

Figure 15-3

Also note that the Web Test Recorder window is docked within Internet Explorer. As you conduct your usage scenario, the steps taken are listed as each request is submitted. You have several options while recording. The Pause button temporarily suspends recording and timing of your interaction with the browser, enabling you to use the application or get a cup of coffee without affecting your web test. Click the X button to clear your recorded list. The other button, Add a Comment, enables you to add documentation to your web test, perhaps at a complex step. These comments are very useful when you convert a web test to a coded web test, as you'll see later.

Calls to web pages are normally composed of a main request followed by a number of dependent requests. These dependent requests are sent separately to obtain items such as graphics, script sources, and stylesheets. The web test does not record these dependent requests. You'll see later that all dependent requests are determined and processed automatically when the web test is run.

Configuring web test run settings

When you're done recording your web test, click Stop and the browser will close, displaying the Web Test Editor with your recorded web test, as shown in Figure 15-4.

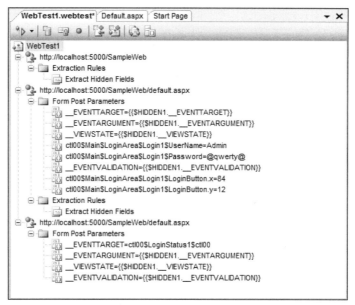

Figure 15-4

The Web Test Editor displays your test as a series of requests to be sent to the web application. Notice that, just as you saw in Figure 15-3, there are three distinct requests. These are the three requests you submitted through the browser: the initial page, the login request, and the logout request.

Frequently, you'll need to use the Web Test Editor to change settings or add features to the tests you record. This may include adding validation, extracting data from web responses, and reading data from a source. We'll cover these topics later in the chapter, but for now, we'll use this test as recorded.

Parameterizing the web server

You may recall from the earlier "Configuring the sample application for testing" section that using the ASP.NET Development Server, while convenient, poses a slight challenge because the port it uses is selected randomly with each run. While you could set your website to use a static port, there is a better solution.

Using the Web Test Editor, click on the rightmost button, labeled Parameterize Web Servers. You could also right-click on the web test name and choose Parameterize Web Servers. In the resulting dialog, click the Change button. You will see the Change Web Server dialog, shown in Figure 15-5.

Use this dialog to configure your web test to target a standard web application service, such as IIS, or to use the ASP.NET Development Server. In our example, we are using the Development Server, so choose that option and enter or browse to the location of the SampleWeb site. The Web application root in this case is simply the name of the site, /SampleWeb. Click OK and you'll see a new context parameter in the list.

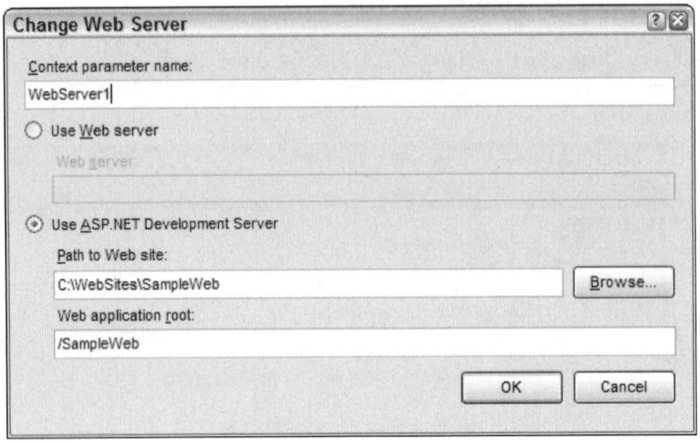

Figure 15-5

Close the Parameterize Web Servers dialog. You will notice the Web Test Editor has automatically updated all request entries, replacing the static web address with a reference to this context parameter, using the syntax `{{WebServer1}}`. In addition, the context parameter `WebServer1` has been added at the bottom of the web test under Context Parameters. Refer to Figure 15-10 to see the effect of this on our sample web test.

> *Context parameters, named variables that are available to each step in a web test, are described in the "Extraction rules and context parameters" section, later in this chapter.*

Now you can run the web test and Team System will automatically find and connect to the port and address necessary when the ASP.NET Development Server is started. If you have more than one target server or application, you can repeat this process as many times as necessary, creating additional context parameters.

Web test run settings

Before you run a web test, you may wish to review the settings that will be used for the test's runs. Choose Test ➪ Edit Test Run Configurations, and then select the Local Test Run option. Select the Web Test entry from the list on the left side and you will see the options shown in Figure 15-6.

The option group "Number of run iterations" enables you to specify a specific number of times your web tests will be executed when included in a test run. Note that you should not enter a large number here to simulate load through your web test. Instead, you will want to create a load test, covered later in this chapter, referencing your web test. Also, if you assign a data source to your web test, you may instead choose to run the web test one time per entry in the selected data source. We cover data-driven web tests in detail later in this chapter.

The Browser Type setting enables you to simulate using one of a number of browsers as your web test's client. This will automatically set the user agent field for requests sent to the web test to simulate the selected browser. By default, this will be Internet Explorer 6.0, but you may select other browsers such as Netscape or a Smartphone.

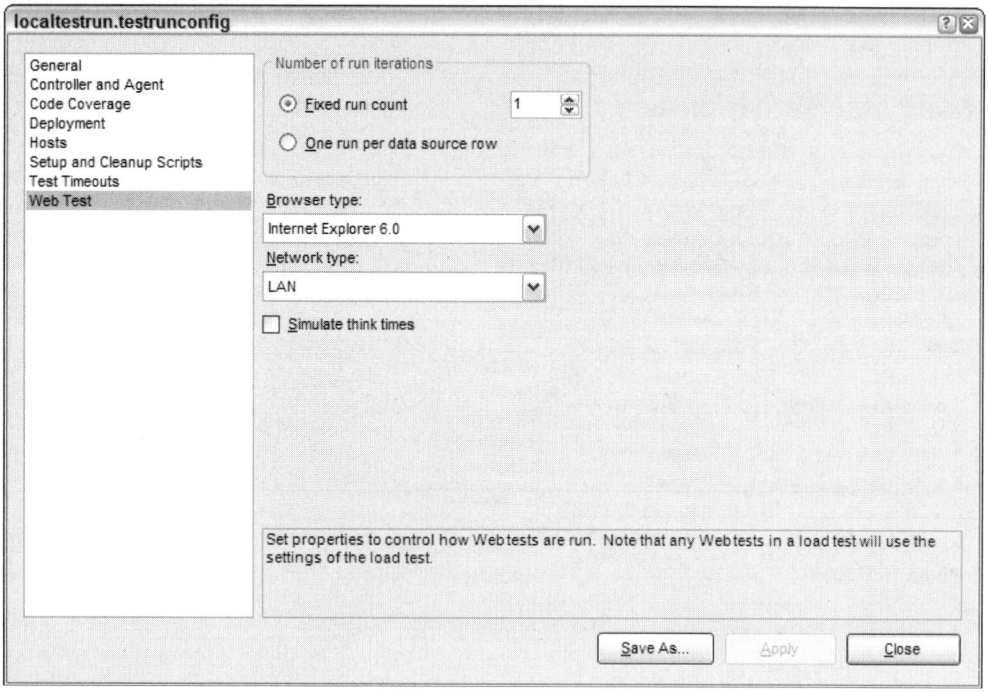

Figure 15-6

Similar to the Browser Type setting, Network Type is used to simulate the type of connection a user has when accessing the web application. This can be used to simulate local LAN users down to 28.8k dial-up modem users.

> *If you want to test more than one browser and/or network type, you'll need to run your web test multiple times, selecting a different browser and network each time. However, you can also add your web test to a load test and choose your desired browser and network distributions. This will cause each selected type to be simulated automatically. You'll learn how to do this in the "Load Tests" section of this chapter.*

The final option, Simulate Think Times, enables the use of delays in your web test to simulate the normal time taken by users to read content, modify values, and decide on actions. When you recorded your web test, the time it took for you to submit each request was recorded as the Think Time property of each step. If you turn this option on, that same delay will occur between the requests sent by the web test to the web application. Think times are disabled by default, causing all requests to be sent as quickly as possible to the web server, resulting in a faster test. You will see later in this chapter that think times serve an important role in load tests.

> *Note that these settings affect every run of this web test. You'll see later that the Web Test Run Settings dialog enables you to override these settings for a single run.*

Running a web test

To run a web test, click the Run button, the leftmost button on the Web Test Editor toolbar, as shown in Figure 15-4. As with all other test types in Team System, you can use the Test Manager and Test View windows to organize and execute tests. See Chapter 13 for full details on these windows.

You can also run web tests from the command line. See the "Command-line Test Execution" section later in this chapter.

Observing test execution and results

When the test run is started, a window specific to that web test execution will appear. If you are executing your web test from the Web Test Editor window, you will need to click the Run button in this window to launch the test. The results will automatically be displayed, as shown in Figure 15-7. You may also choose to step through the web test, one request at a time, by choosing Run Test (Pause Before Starting), available via the drop-down arrow attached to the Run button.

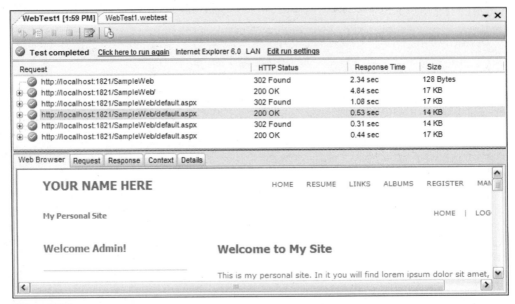

Figure 15-7

Note that if you choose to run your web tests from Test View or Test Manager, the results will be summarized in the Test Results window, docked at the bottom of the screen. To see each web test's execution details, as shown in Figure 15-7, double-click on the web test's entry in the Test Results window.

This window displays the results of all interactions with the web application. A toolbar, the overall test status, and two hyperlinked options are shown at the top. The first will rerun the web test and the second allows you to change the browser type and network settings via the Web Test Run Settings dialog.

Changes made in this dialog will only affect the next run of the web test and will not be saved for later runs. To make permanent changes, modify the web test's run configuration using Test ➪ Edit Test Run Configuration.

Below that, each of the requests sent to the application are shown. You can expand each top-level request to see its dependent requests. These are automatically handled by the web test system and can include calls to retrieve graphics, script sources, cascading stylesheets, and more.

Each item in this list shows the request target as well as the response's status, time, and size. A green check indicates a successful request and response, whereas a red icon indicates failure.

Identifying which requests failed and why can be difficult if you have a large number of requests. Unfortunately, there is no summary view to see only failed requests with the reason for failure (for example, violating a validation rule). For large web tests, you will need to scroll through all of the requests and open failed requests to see failure details.

The lower half of the window enables you to see full details for each request. The first tab, Web Browser, shows you the rendered version of the response. As you can see in Figure 15-7, the response includes "Welcome Admin!" text, indicating that you successfully logged in as the Admin account.

The Request tab shows the details of what was supplied to the web application, including all headers and any request body, such as might be present when an HTTP POST is made.

Similarly, the Response tab shows all headers and the body of the response sent back from the web application. Unlike the Web Browser tab, this detail is shown textually, even when binary data such as an image is returned.

The Context tab lists all of the context parameters and their values at the time of the selected request. Finally, the Details tab shows the status of any assigned validation and extraction rules. This tab also shows details about any exception thrown during that request. We describe context parameters and rules later in this chapter.

Editing a web test

You'll often find that a recorded web test is not sufficient to fully test your application's functionality. You can use the Web Test Editor, as shown in Figure 15-4, to further customize a web test, adding comments, extraction rules, data sources, and other properties.

> **We recommend that you run a recorded web test once before attempting to edit it. This will verify that the test was recorded correctly. If you don't do this, you might not know whether a test is failing because it wasn't recorded correctly or because you introduced a bug through changes in the Web Test Editor.**

Setting request properties

Right-click on a request and choose Properties. If the Properties window is already displayed, simply selecting a request will show its properties. You will be able to modify settings such as cache control, target URL, and whether the request automatically follows redirects.

The Properties window also offers a chance to modify the think time of each request. For example, perhaps a co-worker dropped by with a question while you were recording your web test and you forgot to pause the recording. Use the Think Time property to adjust the delay to a more realistic value.

Adding comments

Comments are useful for identifying the actions of a particular section of a web test. In addition, when converting your web test to a coded web test, your comments will be preserved in code.

Because the requests in our example all refer to the same page, it is helpful to add comments to help distinguish them. Add a comment by right-clicking on the first request and choosing Insert Comment. Enter **Initial site request** as the comment text. Add comments to the other two requests, such as **Login as Admin** and **Logout**.

Adding transactions

A *transaction* is used to monitor a group of logically connected steps in your web test. A transaction can be tracked as a unit, giving details such as number of times invoked, request time, and total elapsed time.

> *Don't confuse web test transactions with database transactions. While both are used for grouping actions, database transactions offer additional features beyond those of web test transactions.*

To create a transaction, right-click a request and select Insert Transaction. You will be prompted to name the transaction and select the start and end request from drop-down lists.

Transactions are primarily used when running web tests under load with a load test. You will learn more about viewing transaction details in the "Viewing and interpreting load test results" section later in this chapter.

Extraction rules and context parameters

Extraction rules are used to retrieve specific data from a web response. This data is stored in special parameters, called *context parameters,* that live for the duration of the web test. Context parameters can be read from and written to by any request in a web test. For example, you could use an extraction rule to retrieve an order confirmation number, storing that in a context parameter. Then, subsequent steps in the test could access that order number, using it for verification or supplying it with later web requests.

> *Context parameters are similar in concept to the* `HttpContext.Items` *collection from ASP.NET. In both cases, you can add names and values that can be accessed by any subsequent step. Whereas* `HttpContext.Items` *entries are valid for the duration of a single page request, web test context parameters are accessible through a single web test run.*

Referring to Figure 15-4, notice that the first request has an `ExtractHiddenFields` entry under Extraction Rules. This was added automatically when we recorded our web test because the system recognized hidden fields in the first form we accessed. Those hidden fields are now available to subsequent requests via context parameters.

A number of context parameters are set automatically when you run a web test, including the following:

- ❑ `$TestDir`: The working directory of the web test.

- ❑ `$WebTestIteration`: The current run number. For example, this would be useful if you selected more than one run in the Test Run Settings and needed to differentiate the test runs.

- ❑ `$ControllerName` and `$AgentName`: Machine identifiers used when remotely executing web tests. You'll learn more about this subject later in the chapter.

A significant limitation of web test contexts is that they cannot be shared between web tests. For example, you may have several web tests, each of which performs a common action on your site, such as "Create new user," "Log user in," and "Delete user account." Ideally, you would like to have the ID of the user created in the first web test automatically flow into the context of the "Log in user" web test. Unfortunately, this is not supported, even if you wrap the web tests with an ordered test. The suggested workaround for this is to convert the web tests to coded web tests, and then use a controlling coded web test to launch each of the web tests, enabling them to access the context of the previous tests.

To add an extraction rule to a web test, right-click on any request and select Add Extraction Rule. The dialog shown in Figure 15-8 will appear.

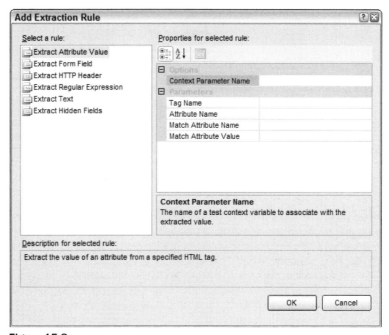

Figure 15-8

The built-in extraction rules can be used to extract any attribute, HTTP header, or response text. Use ExtractRegularExpression to retrieve data that matches the supplied expression. Use ExtractHiddenFields to easily find and return a value contained in a hidden form field of a response. Extracted values are stored in context parameters whose names you define in the properties of each rule.

You can add your own custom extraction rules by creating classes that derive from the ExtractionRule class found in the Microsoft.VisualStudio.TestTools.WebTesting namespace.

Validation rules

Generally, checking for valid web application behavior involves more than just getting a response from the server. You need to ensure that the content and behavior of that response is correct. Validation rules offer a way to verify that those requirements are met. For example, you may wish to verify that specific text appears on a page after an action, such as adding an item to a shopping cart. Validation rules are attached to a specific request and will cause that request to show as failed if the requirement is not satisfied.

Let's add a validation rule to our test to ensure that the welcome message is displayed after we log in. Right-click on the second request and choose Add Validation Rule. You will see the dialog shown in Figure 15-9.

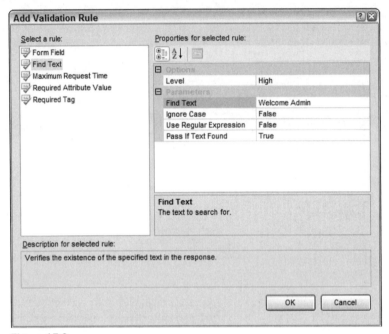

Figure 15-9

As with extraction rules, you can also create your own custom validation rules, by inheriting from the base `ValidationRule` class, found in the `WebTestFramework` assembly, and have them appear in this dialog. Choose the Find Text rule and set the value Welcome Admin to the Find Text parameter. Set Ignore Case to `false`, and Pass If Text Found to `true`. This rule will search the web application's response for a case-sensitive match on that text and will pass if found. Click OK and the web test should appear as shown in Figure 15-10.

Verify that this works by running or stepping through the web test. You should see that this test actually does not work as expected. You can use the details from the web test's results to find out why.

View the Details tab for the second request. You'll see that the Find Text validation rule failed to find a match. Looking at the text of the response on the Response tab shows that instead of "Welcome Admin" being returned, there is a tab instead of a space between the words. You will need to modify the validation rule to match this text.

To fix this, you could simply replace the space in the Find Text parameter with a tab. However, you could use a regular expression as well. First, change the Find Text parameter to `Welcome\s+Admin`. This indicates you expect any whitespace characters between the words, not just a space character. To enable that property to behave as a regular expression, set the Use Regular Expression parameter to `true`.

Save your web test and rerun it. The web test should now pass.

The functionality that extraction and validation rules provide comes at the expense of performance. If you wish to call your web test from a load test, you might wish to improve performance at the expense of ignoring a number of extraction or validation rules.

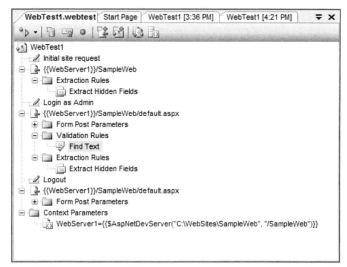

Figure 15-10

Each rule has an associated property called Level. This can be set to Low, Medium, or High. When you create a load test, you can similarly specify a Validation Level of Low, Medium, or High. This setting specifies the maximum level of rule that will be executed when the load test runs. (*Note that this means High level rules are run in fewer cases than Low and Medium rules.*) For example, a validation level of Medium will run rules with a level of Low or Medium, but will exclude rules marked as High.

Data-driven web tests

You can satisfy many testing scenarios using the techniques described so far, but you can go beyond those techniques to easily create data-driven web tests. A *data-driven web test* connects to a data source and retrieves a set of data. Pieces of that data can be used in place of static settings for each request.

For example, in your web test, you may wish to ensure that the login and logout processes work equally well for all of the configured users. You'll learn how to do this next.

Configuring a data source

The first step in creating a data-driven web test is to define a data source. Using the Web Test Editor, you can either right-click on the top node of your web test and select Add Data Source or click the Add Data Source button on the toolbar.

Configure the connection to your data source. Be certain to use the Test Connection option to verify your connection before continuing. Once the connection is established, you will be prompted to select one or more tables or views from the source. When the data source is added, you will see it at the bottom of your web test in the Web Test Editor.

Expand the data source to see the selected table(s). Click on a table and view the Properties window. Notice that one of the settings is Access Method. This has three valid settings:

- ❑ **Sequential:** Reads each record in first-to-last order from the source. This will loop back to the first record and continue reading if the test uses more iterations than the source has records.

- ❑ **Random:** Reads each record randomly from the source and, like sequential access, will continue reading as long as necessary.

- ❑ **Unique:** Reads each record in first-to-last order, but will do so only once.

Use this setting to determine how the data source will feed rows to the web test.

Binding to a source

Several types of values can be bound to a data source, including form post and URL query parameters' names and values, HTTP headers, and file upload field names. To bind a name or value to a data source, select the item in the Web Test Editor and view the Properties window. Click the appropriate setting and then click on the down arrow that appears in the box.

You will then see the data binding selector, as shown in Figure 15-11.

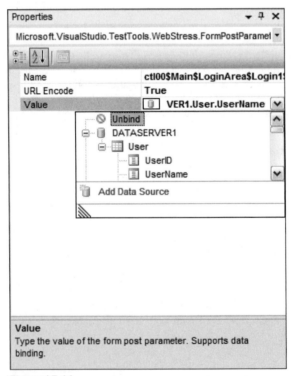

Figure 15-11

Expand the desired data source, choose the correct table or view, and then click on the column you wish to bind to the current property. A database icon will appear in that property indicating that it is a bound value. You can select the Unbind entry to remove any established data binding.

Binding to the results of stored procedures is not supported for web tests.

Before you run your web test, you need to indicate that you want to run the test one time per row of data in the data source. Refer back to the Configuring Web Test Run Settings section and Figure 15-6. In the web tests section of your test run settings, choose the "One run per data source row" option of the "Number of playback runs" panel.

The next time you run your web test, it will automatically read from the target data source, supplying the bound fields with data. The test will repeat one time for each row of data in the source.

Coded web tests

As flexible as web tests are, there may be times when you need more control over the actions that are taken. Web tests are stored as XML files with `.webtest` extensions. Team System uses this XML to generate the code that is executed when the web test is run. You can tap into this process by creating a coded web test, enabling you to execute a test from code instead of from XML. Coded web tests enable you to perform actions not possible with a standard web test. For example, you can perform looping and branching. Essentially, a coded web test is limited only by your ability to write code. The language of the generated code is determined by the language of the test project that contains the source web test.

A coded web test is a class that inherits from either a base `WebTest` class for C# tests or from a `ThreadedWebTest` base for Visual Basic tests. These classes can be found in the `Microsoft.VisualStudio.TestTools.WebTesting` namespace. All of the features available to web tests that you create via the IDE are implemented in classes and methods contained in that namespace.

> *While you always have the option to create a coded web test by hand, the most common, and the recommended, method is to generate a coded web test from a web test that was recorded with the Web Test Recorder and then customize the code as needed.*

You should familiarize yourself with coded web tests by creating a number of different sample web tests through the IDE and generating coded web tests from them to learn how various web test actions are accomplished with code.

Using the example web test, click the Generate Code button (the next to last button on the Web Test Editor toolbar). You will be prompted to name the generated file. Open the generated file and review the generated code.

Here is a segment of the C# code that was generated from our web test (some calls have been removed for simplicity):

```
public override IEnumerator<WebTestRequest> GetRequestEnumerator()
{
   // Initial site request
   ...
   yield return request1;

   // Login as Admin

   WebTestRequest request2 = new WebTestRequest
     ((this.Context["WebServer1"].ToString() + "/SampleWeb/default.aspx"));
   request2.ThinkTime = 10;
   request2.Method = "POST";
```

```
        FormPostHttpBody request2Body = new FormPostHttpBody();

        request2Body.FormPostParameters.Add("ctl00$Main$LoginArea$Login1$UserName",
                                    "Admin");
        request2Body.FormPostParameters.Add("ctl00$Main$LoginArea$Login1$Password",
                                    "@qwerty@");
        request2.Body = request2Body;
        if ((this.Context.ValidationLevel >=
           Microsoft.VisualStudio.TestTools.WebTesting.ValidationLevel.High))
        {
           ValidationRuleFindText rule2 = new ValidationRuleFindText();
           rule2.FindText = "Welcome\\s+Admin";
           rule2.IgnoreCase = false;
           rule2.UseRegularExpression = true;
           rule2.PassIfTextFound = true;
           request2.ValidateResponse += new
               EventHandler<ValidationEventArgs>(rule2.Validate);
        }
        ExtractHiddenFields rule3 = new ExtractHiddenFields();
        rule3.ContextParameterName = "1";
        request2.ExtractValues += new
           EventHandler<ExtractionEventArgs>(rule3.Extract);
        yield return request2;

        // Logout
        ...
        yield return request3;
    }
```

This `GetRequestEnumerator` method uses the `yield` statement to provide `WebTestRequest` instances, one per HTTP request, back to the web test system.

Visual Basic test projects generate slightly different code than C# tests because Visual Basic does not currently support iterators and the `yield` statement. Instead of having a `GetRequestEnumerator` method that yields `WebTestRequest` instances one at a time, there is a `Run` subroutine that uses the base `ThreadedWebTest.Send` method to execute each request.

Regardless of the language used, notice that the methods and properties are very similar to what you have already seen when creating and editing web tests in the Web Test Editor. You'll also notice that the comments you added in the Web Test Editor appear as comments in the code, making it very easy to identify where each request begins.

Taking a closer look, you see that the Find Text validation rule you added earlier is now specified with code. First, the code checks the `ValidationLevel` context parameter to verify that you're including rules marked with a level of High. If so, the `ValidationRuleFindText` class is instantiated and the parameters you specified in the IDE are now set as properties of that instance. Finally, the instance's `Validate` method is registered with the request's `ValidateResponse` event, ensuring that the validator will execute at the appropriate time.

You can make any changes you wish and simply save the code file and rebuild. Your coded web test will automatically appear alongside your other tests in Test Manager and Test View.

Another advantage of coded web tests is protocol support. While normal web tests can support both HTTP and HTTPS, they cannot use alternative protocols. A coded web test can be used for other protocols, such as FTP.

For detailed descriptions of the classes and members available to you in the `WebTesting` namespace, see Team System's Help under "Team Test API" and "Microsoft.VisualStudio.TestTools.WebTesting Namespace."

Load Tests

Load tests are used to verify that your application will perform as expected while under the stress of multiple concurrent users. You configure the levels and types of load you wish to simulate and then execute the load test. A series of requests will be generated against the target application and Team System will monitor the system under test to determine how well it performs.

Load testing is most commonly used with web tests to conduct smoke, load, and stress testing of ASP.NET applications. However, you are certainly not limited to this. Load tests are essentially lists of pointers to other tests, and they can include any other test type except for manual tests.

For example, you could create a load test that includes a suite of unit tests. You could stress-test layers of business logic and database access code to determine how that code will behave when many users are accessing it concurrently, regardless of which application uses those layers.

As another example, ordered tests can be used to group a number of tests and define a specific order in which they will run. Because tests added to a load test are executed in a randomly selected order, you may find it useful to first group them with an ordered test, and then include that ordered test in the load test. You can find more information on ordered tests in Chapter 13.

Creating and configuring load tests

In this section, we describe how to create a load test using the New Load Test Wizard. You'll examine many options that you can use to customize the behavior of your load tests.

As described in the web testing section of this chapter, a test project is used to contain your tests, and like web tests, load tests are placed in test projects. You can either use the New Test option of the Test menu and specify a new or existing test project or you can right-click on an existing test project and choose Add ➪ Load Test.

Using the New Load Test Wizard

Whether from a test project or the Test menu, when you add a new load test, the New Load Test Wizard is started. This wizard will guide you through the many configuration options available for a load test.

Scenarios and think times

A load test is composed of one or more *scenarios*. A scenario is a grouping of web and/or unit tests along with a variety of preferences for user, browser, network, and other settings. Scenarios are used to group similar tests or usage environments. For example, you may wish to create a scenario for simulating the creation and submission of an expense report by your employees, whereby your users have LAN connectivity and all use Internet Explorer 6.0.

When the wizard is launched, the first screen describes the load test creation process. Click Next and you will be prompted, as shown in Figure 15-12, to assign a name to your load test's first scenario.

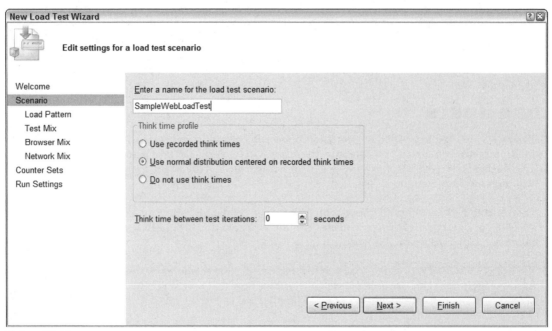

Figure 15-12

Note that the wizard only supports the creation of a single scenario in your load test, but you can easily add more scenarios with the Load Test Editor after you complete the wizard.

The second option on this page is to configure think times. You may recall from the "Web Tests" section earlier that think time is a delay between each request, which can be used to approximate how long a user will pause to read, consider options, and enter data on a particular page. These times are stored with each of a web test's requests. The think time profile enables you to turn these off or on.

If you enable think times, you can either use them as is or apply a normal distribution that uses the stored times as a basis. We recommend using the normal distribution if you want to simulate the most realistic user load, based on what you expect the average user to do.

You can click on any test step on the left-hand side to jump to that step. Click Next to advance to each next step. Click Finish when you are satisfied with the settings and wish to create the load test.

Load patterns

The next step is to define the load pattern for the scenario. The load pattern, shown in Figure 15-13, enables simulation of different types of user load.

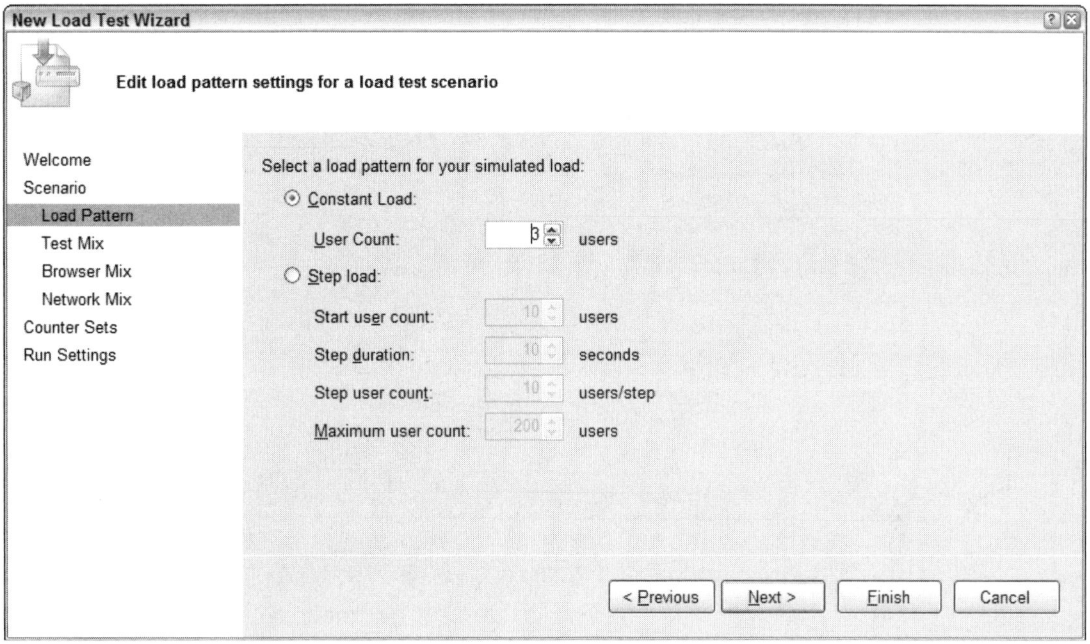

Figure 15-13

In the wizard, you have two load pattern options: Constant and Step. Constant load enables you to define a number of users that will remain unchanged throughout the duration of the test. Use a constant load to analyze the performance of your application under a steady load of users. For example, you may specify a baseline test with 100 users. This load test could be executed prior to release to ensure that your established performance criteria remain satisfied.

A step load defines a starting and maximum user count. You also assign a step duration and a step user count. Every time the number of seconds specified in your step duration elapse, the number of users is incremented by the step count, unless the maximum number of users has been reached. Step loads are very useful for stress-testing your application, finding the maximum number of users your application will support before serious issues arise.

> A third type of load profile pattern, called "Goal Based," is available only through the Load Test Editor. See the section "Editing load tests" for more details.

We recommend you begin with a load test that has a small constant user load and a relatively short execution time. Once you have verified that the load test is configured and working correctly, increase the load and duration as you require.

Test Mix

Now select the tests to include in your scenario, along with the relative frequency with which they should run. Click the Add button and you will be presented with the Add Tests dialog shown in Figure 15-14.

By default, all of the tests, except manual tests, in your solution will be displayed. You can constrain these to a specific test list with the "Select test list to view" drop-down. Select one or more tests and click OK. To keep this example simple, only add the web test you created earlier in this chapter.

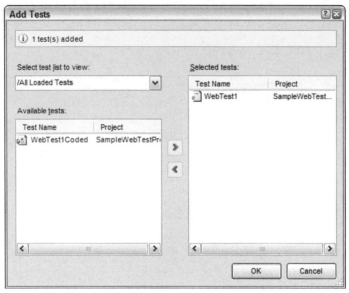

Figure 15-14

Next, you will return to the Test Mix step to assign frequencies for each test, as shown in Figure 15-15.

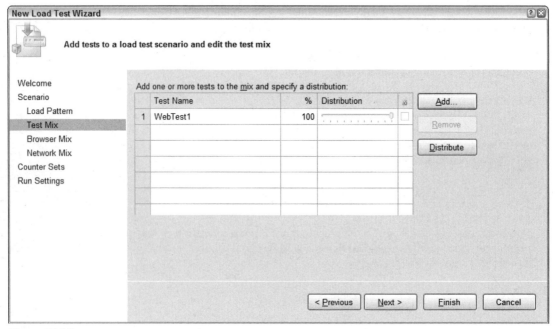

Figure 15-15

Use the sliders to assign the chance, in percentage, that a virtual user will select that test to execute. You may also type a number directly into the numeric fields. Use the lock checkbox to freeze tests at a certain number, while using the sliders to adjust the remaining "unlocked" test distributions. The Distribute button resets the percentages evenly between all tests.

> *Remember that distribution percentages do not indicate how much time will be devoted to each test. Whenever a new virtual user "runs" during the load test, one test is randomly selected from the mix according to these percentages.*

For example, assume you have a few tests and distribute percentages evenly between them. If one of those tests takes considerably longer than the others, your load test will spend more time running that test even though the number of times each test runs will be similar. Keep the time that each test takes to run in mind as you assign distributions.

Browser Mix

The next step, applicable only when web tests are part of the load test, is to define the distribution of browser types that you wish to simulate. Team System will then adjust the headers sent to the target application according to the selected browser for that user.

As shown in Figure 15-16, you may add one or more browser types and then assign a percent distribution for their use. Like the Test Mix step described earlier, you can use sliders to adjust the percentages, lock a particular percent, or click the Distribute button to reset to an even distribution.

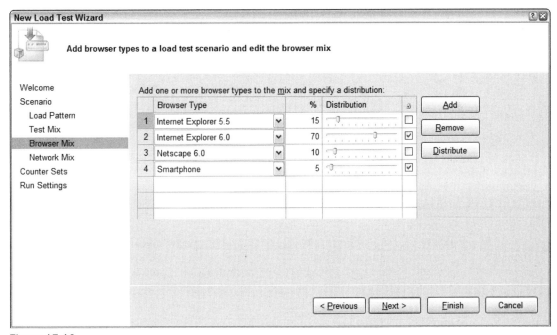

Figure 15-16

As with the Test Mix settings, each virtual user will select a browser type at random according to the percentages you set. A new browser type is selected each time a test is chosen for execution. This also applies to the Network Mix described next.

Network Mix

After selecting the browser type(s) you wish to simulate, you then specify the kinds of network connectivity you expect your users to have. This step is shown in Figure 15-17.

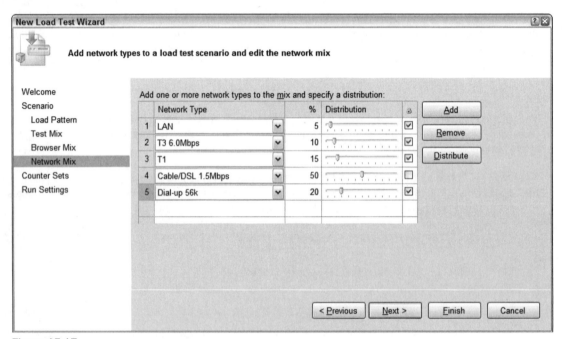

Figure 15-17

Select one or more network types, such as LAN, T1, and Dial-up, and then assign a percentage distribution, as with the browser mix.

Performance counter sets

A vital part of load testing is the tracking of performance counters. You can configure your load test to observe and record the values of performance counters, even on remote machines. For example, your target application is probably hosted on a different machine from the one on which you're running the test. In addition, that machine may be calling to other machines for required services such as databases or Web services. Counters from all of these machines can be collected and stored by Team System.

A counter set is a group of related performance counters. All of the contained performance counters will be collected and recorded on the target machine when the load test is executed.

Once the wizard is complete, you can use the editor to create your own counter sets by right-clicking on Counter Sets and selecting Add Custom Counter Set. Right-click on the new counter set and choose Add Counters. Use the resulting dialog box to select the counters and instances you wish to include.

Select machines and counter sets using the wizard step shown in Figure 15-18. Note that this step is optional. By default, performance counters are automatically collected and recorded for the machine running the load test. If no other machines are involved, simply click Next.

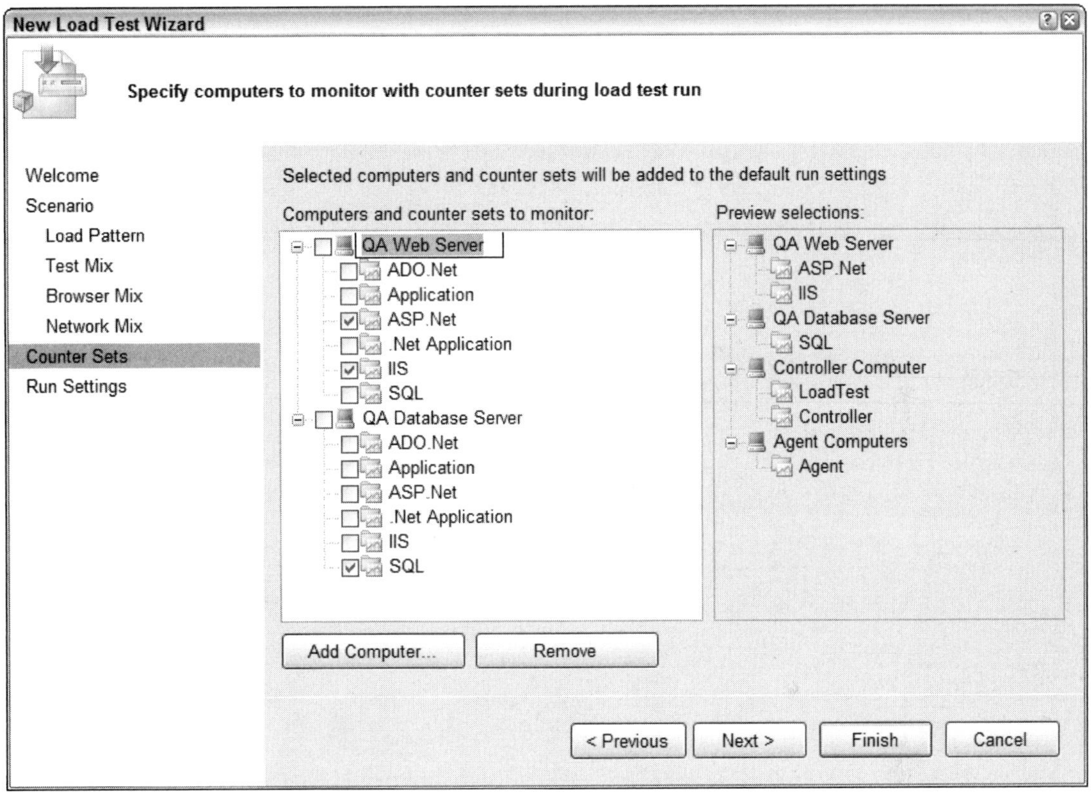

Figure 15-18

To add a machine to the list, click Add Computer and enter the name of the target machine. Then, check any counter sets you wish to track to enable collection of the associated performance counters from the target machine.

Run settings

The final step in the New Load Test Wizard is to specify the test's run settings, as shown in Figure 15-19. A load test may have more than one run setting, but the New Load Test Wizard will only create one. In addition, run settings include more details than are visible through the wizard. We cover these aspects of run settings in the section "Editing load tests" later in this chapter.

First, select the timing details for the test. Warmup Duration specifies a window of time during which, although the test is running, no information from the test is tracked. This gives the target application a chance to complete actions such as just-in-time compilation or caching of resources. Once the warmup period ends, data collection begins and will continue until the Run Duration value has been reached.

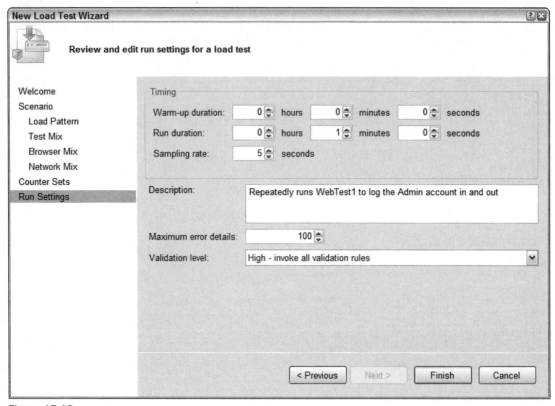

Figure 15-19

The sampling rate determines how often performance counters will be collected and recorded. A higher frequency (lower number) will produce more detail, but at the cost of a larger test result set and slightly higher strain on the target machines.

Any description you enter will be stored for the current run setting. You can also use the Maximum Error Details field to specify how many identical errors will be stored before truncation occurs.

Finally, the Validation Level setting indicates which web test validation rules should be executed. This is important because the execution of validation rules is achieved at the expense of performance. In a stress test, you may be more interested in raw performance than you are that a set of validation rules pass. There are three options for validation level:

❑ **Low:** Only validation rules marked with Low level will be executed.

❑ **Medium:** Validation rules marked Low or Medium level will be executed.

❑ **High:** All validation rules will be executed.

Click Finish to complete the wizard and create the load test.

Editing load tests

After completing the New Load Test Wizard, or whenever you open an existing load test, you will see the Load Test Editor, as shown in Figure 15-20.

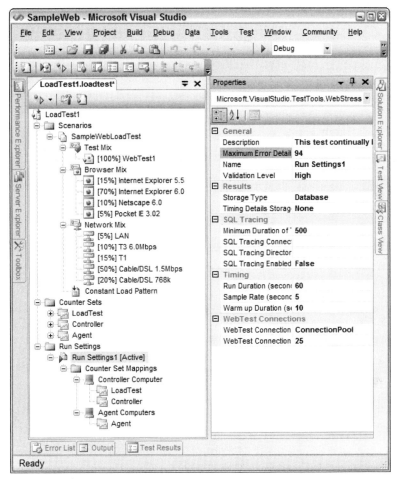

Figure 15-20

The Load Test Editor displays all of the settings you specified in the New Load Test Wizard. It allows access to more properties and options than the wizard, including the capability to add scenarios, create new run settings, configure SQL tracing, and much more.

Adding scenarios

As you've already seen, scenarios are groups of tests and user profiles. They are a good way to define a large load test composed of smaller specific testing objectives.

For example, you might create a load test with two scenarios. The first includes tests of the administrative functions of your site, including 10 users with the corporate-mandated Internet Explorer 6.0 on a LAN. The other scenario tests the core features of your site, running with 90 users who have a variety of browsers and connections. Running these scenarios together under one load test enables you to more effectively gauge the overall behavior of your site under realistic usage.

The New Load Test Wizard generates loads tests with a single scenario, but you can easily add more using the Load Test Editor. Right-click on the Scenarios node and choose Add Scenario. You will then be prompted to walk through the Add Scenario Wizard, which is simply a subset of the New Load Test Wizard that you've already seen.

Run settings

Run settings, as shown on the right-hand side of Figure 15-20, specify such things as duration of the test run, where and if results data is stored, SQL tracing, and performance counter mappings.

A load test can have more than one run setting, but as with scenarios, the New Load Test Wizard only supports the creation of one. You might want multiple run settings to enable you to easily switch between different types of runs. For example, you could switch between a long-running test that runs all validation rules and another shorter test that runs only those marked as Low level.

To add a new run setting, right-click on the Run Settings node or the load test's root node and choose Add Run Setting. You can then modify any property or add counter set mappings to this new run setting node.

SQL Tracing

You can gather tracing information from a target SQL Server or SQL Express instance though SQL Tracing. Enable SQL Tracing through the run settings of your load test. As shown in Figure 15-20, the SQL Tracing group has four settings.

First, set the SQL Tracing Enabled setting to True. Then click the SQL Tracking Connect String setting to make the ellipsis button appear. Click that button and configure the connection to the database you wish to trace.

Use the SQL Tracing Directory setting to specify the path or UNC to the directory in which you want the SQL Trace details stored.

Finally, you can specify a minimum threshold for logging of SQL operations. The Minimum Duration of Traced SQL Operations setting specifies the minimum time, in milliseconds, that an operation must take in order for it to be recorded in the tracing file.

Goal-based load profiles

As you saw in the New Load Test Wizard, you had two options for load profile patterns: Constant and Step. A third option, Goal Based, is only available through the Load Test Editor.

The goal-based pattern is used to raise or lower the user load over time until a specific performance counter range has been reached. This is an invaluable option when you want to determine the peak loads your application can withstand.

To access the load profile options, open your load test in the Load Test Editor and click on your current load profile, which will be either Constant Load Profile or Step Load Profile. If the Properties window is not already open, press F4 or right-click on the node and choose Properties.

In the Properties window, change the Pattern value to Goal Based. You should now see a window similar to what is shown in Figure 15-21.

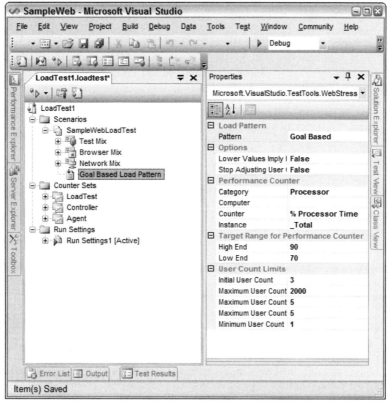

Figure 15-21

First, notice the User Count Limits section. This is similar to the step pattern in that you specify an initial and maximum user count, but you also specify a maximum user increment and decrement and minimum user count. The load test will dynamically adjust the current user count according to these settings in order to reach the goal performance counter threshold.

By default, the pattern will be configured against the % Processor Time performance counter. To change this, enter the category (e.g., Memory, System, etc.), the computer from which it will be collected (leave this blank for the current machine), and the counter name and instance—for example, if you have multiple processors.

You then need to tell the test about the performance counter you selected. First identify the range you're trying to reach using the High End and Low End properties. Set the Lower Values Imply Higher Resource Utilization option if a lower counter value indicates system stress. For example, you would set this to True when using the system group's Available MBytes counter. Finally, you can tell the load test to remain at the current user load level when the goal is reached with the Stop Adjusting User Count When Goal Achieved option.

Storing load test run data

A load test run can collect a large amount of data. This includes performance counter information from one or more machines, details about which test passed, and durations of various actions. You may choose to store this information in a SQL Server or SQL Express instance or an XML file.

To select a results store, you need to modify the load test's run settings. Refer back to Figure 15-20. The local run settings have been selected in the Load Test Editor. In the Properties window is a setting called Storage Type. The valid settings for this are None, Database, and XML.

In order to use the Database option, you must first configure an instance of SQL Server or SQL Express using a database creation script. The script, `LoadTestResultsRepository.sql`, is found under the `\Common7\IDE` directory of your Visual Studio installation directory. You may run this script any way you choose, such as with Query Manager or SQL Server 2005's SQLCMD utility.

Once created, the new LoadTest database can be used to store data from load tests running on the local machine or even remote machines. Running remote load tests is described later in the "Distributed Load Tests" section of this chapter.

Executing load tests

There are several ways to execute a load test. You can use various windows in Visual Studio Team System, the Load Test Editor, Test Manager and Test View, or you can use command-line tools. For details on using the command line, see "Command-line Test Execution."

In the Load Test Editor, you can click the Run button at the upper-left corner or right-click on any load test setting node and select Run Load Test.

From the Test Manager and Test View windows, check or select one or more load tests and click the Run Tests button. In Test View, you may also right-click on a test and select Run Selection. See Chapter 13 for more information on the Test Manager and Test View windows.

Viewing and interpreting load test results

If you ran your test from either Test Manager or Test View, you will see the status of your test in the Test Results window, as shown in Figure 15-22.

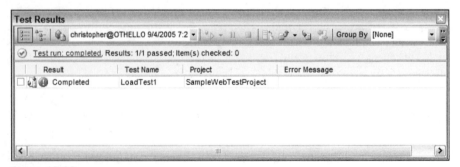

Figure 15-22

Once the status of your test is In Progress or Complete, you can double-click to see the Load Test Monitor window, shown in Figure 15-23. You may also right-click and choose View Test Results Details. When a load test is run from the Load Test Editor, the Test Results window is bypassed, immediately displaying the Load Test Monitor.

You can observe the progress of your test and then continue to use the same window to review results after the test has completed.

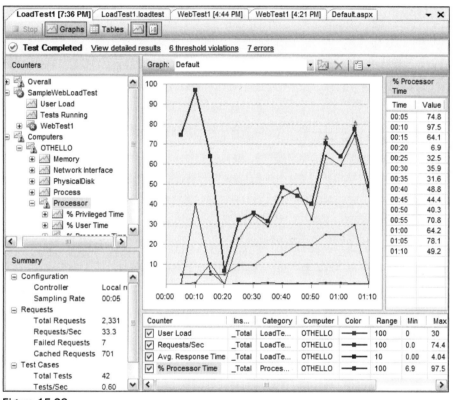

Figure 15-23

At the top of the screen, just under the file tabs, is a toolbar with several view options. First, you can select between Graphs and Tables view. We describe each of these views in a moment. The Show Counters Panel and Show Summary Panel buttons are used to toggle those panels on and off.

Graphs View

The most obvious feature of the Load Test Monitor is the graph, which is selected by default. This plots a number of selected performance counters over the duration of the test.

The tree in the left-hand, or Counters, pane, shows a list of all available performance counters, grouped into a variety of sets — for example, by machine. Expand the nodes to reveal the tracked performance counters. Hover over a counter to see a plot of its values in the graph. Double-click on the counter to add it to the graph and legend.

Selecting performance counters and knowing what they represent can require experience. With so many available counters, it can be a daunting task to know when your application isn't performing at its best. Fortunately, Microsoft has applied their practices and recommendations to predefine threshold values for each performance counter to help indicate that something might be wrong.

As the load test runs, the graph is updated at each snapshot interval. In addition, you may notice that some of the nodes in the Counters pane are marked with a red error or yellow warning icon. This indicates that the value of a performance counter has exceeded a predefined threshold and should be reviewed. For example, Figure 15-23 indicates threshold violations for the % Processor Time counter. In fact, you can see small warning icons in the graph itself at the points where the violations occurred. We'll use the Thresholds view to review these in a moment.

The list at the bottom of the screen, called the *legend*, shows details of the selected counters. Those that are checked appear in the graph with the indicated color. If you select a counter, it will be displayed with a bold line.

The right-hand table, called the Plot Points pane, shows the value of the currently selected counter at each sampling interval during the test. *Remember, you can adjust this interval using the Load Test Editor by changing the Sample Rate property under Run Settings.*

Finally, the bottom-left view, or Summary pane, shows the overall results of the load test.

Tables View

When you click the Tables button, the main panel of the load test results window changes to show a drop-down list with a table. Use the drop-down list to view each of the available tables for the load test run. Each of these tables is described in the following sections.

Tests table

This table goes beyond the detail of the Summary pane, listing all tests in your load test and providing summary statistics for each. Tests are listed by name and containing scenario for easy identification. You will see the total count of runs, pass/fail details, as well as tests per second and seconds per test metrics.

Pages table

The Pages table shows all of the pages accessed during the load test. Included with each page are details of the containing scenario and web test along with performance metrics. The Total column shows the number of times that page was rendered during the test. The Page Time column reflects the average response time for each page. Page Time Goal and % Meeting Goal are used when a target response time was specified for that page. Finally, the Last Page Time shows the response time from the most recent request to that page.

Transactions table

A transaction is a defined subset of steps in a web test that are tracked together. For example, you can wrap the requests from the start to the end of your checkout process in a transaction named Checkout for easy tracking. For more details, see the section titled "Adding Transactions" under "Editing a web test" earlier in this chapter.

In this table, you will see any defined transactions listed, along with the names of the containing scenario and web test. Details include the count, response time, and elapsed time for each transaction.

SQL Trace table

The SQL Trace table will only be enabled if you previously configured SQL Tracing for your load test. Details for doing that can be found in the "SQL Tracing" subsection of "Editing load tests" earlier in this chapter.

This table shows the slowest SQL operations that occurred on the machine specified in your SQL Tracing settings. Note that only those operations that take longer than the Minimum Duration of Traced SQL Operations will appear.

By default, the operations are sorted with the slowest at the top of the list. You can view many details for each operation, including duration, start and end time, CPU, login name, and others.

Thresholds table

The top of Figure 15-23 indicates that there are "6 threshold violations." You may either click on that text, or select the Threshold table to see the details. You will see a list similar to the one shown in Figure 15-24.

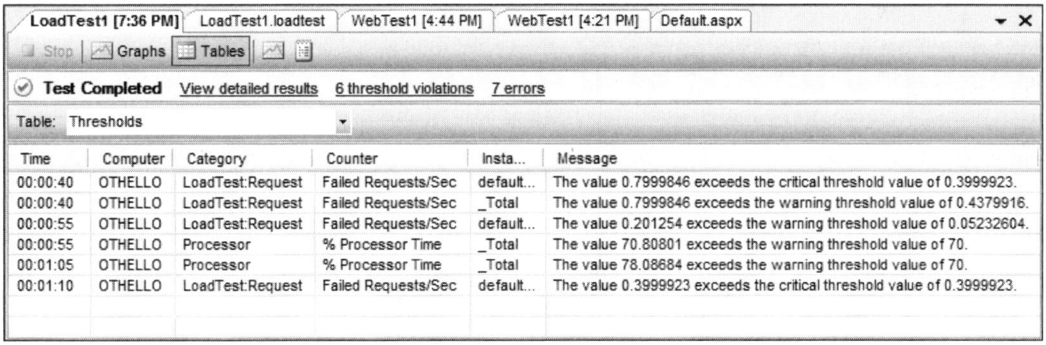
LoadTest1 [7:36 PM]
LoadTest1.loadtest
WebTest1 [4:44 PM]
WebTest1 [4:21 PM]
Default.aspx
Stop
Graphs
Tables
Test Completed
View detailed results
6 threshold violations
7 errors
Table: Thresholds
Time | Computer | Category | Counter | Insta... | Message
00:00:40 | OTHELLO | LoadTest:Request | Failed Requests/Sec | default... | The value 0.7999846 exceeds the critical threshold value of 0.3999923.
00:00:40 | OTHELLO | LoadTest:Request | Failed Requests/Sec | _Total | The value 0.7999846 exceeds the warning threshold value of 0.4379916.
00:00:55 | OTHELLO | LoadTest:Request | Failed Requests/Sec | default... | The value 0.201254 exceeds the warning threshold value of 0.05232604.
00:00:55 | OTHELLO | Processor | % Processor Time | _Total | The value 70.80801 exceeds the warning threshold value of 70.
00:01:05 | OTHELLO | Processor | % Processor Time | _Total | The value 78.08684 exceeds the warning threshold value of 70.
00:01:10 | OTHELLO | LoadTest:Request | Failed Requests/Sec | default... | The value 0.3999923 exceeds the critical threshold value of 0.3999923.

Figure 15-24

Each violation is listed according to the sampling time at which it occurred. You can see details about which counter on which machine failed as well as a description of what the violating and threshold values were.

Errors table

As with threshold violations, if your test encountered any errors, you will see a message such as "4 errors." Click on this text or the Errors table button to see a summary list of the errors. This will include the error type, such as Total or Exception, and the error's subtype. SubType will contain the specific Exception type encountered — for example, `FileNotFoundException`. Also shown are the count of each particular error and the message returned from the last occurrence of that error.

If you configured a database to store the load test results data, you can right-click on any entry and choose Errors. This will show the Load Test Errors window, as shown in Figure 15-25.

This table displays each instance of the error, including stack and details if available, according to the time at which they occurred. Other information, such as the containing test, scenario, and web request, is displayed when available. Hover over any error to see the error's full text.

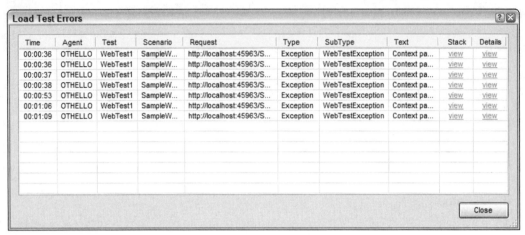

Figure 15-25

Command-line Test Execution

To execute a web or load test from the command line, first launch a Visual Studio 2005 command prompt. From the Start menu, select Programs ➪ Microsoft Visual Studio 2005 ➪ Visual Studio Tools ➪ Visual Studio 2005 Command Prompt. This version of the command prompt sets environment variables that are useful for accessing Visual Studio utilities.

The MSTest.exe utility is found under the \Command7\IDE directory of your Visual Studio installation directory but will be available from any directory when using the Visual Studio command prompt.

Executing tests

From the directory that contains your tests, use the MSTest program to launch the test as follows:

```
MSTest /testcontainer:<Name>.<extension>
```

The target can be a web test, a load test, or an assembly that contains tests such as unit tests. For example, to execute a load test named LoadTest1, enter the following command:

```
MSTest /testcontainer:LoadTest1.loadtest
```

This will execute the specified test(s) and display details, such as pass/fail, which run configuration was used, and where the result were stored.

Executing test lists

You can also run tests that are grouped into a test list. See Chapter 13 for a full description of Test Manager and test lists. First, specify the /testmetadata:<filename> option to load the metadata file containing the test list definitions. Then, select the test list to execute with the /testlist:<listname> option.

Other test options

Remember that tests can have more than one run configuration. Specify a specific run configuration using the `/runconfig:<filename>` option.

By default, results are stored in an XML-based file called a *TRX file*. The default form is `MSTest.MMDDYYYY.HHMMSS.trx`. To store the run results in an alternate file, use the `/resultsfile:<filename>` option.

More options are available. To view them, run the following command:

```
MSTest /help
```

Distributed Load Tests

In larger-scale efforts, a single machine may not have enough power to simulate the number of users you need to generate the required stress on your application. Fortunately, Team System load testing includes features supporting the execution of load tests in a distributed environment.

There are a number of roles that the machines play. *Client* machines are typically developer machines on which the load tests are created and selected for execution. The *controller* is the "headquarters" of the operation, coordinating the actions of one or more *agent* machines. The controller also collects the test results from each associated agent machine. The agent machines actually execute the load tests and provide details to the controller. The controller and agents are collectively referred to as a *rig*.

There are no requirements for the location of the application under test. Generally, the application is installed either on one or more machines either outside the rig or locally on the agent machines, but the architecture of distributed testing is flexible.

Installing controllers and agents

Before using controllers and agents, you must install the required Windows services on each machine. The Visual Studio 2005 Team Test Load Agent package includes setup utilities for these services.

The Team Test Load Controller Setup utility is started with `setup.exe` under the `VS\Controller` directory of the Team Test Load Agent package. This will install a Windows service for the controller and will prompt you to assign a Windows account under which that service will run. SQL Express will also be installed for data collection, but you may later configure the controller to use a different database for storage, such as SQL Server.

> *Install your controller and verify that the controller Windows service is running before configuring your agent machines. This will allow your agent machines to automatically register with the controller.*

After the controller service has been installed, run the Team Test Load Agent Setup on each agent machine, specifying a user under whom the service should run and the name of the controller machine. The agent installation program, `setup.exe`, can be found in the `VS\Agent` directory of the package.

Configuring controllers

Once you have run the installation packages on the controller and agent machine(s), configure the controller by choosing Test ➪ Administer Test Controllers. This can be done from any machine and does not need to be done on the controller machine itself. You will see the Administer Test Controller dialog, as shown in Figure 15-26.

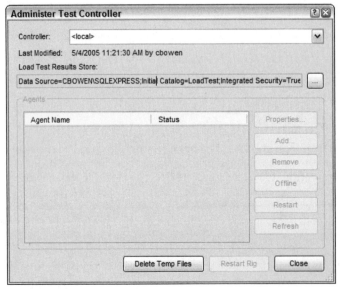

Figure 15-26

Type the name of a machine in the Controller field and press Enter. Ensure that the machine you specify has had the required controller services installed. The Agents panel will then list any currently configured agents for that controller, along with each agent's status.

The Load Test Results Connection String points to the repository you are using to store load test data. Click the ellipsis button to select and test a connection to your repository. If you have not already configured a repository, refer to the "Storing load test run data" section earlier in this chapter.

To add an agent, click on the Add button and specify a machine on which you've previously run the agent installation package. Temporarily suspend an agent from the rig by clicking the Offline button. Restart the agent services on a target machine with the Restart button.

You also have options for clearing temporary log data and directories as well as restarting the entire rig.

Configuring agents

Using the Administer Test Controller dialog just described, select an agent and press the Properties button. You will be able to modify several settings, described in the following sections.

Weighting

When running a distributed load test, the load test being executed by the controller has a specific user load profile. This user load is then distributed to the agent machines according to their individual weightings.

For example, suppose two agents are running under a controller that is executing a load test with 10 users. If the agents' weights are each 50, then five users will be sent to each agent.

IP Switching

This indicates the range of IP addresses to be used for calls from this agent to the target web application.

Attributes

You may assign name-value attributes to each agent in order to later restrict which agent machines are selected to run tests. There are no restrictions on the names and values you can set.

You will learn how to leverage these attributes in the next section.

Test run configuration

Once your controller and agents have been installed and configured, you are ready to execute a load test against them. You specify a controller for the test and agent properties in the test run configuration. You may recall seeing the test run configuration when we covered web tests.

Open your test run configuration by choosing Test ⇨ Edit Test Run Configurations, and select the appropriate configuration. Then, choose the Controller and Agent entry from the left-hand list. You should see the dialog shown in Figure 15-27.

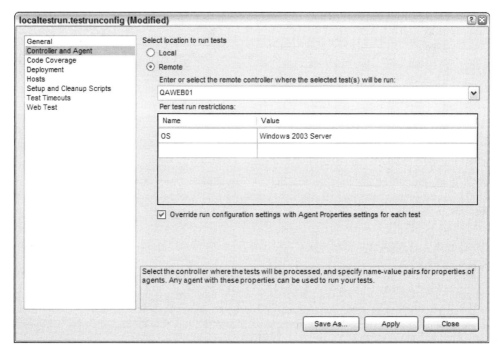

Figure 15-27

Under "Select location to run tests," choose Remote, and then enter or select the name of a valid controller machine.

You may then wish to specify restrictions for the agent machines that will run the tests. In the "Per test run restrictions" section, enter name-value pairs to qualify the agents that will be selected to run tests. For example, you could enter OS with a value of Windows 2003 Server to ensure that the tests ran only on agent machines with this matching attribute, as shown in Figure 15-27.

When you have finished making your changes, you may wish to create a new test run configuration especially for remote execution. To do so, choose Save As and specify a new file.

Running a distributed load test

Now that you have installed and configured your rig (a controller and at least one agent machine) and modified your test run configuration to target the controller, you may execute the load test. Execute the test using any one of the options described in the "Executing load tests" section earlier in this chapter, ensuring that the correct test run configuration has been selected.

The controller will then be signaled to begin the test. The controller will contact the (qualifying) agent machines and distribute tests and load to each. As each test completes, the controller collects test run details from each agent. When all agents have completed, the controller finalizes the test and the test run ends.

Viewing a distributed load test

To view the progress of your distributed load test, open the Test Runs window via the Windows option under the Test menu. You will see a window similar to the one shown in Figure 15-28.

Figure 15-28

Select the controller and press the Connect button. The window will then show details of any running, waiting, and completed runs on that controller. You may also select a run and start, stop, or temporarily suspend its execution.

Summary

This chapter described web and load tests in detail. You first learned how to use the Web Test Recorder to easily record a new web test. You then learned how to use the Web Test Editor to finely tune the web test, adding features such as validation and extraction rules. You also looked at coded web tests, which enable you to create very flexible tests in any .NET language.

The next section introduced load tests, which can be composed of any automated testing type, such as web and unit tests. You learned how to use the New Load Test Wizard to create an initial load test. You then used the Load Test Editor to add scenarios, SQL tracing, and other options not available through the wizard. You also looked at various options for executing load tests, including the command-line tool `MSTest.exe`.

You then saw the power of the Load Test Monitor, used to graphically view performance counter details as well as errors, transactions, SQL operations, and more.

Finally, you learned how to run load tests in a distributed environment. You now know how to install and configure the controller and agent machines and how to use the controller to parcel out load to the agent machines, collecting results in the test repository.

In the next two chapters, we continue our coverage of the various test options supported by Visual Studio Team Edition for Software Testers.

16

Manual Testing

Software test engineers use manual testing techniques to find and document bugs so that they can be reproduced at a later date by the developer. The quality of a manual test often depends on the thoroughness and precision of the tester. The manual testing process is an important part of any test cycle — some tasks are impossible to automate, such as verifying the usability and functional requirements of an application. Plus, in some cases, it will take more time to automate a manual test than actually running through the test by hand. Manual tests are also very inexpensive and easy to implement — all you need is a qualified tester, a word processing program (or paper and pencil), and a set of use cases and test cases.

Microsoft still uses manual testing in the development of their products, but there has been a gradual shift away from this method because of the time and effort required to build and complete tests for the complexity of Microsoft products. The Microsoft Visual C++ IDE Team used 15 testers for a period of two to three weeks to run all of the required manual tests for the Visual C++ IDE! For insights on Microsoft's internal testing practices, visit the Microsoft Visual C++ Testers weblog (`http://blogs.msdn.com/fivetestersfromvc`).

How do you decide when to opt for automated as opposed to manual tests? The key is strategy — you must make a careful, informed decision based on set criteria. In this chapter, we will cover all the basics of manual testing. The next section covers various scenarios to help you evaluate how to choose the right tests for the right circumstances. You will also learn how Team System facilitates the process and enables you to create, manage, and share test results within your team.

Test Automation versus Manual Testing

All software development projects have a finite schedule and budget. It is up to the software test engineers and the project managers to decide what tests to implement to reach the goal of producing stable and reliable software.

There is quite a bit of debate within the developer community as to the merits of manual testing versus automated testing. Extreme Programming (XP) practitioners typically favor automated testing in the interest of saving time. Automated tests can verify results, but are constrained within a set of predefined problems. Manual testing can undoubtedly uncover problems that are not easily found using standard testing tools.

We will look at the features of both automated tests and manual tests. You can then make an informed decision as to what tests will give you the best results for the projects on which you are working.

Test automation

Automated tests are very handy because you can implement them as part of the build process using Team Foundation Build (you can learn more about Team Foundation Build in Chapter 24). For obvious reasons, manual tests are not designed to be used within an automated test environment. Team System has several built-in automated tests, including load tests, generic tests, and unit tests. Test automation makes a great deal of sense for medium to large software projects.

Automated tests are easily deployed, can quickly be executed by the build server, and are highly suited for repetitive tasks (you can run automated tests hundreds of thousands of times with ease). Therefore, it makes regression testing a snap. (Regression testing is the process of retesting your application to make sure you don't introduce bugs while in the process of fixing other bugs.) Automated tests hook into Team Foundation Build, enabling you to focus on other tasks. You can have a farm of build servers running through a battery of automated tests, enabling your testers to deal with "show-stopping" problems.

However, testing is an iterative process — you should constantly look at the effectiveness of your tests and adjust as needed during the lifetime of your project. By refining the test process, you can document best practices to carry forward in future projects.

Test automation works really well for long-term projects. One of the main reasons for this is cost — designing an automated test framework and elaborate test cases takes a lot of work hours to implement. This is not to say that it isn't a good idea to automate tests in smaller projects. In fact, many Agile practitioners swear by automation. In some cases, a manual bug fix may take just a few minutes to correct. In the end, the decision should be based on the effective prioritization of your time and cost.

Use automated tests to review your application structure and code. Automated tests are not really effective for usability (and other user-centric issues). It would be very difficult (and impractical) for a human tester to manually generate a code coverage report for an application with millions of lines of code (such as the Windows operating system). This is an area where automated tests really shine — machines can perform tests such as code coverage and static and dynamic code analysis with little to no personnel required.

There are, however, tools that bridge the gap. One example is the Framework for Integrated Testing (FIT) by Ward Cunningham and related tools (such as FITnesse). FIT excels at running acceptance and regression tests. FIT allows a customer or tester to use a Microsoft Word document to model how an application should behave. Using "fixtures" (code written by programmers), FIT compares the values in the HTML table with the software. It makes it easy for a nontechnical user to interact with a complex application. You can learn more by visiting the following website: http://fit.c2.com/.

Here is a short list of some of the processes you may want to automate:

❑ **Web and load testing:** Web and load testing enable you to automatically test the performance of your web application using different browser, traffic, and network simulations, bandwidth profiles, server load scenarios, and other environmental factors. Web and load tests can also be used to implement functional and smoke testing. You can find more information about these tests in Chapter 15.

❑ **Structural testing:** Some tests are best left to a computer. For example, in Chapter 10, you learned that the Application Verifier can dynamically detect memory-handling errors. Some of the errors are far from intuitive (a stack corruption may cause errors and instability in your system long after a defect has been injected in your code). Structural testing can help you uncover these errors and issues.

❑ **Performance testing:** Performance testing (and tuning) is an essential part of any application development cycle. You can test your application using both the sampling and instrumentation methods, and the best part is that both can be automated. Performance testing is covered in depth in Chapter 12.

❑ **Regression testing:** Using automated tests, you can easily verify that the code that is checked in meets a certain level of quality. If you uncover specific errors using automated tests, it is quite easy to rerun the tests to make sure the problems have been corrected.

❑ **Generic tests:** Team System offers great extensibility features, including the capability to formulate new kinds of tests and bring in external test results that are handled with the same instrumentation and tools as your built-in tests. Generic testing is discussed at length in the next chapter.

❑ **Stress testing:** You can simulate the stress of thousands of users accessing your application. This is not possible using manual testing (unless you have thousands of testers on staff!).

Manual testing

Manual testing is the process of testing software by hand and writing down the steps to reproduce bugs and errors. Before you start manually testing an application, you should formulate a solid set of test cases. Automated tests are predefined in scope, and can only confirm or deny the existence of specific bugs. However, an experienced tester has the advantage of being able to explore facets of the application and find bugs in the most unlikely places. Because software isn't completely written by machines (yet), human error can creep into the design and structure of an application. It takes the eye of a good tester to find these flaws and correct them.

Accuracy is one of the main challenges of running effective manual tests. If your tester isn't using careful documentation and a solid methodology, he or she may miss bugs. Manual tests are well suited for small or one-shot development projects. Again, cost becomes an issue; due to small budgets and lack of resources, it may be impractical to implement large-scale custom testing frameworks. Small projects usually have aggressive development schedules, so you have to make the best use of your time.

Even if you are an Agile developer, you shouldn't disregard manual testing. As mentioned before, some tasks shouldn't be automated. For example, the most effective way of tracking down user interface and usability problems in your application is by using manual testing techniques.

In most development environments, manual tests are performed as a prelude to automated tests. Manual testing practices may also be incorporated into the bug documentation process. Here are some of the tasks you can't easily automate:

❑ **Error management:** Does your application behave well when an error is encountered? Are the error messages presented to the end users descriptive enough to help guide them through your application? Unit testing should be used as your first line of defense. Error management testing looks at the interaction between the user and your application once it has been compiled.

❑ **Deployment, configuration, and compatibility testing:** How easily does your application deploy? Will your application work with all versions of the .NET Framework? Deployment testing involves testing an application with a variety of platforms, systems, and hardware configurations, and in production environments. The deployment manager role usually handles this task (see Chapter 22 for more details).

❑ **Quality assurance (QA)/user acceptance testing:** In any development process, the client (or business analyst) has to sign off on features. To ensure that these requirements are met, user acceptance testing is required. Quality assurance testing involves ensuring that all procedures and requirements have been followed, tests have been performed, and the end product meets a set standard of quality.

❑ **Localization testing and requirements:** Does your application behave correctly when it's localized in another language? Will fonts and words disappear or align incorrectly? Does it support bi-directional positioning? If you are writing software for a global market, you should be manually testing your application under many globalization scenarios and conditions.

❑ **User interface testing:** A lot of work is being done with automated user interface test frameworks. However, nothing can replace a good tester who can evaluate whether the application meets accessibility and visual requirement guidelines.

❑ **Usability testing:** Does the user have to perform unnecessary steps to access a feature? Is the application intuitive (or counterintuitive)? What's most important in usability testing is setting up a proper test methodology. Some of the tests that fall under this category include exploratory, assessment, comparison, and validation testing.

❑ **Black-box (or functional) testing:** Black-box tests are performed by testers, and will sometimes yield unexpected results. How will your application behave if you enter a very large amount of text in a text field? All inputs in your application are tested without knowledge of the code or the expected output. One of the popular functional tests you can try on your application is a *smoke test* — a run-through of a piece of software after a major build or update. (The term "smoke test" comes from hardware testing — if your electronics project starts to spark or produce smoke, you know you have a problem!)

❑ **Recovery and fail-over testing:** If an application crashes, is there any way for end users to recover their data? Recovery testing looks at how your application copes with disastrous scenarios.

❑ **Security testing:** Will the application work under a least-privileged user account? Does your application violate basic Windows security principles (such as writing to HKEY_LOCAL_MACHINE)? The Application Verifier component of Team System can automatically uncover many types of security violations. The best way to implement security in your development environment is by enforcing best practices (using check-in policies), writing good inline documentation, and performing regular manual audits on your code.

Test Cases

One of the problems with most software companies (especially smaller ones) is that they take an ad hoc approach to testing. The result is inconsistencies in the product, both in terms of quality and robustness. If you are building commercial or enterprise software, you can't afford to fly by the seat of your pants.

A test case is documentation that defines the input, the expected output, and the steps to complete a test. This documentation is needed for both automated and manual tests. In the case of automation, the case will have a huge impact on how the test code will be written and implemented. If you are interested, Chapter 17 explores the topic of test case management in more detail.

Using test cases, you can easily manage and document the tests in your project. You can also track whether your application is functioning as expected and all of your customer requirements have been met. In a nutshell, test cases help the developer to reproduce a bug or problem during debugging

Manual tests and test cases go hand-in-hand. The following table contains an example of a couple of test cases. Test cases usually have two possible outcomes: Pass or Fail.

Table 16-1

Requirements	Pass	Fail
Does the application install under the Guest account?		
Can the user run two instances of the application at once?		

Many Microsoft logo programs use test cases, which you can use to evaluate whether your application meets the expected requirements. For example, the "Designed for Windows XP" program has an Application Test Framework that uses test cases to help you evaluate the eligibility of your application. You must pass all requirements to get the logo designation.

Microsoft internally uses a Test Case Manager code-named "MadDog." You can view screenshots and learn about Microsoft's test case methodologies from the following post on Scott Guthrie's weblog: `http://weblogs.asp.net/scottgu/archive/2004/10/28/249458.aspx`.

Many professional test case products are available on the market. If you want a free basic tool to manage your test cases, be sure to check out the PBSystems Test Case Manager (please note that this application requires Microsoft Access 2000): `www.matpie.drw.net/PBSystems/products/tcm/tcm.htm`.

Planning Your Manual Tests

The first step in designing an effective test process is the planning stage. In this step, you must identify and isolate all of the important features of your application. You can then compose a detailed plan to cover individual use cases and scenarios.

Let's say you are writing a manual test plan to test Internet Explorer. First, you would need to identify important features (such as Add Favorites). Then, you should identify a set of specifications for each feature. For example, what should be happening when the user clicks Favorites ➪ Add to Favorites?

> *A rule of thumb is to use context awareness while you are building Test Cases. You must apply the "Big 5 W" questions: who, what, where, when, and why (plus how).*

Keep in mind that your test plan does not need to be limited. You can outline features that are not being tested, and look at issues such as security and globalization. You can also apply edge cases to your application. That is one of the core advantages of manual testing — there are no constraints per se. The final step is creating a checklist, which enables you or another developer/tester to reproduce the errors.

Using Team System, you can classify bugs and defects using a variety of scales that reflect real-world test outcomes. In fact, prioritization is key if you want to lower your development costs and focus on bugs that affect the most important features in your software. Here is a prioritization scale listed in order of severity. Please note that this list is not the "be all, end all" solution — you can flexibly add and remove prioritization levels according to your needs. As you can see, the time frames reflect a formal methodology-style approach. If you prefer a more Agile approach, you can adapt this scale by modifying the requirements and escalation:

❑ **Critical:** This is literally a showstopper. Bugs that are classified "critical" should be handled right away. Usually, critical bugs affect important and commonly used features in your software. You must repair the bug before reintroducing your code into the daily build process.

❑ **Severe:** This is an important bug that affects the secondary features in your software. This bug or defect should be corrected before the next weekly build.

❑ **Medium:** This bug needs to be fixed before the next milestone. It affects a tertiary feature in your software. The problem must be repaired by month's end.

❑ **Minor:** This error should be fixed before the next release of the product. The error affects a noncritical portion of your application.

❑ **Cosmetic:** This is a minor bug affecting a visual element or nonfunctional element of the application. These cosmetic bugs are the lowest priority and should be corrected before the next release of your product.

Manual Testing in Team System

Manual tests are first-class citizens in Team System — you can run automated tests and manual tests side by side. You can track the progress of a test in the Test Results window, use import/export functions, and drill down into any tests at any time. You can also generate metrics and reports derived from manual tests.

To use the manual testing features of Team System, you should install and use the Team Edition for Software Testers or Team Suite version of the product. Microsoft Word is not necessarily required to create manual tests (you can create plaintext-based manual tests), but overall, it provides a better experience by allowing you to flexibly format the content.

Traditionally, manual testing has been a "paper-based" process. You can also find third-party applications that can manage manual tests. The main advantage Team System offers is integration with Visual Studio 2005 and Team Foundation Server. Team System provides a framework in which the software test engineer can focus on test planning and generating requirements, rather than having to worry about learning a new toolset because the tester is primarily working with Word or text documents.

Creating manual tests

Creating a manual test in Team System is quite easy. Simply open your target project, right-click on the project name in the Solutions Explorer and select Add Test Project. You can also add a project by clicking File ➪ New ➪ New Project. Then you must select the Test Project type. Figure 16-1 shows a screenshot of the New Project dialog box.

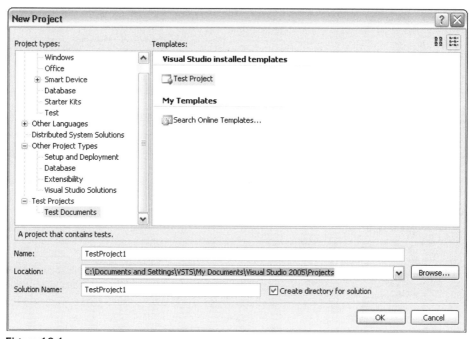

Figure 16-1

Once you have created the test project, you can add new manual tests by right-clicking on the test project within the Solutions Explorer and selecting Add ➪ New Test. This option to add a new test is also accessible from the Test menu within the Visual Studio 2005 IDE. The manual test will automatically appear within your test project in the Solutions Explorer.

As a shortcut, you can also add a manual test (Word format) directly, without going through the wizard, by right-clicking on your project in the Solution Explorer and selecting Add ➪ Manual Test (Word Format).

Figure 16-2 shows the Add New Test Wizard. Clicking on any of the tests in the Templates pane will give you a more detailed explanation in the Description pane on the right.

Configuring manual test options

When you create a test project, two tests are added by default: a unit test and a Word-based manual test. You can modify your default test project to include manual tests by clicking Tools ⇨ Options ⇨ Test Tools ⇨ Test Project. The test project Options window is shown in Figure 16-3.

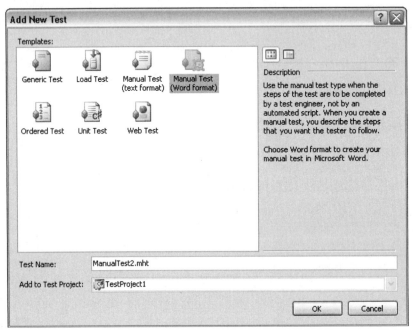

Figure 16-2

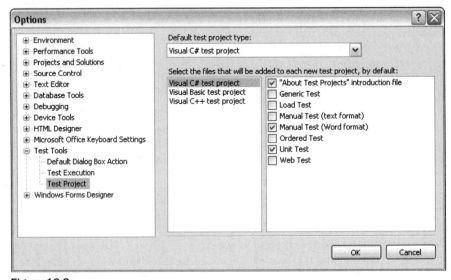

Figure 16-3

To add the manual test file to the default test project, simply check the Manual Test (text format) check-box and click the OK button. You can set individual test project settings for any development language, including Visual C#, Visual Basic, or Visual C++.

You can also control the behavior of manual tests by accessing the Default Dialog Box Action options (see Figure 16-4). To access the options, simply click Test ➪ Options ➪ Test Tools ➪ Default Dialog Box Action.

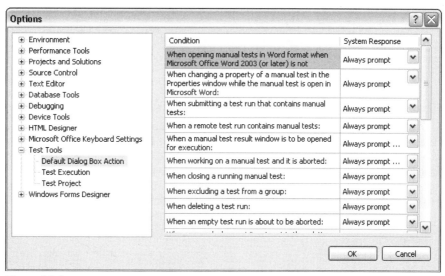

Figure 16-4

Some of the manual testing options you can configure include the following:

❑ **When opening manual tests in Word format when Microsoft Word 2003 (or later) is not installed**: Team System requires Microsoft Word 2003 because it embeds special metadata inside the document to identify it as a test (see the section entitled "Creating a Visual Studio 2005 test template" for more details). The two options you have at your disposal include "Always prompt" and "Always view the manual test in read-only mode."

❑ **When changing a property of a manual test in the Properties window while the manual test is open in Microsoft Word**: Because Microsoft Word is an external program, any changes to the properties window within Visual Studio will not automatically propagate to your Word document when it is open. To get around this problem, you can set one of two options in the Default Dialog Box Action window: "Always prompt" or "Always save the manual test."

❑ **When submitting a test run that contains manual tests:** Your options are "Always prompt" or "Don't prompt." Because manual tests require the intervention of a tester, you will definitely want to set this option to "Don't prompt" if you are planning to deploy manual tests in a test run on the build server. By setting "Don't prompt," Team Foundation Build will skip over the manual tests and continue with the automated tests. Otherwise, you will get the prompt shown in Figure 16-5.

❑ **When a remote test run contains manual tests:** You have three options: "Always prompt," "Always remove manual tests from test run and continue," or "Always abort the test run." These options are quite important if you want to automate the tests on your build server. Otherwise, you will either receive a prompt that will stop the automated tests dead in its tracks or the test run will be aborted. In most cases, you will want to select "Always remove manual tests from test run and continue."

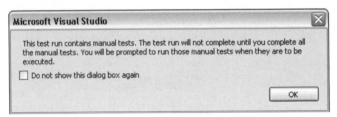

Figure 16-5

❑ **When a manual test result window is to be opened for execution:** When you include manual tests in your test project, Visual Studio will pop up a series of dialog boxes to prompt the tester. You can choose to disable some of these prompts to streamline the testing process. The two options you can set include "Always prompt and disable the manual test result window" or "Always directly disable the manual test result window."

❑ **When working on a manual test and it is aborted:** If a manual test is aborted for any reason whatsoever, you can choose whether to allow Visual Studio to prompt the tester to enter a test result or skip over the test completely. The options for this include "Always prompt and disable the manual test result window" or "Always directly disable the manual test result window."

❑ **When closing a running manual test:** If you close a manual test mid-run, you can set whether the test will abort or whether the tester can enter a test result before shutting it down. The two options for this scenario are "Always prompt" or "Always abort the test."

Manual test templates

Team System provides two default manual test templates: a Microsoft Word template and a Text template. These default tests can be found as part of the Team Suite and Team Tester SKUs. All of the test templates are located in the following program directory:

```
Program Files\Microsoft Visual Studio 8\Common7\IDE\ItemTemplates\<Language>\1033\
```

The default manual tests are available for a variety of programming languages, including Visual C#, Visual Basic.NET, Visual J#, and Visual C++. The manual test templates are located in two .zip files:

❑   ManualTestWordFormat.zip

❑   ManualTestTextFormat.zip

Each of these .zip files contains two files:

- ❏ `ManualTest.mtx` (or `ManualTest.mht`): The actual test template files
- ❏ `ManualTest.vstemplate`: Used to create project items, which can be consumed by Visual Studio 2005 and shown in the Add New Test Wizard (see Figure 16-2)

Only Microsoft Word and text-based manual tests are supported in the current version of Team System. Other file types (such as Excel) are not supported.

Creating custom manual test templates

There are several ways to create custom manual test templates: add a modified manual test in your project, export your manual test template as a new item, or package up a new manual test template for the Visual Studio 2005 IDE. Please note that the third option is the most complex and prone to errors.

Adding a custom manual test in your project

You can add a custom manual test in your project by following these steps:

1. Create a new test project.
2. Take the default manual test template and create a copy of it.
3. Add the copy to your project and launch the Word or text file to edit the contents of the manual test.
4. Once you are done, rename the file (give it a filename such as `CustomManualTest.mht`) and save it. You can then copy and reuse the new template as you like.

Exporting your custom manual test as a new item

You can export a custom manual test as an item template. That way, users will be able to import it using the Add New Item dialog box. Here are the steps to create a new item template:

1. Open your test project. Make the modifications you want to your test.
2. Click File ➪ Export Template.
3. The Export Template Wizard will appear, as shown in Figure 16-6. Select the Item template option and the appropriate test project.
4. Select the manual test(s) you would like to export (see Figure 16-7).
5. You will then arrive at the Select Item References page (as shown in Figure 16-8). You don't have to select any of the options because manual tests don't require special assembly references to run. Click Next.
6. During the final step, you can select an icon, a name, and description for your project (shown in Figure 16-9). If you check "Automatically import the template in Visual Studio," the template will be made available locally every time you launch the IDE. Checking the "Display an explorer window on the output files folder" option will show you all your templates (including the one you just created) in the following directory: `C:\Documents and Settings\...\My Documents\Visual Studio 2005\My Exported Templates`.

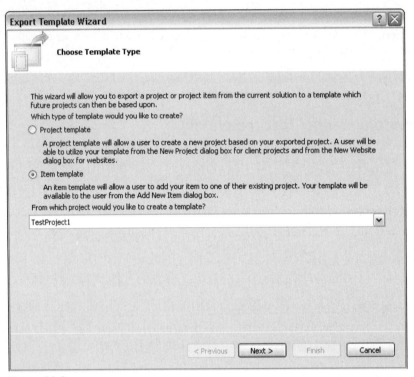

Figure 16-6

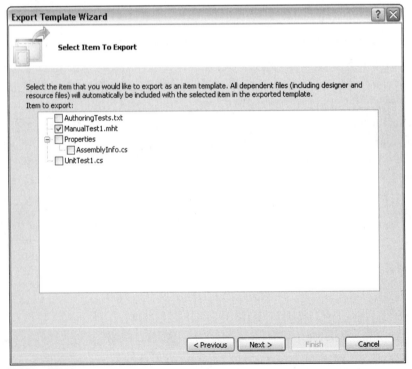

Figure 16-7

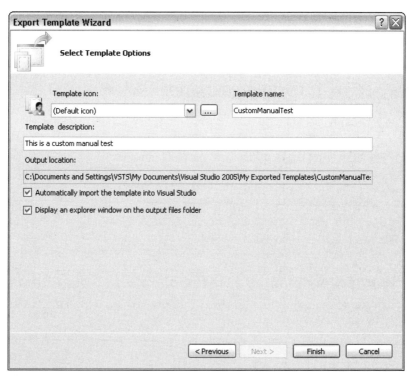

Figure 16-8

Figure 16-9

Creating a Visual Studio 2005 test template

Of all the methods outlined so far, this is by far the trickiest. The advantage of creating a Visual Studio 2005 template is that it is conveniently added with the other templates in the Add New Test dialog.

1. Copy `ManualTestWordFormat.zip` on your desktop and extract `ManualTest.mht`. Customize it to your liking using Microsoft Word. Assuming you installed Visual Studio 2005 on your C: drive, the path to the zip file should be `C:\Program Files\Microsoft Visual Studio 8\Common7\IDE\ItemTemplates\<language>\1033\ManualTestWordFormat.zip`.

2. Please note that `TestID` and `TestType` are required custom Word properties that enable your document to be recognized as a manual test within the IDE. To manually set the `CustomDocumentProperties`, edit the source of the `.mht` file (using a text editor other than Word) and add the values highlighted below.

    The `TestType` value should always remain `Manual Test`. Otherwise, Visual Studio may not recognize your document as part of a manual test. The `TestID` Globally Unique Identifier (GUID) should be left at the value of `$guid1$`. Visual Studio will automatically populate this field with a new GUID once a test is created within the IDE, to uniquely identify each manual test in the test results.

    ```
    <html xmlns:o="urn:schemas-microsoft-com:office:office"
    xmlns:w="urn:schemas-microsoft-com:office:word"
    xmlns:dt="uuid:C2F41010-65B3-11d1-A29F-00AA00C14882"
    xmlns="http://www.w3.org/TR/REC-html40">

    <head>
    <meta http-equiv=Content-Type content="text/html; charset=us-ascii">
    <meta name=ProgId content=Word.Document>
    <meta name=Generator content="Microsoft Word 11">
    <meta name=Originator content="Microsoft Word 11">
    <link rel=File-List href="ManualTest1_files/filelist.xml">

    <title>To do: set description</title>
    <!--[if gte mso 9]><xml>

      <o:CustomDocumentProperties>
       <o:TestType dt:dt="string">Manual Test</o:TestType>
       <o:TestID dt:dt="string">$guid1$</o:TestID>
      </o:CustomDocumentProperties>

    </xml>
    ...
    </head>
    ```

3. Once you are done, replace the `.mht` file in `ManualTestWordFormat.zip` with the one you just edited. Rename `ManualTestWordFormat.zip` to a filename of your choice (such as `CustomManualTest.zip`) and paste it into the following directory: `C:\ProgramFiles\Microsoft Visual Studio 8\Common7\IDE\ItemTemplates\<language>\1033\`.

Integrating your custom manual test template into Visual Studio 2005

Once the custom test has been added in the correct directory, you can refresh the `ItemTemplatesCache` directory using the following command:

```
devenv /setup
```

Team System and Visual Studio 2005 doesn't have a mechanism to enable you to deploy manual tests to multiple users. Here are a few solutions to get around this problem:

❑ **Custom MSI:** You can create an installer that will place the template in the right directory. You can then silently install them on any of your team members' computers using Group Policies and a solution such as Systems Management Server. See the section entitled "Distribute Visual Studio Templates and Policy Wizards in a Deployment Project" in the MSDN Documentation for more information. For information on how to deploy files in your infrastructure, visit the Microsoft TechNet website at `http://technet.microsoft.com`.

❑ **Project Portal:** You can add the `.zip` file in your custom process and request that your team members install them manually.

❑ **Source Control:** You can both check the files into source control and request that your team members use them, or map the source control system with the Visual Studio Templates directory. Once your team members retrieve the latest source code updates, the templates will also be updated.

Opening test templates using the Open With wizard

To open a test template using the Open With Wizard, simply right-click on the file in the Solutions Explorer and select Open With. Figure 16-10 shows a screenshot of the Open With Wizard (listing an assortment of editors you can pick from to manipulate your manual tests).

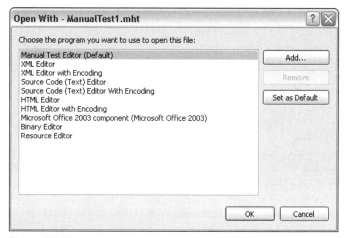

Figure 16-10

If you choose any editor other than the Manual Test Editor (Default), your test may be rendered as HTML tags, rather than an editable test template.

Microsoft Word format template

The Microsoft Word version of the manual test template has an `.mht` file extension (which denotes that it is a Microsoft HTML document). If you have Microsoft Word installed on your system, you should select this template type because it will enable you to nicely format your test.

You can also embed screenshots, photos, and other rich content. Figure 16-11 illustrates the layout of a Word-based manual test template.

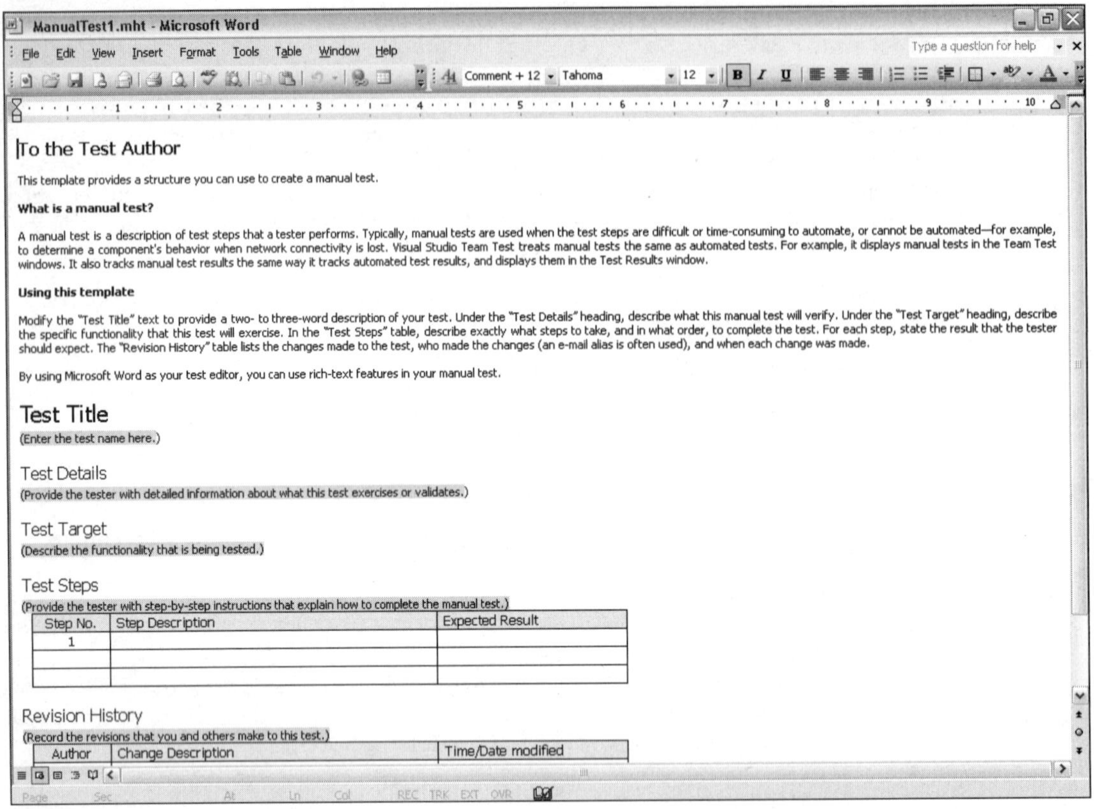

Figure 16-11

Text Format template

The Text Format template has an `.mtx` extension (a Microsoft Text document — not to be confused with the Twain device driver). The Text Format template is a great deal simpler than its Microsoft Word counterpart. On the downside, you can't embed any rich content such as pictures. On the upside, it doesn't require Microsoft Word to be viewed and edited. Figure 16-12 shows a screenshot of a Text Format Manual Test template displayed in the Manual Test Editor in Visual Studio 2005.

Manual test structure

All manual test templates are structured the same way. There are five main sections in a manual test:

- ❑ Test Title
- ❑ Test Details
- ❑ Test Target
- ❑ Test Steps
- ❑ Revision History

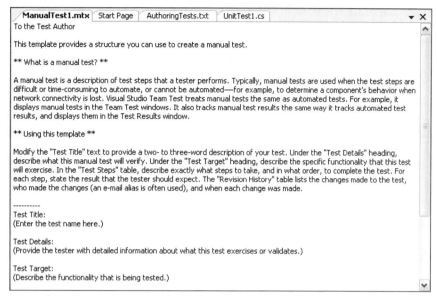

Figure 16-12

The Test Title and Test Details sections describe what kinds of tests are being performed on your application. This is an important step because the test will have to be reproduced in the future, so be detailed in your wording. You can only enter two to three words in the title.

The Test Target section describes the specifics of the functionality covered by your test. The Test Steps section describes in detail what steps are needed to accomplish the test. Each step is numbered with a description of the step and the outcome. It is crucial that the test be sufficiently documented in order to be reproducible. In addition, try to minimize the number of steps to reproduce.

Finally, the Revision History section tracks when the test was revised and by whom. You can enter the author's name (or e-mail alias), a description of the revisions made to the test, and the current date and time. The data entered on this template is handled and measured the same as any other test in Team System, using the same underlying framework.

Don't feel you have to stick to these five elements. You can expand on it, add other sections, and remove sections. Team System does not parse the contents of your manual test document, so you have a lot of flexibility in the way you structure your content in the document. In fact, grouping manual tests can be as simple as cutting and pasting several tests into one document.

Managing Manual Tests

Team System offers powerful collaboration features. Manual tests can be shared with any member of a development team using work items. The following section (and subsections) will show you how to run manual tests and export the results on Team Foundation Server.

Using the Test Manager

To start the test run, go to the Solution Explorer on the right side of the interface, right-click on your project and select Debug ⇨ Start New Instance. You can also run a test by going to the Test View window and selecting Run Tests. Right-clicking on any of the tests in the Test View window also gives you the option of running individual tests (as opposed to the entire test grouping). Simply select the Run Selection option to execute an individual test.

You can differentiate each test type using the Group By drop-down selector. This option is very useful for isolating the manual tests from the other tests. When you execute a manual test, the initial status is always Pending in the Test Results window. Figure 16-13 illustrates the Test Results.

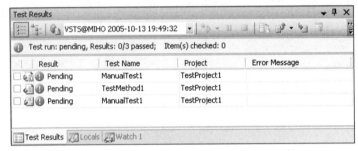

Figure 16-13

To do a test run, simply check off the desired test (or tests) in the Test Results view, select the drop-down list above the test results and select Run (as shown in Figure 16-14). You can also individually right-click on any test in the Test View window and select Run Selection (which will have the same effect).

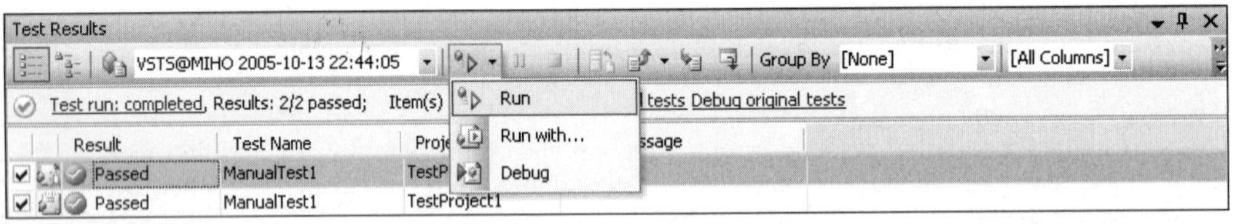

Figure 16-14

> *As with all tests, clicking Delete will remove the test from the Test Results window but not remove it from the project.*

The edited tests will then appear in the IDE for running, along with a Pass/Fail window. Microsoft Word will only appear when you invoke editing from the Test View or the Test Manager and right-click.

Once you are done, you can evaluate whether or not the test was successful by clicking Pass or Fail, inserting any applicable comments, and then selecting Apply in the Test Results pane. Figure 16-15 shows you how you can select a pass or fail grade on the manual test. You can also add comments relating to the test results.

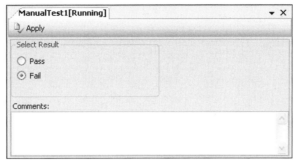

Figure 16-15

You can save your manual test results by closing the file. The Test Results window will confirm the Pass or Fail status of your test. If you want to cancel all manual tests in the Test Results window, right-click on any of the tests and select Delete Test Run.

> *Here is a handy tip: Group manual tests together using test projects to differentiate these tests from the others when viewing your test results on the Team Project portal.*

If the test fails, the software test engineer can associate it with a bug report work item.

Logging your manual test as a bug work item

Once the manual tests have been executed, you can log any resulting test failures as bug work items. To do this, simply right-click on the test that failed and select Create Work Item ➪ Bug. You can also add the results to an existing work item by using the Add to Work Item option.

Many of your manual test details will be associated with the bug work item, including the following:

❑   Test name

❑   Test ID

❑   Physical path to the manual test

❑   An attachment containing the manual test results in a Test Results XML file (.trx). The .trx file will re-create the test results for anyone wanting to view and diagnose the test results.

Figure 16-16 shows the bug work item instance that is automatically generated. The middle of the bug work item form enables you to change the assignment, iteration, priority, state, and so forth. The bottom half of the bug work item provides information about the test, including a summary, links, file attachments, and details.

> *The bug title is critically important: Notice in Figure 16-16 that the columns indicate information provided by default in a Work Item query including the unique ID, Work Item Type, State, Assigned to, and Title. When a work item is generated from a manual test, the name of the manual test is automatically added to the title, but if you don't add a more descriptive title, you will have a hard time finding a specific bug, especially if there are hundreds of nondescriptive titles like "manualtest1" in the work item database. Take the time to briefly describe the issue — for example: "Manual Test: UI Crash on Web Configuration Page."*

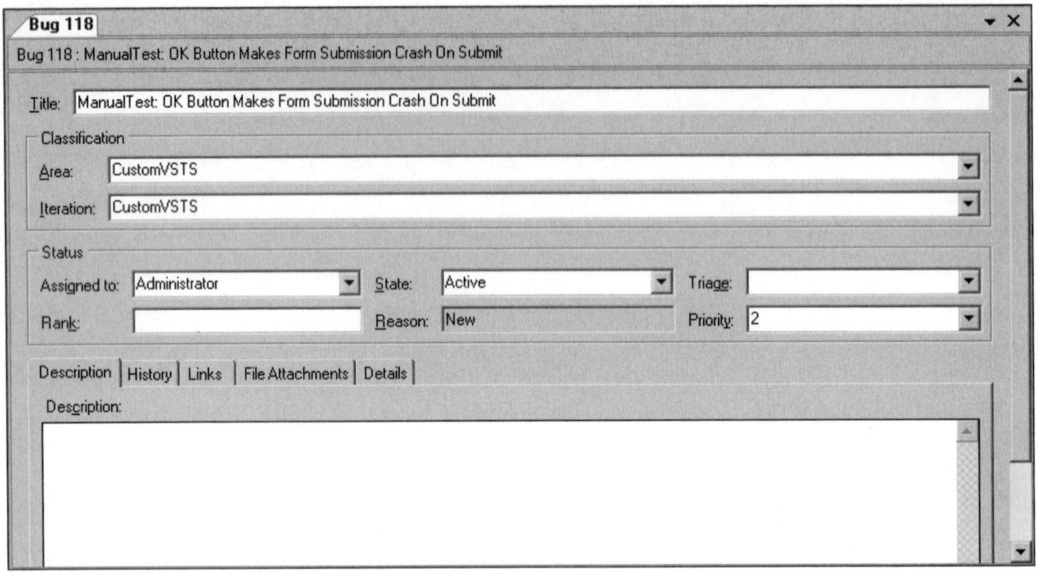

Figure 16-16

Publishing the test results on Team Foundation Server

Once your test run has been completed, you can share the results with the rest of the team by publishing them on Team Foundation Server. After the test results are published, the project manager or test lead can look at test reports (using the SQL Server Reporting Services — see Chapter 19 for more details). The project manager can also assign and manage any new bug work items.

You can publish test results by right-clicking on a test and selecting the Publish icon. The Publish Test Results window will appear (as shown in Figure 16-17), with the name of your test run, the owner, the file size of the results, and the date.

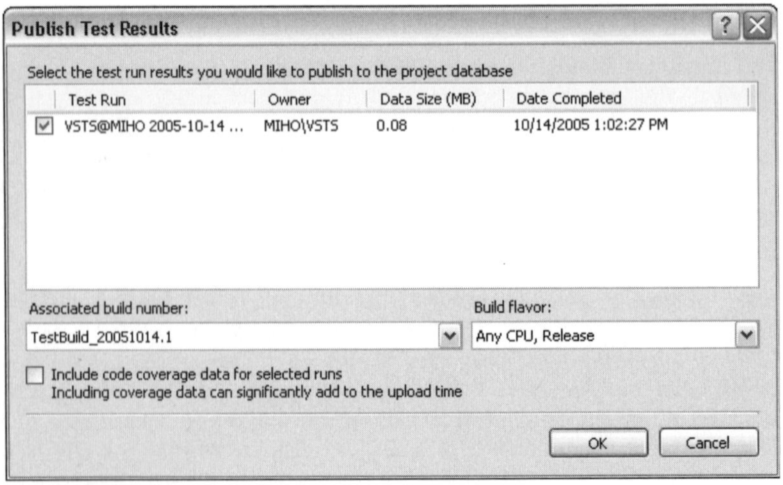

Figure 16-17

The Team System data store contains an OLAP database with cubes (in other words, multi-dimensional data constructs in SQL Server) that contains data-based representations for tests and work items. Several tables contain work item information, including `tfsWorkItemTracking` and `tfsWorkItemTrackingAttachments`.

As an administrator, you don't need to dig into the database to get this information. You can also query all work items using Team Explorer (or you can query the work items using the reporting site), as shown in Figure 16-18.

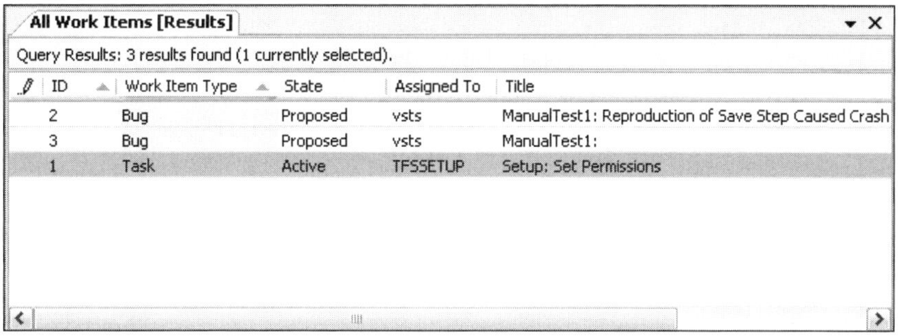

ID	Work Item Type	State	Assigned To	Title
2	Bug	Proposed	vsts	ManualTest1: Reproduction of Save Step Caused Crash
3	Bug	Proposed	vsts	ManualTest1:
1	Task	Active	TFSSETUP	Setup: Set Permissions

All Work Items [Results]
Query Results: 3 results found (1 currently selected).

Figure 16-18

You can also export the test results in a Visual Studio Test Results File (`.trx`). This file contains an XML representation of the entire test run data, including the execution time, the name of the host machine, the test type, and much more.

Once the results are exported, it is easy to share them with other members of your testing team, developers, and project leads. The key here is to create reproducible results that anyone can use to eliminate bugs.

You can also import manual tests from Team Foundation Server. You can then open the tests within Test View, which enables you (or anyone else) to reproduce the steps and find the bugs or defects within your target application.

Summary

In this chapter, you learned how manual testing compares to automated testing. You must make informed decisions with regard to your testing strategy because it greatly affects your bottom line in terms of time and resources,

You also learned how to plan and map out the test cases specific to manual tests. You then explored the manual test support in Team System, including how to generate tests in the IDE, creating custom test templates, running manual tests, and communicating the results with Team Foundation Server.

If you are interested in alternative testing methodologies, Michael Hunter (a Microsoft Test Technical Lead) has compiled a useful list of application tests you can use to create a comprehensive test plan. Visit `http://blogs.msdn.com/micahel/articles/175571.aspx`.

In the next chapter, you'll learn how to create custom generic tests that integrate external third-party testing tools seamlessly with Team System's test framework.

17

Generic Testing

Generic tests enable you to reach outside of the test framework by running external executables, which return results back to Team Test. Generic tests are useful for supporting current test processes that you may already have in place by wiring them to Team Test. They are also useful when there are complex steps to be performed by third-party tools, or when you want to create your own external testing tools.

Generic tests offer easy extensibility to the Visual Studio Team Test toolset, enabling easy integration of external tools to the test framework. No code is required to step outside the boundaries of Visual Studio and integrate with custom tools. Generic tests use the same test framework as the other test types, but instead of producing test results, they return the results of an externally run application to the test framework.

During the execution of a generic test, an external application is run. The application can return a simple pass or fail by setting its *exit code*, also known as the *ErrorLevel*, or it can return an XML file with the specific results of any number of tests that were run as part of the external application.

Figure 17-1 shows the integration of generic tests and Visual Studio Team Test. Notice that the generic tests are part of the Visual Studio Team Test system, but run external applications.

You can create your own test types using the test framework's extensibility, but this is such a complex process it deserves a book of its own. By using a generic test, you can obtain almost instant extensibility by creating your own external applications to perform any custom test or operation and then report the results back to the generic test.

Additional tools for extending the test tool framework are available as part of the Visual Studio 2005 Team System Extensibility Kit available for download from MSDN (`http://msdn .microsoft.com/vstudio/extend/SDKDownload`).

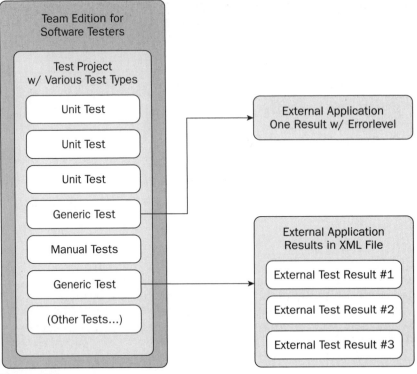

Figure 17-1

Creating and Running a Generic Test

In the following sections, you will create a new generic test, see how it runs, and view the results of the test. In the process, we will discuss *exit codes* (otherwise known as *ErrorLevels*).

Creating a generic test

For this example, let's assume that you have a simple C# app that runs a web search engine query. You have half a dozen unit tests to test your code, but before they kick off you want to verify that the server exists. One possible solution would be to write a unit test with code that tries to hit the server. Another possible solution is shown in the following example, which uses the ping.exe utility included with Windows.

To begin, start Visual Studio Team System. Select File ➪ New ➪ Project. This will bring up the New Project dialog. Select the Test Documents under the Test Projects type and the Test Project template, give it a name, and click OK (see Figure 17-2).

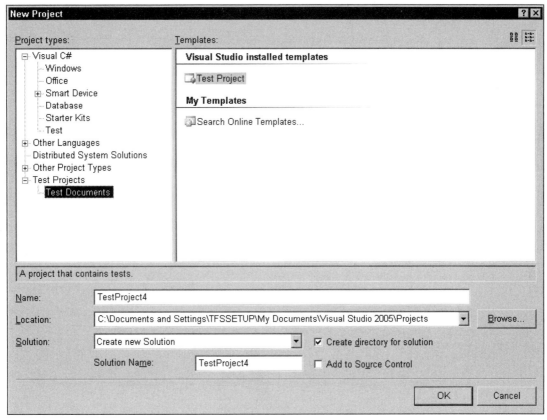

Figure 17-2

A new test project will be created with a text file of notes (`AuthoringTests.txt`), a manual test (`ManualTest1.mht`), and a unit test (`UnitTest1.cs`). These can all be deleted from the project for the sake of this example.

This is where we use a generic test. Right-click on the project name to bring up the context menu and select Add ➪ New Test. Select New Test instead of Generic Test so that you can give the test a name using the Add New Test dialog shown in Figure 17-3.

> *If you select Generic Test from the context menu, a file will be immediately added to the project, but giving the file a meaningful name is a more involved process. First the file would be renamed (by right-clicking the file and choosing Rename or pressing F4), but this would not affect the actual displayed verbose name of the test. You would need to view the Test Manager window, select the new test, view the Properties window, and then edit the Test Name property. All this is done for you using the Add New Test dialog, so the process is not shown here.*

Name the file `Ping.GenericTest` and click OK. As you can see, a generic test is just one of the several built-in test types available. Other types include load test, manual test, ordered test, unit test, and web test and are discussed in other chapters of this book.

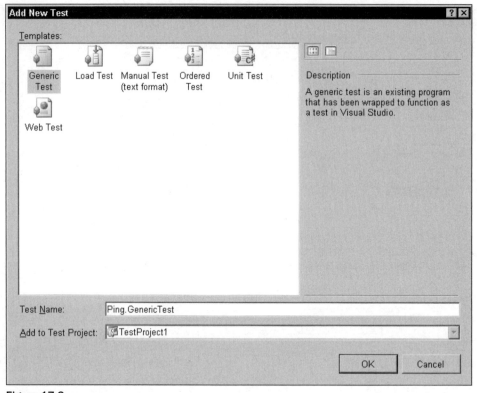

Figure 17-3

Next, the generic test editor will appear (see Figure 17-4). This editor contains the main properties of the generic test. Other properties can be accessed using the Property window, as described in the section "Running the generic test."

In the text box at the top of the editor under the "Specify an existing program to wrap as a generic test:" label, enter the location and name of the program. In our case, C:\WINDOWS\system32\ping.exe. The option of selecting a program by clicking on the ellipsis located next to the text box is also available. Under Run settings, in the "Command line arguments" text box, enter -n 1 google.com. Now save your entries (Ctrl+S) and close the editor for this generic test (Ctrl+F4).

The -n 1 tells ping.exe to attempt to reach the server only once. ping.exe sets an ErrorLevel of 0 for success (Passed) and 1 for failure (Failed), which is what the generic test type expects.

The filename of the generic test does not affect the displayed name of the test. To rename the test, view the Test Manager by selecting Test ➪ Windows ➪ Test Manager.

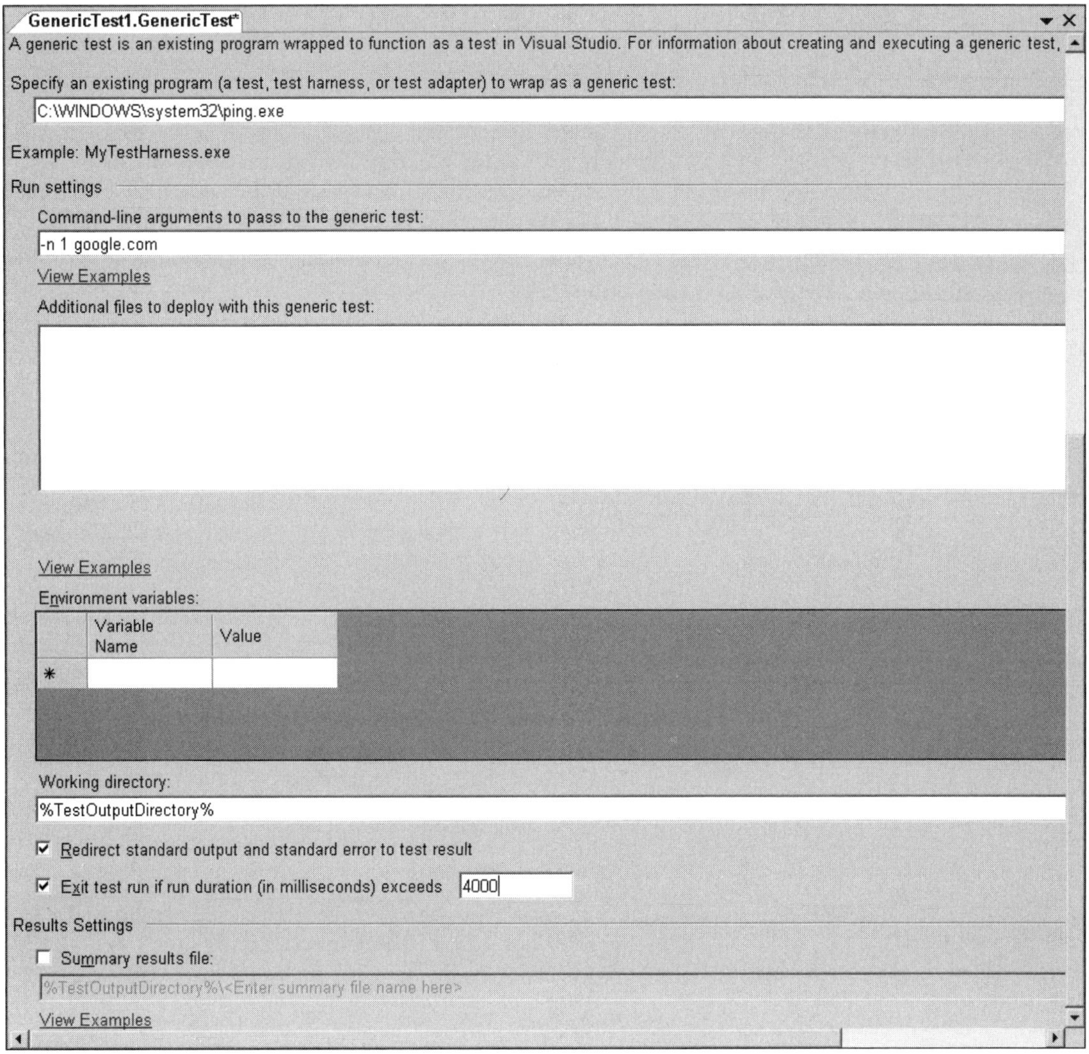

Figure 17-4

Figure 17-4 also shows a number of options that you can configure in the generic test properties dialog box:

❑ **Specify an existing program to wrap as a generic test:** The first text box is the full path to the executable to be run. When the generic test is run, the executable will be run one time. The test engine will use the executable's output (ErrorLevel or XML) to determine whether the test was successful.

This file must be either a Win32 Windows (GUI) or a Win32 Console application. Scripts, such as JScript or VBScript, are executed by `cscript.exe`, a Win32 console application. It cannot be a DOS command or a 16-bit app, because the test engine tracks the state of the thread during execution and captures the resulting ErrorLevel, which requires a Win32 proc.

> **To run a batch file, use the syntax** `C:\windows\System\cmd.exe/c[batchfile]`.

❑ **Command-line arguments to pass to the generic test:** The second text box (the first under the Execution Settings area) is used to provide additional arguments to be passed to the executing app. As with all command-line arguments, filenames with spaces anywhere in the path must be contained in quotes — for example: `"C:\Program Files\Internet Explorer\iexplorer.exe"`.

❑ **Additional files to be deployed with this generic test:** You can select files that will be deployed along with the tests. These files will be copied to the directory stored in the `testdeploymentdir` environment variable. These are usually files that your code under test requires to run properly.

❑ **Environment Variables:** You can add additional environment variables to the process in which the external application is run. These variables will only be available to the application when it is started and run by the generic test. The following table describes the additional available environment variables that the test engine sets.

In the example values in the following table, NOAHC *refers to the name of the computer on which the test is being executed;* MySolution *is the directory containing the solution file; and* find guts.generictest *is the name of the currently running test.*

Variable	Purpose
Testdir	Directory to which this test generic test was deployed. Example value: C:\MySolution\TestResults\Noahc_NOAHC 9_2_2005 2_28_20 AM\Out\find guts.generictest
Testlocation	Directory that contains the original source .GenericTest file.
Testlogsdir	Directory that will contain log files, code coverage data, etc.
Testdeploymentdir	Directory to which the files the user selected to be deployed are copied. Example value: C:\MySolution\TestResults\ Noahc_NOAHC 9_2_2005 2_28_20 AM\Out\find guts.generictest
Testoutputdirectory	Directory to which any output from the application should be copied so that it is picked up by the test engine and made available in the reports. Example value: C:\MySolution\TestResults\ Noahc_NOAHC 9_2_2005 2_28_20 AM\In\NOAHC\ c1953ae8-40bf-42b7-aef1-f55c78451713

If you created a .NET executable being run by the generic test, you can obtain the value of the environment variables in your code using the `Environment` class:

```
string dir = Environment.GetEnvironmentVariable("testlocation");
```

❑ **Redirect standard output and error to test result:** If checked, the test engine captures the process's output and error streams and saves them as part of the test run's report.

❑ **Display execution application (window or console) at runtime:** When checked, this will display the app to the user. The preceding checkbox must be unchecked if the user is to see any output on the console.

❑ **Exit test run if run duration (in milliseconds) exceeds:** The test will terminate with a Failed result if the time elapses. If this is unchecked, the test run may be permanently frozen until the test run is manually shut down.

Back in the Microsoft DOS days, an executing application could leave a trail when it exited by returning a single integer back to the operating system as an exit code. This exit code was called an ErrorLevel because it was designed to report an error, and, if so, a value indicating the type of error. In batch files, this ErrorLevel could then be used to test the result of an execution, and branch if there was an error. An ErrorLevel of 0 indicated a success, and anything else was some form of an error. The DOS batch `if errorlevel [x]` statement would result to `true` if the last statement's ErrorLevel was equal to or greater than `[x]`. For example:

```
@echo off
rem QuickTest.bat
ping -n 1 google.com
if errorlevel 1 goto problem
echo Success!
goto end

:problem
echo There was a problem, batch aborted.
echo ErrorLevel: %errorlevel%
goto end

:end
```

The environment variable `errorlevel` is set by the command shell to the exit code of the application. This would branch on any ErrorLevel greater than 0. The only common standard is that 0 indicates a success and anything else is a failure. The ErrorLevel is a standard integer with possible negative and positive values. The interpretation of what type of error occurred within the application by the resulting ErrorLevel is determined by the application. One would have to read the application's documentation, view its code, or deduce by trial and error what exit code was produced by what error.

You can easily return an exit code from a .NET console application. Most importantly, change the `Main` method from returning `void` to returning an `int`. The following short example will return the exit code provided on the command line. Its only "output" is the ErrorLevel code:

```
class SimpleExitCode
{
  static int Main(string[] args)
  {
    int exitcode = 0;

    // No argument specified
    if (args.Length == 0) return 1;

    // Could not parse command line argument
    if (!int.TryParse(args[0], out exitcode)) return 2;

    return exitcode;
  }
}
```

Another approach, which works from within a console application or a Windows application, is setting the `Environment.ExitCode` property:

```
// Set the errorlevel to success
System.Environment.ExitCode = 0;
```

Exit codes can be negative, but negative values are reserved for system ErrorLevels and should typically be avoided. For example, an ErrorLevel of -1073741510 is returned if the keyboard combination of Ctrl+Break is used during execution of a .NET console application.

Running the generic test

The next step after creating the generic test is to run the test and try it out. The Test View window provides a quick and easy way of running a set of tests. To view the available Team Test windows, from the main Visual Studio menu, select Test ⇨ Windows. Select Test View.

Select the Ping generic test from the list and click the Run Tests button to execute the test (see Figure 17-5).

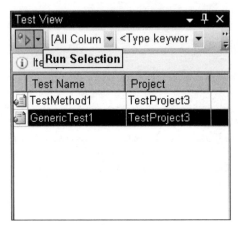

Figure 17-5

As the test is run, the Test Results dialog appears, as shown in Figure 17-6.

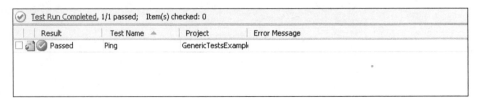

Figure 17-6

You know that the test pings google.com, so the test should pass. If we double-click on the test line that has just passed in the Test Results window, a report of the test run will display. Figure 17-7 shows the output captured from `ping.exe`. The fields Internal Test Name and Detailed Results File are not applicable to a simple generic test with only a return result and are discussed in the section "Extended Return Results."

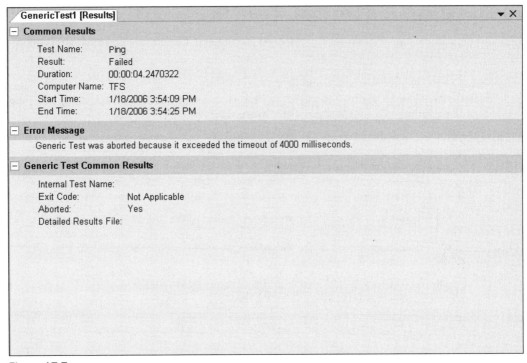

Figure 17-7

Let's see what happens when a test fails. Go back to the Generic Test properties document (Figure 17-4) by double-clicking the `Ping.GenericTest` file in the Solution Explorer. Change `google.com` to `nowhere.xyz`, save it, and close the editor. Re-run the test from the Test View window (refer to Figure 17-5), and this time the test will fail, as shown in Figure 17-8. Notice that the exit code is 1, which is not 0 and thus indicates a failure.

Quick links are visible on failed test results that conveniently allow you to re-run or debug the original test directly from the Test Results window.

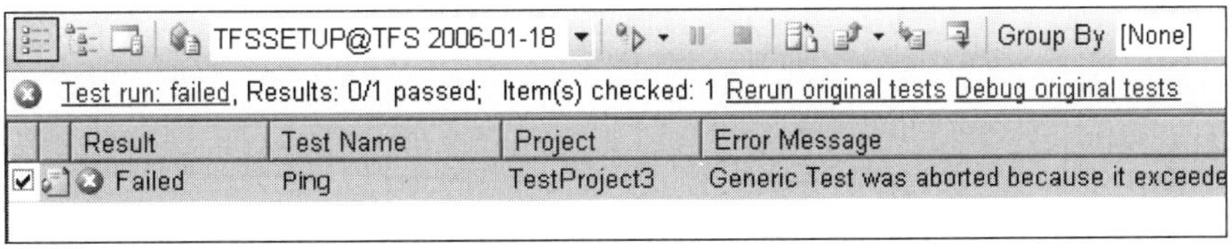

Figure 17-8

This example has demonstrated how to leverage an existing application to quickly create a test, how to run the test, and how to see the results when it passes or fails. Now you may want to create your own external applications to wrap in a generic test.

Creating an External Testing Tool

Here are some of the scenarios for which it may be useful to create your own external application, rather than write a unit test or other test type:

❑ **Supporting legacy test applications:** You have already devoted resources to creating your own test tools. These tools now need to be modified to interact with Team Test. Using this code, you can easily modify your existing test environment.

❑ **Developing new external test applications:** You may need a test application completely independent of Visual Studio. This is common when a test needs to be run on large amounts of code or when you want to provide custom testing tools for customers who do not have Visual Studio. For example, you could use this to create a tool to verify that assemblies are all marked with the same version number.

❑ **Logging test run data:** If you just want to report data to the test run results log without actually putting any code under test, you can quickly create a console app that writes to the console. An example would be reporting all the files, dates, and times in the solutions' directory. The console output will be part of the test results.

❑ **Wiring other test systems to Team Test:** If you already have a large test base in another test framework and you want to continue using these coded tests, you can create a simple conversion application to translate the results of the existing test framework into results that Team Test can understand. This is covered in the section "Wiring to Existing Test Systems" later in the chapter.

Scripting Host example

The Windows Scripting Host provides a quick and easy way to create specialized external applications for generic tests. You can use these scripts to set the stage for other generic tests or perform set up for unit tests that are to follow, such as copying files, installing an application, verifying that certain disk resources are available, or much more.

The advantages of using a script as a generic test target are that they are quick to create, are easily modifiable, do not require .NET expertise, and are easy to interoperate with many different objects on a system. They are also useful as a more advanced equivalent to DOS batch files.

Microsoft's Developer's Network has a great scripting reference with information on all the objects used here. See `http://msdn.microsoft.com/library/en-us/script56/html/ vtoriMicrosoftWindowsScriptTechnologies.asp` for more information.

To use this example:

1. Copy the code into a file titled `QuickTest.js` under the `C:\Temp` folder.

2. Create a new generic test.

3. In the "Specify an existing program..." field, use the command-line Windows Script Host application `C:\WINDOWS\system32\cscript.exe`.

4. In the "Command line arguments..." field, provide the path to your script—for example, `/nologo "C:\Temp\QuickTest.js"`.

5.   Close and save the generic test editor document.

6.   Run the test from the Test View window.

7.   Double-click the test in the Test Results window. You will see the standard command-line output at the bottom of the test results.

Here is the code:

```
// Instantiate scripting shell support
var WshShell = WScript.CreateObject("WScript.Shell");

// Intantiate file system support
var fso = WScript.CreateObject("Scripting.FileSystemObject");

// Obtain the collection of environment variables available to this process
var WshSysEnv = WshShell.Environment("PROCESS");

// Retrieve the env var that points to the tests' output directory
var TestOut = WshSysEnv("TestOutputDirectory");

// If the environment variable is not set, quit with an error
if (TestOut == "") WScript.Quit(1);

// Report the date & time the directory was created
WScript.Echo("%TestOutputDirectory% = " + TestOut);
WScript.Echo(fso.GetFolder(TestOut).DateCreated);

// Return Successful, this script is just for reporting data
WScript.Quit(0);
```

Managed Code example

The scenario here is that your company, which has 20 developers working on five different projects, wants to ensure that all of its assemblies are marked with the correct company name. Because projects come and go and all teams must run this verification, it is advantageous to place the code to perform the verification across .NET assemblies in a separate, standalone executable.

The standalone application can then be easily run from the command line, tied to a series of other such command-line applications with scripts, added as part of a build process, or added to a suite of tests with a generic test.

This particular code example uses the following command-line syntax:

```
AssemblyCompanyNameVerifier "Your Company Name" file [file|directory...]
```

For this example, `"Your Company Name"` should match the line `[assembly: AssemblyCompany ("Your Company Name")]`, usually in `AssemblyInfo.cs`, with quotes. `file` is a .NET assembly file to be verified, and `directory` can be a directory containing `.dll` .NET assemblies to be verified.

The possible errors and resulting ErrorLevel exit codes are defined in the `ExitCode` enumeration. An exit code of 0 indicates success.

```
#region Namespace Inclusions
using System;
using System.IO;
using System.Diagnostics;
using System.Reflection;
using System.Collections.Generic;
#endregion

namespace AssemblyCompanyNameVerifier
{
  class Program
  {
    // ErrorLevel codes to be set as the exit code
    public enum ExitCode { Success = 0, WrongArguments = 1, FileNotFound = 2,
                           WrongName = 3, CantLoadAssembly = 4,
                           CompanyNameNotFound = 5 }

    static int Main(string[] args)
    {
      // Verify the minimum number of arguments are passed
      if (args.Length < 2) return ErrorLevel(ExitCode.WrongArguments);

      // Obtain the company name from the command line which will be used to verify
      // assemblies against
      string CompanyName = args[0];

      // Create a list to contain the files to be verified
      List<string> AssemblyFiles = new List<string>();

      // Traverse the remaining command line arguments
      // If they point to a directory, add the *.dll files in the directory
      // If they point to a file, add the individual file
      for (int i = 1; i < args.Length; i++)
        if (Directory.Exists(args[i]))
          foreach (string file in Directory.GetFiles(args[1], "*.dll"))
            AssemblyFiles.Add(file);
        else if (File.Exists(args[i])) AssemblyFiles.Add(args[i]);
        else return ErrorLevel(ExitCode.FileNotFound);

      foreach (string file in AssemblyFiles)
      {
        // Track if the CompanyName attribute is found
        bool FoundName = false;

        // Attempt to load this file as a .NET assembly
        Assembly a = null;
        try { a = Assembly.LoadFile(file); }
        catch (BadImageFormatException)
        { return ErrorLevel(ExitCode.CantLoadAssembly); }

        // Traverse each company name assembly attribute
        // and make sure the name matches
        foreach (AssemblyCompanyAttribute attrib in
                a.GetCustomAttributes(typeof(AssemblyCompanyAttribute), true))
```

```
        {
          if (attrib.Company == CompanyName) FoundName = true;
          else { ValidName = false; return ErrorLevel(ExitCode.WrongName); }
        }

        // If the company attribute was not found, return the appropriate error
        if (!FoundName) ErrorLevel(ExitCode.CompanyNameNotFound);
      }

      // The correct name was found in each assembly
      return ErrorLevel(ExitCode.Success);
    }

    public static int ErrorLevel(ExitCode code)
    {
      // Create a simple little report
      string report = "Result: " + code.ToString();

      // Send the output to the console and debug terminal
      Console.WriteLine(report);
      Trace.WriteLine(report);

      // Return the Exit Code
      return (int)code;
    }
  }
}
```

The primary output from this app, other than the name of the `ExitCode` enumeration value, is the ErrorLevel (or exit code) returned from the `Main` method.

Extended Return Results

A basic external application that is run by a generic test communicates back to the Team System test engine by means of a single exit code indicating a passed or failed result. A more advanced alternative is for your application to create an XML file as part of its output, with detailed results of its run that conforms to the `SummaryResult.xsd` scheme. If you use an XML results file, you can pass back more information regarding the state of the external application's test run.

An XML results file adds the following additional fields:

❑   Return types—values include `Passed`, `Completed`, `PassedButRunAborted`, `Pending`, `InProgress`, `Warning`, `Disconnected`, `NotExecuted`, `NotRunnable`, `Failed`, `Inconclusive`, `Error`, and `Aborted`

❑   Path to an additional log file

❑   Verbose test name

❑   Custom error message

❑   Inner Tests, each with its result

To specify that your generic test will return an XML results file that conforms to the `SummaryResult.xsd` scheme (more about this below), enter the name of the file in the Results Settings section at the bottom of the Generic Tests properties page and check the Summary Results File checkbox. A typical entry here would look like `%TestOutputDirectory%\GenericTestOutput.xml`, where `%TestOutputDirectory%` will be replaced with the appropriate directory used in the running of the external application. Be sure to store your output file using this environment variable's path in your application.

Summary report XML schema

The schema for the results file is shown in the following code. This schema file, part of the standard files installed with Visual Studio Team System, is called `SummaryResult.xsd` and is placed in the `Microsoft Visual Studio 8\Xml\Schemas` directory.

```xml
<?xml version="1.0" encoding="UTF-8"?>
<xs:schema xmlns:xs="http://www.w3.org/2001/XMLSchema"
 xmlns:msdata="urn:schemas-microsoft-com:xml-msdata" elementFormDefault="qualified"
 attributeFormDefault="unqualified">
  <xs:element name="SummaryResult">
    <xs:annotation>
      <xs:documentation>Describes summary result for tests</xs:documentation>
    </xs:annotation>
    <xs:complexType>
      <xs:sequence>
        <xs:element name="TestName" type="xs:string" minOccurs="1" maxOccurs="1" />
        <xs:element name="TestResult" type="testResultType" minOccurs="1"
         maxOccurs="1" />
        <xs:element name="ErrorMessage" type="xs:string" minOccurs="0"
         maxOccurs="1" />
        <xs:element name="DetailedResultsFile" type="xs:string" minOccurs="0"
         maxOccurs="1" />
        <xs:element name="InnerTests" minOccurs="0" maxOccurs="1">
          <xs:complexType>
            <xs:sequence>
              <xs:element name="InnerTest" minOccurs="0" maxOccurs="unbounded">
                <xs:complexType>
                  <xs:sequence>
                    <xs:element name="TestName" type="xs:string" minOccurs="1"
                     maxOccurs="1"/>
                    <xs:element name="TestResult" type="testResultType"
                     minOccurs="1" maxOccurs="1" />
                    <xs:element name="ErrorMessage" type="xs:string" minOccurs="0"
                     maxOccurs="1" />
                    <xs:element name="DetailedResultsFile" type="xs:string"
                     minOccurs="0" maxOccurs="1" />
                  </xs:sequence>
                </xs:complexType>
              </xs:element>
            </xs:sequence>
          </xs:complexType>
        </xs:element>
      </xs:sequence>
    </xs:complexType>
    <xs:key name="InnerTestNameMustBeUnique" msdata:PrimaryKey="true">
```

```
        <xs:selector xpath=".//InnerTest" />
        <xs:field xpath="TestName" />
    </xs:key>
</xs:element>

<xs:simpleType name="testResultType">
    <xs:restriction base="xs:string">
    <xs:enumeration value="Aborted"/>
    <xs:enumeration value="Error"/>
    <xs:enumeration value="Inconclusive"/>
    <xs:enumeration value="Failed"/>
    <xs:enumeration value="NotRunnable"/>
    <xs:enumeration value="NotExecuted"/>
    <xs:enumeration value="Disconnected"/>
    <xs:enumeration value="Warning"/>
    <xs:enumeration value="InProgress"/>
    <xs:enumeration value="Pending"/>
    <xs:enumeration value="PassedButRunAborted"/>
    <xs:enumeration value="Completed"/>
    <xs:enumeration value="Passed"/>
    </xs:restriction>
</xs:simpleType>
</xs:schema>
```

In a single summary result file, there must be a `TestName` and `TestResult` for the master test and for each (optional) `InnerTest` that exists. All other fields/tags are optional. The simple type `testResultType` defines all the possible results of a test, which obviously provides much more granularity than the two states, Passed and Failed, that are used with exit codes.

Example summary report XML file

Here is an example summary report XML file. Notice that the test can be given a friendly verbose name:

```
<SummaryResult>
  <TestName>Manual Summary Results Example</TestName>
  <TestResult>Inconclusive</TestResult>
  <ErrorMessage>This is the error that caused the test to fail.</ErrorMessage>
  <DetailedResultsFile>C:\Temp\TestOutput\TestOverview.html</DetailedResultsFile>
  <InnerTests>
    <InnerTest>
      <TestName>First Inner Test</TestName>
      <TestResult>PassedButRunAborted</TestResult>
      <ErrorMessage>A bogus test message.</ErrorMessage>
      <DetailedResultsFile>C:\Temp\TestOutput\TestPass01.html</DetailedResultsFile>
    </InnerTest>
    <InnerTest>
      <TestName>Second Inner Test</TestName>
      <TestResult>Passed</TestResult>
      <ErrorMessage>A bogus test message.</ErrorMessage>
      <DetailedResultsFile>C:\Temp\TestOutput\TestPass02.html</DetailedResultsFile>
    </InnerTest>
  </InnerTests>
</SummaryResult>
```

This XML file produces the summary results shown in Figure 17-9.

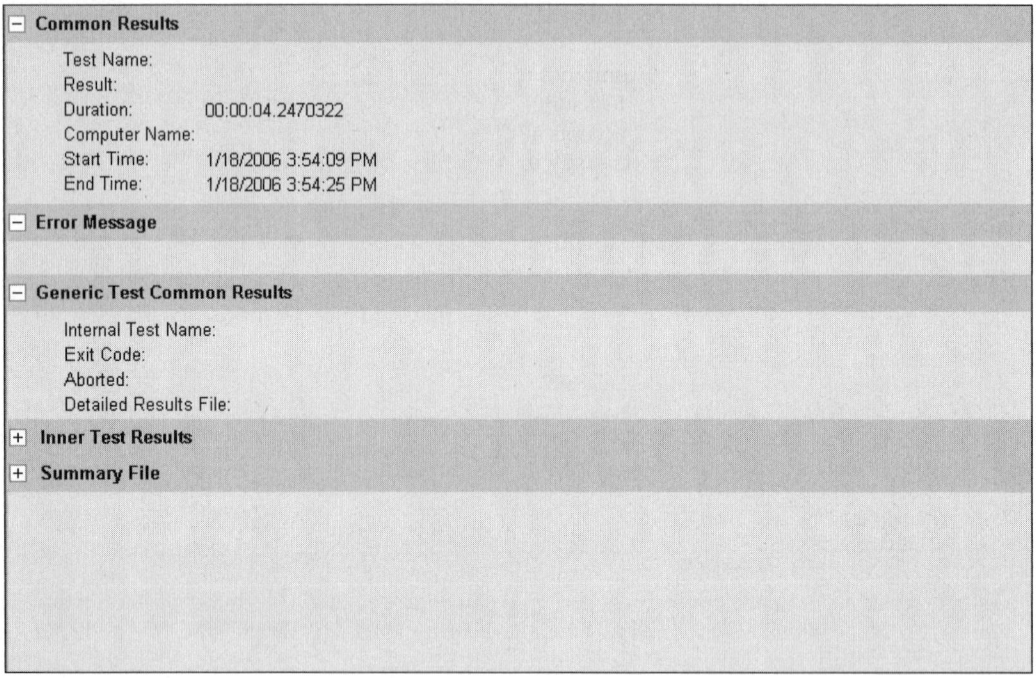

Common Results	
Test Name:	
Result:	
Duration:	00:00:04.2470322
Computer Name:	
Start Time:	1/18/2006 3:54:09 PM
End Time:	1/18/2006 3:54:25 PM

Error Message

Generic Test Common Results	
Internal Test Name:	
Exit Code:	
Aborted:	
Detailed Results File:	

Inner Test Results

Summary File

Figure 17-9

When an inner test is selected with a detailed results file (as defined in the `<DetailedResultsFile>` tag) the contents will be displayed in the embedded Internet Explorer under "Summary File." Because the file is displayed in an IE control, it can be a full HTML file or XML with XSL for rich display results (including images, like screen shots). A common way of producing a summary file is to perform an XSL transform over your results to create a nicely formatted HTML report. An example of this is included in the book's source code.

> **The detailed results file for the entire test (the line containing** `TestOverview.html`**) is shown only as a property of the generic test and is not rendered inside the test result's IE control. So it is recommended that this property is not used and you use the** `DetailedResultsFile` **tag inside the Inner Test instead.**

Wiring to Existing Test Systems

Supporting existing test frameworks by linking a generic test to the other test framework is one of the scenarios mentioned in the section "Creating an External Testing Tool," above. If you already have a test framework in place and you want to use it with Team Test, you need a tool for converting the result output from the existing test framework to a format the generic test engine recognizes.

As time progresses, more conversion tools will be made available online. Until one is available for the test framework you're currently using, you may need to manually create one. Thankfully, most test frameworks can produce XML output that can be transformed into the generic test results schema.

The example provided in this section combines the "Script Host Example" and "Extended Return Results" to wire together an NUnit 2.0 test suite to a generic test. Because NUnit produces an XML results file, and the generic test engine accepts an XML file as results, all you need is an XML transformation from one schema to another. This is easily implemented with some JScript and an XSL file.

This is an example and is not intended to be an all-encompassing transformation solution. You may encounter more complex results that cannot be easily transformed by an XSL. In this case, you'd need an interpreter application that reads one format, interprets the results, and produces the resulting XML file. The tool could also create elaborate reports that could be added to the `<DetailedResultsFile>` tag and shown in the summary report, shown in Figure 17-10.

Creating a wire to NUnit

To see a generic test run an NUnit test suite and then convert the NUnit results to a generic test XML result, just follow the steps outlined in the following sections. Each step reflects material drawn from various earlier parts of the chapter.

Flow of operation

This example is designed to use all the extensible points in the generic test properties document (see Figure 17-10).

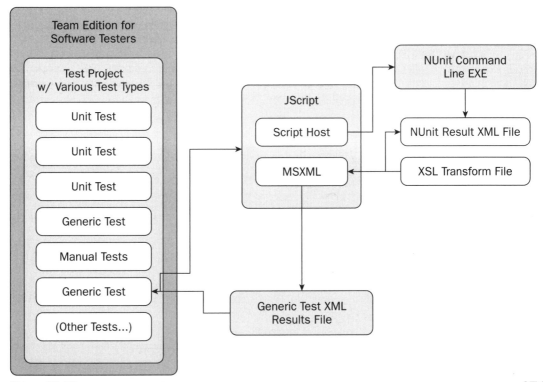

Figure 17-10

Here is what happens in this example:

1. Team Test starts the generic test.

2. Team Test sets up the process's environment by setting the environment variables and copying the deployment files.

3. The generic test starts the Windows Scripting Host, which executes the JScript file.

4. The script runs NUnit with the appropriate command-line options.

5. NUnit performs its tests and outputs an XML file with its test run results.

6. The script uses MSXML to pull in the NUnit XML file and the XSL transform file and perform the transformation.

7. An XML file conforming to the generic test results scheme is written to disk as `Generic Test XML Results.xml`.

8. The script ends.

9. The generic test reads the results from `Generic Test XML Results.xml` file.

10. The generic test type returns the results back to the test framework.

11. The test run is complete.

Setup and run

Here's how you would carry out this workflow:

1. Install NUnit 2.0. NUnit is a free download and will install the necessary C# sample files.

2. Run the included NUnit C# Example, designed to be used with Visual Studio .NET 2003. If you want to use Visual Studio 2005 (.NET 2.0), you need to apply a workaround to replace it with a different runtime version (posted on `http://blogs.msdn.com/jamesnewkirk/archive/2004/07/05/173513.aspx`). Load the solution `C:\Program Files\NUnit 2.2\src\nunit.sln` and follow the directions to reset the references and build at least the C# project (the other projects can be removed from the solution).

3. Copy the following below to a deployment directory. For this example, use `C:\Temp\NUnitExample`.

4. Create a new generic test. Follow the steps under "Creating a generic test" earlier in this chapter.

5. Change the properties as outlined in the following table. *Note:* The actual directory NUnit installs in is different depending on what version of NUnit you have installed.

Field/Property	Value
Specify an existing...	`C:\WINDOWS\system32\cscript.exe`
Command line arguments...	`/nologo RunNUnit.js "C:\Program Files\NUnit 2.2\samples\csharp\bin\Debug\csharp-sample.dll"`
Additional files...	`RunNUnit.js`

Field/Property	Value
Environment Variables	
NUnitExe	`C:\Program Files\NUnit 2.2\bin\nunit-console.exe`
XslTransformFile	`C:\Temp\NUnit to Team Test.xsl`
Working Directory	`%TestOutputDirectory%`
Redirect standard output...	Checked
Display execution application...	Unchecked
Exit test...	30000
Summary Results File (checkbox)	Checked
Summary Results File (field)	`%TestOutputDirectory%\Team Test NUnit Results.xml`

6. Run the NUnit Generic Test. For details, see the section "Running the generic test."

7. View the Results Report (see "Example Summary Report XML File" and Figure 17-10). Notice that in this case, there are several Inner Tests because each NUnit "test-case" is translated to an Inner Test.

JScript conversion code

We used JScript in this example because many test frameworks are tied together via scripts like this one. The script deals mostly with files and XML, for which the Windows Script Host is optimized. It can be quickly and easily modified, and deployment is easy with just the one `.js` file.

This simple DOS batch file will sufficiently set the needed environment variables and test the script on the command line, separate from the generic test framework. It is recommended that you get this combination working first from the Windows command line (`cmd.exe`), and then use the script directly from the generic test (without the batch file).

```
@echo off
set TestOutputDirectory=C:\Temp\TestOutputDir
set NUnitExe=C:\Program Files\NUnit 2.2\bin\nunit-console.exe
set XslTransformFile=C:\Temp\NUnit to Team Test.xsl
cscript.exe /nologo RunNUnit.js "C:\Program Files\NUnit
2.2\samples\csharp\bin\Debug\csharp-sample.dll"
```

The script performs the following major operations:

❑ Checks the environment variables and command-line options

❑ Executes NUnit

❑ Transforms the XML output from NUnit to a Generic Test Results XML file conforming to `SummaryResults.xsd` scheme

❑ Writes the result to an output XML file that the generic test framework will pick up to display a complete set of test results

If an error occurs along the way, the app will exit and set the ErrorLevel code. Because it was specified above that a Summary Results XML file would be used, the exit code is just ignored by the test framework. However, it is good practice to set the exit code. This sample could be considerably reduced if the script just ran NUnit, looked at the top-level suite pass/fail result from the resulting XML file, and set the exit code without transforming the XML output for extended result information. This is a good task to try out to become more familiar with the workings of the generic test type.

```javascript
// Runs an NUnit test suite and converts to Team Test

Main();

function Main()
{
  // Obtain access to the Windows Shell
  var WshShell = WScript.CreateObject("WScript.Shell");

  // Collect the environment variables available to this process
  var WshSysEnv = WshShell.Environment("PROCESS");

  // Retrieve the needed parameters from environment variables
  var TestOutDir = WshSysEnv("TestOutputDirectory");
  var NUnitExe = WshSysEnv("NUnitExe");
  var XslFile = WshSysEnv("XslTransformFile");

  // Verify the environment variables are available
  if (TestOutDir == "")
  {WScript.Echo("Error: Could not find %TestOutputDirectory"); WScript.Quit(3);}

  if (NUnitExe == "")
  {WScript.Echo("Error: Could not find %NUnitExe"); WScript.Quit(3);}

  if (XslFile == "")
  {WScript.Echo("Error: Could not find %XslTransformFile"); WScript.Quit(3);}

  // Build the file paths
  var NUnitOut = TestOutDir + "\\NUnit Test Results.xml";
  var TeamTestOut = TestOutDir + "\\Team Test NUnit Results.xml";

  // Make sure the command line arguments are specified
  if (WScript.Arguments.length == 0)
  {WScript.Echo("Syntax: RunNUnit.js TargetDll [TargetDll..]"); WScript.Quit(1);}

  // Build the list of .NET assemblies to be tested
  var args = "";
  for (var i = 0; i < WScript.Arguments.length; i++)
    args += " \"" + WScript.Arguments.item(i) + "\"";

  // Execute NUnit
```

```
   var cmdline = NUnitExe + args + " /xml=\"" + NUnitOut + "\"";
   WScript.Echo("Executing NUnit Test Suite");
   WScript.Echo(cmdline);
   var exe = WshShell.Exec(cmdline);

   // Wait for NUnit to finish
   while (exe.Status == 0) WScript.Sleep(100);

   // If there was an error, abort
   if (exe.ExitCode != 0)
   {WScript.Echo("Error: NUnit execution error: " + exe.ExitCode); WScript.Quit(5);}

   // Perform the XML transformation
   WScript.Echo("Transforming NUnit results to Team Test results.");
   var TransformedResults = PerformTransform(NUnitOut, XslFile);
   if (TransformedResults == "") WScript.Quit(2);

   // Save the transformation output
   WScript.Echo("Writing Team Test XML output.");
   WriteTextFile(TeamTestOut, TransformedResults);
}

// Applies an XSL transform to an XML document
function PerformTransform(xmlfile, xslfile)
{
  // Create the XML data source
  var xml = new ActiveXObject("Msxml2.DOMDocument.3.0");

  // Load the XML source data
  xml.async = false;
  xml.resolveExternals = false;
  xml.load(xmlfile);

  // Verify the XML source data is valid
  if (ParseOkay(xml))
  {
    // Create the XSL utility objects
    var xslt = new ActiveXObject("Msxml2.XSLTemplate.4.0");
    var xslDoc = new ActiveXObject("Msxml2.FreeThreadedDOMDocument.4.0");
    var xslProc;

    // Load the XSL source data
    xslDoc.async = false;
    xslDoc.resolveExternals = false;
    xslDoc.load(xslfile);

    // Verify the XSL source data is valid
    if (ParseOkay(xslDoc))
    {
      // Perform the XSL transformation
      xslt.stylesheet = xslDoc;
      xslProc = xslt.createProcessor();
      xslProc.input = xml;
      xslProc.transform();
```

```
        // Plase the XSL transform output
        return xslProc.output;
      }
    }

    return "";
}

// Write text to a file
function WriteTextFile(filename, contents)
{
    var fso = new ActiveXObject("Scripting.FileSystemObject")
    var f = fso.OpenTextFile(filename, 2, true)
    f.Write(contents);
    f.Close();
}

// Verify that the XML is valid, if not show a message
function ParseOkay(xmldoc)
{
  if (xmldoc.parseError.errorCode != 0)
  {
    var err = xmldoc.parseError;
    WScript.Echo("Parsing Error:\n" + err.url + "\n" + err.reason + "On line " +
      err.line + " at " + err.linepos + "\n" + err.srcText);
    return false;
  }
  else return true;
}
```

See the earlier section "Scripting host example" for a good MSDN Library URL with reference information on all the scripting objects used in the code.

The heart of the operation is the XSL transformation. This is a basic transformation designed for the test suite sample code that ships with NUnit 2.0. Note that NUnit reports a test's "success" as true or false (see the "TestResult" template element), which is easily translated into a Passed or Failed result:

```
<?xml version="1.0" encoding="utf-8" standalone="no"?>
<xsl:stylesheet version="1.0" xmlns:xsl="http://www.w3.org/1999/XSL/Transform">
  <xsl:template match="/test-results">
    <SummaryResult>
      <TestName>NUnit test on: <xsl:value-of select="@name"/></TestName>
      <xsl:for-each select="test-suite[1]">
        <TestResult><xsl:call-template name="TestResult" /></TestResult>
      </xsl:for-each>
      <ErrorMessage></ErrorMessage>
      <DetailedResultsFile></DetailedResultsFile>
      <InnerTests>
        <xsl:for-each select=".//test-case">
          <InnerTest>
            <TestName><xsl:value-of select="@name"/></TestName>
            <TestResult>
```

```
            <xsl:if test="@executed='True'">
              <xsl:call-template name="TestResult" /></xsl:if>
            <xsl:if test="@executed='False'">NotExecuted</xsl:if>
          </TestResult>
          <ErrorMessage>Message: <xsl:value-of select="failure/message"/>
  Stack Trace: <xsl:value-of select="failure/message"/>
          </ErrorMessage>
        </InnerTest>
      </xsl:for-each>
    </InnerTests>
  </SummaryResult>
</xsl:template>

<xsl:template name="TestResult">
  <xsl:if test="@success='True'">Passed</xsl:if>
  <xsl:if test="@success='False'">Failed</xsl:if>
</xsl:template>
</xsl:stylesheet>
```

Combine all these elements and you have a conversion utility that will run an existing test framework and incorporate the results into Team Test. With simple modifications, most existing test frameworks can be run using this same technique.

Summary

Generic tests reach outside of the test framework provided by Team System, by running external applications and incorporating their results. They can be used to leverage existing testing frameworks and even your own independent test tools.

Using scripts, batch files, XML, XSL, and custom-written .NET console applications, one can vastly extend the capabilities of the test framework. Using a generic test is the quickest and easiest way to achieve test framework extensibility. This can be a big time saver and is quick and easy to implement.

An external application can return two types of results. One is an exit code, otherwise known as an ErrorLevel, for which 0 indicates a passed test and any other value is a failed test. The other option is for an external application to return an XML file that conforms to the generic test results schema and provides more test result types and reports on inner (sub) tests.

Part IV
Team Foundation

18

Team Foundation Architecture

Software teams store and manage many kinds of project data in various places. This data ranges from workflow documentation, functional and nonfunctional requirements, project specifications, guidance documentation, checklists, and policies, to the generation of day-to-day project artifacts that often include source code changes, test data, work assignments, reports, and, of course, defects.

Consolidating this information in a single accessible location in preparation for a software project can be a challenge. Managing project artifacts during the life cycle of the project and maintaining meaningful relationships between them can be painful and time consuming. Ensuring that all team members are communicating and collaborating effectively on the project data, within a growing distributed and stove-piped role environment, is increasingly difficult. Moreover, easily extracting accurate and timely project information to assess progress and mitigate risks is likely near impossible.

Nonetheless, the consequence of failing to adequately manage software data and team members is significant. According to the Standish Group's tenth edition of their annual CHAOS report, project success rates are only 34 percent of 40,000 projects tracked. An impressive 51 percent of all projects in the survey are "challenged" — that is, they are over budget, over time, and/or lacking critical requirements or features. Fifteen percent of projects fail outright.

What if these problems could be solved? Enter Microsoft Team Foundation, which enables you to consolidate all your data, configure and track your relationships under version control, quickly and accurately report the status and health of the project at any time, and provide all members of the team with near friction-free collaboration because they have visibility into the right data at the right time.

In this chapter, we'll give you a quick look at some of its tools and introduce you to the Team Foundation architecture, including the Reporting Warehouse.

What Is Team Foundation Server?

Visual Studio Team Foundation is the server part of Visual Studio 2005 Team System (VSTS), and is built on the .NET platform. It is an extensible team collaboration server for managing project assets, progress, and health across the extended IT team. It drives an organization's policies, practices, and processes. It controls access to source files, enables users to create and manage work items, facilitates reporting, automates the process of building applications, and manages releases. It was designed from the beginning with open protocols and an extensible Web services architecture exposed through .NET client APIs. Team Foundation is tightly integrated into the Visual Studio 2005 IDE and supports numerous customizations from third parties and customers.

Team processes

Every project begins with a process. Simply put, a process is the system that your organization uses to get the project done. Team Foundation enables projects to begin and move forward effectively by helping you manage the process for your team. No single process can work efficiently for all projects in your organization. You often need to be able to create new processes or customize existing ones and ensure that the resulting processes remain tightly integrated into your life cycle tools and guidance. Visual Studio 2005 Team System provides that customizable process guidance and integration using Microsoft Solutions Framework.

Microsoft Solutions Framework (MSF)

The Microsoft Solutions Framework (MSF) provides guidance regarding people and processes that enable you to successfully deliver technology solutions to your customers. MSF is a disciplined approach to technology projects based on proven practices related to how Microsoft delivers projects in-house.

Microsoft Solutions Framework (MSF) version 4.0 is the next evolution of the Microsoft Solutions Framework. MSF 4.0 exposes a meta-model (or framework) on which processes are built. Visual Studio Team System integrates this meta-model with a template mechanism to produce *process templates*. Each template defines a set of instructions for setting up a new project. This includes the project's initial tasks, project roles and permissions, document templates, and reports. Each process template can be used as is or customized to fit the needs of one or more projects. After a project has begun, you can further customize many of the process template settings.

Because every organization works differently, Visual Studio 2005 Team System defines two process templates. One is called *MSF for Agile Software Development*. It provides an adaptive, lightweight template for projects with short life cycles and results-oriented teams. The other process template lends itself to a more formal approach and is called *MSF for CMMI Process Improvement*. It targets projects with longer life cycles requiring a more thorough record of decisions made. Both templates follow an Incremental and Iterative Development (IID) approach to software development, called the *Agile* approach.

Both MSF 4.0 templates are available out-of-the-box through Team Foundation Server. As such, they are fully integrated into the Visual Studio 2005 Team System IDE or Team Explorer and provide customizable scenario-driven, context-based software development processes for enabling customers to build new or improve .NET or other platform and architectural-type applications.

Templates are not limited to the MSF approach. Visual Studio Team System process templates can be created to guide the development of projects based on the Rational Unified Process (RUP), Agile Unified Process (AUP), Extreme Programmer (XP), and MSF Waterfall. If you want more detailed information about MSF and process templates, we highly recommend you read Chapters 21 and 22.

Project management guidance

In addition to enabling the right level of process for any given project, Team System also provides guidance that helps you move forward at each step along the way. No longer do you need to hunt around for the right documentation to help solve a problem at hand. Team System not only provides the right guidance at the right time, it exposes the right tools to propel you forward, provides guidance that is well integrated into Visual Studio Team System, is highly customizable, and enjoys updates delivered via MSDN.

An example of integrated project management guidance is the Team System-enabled Microsoft Project. MSF guidance is provided for a number of Microsoft Project–related tasks associated with your project, including defining the project and its work items, organizing the work item tasks into phases, adding documents to the project, and so much more.

After planning your tasks in MS Project, you can review resource guidance on how to build your project's team and assign tasks. Once the project is defined and resources are assigned, Team System provides further guidance on managing the project once it has begun. This includes checking the progress of the project and publishing project information to the web.

Reporting is another area of guidance, including how to report the status of your project and publish these reports to the web.

Armed with an overview of the process templates and guidelines, we can now turn to an overview of the tools of Team Foundation Server that are central to making team processes a reality.

Team Foundation features

Team Foundation provides a number of new tools (some of which were previously only internal to Microsoft) to facilitate team collaboration, communication, and productivity. At a high level, Team Foundation consists of the following:

- ❑ **Version Control:** A new enterprise-class three-tier version control system with powerful merging and branching capabilities. It is designed to effectively manage not only source code, but project files, documents, reports, and templates.

- ❑ **Work Item Tracking (WIT):** A customized version of an internal defect-tracking tool used by the majority of internal Microsoft product groups. It has been expanded beyond defects to support tracking many units of work that need to be performed throughout a project.

- ❑ **Team Portal:** Built on Windows Sharepoint Services 2.0, this is used to facilitate team communication. From this site, it is possible to run reports, review work items and docs, and perform daily builds.

- ❑ **Team Foundation Build:** Out-of-the-box support for daily build management.

- ❑ **Team Reporting:** Provides a systemwide data view of one or more projects residing on TFS. Built on SQL Server Reporting Services.

- ❑ **Project Management:** Integration with Microsoft Office Project 2003 and Microsoft using Visual Studio Tools for Office (VSTO) technology.

- ❑ **Integration Services:** A set of Web service and object models that allow outside tools to integrate into the Team System environment as first-class citizens. The provide customization and extensibility support for each tool offered in Team System.

❑   **Team Explorer:** A thin shell of Visual Studio that supports many of the features of Team Foundation Server. It does not contain any of the development or test tools normally associated with Visual Studio (e.g., languages, compilers, debuggers).

Version control

Team Foundation version control is an industrial-strength change management tool for managing assets and work items. It includes all the facilities for changesets, rich branching, merging, and "diffing" that you'd expect from an enterprise-scale source code control system, as well as innovations around parallel development, atomic check-ins, and remote development. Team Foundation version control is tightly integrated into the development environment, so the developer never needs to leave the VS IDE.

Team Foundation version control is not simply a standalone system for managing source code. It's tightly integrated with Team Foundation's policies, e-mail notification, build automation, data ware-house, and work item tracking system. For detailed information about Team Foundation version control, please refer to Chapter 20.

Integrated check-in

At the heart of Team Foundation version control is the *changeset*. A changeset is a logical container used by Team Foundation Server to store everything related to a single check-in. This container may include files (source code and nonsource code), meta-data associated with the file(s) such as data and time of check-in and the owner's name, and any check-in notes or comments. A changeset may also include links to other artifacts (documents, work items, and so on).

When a set of pending changes are checked in, Team Foundation creates a new changeset in the source repository and assigns it a number that is unique on a given server and always increases by one from one change to the next. In this way, a changeset represents the state or version of the repository at a given point in the past. It's often important to be able to go back and identify these past states, such as identifying a past build. Identification is done by assigning a label to the state of the repository after a build is produced. Using this label, others (e.g., a partner team) can identify, pick up, and use the pub-lished build.

By the way, check-in in Team Foundation is atomic. That is, the operation is all or nothing, so either all the files are checked in or none of them are. Atomic check-in resolves the problem of corrupted reposito-ries. If a network is lost halfway through a 100-file check-in, then all files will be uncommitted and restored to their original state on the workspace and server repository (more about this later). At the time of this writing, being able to back out of a changeset is not yet possible.

This changeset functionality enables revisions to one or more related files, comments, work items, policy, and e-mail to work as a single process. Integrated check-in enables a work item to be associated with a pending check-in by simply adding a link between the two using the UI.When the changeset is checked in, the user has the option of specifying a "check-in action." The default action is to set the state of the bug to Resolved.

When the bug is resolved, revisions of these files are checked in and a new changeset artifact is created with a unique identifier in the source control repository to contain the data and related metadata. Upon check-in, this work item is updated to refer back to the new changeset, maintaining the linkage between the work item and changeset. This links the corrected code to the bug for anyone to see. This type of linkage is not the only scenario, however. Code can be linked to work item types to map other forms of interaction.

Workspaces

A workspace is your client-side copy of the folders and files on the Team Foundation version control server. Any changes (e.g., delete, modify, move, rename) to these folders and files are reflected in your workspace and marked as pending changes. You can edit, build, and test your code without worrying how your activities might affect your teammates or checked-in source code. Once these pending changes are checked in, they will be atomically committed and persisted to the server version control repository. Any subsequent changes to your workspace will not be reflected in the server until the next successful check-in.

Branching and merging

Team Foundation version control enables a team with an existing code base to branch all or part of that code base to facilitate parallel development. After changes to the various branches become stable, they can be integrated back into the original code line. A number of different scenarios are applicable to branching and merging. One is *release branching*, whereby, for example, branching and merging enables a maintenance team to work on a code line for fixing bugs and releasing patches separately from the released product's source code.

Branching in Team Foundation version control is similar to Visual SourceSafe. Both handle branching analogously to a file system copy operation. When a file is branched, it is as if a new file were created with a unique identity. In fact, the Foundation Source Code branching UI in Visual Studio looks very similar to a file copy operation within Windows Explorer. However, there is a notable difference. Unlike file system copies, branching maintains relationships between the files of the original and the new branch. This enables all changes to be easily tracked and "merged" between the two.

Team Foundation version control manages branches holistically. Any type of change within the branch (files added, renamed, deleted, or edited) will be handled when the changes are merged. As discussed earlier, Team Foundation version control uses *changesets* to manage changes to a set of files that are checked in at the same time. These changesets make it possible for the system to automatically identify the set of files that need to be merged for a given change.

Branching in Team Foundation version control is a pending operation. A branch is not actually created until the files are committed to the repository. This affords the user the opportunity to synchronize the new branch to a local workspace. It also enables you to modify, rename, and delete files and folders before the branch is committed to the repository.

Merging gives users an extremely flexible and powerful tool for managing the contents of branches. Merges can be made into a single file or into a tree of related files. Merges can also migrate the entire change history of the specified source files, or an individual changeset or revision that may contain a specific fix or feature that should be migrated without moving other changes from the source in the process.

History

Source control maintains a history of everything that has been merged. This enables you to easily see whether a change exists in a given branch. You can also easily see a generated list of changes in one branch (changesets) that have not been merged and are candidates for a future merge operation. You can "cherry-pick" specific changes, such as a bug fix, and merge it without also pulling over other changes that were made to the same files in earlier revisions. Using changesets provides an atomic (transactional) package, which makes change management a great deal easier.

Shelving

What should a developer do when a manager tells her to drop everything and immediately fix a high-priority bug? She probably can't store her unfinished work on her workstation, as that is likely against company policy. Nor can she check in her changes to the server, as it will likely break the build. With Team Foundation version control the developer can now *shelve* it.

Team Foundation version control provides an archiving command called `shelve` that enables a source control user to store pending changesets on the server without committing it to the Source store. These changesets are called *shelvesets* when used in the context of shelving. Users can use shelving to simply back up the current changes to make it easy to get back to a known state or to move their changes out of their workspaces. Because the changes are saved on the server, they are transferable to other users. This enables sharing changes as well, thereby enabling changes to be reviewed and tested on another machine by other users prior to committing them. The following code is a command-line example of shelving:

```
> tf shelve HelloWorldBuddyReview;Erik c:\myprojects\*.cs /recursive
```

This example creates a new shelveset on Team Foundation Server called `HelloWorldBuddyReview`. It assigns ownership to the user named `Erik` and returns all C# source files under the `c:\myprojects` workspace folder (and subfolders) that are pending.

Proxy support

Team Foundation provides version control proxy support for developers working from remote offices on inadequate network bandwidths and suffering from slow file downloads from the Team Foundation Server. The proxy works by locally caching copies of source control files. This significantly improves the time it takes to download files to a user's workspace, which is a bandwidth-intensive operation, as it uses the LAN instead of the WAN. Proxy support will not change how file uploads and meta-data are exchanged with the Team Foundation Server. Remote office users will still need to communicate across the WAN for check-ins and meta-data exchanges, but this represents a fraction of the data transferred in working with source control. This proxy-supported solution is much less expensive to administer and maintain than source control products offering multi-master solutions.

The most noticeable proxy performance is obtained when the middle tier has a limited bandwidth connection to the client, and both proxy and client are located on a network not challenged by these bandwidth limitations.

Team Foundation version control proxies can make a significant difference in performance over non-proxied cases. Over a single-digit Mb connection, proxies can provide considerable improvement, up to 20 to 30 times faster.

Check-in policies

Visual Studio Team Foundation enables team project administrators to enforce compliance with organizational rules during the check-in process. This is accomplished through a check-in policy. A *policy* is a guideline that governs what conditions must be satisfied before a Software Configuration Management (SCM) operation is performed. A check-in policy is a team-specific source control integration guideline. They are only set at the team-project level. It is used to validate that a developer's changes comply with organizational requirements before a set of pending changes are checked into the repository. When a developer attempts to check in pending changes that are in breach of team policy, a policy warning is raised. Because a policy is considered a reminder, and not a directive, the developer can elect to ignore policy warnings. However, they will be prompted to explain why they have elected to override the check-in policy.

The following check-in policies ship with Team Foundation:

❏   Validating that work items are associated with changes

❏   Unit tests pass successfully

❏   Static analysis has run cleanly on source code

You can write custom check-in policies fairly easily using some of the same interfaces exposed for the check-in policies that ship in the box. You can install a custom source control check-in policy by adding a new string value with the policy's name and the path to the DLL implementing these interfaces at the registry:

```
HKEY_LOCAL_MACHINE\SOFTWARE\Microsoft\VisualStudio\8.0\TeamFoundation\SourceControl
\CheckinPolicies
```

There you will see the policies that are installed at setup. Details on how to create custom check-in policies are provided in the Team Foundation Extensibility Kit.

It is interesting to note there is no check-out policy. To keep track of status, the developer would need to regularly update the status of the "in-progress" work items. Microsoft Project work item integration could be used if the work items have been scheduled in Project.

Migrating from VSS to Team Foundation version control

Team System provides a tool for migrating source code from Visual SourceSafe to Team Foundation using the VSS converter tool (VSSConverter.exe). This tool enables teams to move from a source control tool targeted at professional software developers working in groups of less than five to a change management system that provides integrated version control, process management, and issue tracking for development teams of five to upwards of two thousand users working on a single instance of Team Foundation Server. You'll learn the precise steps of how to migrate your source code in the Team Foundation Version Control chapter. Over time, Team Foundation and/or third parties will provide migration tools from other version control tools.

Work item tracking

Team Foundation's work item tracking capabilities enable a new level of software development life cycle tool integration. It provides the glue that binds the software development team's processes together and enables the team to accomplish the tasks necessary to successfully move a project from envisioning to deployment. Work item tracking (WIT), like source code control, plays a vital part role in successful software teams.

At the center of work item tracking is (of course) work items. A work item can be a bug, a task, a requirement, a risk, a schedule, a Design Change Request (DCR), or essentially any project artifact type any member of the team needs to track. Each work item maintains meta-data such as its owner, area, or the iteration of the project to which it is assigned. Work items may also be linked with other project artifacts. Each work item defines the states it can transition through. For a bug, these states may include (but are not limited to) opening, verifying, triaging, reassigning, and closing a bug. Because every project has its own needs and requirements, these work items can be customized, or new work item types can be created for the project using the Team Foundation Extensibility Kit.

Integration is a driving force behind Team System. This is integration with other tools as well as deep integration among the Team System tools and components. It is the work item tracking system that ties into all aspects of the software development life cycle. Therefore, it is critical that work item tracking be tightly integrated with other enterprise tooling efforts. WIT provides the infrastructure, APIs, and object model that enable testing integrations and project management integrations.

Many tool integrations are brittle or provide a poor user experience because they have no common services for actions such as authorization, linking, eventing, and reporting. WIT uses Team Foundation integration services and a common reporting infrastructure (Warehouse) to avoid these tool integration problems, delivering one of the most integrated software development life cycle tooling solutions on the market. Work item internals and customization are covered in more detail in Chapter 19.

Team Project Portal

The single place to go for high-level project information is the Team System Project site. The Project Portal, built on Windows Sharepoint Services (WSS 2.0), provides lightweight access to all members of the team who may not wish to gain project visibility through Visual Studio. Using the portal, team members can view reports, review specs, and see announcements, among many other things.

The project portal can also be viewed within Visual Studio 2005 Team System via the Documents Node in the Team Explorer. Chapter 19 has more information about navigating and administrating the Team Portal.

Team Foundation Build

Another tightly integrated feature of Team Foundation is Team Foundation Build. Team Foundation Build provides a simple, reliable, and repeatable build process that does not require the help of a dedicated build engineer. It is used by build engineers, developer leads, or testers who are responsible for the public build. A wizard enables users to easily create initial build scripts (MSBuild) that can be activated with a single click.

There is no need to know MSBuild, nor is it necessary to edit MSBuild XML scripts to initiate a simple build. Team Foundation Build is integrated with a number of Team Foundation components to enable an end-to-end build workflow. It not only includes traditional compilation, but also automates the build steps, beginning with initiating a build from a server, synchronizing sources, documenting the build environment, building the application, analyzing generated binaries, executing tests, generating exceptions, calculating code coverage and churn, updating relevant work items, collecting and creating release notes, to finally producing and publishing a centralized build report. For more information about Team Foundation Build, please refer to Chapter 23.

Team Foundation Reporting

Team Foundation Reporting uses SQL Server 2005 Reporting Services to provide the team with a system-wide and historical data view of project metrics stored in the Team Foundation Data Warehouse (discussed later in this chapter). These reports include "stoplight" (red, yellow, green) health reports that clearly show work progress, test effectiveness (code coverage), and requirements stability, and informational health reports that show bug rates, team productivity, test effectiveness over build, work progress over time, requirements stability over time, and code completion. These reports can be viewed from the Team Project Portal Site, either directly from your browser or from Team Explorer.

If a report is not available, you can generate a custom report using Microsoft Excel, Visual Studio, or SQL Reporting Services. Team Foundation Data Warehouse provides the SQL 2005/AS Cube structure to build these. Examples of custom reports may provide support for the following:

❑   The history of a particular test (result)

❑   The difference between the results of two load tests

❑   Status, in terms of testing of a scenario or requirement

If you wish to explore further, please investigate the Business Intelligence Development Tool in SQL 2005. It enables you to diagram facts and dimensions, the things you expect to see in cubes, for your report.

Reporting in version one of Team System provides some benefits for those facing some form of regulatory compliance, such as Sorbanes Oxley (SOX). For many in IT, SOX compliance centers on change management, user access, and segregation of duties. Being able to track who checked what source code in for what set of work items is one example of how Team System will play a larger role in governance. Perhaps future versions of Team System will address this aspect more fully, especially in the area of deployment. Please refer to Chapter 19 for more information about Team Reporting.

Team Foundation core services

Visual Studio Team System was designed with extensibility in mind. In fact, the features we've described so far are all built on an extensibility model that enables integration between Team System components and in-house or third-party-provided process frameworks, components, and services. In addition to the Team Foundation integration services, each of the tools in Visual Studio 2005 Team System may be extended through its own services or public APIs. The API allows you to control Eventing, Linking, Registration, Group Security, and the Common Structure Service.

Team Edition Test Load Agent

Although load tests are integrated into Visual Studio Team Edition for Software Testers, Microsoft enables you to go beyond this capacity using the Team Edition Test Load Agent. The Team Edition Test Load Agent is composed of a test controller and one or more agents. An agent is used to run tests and generate simulated load, and the controller collects the test results. Together, they enable you to set up a group of computers that generate simulated load for testing. The test controller and agent can be installed together on one computer or separately on two computers. One test controller can coordinate the test runs executing on agents installed on any number of computers.

Note that the Test Load Controller and Agent must be purchased separately from Team Foundation Server. If you try load testing on your local machine, you'll find that you'll encounter a practical limit of about 100 users. The Load Test Controller and Agent will allow you to greatly exceed that number.

Team Foundation Architecture

Team Foundation is based on a modern, service-oriented, three-tier architecture comprised of a client, an application tier, and a data tier. The application tier is facilitated by an ASP.NET 2.0 web server hosted in an IIS6 environment. The data tier is supported by SQL 2005. The architecture of Team Foundation is optimized around the following basic assumptions:

Chapter 18

❑ A high bandwidth connection exists between the application and data tier.

❑ The application tier and data tier servers can co-exist on the same side of a switch, which limits the impact their traffic has on the overall network.

❑ Clients may talk to the application tier beyond the switch in possibly remote locations.

❑ A combination of low bandwidth and high bandwidth connections exists between the clients and the application tier.

The following sections briefly look at the clients of the Team Foundation and explore the Team Foundation architecture. Following this, we'll illustrate the tight integration between the components of Team Foundation by walking through the process flow of Team Foundation Build. The data tier will be explored in part by taking a look at the Reporting Warehouse architecture.

Although there are many interesting architecture areas in Team Foundation that can be explored (such as security), this section only addresses a few.

Clients of Team Foundation

Several clients ship with or are supported by Visual Studio 2005 Team System (shown in Figure 18-1).

The principal clients are the "role-based" clients of Team Suite that ship with Visual Studio 2005 Team System. These clients are Windows applications that run on Visual Studio–supported platforms. Additional Microsoft client applications have been integrated into Team Foundation Server, including Microsoft Project and Microsoft Excel. Although these clients are integrated into the Team Foundation server using managed add-ins, they can operate independently. One client that is dependent on Team Foundation is the Team Explorer. Team Explorer is a "bare-bones" Visual Studio–based client application for project management and analysis. As pointed out earlier, it provides user and administrative access to work item tracking, reporting, source code control, team project, and build management capabilities of Team Foundation. Team Explorer does not contain the language features and compilers of Visual Studio, or many of the modeling, development, and testing features of Visual Studio Team Suite. It is not considered one of the role-based clients. Internet Explorer can be used as a client to directly connect to the web-based Team Portal and the Team Reports.

Clients communicate with Team Foundation through a set of publicly available .NET-managed APIs exposed by the various object models of Team Foundation. This Team Foundation client-side architecture also enables third-party clients to easily integrate into Team Foundation.

Team Explorer

Team Explorer is a product with many hats. It's the name of a window in Visual Studio 2005 Team System, an add-in supporting Team Foundation Server functionality, and the name of a standalone client. When Team Explorer is installed in one or more of the role-based clients (e.g., Team Foundation Developers Edition), Team Explorer functionality is surfaced through a number of explorer windows in Visual Studio (e.g., Team Explorer, Source Control Explorer). For those nondevelopers interested in accessing Team Foundation features, a standalone install of Team Explorer is available. This is a thin-shelled Visual Studio-based client application for software project management and analysis and contains many of the same Team Foundation explorers exposed in Visual Studio logical architecture

The Team Explorer window will be discussed in other sections of this book. The remainder of this section covers the client.

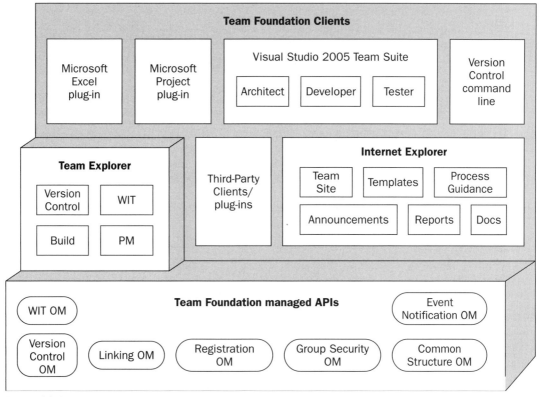

Figure 18-1

The Team Explorer client is targeted at those project leaders and analysts who want access to some or all the Team Foundation Server features but who:

❑ Do not want to install Visual Studio 2005 Team System role-based clients, either due to cost or the install's heavy footprint.

❑ Are developing using Visual Studio 2005 Professional or Standard Editions.

❑ Wish to project-manage non-.NET software projects. Thus teams that may wish to do all their development on, for example, Java but wish to leverage the Project Management office tools, Work Item Tracking, Source Control, SharePoint, and even Team Foundation Build functionalities of Team Foundation Server, can still do so through the Team Explorer client.

❑ Are developing using earlier versions of Visual Studio that do not have a Team Foundation version control Add-in.

Team Explorer provides the user and administration features of Team Foundation Server. Many of these are described as follows:

❑ Reference an existing or create a new Team Project

❑ Import and export process templates

❑ Create, edit, and run queries

- ❏ Connect to Report Server, create and view reports
- ❏ Create and kick-off Team Foundation Build configurations, view Team Foundation Build summaries
- ❏ Add/remove/modify Team Project groups and permissions
- ❏ View and edit Team Project classifications and iterations
- ❏ Launch the Source Control Explorer, edit Team Project SCC settings, view Pending check-ins
- ❏ Add, view, and edit Work Items

*At the time of writing, a Microsoft Source Code Control Interface (MSSCCI) client is available for Visual Studio 6.0. (You can learn more about it on Brian Harry's weblog—*http://blogs.msdn*.com/bharry/.) Microsoft also announced the availability of a MSSCCI client for Visual Studio 2002 and Visual Studio 2003 around the time of Team Foundation Server's release. There are other similar interfaces for other development platforms including Teamprise for Eclipse, which will enable a Java developer to directly interface with Team Foundation Server.*

Team Foundation Server services are exposed as ASP.NET 2.0 Web Services by an Integration Services layer. These Web services are optimized for high-latency networks for access by remote development teams. Each Team Foundation client accesses each Web service through a proxy with an easy-to-use Team Foundation public API, as shown in Figure 18-2.

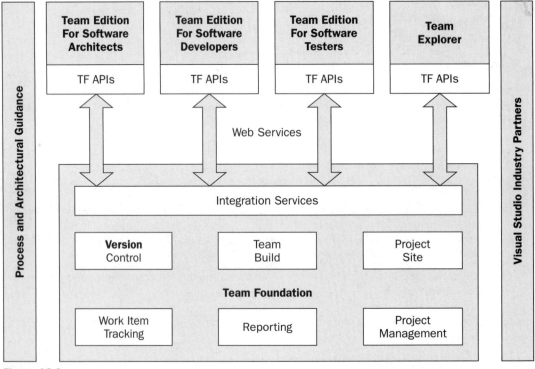

Figure 18-2

Integration between Team System and third-party components and services can be categorized in terms of user interface integration, process extensibility, and data integration:

❑ User interface integration is facilitated through the Visual Studio Industry Partner (VSIP) program. VSIP enables third parties to plug services and products into the Visual Studio Integrated Development Environment (IDE).

❑ Process extensibility is provided through the use of methodology templates. These templates define the process that individual projects will follow. Customers and partners will be able to create new process templates or customize out-of-the-box process templates for their own projects. Process extensibility can include customization of work item types, custom reports, check-in policies, and project management templates. Project Creation Wizard (PCW) plug-ins allow the process to be customized further.

❑ Data integration is handled between the Team Foundation Application tier and its clients using a collection of Team Foundation object model (OM) public interfaces. Each Team Foundation component has a complementary pair of OMs. For example, a WIT client-side OM communicates to an application tier WIT OM using ASP.NET 2.0 Web services. Within the Application tier, a common set of integration services, called the Team Foundation Core Services, ties these components together. The Application tier then communicates the data to the Team Foundation Data tier using MSSQL. Finally, the data is read or written to the appropriate SQL 2005-based data store. The overall Team Foundation Server architecture is illustrated in Figure 18-3.

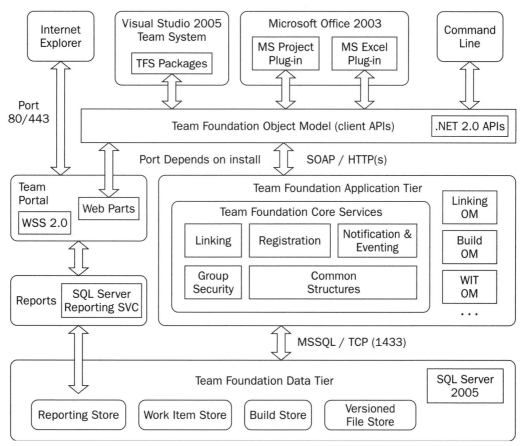

Figure 18-3

All Team Foundation Data Tier data is managed by SQL Server 2005. This means you can use SQL methods to handle backup and recovery and SQL clustering/mirroring for data tier failover. (Note that for data migration between VSTS product versions, VSTS supplied scripts will be necessary.)

A few of the Team Foundation Core Services are particularly notable:

❑ **Notification & Eventing Service:** A publish/subscribe synchronous or asynchronous system for event notification. Users and other tools and services can subscribe to those events it may raise.

❑ **Linking Service:** Enables loosely coupled linking between tools' data using URI-based links

Team Foundation Build

To illustrate the high level of integration between components of Team Foundation Server and Team System role packages, we'll provide a short introduction to the Team Foundation Build architecture and process flow. Before we dig into the features, let's briefly discuss what exactly is Team Foundation Build.

The goal of Team Foundation Build is to provide a "build a lab out-of-the-box" experience. A conventional build covers many steps, such as cleaning the remote build machine, obtaining the sources from the build machine, compiling the source, running tests against the build, either before or after the build, and communicating the results of the build back to the team. Most build scripts cover these steps, but getting a solid build process up and running reliably is often more of a chore than you or your team would like to face. The poor integration of the tools involved in this build process often results in a weak software life cycle experience.

Team Foundation Build solves this problem by automating these traditional build steps using wizards supported by Team Explorer. These wizards enable users to easily generate and kick-off fully extensible XML scripts for the Visual Studio Build engine called MSBuild within a well-integrated infrastructure.

Team Foundation Reporting Warehouse architecture

The Team Foundation Reporting Warehouse is a conventionally organized data warehouse where data from third-party tools and Team System plug-ins (e.g., version control, WIT, builds, testing tools) can be stored. Data from these tools and plug-ins is published, either manually (for test data) or as part of an application tier Team Foundation services, to a number of relational databases, located on the Team Foundation data tier, called operational stores. These operational stores are optimized for online transaction processing and have names like TfsVersionControl and TfsWorkItemTracking. Periodically, data is pulled from these stores through warehouse adapters. Each operational store has its own adapter whose task is to transform and publish data in a standardized format to a relational database, called the Team Foundation Relational Warehouse (TFSWarehouse). On top of the Relational Warehouse is an OLAP cube that further aggregates the data for end user and prebuilt reports.

A number of tools can be used to build reports from this cube. Microsoft Excel can be used by project managers to access the cube directly and build ad-hoc reports, possibly for exploratory analysis. Report Builder is a tool that comes with SQL Server 2005 Reporting Services. It can be used to create reports by dragging and dropping OLAP fields onto a design surface. For specific layout and formatting requirements, the Report Designer tool from Visual Studio 2005 can be used. This tool allows you to interactively design a report by using data from Team Foundation as a data source. The Team Foundation Reporting Warehouse architecture is shown in Figure 18-4.

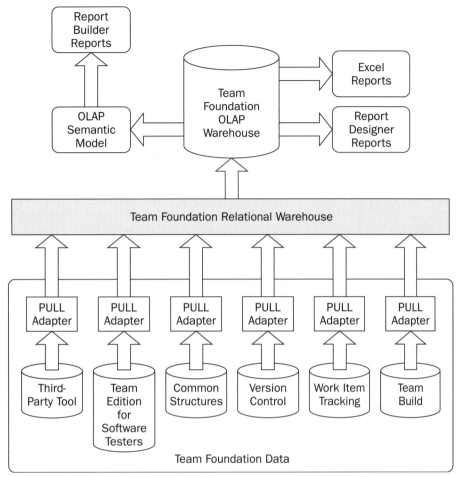

Figure 18-4

The operational stores are organized in a star schema with an OLAP database that draws from the Relational Warehouse schema. A star schema is the simplest data warehouse schema that can be used. At the center of this schema is a "fact" table that lists the core facts that make up the Report query. Each fact is composed of the following: *dimensions*, used to slice the data in a report; *measures*, things that are counted or aggregated; and *details*, the columns that appear in the relational table.

The Reporting Warehouse uses a single OLAP cube with a measure group per fact to assemble the data from the star schema. Examples of measure groups are Work Item History, Test Results, Code Churn, and more. This enables reports drawn from the aggregation of data to end up being simple selects. For complex queries, an answer can be produced in OLAP in about 0.1 percent of the time it takes for the same query on relational data.

The Reporting Warehouse architecture enables each Team System tool to submit data to the warehouse schema and transform the data. For example, when a load test is run, the results are published to a local results store (e.g., SQL Server Express database). The user can elect to manually publish these results (assuming the user has installed Team Foundation Client) to an operational store. This store has a schema that reflects the type of data the Team System load test tool generates. A Reporting Warehouse service on the application tier (called TFSScheduler) periodically sweeps the data stores every hour (by default) and tells the Warehouse Controller service to run adapters. Each of the registered warehouse adapters are then engaged by the Warehouse Controller service through methods on the IDataAAdapter interface. These adapters, represented by managed code running outside of SQL 2005, filter, transform, and move the data to the Team Foundation Relational Warehouse. For example, the LoadTest adapter provides the Team Foundation Relational Warehouse with an "average" of all the counter metrics collected by the operational store.

Team Foundation links work items and code files back to requirements that may be outlined in documents stored in the Reporting Warehouse. This integration enables a modest form of a requirements traceability matrix, essentially coverage analysis that provides a birds-eye view of how much of the requirements are being covered by tests or being worked on in design or development. Such mapping is an important tool for large development shops.

Configuration

You can configure Team Foundation Server deployments on one machine (application and database tier together) or two machines (application and database tier separate). This is illustrated in Figure 18-5. An additional server may be added to the configuration to support building. Another server may be added to enable version control proxy support. As of this writing, a two-server install (separate application and data tiers) with the following configuration will support teams of up to approximately 2,000 users:

❑ **Application tier:** 2P 2.8 GHz 4GB

❑ **Data tier:** 4P 2.7 GHz 16GB

❑ **Disk system:** Direct attach storage, 14-15Krpm RAID 0 spindles

The application tier and data tiers DT servers require Windows Server 2003 SP1, and have a dependency on IIS 6.0, Windows Sharepoint Services 2.0 with SP2, and SQL Server 2005. Team Foundation–enabled clients require Windows 2000 SP4, Windows 2003 SP1, or Windows XP SP2. These clients also will have a dependency on Internet Explorer 6.0, Microsoft Office 11 with SP1 (Office 2003), NET Framework 2.0, and of course Team Explorer.

The Team Foundation Proxy requires Windows XP SP2 or Windows 2003 Server SP1, and .NET FX 2.0.

Please refer to the Team Foundation Server setup instructions for additional hardware and software requirements.

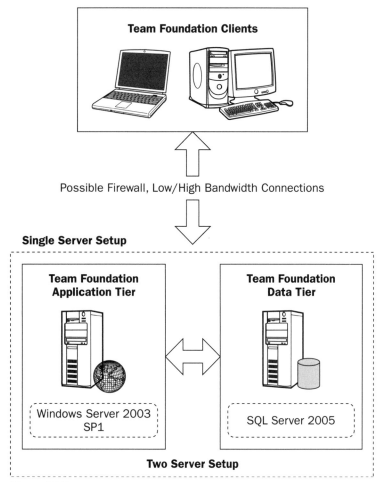

Figure 18-5

Summary

Visual Studio Team Foundation Server provides software teams with the integrated tools and infrastructure they need to more successfully deliver solutions on time and with assured quality. With integrated process guidance, version control, work item tracking, automated builds, and reporting, teams can more effectively configure and track project artifacts and their relationships, enjoy reliable, simple, and repeatable out-of-the-box build processes, and accurately report the status and health of the project at any time. With Team Foundation Server, all members of the team can enjoy nearly friction-free collaboration because they have visibility into the right data at the right time using the Agile software development processes they need.

19

Project Management Tools and Team Reporting

More often than not, the success of a project will be defined by how well a manager organizes and executes the required tasks. In the real world, these skills can vary greatly, which accounts for one of the reasons why certain projects succeed or fail. To minimize this variance and increase the predictability of project outcomes, you can supply a manager with two fundamental things:

❑ **Process Guidance**: Within the context of project management, process guidance is the documentation of a consistent set of operational tasks to guide a project. In most development shops, the process guidance document is located in a thick binder on someone's desk. In Team System, Microsoft provides you with a predefined process guidance document called the *Microsoft Solutions Framework (MSF),* which is based on 30 years of solid software development experience, now integrated and enabled within the Team System development tools.

❑ **Tools**: There are many software tools and packages to help you manage a project, including Microsoft Project, Microsoft Project Server, Exchange, and Outlook. The problem with these tools is that they are lightly integrated. Team System provides a tightly coupled integration between tools. Team System also gets around the issue of managing projects using e-mail. The problem with e-mail is that messages can get lost, miscommunication can occur, and messages are hard to track and manage. Team System provides a centralized store of tasks, requirements, and bugs that are updated in real time by your team members. It makes it very easy to take a snapshot of the project to determine whether things are going well.

No matter what software development project you are working on, the following common tasks keep coming up over and over again. The project manager must do all of the following:

❑ Help define scenarios (along with the business analysts) to map out the features of the software application and ensure that these features provide business value within a limited budget

❑   Create a set of iteration plans based on milestones

❑   Work with team members to define and schedule development and test tasks to successfully implement each scenario

❑   Orchestrate work flow and facilitate communication within your development team, and manage relationships

❑   Continuously monitor the status of the project to avoid bottlenecks and identify possible risks

As a project manager within Team System, you are empowered to do all of these things. Not only can you create and monitor project plans, Team Foundation Server provides a set of tools and the infrastructure to help you communicate and collaborate with other team members, automatically aggregate and collect project health metrics, and centralize all project management operations. For the first time, project managers can now choose to interact with a project on Team Foundation Server using a variety of tools, including Microsoft Excel, Microsoft Project, or an ultra-light version of Visual Studio 2005 called *Team Explorer*. You can pick the tool you feel most comfortable with and run with it.

This chapter focuses on common project management tasks, including the following:

❑   Creating a software project

❑   Administering the project details using work items

❑   Project monitoring using SQL Server Reporting Services

Creating a Software Project

The basis for all projects in Team System is the Team Project. The Team Project holds information about every step of the software development life cycle in a central repository within the Team Foundation Server. This includes requirements management, scheduling, and resources.

There are important differences between a Team Project and a Visual Studio Project — in fact, some people get confused about the meaning of these project types. The Team Explorer enables you to navigate and manage all elements of your Team Project, including your development team, the SharePoint team portal, source code repository, work item database, documents, reports, and templates. The interface of Team Explorer is very similar to that of the Solution Explorer, so you should feel quite at ease using it. To put it in perspective, think of a Team Project in this way: A Solution can contain several Visual Studio Projects. A Team Project, on the other hand, can contain several Solutions. The Visual Studio project is primarily used to organize your code. The Team Project is used to organize all of your software development efforts!

> *If you can't find the Team Explorer option within Visual Studio, you probably forgot to install the client plug-in. Team Explorer is bundled with Team Foundation Server. You can find the installer on the Team Foundation Server DVD/CD media; please refer to Chapter 18 for more details.*

Without helpful software tools like Team System, managing a software development project can be quite a challenge. Here are some common scenarios you might encounter without the help of Team System:

❑   Many development teams use e-mail or some other paper processes as their primary mode of communication. If team members are behind on their mail or a report is lost, then communication problems may occur.

❑ All reporting has to be done manually by project leads. The process of compiling the data can be time-consuming and may not provide enough information to identify trends or problems, especially if you want to manipulate data from a variety of sources. In many cases, you have to buy expensive third-party software to get the job done.

❑ Many project managers use Microsoft Excel or Microsoft Project to create Gantt charts or list requirements. Most project managers update their lists and then have to perform cut and paste operations to bring them into third-party applications.

The prerequisites for the Project Management components of Team System include Team Foundation Server (including an Administrator account), SQL Server 2005, and Microsoft Excel or Microsoft Project (or both).

Currently, the only way to create projects is using the Visual Studio IDE — by using Team Explorer.

In the next section, you will learn the key markers of a successful software project. Then, you will find out how to use the New Team Project Wizard to create and configure your first project within Team System.

Why software development projects fail

Here is a list of common problem spaces and the solutions offered by Team System (as shown in Table 19-1).

Table 19-1

Problem	Solutions Offered by Team System
Lack of standards compliance	Each Team System project must be accompanied by a methodology, which enforces good practices. With the advent of Sarbanes-Oxley (SOX) legislation (which resulted from the Enron scandal), creating an accountable environment that is compliant with standards is especially important. MSF also comes with prescriptive guidance.
Poor understanding of processes	Process guidance is integrated in your project in many ways: as a web site accessible from your team portal and through work items, policies and the help menu.
Communication problems	Work item workflow allows easy inter-team communication. The project manager is always on top of the latest metrics without having to communicate directly with team members. In addition, messages are centralized and are not subject to problems experienced by decentralized systems such as e-mail.
Poor metrics and estimation skills	Metrics are handled via SQL Server Reporting Services. All metrics (including build, test, and performance numbers) flow automatically into the central data store on the Team Foundation Server.
Too much focus on operational details and poor workflow management	Team System takes a lot of the operational tasks out of the process. Reports are gathered and generated automatically based on incoming data. Team System also operates in a paper-free process that enables all members of the team to be more productive. Workflow is automatically handled via work items.

Now that you've looked at the challenges of implementing a project using manual processes, and you have a clear understanding of the points of failure of a software project, the following sections explain how to successfully implement and manage a project using Team System.

Using the New Team Project Wizard

To start a new project, select File ⇨ New ⇨ Team Project. The New Team Project Wizard will appear, as shown in Figure 19-1, prompting you to enter a name for your project. You can alternatively launch the wizard by right-clicking on your server name in the Team Explorer and selecting New Team Project.

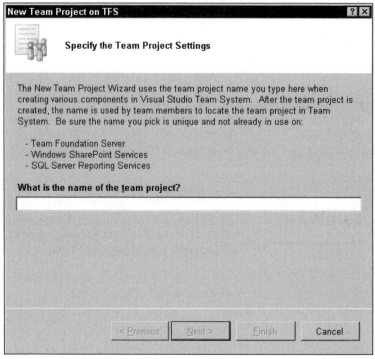

Figure 19-1

The next step involves selecting a process template (as shown in Figure 19-2). Team System comes with two default process templates: MSF for Agile Software Development and MSF for CMMI (Capability Maturity Model Integration) Process Improvement.

The wizard then enables you to add a title and a description to your project portal (see Figure 19-3).

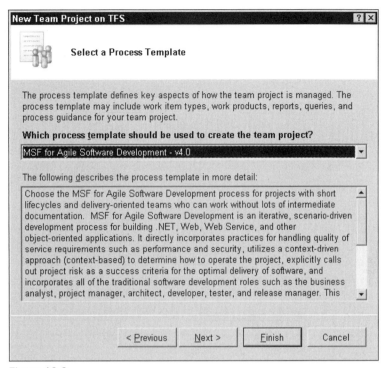

Figure 19-2

Figure 19-3

Use the next page to set the preliminary source control options. You have the choice of creating a source control folder for your project or creating a new branch from an existing source control tree (in case you are creating a project that is derived from another). Figure 19-4 shows the Specify Source Control Settings page.

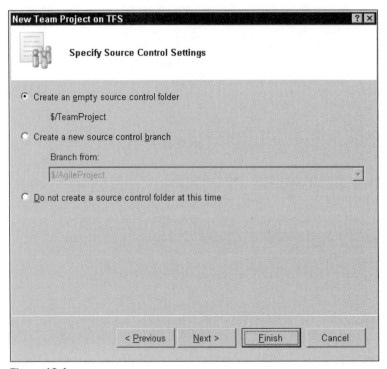

Figure 19-4

Clicking Next completes the wizard. Depending on the template you select, a series of process guidance documents will be generated for your project. The Permissions settings page enables you to set privileges for the groups and users on your team (the next section provides more information on how to secure your project).

Once you click Finish, the wizard will create your Team Project. The process may take a little while (depending on how much RAM your server has). When it is completed, several folders will appear in the Team Explorer (as shown in Figure 19-5). (The figure illustrates the reports and documents you would typically find if you select the MSF for Agile Software Development process).

Your Team Project tree has five primary nodes: Work Items, Documents, Reports, Team Builds, and Source Control. The Work Item node includes predefined queries and custom queries to list the work items associated with your project. The Documents node has Development, Project Management, and Template subnodes to help you map out your development process. The Reports node includes a variety of report types to view the metrics of your project. The Team Builds node offers access to a variety of build types, including custom types. Finally, the Source Control node gives you easy access to your source code tree via the Source Control Explorer (you can also access the Source Control Explorer from the toolbar).

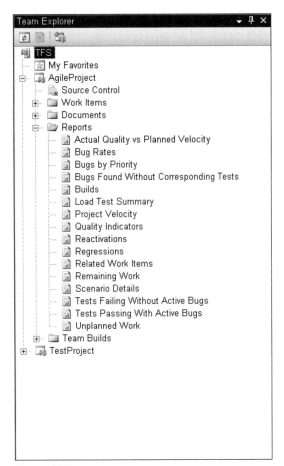

Figure 19-5

Administering Project Details

How effectively you can manage the day-to-day operation of your team is a crucial element to achieving success with any software development effort. Team System offers work items to help you get a handle on the progress of the entire team without having to call meetings. You can also get a handle on metrics such as bugs, requirements, and milestone slips.

Connecting to the Team Foundation Server

Before you can start working with a project, you must first connect to your Team Foundation Server. The Team Explorer enables you to connect to different instances of Team Foundation Server and manage the associated projects. The easiest way to connect to Team Foundation Server is by clicking Tools ⇨ Connect to Team Foundation Server. If the Team Explorer isn't showing up, you can bring it up by clicking View ⇨ Team Explorer.

Once you choose to connect to the server, a window will appear to help you manage your server and Team Projects. Figure 19-6 shows the Connect to Team Foundation Server window. Notice that the team projects have checkmarks next to them — this enables you to narrow down the projects you want to load in the Team Explorer tree view pane (especially useful if you have a ton of Team Projects per server).

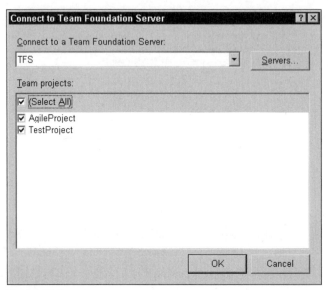

Figure 19-6

To add a new server to the list, click the Servers button. A new window will appear (shown in Figure 19-7) with an Add button. Click the button and enter a server name and URL to complete the process.

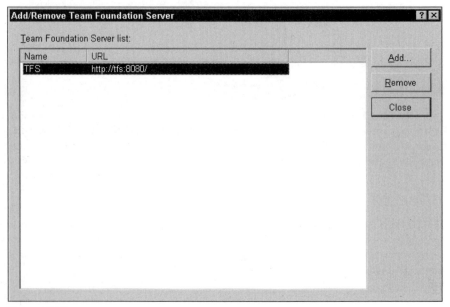

Figure 19-7

Configuring project settings

Once you have created a project, you need to be able to configure it to fit your needs. To access the project properties, right-click the Project name in the Team Explorer and select Properties.

Managing project security

Team Foundation Server has an extensive set of settings and centralized tools to help you create users and groups with predefined permissions, which enables you to efficiently administer and constrain your team members. For example, as a project manager, the last thing you want to do is allow every member of your team access to every report or give them the capability to create projects on the fly, without your authorization. To configure server security (including creating roles), simply right-click the server name in Team Explorer and select *YourServerName* ➪ Team Project Settings ➪ Permissions.

Some processes will automatically create groups when you instantiate a project. For example, the MSF for Agile Software Development process will create a Contributor group right out of the box. Feel free to manipulate the security settings to suit your particular needs. (You will need administrative privileges to view project-level information and to administer builds and test results.) The Project Security dialog box is shown in Figure 19-8.

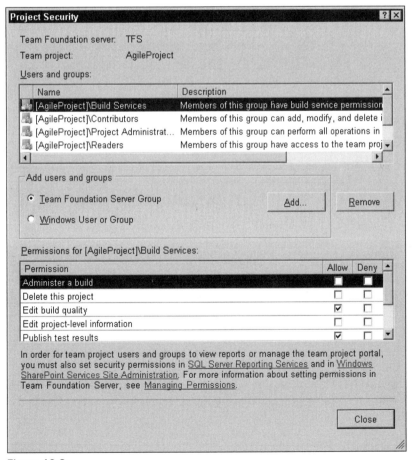

Figure 19-8

You can work with two sets of settings: the Project Security settings (shown in Figure 19-8) and the Group Membership settings (which are accessible by selecting Team Explorer ⇨ *YourServerName* ⇨ Team Project Settings ⇨ Group Membership). Why do you have two ways of manipulating security? Team Foundation Server enables you to assign permissions with three levels of granularity: *serverwide groups* (also called *global groups*), *project groups*, and *users*.

Structuring your project

One of the easiest ways of organizing your work items is by grouping them together logically. In Team System, you can use Iterations and Areas. Most Agile software projects are built in iterative stages. It makes sense to organize work items in iterations, rather than wade through a huge pool of work items for each project.

To access the Areas options, right-click on your project and then select Team Project Settings ⇨ Areas and Iterations. Click on the Iterations tab and you'll notice that there are already predefined iterations in place: Iteration 0, Iteration 1, and Iteration 2 (see Figure 19-9). You can rename these to whatever you like. For example, you can write in a logical sequence such as Alpha, Beta 1, Beta 2, and Release, or subdivide each project as DEV, PROD and QA (as shown in Figure 19-10).

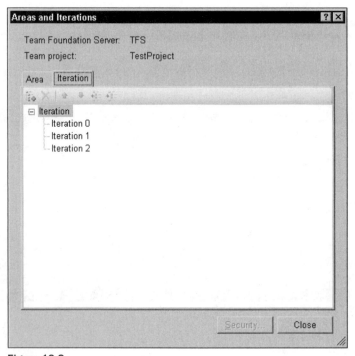

Figure 19-9

To associate a work item with an iteration, simply edit the work item and click on the Iteration drop-down menu below the Title, selecting the iteration you want (see Figure 19-10).

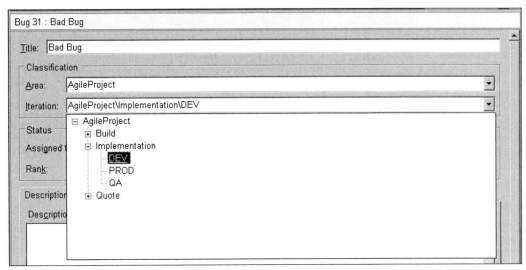

Figure 19-10

Areas offer another way of organizing and classifying your work. Think of Areas as another word for "categories." You can define your own custom areas and assign work items to them. Then it is quite easy to filter the work items by area using work item queries. For example, if you wanted to get all the work items associated with an area called MobileProject, you could enter a query such as the one shown in Figure 19-11.

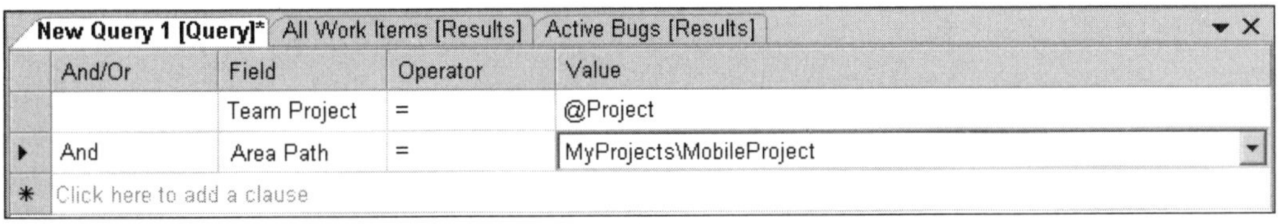

	And/Or	Field	Operator	Value
		Team Project	=	@Project
▶	And	Area Path	=	MyProjects\MobileProject
✳	Click here to add a clause			

New Query 1 [Query]* All Work Items [Results] Active Bugs [Results]

Figure 19-11

To access the Areas options, right-click on your project and then select Team Project Settings ➪ Areas and Iterations. To create a collection of areas, start by right-clicking on the root area node and selecting New. A sub-node called "Area 0" will appear right below the root node (as shown in Figure 19-12). You can rename this node to whatever you like. As you can see in the figure, you can create hierarchies and relationships between the nodes, which can reflect the way you organize your project outside of Team System.

Figure 19-12

To associate a work item with an area, simply edit the work item and select the area you want using the drop-down menu in the Classifications section below the title, and then resave your work item. Figure 19-13 shows a screenshot of the Area field on the work item form.

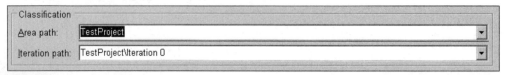

Figure 19-13

Managing version control

Through the project settings, you can easily configure the source control options. Figure 19-14 illustrates how you can set policies. In the example shown, the source code has to build without errors and go through code analysis before it is checked in the repository.

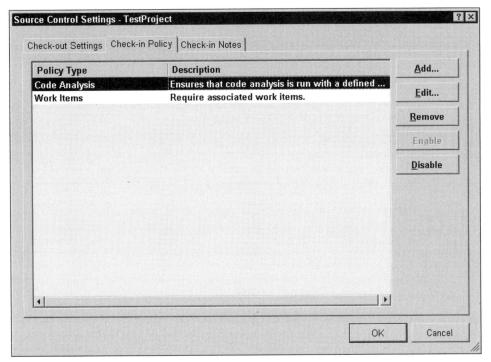

Figure 19-14

For a detailed overview of the Source Control options and features, please refer to Chapter 20.

Working with the Team Project portal

Once your project has been created, a Team Project portal is automatically generated. Currently, the Team System project portals are based on Windows SharePoint Services (which makes them easily extensible using Web Parts). Figure 19-15 shows the layout of a typical project portal (which includes Documents, Process Guidance, and Reports). The front page of the portal includes announcements and links. You can also access some of the important metrics from your project (such as Builds, Remaining Work, Quality Indicators, and Bug Rates).

Project Alerts

Project alerts are e-mail notifications sent to the project manager based on triggered events (such as builds, work item changes, and check-ins). Alerts work on a subscription-based system.

> For the alerts to work correctly, you must provide Team Foundation Server with a valid SMTP server address and credentials during the server installation process.

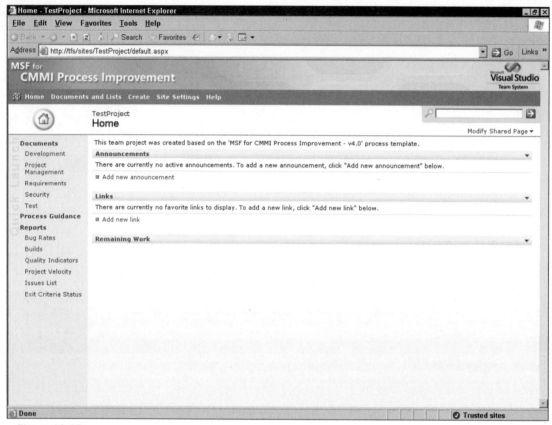

Figure 19-15

You can configure project alerts by clicking on your Team Project title in Team Explorer, and selecting Team ⇨ Project Alerts. The following window will appear (see Figure 19-16):

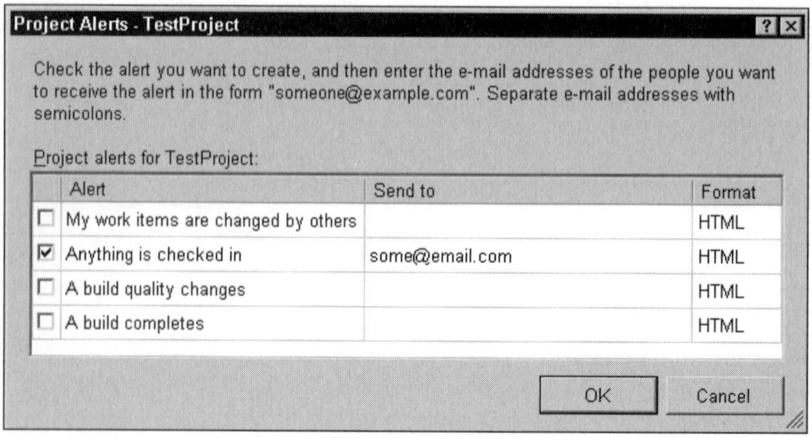

Figure 19-16

There are four default alerts:

- ❏ My work items are changed by others.
- ❏ Anything is checked in.
- ❏ A build quality changes.
- ❏ A build completes.

To add or edit an alert, simply click on the corresponding checkbox, add in your e-mail address and select whether you want to receive an HTML or Text e-mail. In order to view the target e-mail, you may need to have the proper credentials and note that you can view work items associated to alerts by clicking on the work item type and number in the e-mail.

Alerts are defined on a project basis and are sometimes aggregated in one e-mail. You can control on a very granular level what projects should have alerts, and what alerts should be triggered.

You can of course extend and customize the project alerts. Jeff Lucovsky from Microsoft posted some details on how you can do it on his blog: `http://blogs.msdn.com/jefflu/`

Team Portal customization and extensibility

Once you create a Team Project, you'll notice that it has a very specific "look and feel" (based on one of the standard templates available in Windows SharePoint Services 2.0). Windows SharePoint Services has a great administrative interface that allows any user to customize the portal to any specification. For example, you can upload documents, change the graphics on the portal, add web parts and configure the security settings to your heart's content. You can also configure links, announcements, contacts, events, tasks, issues, discussion boards, surveys, and much more.

The problem is, for every Team Project you create, you have to repeat the customization steps over and over again. This can be very tedious and unproductive. Fortunately, you can integrate some of these changes in a process template. Specifically, when you create a project you can pre-populate document libraries on the portal. Chapter 22 has some really useful information on how to work with the process templates. The key to customize the portal is an XML file called `WSSTasks.xml`:

```xml
<?xml version="1.0" encoding="utf-8" ?>
<tasks>
<task id="SharePointPortal"
      name="Create Sharepoint Portal"
      plugin="Microsoft.ProjectCreationWizard.Portal"
      completionMessage="Project site created.">
<dependencies/>
<taskXml>
<Portal>
<site template="TeamDocs#1" language="1033"/>
<documentLibraries>
<documentLibrary name="Security" description="Architecture Documents"/>
<documentLibrary name="Testing" description="Testing Documents"/>
...
</documentLibraries>
```

So far, we've looked at customization. What about extensibility? You have the option to create new web parts which can be integrated into the portal using the Microsoft Windows SharePoint Products and Technologies SDK. web part creation is a bit out of scope for this book, but we recommend that you refer to the SDK and the MSDN documentation for code, tips, and examples.

Here are the steps to add a new web part to an existing page (including a custom web part):

1. Click Modify Shared Page ⇨ Design This Page.

2. Click Modify Shared Page ⇨ Add web Part. You will then be presented with the following options: Browse, Search and Import.

3. Select Browse and then select the Page Viewer web part.

4. You can then drag the part to the left portion of the screen.

5. Click the down arrow at the corner of the web part and select Modify Shared Web Part.

6. In the Link section on the right, enter `http://<servername>/Reports/`.

7. Click OK.

The reporting site will now appear in the web part on the team portal (as shown in Figure 19-17).

> One of the most requested site-customization questions I've been asked is how to change the "look and feel" of the site portal (for example, change the logo and colors on the main portal page). You can easily modify the Team Portal by using FrontPage 2003. Simply connect to the site (File ⇨ Open Site) using FrontPage. (You may be prompted to enter your Team Foundation Server administrator credentials.) You can then import your logo (using File ⇨ Import) and drag and drop it on the page. You can also change the colors on the site by modifying the style sheets in the "themes" directory.

Deleting a Team project

When you first start working with Team Foundation Server, experimenting, creating multiple projects you might find that your server will start looking cluttered. Thankfully, Team Foundation Server comes with a handy tool called `TFSDeleteProject` which comes to the rescue. `TFSDeleteProject` is located in the `C:\Program Files\Microsoft Visual Studio 8\Common7\IDE\PrivateAssemblies\` directory. You can delete a project using the following syntax:

```
TFSDeleteproject /TeamFoundationServer:TFS TestProject
```

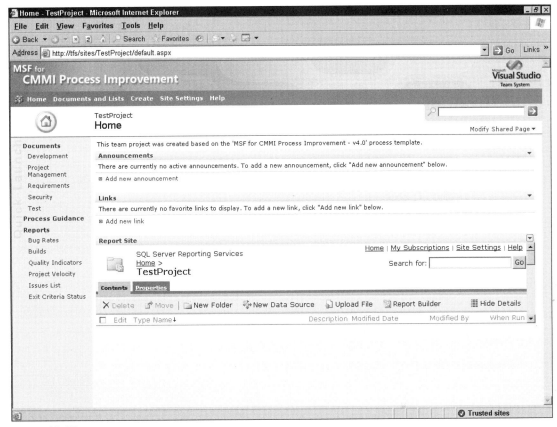

Figure 19-17

In the preceding example, TFS denotes the name of your Team Foundation Server, and TestProject is the name of the project you want to delete. TFSDeleteProject comes with several useful parameters, as shown in Table 19-2.

Table 19-2

Parameter	Description
/force	The application will attempt to delete all parts of a Team Project even if problems occur.
/TeamFoundationServer	You can specify the name of the server using this parameter. It is especially useful if you are running multiple instances of Team Foundation Server.
/q	Run the project delete tool in "quiet" mode. You won't receive any confirmations or prompts during the deletion process.

Please note that once you delete a project, you can't recover it — the process is irreversible. Parts of the Team Project, however, will remain in the data warehouse.

Work Item Tracking

Work items are the drivers behind Team System's task management and time-tracking capabilities. In this section, you'll learn a little about work item internals, including how to create and manage work items in your development projects and how to design custom work item types (WITs).

Anatomy of a work item

In Team System, five kinds of work items are available by default (in the MSF for Agile Software Development process): Bug, Quality of Service Requirement, Risk, Scenario, and Task. In the MSF for CMMI Process Improvement process, there are seven default work item types: Bug, Change Request, Issue, Requirement, Review, Risk, and Task. All of the work items in your project are stored in the work item database (formerly code-named "Currituck") and accessible via the Team Foundation Server.

> **The Team System work item management system is loosely based on an internal Microsoft bug tracking product called Product Studio.**

Table 19-3 describes some of the important fields found in work items (please note that this is by no means an exhaustive list).

Table 19-3

Name	Description
ID	Uniquely identifies each work item within the work item database.
Status	Describes the status of a work item. The default setting is Active.
Type	Depending on the process template you select, several default work item types are made available within a Team Project. Some examples include Task, Requirement, Scenario, or Bug Request. You can also define your own work item types. (See the section later in the chapter entitled "Creating and customizing work item types.")
Priority	Indicates the priority order for your work items. This enables your team members to prioritize their workload and rank work items in order of importance. Team System can also queue work items based on their priority level.
Title	The title of the work item. Make sure you create a descriptive title because it is the first thing you will see when you design a work item query. For example, simply writing "Bug" will not help you assess the type or importance of the bug in the system.

Name	Description
Assigned To	The team member to whom the work item is assigned. You can change the value of this field when you want to reassign a work item to another team member.
Revision	The work item version. As you will see later, you can add fields and customize existing work items. The Revision field helps you maintain a parity match between versions.
State	The current state of a work item.

Work items can also contain durations (including a start date and end date) and descriptions (this feature is especially useful if you need to include lengthy steps to re-create a bug, for example). You can also associate a work item with a Structure node or iteration to indicate when it should be worked on. Work items contain a Sync field to indicate whether the work item has been synchronized with the database. All of the fields are contained on an easily accessible work item form that simplifies the task of entering the data.

Once you create a Team Project using one of Team System's default process templates, the process template will automatically populate your work item list with common tasks related to the process.

Creating work items using Visual Studio

Suppose you wanted to create a Bug work item in Visual Studio 2005. All you would need to do is go to your project in Team Explorer, right-click Work Items, and select Add Work Item ⇨ Bug. You can also click the Team option in the Visual Studio menu and select Add Work Item ⇨ Bug.

A New Bug form, shown in Figure 19-18, will appear. Simply fill out the form and click Save (the little floppy disc icon). The bug will automatically be saved in the work item store and will be accessible to everyone on the team project.

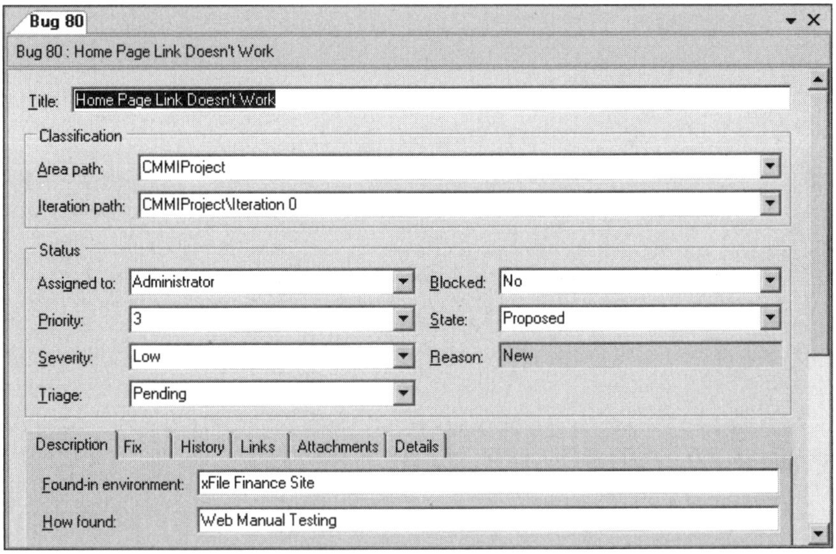

Figure 19-18

By default, anyone on your team can change a work item. There may be scenarios where you may want to prevent developers from reassigning their work to someone else or changing other users' work items. Fortunately, there are two ways of controlling access to work items. First, you can specify security permissions by Area, restricting who can access them. By changing the Area path of a particular work item, it will inherit the permissions you've assigned to it. Another way of controlling access to a work item is by customizing your work item types and adding READ-ONLY rules to the work item fields. This process is documented on the Microsoft Forums at the following link: `http://forums.microsoft.com/` `MSDN/ShowPost.aspx?PostID=172323&SiteID=1`.

To reassign a work item to another team member, in Team Explorer simply double-click the Work Items ⇨ All Work Items query. A split window will appear, with a work item list on the top and a preview pane at the bottom (see Figure 19-19).

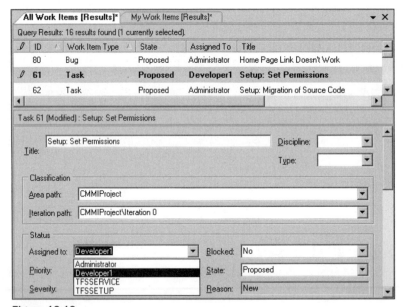

Figure 19-19

As soon as you select a work item in the top pane, you can edit the work item in the bottom pane. Change the assignment to another member of your team and click the Save button. Regular work item management tasks are covered later in the chapter in the section "Creating and assigning work items using Microsoft Office."

Creating and running work item queries

To create a work item query, go to the Team Explorer pane. Right-click on Work Items ⇨ Team Queries and select Add Query. In the query area, simply change the And/Or, Field, Operator, and Value fields.

Figure 19-20 features an example query. These queries are used to filter through your work item list to help you find specific work items. This feature is quite useful for organizing your work items in logical ways. For example, if you select the TeamProject field, the = operator, and the name of your project (@Project indicates the current project), you can filter the work items associated with your projects.

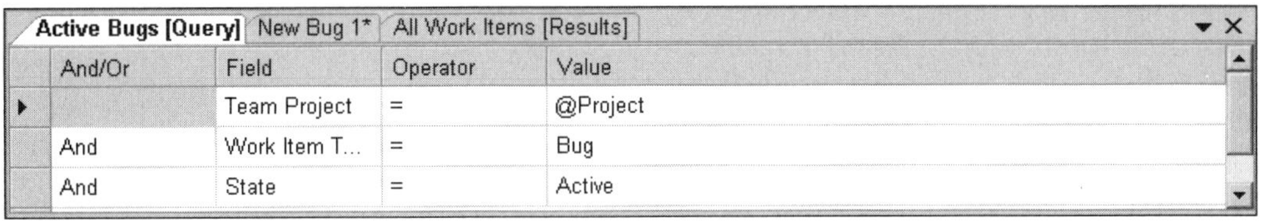

	And/Or	Field	Operator	Value
▶		Team Project	=	@Project
	And	Work Item T...	=	Bug
	And	State	=	Active

Active Bugs [Query] | New Bug 1* | All Work Items [Results]

Figure 19-20

To run a work item query, simply select a query in the Team Explorer, right-click, and select View Results. Queries are useful for creating a triage of important tasks or bugs during team meetings.

> **Once you save a query, you will be prompted whether you want to make it visible to everyone on the team, visible only to yourself, or save it as a file. If you choose to make it visible to everyone on your team, the query will appear in the Team Queries folder in Team Explorer (and everyone on your team will be able to run it). If you choose to save it for yourself, it will appear in the My Queries folder in Team Explorer (and it will not be visible to the rest of your team). Personal queries are useful to organize your work items in useful views (for example, all the personal Tasks that were assigned by a particular project manager). If you are working on a customized process template, the Save as a File option is useful to extract queries as WIQ files.**

Creating and assigning work items using Microsoft Office

Microsoft has created two Office add-ins to enable project leads to manage scheduling and issue tracking using familiar tools such as Microsoft Excel and Microsoft Project. It's a smooth transition: Most project management specialists use spreadsheet tools such as Excel to create Gantt charts and trace milestones.

> **Team System only integrates with Microsoft Office 2003 or later. The add-in is installed during the installation of Team Explorer. Therefore, you must install Microsoft Office before Team Explorer.**

Microsoft Excel

You can use Microsoft Excel to track and manage work items within your project. Your work item list (including tasks, scenarios, and bugs) is synchronized with the work item database tied to the Team Foundation Server (TFS). Excel is suitable for ad hoc or loose projects; you can easily update the status of each item. The main advantage is that the organization is not only visual, but also functional. All of the changes you make propagate throughout the project team.

The Excel add-in works in conjunction with the list object. You can output the results of the query into Excel or Project by right-clicking All Work Items and selecting Open in Microsoft Excel or Open in Microsoft Project from within the context menu.

To create a brand-new work item list, select the Add New List button within Excel, and then select a Team Project using the Team Project button. Pressing the Sync button will synchronize the changes you have made locally with the Team Foundation Server. Figure 19-21 illustrates the Excel add-in options and the basic structure of a work item list.

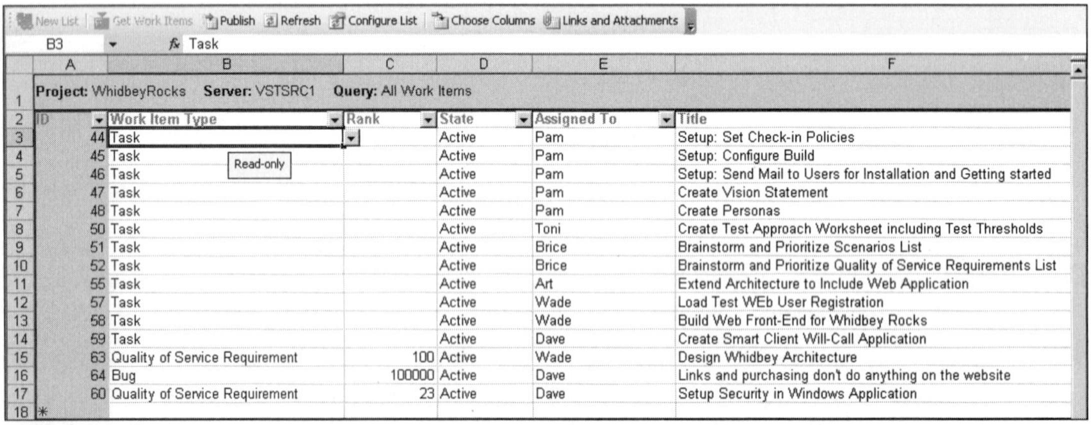

Figure 19-21

Once you click the Sync button, you'll get a dialog box to confirm that the synchronization process was successful. One of the core advantages of using Microsoft Excel as a project management tool is the fact that it is ubiquitous and easy to use. You would be hard-pressed to find a Windows desktop without a copy of Microsoft Office (including Excel). If you are comfortable with Excel, you can create visual representations such as reports and graphs using local work item data. Excel is also appropriate for bulk adding and editing work item data.

> **You don't have to be connected to the Team Foundation Server to work on work items. Simply import them into Excel or Project, work on them offline, and then synchronize back to the server once you are in a connected state.**

You will sometimes encounter conflicts when you synchronize work items with the Team Foundation Server. By double-clicking each conflict, you can resolve whether the changes should cascade to the server or vice-versa. The dialog box shown in Figure 19-22 appears during the process.

Each work item has a schema with rules dictating required fields, workflow rules, and behaviors. When a work item appears that doesn't validate against the schema, you will receive a validation error. A dialog box will appear stating the cause of the error, and you will get the opportunity to add missing fields.

You must select a reason for the conflict (using a drop-down menu). Work item validation is a useful mechanism for maintaining the integrity of your data in the work item database.

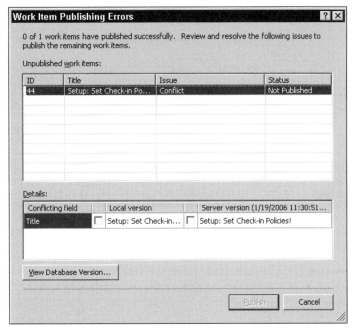

Figure 19-22

> Ideally, you should use the Project Checklist query to get a holistic view of your work load if you are using the MSF for Agile Software Development process. (The process comes with a handy "Project Checklist.xls" work product to manage your project.) Using MSF for CMMI Process Improvement, you can use a variety of queries to manage your workflow. CMMI comes with a MSF CMMI Reference (MSF CMMI Reference.xls) work product as a checklist to implement CMMI based on set workstreams, activities, levels, and goals.

Microsoft Project

Microsoft Project enables you to manage your project with more granularity and richness of information than Microsoft Excel. Microsoft Project excels at scheduling and breaking down tasks, and has been specifically designed to work out project plans. In terms of functionality, you can add and edit work items with the same ease as Microsoft Excel. You can also do *project column mapping* and track the entire project to a baseline. Figure 19-23 illustrates work items imported into Microsoft Project.

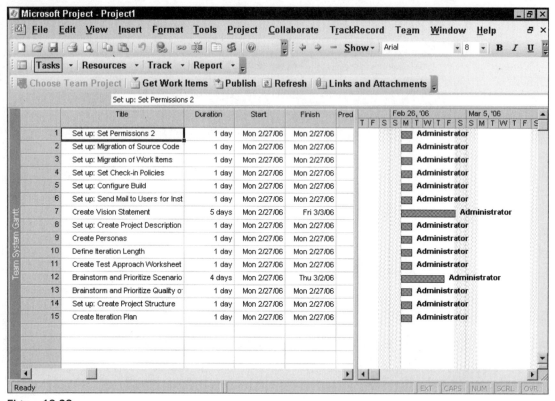

Figure 19-23

There are several ways you can organize your work items in Project. The first method is by using Summary Tasks. This approach is well outlined in the MSDN documentation. Another approach is by using the Group By option, specifically grouping by Iteration. To group your work items, select Project ⇨ Group By ⇨ Customize Group By. In the drop-down box to the right of Group By, select Iteration Path (Outline Code 10) and click OK. Your work items will then be sorted by iteration and will be easier to manage.

Creating and customizing work item types

Custom work items are created using templates that define the behavior. If you edit a work item type, you will notice that the structure is defined using human-readable XML. You can easily add new fields, add restrictions, and rename fields. To edit work item types, the Edit Domain-level Information permission must be enabled on your account (please refer to the "Managing project security" section at the beginning of the chapter for more details).

You have two options for configuring your account to manipulate work items: place yourself in the Namespace or Project Administrator Group.

The work item types can be edited in any XML editor, including the built-in Visual Studio XML editor or Notepad/Wordpad. The following example shows the structure of a "vanilla" work item type. The first node is the Work Item Type Definition (WITD). In this particular instance, we've defined the authoring application as hand edit (you can change this value to your liking):

```
<WITD application="hand edit" version="1.0">
```

Next, name the work item type and give it a description:

```
<WORKITEMTYPE name="Vanilla WIT">
<DESCRIPTION>This is an example of a simple Work Item Type</>
```

Then define the structure and field type that will appear in the work item:

```
<FIELDS>
    <FIELD refname="ProVSTS.title"
           name="Title" type="String"></>
</FIELDS>
```

Now you need to establish a workflow (which includes states and transitions). In this example, we indicate that the default state of the work item is Active (a work item would transition to Active when a new work item is generated). Depending on the work item type, a work item can have several states, including Active, Resolved, and Closed (among others):

```
<WORKFLOW>
   <STATES>
      <STATE value="Active" />
   </STATES>
   <TRANSITIONS>
      <TRANSITION from="" to="Active" />
      <REASONS>
         <DEFAULTREASON value="New">
      </REASONS>
   </TRANSITIONS>
</WORKFLOW>
```

Next, you have to define the physical layout of the work item form. You have many controls at your disposal, including the FieldControl, ExtendedComboBox, and LinkControl. The best way to learn about the different controls is by editing existing work items and comparing the XML with the physical layout of the fields when the work item is in edit mode. In the following example, the work item physically contains a single field named Title:

```
<FORM>
   <LAYOUT>
   <Control Type="FieldControl" FieldName="Title"/>
   </LAYOUT>
</FORM>
</WORKITEMTYPE>
</WITD>
```

Custom work item types can be deployed in two ways: You can create/add your new work item type within a new process template, or you can import/export preexisting work item types (such as a task) and customize them by adding new features.

> You can use the `witimport` and `witexport` to add and modify work items on the server in an existing project. The Visual Studio 2005 SDK has great documentation on how to use the tools. You can download the SDK at www.vsipdev.com.

The best way to get comfortable with customizing work item types is by examining the structure of preexisting types (such as the bug or requirement). Then you can get a feel for where your new fields are and how behaviors can be added.

Team Foundation Server Reporting

Reporting is one of the most powerful features of Team System. Any data stored in the data warehouse can be viewed as a report, which enables you to view and organize project metrics very easily. This includes work item tracking (tasks, bugs, and requirements), test results (unit, static, and dynamic tests), quality indicators (performance and code coverage), build reports, schedule reports, and overall project health reports. You can also create customized reports for your clients or business analysts, and the best part is that you don't have to invest a lot of money in third-party tools to get quick and cost-effective results.

The reporting tools are not only useful for project managers, but also for team members in every role. For example, a developer can look at test results and home in on specific bugs. At the heart of the reporting features is SQL Server 2005 Reporting Services. (You will learn more about this feature later in the chapter.)

Working with Team Reports

Team System has many public reports available right out of the box (19 reports duplicated across both MSF for Agile Software and MSF for CMMI Process Improvement process templates). From a project management perspective, one of the great advantages of using Team System is that you don't have to manually correlate data from a host of third-party sources. All reports are available in a tightly integrated fashion within the report site, which is accessible using Team Explorer and through your web browser.

Managing Reports using Team Explorer

You can access project reports in Visual Studio using the Team Explorer. The reports listed in Figure 19-24 are part of the MSF for Agile Software Development process and can be found in the tree under Reports ➪ Public. To view a report, simply click on it; the results will appear in the middle pane.

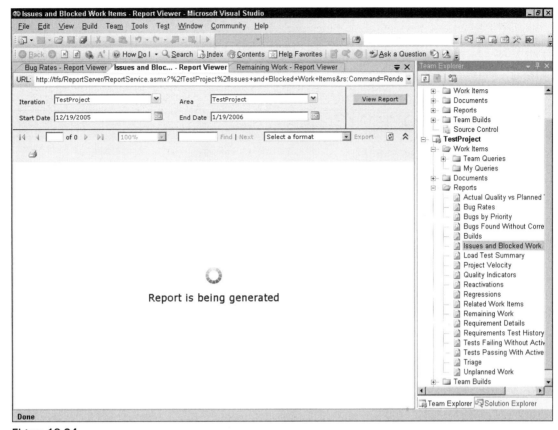

Figure 19-24

Managing Reports using the Reporting Services Report Manager

You can also access the default (and custom) reports using the project portal. In Team Explorer, expand your project and right-click on Reports. To view the available reports, select Show Report Site. You can also manually access the portal by typing the following link in your browser: http://<Application Tier Name>/Reports/. You'll see a page very similar to the one shown in Figure 19-25.

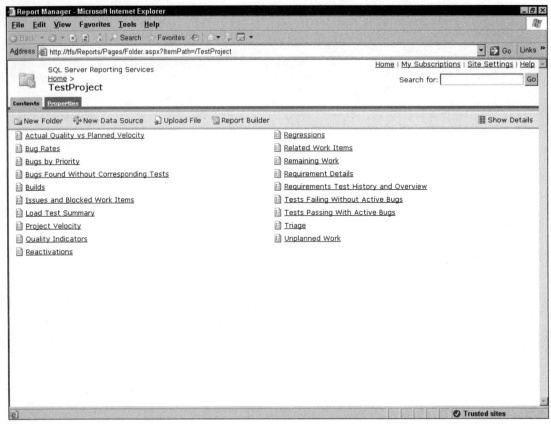

Figure 19-25

Figure 19-26 illustrates a typical Bug Rates report. As you can see, the Active Bugs Backlog is decreasing at a healthy rate, while the bugs are getting resolved and activated at a constant rate. This particular report indicates that the project is in good health (at least you are effectively finding, fixing, and closing bugs).

Analyzing trends within a project

Once you have the data, you need to be able to correctly interpret the metrics in order to make high-level decisions for your project. Let's look at a few case studies to get a handle on how data is presented in a report and how to interpret the results. Figure 19-27 shows a typical Velocity report.

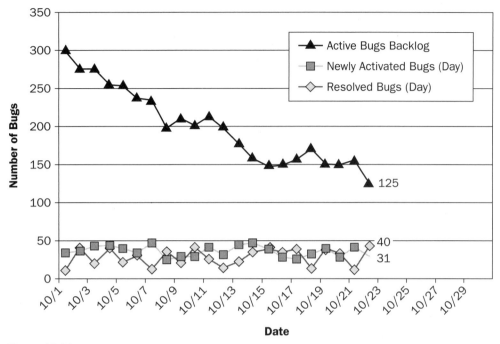

Figure 19-26

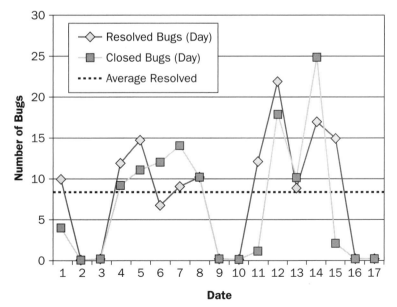

Figure 19-27

The Resolved Bugs rate (represented by the lines with diamonds on the graph) indicates that a variable number of bugs are being fixed. The Closed Bugs Rate (represented by the line with squares) also shows a variable number of bugs being closed. This lack of consistency on the graph indicates that your developers are inconsistently resolving bugs. The problem can be solved by better planning and implementing a formalized methodology on the prioritization and elimination of bugs.

Another example is the Remaining Work report, shown in Figure 19-28.

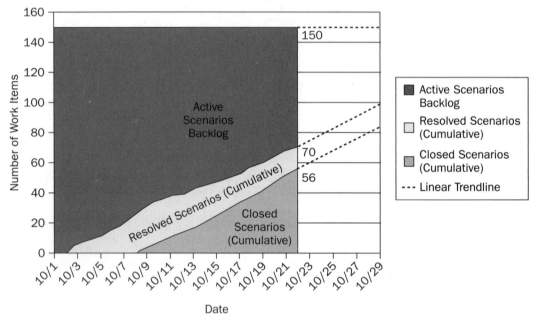

Figure 19-28

There is a predominant negative trend indicated on this report. The Active Scenarios Backlog will not be resolved by the end of the project as indicated by the dotted line. Based on this trend, it would be important to re-evaluate the distribution of work, perhaps allocating more personnel to work through scenarios.

A final example is the Unplanned Work report, shown in Figure 19-29.

As you can see in the diagram, there are a number of planned and unplanned work items in play. The amount of planned work is decreasing, which is a healthy trend. However, the darker area representing the unplanned work is also increasing a bit. The report provides a way to figure out in advance what buffer is required to make sure that your team doesn't get overwhelmed.

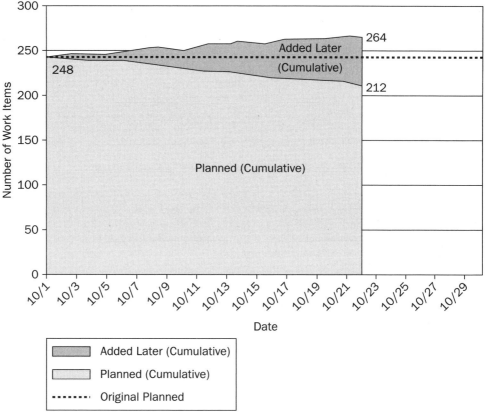

Figure 19-29

Viewing reports using Microsoft Excel pivot tables

You can view your project data using an Excel pivot table. One of the key advantages of using a pivot table is simplicity — Microsoft Excel mines the data warehouse directly and has the built-in capability to display rich graphs and charts. (See Figure 19-30 for an example of data imported into Excel.) Here is how you can set up Excel to view your project data:

1. Open Microsoft Excel.
2. Select Data ➪ PivotTable and PivotChart Report.
3. Select External Data Source and Pivot Table and then click Next.
4. Click the Get Data button.
5. Select the OLAP Cube tab, select New Data Source, and then click OK.
6. Write a custom name for your data source. (If you are unsure, write in something like TFS-DATA.) To use Pivot Tables, you need to first download the OLEDB 9.0 drivers. If you want to

install the drivers without having to install all of the SQL client tools, please refer to this package: www.microsoft.com/downloads/details.aspx?FamilyID=D09C1D60-A13C-4479-9B91-9E8B9D835CDC&displaylang=en.

> If the OLEDB drivers have been installed and you encounter an "Initialization of the data source failed" error, simply go to Start ⇨ Run, and type Regsvr32 "C:\Program Files\Common Files\System\Ole DB\msolap90.dll".

7. Select the Microsoft OLE DB Provider for Analysis Services 9.0 and click Connect.

8. A new window entitled Multidimensional Connection 9.0 will pop up.

9. Select Analysis Server; under Server, enter (local).

10. Enter the credentials you used for TFSSETUP in the User ID and Password fields. (The wizard will warn you if your credentials are invalid.) Theoretically, you should not need credentials, but you need to be a member of the TFSDataWarehouseReader role on the cube. You can set this up using the SQL Server Management Studio.

> If you enter incorrect credentials or credentials that don't have sufficient permissions to access the cube, you may receive an "error occurred in the transport layer" message. You can avoid the error message by entering valid user names and passwords.

11. Select the TFSWarehouse database and click Finish.

12. Select Team System, check Save My User ID and Password, and click Yes. You may get a warning that your user name and password will not be encrypted. The wizard will not allow you to move forward until you accept the warning. It's an important consideration if you are not in a secure environment (i.e., working from a coffee house hotspot).

13. Click OK in the Create New Data Source dialog box; click OK once more.

14. Click Finish in the PivotTable dialog box.

At this point, you can select any fields you want to view in the pivot table. Select the items that interest you and drag them into the Pivot Table. For example, you may be interested in seeing ChangeSet information. The information will auto-magically appear in the Excel spreadsheet within the pivot table. You can then save the sheet or choose to manipulate it at will.

Building custom reports

Microsoft provides you with a good variety of reports to help you evaluate the health of your project. However, sometimes you will want to create custom reports to view your data in different ways, based on business requirements. The good news is that, like many other parts of Team System, the reporting feature is completely customizable and extensible. All of the default reports included in the process templates are written as Report Definition Language (.rdl) files. These files are defined by an XML-based schema that makes them interoperable with a variety of tools, including Visual Studio. For more information about the Report Definition Language file specifications, please visit the following link: www.microsoft.com/sql/reporting/techinfo/rdlspec.mspx.

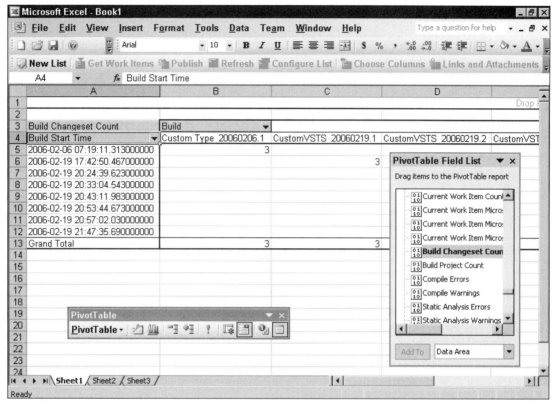

Figure 19-30

Of course, you don't need to write low-level XML to create reports. Team System comes with a variety of tools, including the Report Builder, the Report Designer, the Business Intelligence Development Studio (BIDS), and even Microsoft Excel. The Report Designer and the Business Intelligence Development Studio are add-ins for Visual Studio 2005. Once you have created your custom reports, they can easily be bundled with your process template to be redeployed whenever you want to create a new project. Chapter 22 has useful information about how to incorporate reports as documents (also known as *work products*) within a process template.

Creating custom reports using the Report Builder

Report Builder is a ClickOnce application that is integrated in SQL Reporting Services. It's designed for business analysts and developers who wish to create custom reports quickly and easily. You can launch it by clicking the Report Builder option on the Report Manager menu bar. (You can bring up the Report Manager by right-clicking a project Reports folder in Team Explorer and selecting Show Report Site.)

Before you can access Team System data, you'll have to create a Semantic Model Definition Language (SMDL) model. As complicated as that sounds, creating the model is actually a simple process:

1. Go to the Home page of SQL Reporting Services. (The URL is `http://<your application tier>/Reports/`.)

2. Click the TfsReportDS data source link.

3. At the bottom of the next page, you will see a button that says Generate Model. Click the button.

4. You'll then be prompted for a Name, Description, and Location. Name the model "TfsReportDS".

5. Once you are finished, you are ready to start building a report. Launch the Report Builder by clicking the link from the front page of the Report Manager site. (You can access the Report Manager by right-clicking your Team Project reports folder in Team Explorer.)

6. Once the application launches, you can choose whether your report is a matrix, chart, or columnar table. Select the "TfsReportDS" model and select your report type; then click OK.

7. A report template will appear with an area where you can drag and drop data fields onto it. To create a build report, click the Build entity and select the fields you want to appear on the report. You can also drag and drop entities. (*Entities* are a logical collection of fields and other data type.) You can then save your report by selecting File ⇨ Save. Once you click Save, you'll have the option of placing your report in any Team Project you want.

You can mix and match the entities and fields to get unique views of your project data — for example, mixing your build data with changeset data.

Viewing and running your custom reports

There are many different ways you can access and view reports in Team System. You can use Team Explorer or the Team Project report site, or use Microsoft Excel templates or pivot tables. Here are the steps you follow to view the report in Visual Studio using the Team Explorer:

1. Go to the Team Explorer pane.

2. Select *YourProjectName* ⇨ Reports.

3. Right-click on any project you want.

4. Select the Open option. The report will open in Visual Studio.

You can also access reports via the Team Project report site. Here are the steps to access and launch the reports in a web browser:

1. Go to the Team Explorer pane.

2. Right-click on Reports within one of your projects.

3. Select Show Report Site.

Alternatively, you can access the report site by clicking Team ⇨ Show Report Site (note that you have to be connected to your Team Foundation Server for this to work). To learn more about creating reports and fully leveraging the reporting features of SQL Server 2005 Reporting Services, please visit the SQL Server Developer Centre at the following link: http://msdn.microsoft.com/SQL/sqlwarehouse/ReportingServices/default.aspx.

Report site security

The SharePoint project portal and the Team Reporting sites have to be configured separately from the rest of Team Foundation Server. As with Team Foundation Server, you can simply add server groups to the report site to provide easy administration. Or you can opt to add individual users to provide a higher level of granularity in your security approach per report.

You can access the security setting for your site by first opening up the reports site. Right-click on Reports in Team Explorer and select View Report Site. Once the Report Site appears, click on the Site Settings link on the upper-right corner of the page. At the bottom of the new page, you will have the option of configuring site-wide security, configuring item-level role definitions, and configuring system-level role definitions (as shown in Figure 19-31).

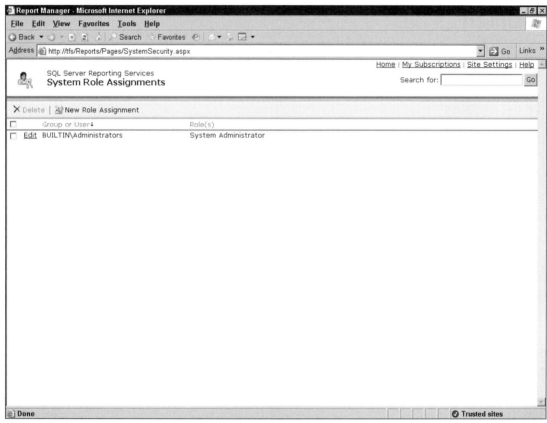

Figure 19-31

Summary

So far, you have learned how to create a Team Project using the New Team Project Wizard, setting up the architecture and configuring various aspects of the project, including the security roles and the source control repository. You also learned about work item tracking. You found out how work items are configured, how to assign and manage them within a project, and the steps for designing your own work item types. The last bit we covered was Team Reporting, including how to access project metrics, analyze trends, and create your own reports.

One of the important features of Team System for your developers and testers is the source control repository. In the next chapter, you'll examine how to leverage Team Foundation Source Control to effectively manage and administer code within an enterprise development environment.

20

Team Foundation Version Control

If you are a developer or a tester, you are basically living in source code. When you have more than one person working on a project, versioning becomes an issue. If two developers work on the same assembly, how do you merge their code together? How do you prevent accidentally over-writing files? Incredibly, many of the organizations I've consulted for still use file shares to store source code. I've seen others push Microsoft Visual SourceSafe to the limit with 150 active users or more. Others use third-party solutions or open source solutions that integrate poorly with Visual Studio.

One of the key features of Team Foundation Server is its version control management system (formerly code-named "Hatteras"). It includes a number of features, including the capability to branch, merge, and shelve your source code, atomic check-ins, policies, security — all the features you would expect from an enterprise version control solution. The core engine for this tool is Microsoft SQL Server 2005. As such, the performance of Team Foundation version control will greatly depend on your server's hardware and the size of your SQL Server 2005 database.

> You'll notice that the title of the feature is Team Foundation version control. However, when you start using the feature, a lot of the tools and windows will say "source control" such as the "Source Control Explorer." The version control title is there to indicate to you that the product can handle much more than source code. You can upload manual tests, work products, build files — anything you want, really.

Once you install Team Explorer alongside Visual Studio 2005, you will get access to a nicely inte-grated Source Control Explorer. You can also manipulate the source control system using the Team Foundation command-line client called tf.exe. In this chapter, you will learn how to effectively use both tools.

> The version control system is named after the Cape Hatteras Lighthouse on Hatteras Island, situated on the Outer Banks of North Carolina. The lighthouse has the reputation of being one of the tallest in North America. Hatteras is near Ocracoke Island, which coincidentally happens to be the code name for the Team System Web Testing Tools.

In this chapter, you will learn about features such as branching and merging, how to check in and check out code, setting check-in policies, and temporarily shelving your code for easy access at a later date. The Team Foundation version control system also supports a number of other features, such as atomic check-ins, workplaces, and changesets. Using Team Foundation proxy server, you can also scale out your source control system to distributed teams.

One of the common misconceptions about Team Foundation Source Control is that it is a new version of Microsoft Visual SourceSafe. This is completely untrue — Team Foundation Source Control has been written from scratch just for Team System; and unlike SourceSafe, it has been designed to scale well to a large number of developers (more than 2000). They are completely different products.

Comparing Team Foundation Source Control and Visual SourceSafe (VSS) 2005

One of the key reasons for examining both products is to determine which one is the most appropriate for your environment. In most cases, your best bet is to move over to Team Foundation version control because you can also pick up the integration with the rest of Team System. In other words, you can now run automated tests on your code, build the source using Team Foundation Build, create work items to monitor bugs, receive automated alerts, apply check-in policies, apply a very granular level of security and generate detailed reports on everything from code churn, bug rates, and build results. Team Foundation version control is part of a greater Software Configuration Management (SCM) solution. Unlike Visual SourceSafe, Team Foundation version control is designed to scale to large development teams and can support distributed and outsourced teams in remote locations. Plus you will avoid problems such as the occasional corruption of your source code files (since the data is written to a database rather than flat files).

Microsoft Visual SourceSafe 2005 retains a role for smaller development teams. It has a few enhancements such as HTTP support, a better lock-contention mechanism, better performance over a network, and internalization support. Visual SourceSafe 2005 is available for a fee and is bundled in select versions of Visual Studio 2005.

As a rule of thumb, if you need Team System to manage your development projects, you should seriously consider migrating your code to Team Foundation version control. Let's quickly compare the features of both products in Table 20-1.

Table 20-1

Team Foundation Version Control	Visual SourceSafe (VSS) 2005
Supports up to 2000+ concurrent users	Supports a small number of users
Has no support for Sharing and Pinning. It will replace a pin with a label during the migration process.	Supports Sharing and Pinning
Supports Atomic and Transactional check-ins. Nothing is committed to the repository until the transfer has been completed successfully.	No rollback capabilities. File integrity can be compromised if there are connectivity issues.
Server-based source repository. Your source code is stored in SQL Server 2005 and accessed by Team Foundation Server via XML Web Services.	Encrypted file-based source repository, usually stored on a network
Project and feature security is tied directly to Windows user accounts and security can be set on a more granular level for different features of Team Foundation Server.	Rights are separate from Windows permissions. All SourceSafe users have access to the shared folder and source code.
Considerably faster than Visual SourceSafe	Speed limited by file access constraints and network latency
Access rights controlled using Windows user accounts and NTLM authentication. Team Foundation version control also supports Basic Authentication, which is useful when providing HTTPS access over the Internet.	Access rights set within VSS and Windows file sharing
Creates changesets, which bundle your source code, comments, and other data for easy future access	Does not support changesets
Supports Team System–specific features such as work items, Team Build, etc.	Does not support work items and does not integrate directly with the Team Build system
Supports check-in policies, auditing, and locking	Does not support check-in policies, auditing, or locking

Microsoft has developed a migration tool called `VSSConverter` to enable you to migrate your Visual SourceSafe code to Team System. The migration can be broken into two phases: In the first phase, you analyze the VSS database, and in second phase, you do the actual migration from the VSS database to Team Foundation version control.

The first phase, or the *analysis phase*, is going to generate some reports for you, indicating the potential data loss that may occur during the migration. Using these reports, you should be able to configure some of the migration options to minimize this loss. Be aware, however, that some data loss is unavoidable. This is due to some aspects of the VSS data not being mapped into Team Foundation.

Once you are satisfied with the results from the first phase, you can proceed with the *actual migration*. Once the migration is complete, you will again receive a report, detailing any errors or warnings encountered during the migration.

While a detailed walkthrough of the conversion process is outside the scope of this book, we will present a high-level overview, as well as refer you to where you can obtain more detailed information. The following paragraphs describe the general process for migrating from VSS to Team Foundation version control.

First, you need to install VSS on the machine on which you will be doing the conversion. Remember, the VSS database that you will be migrating to must be version 6.0. If it is an older version, please use the DDUPD utility (at `http://msdn.microsoft.com/library/en-us/guides/html/vstskupgradingvisualsourcesafe.asp`) to upgrade the database. Make sure that you install VSS 2005 on the conversion machine as well. To decrease the migration time, it is recommended that you copy the VSS database to a local directory on the conversion machine. Also, running the `Analyze.exe` application (at `http://msdn.microsoft.com/library/en-us/guides/html/vsgrfss_analyze.asp`) can help you find and fix any integrity and corruption issues before you begin the analysis and migration of the database.

The `VSSConverter` application uses SQL Express in the migration process. SQL Express needs to be installed on the conversion machine, before the analysis and migration are started. Make sure that you have administrator rights on SQL Express before you continue. Also, make sure that you install Team Explorer on the conversion machine. The VSS converter application is part of the client portion of Team Explorer. Before you start the migration, make sure that you are a member of the Team Foundation Administrator group on the Team Foundation Server.

At this point, you are ready to run your analysis. Remember, the migration process is going to be time consuming, depending on the amount of data involved. One recommendation is to migrate sources one project at a time, which will typically be one folder. Once you know which folders to migrate, you will create the settings file. This is an XML file containing all the options for the migration. Once this file is ready, you run the VSS Converter application to begin your analysis. For more detailed information on the analysis phase, please refer to the MSDN Library: Preparing To Migrate From Visual SourceSafe to Team Foundation (`http://msdn2.microsoft.com/en-us/library/ms181246`).

After the analysis is finished, a report file is generated. This file indicates some of the conversion issues that will occur during the migration. Here is a brief list:

❑ Sharing isn't supported in Team Foundation version control. As a result, a copy of the file(s) will be made to the destination folder from the point in time the file(s) were shared.

❑ As branches in VSS require sharing, the file(s) will be copied, and any changes in a branch will also be copied over to the corresponding branch in Team Foundation version control.

❑ Pinning isn't supported in Team Foundation version control. In the migration process, the converter will add "PINNED" in the label of your pinned files.

❑ The check-in dates in Team Foundation version control won't match the check-in dates for Visual SourceSafe. The original SourceSafe timestamp is typically appended in the comments.

The analysis phase will also generate a user map file. This file shows all the users who have performed any sort of operation on the folders that were analyzed. This file is also used to map Visual Studio users to Team Foundation users. (Take note that this step is optional.)

Before you can move over the source code, you must create a Team Project that matches the name of your VSS repository. The VSS files will subsequently be moved over to the corresponding branch on Team Foundation version control.

Finally, you are ready to perform the actual migration. Before you begin, make sure that you have identified the destination folders in Team Foundation version control for each folder in VSS. If the destination folder already exists, it must be empty. If the destination folder does not exist, the VSS Converter application will create it automatically. Next, you need to make modifications to the settings file (for example, map the VSS users with the Team Foundation server users) to prepare it for migration. At this point, you are ready to run the VSS Converter application, and migrate the database. For more detailed information on the migration phase, please refer to the MSDN Library: Migrating From Visual SourceSafe to Team Foundation (`http://msdn2.microsoft.com/en-us/library/ms181247`).

Once the VSS Converter application is finished, you need to review the report file to see what errors and warnings occurred during the migration. You will also need to change the source control bindings of the solution files from VSS to Team Foundation. (See `http://blogs.msdn.com/akashmaheshwari/` for more information.)

If you work in both Visual SourceSafe and Team Foundation Source Control, you can select what version control system you want to use. Visual Studio 2005 has a plug-in selection option that can be accessed by clicking Tools ➪ Options and then Source Control ➪ Plug-In Selection. The default plug-in is Visual Studio Team Foundation Server. (Team System supports an extensible plug-in architecture.) You also have the option of connecting to another source control application such as Microsoft SourceSafe 2005. Figure 20-1 illustrates the Source Control ➪ Plug-in Selection Window.

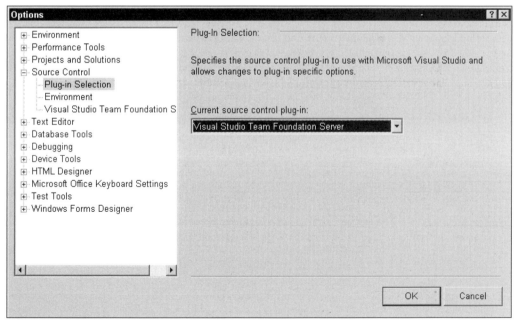

Figure 20-1

Source code migration

Visual Studio 2005 and Team Foundation Build are primarily designed to support software written using the .NET Framework 2.0. Team Foundation version control supports any programming language, format, and file type. (In essence, if you can save it to disk it can be stored in the repository.) An interesting challenge comes up if you are storing source code using the .NET Framework 1.0, 1.1, Visual Studio 6.0 (or even on other platforms). Team Foundation version control is naturally designed to integrate with Team Foundation Build. Since Team Foundation Build builds .NET 2.0 code by default, you may need to customize your build scripts and use alternative tools to manage your source code. Table 20-2 is a matrix covering the common scenarios you may encounter.

Table 20-2

Scenario	Action
You have VB 6.0 or VC++ 6.0 you would like to import into Team Foundation version control	You can choose to run Visual Studio 6.0 side-by-side with Visual Studio 2005. You can then import Visual Studio 6.0 projects into Team Foundation version control using the command-line tool or the MicroSoft Source Code Control Interface (MSSCCI) client. For more information, visit http://msdn.blogs.com/bharry/archive/2006/02/21/535985.aspx.
	You can quite easily add any files by Visual Studio 6.0 to the repository by creating a workspace and using the Add File. The problem occurs when you try to check out the files — Visual Studio 2005 will "assume" that you want to upgrade and then will launch the Upgrade Wizard.
	Another option is converting your code from VB or VC++ 6.0 to the .NET Framework 2.0. For example, if you attempt to open a VB 6.0 project in Visual Studio 2005, the Upgrade Wizard will appear. There is also a lot of migration documentation on the MSDN website: http://msdn2.microsoft.com/en-us/library/.
You would like to import and build .NET 1.0 or 1.1 code in Team System	In most cases, attempting to open and save a .NET 1.0 or 1.1 solution in Visual Studio 2005 will result in a solution that will no longer open in Visual Studio 2002 or 2003. The reason is that Visual Studio 2005 only supports the .NET Framework 2.0.
	So what are your options? You can install Visual Studio 2002/2003 and Visual Studio 2005 side-by-side. By opening your older solutions in the older versions of Visual Studio, you will avoid any migration issues.
	To download the MSSCCI plug-in to connect Visual Studio 2002/2003 with Team Foundation version control, please refer to the following link: http://go.microsoft.com/fwlink/?LinkId=58454.
	Another option is upgrading your application to the .NET Framework 2.0. This is facilitated by the built-in Upgrade Wizard. The downside is that you will have to deal with migration issues; however, the upside is that you will be able to import and export your source code using Team Explorer.

Scenario	Action
	There are two tools available to build .NET 1.1 within Team Foundation Build. The first tool is called MSBuild Toolkit and is available on the following website: `http://downloads.interscapeusa.com/MSBuildToolkit_v2_RC.msi`. The second tool is called MSBee - MSBuild Everett Environment. It is being developed by Microsoft — more information is available on the following site: `http://blogs.msdn.com/clichten/`.
You would like to migrate ASP.NET 1.0 or 1.1 code	The Upgrade Wizard will help you migrate your application to ASP.NET 2.0. By experience, the easiest way to migrate 1.0 Web services is to recreate them in 2.0 and copy and paste your source code. Keep in mind that launching ASP.NET 2.0 websites will automatically launch the local Cassini Web Developer server by default. You should configure the virtual directory in your IIS server to host your application and set Visual Studio to launch without Cassini if you are developing web applications alongside Web services. ASP 3.0 applications are compatible but will not compile under Team Foundation Build.
You would like to import source code from another platform (such as Java code) into Team Foundation version control	There may be circumstances where you will be need to deploy Team System in a mixed development environment. For example, half the company may be using PowerBuilder, the other half .NET. Team Foundation version control is quite versatile and can store different file types including projects on other platforms (such as Java projects). Obviously, code from other platforms will not integrate as nicely with the testing tools and the build engine. However, it is possible to launch remote builds using the Windows Task Scheduler, programmatically hooking it into the Team Foundation Eventing Service — you have a lot of possibilities at your disposal. Teamprise (at `www.teamprise.com`) has developed a plug-in to enable Windows, Mac, and Linux to integrate with Team Foundation version control and Team Foundation's work item tracking system. Teamplain (at `www.devbiz.com/teamplain/`) also a web-based application that enables you to manipulate the work item database. (In fact, it provides access to any part of Team Foundation Server accessible to Team Explorer including the build system and work items.) This web application will work on any platform, including the Mac OS and Unix-based systems.

Setting Up Version Control

Assuming you've never used a source control system, where do you start? Even if you have used other version control systems, how to do you effectively set up and use Team Foundation version control? We will walk you through the process step-by-step.

When you start up a new Team Project (by clicking on File ➪ New ➪ New Team Project—you have to be connected to a Team Foundation Server for this option to show up), you will be provided a series of options. You'll get three source control options to set up a new parent folder (as shown in Figure 20-2).

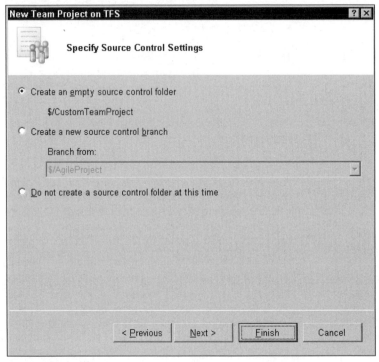

Figure 20-2

In this window, you have the following three options:

- ❑ You can create a brand-new parent source control folder (based on the name of your project).

- ❑ You can create a branch based on a pre-existing project. This option is especially compelling if you want to create another version of an existing application or implement a new process to develop an existing application.

- ❑ You can also skip the source control folder creation process. Note that it isn't possible to create root level folders other than by creating Team Projects. Interestingly enough, you can't get rid of a root level folder without deleting a Team Project also.

Setting up security roles

Before you can start using the version control feature, you should determine who on your team will take on the responsibility of Administrator. The rest of the individuals on your team will be typically classified as Contributors. Keep in mind that the way you organize your roles should be determined by a matter of convenience and organizational requirements. For example, if you are in a small team, you might want to make everyone an administrator to maintain as much flexibility as possible. The roles and responsibilities shown in the following list are a configuration appropriate for a large organization:

- ❑ **Administrator:** The administrator is responsible for setting up version control permissions for each contributor (either directly or through the IT staff). He (or she) also sets the security and policies around your code check-in and co-ordinates with the build team.

- ❑ **Development or Test Lead:** The lead could be granted certain additional permissions above a contributor, but still less than an administrator.

- ❑ **Contributor:** The contributor's role is as an end user, to check-in and check-out code, shelve and create changesets. Typically, you would assign this role to a tester or developer.

Setting up your workspace

Think of a workspace as simply your personal local folder to work on source code. A workspace is associated to a folder in Team Foundation version control. Whenever you check-out code, the code from the repository is placed in your workspace and vice-versa. The core advantage is isolation—workspaces allow you to work on an application without affecting any changes the rest of your team might be making.

There are two primary restrictions in setting up your workspaces. You can't map two local folders to one folder in the repository. Likewise, you can't map two repository folders to a single local folder. As a rule of thumb, stick to one local folder mapped to a single folder in the version control system.

To set up a new workspace, click on File ⇨ Source Control ⇨ Workspaces. You'll get the Manage Workspaces window (as shown in Figure 20-3).

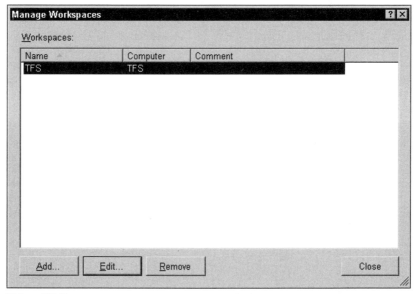

Figure 20-3

The next step involves adding a new workspace. Note that within each workspace, you can create several one-to-one mappings between local folders and repository folders. Clicking the Add button on this window opens the Add Workspace window, as shown in Figure 20-4.

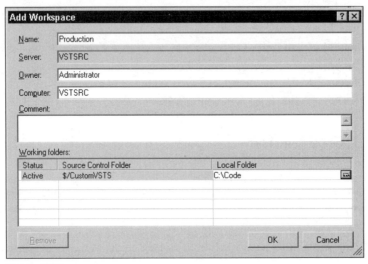

Figure 20-4

In the preceding example, the Code folder on your local C: drive will synchronize with the CustomVSTS folder in Team Foundation version control.

Notice that you have a Status field next to the Source Control Folder path. There are two statuses that can be set — Active and Cloaked. When you cloak a folder, you exclude it from certain synchronization tasks (such as add, get, and others). Note that cloaking is not an alternative to deleting a workspace. It's a way to cut down on the amount of disk space used as well as bandwidth for files that you don't have an interest in or need for. It will also provide better performance because only Active mappings are synchronized.

Using the Source Control Explorer

The Source Control Explorer is similar to other explorers in Visual Studio. It enables you to browse and manage entire projects and individual folders in the repository. You can add and delete files; check in, check out, and view any of your pending changes; and view the status your local code compared to the code in Team Foundation version control. Think of it as your master control area for all tasks related to source code management. Some of the important tasks it will allow you to do include:

❑   **Creating Shelvesets.** A shelveset is a collection of changes stored in a "shelf," or area, to temporarily store your source code without committing it to the repository.

❑   **Locking and unlocking files and folders.**

❑   **Resolving conflicts.**

❑ **Branching and Merging.**

❑ **Viewing Historical Data.**

❑ **Labeling your files and folders.**

We will cover many of these topics later in the chapter. To access the Source Code Explorer, simply click View ➪ Other Windows ➪ Source Control Explorer.

Another way you can open your source code is by clicking File ➪ Source Control ➪ Open from Source Control. Visual Studio will then prompt you to connect to the Team Foundation Server and select the source code repository of your choice if you are not connected.

The Source Control Explorer interface is pictured in Figure 20-5. It is divided into three main areas: the source tree view on the left (which enables you to navigate and select source files from your project), the details view on the right, and the Source Location bar. The Workspace drop-down list enables you to easily jump from one workspace to another. You will examine workspaces in more detail in the next section.

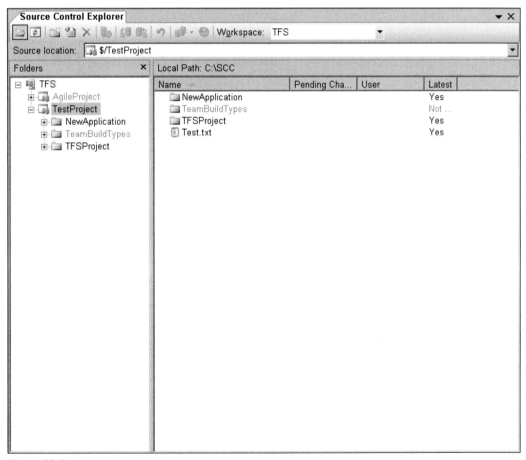

Figure 20-5

Workspaces

When you create a project or solution, you can automatically add it to Source Control (as shown in Figure 20-6). Please note that a workspace is created *only* if you don't already have one. Think of the workspace as your local copy of the source files and folders contained on the server. It enables you to work on an application without affecting any changes the rest of your team might be making.

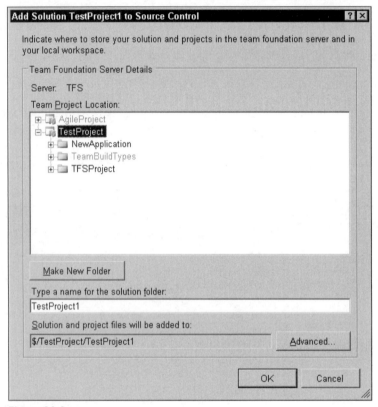

Figure 20-6

Each of the changes you make to these files will be pending until you check them in or undo them. Once they are checked into the repository, they will be committed into the main repository.

You can manipulate your workspace using the Team Foundation command-line tool. You can also manipulate it from the GUI by selecting File ➪ Source Control ➪ Workspaces. For example, to create a new workspace, simply type the following command:

```
> tf.exe workspace /new MobileExplorerProject
```

In the preceding example, a new workspace is created called MobileExplorerProject. Anyone can create his own workspaces, but you must be logged in as an administrator to create and assign workspaces for other people. Table 20-3 describes common workspace options.

Table 20-3

Workspace Options	Description
/comment	Tag a workspace with a comment.
/computer	Specify the target computer for the workspace.
/delete	Delete a workspace.
/new	Create a new workspace.
/newname	Rename an existing workspace.
/noprompt	Execute workspace commands without prompts.
/template	Specify a workspace to be used as a template to create brand-new workspaces.

The workspaces (plural) command provides you with a holistic view of the workspaces on your Team Foundation Server. Note that the workspaces command will update the local cache file. It will cause the server to update its user cache when /updateUserName is used. The /updateComputerName option will change the computer name that is associated with the workspace on the server.

Table 20-4

Workspaces Options	Description
/computer	Indicate what workspaces you want to view or manipulate from the repository, filtered by computer name.
/format	Specify the format in which you would like to see the reports. You have two possible values at your disposal: Brief or Detailed. The default value is Brief.
/owner	Specify the creator of the workspace.
/s	Specify the name of the Team Foundation Server.
/updateComputerName	Instruct Team Foundation Server to refresh because the client computer has changed name. It is typically written out as /updateComputerName:oldComputerName. The oldComputer-Name is the name that the computer had previously.
/updateUserName	Instruct Team Foundation Server to refresh because one (or more) network users have changed names.

In addition to the command line, you can also use Visual Studio to manage your workspaces. Figure 20-7 shows the Manage Workspaces window. You can access this window by clicking File ⇨ Source Control ⇨ Workspaces.

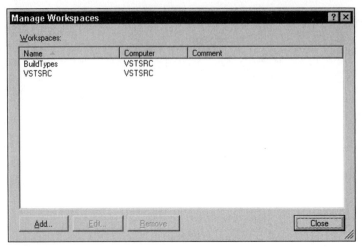

Figure 20-7

Adding Projects to the Source Repository

Once you have created workspaces, you can import the associated source files into the repository. The process of putting code in Team Foundation Server is called *checking in*. (You'll learn more about the check-in/check-out process in the next section.) To open the Add to Source Control window, simply right-click your solution in the Solution Explorer and select Add Solution to Source Control.

First, select which Team Foundation Server project, workspace, and folders will end up in the repository. The combination of these elements makes up the solution. Click the Advanced button to invoke a window in which you can specify the project locations, as shown in Figure 20-8.

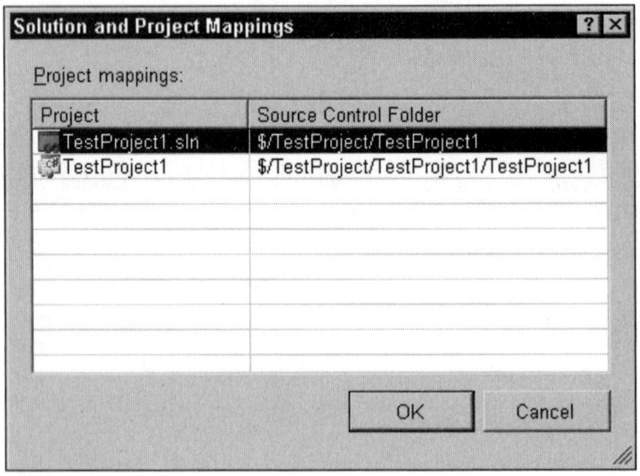

Figure 20-8

In the next section, you will learn how to effectively check in and check out code from the source repository. You also find out about changesets and how to configure team check-in policies.

Check-in and Check-out

Daily check-ins and check-outs are an essential part of a developer's workflow. *Checking out* simply means that you are operating with the files you already have in your personal workspace. *Checking in* refers to items that are re-inserted into the repository. The source code is represented as a tree structure, with branches and other logical elements.

> **Unlike Visual SourceSafe, Team Foundation version control does not necessarily retrieve files from the source repository. This is an important point to consider.**

Checking in an item

A *changeset* contains all of the information related to a check-in, such as work item links, revisions, notes, policies, and owner and date/time details. Team Foundation Source Control bundles all of the information together into this container. A changeset is created once you check code into the repository, and as a container it reflects only the changes you checked in at a particular date and time. You can also view it as the state of the repository at a particular time and date. The usefulness of a changeset comes from the fact that you can, on a very atomic level, return to any point in time and troubleshoot your code.

> *Team Foundation Server contains four types of artifacts: work items, changesets, source code files, and builds. For example, you can associate a work item to a source code file. You can also link builds to work items if you wish. This is a really powerful concept — imagine that you are having trouble with a build. You can automatically call up the changeset with the problem code. You can also generate a work item to get a developer to fix the problem. The integration possibilities are endless.*

All developers forget to check-in their code at one point or another. You can implement automatic check-ins by changing the environment settings in your project. Specifically, you can check an option called Check-in Everything When Closing a Solution or Project.

The Pending Changes window enables you to view all of the checked-out files in your project. After your solution has been added to version control, the window shown in Figure 20-9 will appear on the bottom half of the screen.

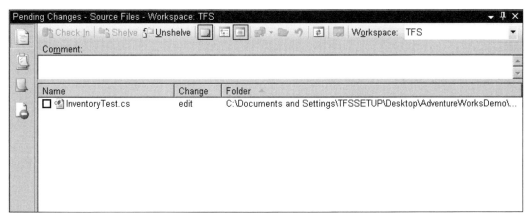

Figure 20-9

Checking out an item

Checking out an item means that you are working with your local repository for the purpose of editing or manipulating it. There are several ways you can check out an item within Visual Studio 2005. Items that are checked in are represented in the Solution Explorer with small padlocks at the left of the program icon, as shown in Figure 20-10.

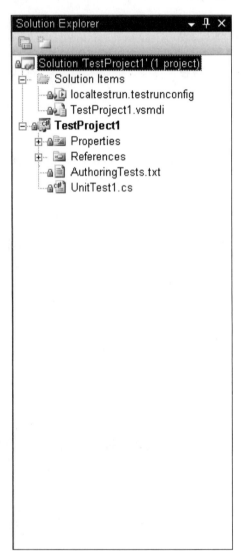

Figure 20-10

As soon as you select files and click the Check Out button, the Solution Explorer replaces the blue lock icon with a checkmark icon. This visually confirms that all the files have been checked out. There are three lock options you can configure:

❑ **Check-In:** This option allows other users to check out the files, but they can't check them in.

❑ **Check-Out:** This option prevents other users from checking in/out the corresponding source files.

❑ **None:** This option allows other users to pend changes to the source files.

Creating and administering check-in policies

Check-in policies enable project managers and development leads to control the source management process within a team. Three types of policies are available by default in Team System: Code Analysis, Testing Policy, and Work Items.

To configure your check-in policies, right-click on your Team Foundation project and select Team Project Settings ➪ Source Control. Under the Check-in Policy tab (see Figure 20-11), there are several options for modifying the check-in policy.

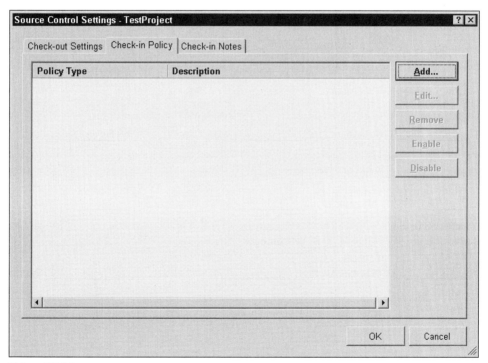

Figure 20-11

If you click the Add button in the Source Control Settings dialog box (refer to Figure 20-11), you will be prompted to select a check-in policy type. Select one of the three options (shown in Figure 20-12) and click the OK button. The default policy types included in Team Foundation Source Control are as follows:

❑ **Code Analysis.** This option will add a static code analysis quality check before source code can be inserted into the code repository. The code analysis check will be dependent on the project level settings. For example, if you selected code analysis for C/C++ in your project, the engine will automatically use that test as a "quality gate" or quality assurance before code is reintroduced into the source.

❑ **Testing Policy.** You can apply testing policies to check the correctness of your code before it is checked in. For example, you may want to require Unit Testing to verify the default values in your application. For more information about testing policies, please refer to the testing chapters in the book.

❑ **Work Items.** You may want to require that a work item needs to be associated to every check-in. That way, changes can be documented, which will make it easier to track any problems.

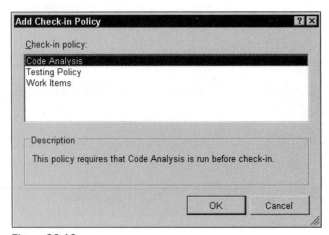

Figure 20-12

Once the check-in policy has been created, try checking in code without complying with the new policies. The Policy Failure window, shown in Figure 20-13, will appear. At this point, you will have the option to override the policy requirement and comment on the failure.

If you click on the Cancel button, the Pending Changes – Policy Warnings window will appear (with a detailed explanation of each warning, as shown in Figure 20-14).

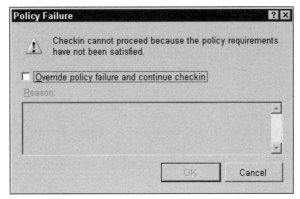

Figure 20-13

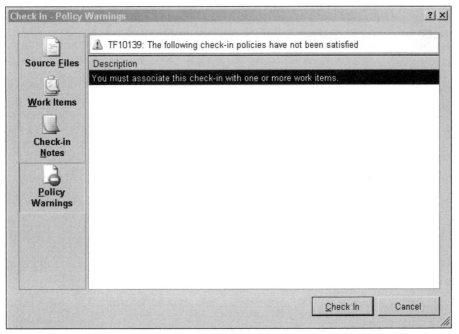

Figure 20-14

Branching and Merging

Branching and Merging are two important functions of any source control system. During the process of building a piece of software, you may find the need to release a stable version for Beta testing, or you may want to work in parallel on bug fixes without interrupting the main process of development process. In order to better manage this process, you can create many development versions of the same code base (called branching) and re-integrate them into the Main tree (merging). You might have heard of the terms Forward Integration and Reverse Integration. Here is what they mean in the context of branching and merging. Forward integration is the process of merging changes from the main development line into a branch. Reverse integration is the complete opposite — you integrate or merge the changes in your branches back down to the Main branch. Figure 20-15 shows a few common scenarios you might encounter where you would need branching and merging.

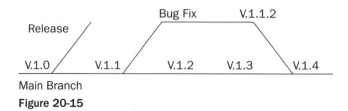

Figure 20-15

A branch was created from version 1.0 of the application to create a release or preview version for customers or beta testers. In version 1.1, a critical bug was found and a separate branch was created with incremental fixes. The fixes were completed in version 1.1.1.2 and reintegrated into version 1.4 of the main branch.

Branching

Branching enables you to create copies of your source files, but also maintains a history of your changes in case you want to do a merge in the future. You can use the Source Control Explorer to navigate between different branches. To create a branch, simply right-click your solution in the Source Control Explorer and select Branch from the context menu — the dialog box shown in Figure 20-16 will appear on-screen.

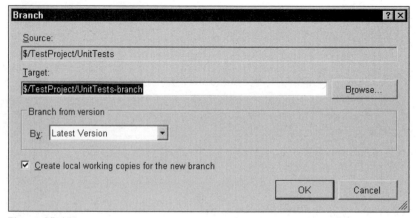

Figure 20-16

The main branch dialog box has several options: The Target field enables you to set the name of your branch. The Branch From version option enables you to select which version of the branch you would like to use (the latest version or an older version). You can opt to create a local copy of a branch by selecting the Create Local Working Copies for the New Branch option. It will download the newly created branch files to your workspace.

Everyone has his or her own way of organizing source code. One of the popular models is the development/main/release model, as shown in Figure 20-17.

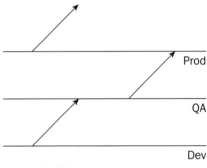

Prod

QA

Dev

Figure 20-17

As you can see in the figure, development, main and release is running in parallel. Once work is stabilized in development, it is integrated into the main branch. As code moves up to the release branch, its quality increases to the point it can be released publically.

Merging

Merging means to combine changes from two or more branches. This functionality is very useful for teams of developers working in parallel. During a merge, many changes are integrated, including add/edit/delete operations. If there are merge conflicts between branches, you can resolve them in a variety of ways, including the use of a diff-merge tool. There are two ways you can merge files: using the Source Control Explorer and via the command line. You can also specify whether you want to incorporate all the changes or just specific versions.

When you merge, Team Foundation version control will use the history behind the scenes to try to branch files and folders that have been added to another branch. Changes that don't exist in the target branch will be merged. If any of the files or folders have been changed in the target branch, a merge conflict will occur.

You can access the Merge Wizard by right-clicking the folder (in the Source Control Explorer) that you want to merge. If you click the Merge option on the pop-up menu, you will be presented with the Source Control Merge Wizard, as shown in Figure 20-18.

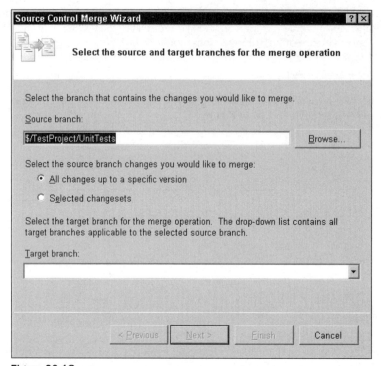

Figure 20-18

The Version Control Merge Wizard will present you with a preset list of target branches you can merge to and give you the option to commit all changes in the source branch or only selected changes. Once you click the Next button, you will be presented with the option to select the changes you want to merge, as shown in Figure 20-19.

Once all of the options have been set, all you need is to click the Finish button to execute the merge process.

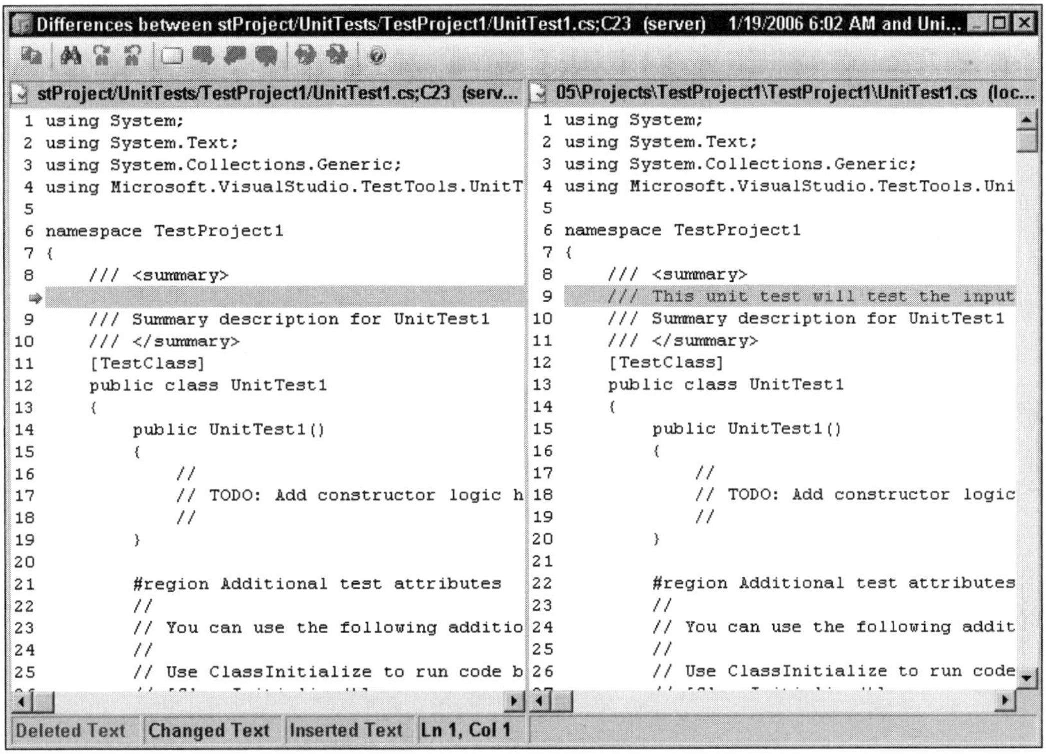

Figure 20-19

Shelving

There are times when you won't be ready to commit your source code into the core repository. For example, say that you are working on solving a bug and you haven't completed the task by the end of the workday. Shelving enables you to store files and code aside on a temporary basis. The collections of stored pending changes that haven't been committed to the server are called *shelvesets*.

> The security settings for a shelveset are determined by the item permissions. You must have read and pending change permission for the item changes you wish to unshelve.

The process of creating a shelveset is fast and easy. To begin, access the Pending Checkin window by clicking View ➪ Other Windows ➪ Pending Changes, as shown in Figure 20-20. Check the item you want to shelve and click the Shelve button.

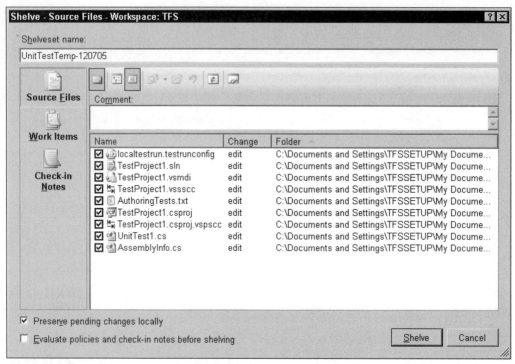

Figure 20-20

The Shelve dialog box will appear with the files you have selected. (Be sure to give it a descriptive name to differentiate it from the other shelvesets.) You now have the option of unchecking the items, preserving pending changes locally, or clicking the Shelve button. You also have the option of evaluating policies and check-in notes before shelving. Shelvesets contain the same level of information as a changeset, including associated work items, comments, and check-in notes. Keep in mind that, unlike with a changeset, the changes are not versioned. Shelvesets can be permanently deleted (which is something you can't do with changesets). You can't link directly to a shelveset from a work item and policies can't be enforced on shelving.

When would you want to use this feature? There are a few scenarios: Say that a project manager asks you to drop what you are doing and work on a bug fix. Your current work can be set aside temporarily. Say that you have code that isn't quite ready to be checked in but needs a code review. You can shelve your pending changes to allow other team members to work with it. Shelving is also useful as a backup mechanism and is used as a way to reassign unfinished code to another team member.

Shelvesets are available to individual users and to administrators. That means if you fall off the planet, the administrator will be able to take your work and reassign it to another developer, thus assuring business continuity. Any user can also create as many shelvesets as the user wants.

Unshelving source files is as easy as shelving. First, bring up the Pending Changes window (as shown at the beginning of this section) and click the Unshelve button. The Unshelve window will appear with the option to select an owner and the name of a shelveset (see Figure 20-21). You also have the option of deleting shelvesets or reading more details.

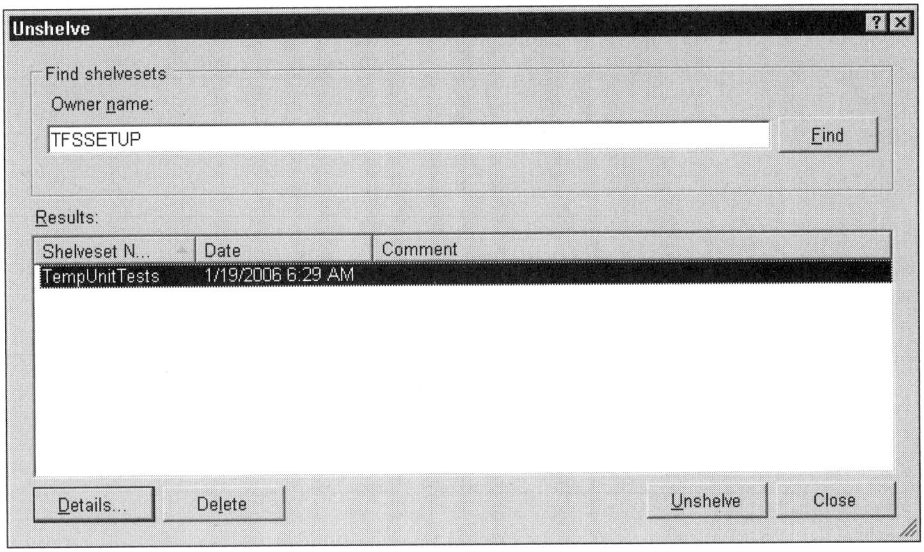

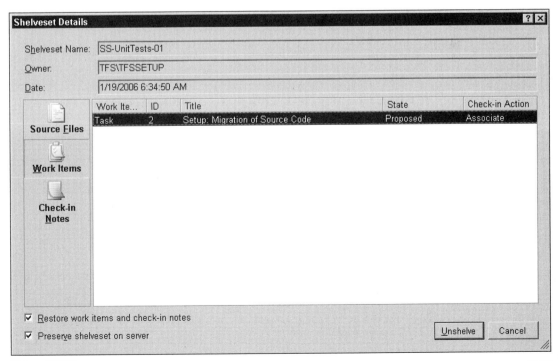

Figure 20-21

Once you select a shelveset, you then have the option of preserving the shelveset on the server. You can also choose whether you want to restore the work items and check-in notes (see Figure 20-22). When you unshelve your code, all the pending check-in information is also restored. If you made any changes to your workspace (for example, renamed or moved a folder in your workspace), the unshelved folder will also be renamed and moved. Shelved files that are marked for deletion are deleted in the workspace.

Figure 20-22

Command-line Tools

You can manipulate any part of the version control system using the Team Foundation command-line tool. The tool itself is called `tf.exe` (short for Team Foundation). For example, to create a new workspace, simply type the following command:

```
> tf.exe workspace /new MobileExplorerProject
```

In the preceding example, a new workspace is created, called `MobileExplorerProject`. You can exercise a great deal of control over the source control system using the tool. For example, you can manipulate workspaces and workfolders, permissions, changesets, labels, and much more.

You can also use the command-line tool to monitor how long files have been checked out. To get a report about the changes in your workspace, simply type the following:

```
> tf.exe status /server:YourTFSServerName /format:detailed
```

The Team Foundation version control command-line tool will enable you to perform operations that you can't perform using the Source Control Explorer. One such operation is the baseless merge (`merge` command). A baseless merge enables you to relate and merge two version control branches (when they aren't directly branched).

If you want to bundle several commands together, you can use a command file. A command file is a text file with the `.tfc` extension (similar in concept as a DOS batch file). You can insert remarks (`rem`) and use commands such as cd (to change directories) and `exit` (to escape the command file — you can also use `quit`).

> Note that the special `rem`, cd, and `quit` commands are supported only within command files. They aren't supported in other version control operations.

Here is the source code for `CheckoutCode.tfc`:

```
get %1
checkout %1
get %2
checkout %2
rem manipulate the code as you wish
checkin
```

You can execute the command file by using the following syntax:

```
> tf.exe @CheckoutCode.tfc source1.cs source2.cs
```

In the preceding example, `source1.cs` is checked out of version control and then `source2.cs` is checked out. You can then add a variety of commands to manipulate the files (such as branching and merging).

Rather than completely rewrite all of the commands in this chapter, we highly recommend you refer to the MSDN documentation either online or as part of your Team System install. Buck Hodge's blog (`http://blogs.msdn.com/buckh`*) is also a great source for Team Foundation version control information, hints, and tips.*

Summary

In this chapter, you found out the core differences between Visual SourceSafe and Team Foundation Source Control. You examined the configuration options for the Team Foundation Source Control module.

You found out how to use the Source Control Explorer and how to check in and check out code, showing you the concepts of workspaces and changesets. The chapter also covered advanced concepts such and branching/merging and shelving.

Finally, you got a good overview of the source control migration tools available in Team System. These tools and technologies were designed to help teams of developers to organize and manage software assets in robust and predictable ways. Version control is an important tool to help you manage your development process by providing an effective way of organizing your source code. In the next chapter, you will learn how the Microsoft Solutions Framework includes a consistent set of best practices and a process to organize the roles, tasks, and flow of your software development projects.

21

Microsoft Solutions Framework

The Microsoft Solutions Framework (MSF™) is a proven set of principles and best practices to help guide software development projects. It incorporates guidance from a wide variety of sources inside the Microsoft product groups; customers; consultants; and partners. MSF deeply integrates with Team System, manifesting itself as process guidance within the Team Portal and through automation via work items and work products. In addition, it is highly customizable and will scale to any development environment. Team System is the first product to be bundled with the Microsoft Solutions Framework. It includes two default process instances:

❏   MSF for Agile Software Development

❏   MSF for CMMI (Capability Maturity Model Integration) Process Improvement

Third-party process templates are being developed by many Microsoft partners as we speak, including global system integrators, ISVs, and service providers. Your custom in-house processes (usually a combination of an established development process and policies, processes, and conventions used within your own company) can also be integrated into Team Foundation Server. That means you can work within a recognizable framework, making it super easy for your team to adapt to Team System.

This chapter will survey a high-level overview of both Agile and CMMI process methodologies, after which we will drill down into MSF components shared by both methodologies — providing you with practical information and a "real-world" context.

This chapter is part one of a two-part series. Once you have a firm grasp of the Microsoft Solutions Framework, you can then move on to part two (Chapter 22, "Process Templates"), which details how to customize processes to make them work within your company's development environment.

Please note that the content of this chapter is based on Build 100 of the MSF processes which ships in Team Foundation Server RTM. Keep in mind that MSF is constantly being refined. If you want the latest information on the Microsoft Solutions Framework, please refer to the official Visual Studio Team System Workshop website found at the following address: `http://msdn.microsoft.com/vstudio/teamsystem/msf/`.

About the Microsoft Solutions Framework

One of the problems with process is that it is inherently disconnected from your day-to-day activities. Without Team System, you have to rely on a traditional process binder (or CD-ROM) in the hands of your project manager. Processes are usually stored in thick paper-based documents that you have to manually refer to when needed. If you are using third-party Enterprise Project Management (EPM) software to manage your project management, there is an inherent disconnect between your tools (Visual Studio) and your project management framework. Team System aims to remove that limitation by providing an unprecedented level of integration between all aspects of the software life cycle.

One of the major obstacles with adopting process-driven development is the lack of process integration with your environment and tools. Originally, tools and process did not go well together. The original intent of the Agile Manifesto was to bypass the deficiencies inherent in the development tools and move away from documentation because, frankly, it prevented developers from doing what they should be doing — coding software! Yet if you work within a corporate environment, you need the documentation and the predictability to effectively run your project — especially when governance requirements set a high bar of accountability. Where, then, is the middle ground?

Fortunately, the tools have improved considerably. Team System promotes agility by automating many of the tasks that a developer would have to implement or document by hand. For example, during the course of a project, a developer can document a bug with a few simple button-clicks and keystrokes. The bug is then transmitted to the Team Foundation Server, where the bug results are aggregated and organized as a report for the project manager. Compare this to a tedious manual form-filling process and you can immediately see the productivity gains. More important, as a project manager you can very quickly get a view of the project health and progress.

Why is MSF such an important and key piece of Team System? Well, if you consider that Microsoft drives some of the largest and most ambitious software projects on the planet, you can assume that Microsoft has a great deal of experience in organizing projects, identifying common tasks, and defining optimal workflow patterns.

Consider one of the important concepts in examining development processes within Team System: The Microsoft Solutions Framework provides process guidance templates integrated with Team System, and it also provides customization and tailoring features so that you can develop your own process, capturing best practices for your teams. From a practical standpoint, some companies will find value in Team System's "out-of-the-box" process templates. However, in most cases, the template will have to be modified to fit in all your requirements.

For example, MSF for Agile Software Development has been designed with six primary roles. However, if you don't need all of the roles, you can selectively take some out. Alternatively, you can add new roles within a process. The framework has been designed to scale well to almost any circumstance and it can be flexibly extended to fit your needs. Process and guidance are necessary parts of any software development life cycle.

Can Team System function without a process? Theoretically, yes, but why would you want to? Processes provide a number of benefits, including helping you organize your team and workflow, and document your best practices (so you can avoid repeating mistakes in the future). In addition, processes provide insight about how a project is succeeding (or failing). The last point is a key consideration: If you are running without a process, it is very difficult to know how well you are doing. In fact, it's almost impossible to evaluate your progress if you don't gather any empirical data. If your processes are mostly ad hoc or nonexistent, Team System will help bring order and organization to your projects—making project management a whole lot easier.

A conceptual overview of MSF

The Microsoft Solutions Framework contains a consistent meta-model for software development processes. This model is shared across both MSF for Agile Software Development and MSF for CMMI Process Improvement. This section describes the key concepts, structures, and activities in MSF (represented in the diagram shown in Figure 21-1).

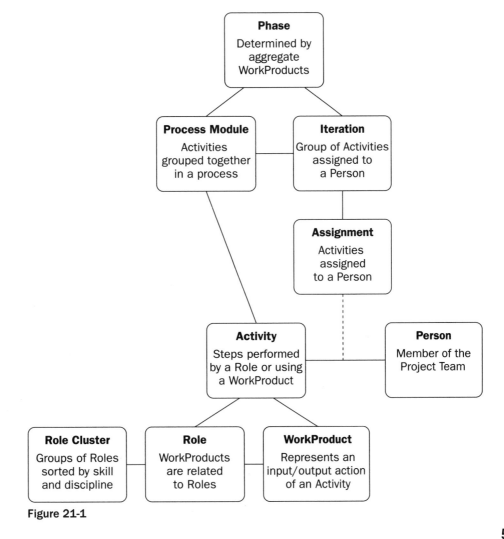

Figure 21-1

The *project* is composed of your team of peers, tracks (the iterative process of envisioning, planning, building, stabilizing, and deploying software on a continuous basis), and the Team Project (which is the physical manifestation of your project components and tools).

The *team* is composed of a collection of roles (including architects, developers, testers, and project managers). Each role has a distinctive collection of activities that are grouped into workstreams. The team is unified by the features of Team Foundation Server (work item tracking, version control, the build environment) and the Team Portal.

The team members assume equal responsibility vis-à-vis the project, but the demands are based on what role the team member plays within the larger team. Work items can be defined as a subset of activities — the project manager has to break down the activities into component parts that are then assigned to members of the team in order to reach a common goal. Work products are documents and templates that assist in the completion of a task. For example, a project manager may map out an iteration plan using a Microsoft Project template available on the Team Portal. The work items generated using the spreadsheet can then be modified and synchronized with Team Foundation Server, providing other members with a just-in-time view of their workflow.

The Microsoft Solutions Framework only represents but one piece of the puzzle. The development framework is designed to interact with the Microsoft Operations Framework (MOF) to provide not only guidance in the development of software, but also the deployment and long-term maintenance of software development projects. In a nutshell, think of the MOF as the IT Professional piece of the puzzle once your software project has been deployed. The MOF specifications are available on the Microsoft TechNet website at: www.microsoft.com/technet/.

Obtaining the Microsoft Solutions Framework

The Microsoft Solutions Framework 4.0 is currently available from two sources. If you intend to deeply customize the process, we recommend you download the target process from the MSDN website:

❑ You can obtain the MSF process templates and guidance directly from Team Foundation Server. To download the files to your desktop, launch Team Foundation Server and select Team ⇨ Team Foundation Server Settings ⇨ Process Template Manager. Simply click on one of the templates and click Download. A dialog box will prompt you for a location for the files on your hard drive and the transfer will begin. The download function is designed to enable your developers to locally modify any process template to make it fit the needs of your software development team (for example, to create new roles, incorporate new work products, and set up custom default tasks). For more information about process template customization, please refer to Chapter 22.

❑ MSF process guidance is also available on MSDN at www.microsoft.com/msf/ and is updated on a regular basis. Please note that the process templates and integrated feature set with tools are only available via Team Foundation Server.

MSF for Agile Software Development

Unlike many other process frameworks, MSF for Agile Software Development is based on scenarios and context-driven actions. This makes a great deal of sense if you think about it, because most development processes have universally recognized tasks and activities — for example, releasing a product or closing a bug. It enables you to create guidance while remaining very flexible in the development of your processes.

MSF for Agile Software Development is primarily designed for an agile development team that doesn't need to focus on the CMMI maturity levels. Here are a few key characteristics of this process:

- ❑ **Open communication between team members.** Freely sharing information within the team is a marker of project success. The work item infrastructure, SQL Reporting Services, and the Team Model all work together to open channels within your team.

- ❑ **Shared vision.** Everyone on your team has to have the same vision of the project. Team System's project management tools and the open Team Model help achieve this goal.

- ❑ **Agility and adaptation.** The capability to document every possible event that might occur within a software development project would result in volumes of documentation. Adaptation uses the mindsets and principles as a basis for dealing with unlikely or infrequent events.

- ❑ **Focus on the customer.** Communicating with the customer is key to achieving the business goals in any software project. The Business Analyst role is designed to facilitate this focus.

- ❑ **People come first.** Tools and process will only get you so far. The most important factor in any project is the people involved — your team members. Team System increases the productivity of your team by organizing your process in a central Team Portal, tracking workflow using work items, and providing an easy work environment by facilitating process through tool-process integration. If you want a project to succeed, the best thing you can do is create an empowering environment for your team.

- ❑ **End-to-end quality.** Quality can be achieved in Team System using the iterative process and artifacts such as the Quality of Service Requirements and tests to maintain the highest levels of security and performance. You can also enforce quality by setting tool-driven *quality gates* in your development process. Quality gates are policies that ensure that your code meets a certain standard (mostly through extensive testing) before it can be checked into the source tree.

- ❑ **Frequent deployment.** The best software products are designed out of a need to maintain the highest level of quality. Highly iterative processes and frequent testing will help in reaching that goal. The product should be used internally and fit the customer's requirements. Tools such as the Unit Test Framework and Team Build can drive your team to reach a high caliber of quality.

- ❑ **Customize MSF to your needs.** As explained earlier, MSF is designed to be a base framework. There is no doubt that guidance is required for any successful project, but MSF gives you the option to integrate as much or as little as you want.

- ❑ **Value.** The important factor that needs to follow through the implementation of software is value. Iterate often, communicate, and work on those features that are important for high return on investment.

Figure 21-2 shows the main page of the MSF for Agile Software Development process guidance.

Within your project, you can access the process guidance from the help menu (in Microsoft Excel or Microsoft Project) or from within Team Explorer.

Figure 21-2

About Agile development

The Agile "movement" started around 2001. This movement consisted of an outspoken group of professional developers that met at a workshop in Snowbird, Utah, to discuss new software development methodologies. At the time, developers were bogged down with formal processes and the need to extensively document their work. Projects were doomed to fail before they began because key features or issues were not identified at the start of the process, and there was no way to change them midprocess.

Many evolutionary processes were in development in the 1990s that focused on small teams, close interaction between programmers and business analysts, quick iterative programming cycles, and a move away from requirements.

The proponents of these new development methodologies came up with the term "Agile" and composed the Manifesto for Agile Software Development (you can read it in its entirety at www .agilemanifesto.org).

One of the key concepts behind the Agile movement is the idea that people are more important than process. The *agile alliance* was created from the emerging work of several Agile software development processes, including Extreme Programming (XP) and SCRUM.

For general information, articles, books, and other resources relating to Agile development, check online at www.agilealliance.org.

MSF for CMMI Process Improvement

The Microsoft Solutions Framework also has a more formal instance called "MSF for CMMI Process Improvement." Capability Maturity Model Integration (CMMI) was originally developed by the Carnegie Mellon Software Engineering Institute (www.sei.cmu.edu/cmmi/) to assess defense, aerospace, and government contractors in a regulated environment. The MSF version of CMMI is partially based on the work of W. Edwards Deming, a renowned statistician in the area of quality control and statistical process.

Deming popularized statistical process control in the field of business and manufacturing in his *theory of profound knowledge*. To properly implement process controls, you must be able to identify the difference between common cause variations (CCVs) and special cause variations (SCVs): Common cause variations are natural fluctuations found in any process. Special cause variations are caused by special occurrences, environmental factors, and problems that affect a process. The challenge as a project manager is to correctly identify an instance of a special cause variation and reduce it. Complicating this goal is the fact that these variations usually occur on a random basis. The reporting component of Team System provides visual metrics to measure factors such as project health. These charts can help you determine whether the Upper Control Limits (UCLs) and Lower Control Limits (LCLs) are within operational boundaries. Figure 21-3 illustrates the two varieties of variation and the attainment of process improvement.

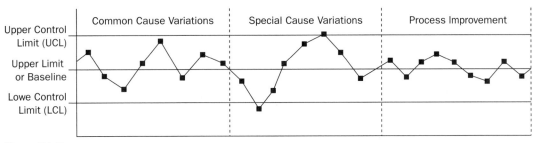

Statistical Process Control

Figure 21-3

Another principle that influenced the development of MSF for CMMI Process Improvement is the Theory of Constraints (TOC) documented by Dr. Eliyahu M. Goldratt in his novel *The Goal* (North River Press, 2004). The focus behind the theory is the goal of *constant improvement*. Constraints (as defined by Goldratt) are bottlenecks preventing you from reaching a specific goal. By identifying physical and nonphysical constraints, you can focus your energies on eliminating (or reducing) the constraints, making your process more effective.

Team System is Microsoft's foray into the Application Lifecycle Model (ALM). The ALM was developed in response to the inefficiencies of software development projects such as budget overruns, delivery delays, and so forth (in other words, special cause variations). Process within a project is vitally important to bring down costs and increase productivity, which is why you are currently unable to create a project in Team System without first selecting a process template.

> Some of the working titles for MSF for CMMI Process Improvement include MSF
> Complete and MSF Formal. For in-depth insight on the development of MSF for
> CMMI Process Improvement, be sure to visit David J. Anderson's blog at
> `www.agilemanagement.net`.

System and hardware engineering processes have matured over the decades. Relative to manufacturing, software engineering is still in its infancy. CMMI is based on quality assurance ideas that came out of manufacturing. This makes sense from an operational perspective—most hardware manufacturing companies rely on software on the production line. For that reason, there are many varieties of CMMI specifications.

In a nutshell, CMMI is used to track the maturity of any software design organization, from requirements to validation. The CMMI has six maturity capability levels outlined in Table 21-1.

Table 21-1

Capability Level	Description
0	**Incomplete Process**
1	**Performed Process**. You have little to no controls in your project. The outcome is unpredictable and reactive. Frequent instances of Special Cause Variations. All of the process areas for performed process have been implemented and work gets done. However, the planning and implementation of process has not yet been completed.
2	**Managed Process**. You have satisfied all of the requirements for the implementation of a managed process. Work is implemented by skilled employees according to policies. Processes are driven according to specific goals such as quality and cost. Planning and review are baked into the process. You are managing your process.
3	**Defined Process**. In the defined process, you have a set of standard processes (or processes that satisfy a process area) within your organization that can be adapted according to specific needs.
4	**Quantitatively Managed Process**. All aspects of a project are quantitatively measured and controlled. Both your operational and project process are within normal control limits.
5	**Optimizing Process**. Continuous project improvement. CMMI Level 5 focuses on constant process improvement and the reduction of special cause variations. The project process is under constant improvement.

> There are two models for implementing CMMI: the *continuous model* and the *staged model*. In the continuous model, elements such as Engineering, Support, Project Management, and Process Management are each composed of a set number of process areas. A *process area* is a description of activities for building a planned approach for improvement. Using the staged model, the process areas are set up according to the five maturity levels. MSF for CMMI Process Improvement was designed to support the staged model.

Capability Level 3

The CMMI template included in Team System is designed to help you accelerate the appraisal to Level 3 compliance. The CMMI specifications are quite detailed (more than 700 pages long). Here are the characteristics of CMMI Level 3 (boiled down to three main points):

- ❏ Customized to the organization's set of standard processes according to the organization's guidelines

- ❏ CMMI Level 3 has a process description that is constantly maintained. This is implemented in Team System using work items and iterations.

- ❏ CMMI Level 3 must contribute work products, metrics, and other process improvement information to the organization's process assets. Process templates and the Project Site enable project managers to share metrics and documents with the rest of the team.

Business analysts, project, and release managers

Business analysts and managers can benefit from utilizing pre-established planning and management processes, based on lessons learned and best practices. Projects contain templates and historical metrics that apply regardless of what project you are working on, which help in the estimation phase of the project. You can detect and reduce defects early in the process and before you ship. From a business perspective, you can establish a project schedule and measure costs, which enables you to negotiate better contracts with your clients.

Developers, testers, and architects

CMMI Level 3 provides a solid process framework for developers, testers, and architects. With process, the knowledge and experience gathered during the project is quantifiable. That means any lessons learned can help improve the process, bugs are avoided, and code is enhanced. All of this information can then be leveraged on future projects. This also builds processes that are derived from best practices, much like MSF is derived from Microsoft's collective experience.

In a process-driven environment, the roles and tools are better defined because it is a more detail-oriented methodology. This helps team members stay focused within your organization. CMMI provides a focus on process and project management — in fact, the entire team shares the responsibility of making decisions, managing risk, and shaping and meeting requirements. CMMI emphasizes training and integrated teams to create an environment that facilitates the integration of end-to-end features and a verification process to lower bugs and keep the project on track in terms of QA and feature requirements.

CMMI Level 3 versus MSF for CMMI process improvement

Formal processes have a reputation of being too bureaucratic and lacking agility. The traditional way of planning software is using the *waterfall method* (see the section "Team Model" for more details). The plan is central to the process and usually a lot of ceremony is attributed to the handing off of the project (for example, a project plan sent to developers for a coding phase).

The Microsoft Solutions Framework will enable your team to operate at CMMI Level 3. MSF for CMMI Process Improvement adds work items such as Risk, Change Requests, and Issues (building on the work items already available through MSF for Agile Software Development). MSF for CMMI will also include additional reports to the base spec.

MSF CMMI is designed to be flexible. In fact, MSF CMMI out of the box will not "automagically" transform an organization into Level 3 — it needs to be augmented with the other parts of MSF not in Team System. (For example, some components not included in MSF, such as training, are required to reach that goal.) If you need a formal process architecture, MSF for CMMI Process Improvement provides a light and flexible meta-framework you can customize to your needs.

MSF for CMMI Process Improvement provides an example of an agile interpretation of CMMI when more often than not the interpretation is traditional, waterfall, command and control, and documentation centric. It is designed to be light, with almost no overhead or bureaucracy. David J. Anderson (one of Microsoft's leading architects for the CMMI for Process Improvement Framework) describes this hybrid in his book *Agile Management for Software Engineering* (Prentice Hall, 2003) as "the Learning Organization Maturity Model." The CMMI version of MSF has the following characteristics:

❑ It is geared toward larger-scale projects with a greater emphasis on breaking a project into phases and groups. MSF for Agile Software Development, conversely, is designed for smaller groups with quicker iterations.

❑ It is designed to conform to a process, rather than plans and specifications. Process improvement is implemented in two ways: by reducing variations within baseline operating conditions and instituting constant improvement using cyclical process structures.

❑ It does not support project management artifacts by default, such as time tracking. However, the specification can be extended to include *earned value (EV)*, the *critical path method (CPM)*, and other Enterprise project management features into the framework.

❑ Everyone on the development team is responsible for issue and risk management. The goal is to eliminate special cause variation.

❑ MSF for CMMI Process Improvement focuses on automation through Team System's toolset and the CMMI appraisal model via the reporting tools to measure quality, velocity, and productivity.

❑ It uses the Team Model whereby all team members are empowered to make decisions and take responsibility for the success of a project. This includes standup meetings and log, risk, and operations reviews.

❑ All software development contains constraints. They include time, personnel, functionality, resources, and budget. MSF for CMMI Process Improvement has the means to help you buffer uncertainties (SCVs) within your project, and measure events and activities outside the scope of your project. The MSF for CMMI model is geared to reduce variation.

❑ MSF for CMMI Process Improvement expands on CMMI with the concepts of release management, risk management, and iterative cycles.

❑ It includes custom work items, reports, and process guidance. Like its Agile counterpart, the framework is highly extensible and customizable.

❑ This version of MSF uses metrics such as remaining work (or cumulative flow) and iteration velocity (measuring work in progress to track project health).

❑ Microsoft is working with SEI and other partners to build the specifications.

In future versions of MSF, Microsoft is aiming for Level 5 compliance. They are also investigating making the process Sarbanes-Oxley (SOX) compliant. CMMI is required for dealing with government agencies and larger software companies (see Figure 21-4).

Please refer to the Microsoft Solutions Framework website for more detailed guidance and technical information about the MSF for CMMI Process Improvement specifications, at http://msdn .microsoft.com/vstudio/teamsystem/msf/msfcmmi/.

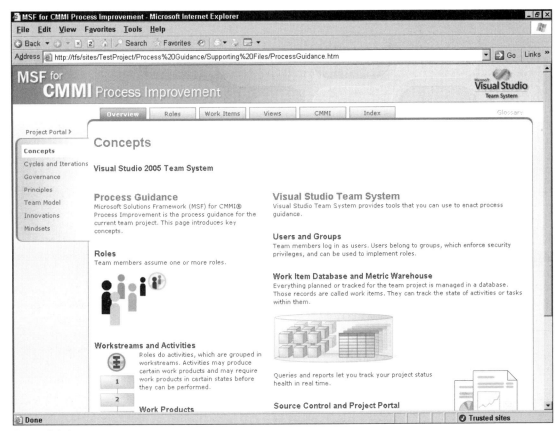

Figure 21-4

One of the key principles behind MSF is the concept of trust. A lot of the mechanics behind formal processes are designed for the purpose of accountability and conformance to specification — in other words, documenting, evaluating, and auditing each step of the process to make sure the quality of the end product remains high. In Agile methodologies, trust is inherent in the process — you have to trust that your developers will build quality features and build trust with your customers. MSF Agile and CMMI® both foster agility by allowing your team members to focus on their core activities, automating documentation and policies, and most importantly building quality within the process.

Choosing the Right Process

Of course, the key question is how to evaluate which process to use in an environment. Table 21-2 shows a side-by-side comparison of both processes.

Table 21-2

MSF for Agile Software Development	MSF for CMMI Process Improvement
Enables agility in your software development process	Extends MSF for Agile Software Development with support for auditing, verification, and formal processes
People are more important than process	Focus on organization
Improvement from iteration postmortems and other informal reviews	Formal continuous improvement and quality assurance
Relies on skill and abilities of individual developers	Relies on process and conformance to process, not specifications
Based on the Agile Manifesto	Based on the works of W. Edward Deming and Philip Crosby
Project-centric	Organization-centric

Fundamental Concepts

MSF is built around the concept that process should enable you, rather than hinder you. If you implement too little process, you have to take great steps to stay on track. The inroads you make on a project will fully depend on the organizational skills of your team. The infrastructure will not support or enforce your process. Too much process inhibits productivity and velocity. MSF is the marriage of process and agility. The following sections take a look at the components that enable process within Team System.

Process template components

MSF comes with many principal template components to support a software development process including *work products and work item queries.*

Work products

Work products are the tangible assets that support the framework. They include documents, spreadsheets, binaries, and specifications necessary to support the process flow. These work products are usually included in process templates and are included in a new project when a process is selected.

Queries

Work item queries are important for gathering and supporting information about your activities and the activities of your team. They include some of the following:

❑ **Active Bugs.** Returns all of your active bugs (which you can export to Microsoft Excel).

❑ **All Work Items.** Returns active work items for your project. You can also use this query to schedule and manage work items.

❑ **All Quality of Service Requirements.** Returns all active project QoS requirements lists (which you can export into Microsoft Excel).

❑ **All Scenarios.** Returns a scenario list for your project (which can be imported into Excel).

❑ **All Tasks.** Returns all active tasks within your team project. The output from the query can be exported to Microsoft Excel or Project.

❑ **All Work Items.** Returns all of your project team's work items.

❑ **My Work Items.** Returns a list of your work items.

❑ **Project Checklist.** Returns a work items list for which the exit criteria field has a value of Yes.

❑ **Resolved Bugs.** Returns a list of resolved bugs.

Iterative process

The Microsoft Solutions Framework can handle quick multi-iterations to help you refine your code, wring out any bugs, and create better software. MSF includes a four-step cycle that enables you to incrementally develop and stabilize your application. Each iteration focuses on a different feature or bug fix. Smaller iterations are recommended for accurate project timelines. Here is an overview of the four iterative steps:

❑ **Iteration 0:** Plan and set up project

❑ **Iteration 1:** Plan, develop, and test application

❑ **Iteration *n*:** Plan, develop, and test application

❑ **Final Iteration:** Develop, test, and release product

Figure 21-5 illustrates the MSF iterative process in a nutshell. Team System supports quick iterations with continuous improvement. These iterations may overlap at times and the iterative process may be modified to fit your custom process. Iterations are supported in the product using the Areas and Iterations classification features (covered in Chapter 19). Using project management tools such as Team Explorer and Microsoft Project, you can organize your work items by iteration and map out the amount of time the iteration should take. On top of that, you can modify the process template to define default iterations as soon as a project is created. These are some of the ways Team System functionally support an iterative process.

Cycles

Cycles represent the process of building a software project and its associated tasks and activities. Cycles are another way of describing phases in a software development project that are not neccesarily sequential. Some of the most common cycles include the following:

❑ Check-in

❑ Daily Build

❑ Accepted Build

❑ Iteration

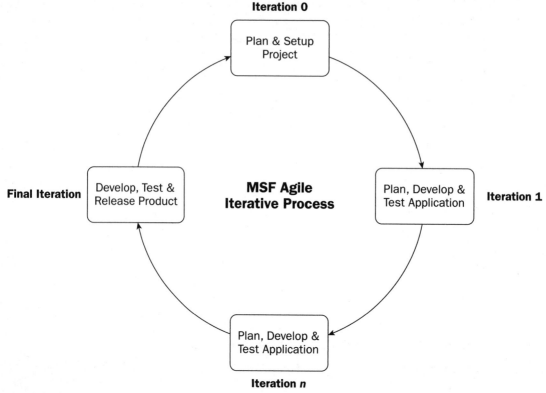

Figure 21-5

Smaller iterations enable you to quickly build features and reduce estimation errors, and they provide an effective feedback loop. Each iteration cycle should result in a solid feature in your product.

Cycles and iterations are loosely coupled. For example, a check-in may occur several time a day during a particular iteration of a project. Cycles represent a cross-section view of the MSF specifications. For more information about this view, please refer to the default process guidance documentation.

Personas

Personas are used to describe groups of users or customers. Instead of dealing with abstractions, you can tailor software to the needs, skills, abilities, and lifestyle of a fictional person. Personas should not be constructed in a vacuum; you must try to gather metrics to determine your audience and build a profile based on your gathered data. Personas are not a substitute for customer interaction. They are merely a way of communicating with customers.

> *Kim Goodwin (who works for Alan Cooper's firm Cooper Interactive Design) is the originator of personas. Alan Cooper made personas famous in his book* The Inmates are Running the Asylum *(Sams, 2004). You can read an article on the origins of personas on his personal website at* www.cooper.com.

"Bob" is an example of a simple persona:

- ❑ **Role:** New user.
- ❑ **Motivation:** Wants guided search results.
- ❑ **Usage:** Bob is unfamiliar with the web and related technologies. He types in the URL for the search engine looking for guidance. Fortunately, the search engine provides a portal categorized by topic to allow unfamiliar users to find what they want.

"Jill" is another example of a persona:

- ❑ **Role:** Power user.
- ❑ **Motivation:** Wants quick search results.
- ❑ **Usage:** Jill is familiar with search engines and types in her keyword query. The search engine returns highly relevant results that enable her to gather research for a term paper.

Personas are used widely at Microsoft. For example, "Mort Gaines" is the personification of a hobbyist VB developer, as opposed to Elvis (a C# developer) and Einstein (a C++ developer). You can find photos and profile information about Mort on presentation materials such as Microsoft PowerPoint slides and internal posters.

Governance, tracks, and activities

Governance measures value based on budget and scheduling. MSF for Agile Software Development has five tracks (not to be confused with the Track view) relating to work cycles and iterations. The five general questions (or checkpoints) you should be asking yourself are as follows:

- ❑ What are our current objectives?
- ❑ Are we making the necessary progress?
- ❑ Are we on track for designing a quality product?
- ❑ Are we addressing the risk?
- ❑ Are we ready to deploy?

These checkpoints are defined from within MSF. To measure these governance checkpoints, you must evaluate whether the project is on target from both a business and operational perspective at all stages of the software life cycle. The CMMI for Process Improvement incorporates the following five tracks of the software development lifecycle:

- ❑ Envision
- ❑ Plan
- ❑ Build
- ❑ Stabilize
- ❑ Deploy

Using tracks, you can organize activities to address matters of governance. Different tracks can overlap with each other. They don't have to describe specific tasks — they are meant to be conceptual "buckets" to organize how you approach your process. Each track corresponds to a governance checkpoint.

Activities describe a collection rather than an ordering of tasks undertaken to perform a single action. There are defined activities for each role, and they may overlap with other roles. You can track an activity using work items or create work products to support them. Within most tracks, you'll find a variety of activities, including:

- Analysis
- Create Solution Architecture
- Develop Documentation
- Establish Environments
- Establish Project Process
- Fix a Bug
- Implement a Development Task
- Release a Product
- Test a Customer Requirement
- Verify a Product Requirement

The Develop Documentation and Verify a Product Requirement activities are examples of activities that provide a level of verification and accountability in the process. Tracks enable you to judge whether your process is on "track" — are we properly envisioning the project? Do we have a clear idea of what the software will do? What exactly are we building? By following the tracks and incorporating the right activities per track, we can avoid being led astray.

> Both MSF for Agile Software Development and MSF for CMMI Process Improvement have consistent views, including disciplines, qualities of service, cycles, and tracks. The chapter provided a very cursory examination of the tracks for MSF for Agile Software Development. If you look closely at the Agile documentation, you'll notice that the information presented under Governance and Tracks is identical. For more information, please refer to the process guidance documentation.

Work item types

Team Foundation Server uses work items to track assignments and work. MSF for Agile Software Development contains five work items: bugs, risk, tasks, scenarios, and quality of service requirements. Figure 21-6 shows a view of the Work Items window.

> SCRUM (one of the Agile methods) popularized a key innovation called the Product Backlog to track work progress. Product Backlog loosely inspired the Work Item Tracking functionality in Team System. In MSF, the product backlog is contained in two work products. The scenario list is the list of scenarios waiting to be implemented. The quality of service requirement list contains a list of quality of service requirements.

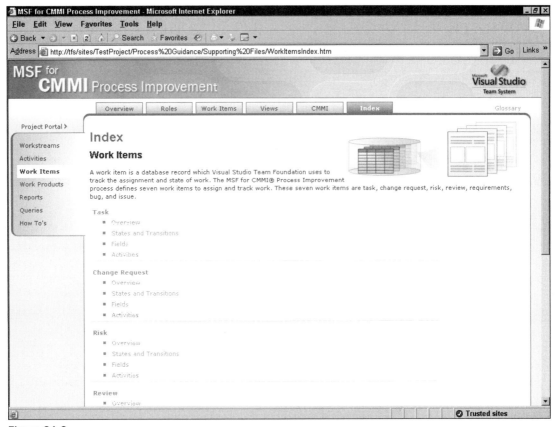

Figure 21-6

Please refer to Chapter 19 for more detailed information on the work item schema and how to customize work items within a team project.

Bug

A *bug* is a work item used to track and monitor problems within a software product. In order to be effective, a bug must be well documented, including the steps to reproduce the issue. A clear description of the bug is key to the process of "bug bashing" and will result in a higher-quality product. From the work item, the impact of the bug should be easily and clearly recognized. In MSF for Agile Software Development, bugs have four defined states:

❑ **New:** All new bugs need to be added to the work item database and documented as soon as possible.

❑ **Active:** This is the default state of a bug. An active bug means that the bug has been documented but not yet dealt with.

❑ **Resolved:** A resolved state means that a bug has been handled by a developer or tester. Once resolved, a bug can be classified as "Fixed" or included "By Design."

❑ **Closed:** A closed status means that the bug has been completely dealt with, including a verification process.

Figure 21-7 shows a state diagram illustrating how a bug might transition in a practical scenario.

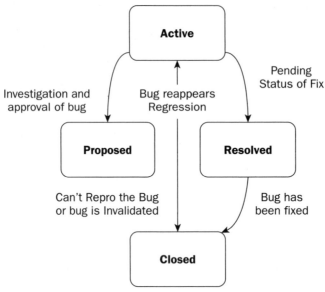

Figure 21-7

Quality of service (QOS) requirement

Quality of service is central to the MSF for Agile Software Development process. The mindset should be reflected from all roles represented on the project team and all tracks of the software design process. (See the "Mindsets," "Tracks," and "Roles" sections near the end of this chapter for more details.)

In particular, quality of service focuses on user experience, security, and performance. You can measure these factors using functional testing (stress and load testing, performance testing). Quality of service requirements set a high quality bar for your application. These requirements contain four default states:

❑ **New:** You can create a new quality of service requirement using the `Requirements` folder in the document library. You can also create a new work item in Team Explorer by right-clicking the `Work Items` folder.

❑ **Active:** Like many other work Items, quality of service requirements are by default "Active." The requirements are originally designed by a business analyst. Then the requirements are passed along to the developer team to write the necessary code. The requirements stay in Active mode during the coding process.

❑ **Resolved:** You can resolve a quality of service requirement when code has been written to implement it. A tester is then assigned to test the code to determine whether it adequately fills the requirement.

❑ **Closed:** Once a quality of service requirement passes testing, it is assigned the "Closed" status. A requirement can also be Removed, Deferred, or Split into two or more requirements.

For example, a load test might have to be performed for every build of a web application. This requirement might be enforced constantly throughout the development of an application. Once the load tests have been designed, they may be transitioned to "Resolved." Once the load tests have been performed and have passed testing, you can "Close" and complete the requirement.

Scenario

Scenarios take the place of use cases in MSF for Agile Software Development. They are built to determine a set of goals for each defined persona you establish in your project. Scenarios are used because they represent smaller pieces of functionality, a requirement to keep the iterations small. You must then figure out how to prioritize the list by looking at the outcomes. Will the customer be dissatisfied? If so, how much? Scenarios may take into consideration quality of service requirements.

> **Scenarios should be written jointly with the customer wherever possible.**

For each goal, create a list of successful and unsuccessful scenarios. In other words, try to figure out how the persona will reach the goal. These scenarios will be recorded as work items in Team System and will serve to help you anticipate problems and bottlenecks.

The scenario work item has four states:

- ❑ **New:** You can create scenarios using the Quality of Scenarios list found in the `Requirements` folder of your project. You can also create a new work item in Team Explorer by right-clicking on the `Work Items` folder.

- ❑ **Active:** Scenarios are usually designed by business analysts and are "Active" by default. They are then assigned to the development team and implemented as code.

- ❑ **Resolved:** Once the scenario has been coded, the developer (or developer lead) will change the status to "Resolved." It is then reassigned to a tester to confirm that it meets all criteria.

- ❑ **Closed:** Once testing is successfully completed, the tester can close a scenario. It can also be closed if it's Removed, Deferred, or Split into two or more scenarios.

Risk

A risk is a new work item type introduced in Team System (risk is not usually measured in the Agile development process). It can be defined as an outcome that can adversely affect a project. Each role within a development team should submit risks as work items, including as much information as possible to identify and mitigate it. It is important that you establish an open environment within your team to enable all members of your team to submit risk documentation.

A risk can be technical or organizational in nature. As you will learn, risk mitigation will help lower special cause variation within your project. The risk work item has three states:

- ❑ **New:** Any team member can create a work item once a new risk has been identified. A full detailed description of the risk should be written down, including negative effects and the impact to the project. Depending on the source of the risk, it should be reassigned to another team member. For example, solution or architectural risks should be assigned to the solutions architect.

❑ **Active:** By default, a new risk is set to "Active" once it is created. An active risk can pose a problem to your project and should be dealt with.

❑ **Closed:** A risk that has been dealt with is classified as "Closed." It should be re-examined during periodical team operations or risk reviews.

Risk can be found in the Identify Risk and Create Architectural Prototype workstreams.

Task

Tasks are created within a project to assign and complete work. Tasks can be specific to each role, such as development tasks and test tasks. When you create a task work item, it will be formatted (fields will be added and omitted) depending on the corresponding role. A task work item has three states:

❑ **New:** You can create a new task work item in Team Explorer by right-clicking on the `Work Items` folder. There are three varieties of tasks: Development, Test, and Generic.

❑ **Active:** Once a new task work item is created, it is automatically set to "Active." The Active status denotes that there are work requirements that need to be completed. Tasks can be reassigned to other team members depending on the role.

❑ **Closed:** The "Closed" state means a task has been completed. Development tasks are completed once code updates have been implemented. Test tasks are completed when all tests have been executed for a specific feature or component.

Reports

Reports provide you with valuable metrics to measure the success and health of a software development project. In Team System, reporting is tightly integrated with the Team Foundation version control repository, the work item database, Team Foundation Build, and the test components of Visual Studio 2005. In MSF, reports provide snapshots of your project progress within each iteration; a progress meter on quality metrics; and a means to track and measure the effectiveness of each role within your software development team. For more information about reporting, please refer to Chapter 19 and the MSF for Agile Software Development documentation.

Team Model

Team communication is key to the success of any project. One of the most common logical structures used in an organization is the *Hierarchy structure*. At the top are the managers and business analysts, followed by your team leads and the team members. Figure 21-8 illustrates the Hierarchy structure.

The problem with this structure is that there is a disconnect between the higher-level management and staff. For example, testers typically have to communicate through their leads to reach the business analyst. This reduces the agility of your team. The MSF Team Model assumes that all members of your team are working as peers toward the same goal, each role is set up as an advocacy group. In effect, you are leveraging the experience and collective mindset of your group. Figure 21-9 shows the structure of the MSF Team Model within the MSF for Agile Software Development process. (The CMMI version doesn't differ very much — it simply adds the user experience advocacy role.)

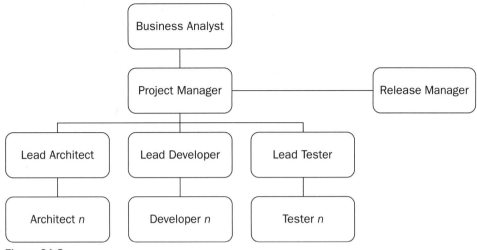

Figure 21-8

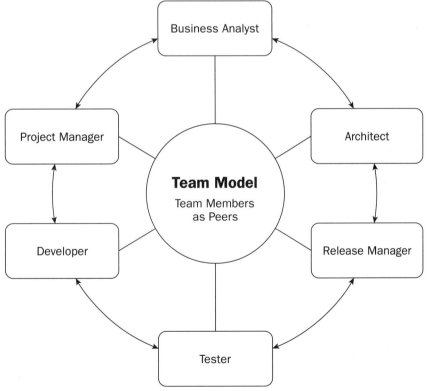

Figure 21-9

The MSF Team Model was created as a mix of waterfall and cyclical models. This model isn't just theo-retical; it outlines a structure in which you can effectively organize your software team.

Here are the primary outcomes of the Team Model:

❑ **Accountability:** Each member of the team is accountable for his or her actions and the outcome of the project. The effectiveness and quality of a project depends on collective responsibility and communication. This concept is also called the *team of peers.*

❑ **Scalability:** To solve problems, teams may scale in or out. Teams must refine themselves based on the requirements of the project. MSF calls this "stretch to fit."

❑ **Advocacy:** See the following section for further details.

> **The Team Model is essentially a risk-management strategy. The formerly named "Role Clusters" are now "Constituencies of Concern" (or Risk). Roles in MSF "advocate" for these constituencies, with a role typically advocating for only one constituency, but often several roles have a responsibility to advocate for the same constituency.**

Advocacy

Advocacy provides a balanced view of the project by all members of the software development team and the stakeholders in a project. A strong advocacy within your group will provide a framework that enables you to avoid operational and functional errors, miscalculations, and bad decisions. Each role within your team has a mandate to ensure that your project plans meets practical and functional expectations.

MSF for CMMI® Process Improvement includes functional areas within Advocacy Groups by adding managers, auditors, and officers to make it easier to monitor each stage of the development of a project. This process also includes a new advocacy group, User Experience, which accounts for a portion of the training requirement of CMMI — for example, the role of a Technical Writer who can carefully document the product for the end user. There are seven advocacy groups found in MSF for CMMI® Process Improvement, as follows:

❑ **Product managers:** The customer wants a software product that effectively solves a problem. The product has to fulfill the customer's needs. Usability is a consideration that all team members have to understand and strive for. The product manager is the advocate in MSF for "Customer Business."

❑ **Business analyst:** This role advocates for the customer. This team member's mandate is to make sure the solution meets the customer's business needs.

❑ **Program manager:** This is an advocate for product delivery. The PM's mandate is to ensure that the software solution is delivered on time and on budget. The customer's needs and expectations have to be met and managed. Program managers in MSF are advocates for the "Solution Delivery."

❑ **Architects:** This advocate is for the solution. The mandate of the architect is to map out the solution infrastructure, interoperation between system components, quality of service, and long-term viability. Architects are the advocates for the "System in the Large."

❑ **Developers:** This role advocates for the most effective technical approach. The mandate for the developer is to design a clean infrastructure, effectively estimate project parameters, and create high-quality code. According to MSF, the developer is the advocate for the "Technical Solution."

❑ **Testers:** These team members are advocates for the customer and the quality of the end product. The mandate of the tester is to report any issues that may affect the customer in terms of quality or usability. MSF calls the tester the advocate for "Solution Quality from the Customer Perspective."

❑ **User experience**: This person is an advocate for the needs of the end users and the usability of a software product. MSF states that the user experience expert is the advocate for "the most effective solution in the eyes of the intended users."

❑ **Release managers:** These team members advocate for the smooth deployment of a solution through any number of delivery channels. The release manager in MSF is the advocate for "the smooth delivery and deployment of the solution into the appropriate infrastructure."

Mindsets

Mindsets enable your team members to deal with situations in a consistent way. They should be enforced early in the project life cycle and maintained right through to completion. Mindsets can help your team members to correctly manage their work and interactions. This part of MSF isn't tool driven — it's behavioral. One of the key concepts of any Agile methodology is that the process should be "people-centric." This part of MSF includes best practices to set up and manage a team on an interpersonal level.

Roles

The role is a very important concept in Team System regardless of which process you decide to implement. The underlying process and tooling is built around the interplay between project managers, architects, developers, and testers. To enforce this concept, Microsoft has designed different versions of Visual Studio that play on the strengths of each of the principal roles. MSF for Agile Software Development defines six primary roles:

❑ Business analyst

❑ Project manager

❑ Architect

❑ Developer

❑ Tester

❑ Release manager

> **In recap, MSF for Agile Software Development has six defined roles. MSF for CMMI Process Improvement has seven defined roles. In the following section, we will look at all seven roles.**

What if you have a very small team or the members of your team take on several roles? Microsoft took this into account in the creation of the *Team Suite,* a version of Team System that incorporates all of the primary roles within a software development team. Moreover, you aren't limited to the roles defined in

MSF for Agile Software Development or CMMI. You can modify the process to remove roles and incorporate your own custom roles. For example, if your team has members that are both developer and tester, you can create a new role called DevTest.

When you are looking at the process guidance documentation, you'll notice that there is a Set as Start Page option with a checkbox on the top-right side of the screen (once you click a specific role). Selecting the checkbox will set your home page to the role description and bookmark the tasks and other useful information pertinent to your role.

MSF is quite flexible regarding the definition of a role. For example, if you are both an architect and a developer, the only requirement set in place is that you have the expertise to effectively perform tasks within each role, and act as advocates for the technical solution.

The following sections provide an overview of the roles on a software team as defined by both versions of MSF. For greater detail about a specific role, we recommend that you refer directly to the MSF documentation.

Business analyst

The goal of a business analyst is to analyze the business requirements and opportunities and outline the applications that will help the company reach their business goal. The analyst has to translate the business requirements from stakeholders and customers into requirements for the development team.

The business analyst advocates for the customer and should provide direct customer contact to the other roles in the development group whenever it is needed and where possible. Often, there are quintessential customers willing to work directly with the development team. The business analyst is responsible for managing these relationships and making these folks available to the project team to create maximum agility.

From a business perspective, business analysts manage customer expectations and act as an advocate for the customer. They play an integral role in the planning stage of the product — especially in terms of building business cases, a communication plan, marketing and evangelism, defining and managing the customer requirements, and driving business value in a software development project. A business analyst will also help the project manager balance resources, scheduling, and features.

Within a software development process, the business analyst's role is to help determine quality of service requirements (QoS), create use cases and scenarios, and define personas. MSF for Agile Software Development provides a business analyst with three primary workstreams:

- ❏ Capturing the project vision
- ❏ Creating scenarios
- ❏ Creating quality of service requirements

Once the project vision report and scenario are completed, they are typically published to the project portal. You can also publish the quality of service requirements to the project site and create quality of service and scenario work items to relate to your project plan. Examples of quality of service requirements include load and stress testing, security, platform, and performance.

MSF for CMMI Process Improvement adds four extra roles to the mix: the *sponsor* provides the funding and governance for the project and helps define the feature spec of an application. The *subject matter expert* provides input on the technical requirements of an application. For example, Microsoft uses most valuable professionals (MVPs) as valued customers and experts when they define technical feature sets for their products. Both these roles provide a "reality check" to determine whether the software will meet business and real-world requirements. The *auditor* also plays an important part in the process, verifying that the project is within budget and meets the business requirements. Finally, the *product manager* will take the vision statement and specifications and work closely with the project managers in the implementation phase of the project.

Project manager

The project manager (or project lead) is responsible for coordinating and facilitating software development projects — from scheduling to the overall budget. Project managers usually create project and iterative plans and analyze reports to identify and correct problems before they happen.

They are the connective glue within a team. PMs communicate with business analysts to ensure that a project is hitting all business requirements. Alongside the analysts, they are the primary architects for the project.

Project managers also handle implementation details such as administrative tasks, negotiation, and communication within a software development team. They are responsible for managing the project specs, quality assurance, and risk. They also have to interface with *solution and operation architects, developers,* and *testers* to correctly estimate, deploy, and maintain the project plan and scheduling.

For a detailed overview of the project management features of Team System, be sure to take a look at Chapter 19 and the MSF for Agile Software Development documentation. In MSF for Agile Software Development, a project manager performs three workstreams:

❑   Planning iterations

❑   Guiding projects

❑   Guiding iterations

Within MSF for CMMI Process Improvement, there are two advocacy roles: the project manager and the integrated project management (IPM) officer. The IPM officer is an executive who is responsible for a collection (or portfolio) of projects (a project manager is typically responsible for a single project at a time). The IPM officer can manage multiple project managers, distribute resources across multiple projects, and involve stakeholders during set milestones in the project.

Architect

An architect's role is to model the structure and foundation of a software application. Using the Team Suite for Architects tools, an architect can define the physical and logical structure of a service-oriented system and the operational constraints of a network. Based on the quality of an architecture, the system will be usable, scalable, secure, and performable. For a more detailed overview of the resources available for an architect in Team System, please refer to Chapters 1 through 7. In MSF for Agile Development, the architect has a single workstream: to create a *solution architecture*.

Within the MSF for CMMI Process Improvement process, the architecture role is divided in two:

- Infrastructure architect
- Solution architect

The infrastructure architect is responsible for creating a system design (in other words, mapping out the logical topology). The solution architect can then validate his or her solution design against the topology. This is a great way to identify security issues, and other real-world scenarios before the application moves on to the coding phase.

Developer

Developers are responsible for the implementation of a software application in code within certain constraints (such as schedule). In the MSF for Agile Software Development framework, developers contribute to the modeling of the project infrastructure, requirements, and features. As subject matter experts, they can provide invaluable input on the selection of the proper technological approach.

Developers build the features with an eye on maintaining quality and mitigating risk, and they set up the deployment details. They can also provide services writing documentation and consulting. Here are the important workstreams associated with a developer:

- Implementing development tasks
- Fixing bugs
- Building products

To learn more about Team System's development tools, please refer to Chapters 8 through 12. The development advocacy group in the CMMI for Process Improvement process is split up into four key roles to ensure predictability and accountability:

- Developer
- Lead developer
- Development manager
- Build engineer

Tester

Testers have an important role within the software team. They must create and update test plans and strategy, and perform a battery of tests to uncover problems within code. There is a wide spectrum of tests to implement, including functional, usability, quality, documentation, and many others. Once a bug or issue is found, it must be addressed and communicated to the rest of the team in an effective way.

The tester has to have a deep understanding of project requirements to provide the team with actionable information about a bug. Once the tests have been performed, the tester has the responsibility of signing off on a feature and approving a release. If the quality of a product is not up to par, the entire project suffers. The tester has to document and create workarounds, re-create the steps to reproduce a bug, and ideally try to discover new bugs within a product.

Finally, a tester must comprehensively report on all issues for the rest of the team. Here are the workstreams associated with the tester:

❑   Testing scenarios

❑   Testing quality of service (QoS) requirements

❑   Closing bugs

For more in-depth information about the Team System testing tools, please refer to Chapters 13 through 17. MSF for CMMI Process Improvement adds the *test manager* role, in order to track and measure progress of the testing phase of a project.

Release manager

Not all teams have a release manager: In some instances, your developer or project manager may handle release details. If your team is large enough, the release manager's main responsibility is deploying a product. The release manager must create deployment plans and coordinate the transfer of products to media (such as CD-ROM, DVD, online distribution or other delivery channels), the shipment details, and rollout plans (if applicable). If a product is to be rolled out, the release manager must prepare the target site.

Release managers use quality reports to ascertain the readiness of a product release. They are also responsible for the smooth ongoing operation of software after deployment, including coordination with operations personnel. A release manager has but one workstream: releasing a product. For more information about product deployment, be sure to read Chapter 24. Both MSF for Agile Software Development and MSF for CMMI Process Improvement include the release manager role.

User experience

The user experience advocacy group is unique to MSF for CMMI Process Improvement. It incorporates two advocacy roles: a user experience architect and a user architect specialist. The architect will constantly evaluate the overall usability of an application, whereas the specialist will work on design elements, prototypes, and technical documentation related to facilitating the product's use. The user experience experts are user education specialists — for example, technical writers.

Workstreams

MSF for Agile Software Development is composed of 14 different workstreams. Fundamentally, workstreams are activities composed of other activities and are primarily role based. Workstreams are described using the Entry, Task, Verification, and Exit (ETVX) process initially developed by IBM.

MSF for Agile Software Development has more than 70 different activities (not including workstreams). Each workstream has about five activities and each role has approximately two and one-third workstreams. Most workstreams don't span multiple roles.

For example, a tester has three workstreams in MSF for Agile Development: Test a Scenario, Test a Quality of Service Requirement, and Close a Bug. To test a scenario, a tester must go through several activities including defining a test approach, writing validation tests, selecting and running test cases, opening bugs and conducting exploratory testing. These activities are iterative and don't neccesarily have to be executed sequentially. The tester can use the Manual Testing capabilities to write test cases, the Unit Test Framework provides the tester with the capability to write validation tests and much more.

The architect on the other hand has only one workstream: Create a Solution Architecture. This workstream is composed of six different activities including partitioning a system, designing interfaces, developing threat models, developing performance models, creating architectural prototypes, and creating an infrastructure architecture. The design component of the architect's activities is nicely supported by Team Edition for Software Architects. Other models can be designed using Visio and tracked using work items.

Figure 21-10 shows how workstreams, tracks, and activities interrelate.

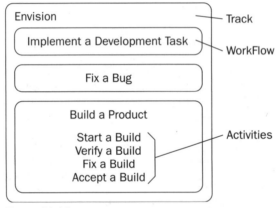

Figure 21-10

Summary

In this chapter, you got an overview of MSF for Agile Software Development and MSF for CMMI Process Improvement. We delved into the inner workings of MSF and the important elements of the underlying meta-model. MSF is designed to help you structure your process, especially if you have none in place. Now that we have a good understanding of the process framework, we can look at how to design, create, and deploy a process template within Team System.

Process Templates

In the previous chapter, you learned how the Microsoft Solutions Framework can be used as a framework to help you define all parts of your process. But how do you enact that process within Team System? Process templates enable you to work out a custom methodology that works for you. Your process can appear within Team System in many forms:

❑ Your process guidance provides all your team members with policies and best practices tailored to your company's need.

❑ Work products, such as project plans, enable you to further support your process.

❑ Your project workflow is driven by work items, iterations, and areas.

❑ Reports provide a window to accurately and predictably assess the health of your project.

> **To create and modify process templates, you must have an account within the Team Foundation Administrator group on Team Foundation Server.**

Unless you are very familiar with the schema, or you are using third-party tools that validate your templates on the fly, we strongly recommend that you use an existing process template as the prototype for your customizations. Template customization can be an error-prone process due to the complexity of the XML files.

The Visual Studio 2003 enterprise templates vary a great deal from Team System process templates. Team System process templates can span many projects to many members of your team. Enterprise templates are designed to enable you to create policies, frameworks, and process guidance on a per-project basis, and be installed locally to appear in the New Project dialog box. The Team System process templates are also centrally available via the Team Foundation Server.

> While reading and navigating documentation on the web, you may encounter both the term "process template" and the term "methodology template." In most cases, both terms mean the exact same thing. In this chapter, we consistently refer to the process configuration files as a process template.

New Team Project Wizard

In creating new customized process templates, you must understand how the New Team Project Wizard works. Chapter 19 has an overview of the project creation process. Under the covers, once a project manager selects a project type, a series of plug-ins will launch to create the required project files. The plug-ins will set up the following project elements:

❑ Process guidance

❑ Iterations, groups, and permissions

❑ Default report directory and reports

❑ Version control folders with default check-in notes and permissions

❑ Work item types, queries, and tasks

❑ Team Portal and associated files

❑ Other extensibility points

Unlike other process management systems, when you customize a process template, you are not only customizing the documentation, but also modifying the behavior of both Team Foundation Server and Visual Studio 2005. The integrated process methodology and guidance facilitates adoption and drives the generation and collection of project metrics.

This chapter is divided into three distinct sections: In the first section, you'll learn about the tools you need to work with process templates and files. You'll then learn how to tailor your process guidance. In the last part of the chapter, you will learn how to customize your process templates to fit your needs and environment.

> *For complete information on customizing process templates, see the Process Template Customization Guide, which can be downloaded from the Visual Studio Extensibility Center:* `http://msdn.microsoft .com/vstudio/extend/`. *We encourage you to explore the XML files within your process as one of the best ways of learning how to work with a custom process.*

Customization Tools

A variety of file types are included in your process template, including HTML, XSL, and XML. There are also a variety of tools you can use to customize these files:

❑ XML/XSL editors

❑ Microsoft InfoPath 2003

❑   MSF HTML Build Utility

❑   Third-party tools

The following subsections describe the features and functions of each of these tools.

XML/XSL editors

The process guidance portion of the template contains several XML and XSL files, especially in the `\Windows SharePoint Services\Process Guidance\Supporting Files\XSLs` or the `\Windows SharePoint Services\Process Guidance\Supporting Files\XML` directories. Visual Studio 2005 has a built-in XML editor. You can also use Notepad, Wordpad, or third-party solutions.

Microsoft InfoPath 2003

Microsoft InfoPath is a useful tool for editing the process guidance portion of your process templates. It is available in Microsoft Office 2003 and is primarily used to edit and validate `.xsd` and `.xsn` documents. However, you can incorporate XML files by creating a new form and using an XML document or schema as your data source.

> You must completely exit InfoPath before trying to render your process guidance files in the browser. By default, InfoPath will place a file lock on open documents and prevent you from looking at your updates.

You can also use the default InfoPath template file located at the following location:

`\Windows Sharepoint Services\Process Guidance\Supporting Files\XML\template.xsn`

Figure 22-1 shows a screenshot of `template.xsn` edited in the InfoPath tool.

InfoPath can manage several file types included in Table 22-1.

Table 22-1

File Extension	Description
.xml	Extensible Markup Language file
.xsd	XML Schema Definition file
.xsf	InfoPath Manifest file
.xsl	Extensible Stylesheet Language Template file
.xsn	InfoPath Form Template file

InfoPath is designed to facilitate the process of creating and filling out forms. It has two specific modes to match up with these tasks: form filling and design mode. The form-filling mode was designed to prevent casual users from changing the schema. As opposed to a tool like Wordpad, InfoPath can validate your schema and ensure that it is well formed.

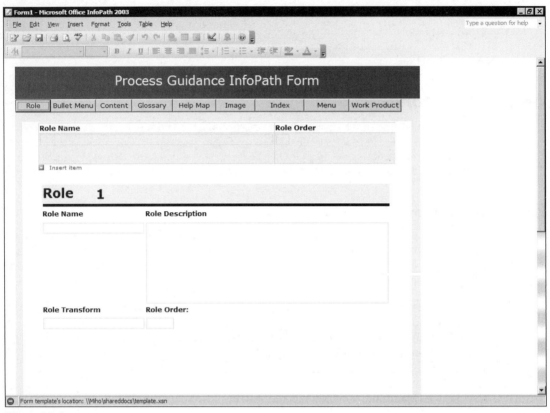

Figure 22-1

> We highly recommend that you install InfoPath 2003 Service Pack 1 before attempting to edit your process guidance files.

MSF HTML Build utility

The MSFWinBuild tool is used to compile your process guidance from XML to HTML pages. This compilation process is necessary for performance and zone security reasons. You can download the tool at the following link (the documentation is included):

    www.gotdotnet.com/workspaces/workspace.aspx?id=c0ce8992-2955-4371-904b-1f93a9efffe6

Please refer to the MSDN help file (http://msdn.microsoft.com) for more detailed information on how to compile your process guidance files using the tool.

Third-party tools

At the time of writing, a few preliminary process template–related offerings are on the market:

- ❑ Joel Semeniuk, a Canadian Microsoft Regional Director, has released a process template editor on GotDotNet dubbed the "VSTS Customization Toolkit." Please note that at the time of writing, this toolkit is still in pre-release stages and should not be run or installed on a production system. Please visit GotDotNet.com or Joel's weblog for more details: `http://weblogs.asp.net/Jsemeniuk/`.

- ❑ Brightworks has several commercial MSF management tools for SharePoint. You can learn more about them at `www.brightworks.com`.

- ❑ Osellus, Inc., has released a commercial VSTS process template editor called the IRIS Process Author that is available as a standalone tool and as a software-as-service. Check out the following website for details: `www.osellus.com`.

Customizing Process Guidance

This section presents an architectural overview of your process guidance. You should take your documented processes (roles, workstreams) and integrate them into your primary XML data source (`ProcessGuidance.xml`). Then you can use the MSF Build tool to create HTML versions of the process guidance files. These HTML files can then be placed on the Team Portal and displayed using Internet Explorer or any of the Visual Studio 2005 Team editions.

To customize the process guidance, you must first download the full process template (rather than use the Process Template Manager within Team Explorer). The full process template is available at `http://msdn.microsoft.com/msf`.

> **Be sure to make a backup copy of** `ProcessGuidance.xml` **before making any customizations or changes.**

You must use the XML files to make any changes to the process guidance. When in Edit mode, Windows SharePoint Services will dynamically render the process guidance using a series of XSL queries. The source files are contained in the Source folder (`\Process Guidance\Source\XML\`). When in Run Mode, the source files are precompiled using the MSF HTML Build utility. In Run mode, SharePoint Services will launch `ProcessGuidance.htm` *(found in* `\ProcessGuidance\Source\`*). One of the key advantages of precompiling your process guidance is performance — the server won't have to prerender and transform the pages on every call.*

Anatomy of process guidance (ProcessGuidance.xml)

Each content item in your process guidance has four common sections (each activity or workstream requires that these sections are complete):

- ❑ **Parts.** Within a workstream, a part refers to an activity. Within each activity, a part refers to a step within an activity.

- ❑ **Responsible/Accountable/Consulted/Informed (RACI).** This pinpoints a role and level of involvement (an example of a Responsible role is the project manager or administrator).

- ❑ **Criteria.** Mandatory conditions.
- ❑ **Cross Reference.** Links to internal or external resources.

Creating workstreams and activities

Workstreams can be defined as a series of activities tied to a specific role (you can learn more about workstreams in Chapter 21). The following sections explain how to define and create new workstreams and integrate them into your custom process guidance.

Creating new workstreams

Here are the four steps to create a new workstream. In fact, all elements of the process guidance will be documented in Chapter 21 and in the MSF process guidance itself.

1. Open your process guidance file (`ProcessGuidance.xml`) using InfoPath.
2. Insert a new content item by selecting the Insert Item menu, and then selecting Section ⇨ ContentItem.
3. Change the Content Type to Workstream. Give your workstream a unique name and description.
4. Save your work and close InfoPath (InfoPath has to be shut down before you can open Internet Explorer and evaluate your updates).

Assigning roles to workstreams

Once your workstream has been created, you have to associate it to a role. The RACI scale enables you to assign a functional level of responsibility and involvement for each role. You can add a RACI role to a workstream by following these five steps:

1. Open your process guidance file (`ProcessGuidance.xml`) using InfoPath.
2. Insert a new RACI Section (if none exists) by selecting the Insert item menu at the end of the Parts node as it appears in InfoPath.
3. Update the RACIType field to the appropriate value. (Chapter 21 has a good overview of the significance of each value.)
4. Add to the Content Name field the exact value found in the Role Name field. For example, a role called "BusinessAnalyst" should appear the same in both fields to establish the relationship between the RACI level and the ownership of the workstream.
5. Save your work and close InfoPath.

Entry and exit criteria in workstreams

You can define entry and exit criteria in your workstreams. Events such as time or dependencies can be set as conditions to initiate or end a workstream. Here is how you can create entry criteria for a workstream in five steps:

1. Open your process guidance file (`ProcessGuidance.xml`) using InfoPath.
2. Pick any workstream and find the Entry Criteria section.

3. Add a Dependency Name and Description. You can also insert timed events in the When field. A dependency is a list of activities that are pre-required in order to proceed with the workstream. To view a dependency in the Agile process guidance, click on a Role. Then click the step-by-step scenario link, and a description of the workstream's dependencies should appear.

4. Add a new Criteria Type (by using Insert Item under the Cross Type section) and give the Criteria Type field a value of Entry. Provide a Name and Description for your criteria.

5. Save your work and close InfoPath.

> **You are not limited to one dependency or criteria. If you have several in your spec, simply use the** `Insert DependencyItem` **or** `Insert CriteriaItem` **options to complete and fill out your criteria.**

Adding exit criteria is just as easy. Simply add a new criteria type (as shown above) and set the Criteria Type field to Exit.

Referencing work products

Work products are documentation to support your process. You can associate and reference work products from your workspaces (this will make the appropriate documents appear in your process guidance). You can also create references between work products and activities (for more information on work products, please refer to Chapter 21). The following list describes the three steps to take in order to create an association between a work product and a workstream (you can use the same steps to associate a work product with an activity):

1. Open your process guidance file (`ProcessGuidance.xml`) using InfoPath.

2. Update the Cross Type field (in the Cross Type section) to the type of work product you want to add (Word, Excel, etc.); and in the Cross Name field, add the name of your work product as indicated in the ContentName field.

3. Save your work and close InfoPath.

> **WorkProduct-PPT stands for Powerpoint, and WorkProduct-VS stands for Visual Studio 2005 Team System. Other default work product files include Word (WorkProduct-Word), Excel (WorkProduct-Excel), and Project (WorkProduct-Project). All of the process guidance CrossTypes are enumerated in the schema found at** `Windows SharePoint Services\Process Guidance\Source\Schema\.`

To validate and view your work, make sure that InfoPath has been shut down and you have set your process guidance to Edit mode. Open Internet Explorer, click on `ProcessGuidance.htm` and make sure that the Workstreams portion of the guidance appears as it should and has been properly updated.

Creating new activities

Activities are a series of steps to attain a desired result. For detailed information about activities, check out Chapter 21. The following steps outline how you can create a new activity:

1. Open your process guidance file (`ProcessGuidance.xml`) using InfoPath.
2. Insert a new ContentItem using the Insert menu, and set Content Type to Activity.
3. Give your activity a unique name and description using the Content Name and Content Description fields.
4. Save your work and close InfoPath.

Adding steps to activities

Each activity is composed of a series of steps. Here's how you can add additional steps to your activities:

1. Open your process guidance file (`ProcessGuidance.xml`) using InfoPath.
2. Click the Insert Item link beneath the Entry Criteria section (in the Part section) and add "Step" to the Part Type field. You can add as many steps as required by your process.
3. Add the pertinent information in the Part Name, Sequence, Is Required, and Part Description fields.
4. Save your work and close InfoPath.

Associating activities to workstreams

You can associate several activities to one (or many) workstreams. Here are the steps to associate an activity to a workstream:

1. Open your process guidance file (`ProcessGuidance.xml`) using InfoPath.
2. Insert a Part section and add "Step" to the Part Type field.
3. Add appropriate values to the Part Name, Sequence, Is Required, and Part Description fields. As with other links, the Part Name has to match with the Content Name.
4. Save your work and close InfoPath.

Assigning roles to activities

The process of assigning a role to an activity is very similar to that of assigning a role to a workstream. Here is the five-step process:

1. Open your process guidance file (`ProcessGuidance.xml`) using InfoPath.
2. Pick an activity and set up a RACI section using Insert Item.
3. Select a value for RACI Type (Responsible, Accountable, Consulted, or Informed).
4. Select a role name (it has to match exactly the role names defined in the role's Content Name field.
5. Save your work and close InfoPath.

To validate the work you have done so far, simply launch the HTML version of the process guidance and look at the workstreams and activities by clicking the Index tab. Your activities should display descriptions, steps, and entry/exit criteria.

Creating work item documentation

Work items enable you to document specific tasks within your process (to learn more about work items, be sure to look at Chapters 19 and 21). You can easily add a new work item in your process using InfoPath:

1. Open your process guidance file (`ProcessGuidance.xml`) using InfoPath.

2. Add a new `ContentItem`. Select `WorkItem` under Content Type.

3. Add a name for your new work item in the `ContentName` field.

4. Add a description for the new work item in the Content Description field. You can use the existing descriptions as a template for the wording and format.

5. Save your work and close InfoPath.

Customizing work item elements

Once your new work item has been created, you'll notice new sections, including Fields, States, and Transitions (you can learn more about these concepts in Chapter 21). Here is how you can customize these work item elements:

❑ Fields can be added by first creating a Part. Set the Part Type field to "Field" and give the field a Part Name, a Part Description, and a Sequence Number, and indicate whether the field is required.

❑ To add a new state, you must select the States, Transitions, and Reasons section. Create a new work item and add a name for your state, along with a unique identifier in the Sequence Number field.

❑ Transitions can be added by jumping to the States, Transitions, and Reasons section. Select a state. Change the Transition Type to "Reason" and then add a Name and Sequence Number.

Linking to workstreams and activities

You can create links within your work items to workstreams and activities. Once the link is clicked, you get a graphic outlining the relationship between activities/workstreams and work items. Use the following steps to link them together:

1. Open your process guidance file (`ProcessGuidance.xml`) using InfoPath.

2. Beneath the last Verification section, create a new Cross Type section and set the Cross Type field to WorkItem.

3. Enter the name of the work item in the Cross Name field exactly as is indicated within your process. Add the state in the Cross Description field. The state name must match a state that exists within your process.

4. Save your work and close InfoPath.

> **Work item links to activities also cascade to parent workstreams.**

To verify your work, open your custom process guidance in Internet Explorer and make sure that the work items appear as they should under the Work Item tab. In addition, check all the work item parts.

Creating custom roles

Your team may include roles that are not defined in the default MSF templates, or you may have overlap between roles. You can modify your process guidance to consolidate roles, delete roles, and create new roles. Please refer to Chapter 21 for more in-depth information about roles.

Here are the steps for adding a new role in your process guidance:

1. Open your process guidance file (`ProcessGuidance.xml`) using InfoPath.

2. Add a new Content Item. Select Role under Content Type.

3. Add a name for your new role in the Content Name field.

4. Add a description for the new role in the Content Description field. You can use the existing descriptions as a template for the wording and format.

5. Save your work and close InfoPath.

Once your role has been created in the process template, you must determine whether RACI information has to be added to an associated activity or workstream. To verify your work, open `ProcessGuidance.htm` and confirm that the role and description appear under the Role tab.

Cross-references

Cross-references enable you to access internal content and content from outside sources. If you look at MSDN or any Microsoft-supplied help file (such as MS Help 2.0), you'll notice that cross-reference links are available at the bottom of each page to direct you to additional resources. You can build three types of cross-references in your process guidance:

❏ **Next Step references.** Next steps are activities that should follow the current activity.

❏ **See Also references.** See Also references provide additional information about a topic.

❏ **Patterns & Practices references.** These provide additional process guidance information about a particular item.

Here are the steps to create a cross-reference in your documentation:

1. Open your process guidance file (`ProcessGuidance.xml`) using InfoPath.

2. If a Cross Type section doesn't exist for the item on which you are working, you can insert one by selecting Insert Item.

3. Depending on the type of cross-reference you want to create, select `NextStep`, `SeeAlso`, or `PatternPractices`.

4. Add a name in the Cross Name field to describe your cross-reference. If you are creating a Next Step reference, you must enter the exact `ContentName` of the activity or workstream you are referencing.

5. For See Also and Patterns & Practices references, add a URL in the Cross Link field.

6. Save your work and close InfoPath to view your changes.

Viewing your custom guidance

After all your changes have been completed, you can re-upload your process guidance to the Team Foundation Server. That means once you create a new project, each team member will be able to access and adhere to your documentation.

Using the `MSFWinBuild` tool (mentioned earlier in the chapter), you can compile all the changes you have made into pre-formatted HTML files. If you don't, you will likely encounter the error "Error Code 0 - The download of the specified resource has failed" when you try to create a new project and view your work. The error occurs because your files are still in Edit mode, rather than Built mode — Edit mode files cannot be accessed using HTTP. However, you can view the changes locally using Internet Explorer.

The `MSFWinBuild` tool reads the `ProcessGuidance.xml` manifest and creates the compiled version of your HTML files. All the target filenames and directories are contained in `WssTasks.xml`. If you have made any changes (added or removed process guidance files), you will have to update the .xml file or your changes will not render correctly.

Customizing Process Templates

In order to create a Team Project, you must first select a process template. In fact, Microsoft included two MSF templates available by default: MSF for Agile Development and MSF for CMMI Process Improvement (you can learn about these frameworks in Chapter 21).

These default templates are usually stored in Team Foundation Server and are retrieved using the New Team Project Wizard. It is highly doubtful that these default templates will fit your needs perfectly. Like many other parts of Team System, process templates are customizable and extensible. In this section, you'll get an end-to-end overview on how to export, design, and import your own process templates.

The workflow process of customizing templates is quite straightforward. At this stage, all that is required to modify process templates is a text editor. To upload your work, you can use the Process Template Manager. To access the Process Template Manager, simply select Team ⇨ Team Foundation Server Settings ⇨ Process Template Manager. You can also access the Process Template Manager by right-clicking your Team Foundation Server icon in the Team Explorer and selecting Team Foundation Server Settings ⇨ Process Template Manager. The window that appears will provide you with several options, including Upload, Download, Make Default, or Delete.

Downloading a process template to your desktop

To modify a process template, you must first export it from the Team Foundation Server to a local drive (your desktop, for example). The key tool for all upload/download operations is the Process Template Manager. The Process Template Manager is made available by installing the Team Explorer as a stand-alone tool or within Visual Studio. The Process Template Manager will export and uncompress all the source files for editing. Here are the required steps to export a process template:

1. Select Team ⇨ Team Foundation Server Settings ⇨ Process Template Manager.
2. The Process Template Manager will open (as shown in Figure 22-2).

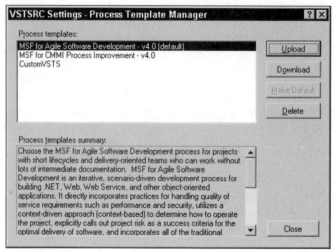

Figure 22-2

3.   Select MSF for Agile Software Development – v4.0 (default).

4.   Click the Download button on the right.

5.   Navigate to your desktop and click Save. Your process template will download to your desktop
      and you will receive the following message: "Process Template downloaded successfully"
      (as shown in Figure 22-3).

*The "Full Process" version of MSF is your best bet if you want to integrate both process and template
customizations. As mentioned in the section "Obtaining the Microsoft Solutions Framework," in
Chapter 21, you can download the full process template on the Team System MSF website* (http://
msdn.microsoft.com/msf).

Navigating a process template

Once your files have been exported, they will appear as shown in Figure 22-4. All the exported files are
part of the Process Template Definition.

Figure 22-3

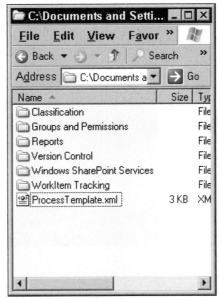

Figure 22-4

The following are the components of a Process Template Definition. In the section that follows, you'll learn how to manipulate all parts of the Process Template Definition to make it suit your custom or in-house process:

- ❑ **ProcessTemplate.xml.** Base template definition of the process itself that consists of configurable elements such as the Project Portal and the reports site, for example.

- ❑ **Classification.** Project definitions.

- ❑ **WorkItem Tracking.** Work item types and query definitions.

- ❑ **Groups and Permissions.** Groups and permissions definitions.

- ❑ **Reports.** Report definitions.

- ❑ **Version Control.** Version control definitions.

- ❑ **Windows SharePoint Services.** SharePoint Portal Stylesheet definitions, including process guidance.

Modifying template definitions

ProcessTemplate.xml contains three pieces of information about your process: the name, the description, and the plug-ins required to create a project. Plug-ins are used to extract Work Products (Word, Excel, Project, or Visual Studio documents), directories, and other important files from compressed process templates (stored as binary objects) on Team Foundation Server.

To add a unique name for your new process template, edit ProcessTemplate.xml. At the beginning of the file, you'll find two nodes: name and description. name is a required element. The description should explain the process template in a short paragraph and distinguish it from other processes. Simply edit the nodes as follows:

```
<?xml version="1.0" encoding="utf-8" ?>
<ProcessTemplate>
<metadata>
<name>My New Process</name>
<description>This custom process is used in the development team at company
XYZ.</description>
```

The name will appear on the process template list in the Create New Project Wizard. The description will appear right below. Figure 22-5 shows how the information appears in the New Project Creation Wizard.

The next part of the XML file contains a list of the required plug-ins in your process template. Let's say that your process requires no changes to the SharePoint Team Site. You could then omit the following line from the list of plug-ins:

```
<plugin name="Microsoft.ProjectCreationWizard.Portal" wizardPage="false"/>
```

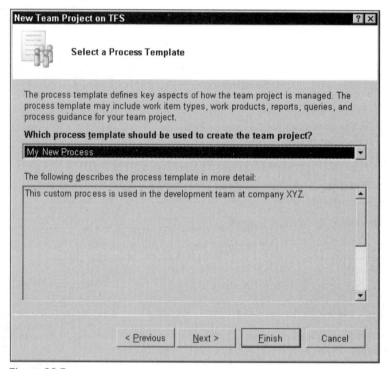

Figure 22-5

Here are the default plug-ins you will find in any Team System process template:

```
<plugins>
<plugin name="Microsoft.ProjectCreationWizard.Classification" wizardPage="false"/>
<plugin name="Microsoft.ProjectCreationWizard.Reporting" wizardPage="false"/>
<plugin name="Microsoft.ProjectCreationWizard.Portal" wizardPage="true"/>
<plugin name="Microsoft.ProjectCreationWizard.Groups" wizardPage="false"/>
<plugin name="Microsoft.ProjectCreationWizard.VersionControl" wizardPage="true"/>
```

```
<plugin name="Microsoft.ProjectCreationWizard.WorkItemTracking"
wizardPage="false"/>
</plugins>
</metadata>
```

This plug-in section is extremely important because it defines what parts of your process template will be enabled in your project. The purpose of each plug-in will be covered throughout the chapter.

This part of the process template is comparable to a .NET build manifest. It contains all of the necessary steps to define a complete Team project. When you transfer this file to Team Foundation Server, it is automatically zipped (along with the files associated with your process). The `MetaData.xml` file is used to provide information about your process.

The core template

The rest of the process template contains similar information as the meta-data portion of the file, with one important difference: it outlines the dependencies between plug-ins. A plug-in is an agent that extracts and sets up the files required for part of your process guidance. Each plug-in will use an associated `Task.xml` file to correctly build your process guidance within a Team Project. For example, once a Team Project is generated, the `Microsoft.ProjectCreationWizard.Classification` plug-in will access the `Classification.xml` file within the Classification directory and perform all associated tasks. `wizardPage` is a required attribute that indicates whether the plug-in requires a configuration page in the wizard.

Some plug-ins are dependent on others to be able to run — in particular, when security settings or permissions are required. For better manageability, you should order your tasks and dependencies in the same order. Table 22-2 outlines the dependencies between plug-ins.

Table 22-2

Plug-in Name	Dependencies
Microsoft.ProjectCreationWizard.Classification	Has no dependencies but is required to set up a project
Microsoft.ProjectCreationWizard.WorkItemTracking	The WorkItemTracking plug-in relies on the Classification plug-in and Groups plug-ins. WorkItemTracking is a non-required plug-in (that is, you can use third-party work item management tools to manage your life cycle).
Microsoft.ProjectCreationWizard.Groups	The Classification plug-in is required to use the Groups plug-in. The Groups plugin is non-required.
Microsoft.ProjectCreationWizard.Reporting	The Reporting plug-in requires the Classification and the Groups plug-ins. Otherwise, it is a non-required plug-in.

Table continued on following page

Plug-in Name	Dependencies
Microsoft.ProjectCreationWizard.VersionControl	The Classification plug-in is required to use the Version control plug-in. The Version control plug-in is non-required (i.e., you can use third-party version control tools and/or repositories to manage source code).
Microsoft.ProjectCreationWizard.Portal	The Portal plug-in has no dependencies and is not required to create a Team Project.

The plug-in dependencies are outlined in the `group` portion of the `ProcessTemplate.xml` file. In the following example, the `WorkItemTracking` plug-in is dependent on the Classification plug-in and the Groups plug-in:

```
<group id="WorkItemTracking"
        description="Workitem definitions uploading."
        completionMessage="Workitem definitions uploaded.">
        <dependencies>
            <dependency groupId="Classification"/>
            <dependency groupId="Groups"/>
        </dependencies>
        <taskList filename="WorkItem Tracking\WorkItems.xml"/>
    </group>
```

All plug-in groups are organized as one task group for every plug-in. A `taskList` defines work or configurations within a Team Project, such as creating a new report type, adding new Team Portal files, and so forth.

In the following example, the version control plug-in will set default permissions, check-in notes, and exclusive check-out settings using the version control task file (`VersionControl.xml`):

```
<?xml version="1.0" encoding="utf-8" ?>
<tasks>
    <task id="VersionControlTask"
        name="Create Version Control area"
        plugin="Microsoft.ProjectCreationWizard.VersionControl"
        completionMessage="Version control Task completed.">
        <dependencies/>
        <taskXml>
            <permission allow="Read, PendChange, Checkin, Label, Lock, ReviseOther,
UnlockOther, UndoOther, LabelOther, AdminProjectRights, CheckinOther"
identity="[$$PROJECTNAME$$]\Project Administrators"/>
            <permission allow="Read, PendChange, Checkin, Label, Lock"
identity="[$$PROJECTNAME$$]\Contributors"/>
            <permission allow="Read" identity="[$$PROJECTNAME$$]\Readers"/>
            <permission allow="Read, PendChange, Checkin, Label, Lock"
identity="[$$PROJECTNAME$$]\Build Services"/>
            <checkin_note label="Code Reviewer" required="false" order="1"/>
            <checkin_note label="Security Reviewer" required="false" order="2"/>
```

```
                  <checkin_note label="Performance Reviewer" required="false" order="3"/>
                  <exclusive_checkout required="false"/>
            </taskXml>
      </task>
</tasks>
```

The next section describes in greater detail how to control the setup of Team Foundation Version Control.

Team Foundation version control

The primary file to control the Team Foundation version control settings within your process is called `VersionControl.xml`. The version control plug-in (`Microsoft.ProjectCreationWizard.VersionControl`) will enable you to set up features such as permissions, check-in notes, and check-out policies.

You first define a task to create the source code repository in your project:

```
<?xml version="1.0" encoding="utf-8" ?>
<tasks>

    <task id="VersionControlTask"
          name="Create Version Control area"
          plugin="Microsoft.ProjectCreationWizard.VersionControl"
          completionMessage="Version control Task completed.">

        <dependencies/>
```

Then you can programmatically set the permissions for each of the security groups on Team Foundation Server (for more information on configuring Team Foundation security groups, please refer to Chapter 19):

```
<taskXml>
   <permission allow="Read, PendChange, Checkin, Label, Lock, ReviseOther,
UnlockOther, UndoOther, LabelOther, AdminProjectRights, CheckinOther"
identity="[$$PROJECTNAME$$]\Project Administrators"/>
   <permission allow="Read, PendChange, Checkin, Label, Lock"
identity="[$$PROJECTNAME$$]\Contributors"/>
   <permission allow="Read" identity="[$$PROJECTNAME$$]\Readers"/>
   <permission allow="Read, PendChange, Checkin, Label, Lock"
identity="[$$PROJECTNAME$$]\Build Services"/>
```

If you want to give your contributors the rights to read their peer's source code, you can easily add `ReviseOther`, `UnlockOther`, `UndoOther`, and `Checkin` rights to the Contributor role in the XML file:

```
<permission allow="Read, PendChange, Checkin, Label, Lock, ReviseOther,
UnlockOther, UndoOther, LabelOther, CheckinOther"
identity="[$$PROJECTNAME$$]\Contributors"/>
```

The next part of the XML file enables you to set the check-in notes. First, preliminary roles are set up corresponding to the groups responsible for governance. For example, a code reviewer may be responsible for verifying the integrity of code (in a peer programming environment), or a manager has to check the source code before it is checked into an important part of the version control tree. You can view the check-in note configuration page via the Source Control settings within your Team Project. (Right-click your project in the Team Explorer and select Team Project Settings ⇨ Source Control ⇨ Check-in Notes.) The required field indicates whether notes are absolutely required (and from whom) when code or files are checked in:

```
<checkin_note label="Code Reviewer" required="false" order="1"/>
<checkin_note label="Security Reviewer" required="false" order="2"/>
<checkin_note label="Performance Reviewer" required="false" order="3"/>
```

Unfortunately, most source code control policies can't be set by default using a custom process template. You must create policies and manually enable them within your Team Project. You can learn more about source control policy customization by looking at the Team System Extensibility SDK. James Manning has a great code sample and article on how to scan the history for the changesets that had policy overrides. You can read more about it here: http://blogs.msdn.com/jmanning/archive/2005/ 11/04/489193.aspx. *Marcel de Vries (a Team System MVP) also has a blog post on how to receive e-mail on a Team Foundation check-in policy violation:* http://blogs.infosupport.com/ marcelv/archive/2005/10/18/1635.aspx.

Check-in notes are used to explain the reasons why source code has been checked in. Several scenarios are possible, including doing a code review or fixing a special bug. You can add a check-in note using the following syntax:

```
<checkin_note label="Custom Review" required="true" order="1" />
```

You can use the exclusive check-out element to specify whether one developer or several developers can simultaneously check out source files. If you set the attribute to "true", you limit the number of people that can access a source file to one per file! A "false" value will allow multiple developers to check out files and manage the changes once the files are checked out. Here is an example of the code to enable exclusive check-out:

```
<exclusive_checkout required="true"/>
</taskXml>
</task>
</tasks>
```

Several states are available for source code file permissions. Table 22-3 outlines the important permissions and their associated descriptions.

Table 22-3

Permission	Description
AdminProjectRights	The user can configure source code control security.
Checkin	The user can check in updated source code.
CheckinOther	The current user can check in using another user's credentials. You must have the required credentials to use conversion tools.
Label	The user can add a label to a source code item.

Permission	Description
LabelOther	The current user can change a label created by another user.
Lock	The current user can lock source code items, preventing other users from manipulating them.
PendChange	The user is given the capability to manipulate a changeset, and can branch, merge, delete, undelete, add, check out, and perform other relevant activities.
Read	The user can read any source code file or associated folder.
ReviseOther	The current user can manipulate another user's check-in notes and comments for a changeset.
UndoOther	The current user can undo a pending change created by another user.
UnlockOther	The current user can remove another user's lock.

The Team Foundation version control folder is created using the New Team Project Wizard.

When you create a Team Project, you can check the custom settings you've added to your process template. To verify that all features and configuration work as advertised, follow these steps:

1. Upload your process template (as described at the end of the chapter in the section "Uploading process templates in Team Foundation Server").

2. Start a new Team Project using your new process template.

3. Right-click on your Team Project and select Team Project Settings ➪ Source Control.

4. Make sure that your Exclusive Checkout settings have been successfully configured.

5. Pick the Check-in Notes tab and make sure that the check-in notes have been added.

6. Now you have to test the line command functionality of your custom source repository. Open a Visual Studio command prompt.

7. Type the following command:

```
tf.exe workspace /new /s:servername
```

Substitute *servername* with the name of your Team Foundation server. Enter a new name for your workspace in the dialog box and click the OK button.

8. To look at a complete list of all the security permissions for your Team Project folders, type in the following command:

```
tf.exe permission /recursive
```

Work items

The Work Item plug-in (`Microsoft.ProjectCreationWizard.WorkItemTracking`) handles all work item tasks, including types, instances, and queries. During project creation, the plug-in has the task of instantiating all the documents you need within a process.

The primary file you will be editing is called workitems.xml, located in the WorkItemTracking folder within your process template folder. The WorkItemTracking folder contains two main directories: one containing queries and one for your project type definitions.

You can customize type definitions to handle tasks such as time tracking and other tasks. The schema is quite extensible and enables you to track any type of information you need within a project.

Work item types (WIT)

Work item types are quite important because they enable you to define what a work item will do. For example, you can set fields, transitions, and rules to fit a new bug type or requirement. You can find all of the work item type information in the TypeDefinitions folder of your WorkItem Tracking directory. The naming conventions are quite simple: for example, a bug schema is located in a file called Bug.xml, and so forth.

To create a new work item type, you must first define it within the workitems.xml file using your XML editing tool of choice. This file is divided into three parts: work item types, tasks, and queries. The work item type portion of the file looks like this:

```
<task
    id="WITs"
    name="WorkItemType definitions"
    plugin="Microsoft.ProjectCreationWizard.WorkItemTracking"
    completionMessage="WorkItemTypes created"
    completionDescription = "Processing work item types used by work item tracking">
  <taskXml>
    <WORKITEMTYPES>
      <WORKITEMTYPE fileName="WorkItem Tracking\TypeDefinitions\Bug.xml"/>
      <WORKITEMTYPE fileName="WorkItem Tracking\TypeDefinitions\Task.xml"/>
      <WORKITEMTYPE fileName="WorkItem Tracking\TypeDefinitions\Qos.xml"/>
      <WORKITEMTYPE fileName="WorkItem Tracking\TypeDefinitions\Scenario.xml"/>
      <WORKITEMTYPE fileName="WorkItem Tracking\TypeDefinitions\Risk.xml"/>
    </WORKITEMTYPES>
  </taskXml>
</task>
```

Simply add a new work item type using the WORKITEMTYPE element to point to the specific type definition for your custom type. For example, if you were building a Time Tracking type, then you would insert the following within the WORKITEMTYPES node:

```
<WORKITEMTYPE fileName="WorkItem Tracking\TypeDefinitions\TimeTracking.xml"/>
```

You then must create a file called TimeTracking.xml within your TypeDefinitions folder. You have the choice of copying the fields and layout of an existing work item and customizing it to your needs, or, if you are adventurous, you can create a work item from scratch.

Please refer to Chapter 19 for more information on the anatomy of a work item and how to build custom work items for your project.

Work item queries

Work item queries function to group together work items by criteria such as category or by the value of a specific field. All the work item queries can be found in the `Queries` folder within the `WorkItem Tracking` directory. All work item queries files end with a `.wiq` extension. Here is an example of the All Work Items query located in `AllWorkItems.wiq`:

```xml
<?xml version="1.0" encoding="utf-8"?>
<WorkItemQuery Version="1">
    <Wiql>SELECT [System.Id], [System.WorkItemType], [Microsoft.VSTS.Common.Rank],
[System.State], [System.AssignedTo], [System.Title] FROM WorkItems
        WHERE [System.TeamProject] = @project AND [System.State] &lt;&gt; 'Closed'
        ORDER BY [Microsoft.VSTS.Common.Rank], [System.WorkItemType], [System.Id]
    </Wiql>
</WorkItemQuery>
```

If you want to create custom queries from scratch using an editor, we recommend you study the `WorkItemType` data constructs within SQL Server 2005.

From a practical perspective, work item queries can be accessed by anyone on your team because they are an integral part of your project. Team Explorer is the easiest tool to use when you create a customized work item query. You can then save the work item query (into a .wiq file) using the following steps:

1. Right-click on a query in Team Explorer and select Query View.

2. Choose Save As in the File menu and select a name.

3. Select a location and name for your .wiq file.

4. Copy your new query file into the `Queries` folder within the `WorkItem Tracking` directory of your custom template.

You then have to add the query to your template. The `QUERIES` portion of the `workitems.xml` file has the following structure:

```xml
<task
 id="Queries"
 name="Stored Query Definitions"
 plugin="Microsoft.ProjectCreationWizard.WorkItemTracking"
 completionMessage="Queries uploaded"
 completionDescription = "Processing the stored queries used by work item
tracking">
<dependencies>
    <dependency taskId="WIs" />
    <dependency taskId="WITs" />
</dependencies>
<taskXml>
<QUERIES>
<Query name="My Work Items" fileName="WorkItem Tracking\Queries\MyWorkItems.wiq" />
<Query name="All Tasks" fileName="WorkItem Tracking\Queries\AllTasks.wiq" />
<Query name="Active Bugs" fileName="WorkItem Tracking\Queries\ActiveBugs.wiq" />
...
</QUERIES>
</taskXml>
</task>
```

Simply insert the following line of code within the QUERIES element to include your custom work item query:

```
<Query name="Custom Query" fileName="WorkItem Tracking\Queries\CustomQuery.wiq" />
```

Work item instances

You can define what work items should be instantiated when a Team Project is created. If you look at the workitems.xml file, you'll notice a lengthy section within the task element. This block of XML code will create an instance of a task work item. The first part of the code block defines what plug-in to use, a completion message, and a task description. You can customize these messages as you see fit:

```
<task
 id="WIs"
 name="WorkItems"
 plugin="Microsoft.ProjectCreationWizard.WorkItemTracking"
 completionMessage="Work items uploaded"
 completionDescription = "Processing the actual work items used by work item
 tracking">
<dependencies>
 <dependency taskId="WITs" />
</dependencies>
```

The next part of the code block enumerates the work items to be included by default in a project. Here is an example of the "Set Permissions" task:

```
<WORKITEMS>
<WI type="Task">
<FIELD refname="System.Title" value="Setup: Set Permissions" />
<FIELD refname="System.IterationPath" value="$$PROJECTNAME$$\Iteration 0" />
<FIELD refname="System.State" value="Active" />
<FIELD refname="System.Reason" value="New" />
<FIELD refname="Microsoft.VSTS.Common.Issue" value="No" />
<FIELD refname="Microsoft.VSTS.Common.ExitCriteria" value="Yes" />
<FIELD refname="System.Description" value="Using the admin UI in VS add users to
one of the 3 groups: Project administrators, Contributors or Readers." />
</WI>...
</WORKITEMS>
</taskXml>
</task>
```

You can use the WI element to define the work item type and the FIELD element to specify the attributes and values assigned to your work item. The attributes outlined in the preceding example are required fields.

We can't emphasize enough how important it is to define the correct structure for your work items. In most cases, try to clone a preexisting work item and tailor it to your needs. Otherwise, problems may occur — for example, when you try to map work item fields to Microsoft Project columns.

Testing your changes

The last step you must take to verify that your queries, instances, and type definitions are valid is uploading a new process template and trying to create a Team Project using your customized template. To test your work item customizations, follow these steps (you may need to repeat some of these steps for each work item type, instance, and query you have created):

1. Upload your custom process template to the Team Foundation Server. (See the section "Uploading process templates in Team Foundation Server" at the end of the chapter.)

2. Create a new Team Project using your template. The Team Project creation process is outlined in detail in Chapter 19.

3. Within the Team Explorer, right-click the Work Items node.

4. Choose the Add Work Item option and select one of your custom work items.

5. Verify the structure and layout of fields in your custom work item.

6. Run usability tests on your work item. Try out all of the field states and conditions.

7. Verify whether your query exists in the My Queries node inside Team Explorer.

8. View the results of a query by right-clicking on it and selecting View Results. Make sure that the results are the ones you are expecting!

9. Run the All Work Items query. Make sure your custom work items appear.

You can also modify work items on existing projects using the `witimport` and `witexport` tools. Please refer to the Visual Studio 2005 SDK for more information (available at `www.vsipdev.com`).

Windows SharePoint Services team portal

From within the process template, you can define elements such as process guidance, document templates, SharePoint templates, and other important files stored on the Team Project Portal. Windows SharePoint Services artifacts are created using the Windows SharePoint plug-in (`Microsoft.ProjectCreationWizard.Portal`).

From within the process guidance folder (Agile or CMMI), the `Windows SharePoint Services` directory contains all the files you need to manipulate the portal guidance and template. Within this directory, you will find several folders:

❑ **Process Guidance.** This folder contains HTML and XML versions of your process guidance files. See the section earlier in this chapter entitled "Customizing Process Guidance" for more information on customizing that part of the project.

❑ **Work Product Folders.** These contain work products (templates and supporting files) for `project management`, `security`, `requirements` and `test`.

Any directory, file, or template contained in the `Windows Sharepoint Services` *directory can be updated and customized to fit your process requirements.*

Document template schema

The `WssTasks.xml` file located in the `Windows Sharepoint Services` directory contains an enumeration of all the SharePoint elements found within your custom process. The file is divided into three sections. The first section lists all of the document libraries (including titles and descriptions) related to your process. This is a high-level way of categorizing your documents — you can easily add and remove any of these categories based on your needs. Please note that these libraries are accessible when you click the `Documents and Lists` link on the main page of the project portal.

```xml
<?xml version="1.0" encoding="utf-8" ?>
<tasks>
  <task id="SharePointPortal"
        name="Create Sharepoint Portal"
        plugin="Microsoft.ProjectCreationWizard.Portal"
        completionMessage="Project site created.">
<dependencies/>
<taskXml>
<Portal>
<site template="VSTS_MSFAgile" language="1033"/>
<documentLibraries>
  <documentLibrary name="Security" description="Documents for the architect team"/>
  <documentLibrary name="Test" description="Documents for the test team"/>
...
</documentLibraries>
```

The `folders` node lists all the folders within specific document libraries. The example defines the folders found in the Process Guidance library:

```xml
<folders>
    <folder documentLibrary="Process Guidance" name="Supporting Files"/>
    <folder documentLibrary="Process Guidance" name="Supporting Files/Code" />
    <folder documentLibrary="Process Guidance" name="Supporting Files/CSS" />
    <folder documentLibrary="Process Guidance" name="Supporting Files/EULA" />
    <folder documentLibrary="Process Guidance" name="Supporting Files/HTML" />
    <folder documentLibrary="Process Guidance" name="Supporting Files/images" />
    <folder documentLibrary="Process Guidance" name="Supporting Files/Other" />
    <folder documentLibrary="Process Guidance" name="Supporting Files/Schema" />
    <folder documentLibrary="Process Guidance" name="Supporting Files/XML" />
    <folder documentLibrary="Process Guidance" name="Supporting Files/XSLs" />
</folders>
```

The Files section of `WssTasks.xml` lists all of the files to be included into a Team Project once your process file has been selected. These include process guidance files and work products:

```xml
<files>
<file source="Windows SharePoint Services\Process Guidance\ProcessGuidance.html"
      target="Process Guidance/ProcessGuidance.html" />
<file source="Windows SharePoint Services\Process Guidance\Supporting
      Files\AboutRoles.htm"
      target="Process Guidance/Supporting Files/AboutRoles.htm" />
...
</files>
</Portal>
</taskXml>
</task>
</tasks>
```

Adding new work products to your team portal

Adding a work product within your process is quite easy using XML. Simply define the path to your source file and the target path of the folder on the server (as defined in the `documentLibraries` collection):

```
<file source="Windows SharePoint Services\Templates\YourPolicy.doc"
target="Security/YourPolicy.doc" />
```

Customizing the team portal

There may be circumstances where you will need to modify the "look-and-feel" and structure of the Team Portal. It's important to establish an identity for the site, and doing so will help your team members feel ownership of it. SharePoint customization (such as creating site definitions and custom Web parts) is out of scope for this book. However, we'll provide you with solid, basic instructions to change the look of the site.

Adding your custom logo to the team portal

Here are the steps to add a custom logo to the portal. SharePoint Services site customization is primarily done using FrontPage 2003. You can also use an XML editor to make style changes by hand:

1. Launch FrontPage 2003.

2. Click File ➪ Open Site.

3. Type the URL of the site you want to customize. For example: `http://tfs/sites/MyCustomSite`.

4. You may be prompted for an administrative username/password.

5. The site will come up in the editor.

6. Click the "images" folder in the folder list on the left side of the screen.

7. Use File ➪ Import and select the custom logo you designed. This will upload the logo into the `images` folder.

   You can use a similar technique to upload custom Web Parts (.dwp) files. Before clicking the Import option, open up the folder list and select _catalogs ➪ wp (Web Part Gallery). That will make it available on the site when you select Modify Shared Page on the portal site.

8. Select the current MSF logo and hit the Delete key to remove it.

9. Open the images folder from the treeview on the left side of the screen and drag and drop your new custom logo into the placeholder in the design view of the portal.

10. Save your changes.

Saving your changes will make your customizations automatically appear on the project portal. You can customize everything from site colors to the graphics on the page. Most of the styles are contained in stylesheets in the `themes` directory.

Saving your custom site template

You now have one of two choices: You can customize each site on a one-by-one basis, or you can save your work as a SharePoint site template and associate it to your process template. The latter option makes sense if you are planning to reuse a process template over and over again. It saves you from having to take the manual steps to customize the "look-and-feel" after creating each project portal. Here are the steps to create a site template file.

1. Open your customized Team Portal.

2. Click Site Settings.

3. Click Go to Site Administration on the Administration menu.

4. Under Management and Statistics, click Save Site as Template.

5. You will now have the option of creating a new filename for your custom template (`filename.stp`). You can also add in a template title and description.

> **We recommend that you omit any spaces from your template filename.**

6. There is a checkbox on the form that says "Include content". This will include all the files that are currently part of your team portal. If you think that you will reuse all of the same files on the portal everytime you create a Team Project, click on the checkbox. Otherwise, leave it unchecked.

    Your template has now been saved.

Here are the instructions to obtain a copy of the site template as a `.stp` file. The `.stp` file is actually a `.cab` (Cabinet) file that contains an XML manifest describing the structure of the site and a collection of compressed files with your template's assets. Follow these steps:

1. From the home page of your portal, click Site Settings.

2. Under Administration, click Go to Site Administration.

3. Under Site Collection Galleries, click Manage Site Template Gallery.

4. Click your template and download the `.stp` file to your `C:\` drive.

Now, you need to make SharePoint recognize the new template and modify the process template. Assuming that you put your custom `.stp` file in the root of the C:\ drive, type the following command using the command prompt and hit Enter:

```
> cd C:\
```

Then type the following to add the custom site template to Team Foundation Server:

```
> "C:\Program Files\Common Files\Microsoft Shared\web server extensions\60\bin\
stsadm.exe" -o addtemplate -filename mycustomtemplate.stp -title customtemplate
```

In the preceding example, the filename for your custom template is `mycustomtemplate.stp`. You also designated `customtemplate` as the identifying title for the template. The title is quite important, as it is used to link the site template to your process template. Once your site template has been added, all you need to do is to make a small customization in your process template.

Integrating a site template within a process template

At this point, all you need to do is link the process template to the site template. Here are the steps to integrate both together.

1. Download a copy of a process template to your desktop as described at the beginning of the chapter.

2. Open the `Windows Sharepoint Services` folder and edit `WssTasks.xml` in your favorite XML editor.

3. Update this `site` node, changing the template to your custom template title. For example:

```
<site template="customtemplate" language="1033" />
```

4. Upload your customized process template. (The steps are described in the section "Uploading process templates in Team Foundation Server.") Before you do that, you may want to rename the title of the process.

Now every time you create a new Team Project using your custom process, a Team Portal will be generated with your custom logo and colors.

Verifying your portal customizations

The best way to check your custom SharePoint setting is by creating a brand-new project incorporating your custom process template. To test your customized process template, use the following steps:

1. Upload your custom process template to the Team Foundation Server (see the section "Uploading process templates in Team Foundation Server" at the end of the chapter).

2. Create a new Team Project using your template. The Team Project creation process is outlined in detail in Chapter 19.

3. Select the Show Project Portal option by right-clicking on your Team Project within the Team Explorer window.

4. Select the Documents and List option at the top of your project portal.

5. Click Document Libraries to see whether they were properly created.

6. You can then click on individual files to determine whether they are located in the right document libraries.

SQL Reporting services

You can use the Reporting plug-in (`Microsoft.ProjectCreationWizard.Reporting`) to manage many aspects of Team System's reporting engine, including the creation of the preliminary default reports that appear on the project portal when you use the New Team Project Wizard. All of the configuration information is contained in a file called `ReportsTasks.xml` located in the Reports folder in your process template. Within this file, you can set iterations, groups, and permissions and define what reports will appear on the Project Site.

You can learn how to create custom reports and use tools such as the Report Builder in the "Team Reporting" section of Chapter 19.

Let's take a look at how reporting is configured within your custom process template. You can use the `site` element to define the path of your project's reporting site (the following example indicates the default value):

```xml
<?xml version="1.0" encoding="utf-8" ?>
<tasks>
<task
 id="Site"
 plugin="Microsoft.ProjectCreationWizard.Reporting"
 completionMessage="Project Reporting site created.">
<dependencies/>
<taskXml>
    <ReportingServices>
        <site />
    </ReportingServices>
</taskXml>
</task>
```

Folders can be created for your reporting site using the `folder` element placed inside the `ReportingServices` element. You define the location using a relative path, as shown here:

```xml
<ReportingServices>
<folders>
<folder path="Public"/>
</folders>
</ReportingServices>
```

Reports are represented in the process template as files with an `.rdl` extension. These files can easily be swapped in and out of your template using the `report` element. Here is an example of a Bug Rates report from the MSF Agile process template:

```xml
<report name="Bug Rates" filename="Reports\Bug Rates.rdl" folder=""  cacheExpiration
="30">
    <parameters>
        <parameter name="Project" value="$$PROJECTNAME$$"/>
    </parameters>
    <datasources>
        <reference name="/TfsOlapReportDS" dsname="TfsOlapReportDS"/>
        <reference name="/TfsReportDS" dsname="TfsReportDS"/>
    </datasources>
</report>
```

To create a link between your project property and a report, use the `$$PROJECTNAME$$` value to tell the server to use the current Team Foundation Server. Properties are used to describe characteristics of a report:

```xml
<properties>
    <property name="" value=""/>
</properties>
```

The `datasource` element is one of the most important within a report. It enables you to connect a data source name to SQL Server 2005 (via Team Foundation Server). In the following example, the data source name is `TfsReportDS`:

```
<report name="My Bugs" filename="Reports\My Bugs.rdl" folder="">
  <parameters>
    <parameter name="Project" value="$$PROJECTNAME$$"/>
  </parameters>
  <datasources>
    <reference name="/TfsReportDS" dsname="TfsReportDS"/>
  </datasources>
</report>
```

Verifying your report status

After you customize the portal's custom reports, it is important to ensure that it will create new reports once a project is instantiated. Follow these steps to validate the creation of Team System reports:

1. Upload your custom process template to the Team Foundation Server (see the section "Uploading process templates in Team Foundation Server" at the end of the chapter).

2. Click the Reports folder in your project within Team Explorer.

3. Execute and test each report.

Connectivity is key for the functioning of a report. If any data is missing, the report may not render correctly.

Classification

If you want to control the iterations and items within a project, the Classification plug-in (`Microsoft.ProjectCreationWizard.Classification`) will handle these tasks. The `Classification.xml` file contains all of the config information to allow you to define iteration hierarchies.

```
<?xml version="1.0" encoding="utf-8" ?>
<tasks>
<task
 id="UploadStructure"
 name="Creating project structure"
 plugin="Microsoft.ProjectCreationWizard.Classification"
 completionMessage="Portfolio project structure created.">
<taskXml>
<Nodes>
```

Iterations define how many times a task will be performed within a software project and determines the grouping of work items depending on the phase of the project. The `ProjectLifecycle` node is the root node for all the iterations. The `LifecycleItem` type defines each iteration within the whole:

```
<Node Type="ProjectLifecycle" Name="ProjectLifecycle" xmlns="">
    <Children>
        <Node Type="LifecycleItem" Name="Plan"></Node>
        <Node Type="LifecycleItem" Name="Develop"></Node>
```

```
            <Node Type="LifecycleItem" Name="Test"></Node>
            <Node Type="LifecycleItem" Name="Deploy"></Node>
        </Children>
    </Node>
```

You can also define organizational units (OU) within the Project Team in order to establish subgroups based on specialty. For example, you can have a development group that focuses on business logic, and another that focuses on Web UI. Organizational units are useful for grouping together work items and reports within these subgroups. An organizational unit can be defined using the ProjectModelHeirarchy root node:

```
    <Node Type="ProjectModelHierarchy" Name="ProjectModelHierarchy" xmlns="">
        <Node Type="OrganizationalUnit" Name="Business Logic DevTeam"></Node>
        <Node Type="OrganizationalUnit" Name="WebUI DevTeam"></Node>
    </Node>
</Nodes>
```

If you change the iterations or organizational units in an existing process template, be aware that work item instance tasks may be bound to specific iterations or OUs in workitem.xml.

The Classification plug-in can map work items to specific fields in Microsoft Project. Microsoft Project has a predefined table structure (unlike Microsoft Excel) and targets specific fields. The field map can be enabled to facilitate matching up Project fields with work items. In the following example, the Microsoft Project field map is contained in FileMapping.xml and referenced in the Classification.xml configuration file:

```
<properties>
    <property name="MSPROJ" value="Classification\FileMapping.xml" isFile="true" />
</properties>
</taskXml>
</task>
</tasks>
```

Here is an example of the field/work item mapping inside of FileMapping.xml.

```
<MSProject>
<Mappings>
<Mapping WorkItemTrackingFieldReferenceName="System.Id"
ProjectField="pjTaskText10"
ProjectName="Work Item ID"/>
<Mapping WorkItemTrackingFieldReferenceName="System.Title"
ProjectField="pjTaskName" />
<Mapping WorkItemTrackingFieldReferenceName="System.WorkItemType"
ProjectField="pjTaskText24" />
<Mapping WorkItemTrackingFieldReferenceName="Microsoft.VSTS.Common.Discipline"
ProjectField="pjTaskText17" />
<Mapping WorkItemTrackingFieldReferenceName="System.AssignedTo"
ProjectField="pjTaskResourceNames" />
<Mapping
WorkItemTrackingFieldReferenceName="Microsoft.VSTS.Scheduling.CompletedWork"
ProjectField="pjTaskActualWork" ProjectUnits="pjHour"/>...
</Mappings>
</MSProject>
```

You should be aware of two columns in the list: the link and attachment field (`LinksField`) type indicates whether links and attachments exist for specific rows:

```
<LinksField ProjectField="pjTaskText26" />
```

The synchronization field (`SyncField`) type indicates whether you should use a specific column as a synchronization field:

```
<SyncField ProjectField="pjTaskText25" />
```

From a user perspective, the synchronization field will display "Sync?" in Microsoft Project, which will prompt the user to refresh or publish the row.

Testing your classification customizations

Follow these steps to determine whether your Organizational Units (OU) and iterations have been created successfully:

1. Upload your custom process template to the Team Foundation Server. (See the section entitled "Upload process templates in Team Foundation Server" at the end of the chapter.)

2. Create a new Team Project using your template. The Team Project creation process is outlined in detail in Chapter 19.

3. Right-click on your project and select Team ⇨ Team Project Settings ⇨ Areas and Iterations.

4. Look at the Project tab to make sure that all of your custom Organizational Units are displaying correctly.

5. Look at the Iteration tab to make sure that your custom iterations are displayed correctly.

Groups and permissions

You can create security groups (and associated permissions) for your project using the Group Security Service plug-in (`Microsoft.ProjectCreationWizard.Groups`). All of your configuration tasks are located in `GroupsandPermissions.xml`, and your primary folder is Groups and Permissions.

Within the configuration file, you should define one task for each security group. Let's take a look at the components of the configuration file (`GroupsandPermissions.xml`). Specify a group name. In this example, the group name is `Reader`:

```
<?xml version="1.0" encoding="utf-8" ?>
<tasks>
<task id="GroupCreation1"
    name="Create Groups and Permissions"
    plugin="Microsoft.ProjectCreationWizard.Groups"
    completionMessage="Groups and Permissions created.">
<taskXml>
<groups>
<group name="Reader" description="A group for those with read access project">
```

The `permission` element is then used to assign permissions to the group you created. Exhaustive lists of all `permission` types are available in Team System's help file:

```
<permissions>
<permission name="GENERIC_READ" class="PROJECT" deny="false" />
<permission name="SUBSCRIBE_BUILD" class="PROJECT" deny="false" />
<permission name="GENERIC_READ" class="CSS_NODE" deny="false" />
<permission name="WORK_ITEM_READ" class="CSS_NODE" deny="false" />
</permissions>
</group>
</groups>
</taskXml>
</task>
</tasks>
```

In the preceding example, the `Reader` group has permission to read work items and other project artifacts and to subscribe to project services.

Verifying your custom security settings

The best way of verifying that your custom settings and permissions were created per the specification is by following these steps:

1. Upload your custom process template to the Team Foundation Server (see the section "Uploading process templates in Team Foundation Server" at the end of the chapter).

2. Create a new Team Project using your template. The Team Project creation process is outlined in detail in Chapter 19.

3. Select your Security Settings by right-clicking on your Team Project in Team Explorer.

4. Confirm that your security groups have been created correctly in the Permissions dialog box.

5. Pick one of the security groups and check the permissions to confirm that they are correct.

Uploading process templates in Team Foundation Server

Once you have customized the process template to your liking, you must re-import it into Team Foundation Server to share it with the rest of the project team members. A project manager can share your custom process by creating a new project using your process. Here are the steps to import a custom process template into Team Foundation Server:

1. Select Process Template Manager by clicking Team Foundation Server Settings within the Team menu. The process template Manager will display all the available options (please refer to Figure 22-2).

2. Click the Upload button and select your process template description file (`ProcessTemplate.xml`) using the Upload Process Template dialog box.

3. As soon as you click the Open button, the process template will import into Team Foundation Server and will appear on the list of available processes.

4. Close the Process Template Manager.

Deleting process templates

There will be times when process templates are no longer needed because they have been replaced by newer versions or they have become obsolete. We strongly recommend that you export a copy of the process template you want to delete as a backup before you take the steps to delete it. To delete a process template, simply follow these steps:

1. Choose the Process Template Manager by selecting Team Foundation Server Settings from the Team menu. You will then see a list of all the available process templates.

2. Pick a process template to delete and select Delete.

According to the Visual Studio 2005 SDK documentation, deleting a process template will not affect Team Projects that were created using the template. This is because a copy of all the artifacts from the process template (documents, source code repository, permissions) has been created on the server and the project is no longer tied to the template file.

You can then change the default template by selecting a process and clicking the Make Default button. You can then close the Process Template Manager.

Testing Your Custom Process Template

There are two primary types of tests you would want to undertake with your custom process templates. The first kind is feature (or requirements) testing to determine whether all of the customized features are available within your new template. The second type of testing you would want to undertake is usability testing: Will the feature break in certain circumstances? Does everything work as it should?

The process of designing and deploying custom processes is quite straightforward: You must customize the template, import the process template into Team Foundation Server (using the Process Template Manager), create a new Team Project, and then finally test all of the custom features. Another important recommendation we can make is to create and test your process templates in a test environment before porting them over to a production environment.

Summary

In this chapter, you got a detailed overview of process template customization. You first learned how to create custom process guidance, which integrates with Team System's toolset. Then you learned how to export, customize, and import process templates to and from Team Foundation Server with the goal of leveraging features such as security, work item extensibility, source code control customization, and project design using simple XML editing tools.

23

Team Foundation Build

One of the biggest problems with most software development packages is a lack of integration between the build engine and the rest of the systems. As a project leader, deployment manager, or build manager, a lot of your time is spent writing build scripts and configuring your environment to try to integrate other "closed" systems and tools. Another challenge you might have to face is scalability: The build server has to be able to handle multiple requests from members of your team. MSBuild is meant to be used on a single machine and doesn't scale very well on its own. NAnt is a great .NET build tool, but it hasn't yet reached v.1.0 status at the time of writing (and therefore would not be a likely candidate for an enterprise environment).

When you are using Agile process methodologies, the build step is a key component of your project: The quality of your end *product* (the compiled code) is wholly dependent on the quality of your build. Agile methodologies typically advocate quick iterative cycles with an emphasis on avoiding "build breaks." Builds are produced every hour (depending on your churn and the size of your team, you might be rebuilding several times per hour). The resulting binaries serve as a yardstick for determining the health of a project.

Team System simplifies the integration of Visual Studio 2005 and the build system with Team Foundation Build. What are the differences between Team Foundation Build and MSBuild? MSBuild is a new build engine specially designed for Visual Studio 2005. Team Foundation Build, conversely, is a build automation tool that "wraps" around MSBuild to provide that end-to-end build experience. Using Team Foundation Build, you can automate your build tasks and generate rich metrics.

> **The code name for Team Foundation Build is BigBuild.**

Here is a rundown of the typical execution steps using Team Foundation Build. In most scenarios, you would have to script these steps using other build engines:

❑ New builds are associated with a Team Foundation project and are created using a Wizard in Visual Studio. The Wizard leads you through all the steps necessary to set up a new build type. This includes generating an MSBuild XML file that represents the build script that is later executed, identifying the target location, and naming the build. The build scripts get checked into source control and synchronized with the build server, which may be different from the Team Foundation Server machine. One or more machines in team system environment may be designated as build servers.

❑ The build process is either started from the command line or initiated through the Team Foundation Build Client UI in Team Explorer. Team Foundation Build supports scheduling using the command-line build tool. The command-line options let the process be initiated using NT Scheduler for normal process scheduling. This process uses the StartBuild web method with a half a dozen parameters. Team Foundation Build can also support continuous integration scenarios, which are triggered in response to Source Code check-in events.

❑ The build request is sent to the Team Foundation Server. The builds do not execute on the Team Foundation Server machine, but are handled by the Build Server Machine that is set up to listen on the network for the build process to be run.

❑ The build server uses MS Build and MS Build Tasks to pull down source code and build scripts into a local workspace, carry out a build, and execute test suites. Any test can be run in the build process by defining a test list within the script. This can be done either through the wizard or by editing the wizard-created script directly. The test list and associated tests must be created before performing the build. Test lists can be defined under `<TestingArgs>` in the Team Foundation Build script as follows:

```
<TestingArgs>/testmetadata: $(SolutionRoot)\SimpleApp\SimpleApp.vsmdi
/testlist:BuildVerifyTest</TestingArgs>
```

❑ Test results (static analysis, code coverage) and build results (logged bugs) are sent to an operational data store. Test results are published and reported with the build results. All tests stored must be associated with a Team Foundation Build ID. This requires you to install Team Foundation Build and create and run a Team Foundation Build script in advance of publishing the test. (Team Foundtion Build is only required for test results. Work items, for example, do not require a Team Foundation Build ID.)

❑ Associated work items are then marked with the build number. New work items bugs are created for build failures. (Team Foundation Build maintains links to work items, reports changesets that went into this build, and also maintains links to these changesets.) The default behavior for Team Foundation Build is to stop the build process should any step fail.

❑ The compiled code is copied to a drop location.

❑ A build report is published to the Team Project website using data from the Team Foundation Data Warehouse. The generating build name is based on the local server time.

The tight integration between Team System components provides an added benefit of automating many of your tasks. For example, a build report will be automatically generated and displayed on the Project Site via SQL Reporting Services once a build has been completed. Work items are updated automatically based on the results of a build. The build engine runs through a gamut of tests and enables you to integrate customized or generic tests in the process using Team Test.

These build steps are not etched in stone. You can customize the build process to fit your needs. You can also customize your build settings, tests, and reports. You'll learn more about Team Foundation Build customization later in the chapter.

Team Foundation Build can be launched manually, scripted to provide continuous integration during your development process, or set up to run nightly. Team Foundation Build can also be installed locally on your desktop or installed as part of Team Foundation Server. Using custom tasks and types, you can configure with a very high level of granularity your builds on a per-project basis.

In this chapter, you'll learn the important features of Team Foundation Build. You'll first find out how to set up the build engine, including planning a build strategy and setting up build security. Next, you will learn the tasks for the day-to-day operations of Team Foundation Build, such as creating build types, configuring e-mail notifications, and running builds. You will get a good overview of the command-line tools you can use, and learn how to leverage the tools in setting up your recurring build schedules (such as nightlies and short iterative builds). Team Foundation Build has effective reporting features to help you determine the health of a build. Finally, the chapter covers Team Foundation Build extensibility, and you will learn how to program and configure Team Foundation Build using XML configuration files and the .NET API.

Without further ado, you can begin with the preliminary setup of Team Foundation Build.

Setting Up Team Foundation Build

Team Foundation Build has a straightforward architecture with three distinct layers. On the uppermost layer sits the role-based Visual Studio editions and the Team Explorer. Using these tools, you can tap into Team Foundation Server to manually launch or stop a build, edit build types, or view build run reports and logs. You can also view build reports from the reports node in Team Explorer or set up a Web part on the Team Portal. Visual Studio enables you to manipulate source code, work with work items, and schedule builds. Team Foundation Build's data infrastrure is laid out as follows: There is a data tier layer, which has the build store or the build database, where all the data is stored, and client side reports are generated from it. This data is also pushed to the overall TFS warehouse from which reports are generated using SQL reporting services.

Finally, you have the build server. You can install Team Foundation Build under many scenarios: as a desktop build engine, on the same server as Team Foundation Server, and on a standalone server. Microsoft recommends the standalone server scenario as a good option. This makes sense for several reasons, including the reduction of CPU load on the other components of Team System. If you want to run tests or static analysis, you additionally need to install the Team Edition for Software Testers or the Team Edition for Software Developers, depending on your requirements and the type of tests you need to run. Figure 23-1 illustrates the layout of Team Foundation Build's architecture.

Team Foundation Build's installer can be found in the build *directory on the Team Foundation Server media (on CD or DVD)*

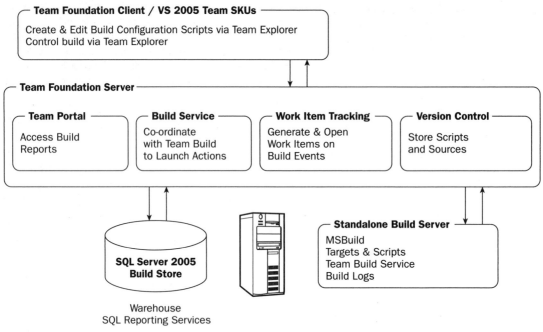

Figure 23-1

Planning a build strategy

Before you can deploy Team Foundation Build, you must first develop a strategy based on your needs. The outcome will determine how Team Foundation Build is configured, including security and build policies. Here are some of the factors you should consider:

❑ **Roles and Permissions.** Within your team, you will have predetermined roles based on the RAPI model (see Chapter 22). Who within your team will be responsible for configuring the build server? You must determine who will have the rights to initiate a build, collect build metrics, change the build process, and so forth.

❑ **Policies.** What is considered a successful build and what is considered an unsuccessful build? How should each of these cases be handled? When and in what way should a team member be notified of build errors? The determination of policies will be based on factors such as internal practices and mandatory standards compliance, such as Sarbanes-Oxley (SOX). Build policies go hand in hand with check-in policies.

❑ **Procedures.** How often will you require a build? If you are a small Agile development team, then most likely you will lean toward frequent builds, every time a check-in is performed. Nightly builds may be suitable if you have a larger shop with millions of lines of code to manage. Do all builds require the same tests? What is your test failure threshold to fail a build?

❑ **Integration.** How will Team Foundation Build integrate with your current development environment? This includes implementing buddy builds or continuous integration (CI). In the section that follows, you'll learn how Team Foundation Build integrates with the rest of Team System.

Setting up your own build lab

Microsoft likes to refer to Team Foundation Build as "your own private build lab." When you install Team Foundation Server, please note that Team Foundation Build is not installed automatically. You must consciously and purposefully install it. The installer is located on the Team Foundation Server installation media. In addition, you need a local administrator account on the target machine in order to install Team Foundation Build.

In the installer, Team Foundation Build is referred to as Team Foundation Server (build)

During the installation process, you have to provide the installer with account information such as the username and password. You should create a dedicated account with sufficient privileges to enable the TfsBuildService to successfully run. If you have misconfigured the build machine account, you can easily add the permission later and the Services Control Panel applet to set the service to run.

To perform test automation, you need to have the appropriate Team System role-based edition installed on the build machine. We recommend installing the Team Edition for Developers, as it contains important automated tests such as unit tests and static code tests.

After the install finishes, create two folders that will be used as part of the build process. The first one is the interim folder, called the *build location,* where Team Foundation Build will extract and build your solution. The second is the *drop location,* a shared folder that must be accessible over the network using the Universal Naming Convention (UNC) format (`\server\shareddropfolder\`). This folder must be given full permissions to the build service account and the Team Foundation service account (`TFSSERVICE`). The reason for this is twofold: First, if you don't share the folder, your team members will not be able to access the builds unless they have physical access to the build machine. Second, the build process will fail primarily because the drop location is the place where all build results, including test results, are published. In a scenario where a tester is manually publishing test results against this build, he or she would need to have permission to publish content on this folder. Hence, it is recommended that everyone have valid permissions on this folder. You can test whether the drop folder has been configured correctly by browsing to the folder over the network.

Team System integration

Team Foundation Build integrates with Team System in several ways:

- ❑ **Work Items Database.** Team Foundation Build automatically creates work items when a build fails or annotates an existing work item with build information.

- ❑ **Team Foundation Version Control.** The main integration points are as follows: to synchronize sources from source control, to label sources that were built, to get information regarding the changesets that went into a particular build, and to store the build type files. Team Foundation version control is the only supported source control system supported in V1. In order to use a third-party solution like Borland's StarTeam, you will build steps and replace the Source Control extraction step that is part of Team Foundation Build.

- ❑ **Team Explorer.** Once a Team Project is created, build configuration and reports are integrated in the Team Explorer tree within a Team Builds folder. Using Team Explorer, you can perform many build tasks, such as initiating a build, creating build types, and viewing build reports.

❑ **Test Integration.** Team Foundation Build integrates deeply with Team System Tests. You can incorporate tests such as unit testing, code coverage, and static analysis in the build process by creating test runs and associating them to a build.

❑ **Reporting Integration.** Team Foundation Build provides holistic information about the health of your data, including how builds rank against historical data. Build information is automatically stored in the Team System data repository, including build configuration, errors, and status information.

❑ **Web Service Integration.** Using the BuildStore and BuildController Web services, you can access status information and control the Team System build engine. These Web services are enabled via the Team Foundation Server. Please refer to the end of the chapter for more information.

Setting up build security

Team Foundation Build has specific security rights and permissions built on top of Team Foundation Server's security groups. In fact, Team Foundation Build has a series of specific privileges to enable (or disable) functionality. The inclusion or omission of permissions will affect the Visual Studio 2005 UI. For example, if you are allowed to perform an action, the corresponding UI command button or option will be enabled. Here are a few of the more important build privileges you should be aware of:

❑ **Start a build.** This allows a specific user to initiate a build using the build command-line tool `tfsbuild.exe` or using the UI. You have the choice of assigning this privilege level to an existing role or creating a specific account for the purpose of starting builds.

❑ **View project level information.** This allows you to view reports and receive e-mail notifications from the build server.

❑ **Edit build status.** This permission set allows you to change the build quality within the reports.

❑ **Administer a build.** This permission set allows you to create, edit, and delete build configurations. When you are logged on to an account with these permissions, corresponding buttons are enabled in the Build Configuration dialog box. This permission set is also required for stopping and deleting builds.

❑ **Update build.** This permission set allows you to add and update build configuration information. Specifically, it gives you write permissions.

For a list of build privileges, please refer to Chapter 19. The MSDN Documentation also offers extensive coverage under the Build Security Rights and Permissions heading.

Using Team Foundation Build

In this section, you will learn how to configure your builds using build types and set up custom build notifications.

Creating build types

If you've ever had the experience of creating custom build scripts, it can be a tedious and time-consuming process. Build types enable you to configure the build environment for your Visual Studio projects and solutions. You can configure what Team Foundation Server and workspace you want to associate to the build type, the tests you want to run, and so forth. The process of creating custom build types is made easy with the Team Foundation Build Type Creation Wizard, which is integrated in Team Explorer. Figure 23-2 shows how the build files appear in Team Explorer.

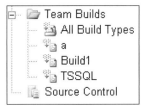

Figure 23-2

Team Build Type Creation Wizard

The New Team Build Type Creation Wizard is pictured in Figure 23-3.

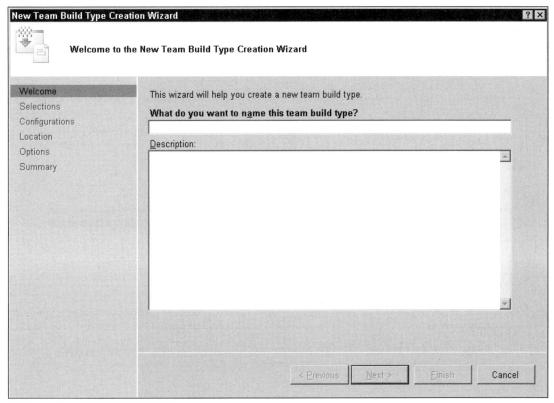

Figure 23-3

Here is how to launch the wizard to configure a build:

1. Create a workspace. You can configure your workspaces using File ⇨ Source Code ⇨ Workspaces.

2. From Team Explorer, right-click on Team Builds and select New Team Build Type. The wizard window will launch as shown in Figure 23-3.

3. The first page of the wizard is the Welcome page. You must define a name and description for your Team Foundation Build type. The build type name is a required field and must contain a unique name.

4. The next page is the Selections page, from which you select a solution to build. If you have several solutions in your workspace, you can choose the ones you want to add to your build. This is a crucial step — you are creating the connective link between your source code and the build engine. If you don't see any workspaces or source code, make sure you have properly configured your Team Foundation version control (see Chapter 20 for more details).

5. Next is the Configurations page, which enables you to configure your build. For example, you can specify whether your build is a debug or release build. You can also define the platform: x86, x64, and so forth. These options must be set for the build to execute properly.

6. Next is the Location page, where you select the build machine on which to execute the build, the Drop location, and the Build directory on the selected machine. Enter the network location of the shared drop folder (`"\\server\share"`).

7. Next is the Options page, where you can configure your build. You can add tests using Test Metadata (.vsmdi) files or enable code analysis. Some of the tests you can enable include static code tests, unit tests, code coverage tests, and custom tests. You can configure these tests using the Team Test or Team Suite SKUs of Team System, save them in a Test Metadata file (.vsmdi) using the Test Manager, and store them in source control. Figure 23-4 shows the Options page.

8. On the Summary page, verify your selections and click Finish.

> *The New Build Type Creation Wizard only supports building Visual Studio solutions in the current version of Team System. Unfortunately, you can't build projects from other platforms such as Java. However, there is an interesting tool called MSBuild Everett Environment (MSBee), which allows you to target the .NET Framework v.1.1 using Visual Studio 2005. Please refer to Craig Lichten's blog for more details:* `http://blogs.msdn.com/clichten/`.

Once you finish the process, the following will happen:

❑ XML build scripts will automatically be generated based on the options you selected. Helper files are also created, and both are checked into Team Foundation version control.

❑ `tfsbuild.proj` will be added to your project. In Team Explorer, you'll notice a new node with the name you selected for your build type.

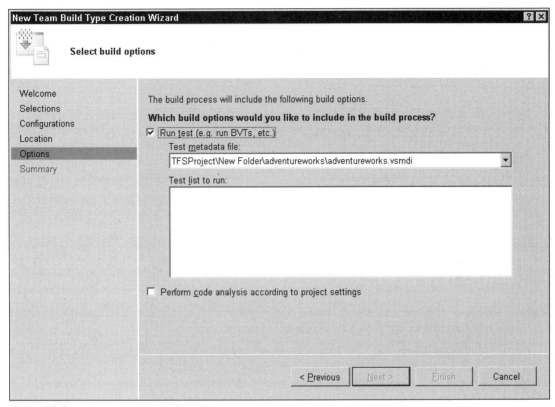

Figure 23-4

You can create an MSI to deploy your Team build types. Please refer to the MSDN documentation for more details.

Editing an existing Team build type

Once you create a Team build type, it will be added to version control in the form of a TFSBuild.proj file (which includes the build type definitions), TFSBuild.rsp (a response file for MSBuild which can incorporate custom MSBuild commands), and a WorkspaceMappings.xml file (which contains your workspace mappings on Team Foundation version control and locally). You must edit the TFSBuild.proj file before you can edit your build type. All of these files are located in Team Foundation version control in the following directory: $(YourProjectName)/TeamBuildTypes/(YourBuildTypeName).

> To edit the files, you should do a "Get Latest Version" on the TeamBuildTypes folder. If you are unsure how to check out a file, refer to Chapter 20. From a security standpoint, make sure the account that is editing the Build Types has the Administer a build rights.

To edit a Team build type, right-click on your Team build type in Team Explorer and select View Team Build Type. An XML description of your Team build type will open in Visual Studio 2005 (or the helper application associated with XML files). To change the description of the file, simply update the `<Description>` node:

```
<Description>A brand new Build Type</Description>
```

You can define what solutions you want to associate with the Team build type using the `Solution ToBuild` nodes. In the following example, you can add, change, or remove path information to Visual Studio 2005 solution files (.sln) to add them into the build process. You can also change the order in which the solutions are built in case one of the solutions depends on another:

```
<ItemGroup>
    <SolutionToBuild Include="$(SolutionRoot)\MEBeta\MobileExplorerBeta.sln" />
</ItemGroup>
```

Next, you can update the Configuration and Platform section. When you created the Team build type, you were prompted to select a configuration and platform. In this section of the XML file, you can manually change these values. For example, you can change the `FlavorToBuild` node from `Debug` to `Release`:

```
<ConfigurationToBuild Include="Debug|Any CPU">
    <FlavorToBuild>Debug</FlavorToBuild>
    <PlatformToBuild>Any CPU</PlatformToBuild>
</ConfigurationToBuild>
```

You can change your target build machine by changing the value of the `BuildMachine` node:

```
<BuildMachine>machine1</BuildMachine>
```

The Team Project to which this Team build type belongs is located in the `TeamProject` node. This value cannot be changed:

```
<TeamProject>Demo_MSF1</TeamProject>
```

You can also specify the path of the build directory, any drop location, whether testing should be implemented in your build, or whether code analysis should be executed or not:

```
<BuildDirectoryPath>C:/drop</BuildDirectoryPath>
    <DropLocation>\\buildmachine\drop1</DropLocation>
    <RunTest>true</RunTest>
    <RunCodeAnalysis>Never</RunCodeAnalysis>
```

Finally, you can specify default states for work items created when a build fails in the `WorkItemFieldValues` node using key-value pairs:

```
<UpdateAssociatedWorkItems>true</UpdateAssociatedWorkItems>
<WorkItemTitle>Build failure in build:</WorkItemTitle>
<DescriptionText>This work item was created by Team Build on a build
failure.</DescriptionText>
<BuildlogText>The build log file is at:</BuildlogText>
<ErrorWarningLogText>The errors/warnings log file is at:</ErrorWarningLogText>
```

To complete your updates on the Team build type file, simply save `TFSBuild.proj` and check-in the file. The next time you run a build, the changes you made will be applied.

Deleting a build type

To delete a Team build type, simply navigate the Team Explorer and click on the Source Control folder. You will launch the Source Control Explorer. Using the explorer, right-click and delete the folder associated with the Team build type. Performing these two tasks will delete all files for that particular Team build type after you check-in the delete operation. Be sure to check-in your pending changes to commit the delete operation.

> *The Administer a Build rights are required on your account in order to delete a build type.*

E-mail notifications

E-mail notifications help you and your teams keep track of the status of your builds and results. The e-mails contain links to view web reports. You can also optionally view the reports in Visual Studio 2005.

The e-mail will contain a variety of details, including the Team Project, build details (when the build started and completed, build machine, and build log), open work items, and custom task events.

You can turn on the build notification e-mail alerts by following these steps:

1. Using the Team Explorer, right-click on your project name node and select Project Alerts, or select the Team menu and click Project Alerts.

2. Select what kind of alert you want to receive. There are two options for Team Foundation Build: You can receive an alert once a build has been completed, or when a tester changes the build quality state on a particular build number in the build view. The following table explains the different build quality states.

Table 23-1

Build Quality State	Description
Initial Test Passed	The build has passed initial testing.
Lab Test Passed	The build has passed lab tests.
Ready for Deployment	The build is ready for deployment.
Ready for Initial Test	The build is ready for initial testing.
Rejected	The build did not pass required tests.
Released	The build has been released.
UAT Passed	The build has passed User Acceptance Testing (UAT).
Under Investigation	The build is under investigation.
Unexamined	The build has been unexamined.

3. Enter the e-mail address for the team member(s) who will be receiving the alerts. You can enter a single e-mail address or a list of recipients. You can also select what type of e-mail should be sent to your team members, plain text or HTML.

4. As soon as you click the OK button, the alerts will be enabled.

Once you receive the e-mail, you will be able to access an overview web page containing your build details. The build details web page is divided into four sections:

❑ **Summary.** The Summary section contains information on the build name, the name of the Team Project, the build type, the build machine name, date and timestamps for the start and completion of the build, the quality of the build, whether a work item was created for this build, and a build log.

❑ **Build Steps.** These steps are associated with the targets in the `Microsoft.TeamFoundation.Build.targets` file. The steps include initialization, getting sources, compiling sources, compiling the solution, compiling the Project(s), getting a list of changesets, updating work items, starting tests, completing tests, dropping binaries and logs to the drop site (or directory), and building completed. Knowing the status of each step of the build will enable you to troubleshoot any problems (if they occur). A detailed explanation of the primary build steps is outlined in the chapter introduction.

❑ **Results Details.** The Results Details section includes information about the build configuration you selected (as part of the build type). You'll get information such as errors, warnings, and tests and coverage results.

❑ **Associated Changesets.** The Associated Changesets section provides information regarding team members that have checked in code and the changesets that were included in the build.

Executing a local build

Executing a build is made easy using the Team Explorer. Simply right-click on a Team build type and select Build Team Project (associated with the name of your project). Then all you have to do is click the Build button and wait for the results. You can also execute a build using the Build menu. Simply click Build ➪ Build Team Project *<your custom project name>*. You can then pick a build type and click the OK button to launch the build. Figure 23-5 shows a view of this screen.

> *Your account needs the "Start a Build" permission set to execute a build. See the section "Setting up build security" for more information.*

You can run builds locally before checking in your code to the team source repository. Keep in mind that local builds will only run the compilation and associated tests. Obviously, steps such as work item updates (and other tasks relying on Team Foundation Server) will not be performed. Please refer to the MSDN documentation if you require more information.

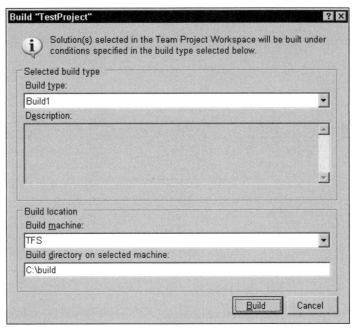

Figure 23-5

Here are the steps to run a desktop build by running MSBuild using the command line:

1. Core components of the build process are the build configuration files (such as your build types). You should first copy these configuration files from the version control repository to your local workspace. The structure of your workspace looks something like the following:

```
C:\MyWorkspace\<the name of your portfolio project>\TeamBuildTypes\<BuildTypeName>
```

2. Launch the Visual Studio 2005 console window (by selecting Start ➪ All Programs ➪ Microsoft Visual Studio 2005 ➪ Visual Studio Tools ➪ Visual Studio 2005 Command Prompt), navigate to the configuration folder, and run MSBuild using the build types you copied locally:

```
MSBuild TFSBuild.proj /p:SolutionRoot=..\sources
```

Getting the Team Foundation Build status

One of the essential operations you will have to perform is assessing the progress and status of your build during the build process. For example, if your build is generating critical errors and it takes an hour to complete it, you might want to abort the build midway to fix problems.

The build status is automatically shown when you start the build. The summary and build steps are refreshed automatically as the build progresses. Another way is to run the build report, which is updated with the latest information about Team builds at each Team System Warehouse refresh.

To view the build summary report, your user account should have a minimum of view project level information privileges.

Command-line interface

Team Foundation Build's command-line functionality is useful for a variety of reasons. It enables you to automatically schedule tasks and administer builds from remote locations. If you are planning to create a build lab, the Team Foundation Build command-line tools will greatly simplify the tasks of managing multiple build servers (rather than manually drilling into each machine using, for example, Terminal Services).

The Windows command console supports a variety of DOS-like commands — for example, md (to create a directory), rd (to remove a directory), and dir (to view a directory listing). To view a list of all the available options for a particular command, simply use the /? or /help option.

To work and operate Team Foundation Build, you would use the command-line tfsbuild executable (tfsbuild.exe).

Starting a build

To start a build, simply use the following syntax (described in the following list):

```
tfsbuild start Teamfoundationserver TeamProject BuildType [/m:buildmachine]
[/b:builddirectory]
```

- ❑   Teamfoundationserver is the server URL on which the solutions being built are checked in.
- ❑   TeamProject is the name of the target Team Project.
- ❑   BuildType is the build type to be used for the build.
- ❑   /m (machine):buildmachine is the machine on which the solutions need to be built. By default, the build machine provided in the build type would be used.
- ❑   /b (builddirectory):builddirectory is the directory in which the build process takes place. By default, the build directory specified in the build type would be used.

Here is an example:

```
tfsbuild start http://TestTFS:8080 TestTeamProject1 BetaBuildType   /m:BuildServer1
/b:C:\build\
```

Deleting a build

To delete a build, use the following syntax (described in the following list):

```
tfsbuild delete Teamfoundationserver TeamProject BuildNumbers [/noprompt]
```

❑   Teamfoundationserver is the server URL on which the solutions being built are checked in.

❑   TeamProject is the name of the target Team Project.

❑   BuildNumbers are the builds that need to be deleted. Multiple build numbers can be provided, delimited by space.

❑   [/noprompt] means do not prompt while deleting the build(s).

Here is an example:

```
tfsbuild delete http://TestTFS:8080 TestTeamProject1 MyBuild_20051027.1 20051027.2
```

Stopping a build

To stop a build, use the following syntax (described in the following list):

```
tfsbuild Stop Teamfoundationserver TeamProject BuildNumber [/noprompt]
```

❑   Teamfoundationserver is the server URL on which the solutions being built are checked in.

❑   TeamProject is the name of the target Team Project.

❑   BuildNumber is the build to be stopped. If the build number has spaces, this needs to be provided within single quotes.

❑   [/noprompt] means do not prompt while stopping the build.

Here is an example:

```
tfsbuild stop http://TestTFS:8080 TestTeamProject1 MyBuild_20051027.3
```

If the server with your drop directory runs out of space, your build will automatically stop.

Setting up a nightly build

There is only one way to configure recurring builds: using the Windows scheduler. With this method, you can configure your build schedule with a high level of granularity; it could be a weekly or daily build or you can set up an hourly build if need be. You can also group together build operations.

To schedule your builds, you can use the Schedule Tasks tool (SCHTASKS.EXE) which is a command-line version of the standard graphical Task Scheduler available by clicking Start ➪ Accessories ➪ System Tools ➪ Scheduled Tasks. Don't use the Schedule Service Command Line Interface (AT.EXE). It's not very configurable and lacks the capability to remotely administer tasks (unlike SCHTASKS).

To configure a recurring (or nightly) build, follow these steps:

1.   Log into your build server. Create a new blank document using Notepad.

2.   Paste the build commands you want to execute (see the preceding section for more information). Please make sure that your drop directory folder and permissions have been preconfigured. Here is an example of the build commands you would write out in your batch file:

```
tfsbuild start http://TestTFS:8080 TestTeamProject1 BetaBuildType   /m:BuildServer1
/b:C:\build\
```

3. Click File ⇨ Save As. Select a name and location for your file (preferably in a location where it can only be accessed by an Administrator and the Team Foundation Build Service). Save the file using the .bat extension and make sure you set the Save As Type field to All Files.

4. Open the Control Panel (by clicking Start ⇨ Control Panel). Double-click the Scheduled Tasks icon.

5. Click the Add Scheduled Task option. The Scheduled Task Wizard will appear. Click Next.

6. Click the Browse button and select the custom batch file you created.

7. Name your task (for example, Nightly Build) and select the frequency with which it should occur. The available options include Daily, Weekly, Monthly, One Time Only, When My Computer Starts, and When I Log On. Select the option appropriate for your project requirements (for example, a nightly build would require the Daily option).

8. Set the time when the build commands should be executed and on what date the process should start.

9. Select an account with the proper credentials to run a build on the machine. You can set the credentials for the task by typing in the username and password. The account you select should have the Team Foundation Server "Start a build" rights to start a build operation. Otherwise, you will not be able to run the build and build commands.

10. Click Next to complete the task configuration process.

You can then view all of your nightly builds using the command-line Task Scheduler SCHTASKS. To view all the build tasks that are scheduled using SCHTASKS, simply type the following in the command-line window:

```
schtasks
```

You will be provided with the task name, the next run time, and the status. SCHTASKS comes with a variety of commands to launch scheduled tasks on demand. For example, to immediately run a scheduled task, use the Run command by specifying the Task Name (/TN). For example:

```
schtasks Run /TN "Nightly Build"
```

You can specify the credentials of the person who wants to launch the build (using SCHTASKS) by using the Username (/u) and Password (/p) options. For example:

```
schtasks Run /u: BuildAccount /p: $crB1dP$$wd! /TN "Alpha Build"
```

Continuous integration (CI)

Microsoft (and many other software development shops) build their products on a daily (or nightly) basis. One of the core principles of SCRUM is "Build early, build often." If you are a practitioner of an Agile methodology, a daily build might not be good enough. Your iterative process may be a lot shorter than that. You may also want to build several times a day (logically, whenever you check in your source code or whenever it has changed).

Continuous integration (CI), a term derived from Extreme Programming, is the implementation of "Build early, build often." By automating your build process as much as possible, integration bugs are found faster and more often. You can also pinpoint compatibility problems. If you incorporate solid testing practices in your build process, your code will be more robust and you'll experience teamwide efficiency gains. Think about it: If you have dozens of developers working on a section of code and it's not well integrated, then you will experience a lot of problems when you try to merge your code. For definitive information about CI, please refer to Martin Fowler and Matthew Foemmel's article at `http://.martinfowler.com/articles/continuousIntegration.html`.

Unfortunately, Team Foundation Build has no built-in support for continuous integration. Using techniques similar to scheduling tasks shown in the preceding section, you can implement CI in your own environment. Khushboo Sharan has posted information and code on implementing continuous integration on her weblog. Visit `http://blogs.msdn.com/khushboo/archive/2006/02/23/537704.aspx`.

You can also refer to a Continuous Integration white paper on MSDN available at `http://msdn.microsoft.com/library/en-us/dnvs05/html/ConIntTmFndBld.asp`.

Team Foundation Build Reporting

Collecting and analyzing reports is an important part of the build process. Examining reports can provide you with a lot of information, such as success/failure metrics, historical trends, the health of your build, and much more. In the build reports, you can find errors and warnings, a changeset list, work items, code coverage results, and test results. The build reports contain links to other resources, such as logs.

Two reports types are available in Team Foundation Build. The first is the Builds report available on SQL Server Reporting Services (see Figure 23-6). When you click each build report, you can obtain more detailed information about each build (see Figure 23-7). The detailed report contains the following information and can be accessed by clicking a build name link in the summary report view:

- ❑ Summary
- ❑ Build steps
- ❑ Result details for Any CPU/Release.
- ❑ Associated changesets
- ❑ Associated work items

The second report type is the build data accessible through the Team Project. Simply double-click a build type to view the reports shown in Figures 23-8 and 23-9.

> *Error messages are intelligently handled in Team Foundation Build. You will not only get a notification and explanation, but also a solution to help you troubleshoot the problem.*

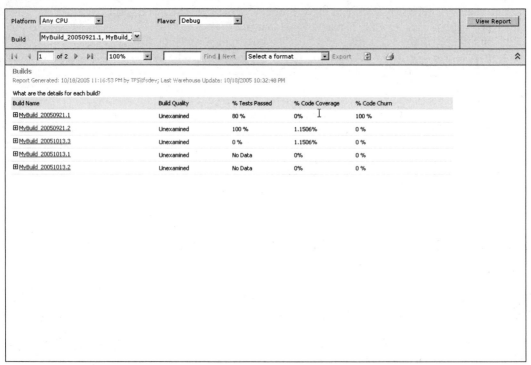

Figure 23-6

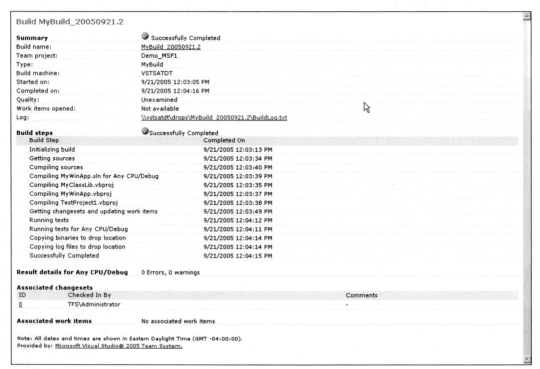

Figure 23-7

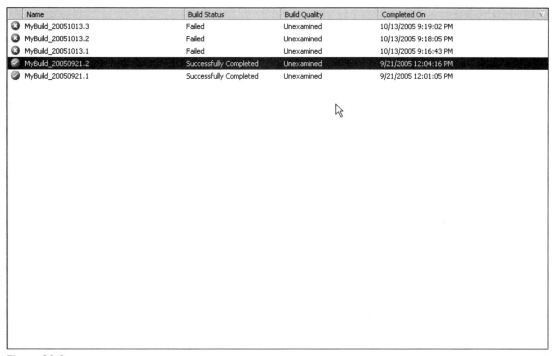

Figure 23-8

	Summary	✓ Successfully Completed	
	Build name:	MyBuild_20050921.2	
	Requested by:	TFS\Administrator	
	Team project:	Demo_MSF1	
	Type:	MyBuild	
	Build machine:	VSTSATDT	
	Started on:	9/21/2005 12:03:05 PM	
	Completed on:	9/21/2005 12:04:16 PM	
	Last changed by:	TFS\Administrator	
	Last changed on:	9/21/2005 12:04:16 PM	
	Quality:	Unexamined	
	Work items opened:	Not available	
	Log:	\\vstsatdt\drops\MyBuild_20050921.2\BuildLog.txt	
	Build steps	✓ Successfully Completed	
	Build Step	Completed On	
	Initializing build	9/21/2005 12:03:13 PM	
	Getting sources	9/21/2005 12:03:34 PM	
	Compiling sources	9/21/2005 12:03:40 PM	
	Compiling MyWinApp.sln for Any CPU/Debug	9/21/2005 12:03:39 PM	
	Compiling MyClassLib.vbproj	9/21/2005 12:03:35 PM	
	Compiling MyWinApp.vbproj	9/21/2005 12:03:37 PM	
	Compiling TestProject1.vbproj	9/21/2005 12:03:38 PM	
	Getting changesets and updating work items	9/21/2005 12:03:49 PM	
	Running tests	9/21/2005 12:04:12 PM	
	Running tests for Any CPU/Debug	9/21/2005 12:04:11 PM	
	Copying binaries to drop location	9/21/2005 12:04:14 PM	
	Copying log files to drop location	9/21/2005 12:04:14 PM	
	Successfully Completed	9/21/2005 12:04:15 PM	
	Result details for Any CPU/Debug	✓ 0 error(s), 0 warning(s), 8 test(s) total, 8 passed, 0 failed	

Figure 23-9

Build Customization and Extensibility

As you start using the product, you'll quickly realize that Team Foundation Build will not necessarily cover all of your build scenarios right out of the box. Team Foundation Build runs through an established process. If you need to add extra steps in the build process (or even change the order of the steps), you can, simply by editing XML files and changing existing properties. Other customization scenarios include specific build numbering or naming requirements or introducing an extra step to obfuscate your executables. Because MSBuild is at the core of the engine, customization is made quite a bit simpler. Some of the reasons you might want to customize a build include integrating a third-party product or shaping the build process to comply with a standards body (such as Sarbanes-Oxley or ISO). Figure 23-10 shows how build configuration event files can be edited in Visual Studio 2005.

Figure 23-10

Creating MSBuild tasks

You can programmatically create a custom MSBuild task using a bit of code. First of all, you must import two namespaces: `Microsoft.Build. Framework` and `Microsoft.Build.Utilities`:

```
using System;
using Microsoft.Build.Framework;
using Microsoft.Build.Utilities;
```

Then you can derive the `Microsoft.Build.Utilities.Task` class. We created a new class called `customTask` that derives from `Task` as the framework for our new MSBuild task:

```
namespace MyTasks
{

   public class customTask : Task
     {
```

We then created a method called `Execute`, which returns a value of `true`:

```
         public override bool Execute()
         {
             return true;
          }
```

Then we created a custom property aptly called `customProperty`. You can define one or many of these properties for each MSBuild task. As you can see, we've added the ubiquitous `get`/`set` options:

```
         private string customProperty;
         public string customProperty
         {
             get { return customProperty; }
             set { customProperty = value; }
         }


      }
   }
```

Once you compile the task, you can access it in your MSBuild targets. Here is what our custom task would look like in an MSBuild target file:

```
<Project xmlns="http://schemas.microsoft.com/developer/msbuild/2003">
   <Target Name="customTarget">

      <customTask customProperty="Value123" />

   </Target>
</Project>
```

In order to use a custom MSBuild task, you must first register your task in your target. You can do this by using the `UsingTask` node to reference your custom task name and assembly:

```
<UsingTask TaskName="customTask" AssemblyName="customTask.dll" Condition="" />
```

For more information about creating custom MSBuild tasks, please refer to the MSDN documentation.

Summary

This chapter explained how Team Foundation Build fits in within your software development process. You learned how to plan and deploy Team Foundation Build and how to perform daily tasks such as starting, stopping, and deleting builds. You also created build types and set up the e-mail notification system.

Essential tools you will use in a multi-server environment are the command-line tools. You looked at how to use the tfsbuild command and then you delved into scheduling. After learning how to schedule daily builds (in a Formal environment) or quick iterative builds (in an Agile environment), you learned how to access the build reports and measure the effectiveness of a build.

Finally, you learned how to extend and modify Team Foundation Build using XML configuration files and MSBuild tasks. In the next chapter, you will learn more about deployment and maintenance strategies for all components of Team System.

24

Deployment and Administration

In previous chapters, you learned how to use the individual features of Visual Studio 2005 Team System. To deploy Team System within a corporate environment, you must know how the components fit together conceptually and the important steps to effectively administer the tools.

Within your development environment, you can also count on your build server, test rigs, and proxies to enable you to connect Team Foundation Server to geographically distributed teams. It is important to note that the current version of Team System has been designed for teams of up to 2,000 users. (See Brian Harry's blog for details about capacity planning and scalability — `http://blogs.msdn.com/bharry/`.) Microsoft is internally introducing Team System within its own product groups, and you can expect future versions of Team System to support and scale to many more users.

If you do have a large number of developers to work with, you can optionally set up several build servers to distribute your builds. The Team Foundation Proxy will help you increase performance by caching your source control files. Finally, you can use the test controllers and rigs to distribute your load tests.

In Chapter 18, you learned a little about the three logical tiers in Team System. In this chapter, you'll get a clearer idea of the interplay between the components and how you can administer the product from an operational perspective. Figure 24-1 shows an overview of the primary logical tiers of Team System and how they interact with each other.

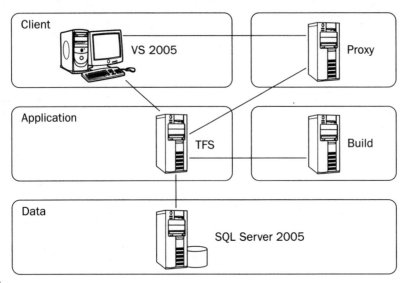

Figure 24-1

> The above diagram is a simplified architectural view. It does not account for situations where you may, for example, want to set up multiple Team Foundation Build servers or set up Team Foundation Build on a client.

Configuring Team System and Team Foundation Server can be quite challenging, especially when you're trying to integrate it within Active Directory, with stringent security requirements and multi-domain network topologies. Many of these topics are out of scope for the book, however; the best source of current information can be found on your CD or DVD media for Team Foundation Server. It includes two useful and detailed guides — the *Team Foundation Server Installation Guide* and the *Team Foundation Server Administrators Guide*.

Next in the chapter, you will find out how to set up your operations team and plan a deployment (using several common scenarios). You'll also get an overview of administrative details such as backup/recovery, tools migration, and general licensing strategies.

A great source of information for all things Team System is Rob Caron's popular blog. (Rob is partly responsible for the Team System documentation.) You can access Rob's site by visiting `http://blogs.msdn.com/robcaron/`.

Setting Up Your Operations Team

You can look at Team Foundation Server administration on four levels: the Enterprise IT Administrator (or Enterprise Architect and quite possibly the Infrastructure Architect), Server Administrator, Project Manager and Users. Figure 24-2 illustrates the groups and the product/role relationship:

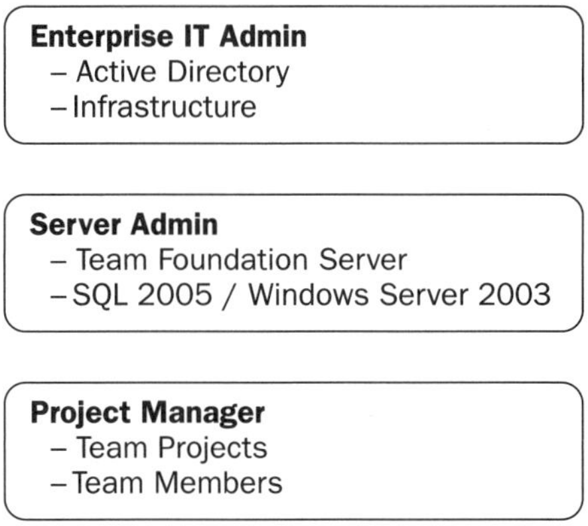

```
┌─────────────────────────────────────────┐
│ Enterprise IT Admin                      │
│  – Active Directory                      │
│  – Infrastructure                        │
└─────────────────────────────────────────┘

┌─────────────────────────────────────────┐
│ Server Admin                             │
│  – Team Foundation Server                │
│  – SQL 2005 / Windows Server 2003        │
└─────────────────────────────────────────┘

┌─────────────────────────────────────────┐
│ Project Manager                          │
│  – Team Projects                         │
│  – Team Members                          │
└─────────────────────────────────────────┘
```

Figure 24-2

Here is a breakdown of the different roles and responsibilities within the group:

❑ **Enterprise IT Administrator:** Responsible for the entire infrastructure. This individual is concerned with the operation of the servers on his/her network. This individual will manage Windows Server 2003 but will usually stay away from the application servers.

❑ **Server Administrator:** The server administrator is responsible for the administration and performance of Team Foundation Server. You typically contact the server administrator to set up new Team Foundation Server roles. It is the responsibility of the server administrator to interact with the enterprise IT adminstrator to make sure that the Active Directory credentials are mapped correctly or that the local accounts are correctly set up on the Windows Server 2003 to be later added into Team Foundation Server.

❑ **Project Manager:** The project manager is concerned with the smooth functioning of a project within Team Foundation Server. The project manager can add and remove users to a project, define policies, and set up the project structure.

❑ **User:** The user has the least amount of privileges. This group can include developers and testers. They can configure their own workspaces, check-in/check-out code and perform other operations which are required for their designated roles.

Planning a Deployment

Installing and deploying a product such as Visual Studio 2005 Team System involves a lot of preplanning and forethought. You must take into consideration variables such as capacity, scale, and the underlying infrastructure.

Some of the key questions you have to ask include whether you'll need one or two Team Foundation Servers (which will depend on the scale of your team). Will you need a proxy server? (In other words, will you support geographically distributed teams?) Do you need more than one build server? If so, where will they be installed? Do you need to create load tests with more than 1,000 simulated users? If so, a test rig may be required. The following section provides a more in-depth look at these variables and how they may affect your implementation of Team System.

Unsupported deployment scenarios

According to Microsoft, the following Enterprise scenarios are not supported on Team Foundation Server:

❑ Application tier network load balancing and clustering — in other words, you can't cluster Team Foundation Server

❑ Dividing Web services from the application tier on several servers

❑ Running several instances of Team Foundation Server on the same box

Capacity planning

The best way to look at capacity planning is by thinking about and looking at scenarios. First, you will look at the performance and scope of a deployment. Next, you will look at deployment on a small and then larger scale.

Performance and scope

Team System was designed to work with a single Team Foundation Server at the core. Microsoft is currently investigating scenarios where multiple Team Foundation Servers are used to scale up to larger-sized teams. However, please note that the product does not currently support clustering and mirroring. (This is, however, supported on the SQL Server 2005 data tier.) The responsiveness of Team System will depend greatly on the amount of memory you have in your server machine. The more memory that you can add in, the better its response will be.

In planning your deployment, you must consider whether you will use a one- or two-Team Foundation Server configuration. Questions you might ask yourself include: How many users will you support? Are Proxy Servers required (for distributed support)? Will you support clusters of remote users? Where on your network is your build server? Do you need a Test Rig (a collection of load test agents and controllers), and how many test users will you simulate? Finally, another question you may want to ask is whether you will integrate with Active Directory.

Small to medium deployments

You have two fundamental scenarios to consider for small to medium deployments. First, we define a small to medium deployment as 1 to 500 users. The first scenario is a single machine to a single user install. The second scenario is a multi-server install for teams of 2 to 500 users.

A one-user scenario may include a customer evaluating a demo version of the product, a consultant giving a presentation on Team System, or even a small learning environment to help a group of users experiment with the product. The one-user version of Team System is usually installed on a single machine and may contain demo or evaluation versions of the product (rather than the full retail version). The single-machine install contains all the components of Team System, including the client tier (CT), build engine, data tier (DT), and application tier (AT).

The second scenario in small to medium deployments is the 2 to 500 user scenario. In this scenario, Team System is installed on a single server and deployed to a small team. Since there are multiple users, the client tier (in other words, Visual Studio) is installed on machines other than the application and data tiers. This enables multiple users to access a single instance of the server. You can also optionally install Team Foundation Build on a separate machine or even on the client's desktop. This deployment model is configured to support workgroups or Active Directory.

Enterprise deployment

There is a single scenario to consider is the very large team of 500 to 2,000 developers, testers, and architects. A large infrastructure requires larger capacity, security, manageability, and support for geographically distributed software teams. Team System supports a large team by dividing up the tiers on different machines. To support such a large number of users, you must use Active Directory. (Otherwise, from an operational perspective, managing the users and the shifting needs will require a lot of overhead from the standpoint of day to day administration.)

> *At the time of writing, Microsoft is internally deploying Team System as a tool to manage ambitious development projects such as Windows or Office. In fact, the Team Foundation Proxy was designed to effectively tackle latency challenges with remote teams.*

For updates regarding how Team System can scale for larger teams, we highly recommend you look at Brian Harry's blog at `http://blogs.msdn.com/bharry/`.

User accounts

Three accounts are required to run and administer Team Foundation Server, as described in Table 24-1.

Table 24-1

User Name	Description
TFSSETUP	This account is used to log on to the different computers and run the installation applications.
TFSSERVICE	This account is used to run the different services that make up the Team Foundation Server. It is also used for different application pools related to Team Foundation Server.
TFSREPORTS	This account is used to access the data sources using SQL Server Reporting Services.

The user names listed in the preceding table are sample names. You can use any name you would like. This book will use these names in discussing the installation and configuration of Team Foundation Server. The TFSSETUP account must be in the local Administrators group on each Team Foundation Server machine. The TFSSERVICE and TFSREPORTS accounts should *not* be in the local Administrators group.

In a multi-server installation, all machines must be a member of an Active Directory domain. The user accounts defined in the previous table *must* be members of that Active Directory domain.

In a single-server installation, the user accounts can either be members of an Active Directory domain or local user accounts on the machine. Also, for a single server installation, you can use the same account for the Team Foundation Server Setup and the Team Foundation Server Service account. The Reporting Services Account must still be a separate account.

Firewall configuration

Table 24-2 contains a list of the ports used by Team System's data and application tiers. These ports should be opened in any intervening firewalls to enable communication in multi-server installs. Please note that firewall ports don't need to be opened on a single-server install.

Table 24-2

Port	Protocol	Reason
80	TCP	Application Tier
1433, 1434	TCP	SQL Server
2382, 2383	TCP	Analysis Services

Network topologies

Depending on your target environment, the network topology may present a special set of challenges. The following sections describe common deployment models which you may encounter.

Single-server deployment (workgroup configuration)

A single-server deployment is the simplest configuration option you can pick. It is advised if you want to deploy Team System for testing purposes or for very small teams. Typically, the single-server deployment is set up using a workgroup configuration (although it is possible to set it up on a domain).

> The MSDN Subscriber Download site includes virtual machine images of a single-server deployment, which makes it very handy for you to test and evaluate Team System in a lab-like environment. You can deploy these virtual machines using either Microsoft VirtualPC or Microsoft Virtual Server.

Please note that the workgroup version of the Team System installation process has a couple of notable limitations. One of the limitations is that the domain users can't log in to the server (see the following section, "Multi-server Deployment," for details). Also, your passwords and user accounts must be synchronized with Team Foundation Server. Otherwise, users cannot log in to the server. Figure 24-3 shows a standard single-server configuration setup.

Multi-server deployment

If you are planning to divide the tiers on separate machines, please note that you should set up your servers on a domain. For your components to access the domain, it is *extremely* important for you to set up your TFSSETUP, TFSREPORTS, and TFSERVICE accounts using domain accounts. Otherwise, TFSSERVICE will be unable to effectively interoperate and authenticate with the domain controller. Figure 24-4 shows a multi-server deployment and the different configuration options you have at your disposal.

For 50 Users or Less
Workgroup or Active Directory

Visual Studio 2005
Office 2003
Team Explorer

Team Foundation Server
SQL Server 2005

Figure 24-3

For 50-2000 Users
Active Directory Only

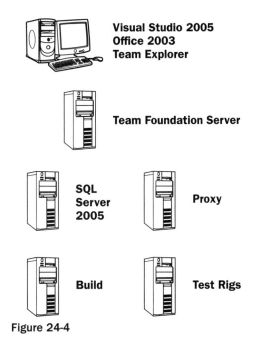

Visual Studio 2005
Office 2003
Team Explorer

Team Foundation Server

SQL
Server
2005

Proxy

Build

Test Rigs

Figure 24-4

Architecting your Active Directory (AD) structure

If you are working within a large infrastructure, Active Directory will be a given for managing your users on Team Foundation Server. Why would you want to use AD over the workgroup configuration, you may ask? First of all, from a convenience perspective you can implement single sign-on. Active Directory has security features that will help prevent scenarios such as unwanted clients or servers running on your network. And, most important of all, is manageability. In Workgroup mode, you have to manually add all users and groups to the server—if you have hundreds of users, this can be a pain from an administrative standpoint, because all changes made to the external network will have to be replicated locally on TFS. For example, if a developer decides to leave a company running Team System, the administrator will not only have to remove that user's privileges from the network, but also on the server.

Team Foundation Server supports Active Directory 2000 and Active Directory 2003. (Windows NT is not supported.) Team Foundation Server will interact with AD 2000 in Native mode—Mixed mode is not supported. Team Foundation Server also supports one-way trusts, full trusts, explicit trusts, and cross-forest trusts.

Team Foundation Server does not support a configuration of the Application and Data tiers on separate domains (or subdomains). You can't mix domains and workgroups either—they have to be on the same domain. Finally, make sure that your network isn't using Windows NT 4.0 Domain Controllers.

Test deployment using virtualization

You can test your deployment using a variety of tools, including Microsoft Virtual PC and Microsoft Virtual Server. There are many advantages to do so, especially in a test environment:

❑　Virtual images created from one product are compatible with the other.

❑　No need to re-install Team Foundation Server. The virtual image can be redeployed to a production server quite easily.

❑　You can create a base installation of Team Foundation Server, which would enable you to restore the server to a pristine state rather than try to clean up the projects.

Almost all the features of Team System work within a virtual environment, with the exception of profiling. The profiler will not work correctly in a virtualized environment because of virtual driver limitations. Think of it, the profiler uses the core system as a baseline to execute the tests—if the core environment is virtualized; it is difficult if not impossible to get accurate performance readings.

> Andy Leonard documented a way to configure a virtual domain controller with Team Foundation Server. You can read the details on his Web site at
> `http://www.vsteamsystemcentral.com/dnn/.`

Creating a test plan

Before you install Team System, you must consider who will be running the tests and the approach that should be taken to implement them. If you are running a large project, you may require additional build and test rigs to support the extra load. Testing can be done manually or as part of a build. You should think about what best practices you want to put into place to create an environment that fosters Test Driven Development (TDD).

All tests will run seamlessly as part of a build with the exception of Manual Tests. As a best practice, you should create dedicated test runs of manual tests. The two reasons are that it will make the tests easier to administer and will not impede the run of automated tests.

You should also take a look at all the tests available in Team System to see which ones you can leverage. Frequent testing will improve the quality of your code and, as a result, improve productivity.

Test rig considerations

If you try to run a load test with more than a few users within Visual Studio 2005, you'll notice that Visual Studio may become unresponsive, or you may experience performance problems at the outset. If you want to run capacity and performance tests, it is best to use a remote test rig (consisting of a test load agent and controller) to run the tests without affecting the overall operating environment.

Using the test runs that you can configure by using Team Edition for Software Testers, you can use a test controller to manage several load agents situated on several machines. By distributing the load, you can most effectively test your applications without loss of productivity. It goes without saying that the larger the project, the more test rigs will be required. Now to take a look at the individual components. Figure 24-5 shows a typical test rig and controller configuration and how it interplays with Team Foundation Server.

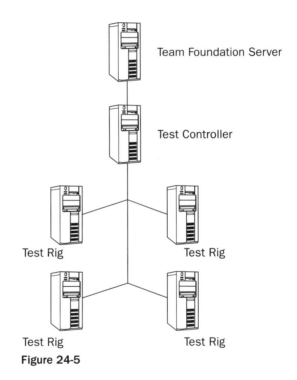

Figure 24-5

Considerations for Migrating and Integrating Your Existing Tools

When you look at how you can work within Team System, you have to consider whether it makes more sense to migrate or integrate your existing tools into Team System. Migration makes a lot of sense if you want to rid yourself of expensive third-party licensing agreements. For example, Team System provides the capability to do large-scale load tests out of the box; therefore, it makes sense to migrate if you are already paying thousands of dollars supporting and licensing a third-party tool because the migration process will result in a cost savings.

Integration is a smart option if you have invested a lot of money on existing tools and you wish to leverage that investment. Integration is a little trickier because it often entails extra configuration and programming steps to make both systems "talk" to and integrate with each other.

In this section "Considerations for Migrating and Integrating Your Existing Tools," we will look at some of the important features of Team Foundation Server and discuss the challenges and resources available to help you migrate and integrate your existing solutions to Team System. This is not meant to be an exhaustive list but will provide you with a good starting point.

> When making a decision about integration or migration, it is important to discuss the implications with a knowledgeable systems integrator or consultant. Whereas a decision may seem straightforward, it may have cost implications. It is important that whoever you decide to work with has a solid background on Team System and your existing tools.

Version control

When looking at source control, the main question you have to ask yourself is whether it makes more sense to maintain the current source control system or to migrate your source projects to Team Foundation version control. If your company has invested tens and hundreds of thousands on a source-control system, it may not be in your best interest from a business perspective to migrate all your code. On the other hand, if you are planning new development using Visual Studio 2005 and the .NET Framework 2.0, starting a project within Team System will be a good decision, as you will be able to leverage the deep integration between Visual Studio and Team Foundation version control.

One of the logical migration paths is moving your code from Visual SourceSafe to Team System. Visual SourceSafe is a good tool for small development projects with a small number of developers. However, it does not scale well if your team grows beyond a dozen developers and testers. Team Foundation version control is designed to manage large teams of developers and provides for the first time concurrent check-ins and rollback capabilities.

> One of the biggest misconceptions about Team System's version control is that it is the new version of Visual SourceSafe. This is completely untrue — Team System version control was written from scratch for Team System and uses SQL Server 2005 as a means of scaling to larger environments and infrastructures.

Microsoft has developed a migration tool called VSSConverter to enable you to migrate your Visual SourceSafe code to Team System. You can find out more details here:
`http://msdn2.microsoft.com/en-us/library/ms253060.aspx`

What if you are using other version-control systems such as CVS or SourceGear? Team System does not support these systems out of the box, but nothing prevents you from using these systems directly. If you choose another source control system, keep in mind that you will not be able to use the build engine. (Team Foundation Build pulls the sources out of source control before building them.)

What if you want to integrate an existing source control system with Team System? Luckily, there are a lot of projects in the works to help you. Team Foundation Server provides a wide variety of APIs to enable you to connect and transmit information from Team Foundation Server to your source control system and vice-versa.

Work-item tracking

Work-item tracking is an important feature of Team Foundation Server for two reasons: One, it provides a way for your team members to track workflow and collaborate right from within Visual Studio. Two, it also provides the important link to implementing your process. For example, if the process you are using has a predefined iterative flow, you can create a series of tasks or requirements that will support and enact the iterations.

Work-item tracking is a baked-in and highly integrated way of managing your work within Team System. But what if you have invested work or budget on other tools? As with any other feature of Team System, you are not forced to use the feature. You can selectively pick what you prefer to use in the end.

If you wish to move over your ClearQuest workflow to the Team System work-item database, Microsoft provides a ClearQuest migration tool called WIConverter to help you out. You can learn more about the migration tool at the following URL: `http://msdn2.microsoft.com/en-us/library/ms253046(en-US,VS.80).aspx`.

You may also be tracking workflow by using Microsoft Office Project Server 2003. Fortunately, there are efforts under way to integrate both Team System and Project Server, using a special connector. You can learn more about the connector at the following URL: `http://www.gotdotnet.com/workspaces/workspace.aspx?id=b9f69ea5-ace1-4a21-846f-6222a507cc9c`.

Reporting

Team System does an amazing thing with reporting — it automatically aggregates project data such as build quality stats, bug counts, work-item completion statistics, and much more. In the past, you had to manually aggregate all your data by hand and import it into Excel to generate such a report. There are also other tools such as Crystal Reports that will provide the capability to generate graphs and other reports from raw data. One of the disadvantages with third-party tools (such as Crystal Reports) is that they can be expensive and complicated to use.

Team System's reporting capabilities are provided by SQL Server Reporting Services. Visual Studio 2005 provides a Report Designer to help you create new kinds of reports that can be viewed on the report site. The main idea here is that, if you can bring external data into SQL Server 2005, you can then mine and view the data in an integrated way within Team System.

Testing tools

Team System incorporates a great number of testing tools, including dynamic analysis, code analysis, manual testing, load testing, unit testing, ordered testing, Web testing, and performance testing.

James Newkirk created a migration tool to port over NUnit tests to Team System called the NUnit Converter. Note that unit testing is fully integrated into the toolset as the Unit Test Framework. Note, too, that this framework is available only in the Team Edition for Software Developers, Team Edition for Software Testers, and Team Suite versions of Visual Studio 2005. The migration tool is available on the NUnit Add-ons workspace on GotDotNet: `http://www.gotdotnet.com`.

The converter tool is integrated in Visual Studio 2005 and requires the installation of the Guidance Automation Extensions to function.

In terms of load testing, Team System comes with an integrated tool. From a practical standpoint, one of the core advantages of the load testing tool is that it is available to the entire software development team and is a great deal less expensive (from a licensing perspective) than other third-party tools. Another advantage is that the Team System load tester can support a great number of concurrent users.

Unfortunately, at the time of writing there aren't any migration tools to help you migrate Mercury Loadrunner tests to Team System. However, it is possible to integrate the Loadrunner tool using a generic test. The generic test enables you to run external executables (with parameters) and import results back into Team System's testing framework.

Backup and Recovery

One of the ways Microsoft has facilitated the administration and deployment of Team System is by putting most of the configuration settings and data on SQL Server 2005. The backup process in Team System can be broken down into three logical steps:

1. Back up Team Foundation Server: One of the easiest ways of backing up Team Foundation Server is by using a third-party solution such as Norton Ghost. You can also back up individual attachments by using the Registration Web service at the following URL:

   http://*your server*:8080/bisserver/Registration.asmx

   Look at the location of the attachments (\VSTS\WorkItemTracking\Attachments). Turn off TFSServerScheduler and Internet Information Server (using iisrest /stop). Then you can easily save your attachments.

2. Back up SQL Server 2005: SQL Server 2005 can't be imaged — otherwise, you will lose the capability to use your logs to recover data. You should use the SQL Server 2005 data backup tools within the SQL Server 2005 Management Studio. Be sure to do a file backup of .bak files to restore later.

3. Back up Windows SharePoint Services: You can back up SharePoint by using the following command:

   ```
   %ProgramFiles%\Common Files\Microsoft Shared\web server extensions\60\bin
   \stsadm.exe -o backup -url http://localhost -filename backup.dat
   ```

   The MSDN documentation also has steps to back up all the individual tables within SQL Server 2005 if you need that extra level of control and schedule your backups.

To restore a Team Foundation Server backup (assuming you have a clean Team Foundation Server install ready to go), follow these steps:

1. Stop your "clean" instance of Team Foundation Server by using the command net stop TFS.

2. On SQL Server 2005, copy the .bak files. Open SQL Server Management Studio and choose Task ⇨ Restore ⇨ Database. Make sure that you overwrite the current database.

3. You should then restart the application and data tiers by using the commands net start TFS (to start up the Team Foundation Server) and iisreset (to restart IIS).

4. Finally, restore the SharePoint site by typing the following command:

```
"%ProgramFiles%\Common Files\Microsoft Shared\web server
extensions\60\bin"\stsadm.exe -o restore -url http://localhost -filename backup.dat
-overwrite
```

> If you choose to use imaging software as part of your backup strategy, be aware that problems may occur if you try to restore on a different computer or server.

Licensing Models

Cost is always one of the key questions that keeps coming up when considering Team System, but unfortunately, the licensing model isn't as clear cut as some other products. In this section, we attempt to provide you with guidance and a simplified view to help you understand the licensing model.

> *The best source of information for licensing is a white paper published on MSDN. To access the white paper, please refer to this URL:* `http://go.microsoft.com/fwlink/?LinkId=55933`

Here are some practical guidelines to consider:

❑ If your team members perform specific roles without overlap, consider obtaining a specific Team Edition version of Visual Studio for each team member. Developers, for example, would obtain the Team Edition for Software Developers. If there is overlap between roles, you should consider obtaining the Team Suite.

> *If you plan to use all the testing feature integration with Team Foundation Build, you should obtain a license for Team Edition for Software Developers and Team Edition for Software Testers (or Team Suite). The combination of these two products will provide the necessary framework to run any of the tests commonly found in Team System. Note that both these products must be installed on the build server.*

❑ Team Foundation Server requires a license, and every computer accessing the server using Team Explorer (or any other client) requires a Client Access License (CAL). In some instances involving a remote "nonemployee," a connector can be purchased to give that person access to the server.

❑ Each instance of Team Foundation Server Proxy requires a Team Foundation Server license. A license is also required for "warm" failover instances of Team Foundation Server.

Where to get Team System

You can obtain Team System three ways from any of the following sources:

❑ Reseller

❑ MSDN Subscriber Downloads

❑ Partner Program

Chapter 24

If you are part of the MSDN Subscriber downloads, you may be able to benefit from substantial savings in upgrading to Team System. You can view more information about each option at the following URL: `http://msdn.microsoft.com/vstudio/howtobuy/`.

Summary

In this chapter, you learned some of Team System's deployment strategies. Then you explored the considerations for migrating and integrating your existing tools. Finally, licensing was discussed, as well as how you can obtain Team System.

Index

U